Fundamental Concepts and Applications

David J. Anspaugh, PED, EdD, CHES

Michael H. Hamrick, EdD, CHES

Frank D. Rosato, EdD

ALL OF THE UNIVERSITY OF MEMPHIS
Memphis, Tennessee

Boston   Burr Ridge, IL   Dubuque, IA   Madison, WI   New York   San Francisco   St. Louis
Bangkok   Bogotá   Caracas   Lisbon   London   Madrid
Mexico City   Milan   New Delhi   Seoul   Singapore   Sydney   Taipei   Toronto

We dedicate this book to

Susan H. Anspaugh   *Dorothy Hamrick*   *Patricia Rosato*

A Division of The **McGraw-Hill** Companies

WELLNESS: FUNDAMENTAL CONCEPTS AND APPLICATIONS

Published by McGraw-Hill, an imprint of The McGraw-Hill Companies, Inc., 1221 Avenue of the Americas, New York, NY 10020. Copyright © 2001 by The McGraw-Hill Companies, Inc. All rights reserved. No part of this publication may be reproduced or distributed in any form or by any means, or stored in a database or retrieval system, without the prior written consent of The McGraw-Hill Companies, Inc., including, but not limited to, in any network or other electronic storage or transmission, or broadcast for distance learning.

Some ancillaries, including electronic and print components, may not be available to customers outside the United States.

This book is printed on acid-free paper.

3 4 5 6 7 8 9 0 VNH/VNH 0 9 8 7 6 5 4

ISBN 0–07–240991–6

Vice president and editor-in-chief: *Kevin T. Kane*
Executive editor: *Vicki Malinee*
Senior developmental editor: *Melissa Martin*
Senior marketing manager: *Pamela S. Cooper*
Project manager: *Rose Koos*
Associate media producer: *Judi David*
Production supervisor: *Enboge Chong*
Coordinator of freelance design: *Michelle D. Whitaker*
Interior designer: *Becky Lemna*
Cover image: *©SuperStock, Inc.*
Senior photo research coordinator: *Carrie K. Burger*
Photo research: *LouAnn K. Wilson*
Supplement coordinator: *Sandra M. Schnee*
Compositor: *Shepherd, Inc.*
Typeface: *10/12 Sabon*
Printer: *Von Hoffmann Press, Inc.*

The credits section for this book is on page 349 and is considered an extension of the copyright page.

www.mhhe.com

Preface

ellness: Fundamental Concepts and Applications assumes that health is not a destination but a journey. Wellness is not a static condition but a continual balancing of the different dimensions of human needs—spiritual, social, emotional, intellectual, physical, occupational, and environmental. Because we are all responsible for our own growth in these areas, this book strives to emphasize the importance of self-responsibility. And because we know that knowledge alone stimulates change for very few people, the reader is challenged to be actively involved in the learning process by constantly assessing how the information presented affects lifestyle from a personal perspective.

Wellness: Fundamental Concepts and Applications is neither a fitness book nor a personal health text. Instead, this text is designed to help students gain knowledge and understanding in a variety of areas, with the goal of taking that information and using it to make behavioral changes that will have a positive impact on their lives. In many cases these changes are necessary if people are to develop the skills, attitudes, beliefs, and habits that will ultimately result in the highest possible level of health and wellness.

Audience

When the fitness and wellness concept appears in university courses and programs, it is usually a scaled-down model of the traditional personal health course or an upscale version of physical fitness courses. In some cases it is a hybrid of personal health and fitness courses, with emphasis on self-participation in the medical marketplace. *Wellness: Fundamental Concepts and Applications* is a hybrid because the physical components of wellness are blended with its many other components. The primary objectives of this text are to present cognitive health and wellness information appropriate for today's college students and to offer suggestions for their application. These suggestions relate to lifestyle behaviors over which people can exert some control. The emphasis is on self-responsibility, and this theme is implemented through a strong self-analysis and assessment component.

Approach

Important features unique to *Wellness: Fundamental Concepts and Applications* distinguish it from other texts.

Balanced approach: Unlike other approaches that emphasize only physical fitness as a route to wellness, *Wellness: Fundamental Concepts and Applications* provides a balanced presentation of the health benefits of exercise, diet, and cardiovascular wellness, along with the management of lifestyle change to achieve lifetime wellness.

Complete lifestyle decision-making information: Goals for Behavior Change, Real-World Wellness boxes, Wellness on the Web Behavior Change Activities, and Assessment Activities help apply the content and encourage responsible student decision making.

Interdisciplinary author team: Two health educators and a fitness educator currently teaching wellness courses have combined their expertise to provide the most balanced presentation possible.

Full-color: A full-color format is used in the photographs, line drawings, and design of the text to increase visual appeal and to enhance the teaching-learning process.

Highlights of This Edition

Features, and issues found in this edition are highlighted here.

Attractive Design and Illustrations

The fresh look, appealing colors, and exciting graphics in this edition will draw students in with every turn of the page. The photographs reflect the diversity of college students of all ages, and the drawings are attractive and informative.

HealthQuest Activities

The HealthQuest CD-ROM that accompanies each new copy of *Wellness: Fundamental Concepts and Applications* contains many useful health and wellness self-assessments. The software is organized into nine modules: Stress Management and Mental Health; Fitness; Weight Control; Communicable Diseases; Cardiovascular Health; Cancer; Tobacco; Alcohol; and Other Drugs. The modules are based on Prochaska's stages of change model, which is presented in Chapter 1 of the text. The HealthQuest Activities complement the Assessment Activities in the text, and they help students get the most from the book and the software.

Goals for Behavior Change

Goals for Behavior Change, listed at the beginning of each chapter, give students objectives that help them apply what they learn in the text. These objectives reinforce the concept of self-responsibility on which the text is based.

Wellness on the Web Behavior Change Activities

The text includes activities in every chapter that take students to quizzes, questions, and self-assessment activities that make surfing the web more interactive and fun for students. Completing these activities will help them assess their current practices and design a more wellness-oriented lifestyle.

Wellness Across the Generations

Many students who take a wellness course are returning to school after some time in the work force. Many of them are raising children or caring for aging parents. Younger students are concerned about how their health will change as they age. New Wellness Across the Generations boxes address wellness concepts throughout the life span by looking at issues such as childhood origins of heart disease, and strength training for older adults.

Nurturing Your Spirituality

Spirituality has become an important focus of the wellness movement. Nurturing Your Spirituality boxes highlight the spiritual dimension of wellness and its effect on overall wellness.

Real-World Wellness

These unique question-and-answer boxes show students how to put wellness concepts into practice. Helpful tips give students practical advice for initiating behavior change and staying motivated to follow a wellness lifestyle. For example, students will learn how to exercise safely in the city and how to choose satisfying, nutrient-dense snacks.

Just the Facts

In every chapter, special material in Just the Facts boxes encourages students to delve into a particular topic or closely examine an important health issue.

Complete, Current Coverage of Nutrition and Weight Control

Chapter 6, "Forming a Plan for Good Nutrition," and Chapter 8, "Achieving a Healthy Weight," include the latest, most comprehensive information available on nutrition and diet. See the next section for a detailed list of topics.

Current Topics

We are committed to making this textbook the most up-to-date wellness text available. Following is a sampling of current topics:

Chapter 1: Wellness and Fitness for Life

- New presentation of the Prochaska stages of change model
- Updated information on the leading causes of death
- New information on the importance of choosing a wellness lifestyle regardless of age and health history
- Greater emphasis on the spiritual dimension of wellness
- New introduction to the benefits of a wellness lifestyle

Chapter 2: Preventing Cardiovascular Disease

- Simplified terminology and more accessible language
- New information on the childhood origins of heart disease
- Greater emphasis on heart disease risk factors and prevention
- New assessment that focuses on CVD risk factors that can be changed

- New discussion of obesity as a major risk factor that can be changed (new AHA classification)
- New information on emerging risk factors for heart disease
- New discussion of heart disease risk among postmenopausal women
- Expanded coverage of stress and personality type
- New discussion of hypertension among African Americans

Chapter 3: Increasing Cardiorespiratory Endurance

- New discussion of managing exercise-related problems
- New information on maintaining cardiorespiratory endurance as we age
- New section on exercising safely in an urban environment
- New tips on choosing home fitness equipment
- New information on ergogenic aids
- Updated information on VO_2 max based on the new ACSM guidelines
- Updated discussion of the health-related and performance-related components of fitness

Chapter 4: Building Muscular Strength and Endurance

- Expanded presentation of the benefits of training
- New discussion of the benefits of strength training for older adults
- Updated recommendations that reflect the 1998 ACSM guidelines
- New discussion of slow-twitch and fast-twitch muscle fibers, myofibrils, and motor units
- New section on ergogenic aids other than steroids, such as vitamins, sports drinks, weight-gain products, creatine, protein supplements, and herbal products
- Updated examples of exercise equipment

Chapter 5: Improving Flexibility

- Expanded coverage of low-back pain, upper-back pain, and neck pain
- New information on exercise to improve flexibility, including among children and the elderly
- New discussion of the emotional and physical benefits of yoga and tai chi
- New explanation of the principles of conditioning as they apply to flexibility
- New discussion of how flexibility exercises should be used during warm-up and cool-down

Chapter 6: Forming a Plan for Good Nutrition

- New food safety tips
- New tips on choosing healthful ethnic foods
- New section on vegetarianism
- Expanded coverage of the importance of water intake
- New section on botanicals, herbs, and phytomedicinals
- Expanded coverage of snacking, fast food, and other convenience foods
- Expanded coverage of vitamins
- New assessment on dietary fat intake
- New section on nutrition and disease prevention
- New section on nutrition during pregnancy
- New discussion of portion sizes
- New coverage of nutrition for activity
- Updated references, with 86 new citations from 1996 to 1999

Chapter 7: Improving Body Composition

- New coverage of body composition of children and adolescents
- New discussion of the importance of setting realistic fitness goals
- New section on subjective ways of determining overweight and body composition
- New information on the latest measurement devices
- New explanation of the margin of error of various measurement techniques
- Coverage of the new BMI guidelines
- New explanation of how to determine a realistic body fat percentage
- Presentation of a new technique used for bioelectrical impedance
- Updated discussion of height-weight tables
- New discussion of the importance of waist circumference alone as a risk for heart disease

Chapter 8: Achieving a Healthy Weight

- New illustration showing locations of body fat deposition
- Updated information on the latest fad diets, including herbal weight loss aids
- New discussion of preventing weight gain and body composition changes as you age
- New information on body image and self-esteem
- New section on recognizing signs of an eating disorder and getting help
- New discussion of exercise as the key to weight maintenance
- New tips for coping with supersize portions
- New tips for evaluating weight-loss schemes
- New section on weight-loss drugs and fasting

Chapter 9: Coping with and Managing Stress

- New "how-to" tips for dealing with stress
- New information on how spirituality affects stress and reduces the likelihood of illness and disease
- New coverage of work-related stress, including a discussion of child-care issues
- Expanded coverage of stress, the immune system, and illness and disease, including an explanation of the term *psychoneuroimmunology*

Pedagogical Features

Wellness: Fundamental Concepts and Applications uses a variety of learning aids to enhance student comprehension.

Key Terms: The most important terms for student retention have been set in boldface type in the text for easy identification.

Chapter Objectives: These are introduced at the beginning of each chapter. They help the student identify the chapter's key topics. Accomplishing the objectives indicates fulfillment of the chapter's intent.

Chapter Summaries: These identify the main parts of the chapter and reinforce the chapter objectives.

Review Questions: Questions are provided to help students review and analyze material for overall understanding.

References: Accurate and current documentation is given at the end of the chapters.

Suggested Readings: Additional current resources are provided for students to obtain further information.

Assessment Activities: Each chapter concludes with at least two Assessment Activities to help students apply the content learned in the chapter to their own decision making. The text is perforated for easy removal of the Assessment Activities.

Appendix: Food Composition Table—More than 1200 common foods and fast foods are analyzed. This comprehensive table will help students complete Assessment Activities in Chapter 6.

Glossary: A comprehensive glossary is provided at the end of the text that includes all key terms, as well as additional terms used in the text.

Supplements

An extensive package is available to adopters of *Wellness: Fundamental Concepts and Applications*. The package has been developed to help the instructor obtain maximum benefit from the text.

Instructor's Manual and Test Bank

Each chapter begins with a brief overview of the content followed by a list of the objectives for that chapter. Detailed lecture outlines and additional class activities have been developed for each chapter, and each chapter concludes with a resource section, including relevant media, software, organization sources, and additional recommended readings. The test bank includes more than 2000 questions. The manual concludes with 65 full-page transparency masters of helpful illustrations and charts.

Computerized Test Bank

This software provides a unique combination of user-friendly aids that enable the instructor to select, edit, delete, or add questions as well as construct and print tests and answer keys. The computerized test bank package is available to qualified adopters of the text in Windows and Macintosh formats.

Overhead Transparency Acetates

A total of 60 of the text's most important illustrations, diagrams, tables, and charts are available as full-color transparency acetates. These useful tools facilitate learning and classroom discussion and were chosen specifically to help explain difficult concepts. This package is also available to qualified adopters of the text.

Fitness and Wellness Supersite

www.mhhe.com/hper/physed/fitness-wellness

At our Fitness and Wellness Supersite, you can find information about our books and telecourse, learn what conventions we plan to attend, and get updates to *Health Net* and *The AIDS Booklet*. The password-protected section of the site includes fitness and wellness news, downloadable personal assessments and lab activities, digitized still images, and a PowerPoint presentation created especially for *Wellness: Fundamental Concepts and Applications*.

McGraw-Hill Online Learning Center

www.mhhe.com/anspaugh

The Online Learning Center for *Wellness: Fundamental Concepts and Applications* is a great resource for you and your students. It offers downloadable ancillaries, such as a PowerPoint presentation that corresponds to each chapter in the book. Students can take on-line quizzes, find updated health information, and log on to interactive web links.

McGraw-Hill PageOut: The Course Web Site Development Center

PageOut is a program that enables you to easily develop a website for your course. The site includes a course home page, an instructor home page, a customizable syllabus, web links, discussion areas, an on-line grade book, student web pages, and sixteen design templates. This program is now available to registered adopters of *Wellness: Fundamental Concepts and Applications*. If you adopt 200 or more copies per year of a McGraw-Hill text, our technology experts will create your website for you in 30 minutes or less. For more information, log on to **www.pageout.net/pageout.html**.

FitSolve Software

This networkable software program helps students design and implement a personalized fitness program based on their unique needs. The program's colorful graphics and easy data entry system let students focus on content and concepts. It includes cholesterol measurement options, treadmill protocols for cardiovascular assessment, the 1.5-mile run test, the Rockport Fitness Walking Test, muscle endurance and flexibility tests, and a variety of body fat measurement options.

NutriQuest™ Software and Diet/Fitness Log

Available for Windows and Macintosh, this nutrient-analysis software allows easy analysis of dietary intake, using an icon-based interface and on-screen help features. Foods for breakfast, lunch, dinner, and snacks can be selected from more than 2250 items in the database. Records can be kept for any number of days. The program can provide intake analyses for individual foods, meals, days, or an entire intake period. Intake analyses can compare nutrient values to RDA or RNI values and to the USDA Food Guide Pyramid and can provide breakdowns of fat and calories sources. An accompanying diet and fitness log motivates students to track their progress. This software can be packaged with the text for a nominal fee.

TestWell: Making Wellness Work for You

TestWell is a self-scoring, pencil-and-paper wellness assessment booklet developed by the National Wellness Institute and distributed exclusively by McGraw-Hill. It adds flexibility to any personal health or wellness course by allowing instructors to offer pre- and post-assessments at the beginning and end of the course, or at any time during the semester.

Diet and Fitness Log

This log helps students assess their diet and physical activity habits. Week-long diet and fitness logs and ten workout strength logs invite students to develop lifelong wellness programs by recording and evaluating their daily choices. Each log offers a brief introduction, followed by an evaluation section in which they can assess their improvements and setbacks.

Health Net: A Health & Wellness Guide to the Internet

This up-to-date booklet is your navigational tool for exploring the vast array of health and wellness resources on the internet. A helpful introduction provides general information about the internet. Each of the following sections in the booklet contains an annotated list of websites to supplement those given in the text.

Video Library

Choose from McGraw-Hill's videotape library, which includes selected Films for Humanities and all videos from the award-winning series *Healthy Living: Road to Wellness*.

The AIDS Booklet

This booklet, by Frank D. Cox, offers current, accurate information about HIV and AIDS: what it is, how the virus is transmitted, how the disease progresses, its prevalence among various population groups, symptoms of HIV infection, and strategies for prevention. Also included are discussions of the legal, medical, and ethical issues related to HIV/AIDS. This booklet ensures that your students have the most current information possible about this important topic.

Berkeley Wellness Letter

Available to qualified adopters, this highly regarded wellness newsletter keeps you informed of the latest developments in the field.

Acknowledgments

We wish to thank the reviewers, whose contributions have added significantly to the text. To the following, a grateful acknowledgement of their expertise and assistance:

Pat Barrett
Radford University

Joel Barton III
Lamar University

Robbi Beyer
University of Wisconsin (Oshkosh)

Evonne Bird
Truman State University

Wilson Campbell
Northeast Louisiana University

Rochelle Caroon-Santiago
McNeese State University

Linda Crawshaw
Kutztown University

Arlene Crosman
Linn-Benton Community College

Randy Deere
Western Kentucky University

Judy Dittman
Dakota State University

Mary Eagan
University of Illinois at Chicago

Betty Edgley
Oklahoma State University

Millard Fisher
DeKalb College

Mimi Frank
California State University at Dominguez Hills

Kathie Garbe
Kenesaw State College

Charles Goehl
Elmhurst College

Rick Guyton
University of Arkansas at Fayetteville

Stephen Horowitz
Bowling Green State University

William Huber
County College of Morris

Margaret Hughes
College of St. Benedict

Tammy James
West Chester University

Cathy Kennedy
Colorado State University

Vicki Kloosterhouse
Oakland Community College

Rebecca Rutt Leas
Clarion University

Mary Mahan
Miami-Dade Community College

Eva W. McGahee
North Georgia College

John McIntosh
Shoals Community College

David Moates
Manatee Community College

Sandi Morgan
San Jacinto College

Brenda Obert
University of Maine–Farmington

Gary Oden
Sam Houston State University

Ken Owen
Manatee Community College

Michael Paul
County College of Morris

Glen J. Peterson
Lakewood Community College

Brian Pritschett
Eastern Illinois University

DawnElla Rust
Stephen F. Austin State University

Steve Sansone
Chemeketa Community College

Russell F. Smiley
Normandale Community College

John G. Smith
Long Beach City College

Rod Smith
Clark College

Kenneth Sparks
Cleveland State University

Sue Stindt
Jackson Community College

James A. Streater, Jr.
Armstrong State College

Frederick Surgent
Frostburg State University

Laurel Talabere
Capital University

Michael L. Teague
University of Iowa

Luke E. Thomas
Northeast Louisiana University

Edith Thompson
Rowan College of New Jersey

Judith Walton
The University of Texas of Brownsville

Randye Williams
Missouri Western State College

Gary L. Wilson
The Citadel

Beverly Zeakes
Radford University

David J. Anspaugh
Michael H. Hamrick
Frank D. Rosato

Brief Contents

1 Wellness and Fitness for Life   1

2 Preventing Cardiovascular Disease   33

3 Increasing Cardiorespiratory Endurance   65

4 Building Muscular Strength and Endurance   97

5 Improving Flexibility   131

6 Forming a Plan for Good Nutrition   153

7 Improving Body Composition   213

8 Achieving a Healthy Weight   233

9 Coping with and Managing Stress   273

Appendix: Food Composition Table   305

Glossary   341

Credits   349

Index   351

Contents

Preface iii

1 Wellness and Fitness for Life 1
Components of Wellness 2
The Wellness Challenge 7
Achieving Lifestyle Change: A Self-Help Approach 11

Assessment Activities
1-1 Lifestyle Assessment Inventory 23
1-2 Health Locus of Control 29
1-3 Assessing Your Health Behavior 31

2 Preventing Cardiovascular Disease 33
Circulation 34
Cardiovascular Disease: A Twentieth-Century Phenomenon 36
Risk Factors for Heart Disease 38
Other Contributing Factors 51
Prevention of Heart Disease 53
Other Possible Risk Factors 54
Medical Contributions 54

Assessment Activities
2-1 What's Your Heart Attack Risk? 61
2-2 A Case Study of Bill M. 63

3 Increasing Cardiorespiratory Endurance 65
The Components of Physical Fitness 66
Cardiorespiratory Endurance 67
Cardiorespiratory Endurance and Wellness 70
Principles of Conditioning 70
Other Exercise Considerations 76
Environmental Conditions 79

Assessment Activities
3-1 The Rockport Fitness Walking Test 85
3-2 The 1.5-Mile Run/Walk Test 89
3-3 The Bench Step Test 91
3-4 Calculating Target Heart Rate 93
3-5 Design an Exercise Program 95

4 Building Muscular Strength and Endurance 97
The Health Benefits of Resistance Training 98
Anaerobic Exercise 99
Muscular Strength 99
Muscle Contraction and Resistance Training 100
Muscular Endurance 111
Principles of Resistance Training 112
Ergogenic Aids 113
Keeping a Daily Training Log 115

Assessment Activities
4-1 Calculation of Strength (Selected Muscle Groups) 119
4-2 Muscular Endurance 121
4-3 Abdominal Muscular Endurance—the Canadian Trunk Strength Test 123
4-4 Assessing Muscular Strength and Endurance with Selected Calisthenic Exercises 125
4-5 Resistance Training Log 129

5 Improving Flexibility 131
Flexibility and Wellness 132
Developing a Flexibility Program 132
When to Stretch 132
Types of Stretching 133

Flexibility Assessment 139
Preventing Back and Neck Pain 139

Assessment Activities

5-1 Sit-and-Reach Test 145
5-2 Shoulder Flexion Test 147
5-3 Sling Test 149
5-4 Trunk Extension 151

6 Forming a Plan for Good Nutrition 153

Nutrition and Health 154
Essential Nutrients 154
Other Nutrients with Unique Health Benefits 170
Putting Nutrition to Work 174
Other Nutrition Issues of Concern 185
Food Labels 190
Changes in American Eating Patterns 192
Planning a Nutrition Strategy for Wellness 193

Assessment Activities

6-1 Assessing Your Carbohydrate and Protein RDA 199
6-2 Assessing Your Maximum Fat and Saturated Fat Intakes 201
6-3 Nutrient Intake Assessment 203
6-4 How Does Your Diet Compare with the Recommended Diet? 207
6-5 Do You Have Fatty Habits? 209
6-6 Eating Behaviors to Consider 211

7 Improving Body Composition 213

Obesity 214
Overweight 214
Regional Fat Distribution 216
Methods for Measuring Body-Weight Status 218
Measurement of Body Fat 219
Selected Methods for Measuring Body Composition 219

Assessment Activities

7-1 Using BMI to Estimate Body-Weight Status and Calculate Desirable Body Weight 229
7-2 Calculating Desirable Body Weight from Percent Body Fat 231

8 Achieving a Healthy Weight 233

Americans' Obsession with Body Weight 234
Defining the Problem 235
Health Aspects of Obesity 236
Weight Loss: A New Attitude Emerges 237
Development of Obesity 237
Causes of Obesity 238
Dieting and Exercise: Strategies for Weight Maintenance or Weight Loss 243
Regular Exercise Is the Key to Weight Management: Make It Fun 254
Eating Disorders 255
Principles of Weight Management: Putting It All Together 258

Assessment Activities

8-1 Assessing Your Body Image 265
8-2 Calculating Caloric Expenditure Through Exercise 267
8-3 Estimating Your Basal Metabolic Rate 269
8-4 Assessing Calorie Costs of Activities 271

9 Coping with and Managing Stress 273

What is Stress? 274
Sources of Stress and Warning Signs 276
Factors Generating a Stress Response 277
Physiological Responses to Stress 277
Self-Esteem and Stress 280
Personality and Stress 282
Dealing with Stress 283
Relaxation Techniques 283
Selecting a Stress-Reducing Technique 288

Assessment Activities

9-1 Life Stressors 291
9-2 How Stressed Are You? 293
9-3 Stress Style: Body, Mind, Mixed? 295
9-4 Identification of Coping Styles 297
9-5 How Hardy Are You? 299
9-6 Time-Management Worksheet 301
9-7 Analyzing Your Use of Time 303

Appendix: Food Composition Table 305

Glossary 341

Credits 349

Index 351

Wellness and Fitness for Life

Key Terms

contracting
countering
health-behavior gap
health disparities
lifestyle diseases
locus of control
psychosomatic diseases
risk factors
self-efficacy
self-help
shaping up
transtheoretical model of behavioral change
wellness

Goals for Behavior Change

- Implement four new health-promoting behaviors.
- Increase physical activity to improve overall wellness.
- Choose and implement three countering strategies.
- Formulate a self-help plan for lifestyle change.

Objectives

After completing this chapter, you will be able to do the following:

- Discuss the wellness approach to healthy living.
- Identify benefits of living a wellness lifestyle.
- Describe the dimensions of wellness.
- Cite evidence of the relationship between physical health problems and social, emotional, and spiritual stressors.
- Identify health disparities that exist in the United States.
- Compare and contrast the major influences on the health of Americans today with those of Americans of the past.
- Identify and discuss the main wellness challenges for Americans.
- Identify obvious and subtle factors that help shape behavior.
- Discuss some of the underlying assumptions of lifestyle change.
- Identify and describe the six stages of change.
- Describe strategies that can be useful in designing and implementing an action plan for change.

ood health is one of our most cherished possessions, one that is often taken for granted until it is lost. Some people convincingly argue that everything else in life is secondary to good health. For many, it is not difficult to recall instances when life's goals, whether academic, career, or family, small or large, immediate or long-range, seemed unimportant because of sudden illness or a long-term debilitating health crisis.

Fortunately, the prospects of good health for Americans have never been better. The extent to which good health is realized is contingent on many factors. Chief among these factors are our actions and the choices we make. We can make choices that will promote health and well-being, prevent or delay the premature onset of many chronic illnesses, and improve our quality of life (see Real-World Wellness: Benefits of Living a Wellness Lifestyle). Staying healthy is not just a matter of common sense. Rather, it is a lifelong process that requires self-awareness, introspection, reflection, inquiry, accurate information, and action. This process relies on the concept of wellness and implies that each of us has the opportunity and the obligation to assume responsibility for factors that are under our control and to shape our health destiny. The wellness approach represents a formidable challenge because the processes leading to today's serious health threats are insidious, often originate in childhood or adolescence, flourish throughout adulthood, and finally culminate in full-blown disease in middle age or later. Lifestyle interventions that are initiated late in life produce limited success, but begun early in life they have maximum effect.

Components of Wellness

Wellness is defined as the continuous, active process of becoming aware of the different areas in one's life, identifying the areas that need improvement, and then making choices that will facilitate attainment of a higher level of health and well-being.[1] Wellness is a process rather than a goal. It means developing attitudes and engaging in behaviors that enhance quality of life and maximize personal potential. Although wellness implies working toward a highly developed level of health, it does not imply making the best choice in every situation or achieving "perfect wellness."

Consider the brief profiles of David, Susan, Carlos, and Maria. How would you rate each of them in terms of health and wellness?

> David is physically active, places a high priority on his social life, barely makes passing grades in school, and engages in binge drinking almost every weekend. Susan is a perfectionist and her grades reflect it. To her, a B means

Real-World Wellness

Benefits of Living a Wellness Lifestyle

I am a full-time student, work twenty plus hours a week, and help with family responsibilities. At the same time, I'm trying to maintain my academic scholarship. There just isn't enough time in the day to be concerned about health and wellness. What am I to gain from a wellness lifestyle?

A wellness lifestyle offers the following benefits:

- Increases energy level and productivity at work and school
- Decreases absenteeism from school and work
- Decreases recovery time after illness or injury
- Supplies the body with proper nutrients
- Improves awareness of personal needs and the ways to meet them
- Expands and develops intellectual abilities
- Increases the ability to communicate emotions to others and to act assertively rather than aggressively or passively
- Promotes the attitude that life's difficulties are challenges and opportunities rather than overwhelming threats
- Acts from an internal locus of control
- Increases ability to cope with stress and resist depression
- Improves the cardiorespiratory system
- Increases muscle tone, strength, flexibility, and endurance
- Improves physical appearance
- Helps prevent or delay the premature onset of some forms of chronic disease
- Regulates and improves overall body function
- Promotes self-confidence
- Delays the aging process
- Promotes social awareness and the ability to reach out to, understand, and care about others

> failure. She spends an inordinate amount of time studying, regularly skips meals, has no physical activity outlet, and rarely socializes. Her family tells her to "get a life." She needs the entire weekend to recover from the stress of academics. Carlos runs 3 miles every day, works out with weights 3 times a week, eats a balanced diet almost every day, has a close circle of friends, refuses to use his seat belt when driving, and smokes an average of two packs

of cigarettes daily. Maria is a worrier. She makes good grades but is rarely satisfied. Her eating practices are exemplary, but she is constantly counting fat grams and calories and rarely looks forward to mealtime. She is self-conscious about her weight and occasionally engages in bulimic practices.

Figure 1-1 depicts how health moves along a continuum from optimal health to premature death. Your position on this continuum is always subject to change and is affected by many factors, including physical health, activity level, nutritional patterns, personal demands, career goals, time of year, and effectiveness in managing stress. The direction you move on the continuum and your place on the continuum at any given time are largely determined by the activities you pursue and your attitudes toward these activities. These activities and attitudes can prevent illness and promote health or can destroy peace of mind and physical well-being. Because your behaviors are intrinsic to your health, you must learn to assume responsibility for your health by developing the skills and acquiring the knowledge to improve it.

In the past, medicine approached wellness from a different perspective. It emphasized the treatment of diseases rather than their prevention. It demanded no more than passive participation by the patient in the decision-making process. Now people are encouraged to become active participants in their health care, to exercise control over wellness **risk factors** (factors or conditions that threaten wellness and increase the chances of developing or contracting disease), to shape their lifestyles to promote health, and to serve as partners with health care providers in making medical decisions. This approach places the responsibility for wellness on the individual.

HealthQuest Activities

- Use the Wellboard to report your life score (number of years out of 114) and the score percentages for each of the eight health areas.
- Fill out the Wellboard using data from a fictional college student. On the first assessment screen, change the demographics to show how gender, ethnicity, age, marital status, and community affect average life expectancy.

Achieving a high level of wellness requires constant balance and maintenance of certain components (figure 1-2): spiritual, social, physical, emotional, intellectual, occupational, and environmental.

Spiritual

Spirituality is a belief in a source of value that transcends the boundaries of the self but also nurtures the self. Everyone has a personal perception of spirituality. The spiritual component provides meaning and direction in life and enables you to grow, learn, and meet new challenges. Spiritual wellness includes developing a strong sense of values, ethics, and morals. It overlaps

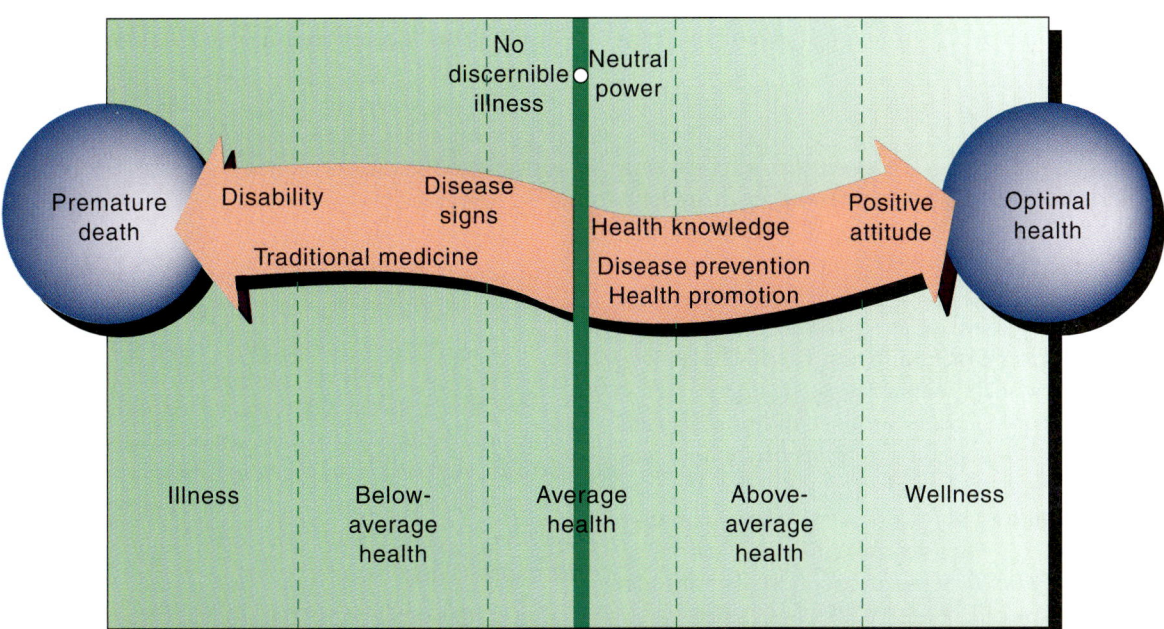

Figure 1-1 The Health Continuum

4 **Wellness** Fundamental Concepts and Applications

Figure 1-2 The Seven Components of Wellness

with the emotional component of wellness (described later). While spirituality may relate to religious precepts, it does not necessarily adhere to any particular religious structure (see Nurturing Your Spirituality: Can Spirituality Improve Your Physical Health?).

Social

Being social means having the ability to interact successfully with people and one's personal environment. Social health is the ability to develop and maintain intimacy with others and to have respect and tolerance for those with different opinions and beliefs. Numerous studies report on the advantage patients who are surrounded by a network of family and friends have over patients without a social support system in recovering from surgery or coping with chronic conditions. Social contacts are even being studied in terms of communicable diseases. Researchers from Carnegie Mellon University gave 276 healthy volunteers nasal sprays containing one of two cold viruses. Volunteers with large relationship networks developed fewer cold symptoms and infections than did people with smaller networks. Researchers pointed out that what mattered was not the total number of friends, but the number of types of relationship. People with six or more relationship types (parents, siblings, schoolmates, coworkers, roommates, and community acquaintances) had 4.2 times fewer colds than did those who had one to three types. The study defined a relationship as speaking with a person at least every two weeks.[2] The investigation revealed that a lack of diverse social contacts is a stronger risk factor for colds than is smoking, low vitamin C intake, or elevated stress hormones.[3]

Physical

The physical component of wellness involves the ability to carry out daily tasks, develop cardiorespiratory and muscular fitness, maintain adequate nutrition and a healthy body fat level, and avoid abusing alcohol and other drugs or using tobacco products. In general, physical health is an investment in positive lifestyle habits. Separate chapters in this text are devoted to many of these physical dimensions of wellness.

Emotional

Emotional wellness is the ability to control stress and to express emotions appropriately and comfortably. Emotional health is the ability to recognize and accept

Chapter 1 Wellness and Fitness for Life 5

Nurturing Your Spirituality

Can Spirituality Improve Your Physical Health?

It's all in your mind. Or is it in your body? Or both? The interconnections between mind and body are the bases for many types of alternative health practices. Spirituality is believing in a source of value that transcends the boundaries of the self but also nurtures the self. Mind-body medicine builds upon spirituality, encouraging methods for improving the body by altering the mind. The National Institutes of Health (NIH) suggests the following spiritual practices:

- *Psychotherapy* focuses on the mental and emotional health of the patient and has been proven to reduce the amount of time required to recover from an illness.
- *Support groups* give patients the consolation that others have endured similar health challenges and survived, instilling hope.
- *Meditation,* formerly associated solely with religious practice, is a self-governed exercise for relaxation. Regular practice of meditation is recommended for reducing blood pressure and anxiety and increasing the quality of life and longevity.
- *Imagery* includes use of all the senses to encourage attitude change, behavior, or physiological responses. Uses of imagery include pain control in cancer patients and increasing immunity in elderly patients.
- *Hypnosis* is an ancient practice molded to fit modern needs. Today physicians, dentists, psychologists, and other mental health professionals utilize hypnosis to help people overcome addictions, control pain, and deal with phobias.
- *Biofeedback* provides patients with a picture of what is occurring physiologically in their bodies and an understanding of how trial-and-error adjustments of mental processes can affect these physiological behaviors. This technique is used in treatment for a wide variety of disorders, such as epilepsy, respiratory diseases, migraines, vascular disorders, and hypertension.

Enjoyable physical activity improves wellness inside and out.

- *Yoga* is a disciplined practice of altering mental and physiological processes previously thought to be outside an individual's control. These alterations, performed on a regular basis, can reduce anxiety, lower blood pressure, treat arthritis, and increase the efficiency of the heart.
- *Dance therapy* uses body movement for therapeutic purposes. It is proven effective for achieving such goals as improving self-concept and self-esteem, minimizing fears, reducing bodily tension, improving circulatory and respiratory functions, promoting healing, and reducing depression.
- *Music therapy* puts to good use the power of music on the psyche. Do you ever listen to music to make you feel better? So do stroke, Parkinson's, brain-injury, cancer, anxiety, cerebral palsy, and burn patients.
- *Art therapy* uses self-expression through art to enhance healing. Art therapy is used with patients who are being treated for burns, emotional problems, chemical addictions, and sexual abuse.
- *Prayer and mental healing* involves communication with some form of higher power. A wide variety of healing techniques fall within this category. Examples are being physically touched by a religious healer or experiencing healing through personal prayer or attendance at church. Studies link regular church attendance with reduced chance of dying from stroke or heart disease, lower blood pressure, lower suicide rates, and reduced depression.

feelings and not be defeated by setbacks and failures. Achieving emotional wellness allows you to experience life's ups and downs with enthusiasm and grace and maintain satisfying relationships with others.[4]

Many studies report on the connection between wellness and emotional health. Anger, for example, is a powerful emotion that has consistently been found to increase the risk of heart attacks. In a recent study of 1305 men, those men who had high anger scores on a personality test were 2.5 times more likely to suffer heart attack symptoms as were their peers with low anger scores.[5] In another study of 1623 patients, 8 percent of heart attack victims had experienced episodes of anger within one day of their heart attacks. Researchers concluded that episodes of anger more than doubled the risk of a heart attack.[6] Irritable bowel syndrome, sometimes referred to as *spastic colon,* is another physical problem thought to have emotional ties.

People with this condition experience various abdominal symptoms ranging from severe cramping to diarrhea and are often subjected to countless diagnostic tests. While traditional treatments include diet therapies and medications, recent studies have shown that treatments aimed at reducing emotional stressors are much more successful.[7]

Many other health problems are rooted in emotional stressors. Health conditions ranging from hives to cancer may have as their origin a breakdown in the body's immune system caused by the body's response to emotional stressors. These stressors, by disrupting the body's delicate balance of powerful hormones, may serve as the triggering mechanism for myriad health problems. The growing acceptance of stress-coping techniques, like those presented in Chapter 9 of this text, is evidence of the trend toward nonphysical strategies for preventing and treating many health problems.

Intellectual

The intellectual component of wellness involves the ability to learn and use information effectively for personal, family, and career development. Intellectual wellness means striving for continued growth and learning to deal with new challenges effectively. It means acting on accepted principles of wellness and assuming responsibility for eliminating the discrepancy between knowledge and behavior, often referred to as the **health-behavior gap.** For example, people know that they should wear their seat belts and that they should not smoke, yet many people do not buckle up and continue to use tobacco products. For wellness to occur, people must internalize information and act on it.

An intellectually well person understands and applies the concepts of locus of control and self-efficacy. **Locus of control** refers to a person's view or attitude about his or her role in wellness and illness. A person's locus of control may be either internal or external. When people view problems concerning their health or other parts of their lives as generally out of their control (when they view themselves as being at the mercy of other people, places, and events), they have an external locus of control. On the other hand, people who have an internal locus of control view their own behaviors as having significant effects, feel that they are at least partially the masters of their fate, and recognize that they can change the course of their health. People with an internal locus of control are more likely to succeed in wellness activities, because they assume the necessary responsibility for their actions. Assessment Activity 1-2 at the end of this chapter will help you determine whether you have an internal or external locus of control.

Another influence on intellectual wellness is self-efficacy. **Self-efficacy** refers to a person's belief in his or her ability to accomplish a specific task or behavior. Perhaps the most important influence on the achievement of a wellness goal is the perception that it can be accomplished. Although the support of others is a source of encouragement, success is likely to require generating a personal sense of competence. Self-efficacy is not earned, inherited, or acquired; it is something you bestow on yourself.

For high-level wellness to be achieved, people must see themselves as successful and believe that they can accomplish a task. Although locus of control establishes an attitude toward one's role in achieving wellness, self-efficacy establishes behavior. Self-efficacy links knowing what to do and actually accomplishing the task. Together, an internal locus of control and a strong sense of self-efficacy are powerful tools in promoting wellness and coping with illness. Evidence of this connection is apparent in a countless number of scientific studies. For example, in a thirteen-year study of 2832 Americans, researchers at the National Center for Health Statistics found that heart disease patients with a more internal locus of control coupled with a strong sense of self-efficacy were 12 times less likely to die of heart disease than were their peers with an external locus of control or a poor sense of self-efficacy or both.[8]

Occupational

Occupational wellness is the ability to achieve a balance between work and leisure time. Attitudes about work, school, career, and career goals greatly affect work or school performance and interactions with others. Striving for occupational wellness adds focus to your life and allows you to find personal satisfaction in your life through work.

Environmental

Environmental wellness is the ability to promote health measures that improve the standard of living and quality of life in the community, including laws and agencies that safeguard the physical environment.

To illustrate the impact of environment on wellness, consider the differences in mortality (incidence of deaths) and morbidity (incidence of sickness) between earlier times and today. At the beginning of the twentieth century, the average life expectancy of Americans was 47 years. Today, at the end of the twentieth century, it is 76.5 years,[9] an all-time high. In 1900, communicable or infectious diseases (diseases that can be transmitted from one person to another) were the major causes of death. Influenza, pneumonia, tuberculosis, smallpox, polio, diphtheria, and dysentery were often fatal and were greatly feared. Only 50 percent of children were expected to reach their fifth birthday. Environmental conditions were appalling; water was dirty and food was often unsafe for consumption. People generally had little control over their health, and prospects for a long life were greatly influenced by fate and circumstance. By comparison, children born today have a 99 percent rate of survival to their fifth birthday. Governmental agencies at the federal, state, and local levels now assume responsibility for protecting health and preventing infectious diseases. Vaccinations have eradicated many dreaded diseases. The world food supply has more than doubled.[10] Adult literacy has increased. Mind-boggling advancements in medical technology have given rise to diagnostic and surgical procedures far beyond the wildest imaginations of early–twentieth–century physicians. Still, even with all of the discoveries of modern medicine, the greatest improvement in the health of Americans is due to a much more basic element of the environment: safe water. No other factor, not even vaccinations or antibiotics, has had as significant an impact on mortality reduction and population growth as safe water.[11]

Today, environmental influences include more than safe water, food, and air. Recent developments in countries such as Russia, where the death rate in 1995 outstripped the birth rate by 1.6 times and the mortality rate was as much as 77 percent higher than it was in 1990,[12] are grim reminders of the effect of the political environment on health and wellness. Here in the United States, subtle influences such as the socioeconomic factors of income, housing, and education play a critical role in the health status of various population groups.

Health disparities (health differences), a term that refers to the disproportionate prevalence of diseases and health problems among certain population groups, have had an important impact on the incidence and severity of many health conditions. The Surgeon General of the United States has identified ninety-three health areas that are related to these disparities (see Just the Facts: Eliminating Health Disparities—Goals for *Healthy People 2010*).

An important assumption of the wellness approach to living is that good health is best achieved by balancing each of the seven components. The body, mind, and spirit are inseparably linked. When they work together in a fully unified, integrated biological system, the body can ward off or overcome many diseases. When any of these components breaks down, wellness is threatened. Although the association between disease and physical causes (such as pathogens) is obvious, some people are reluctant to accept the association between illness and its mental, social, and spiritual aspects.

Nonphysical causes of illness are intangible and difficult to assess. Many people experience poor health because of guilt, anger, hostility, poor interpersonal skills, loneliness, anxiety, and depression. Any of these factors can interfere with the body's immune system and lay the foundation for the disease process. Medical records are replete with examples of **psychosomatic diseases,** in which physical (soma) symptoms are caused by mental and emotional (psycho) stressors. Such symptoms are just as real as if caused by disease-producing germs. Virtually every disease involves interplay among the components of wellness. Fortunately, after a long-standing obsession with medical technology, many health care providers are beginning to focus on treating the whole person, and more people are demanding more than test-tube medical care.

Assessment Activity 1-1 at the end of this chapter provides an evaluation of various aspects of wellness.

The Wellness Challenge

The most serious health problems of today are largely caused by the way people live and are referred to as **lifestyle diseases.** The leading causes of death in the United States among all age groups are heart disease, cancer, and stroke; they account for almost two-thirds of all deaths (table 1-1).[13] These are chronic diseases that are often caused by behaviors established early in life. *Chronic diseases* are health conditions that often begin gradually, have multiple causes, and usually persist for an indefinite time. Heart disease, diabetes, arthritis, and hypertension are examples of chronic illnesses. By contrast, *acute illnesses* come on suddenly, often have identifiable causes, are usually treatable, and often disappear in a short time. Appendicitis, pneumonia, and influenza are examples of acute illnesses.

Diseases are, of course, not the only causes of death. Accidents, homicide, and suicide are the leading killers of Americans between the ages of 15 and 24. Most (77 percent) accidental deaths among this age group involve motor vehicle accidents, many of which are alcohol related. For young adults 25 to 44 years old, accidents, cancer, heart disease, suicide, human immunodeficiency virus (HIV) infection, and homicide are the leading causes of death.

For too many Americans these conditions reflect the dangers of negative lifestyle choices. In spite of this fact, much of Americans' health-related anxiety involves exotic diseases. The current fear that some sort of strangely mutated disease will soon pose the greatest threat to life on Earth ironically coincides with a reduction in attention to chronic diseases that do kill in large numbers. The fear of bizarre pathogens leading to

Just the Facts

Eliminating Health Disparities—Goals for *Healthy People 2010*

Healthy People 2000 is a document that was issued in 1990 by the U.S. federal government. Its purpose was to establish national health goals to be reached by 2000. The document set goals for eliminating disparities (differences) in health status and health risks among population groups. Health objectives were established for racial and ethnic minority groups, women, people with low incomes, people with disabilities, and specific age groups, such as children, adolescents, and the elderly. However, few of these target objectives set out to achieve equity by the year 2000. *Healthy People 2010*, on the other hand, is setting the goal of eliminating these disparities during the next decade.

Despite notable progress in the overall health of the nation, African-Americans, Latinos, American Indians, Alaskan Natives, and Pacific Islanders continue to shoulder more of the burden of illness and death compared with the U.S. population as a whole. These disparities are even greater if comparisons are made between each racial and ethnic group and the Caucasian population:

- Racial and ethnic minorities constitute about 25 percent of the total U.S. population, yet they account for nearly 54 percent of all AIDS cases.
- Infant mortality rates are 12 times higher for Native Americans and 22 times higher for African-Americans.
- Native Americans suffer from diabetes at nearly 3 times the average rate, African-Americans suffer 70 percent higher rates, and the prevalence of diabetes among Latinos is nearly double.
- Vietnamese women suffer from cervical cancer at nearly 5 times the rate of other women.
- African-American men under 65 suffer from prostate cancer at nearly twice the rate of other men.
- African-American men suffer from heart disease at nearly twice the rate of other men.

The demographic changes anticipated over the next decade magnify the importance of addressing health disparities. Groups that currently have poorer health status are expected to grow as a proportion of the total U.S. population; therefore, the future health of the United States as a whole will be influenced by our success in eliminating health disparities. *Healthy People 2010* identified ninety-three health areas in which the disparity is 25 percent or greater between the general population and at least one select population. Following are some of these disparities classified by age, disability, socioeconomic status, geographic location, and race and ethnicity:

Age
- Sedentary lifestyle
- Alcohol-related motor vehicle deaths
- Homicides
- Fall-related deaths
- Motor-vehicle crash deaths
- Drowning deaths
- Residential fire deaths

continued

---

runaway deaths in the United States has been fueled primarily by newspaper headlines, fictional books, and movies. Four recent headlines serve as examples:

- Mad cow disease "jumps" to humans.
- "Bird flu" causes Hong Kong to slaughter every chicken.
- Kenya disease killing humans, animals.
- Fatal, no-name virus leaps from animals to humans.

Although the appearance of an unstoppable, overwhelming disease is possible and the spread of new viruses in a global community is a genuine concern, the real threats to Americans are mundane and are less likely to be featured as the lead stories in the evening news. These threats to health have been the focus of the Public Health Service of the Department of Health and Human Services (DHHS) for more than a decade and are published as objectives in the landmark document *Healthy People 2000: National Health Promotion and Disease Prevention Objectives*. These objectives, which are now being updated, serve as reminders of the health threats most likely to affect Americans.

Healthy lifestyles that involve diet, physical activity, and personal health habits offer the most potential for preventing health problems or delaying them until much later in life. More specifically, the following twelve steps-for-life,[14] developed by the internationally

Just the Facts
continued

- Hip fractures among adults 65 years old and older
- Nonfatal poisoning
- Asthma hospitalizations
- Cervical cancer screenings
- Gonorrhea infection screenings
- Tetanus boosters in the last ten years
- Pelvic inflammatory disease

Gender
- Smokeless tobacco use
- Suicides
- Diagnosis/treatment of depression
- Homicides
- Unintentional injury deaths
- Drowning deaths
- Hip fractures among adults 65 years old and older
- Nonfatal spinal cord injuries
- Oral cancer deaths

Disability
- Sedentary lifestyle
- Overweight

Socioeconomic status (related to income, education, and employment)
- Vigorous physical activity
- Cigarette smoking
- Smoking cessation during pregnancy
- Diagnosis and treatment of dental caries (cavities)
- Complete tooth loss among those 65 years or older
- Breast cancer screenings

Race/Ethnicity
- Coronary heart disease
- Sedentary lifestyle
- Cancer deaths
- Overweight
- Prevalence of diabetes
- Cigarette smoking
- Smokeless tobacco use
- Stroke deaths
- Drug-related deaths
- Teen pregnancies
- Suicides
- Homicides
- Firearm-related deaths
- Residential fire deaths
- Asthma hospitalizations
- Dental caries
- Gingivitis
- Oral cancer deaths
- Infant deaths
- Fetal deaths
- Low birth-weight incidence
- Prenatal care in the first trimester
- HIV infection incidence
- Influenza, pneumonia, tetanus vaccinations

---

renowned Cooper Institute for Aerobics Research, provide the framework for promoting health and improving the quality of life:

1. Exercise regularly.
2. Eat more fresh vegetables and fruit, high-fiber foods, and whole grains and drink more water.
3. Limit animal fat, cholesterol, and sodium in the diet.
4. Supplement the diet with calcium and antioxidant vitamins.
5. Pursue and maintain ideal body weight.
6. Stop illegal drug use and abstain from or limit alcohol consumption.
7. Terminate smoking and use of smokeless tobacco.
8. Avoid excessive sun exposure or wear sunblock.
9. Fasten seat belts.
10. Obtain good prenatal health care.
11. Regularly have medical checkups and perform self-exams.
12. Keep immunizations up-to-date.

Many experts emphasize, in addition to the twelve steps just listed, the need to practice safe sex habits. HIV infections are a serious health problem and one of the leading causes of death in young people. The dramatic drop in the death rate from complications of HIV infections, a nearly 50 percent drop in 1997, has led to a false sense of optimism about the spread of this disease. Most of the drop in HIV-related deaths is due

Table 1-1 Leading Causes of Death for All Ages and for Ages 25–44

	All ages		Ages 25–44	
Cause	Number	Rank	Number	Rank
All causes	2,314,729		133,602	
Heart disease	725,790	1	15,800	3
Cancer	537,390	2	21,555	2
Stroke	159,877	3	3,358	8
Chronic obstructive lung disease	110,637	4	—	—
Accidents	92,191	5	25,477	1
Motor vehicle accidents	42,420	—	13,837	—
Other accidents	49,772	—	11,640	—
Pneumonia and influenza	88,383	6	1,933	10
Diabetes mellitus	62,332	7	2,405	9
Suicide	29,725	8	12,008	4
Nephritis (kidney disease)	25,570	9	—	—
Chronic liver disease and cirrhosis	24,765	10	3,890	7
Septicemia (blood poisoning)	22,604	11	—	—
Alzheimer's disease	22,527	12	—	—
Homicide and legal intervention	18,774	13	8,287	6
Human immunodeficiency virus infection	16,685	14	11,166	5
All other causes*	345,791		27,733	

*Figures are based on weighted data; categories may not add to totals.
SOURCE: Ventura, S. J., R. N. Anderson, J. A. Martin, and B. L. Smith. 1998. Births and deaths: Preliminary data for 1997. *National Vital Statistics Report* 47(4).

to the availability of powerful new drug treatments. Sexual habits remain a serious concern. People must consider the impact of their personal health behaviors on their health, life expectancy, and quality of life.

The risk factor most strongly associated with premature death and chronic disease is cigarette smoking. In studies that try to pinpoint the actual cause of death, tobacco use is responsible for 20 percent of all deaths. Experts state that it is the single most preventable cause of death and disease in the United States. It is followed in descending order by poor diet and lack of exercise, alcohol, infectious agents, pollutants, firearms, risky sexual behavior, motor vehicles, and illicit drug use (see figure 1-3). Donna Shalala, Secretary of the U.S. Department of Health and Human Services, described the seriousness of tobacco use in testimony before the Senate:

> Today, nearly 3,000 young people across our country will begin smoking regularly. Of these 3,000 young people, 1,000 will lose that gamble to the diseases caused by smoking. The net effect of this is that among children living in America today, 5 million will die an early preventable death because of a decision made as a child.[15]

For the smoker, his or her primary wellness challenge is to stop smoking; if that proves impossible, significant reduction in the frequency and duration of smoking will attenuate some of the risk factors that threaten health.

Second in importance to the smoker and first in importance to the nonsmoker as a wellness challenge are improvements in diet and an increase in physical activity. The medical research community has directed considerable attention to the benefits of a diet that conforms to the latest *Dietary Guidelines for Americans*, which were issued in 1995 by the United States Department of Agriculture (USDA). Few diseases escape the influence of nutrition. Evidence is growing that the major threats to wellness are related to dietary habits. Chapter 6 documents the health benefits of diets low in saturated fat and high in fruits, vegetables, and grain products.

The most formidable wellness challenge for Americans of all ages, however, is neither smoking cessation nor improvements in dietary habits. It is related to sedentary lifestyles. More people are at risk due to physical inactivity than to any of the other risk factors.[16] Less than 10 percent of the U.S. adult population reports regular, vigorous physical activity for twenty minutes or longer three or more days per week. Only about 25 percent of adults report physical activity on five or more days per week for thirty

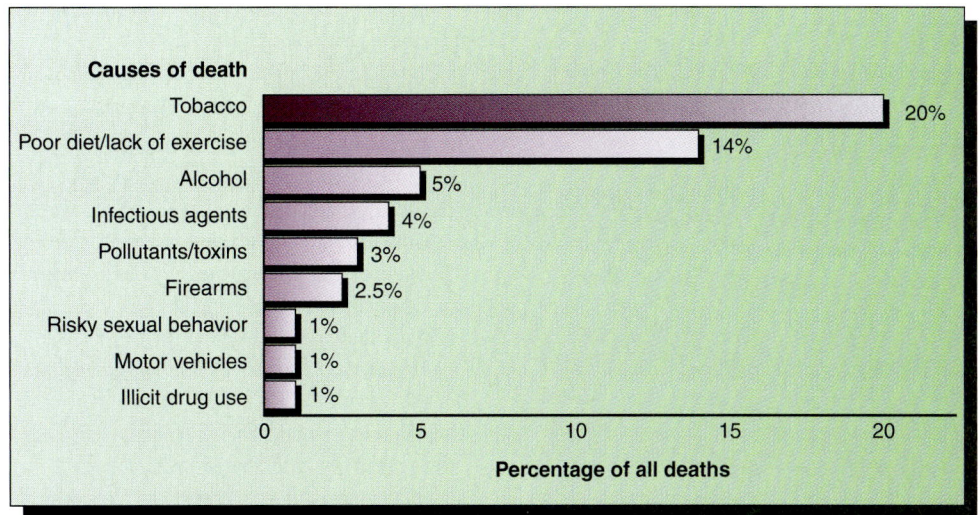

Figure 1-3 Causes of Death in the United States

Running is a challenging activity that builds cardiorespiratory endurance.

minutes or longer, and another 25 percent of adults do not participate in any regular physical activity.[17] Americans' propensity for sedentary lifestyles comes at a time when evidence of the benefits of an active lifestyle is compelling. Physically active people outlive those who are inactive, and physical activity enhances the quality of life for people of all ages. Physical inactivity is regarded by many respected researchers as a risk factor for heart disease that is comparable to cigarette smoking, high blood pressure, and high blood cholesterol.

The Surgeon General's hallmark report *Physical Activity and Health*[17] brought a historic new perspective to exercise, fitness, and physical activity by shifting the emphasis from intensive aerobic exercise to a broader range of health-enhancing physical activity regardless of age (see Wellness Across the Generations: It's Never Too Late for Wellness!). For those who are inactive, even small increases in physical activity are associated with measurable health benefits (see Just the Facts: Physical Activity and Health—Selected Highlights). The benefit of physical activity is the underlying theme of this text and, ideally, will serve as an impetus for you to establish an active lifestyle.

Achieving Lifestyle Change: A Self-Help Approach

A fundamental assumption underlying lifestyle-change programs is that behavior is a learned response. For example, we are not born with a taste for some foods and a dislike for others. And using seat belts is not a function of heredity. Like most other behaviors, health behaviors are learned responses to both obvious and subtle influences. This learning begins at birth and continues throughout life. It is important to remember that this is just as true for behaviors that promote wellness as for behaviors that diminish it.

Wellness Across the Generations

It's Never too Late for Wellness!

"Well, I've been living this way for forty years. I'm too old to change my ways. Why change now?" Does this sound familiar? Do you feel that taking steps toward wellness is only for those younger than you? If so, think again. It is never too early or too late to begin improving your wellness. You can begin changing your behavior today and reap the benefits within a very short amount of time.

If you are a smoker, quitting smoking creates immediate positive results and lasting improvements in your health status. Within twenty minutes of smoking your last cigarette, your blood pressure will drop to its normal level. After eight hours, the amount of carbon monoxide in your blood will return to normal. Within five years, the risk of dying from lung cancer will be cut in half. In fifteen years, your risk of dying from cardiovascular disease will be as low as that of someone who does not smoke.*

People of all ages fall victim to violence and accidental injury. Taking steps to protect yourself from rape, homicide, sexual harassment, and injury caused by car accidents, fires, and falls is a critical part of maintaining your health. These steps are not just for children and young adults; they are for all of us.

Leotards and "meat market" exercise gyms not your style? You might want to consider just going for a walk or riding a bicycle. These wide-ranging benefits of aerobic fitness might persuade you to put on your walking shoes: reduction of the risk of heart disease, prevention of hypertension, strengthening of lungs, control of weight, warding off of infections, improvement of bodily functions, and increase in longevity.

With the average life expectancy reaching well into the 70s, wouldn't you like to still be enjoying life thirty or forty years from now? Making some basic changes in your daily life today will greatly improve your chances of being around for a much longer time. It's never too late to improve your wellness!

*1996. Quitters do win. *Mayo Clinic Health Letter* 14(6):2.

Examples of obvious influences that help shape behavior include parents and family, role models, advertising, and social norms. In many instances these influences are combined to form a single powerful influence on behavior, such as exemplified by an advertisement for cigarettes using "ideal" masculine or feminine models, depending on the brand of cigarettes and the target population. Advertisers are successful not only at marketing products but also at influencing people to think they need those products.

Subtle forces also shape behavior. A good example is *subliminal advertising,* a technique in which messages, words, and symbols are embedded or hidden in the pictures, sounds, or words used in advertisements. Theoretically these messages, though not directly observable, can be perceived by the subconscious mind in such a way as to influence behavior.

Much of our behavior is also motivated by psychological needs. An infant whose main source of attention and stimulation comes during feeding time may learn to associate food with the deeper psychological needs of love and affection. A parent who consistently uses food to appease an unhappy child may be inadvertently establishing a preoccupation with food that will endure far beyond childhood.

Sometimes, behavior is motivated in response to force or coercion. *Reactance motivation,* a theory of behavior that has been associated with drinking among college students, suggests that telling people to abstain completely from doing something often produces the opposite reaction. For many people it isn't difficult to recall instances in their own lives in which they behaved a certain way primarily because they were told that they could not or should not behave that way. Coercion in particular leads to the arousal of reactance, which in turn tends to reduce compliance.

These examples help to explain the myriad complex forces that contribute to behavior and illustrate why successful lifestyle change is so difficult to achieve. The hope and promise of any lifestyle-change program is that, while easier said than done, bad habits can be unlearned and new habits can be learned.

A Self-Help Plan

A **self-help** approach assumes that individuals can manage their lifestyle changes and can learn to control those features in the environment that are detrimental to health. In other words, expensive, long-term, professional help is not a prerequisite for everyone trying to make a lifestyle change. The self-help approach puts you in control of your health, requires your involvement, and permits you to determine what to do and how and when to do it. However, to be successful, this

Just the Facts

Physical Activity and Health—Selected Highlights

Here are selected highlights from the Surgeon General's Report:

- *Mortality:* Higher levels of physical activity are associated with lower mortality rates. Those who are moderately active on a regular basis have lower mortality rates than do those who are least active.
- *Cardiovascular disease:* Regular physical activity decreases the risk of cardiovascular disease. Regular physical activity is comparable to not smoking in decreasing risk of heart disease.
- *Cancer:* Regular physical activity is associated with a decreased risk of colon cancer.
- *Non–Insulin-Dependent Diabetes Mellitus:* Regular physical activity lowers the risk of developing non–insulin-dependent diabetes mellitus.
- *Osteoarthritis:* Weight-bearing physical activity is necessary for maintaining normal muscle strength, joint structure, and joint function.
- *Falling:* Promising evidence suggests that strength training and other forms of exercise in older adults preserve their ability to maintain independent living status and reduce the risk of falling.
- *Obesity:* Low levels of activity, resulting in fewer kilocalories used than consumed, contribute to the high prevalence of obesity in the United States. Physical activity may favorably affect body fat distribution.
- *Mental health:* Physical activity appears to relieve symptoms of depression and anxiety and improve mood. Regular physical activity may reduce the risk of developing depression, although further research is needed on this topic.
- *Health-related quality of life:* Physical activity appears to improve the health-related quality of life by enhancing psychological well-being and by improving physical functioning in people compromised by poor health.
- *Adverse effects:* Most musculoskeletal injuries related to physical activity are believed to be preventable by gradually working up to a desired level of activity and by avoiding excessive amounts of activity. Serious cardiovascular events can occur with physical exertion, but the net effect of regular physical activity is a lower risk of mortality from cardiovascular disease.

Source: U.S. Department of Health and Human Services. 1996. *Physical Activity and Health: A Report of the Surgeon General.* Atlanta, Ga.: U.S. Department of Health and Human Services, Centers for Disease Control and Prevention, National Center for Chronic Disease Prevention and Health Promotion.

---

approach requires considerable time and thought devoted to planning. Successful lifestyle change is almost impossible to achieve without a plan.

The self-help approach that follows is based on the **transtheoretical model of behavior change.**[18] This model of lifestyle change is presented in six stages (figure 1-4), as described next along with recommended strategies. In applying this model of change, it is helpful to remember several important assumptions:

1. Each of the six stages is well defined and entails a series of tasks that need to be completed before moving to the next stage.
2. A linear progression through the stages of change, although possible, is rare. Most people lapse at some point, and it is possible to get stuck at one stage or another. However, the important thing is to formulate a plan and act on it. Even if a relapse takes you back temporarily to an earlier stage, you are twice as likely to succeed during the next six months as a person who never tried at all.[19]
3. A key to successful change is knowing what stage you are in for the health issue or behavior at hand. Behavioral research reveals that people who try to accomplish changes they are not ready for set themselves up for failure. Similarly, too much time spent on a task already mastered—such as understanding your problem—may result in an indefinite delay in taking action.
4. Although nearly all change begins with precontemplation, only the most successful ends in termination. But you cannot skip stages. Most people who succeed follow the same road for every problem. However, you may be at different stages of change for different problems.
5. Successful behavior change does not typically happen all at once; it takes time.

Wellness on the Web Behavior Change Activities

The Health-Behavior Gap
The discrepancy between knowing what behavior is good for your health and actually doing it is called the *health-behavior gap*. The key to striving for high-level wellness is motivation, since no single principle or incident can provide the stimulus necessary to institute change and maintain positive lifestyle habits. Dr. Michael Arloski shares ten suggestions, or tenets, that have emerged from his twenty years of work as a wellness professional. He attempts to answer the critical question, "Why don't people do what they know they need to do for themselves?" Go to www.healthy.net/Library/articles/arloski/tentenets.htm. Read each of the ten tenets, choose five of them, and complete the brief self-evaluation activity for the items you selected.

Your Wellness Profile
An important first step in any lifestyle-change program is to evaluate your health history. For your personal health and wellness evaluation, visit the Wellness-Sources website at www.wellness-sources.com/eval/history.html. Answer all questions using your mouse. It is very important to answer the questions thoroughly and completely. When you're finished, click the Submit button. Then click the Back button of your browser to get to the Test Results Page for your completed evaluation.

Your Life Expectancy
The Longevity Game identifies factors that can help you lead a healthier, longer, more productive life. The game is based on information gathered by the life insurance industry, public health organizations, and scientific studies. Go to the Northwestern Mutual Life website at www.northwesternmutual.com. Scroll down and click on the Longevity Game. After completing the list of questions, click the Submit button to calculate your life expectancy. What lifestyle factors increase your life expectancy? What lifestyle factors decrease your life expectancy? What specific behaviors could you change to increase your longevity?

Stage	1. Precontemplation	2. Contemplation	3. Preparation	4. Action	5. Maintenance	6. Termination
Characteristic	Lack of awareness Denial	Awareness of the need to change Thinking about changing	Planning to change within a month Thinking about the future	Engaging in strategies Commitment to change	Greater difficulty than action stage Duration from six months to a lifetime	Problem behavior no longer an issue
Goal	Feedback on need to change Consciousness raising	More consciousness raising Emotional arousal	Public affirmation of change Development of a plan	Application of strategies Changes in environment Forming of or joining support groups Establishment of rewards Countering	Application of same strategies as in action stage	Exit from cycle of change
Stage	1. Precontemplation	2. Contemplation	3. Preparation	4. Action	5. Maintenance	6. Termination

Figure 1-4 Stages, Characteristics, and Goals of Lifestyle Change

Precontemplation stage

In this stage, individuals have no intention of changing in the near future. Precontemplators may be unaware of the health risks associated with their behaviors. Or they may feel a situation is hopeless; maybe they've tried to change before without success. They often use denial and defensiveness to keep from going forward. They feel safe in precontemplation because they can't fail there.

Strategies. Consciousness raising is a key strategy. Sometimes it comes from a visit to the doctor, a health-threatening diagnosis, a headline news story, or simple feedback from others. One way to encourage consciousness raising is to take an inventory of personal health habits and practices. A good way to start is simply to make a list of your health-promoting behaviors, practices you engage in to maintain or improve your level of wellness (see Just the Facts: Examples of Health-Promoting Behaviors). Make another list of health-inhibiting behaviors, practices that may be detrimental to your health (see Assessment Activity 1-3). If your lists are specific and identify behaviors that relate to wellness in its broadest sense (that is, the physical, social, emotional, and psychological aspects of health), comparing the two should give you insight into and information about your lifestyle.

Detailed, comprehensive lifestyle questionnaires, such as in Assessment Activity 1-1, can provide even more information about specific health practices and behavioral tendencies that can be targeted for change. Many of these questionnaires are similar to those you might complete for your physician. Regardless of the tool you use, remember that the goal is to learn more about yourself.

Contemplation stage

Contemplators have a sense of awareness of a problem behavior and begin thinking seriously about changing it. However, it is easy to get stuck in the contemplation stage for years. Perhaps making a change requires more effort than someone is willing to expend or the rewards or pleasures of the current behavior seem to outweigh the benefits of change. Traps[20] include the search for absolute certainty (nothing in life is guaranteed); waiting for the magic moment (you need to make the moment); and wishful thinking (hoping for different results without changing your behavior).

Strategies. Contemplators need more consciousness raising. Reading, studying, and enrolling in courses are good ways to promote an awareness of the potential problems associated with certain behaviors. (One goal of this text, for example, is to increase your conscious-

Examples of Health-Promoting Behaviors

Specific Behaviors Conducive to Good Health

- I avoid the extremes of too much or too little exercise.
- I get an adequate amount of sleep.
- I avoid adding sugar and salt to my food.
- I include 15 to 20 g of fiber in my diet each day.
- I plan my diet to ensure consumption of an adequate amount of vitamins and minerals.
- I brush and floss my teeth after eating.
- I avoid driving under the influence of alcohol or drugs.
- I drive within the speed limit.
- I wear my seat belt whenever traveling in an automobile.
- I avoid the use of tobacco.
- I consume fewer than two alcoholic drinks per day.
- I know the instructions provided with any drug I take.
- I do my part to promote a clean and safe environment.
- I feel positive and enthusiastic about my life.
- I can express my feelings of anger.
- I can say "no" without feeling guilty.
- I engage in activities that promote a feeling of relaxation.
- I am able to develop close, intimate relationships.
- I am interested in the views of others.
- I am satisfied with my study habits.
- I am satisfied with my spiritual life.
- I am tolerant of the values and beliefs of others.

ness of habits and practices that promote wellness and of risk factors that may threaten your health.) Getting involved in activities that expose you to information about various aspects of health and wellness allows you to focus on the negatives of your current health practices and to imagine the consequences down the line if your behavior doesn't change.

Cognitive dissonance, the internal conflict that occurs when people feel that their behavior is inconsistent with their intentions or values (such as exhibited by a smoking parent who doesn't want his or her child to smoke), helps in this stage. Also, *emotional arousal*, sometimes accomplished by watching a movie or news story on the subject in question (such as about the sudden death of a child caused by drunken driving), spurs someone to action. Social strategies also help. For example, a problem drinker might attend an Alcoholics Anonymous meeting as a way of experiencing social support for behaving differently.

Preparation stage

Most people in this stage are planning to take action within a month. They think more about the future than about the past, more about the pros of a new behavior than about the cons of the old one. Many people motivate themselves by making their intended change public rather than keeping it to themselves. This stage involves developing a plan that is customized to a person's unique circumstances and personality.

Most people make two serious mistakes when starting a lifestyle change. First, they expect miracles and set unrealistic goals. Setting goals that are too ambitious often guarantees failure. For many people the fear of failure easily discourages future efforts at a lifestyle change.

Second, people often view lifestyle change as a temporary goal rather than as a lifetime change. Perhaps more than anything else, this attitude accounts for the high *recidivism* (the tendency to revert to the original behavior) rate of many programs. One of the best examples is weight-loss programs. In weight-loss programs, for example, people typically set a goal, diet until they reach their goal, revert to their original eating habits, and invariably regain the lost weight. The proper way is to change eating habits so that they will endure for a lifetime. When people try to change some aspect of behavior, they have to deny themselves something that feels comfortable or that provides some source of enjoyment or pleasure. Denial often triggers a preoccupation that worsens the health behavior being changed. This is the reason dieters often become more interested in food during a diet. It is important to remember that the real test of a program's success is not how many people reach their goals but how many people successfully maintain that goal for at least two years (see Real World Wellness: Are You Ready for a Lifestyle Change?).

No single strategy for lifestyle change is right for everyone. The key is to get involved in planning your personal program and to use your imagination to create the most suitable plan.

Strategies. In this stage a firm, detailed plan is developed that involves (1) assessing behavior and (2) setting specific, realistic goals.

Assess behavior. Behavior assessment, the collection of data on target behaviors, is the lifeline of any lifestyle-change plan. It involves the process of counting, recording, measuring, observing, and describing. Any behavior that can be qualified is assessed.

Assessment tools are usually daily logs, journals, and diaries. Data should be collected long enough to note behavioral trends, usually for a minimum of one to two weeks.

Sometimes a behavior assessment will prompt a change in behavior without any other action. In most lifestyle-change programs a plan of action is not started until it is clear that assessment alone will not be enough to alter the behavior completely. Bootzin[21] illustrates this point by citing the experience of a friend:

> A friend of mine discovered that he was interspersing the phrase "you know" in almost every sentence he spoke. He decided to try to suppress that behavior. The first step he took—as it turned out, the only step that was required—was to record the number of times he said "you know." Each day that he recorded, his frequency of emitting that phrase decreased. Recording served as a sufficient intervention to bring that verbal behavior under control.

The assessment phase also provides clues to a person's commitment to making a change in lifestyle. A thorough, detailed log is a good sign that a person has the motivation to carry out the plan.

Behavior change, such as following a healthier diet, should be viewed as a lifetime goal, not a temporary fix.

Real-World Wellness

Are You Ready for a Lifestyle Change?

I've started an exercise program four times during the past two years. Each effort resulted in failure. I don't want to start again until I know I'm ready. How will I know that I'm ready to begin a lifestyle-change program?

If you can answer "yes" to the following questions, you are ready to begin a lifestyle-change program:

- Do you view lifestyle change as a lifetime goal rather than as a temporary, short-term goal?
- Are you willing to get personally involved in planning a lifestyle-change program?
- Are you prepared for some disappointments?
- Are you willing to experiment with different ideas?
- Do you have the patience to accept success in small increments stretched over a long period?
- Are you willing to set modest, realistic goals?
- Are you willing to establish some time benchmarks for success?
- Are you willing to make some changes in the way you live?
- Are you willing to tell others about your goals?
- Can you accept a relapse as a temporary setback rather than as a full-blown failure?
- Are you willing to formulate a plan that makes provisions for countering, avoidance, contracting, shaping up, reminders, and support?

When the assessment phase is finished, there should be sufficient information to form a behavioral profile, state specific goals, and customize an intervention program that matches goals and strategies to a person's unique circumstances and personality.

Set specific, realistic goals. Setting specific goals means setting goals that focus on concrete, observable, measurable behaviors. A behavioral goal to overcome shyness is very different from a goal that requires someone to initiate a conversation with a different person each day for the next week. If goals are specific, you know precisely what you are trying to accomplish and where, when, and how often. By using specific goals, you get instant feedback on your progress. Another way to increase specificity is to establish a timetable for achieving goals. A timetable adds structure to the plan and provides a way to evaluate progress.

Realistic behavioral goals are reasonable and relate to personal circumstances. Setting realistic goals also means forming them in the context of correct information. For example, an informed dieter knows that setting a goal to lose 10 pounds in a week is not reasonable. A more achievable goal is 1 to 2 pounds.

When setting goals, starting off small is best. Setting a modest goal initially facilitates some degree of success, which increases confidence. For complex lifestyle changes, behavioral psychologists recommend breaking down an ambitious, long-range goal into a set of intermediate goals, beginning with the easier ones and then moving gradually to more difficult ones. Goals should be structured in moderation. Extreme goals promote the erroneous attitude that lifestyle change is temporary. They create a strong sense of denial, encourage preoccupation with target behaviors, and invariably lead to failure. Exceptions include cigarette smoking, alcoholism, and drug dependence, for which abstinence is still the primary treatment.

Action stage

In this stage a person overtly makes changes in behavior, experiences, or environment. This is the busiest stage of change. It's also the stage most visible to others. New behaviors, such as exercising, not smoking, or actively changing a dietary pattern, can be observed.

Strategies. People in the action stage implement their plan for change. In doing so, they apply their sense of commitment to the change. Rewards and incentives are important elements of this stage. **Countering**, or behavior substitution, in which a new behavior is substituted for the undesirable one, is the most common and one of the most powerful strategies available to people trying to make a change. When this technique is applied, the goal is to think of a behavior that is incompatible with the one being altered. Examples include chewing gum to suppress the urge to smoke, substituting diet colas for sweetened colas, and going for a walk instead of watching television. Some effective countering techniques are summarized in Just the Facts: Countering Strategies.

Making changes in the environment is another key element of the action stage. Avoidance, or the elimination of the circumstances associated with an undesirable behavior, is a fundamental technique of the control process. A smoker cannot smoke if there are no cigarettes, an ice cream binge is not possible if there is no ice cream parlor, and loud music cannot interfere with studying if the radio is put away.

Avoidance is not limited to objects. It may also include jobs, school, and even people. If taking eighteen hours of coursework while working twenty hours per

Just the Facts
Countering Strategies

Here are some countering strategies you can use to replace problem behaviors:

- Exercising
- Cooking
- Playing a musical instrument
- Relaxing (see Chapter 9)
- Cleaning
- Doing crossword puzzles
- Walking
- Reading a book
- Calling a friend
- Going to a movie
- Keeping busy
- Learning to be more assertive
- Learning a new skill
- Joining a fitness club
- Organizing
- Playing a game
- Surfing the internet
- Learning to use new software
- Watching a favorite television show
- Practicing thought stopping (counterthinking) by substituting positive thoughts for negative ones

week is compromising your academics, you may feel justified in dropping several courses or withdrawing from school altogether if a reduction in your workload isn't possible. By the same token it may be necessary to associate less often with people who contribute to a problem behavior.

The use of reminders is also a key element of an action plan. These may be in the form of a daily planner, calendar, clocks, sticky notes, signs on a door, or a to-do list. During times when behavior change is not an issue, the list might read, "call home, 10:00 AM, library, 2:00–4:00 PM, racquetball, 4:30–5:30, dinner date, 6:00–8:30, study time, 9:00–11:00." If you are working on an action plan for lifestyle change, adding action goals is a natural extension. If, for example, you are working on social skills, you might simply add, "initiate a conversation with a classmate," or "eat lunch with someone different." A positive benefit of reminders, in addition to their reinforcement of positive behaviors, is the satisfaction that results from checking something off a list.

Contracting is another common action strategy. Written contracts tend to be more powerful than spoken ones. They usually include a statement of long-range and intermediate health goals, target dates for completion of each goal, intervention strategies, and rewards and incentives, such as "I will deposit five dollars in my new car savings account for every day that I attend all of my classes between now and the end of the semester." These contracts are not legal documents, so simplicity and creativity are in order.

Shaping up is an another essential part of lifestyle change. It requires a person to allow him- or herself opportunities to practice desired behaviors, usually in small increments. The saying "Behavior begets behavior" is the essence of shaping up. This is also true for harmful behaviors. For example, cigarette smokers rarely enjoy their first cigarette; they learn to enjoy smoking by smoking. The same is true for most beer drinkers. Typically, shaping up occurs gradually until it becomes fully integrated into one's behavioral repertoire.

The acquisition of positive health behaviors occurs the same way. A step-by-step approach, with reinforcement following each successive movement, promotes success. In overcoming a fear of flying, a person might first visit the airport; the next step might be to tour an airplane; next the person may take a seat, fasten up, and visualize flying. Each step brings the person closer to flying, each step is reinforced, and any feelings of anxiety are countered with relaxation. People forget that problem behaviors are formed cumulatively and reflect many years of conditioning. It is only reasonable to expect that acquiring a preference for a new behavior will also require considerable time, thought, and reinforcement.

Another good strategy in an action plan is the formation of a support group, which may include a roommate, family, friends, classmates, or someone who can identify with the lifestyle goal. Dieting may be easier and more tolerable when done with a friend. Two people may accomplish their goals more effectively than either can alone. For example, two roommates may be more successful at maintaining their exercise regimen together than separately. Involving someone else in the process of change makes it easier to stick to your action plan, provides a source of encouragement, and holds you accountable for your goals.

Maintenance stage

The goal in this stage is to retain the gains made during the action and other stages and to try hard to prevent a relapse. Change never ends with action. Although people tend to view maintenance as a static stage, it is actually a continuation of the action stage and can last six months to a lifetime. Programs that promise easy change usually fail to acknowledge that maintenance is a long, ongoing process. This is why trendy, extreme programs, such as many diet programs, have a high recidivism rate. People may achieve their weight-loss goal, but they cannot maintain their strategy for losing weight for life. When this happens, a person may erroneously view the action plan as a temporary strategy. This is the opposite of maintenance and lifestyle change.

It is important to remember that most people experience a relapse and return to the precontemplation or contemplation stage of change, maybe several times, before eventually succeeding in maintaining the change. People move through the change process at different paces, and relapse is simply a part of behavior change. It is important to learn from any relapse instead of reacting to it by giving up.

Strategies. Strategies used in the action plan should be continued in maintenance. Provisions for avoidance, reminders, contracting, countering, shaping up, and support groups apply during maintenance just as they do during the action stage.

Termination stage

The termination stage is the ultimate goal for people trying to make a lifestyle change. In this stage the problem behavior is no longer tempting. A person becomes confident that his or her problem behavior will never return; it becomes a nonissue. The cycle of change is exited.

Strategies. Some experts believe that termination is impossible, that the most anyone can hope for is a lifetime of maintenance. The key strategy is to be aware of early warning signs of relapse, such as overconfidence, that can recycle the problem behavior.

Regardless of the results, maintaining the proper perspective about success and failure is important. Many people have the attitude that they either completely succeed or completely fail. This way of thinking can be devastating to a person's motivation. When goals are not fully realized, the proper attitude is to view the shortcoming as justification for making adjustments in the program. The goals may have been too general or unrealistic. The intervention strategies may have lacked relevance. Reshaping goals, setting a more realistic schedule, changing the rewards and penalties, or formulating different intervention strategies may be necessary.

Above all, you should maintain a healthy perspective about yourself and not burden yourself with guilt if you fall short of your goals. What seems important now becomes insignificant when viewed within a broader context. You may consider how significant this event is likely to be to you two years from now. Doing this helps establish the right perspective on your progress. More important than total success are the answers to the following questions: What did you learn from this experience? What did you learn about yourself? What can you do differently? Lifestyle change is a lifelong project that requires insight, skillful planning, and plenty of practice.

Summary

- Wellness is a lifelong process that requires self-awareness, introspection, reflection, inquiry, accurate information, and action. It means assuming attitudes and engaging in behaviors that promote health and well-being.
- Health is a constantly changing state of being that moves along a continuum from optimal health to premature death and is affected by an individual's attitudes and activities.
- Lifestyle diseases represent the major threat to the health and quality of life of Americans.
- Wellness requires the consistent balancing of physical, emotional, spiritual, intellectual, social, occupational, and environmental dimensions.
- An internal locus of control is the attitude that a person is in control of his or her life. An external locus of control is the belief that factors affecting health are outside one's control. An internal locus of control is consistent with the principles of wellness.
- *Self-efficacy* refers to the beliefs people have in their ability to accomplish specific tasks or behaviors. A strong sense of self-efficacy is consistent with the principles of wellness.
- The mind, body, and spirit are inseparably linked. A breakdown in any one of these can threaten health and wellness.
- Psychosomatic diseases occur when physical symptoms are caused by psychological, social, spiritual, or emotional stressors.
- *Healthy People 2010* has as one of its goals the elimination of health disparities that exist among population groups.
- Lifestyle diseases are those that are caused by the way people live. The major lifestyle diseases are heart disease,

- cancer, and stroke. Together these account for almost two-thirds of deaths among Americans.
- Chronic diseases are those that persist for an indefinite time.
- Accidents are the leading cause of death among Americans between 15 and 44 years of age.
- The risk factor most strongly associated with premature death and chronic disease in the United States is cigarette smoking.
- The risk factor that is most prevalent among Americans is physical inactivity.
- Physical inactivity as a risk factor for heart disease is comparable with cigarette smoking, high blood pressure, and high blood cholesterol.
- Lifestyle change is one of the most pervasive human endeavors.
- A fundamental belief in lifestyle-change programs is that health behavior is a learned response and therefore can be changed.
- Health behavior is influenced by many complex forces, including family, role models, social pressure, advertising, and psychological needs.
- The six stages of change are precontemplation, contemplation, preparation, action, maintenance, and termination.
- Action strategies include countering, avoidance, reminders, contracting, shaping up, and support groups.

Review Questions

1. How are the health problems of today different from those of fifty years ago? One-hundred years ago?
2. This book suggests that wellness is a process rather than a goal. What does this mean? What are the implications of this statement?
3. What are the components of wellness? How are they similar? Dissimilar?
4. Define *psychosomatic diseases*. Cite four examples of psychosomatic conditions.
5. Cite some data that confirm the relationship between physical health problems and the spiritual, social, and emotional dimensions of wellness.
6. What are the differences between an internal locus of control and an external locus of control? Which of the two is more consistent with the principles of wellness?
7. Define the concept of self-efficacy. What is the relationship between the concepts of locus of control and self-efficacy?
8. How does the impact of environmental improvements compare with advancements in medical technology in terms of increasing health and longevity among Americans?
9. To what does the concept *health disparities* refer? Give five examples.
10. How do the leading causes of mortality among all Americans compare with those of young adults between the ages of 15 and 24? Between 25 and 44?
11. What do medical experts consider the risk factor most strongly associated with premature death and chronic disease?
12. This book suggests that the most formidable wellness challenge for Americans of all ages is overcoming a sedentary lifestyle. What is the rationale for identifying physical activity as more important than diet or cigarette smoking?
13. Identify six benefits of physical activity as cited in the Surgeon General's Report *Physical Activity and Health*.
14. Identify and briefly describe the six stages of change as presented in the transtheoretical model of behavior change.
15. What are some common mistakes people make in trying to change or modify some aspect of their health behavior?
16. What is a major reason for the high recidivism rate in many lifestyle-change programs?
17. If a college student wants to use countering strategies as a way to cope with compulsive eating, what can he or she do or use?
18. Your roommate wants to improve his or her study habits. Identify for your roommate four strategies that apply the techniques recommended in the action stage of lifestyle change.
19. Give an example of a specific and realistic lifestyle goal.

References

1. National Wellness Institute, Inc. 1997. *Testwell: Making Wellness Work for You*, Madison, Wis.: WCB Brown and Benchmark.
2. New England Journal of Medicine. 1997. Can social contacts prevent colds? *Healthnews* 3(9):7.
3. Harvard Medical School. 1998. Emotions and health: Can stress make you sick? *Harvard Health Letter* 23(6):1.
4. National Wellness Institute, *op. cit.*
5. New England Journal of Medicine. 1996. Grumpiest men have greater risk of heart disease. *Healthnews* 2(17):6.
6. Harvard Medical School. 1996. Anger and heart attacks revisited. *Harvard Heart Letter* 6(6):4.
7. Tufts University. 1997. Irritable bowel syndrome: Treating the mind to treat the body. *Tufts University Health and Nutrition Letter* 15(7):4.
8. Editors of *American Health*. 1996. Pessimism may be hazardous to your health. *American Health* 15(3):54.
9. Ventura S. J., R. N. Anderson, J. A. Martin, and B. L. Smith. 1998. Births and deaths: Preliminary data for 1997. *National Vital Statistics Reports* 47(4).
10. Plotkin S. L., and S. A. Plotkin. 1998. A short history of vaccination. In *Vaccines*, eds. S. A. Plotkin and E. A. Mortimer, Jr. Philadelphia: WB Saunders.

11. Knox, R. 1998. Longevity reshaping the globe. *The Commercial Appeal* 159(132):2.
12. Associated Press. 1997. Racked with ill health, Russia shrinks. *The Commercial Appeal* 158(159):2.
13. Ventura S. J., et al., *op cit.*
14. American Alliance for Health, Physical Education, Recreation, and Dance. 1995. Cooper delivers stirring convention address. *Update* May/June:1–4.
15. U.S. Department of Health and Human Services. 1998. *Targeting tobacco use: The nation's leading cause of death, at a glance—1998.* Atlanta: Center for Disease Control.
16. U.S. Department of Health and Human Services. 1998. *Healthy People 2010 Objectives—Draft for Public Comment.* Washington: U.S. Government Printing Office.
17. U.S. Department of Health and Human Services. *Physical Activity and Health: A Report of the Surgeon General.* Atlanta: U.S. Department of Health and Human Services, Centers for Disease Control and Prevention, National Center for Chronic Disease Prevention and Health Promotion.
18. Prochaska, J. 1994. *Changing for Good.* New York: William Morrow and Company.
19. Prochaska, J. 1996. Just do it isn't enough: Change comes in stages. *Tufts University Diet and Nutrition Letter* 14(7):4–6.
20. Ibid.
21. Bootzin, R. 1975. *Behavior Modification as Therapy: An Introduction.* Cambridge, Mass.: Winthrop Publishers.

Suggested Readings

Rippe, J. M. 1996. *Fit over Forty.* New York: William Morrow and Company.

James Rippe, once an obsessive marathon runner, presents a revolutionary plan to achieve lifelong physical and spiritual health and well-being. It is based on a landmark study that established the first-ever fitness standards for people over 40 and features ten self-tests for evaluating your personal fitness level. It provides the tools needed to custom-design a lifelong fitness program that will enhance total wellness.

Prochaska, J. O., J. C. Norcross and C. C. Diclemente. 1994. *Changing for Good.* New York: Avon Books.

Three acclaimed psychologists studied more than 1000 people who were able to positively and permanently alter their lives without psychotherapy. They discovered that change does not depend on luck or willpower. It is a process that can be successfully managed by anyone who understands how it works. This book offers simple self-assessments, informative case histories, and concrete examples to help clarify the six stages of change.

Benson, H., and M. Stark, 1997. *Timeless Healing—the Power and Biology of Belief.* New York: Fireside.

Drawing on twenty-five years as a physician and researcher, Dr. Benson reveals how affirming beliefs, particularly belief in a higher power, make an important contribution to physical health. This book explains how anyone, with the aid of a caring physician or healer, can use beliefs and other self-care methods to heal many medical problems.

Chapter 1 Wellness and Fitness for Life   31

Name _____ Date _____ Section _____

Assessment Activity 1-3

Assessing Your Health Behavior

Before planning a lifestyle-change program, you should take an inventory of your health behaviors. This reveals important information about your lifestyle and should also help identify areas in need of improvement.

Directions: In this assessment, you are asked to make two lists. In the left column, list the things you do to maintain or improve your level of health. These are your health-promoting behaviors. In the right column, list the things you do that may be detrimental to your health. These are your health-inhibiting behaviors. Try to be specific. Include the things that affect your mental, emotional, social, spiritual, and physical health. If you have a difficult time thinking of specific activities, you can refer to Assessment Activity 1-1.

Health-promoting behaviors
1. I referee and play soccer
2. I eat two pieces of fruit
3. I interact with different people
4. I get regulary sleep
5. I am learning new information from classes
6. I focus on my spiritual well-being
7. weekly/daily
8.
9.
10.
11.
12.
13.
14.
15.

Health-inhibiting behaviors
1. I drink pop
2. I don't get enough excersise
3. I don't deal with stress well enough
4.
5.
6.
7.
8.
9.
10.
11.
12.
13.
14.
15.

Which health-inhibiting behavior would you be willing to change right now? _____

2

Preventing Cardiovascular Disease

Key Terms

aneurysm
atherosclerosis
cerebral hemorrhage
cholesterol
embolus
hypertension
ischemia
lipoprotein
myocardial infarction
sedentary
thrombus

Objectives

After completing this chapter, you will be able to do the following:

- Describe the gross anatomy and function of the heart.
- Trace the development of cardiovascular disease during this century in the United States.
- Identify and differentiate among several types of cardiovascular disease.
- Identify the risk factors for coronary heart disease and discuss ways to reduce them.
- Explain the lifestyle behaviors that contribute to health and longevity.

Goals for Behavior Change

- Choose three high-fat foods that you regularly eat and replace them with low-fat healthier foods.
- Find out what your total cholesterol, LDL cholesterol, and HDL cholesterol are. Select three or four lifestyle behaviors to change to improve your cholesterol profile.
- Find out what your blood pressure is. Select two or three behaviors to change (excluding taking medication) to lower it.
- If you use tobacco products, devise a plan for quitting the tobacco habit.
- If you are not currently active, make a list of physical activities to improve your health status and level of fitness. Determine how many calories you would attempt to expend per week.
- Plan and implement three strategies to help you deal with chronic stress.

ardiovascular disease encompasses a group of diseases that affect the heart and blood vessels. Cardiovascular disease—the leading cause of death in the United States—accounts for 42 percent of all deaths.[1] About 25 percent of Americans (approximately 59 million people) have one or more forms of heart or blood vessel disease. Approximately 1.5 million heart attacks have occurred every year in the last few years, and about 500,000 of these end in death each year. At least 250,000 heart attack victims die within the first hour following the onset of symptoms. They fail to reach a hospital before death occurs. A significant number of these premature deaths could have been prevented with early recognition and treatment.

Of heart attack victims, 50 percent wait an average of two hours before seeking medical attention. Denying the possibility that a heart attack is occurring is the primary reason for the delay. The situation is complicated because the symptoms of a heart attack are similar to those of other physical ailments, and people are more prone to believe that it is one of the other problems than that it is a heart attack.

Although the figures are foreboding, substantial progress has occurred during the last forty-five years. The death rate for cardiovascular diseases has declined by more than 50 percent since 1950.[1] Although an impressive accomplishment, it is somewhat diminished by the fact that cardiovascular diseases remain by far the leading cause of death in the United States. Two types in particular, coronary heart disease and strokes, are the first and third leading causes of death. More than 50 percent of the premature deaths in our society are attributed to lifestyle habits.

Authorities agree that preventive measures emphasizing risk-reduction strategies that involve lifestyle changes will produce the most dramatic benefits in the fight against heart disease.[2] Also contributing to the downward trend in the death rate from cardiovascular disease are more sophisticated diagnostics, improved treatment, and prompt recognition of impending heart attacks.

Circulation

You can understand circulation better if you are familiar with the basic anatomy and function of the heart. The heart consists of cardiac muscle and weighs between 8 and 10 ounces. It is about the size of a fist and lies in the center of the chest. The heart is divided into two halves, or pumps, by a wall (the septum), and each half is subdivided into an upper chamber (the atrium) and a lower chamber (the ventricle). The right heart, or pulmonary pump, receives deoxygenated blood from the tissues and pumps it to the lungs so that carbon dioxide can be exchanged for a fresh supply of oxygen. From the lungs, the oxygen-rich blood is sent to the left heart, or systemic pump, so that the oxygenated blood can be pumped to all the tissues of the body. Both pumps work simultaneously. The systemic pump carries the heavier workload of the two and thus has a more muscular ventricular wall. Figure 2-1 illustrates the circulatory system.

The arteries carry oxygenated blood away from the heart while the veins carry deoxygenated blood to the heart. There are two exceptions, one in the arterial system and one in the venous system. First, the pulmonary artery carries *deoxygenated* blood from the right heart to the lungs to exchange carbon dioxide for a fresh supply of oxygen. Second, the pulmonary vein carries *fully oxygenated* blood from the lungs to the left heart for distribution throughout the body.

The primary function of circulation is to provide a constant supply of blood and nutrients to the cells while removing their waste products. Under ordinary circumstances, the interruption of blood flow for as little as four to six minutes can result in irreversible brain damage due to oxygen deprivation.

The average heart beats seventy to eighty times per minute at rest. Endurance athletes often have resting heart rates in the thirty and forty beat range, whereas

Figure 2-1 The Circulatory System

some overweight and sedentary smokers have resting heart rates in the nineties. The low heart rates of endurance athletes reflect physiological adaptations to training that represent normal values for this group. The Framingham Heart Disease Study showed that a rapid resting heart rate increased the risk of death from heart attack. Mortality increased progressively with higher resting heart rates, especially among men.

The heart is self-regulating; that is, it contains its own conduction system that is fully capable of establishing and maintaining the heart beat without outside neural stimulation. The heart's beating rate and rhythm are established by the sinoatrial node (SA node, or pacemaker), which is located in the right atrium, as shown in figure 2-2. The atria contract, forcing blood into the ventricles as the electrical impulse travels from the SA node to the atrioventricular node (AV node), which is located between the right atrium and right ventricle. The electrical impulse pauses for one tenth of a second at the AV node to allow the ventricles to fill with blood and then resumes down the system and spreads throughout the ventricular walls. The ventricles contract during this time, ejecting blood from these chambers.

Blood that enters the chambers of the heart does not directly nourish the heart muscle because there are no direct circulatory routes from the heart's chambers into its muscular walls. Instead, blood must first be ejected from the heart to the aorta (the largest artery in the body) and then to the coronary arteries that supply the myocardium (heart muscle) with blood and oxygen. The majority of blood is received by the myocardium during diastole (between beats) because the blood vessels dilate during this time, increasing their capacity to accept and deliver blood.

Coronary circulation is illustrated in figure 2-3. The left coronary artery supplies a major portion of the myocardium with blood, whereas the right coronary artery serves less of it. Both vessels divide and subdivide downstream and eventually culminate in a dense network of capillaries (the smallest blood vessels in the body). Blood supply to the myocardium is so important that every muscle fiber is supplied by at least one capillary. The coronary veins return deoxygenated blood to the right atrium so that it can enter pulmonary circulation. The veins bring deoxygenated blood from all tissues back to the right atrium.

Blood plasma is a clear, yellowish fluid that carries approximately 100 chemicals. Plasma represents 55 percent of the blood content. The remaining 45 percent consists of blood solids—the erythrocytes (red blood cells), the leukocytes (white blood cells), and the blood platelets. The red blood cells are the most abundant of the blood solids, composing about 99 percent of the total. These cells carry oxygen and carbon dioxide attached to hemoglobin, which is an iron-rich protein pigment and a main component of red blood cells. The white blood cells are an important part of the body's defense system against invading microorganisms and other foreign substances. The blood platelets are involved in the complex processes that lead to the formation of clots for repairing damaged blood vessels.

Figure 2-2 Electrical Conduction System of the Heart

Figure 2-3 Coronary Circulation

Cardiovascular Disease: A Twentieth-Century Phenomenon

Cardiovascular disease, a relatively rare event 100 years ago, reached epidemic proportions during the middle of the twentieth century. The term *angina pectoris* (chest pain) was introduced into the medical literature by William Heberden, a British physician, in the latter part of the eighteenth century. He was unable to offer any treatment for this strange malady. It was not until 1910 that physicians made the connection between recurrent episodes of angina pectoris and heart disease. Chest pain and other manifestations of a heart attack were not identified with obstructions of the coronary arteries until the early 1900s. An American physician gave the first accurate description of the events associated with a heart attack in 1912. The illness he described, which afflicted a 55-year-old man with no previous evidence of disease, is now a common occurrence in American life. The man died three days after the onset of symptoms. A postmortem examination of the heart revealed that a clot had occluded, or blocked, one of the major coronary arteries. In 1912, this was a medical rarity.

Coronary heart disease is responsible for the majority of heart attack deaths, but other forms of heart disease contribute to disability and death. Congenital heart defects, which exist at birth, affect approximately 32,000 newborns annually. Approximately 5400 of these infants die from their defects. Rheumatic heart disease, caused by a streptococcal infection of the throat or ear, is virtually 100 percent preventable. Antibiotic treatment during the infection stage arrests the processes that could lead to rheumatic heart disease. Congestive heart failure occurs when the heart muscle is so damaged that it can no longer contract with sufficient force to pump blood throughout the body. The leading causes of congestive heart failure are poorly controlled or uncontrolled long-standing hypertension or a history of previous heart attacks or both.

Coronary Heart Disease

Coronary heart disease (also known as *coronary artery disease*) is actually a disease of the arteries that supply the heart with blood and nutrients. A diagnosis of coronary artery disease is made if any artery is narrowed by 60 percent. A heart attack, or **myocardial infarction** (death of heart muscle tissue), occurs when an obstruction or spasm disrupts or blocks blood flow to a portion of the heart muscle. The amount of heart muscle damage is determined by the location of the obstruction or spasm and the speed with which medical intervention is begun. Heart attacks of any magnitude produce irreversible injury and myocardial tissue death. It usually takes five to six weeks to form a fibrous scar around dead cardiac tissue. This area of dead tissue can no longer contribute to the pumping of blood, resulting in a less efficient heart. Massive heart attacks that cause extensive muscle damage result in death.

Although most heart attacks occur after the age of 65, the dysfunctions leading to them often begin before adolescence. These processes occur most often without symptoms and often go undetected until, without warning, a heart attack occurs. The attack is sudden, but the circumstances leading to it develop over many years. In fact, there is considerable evidence that the silent phase of coronary heart disease begins as early as childhood.[3,4]

Risk factors are genetic predispositions, lifestyle behaviors, and environmental influences that increase one's susceptibility to disease. Elevated blood pressure and blood fats (cholesterol and triglycerides) that occur during adulthood can often be traced back to childhood. See Wellness Across the Generations: Childhood Origins of Heart Disease for more information about this connection.

The ongoing Framingham Study, which began in 1949, identified the risk factors connected with heart disease.[9] Cigarette smoking, high blood pressure, elevated cholesterol levels, diabetes, obesity, stress, physical inactivity, age, gender, and family history were found to be highly related to heart attack and stroke. As the risks were discovered, the realization evolved that heart disease was not the inevitable consequence of aging or bad luck but an acquired disease that was preventable. After a few years, researchers realized that preventive efforts should begin in childhood.

Autopsy studies of 18-year-olds who died in accidents have shown a positive relationship between blood cholesterol levels and the prevalence of fatty streaks on the walls of the coronary arteries and aorta. The evidence indicates that the average cholesterol level in children in overfed, underexercised societies such as the United States is too high.

Autopsy studies of American combat battle casualties, whose average age was 22 years, in the Korean and Vietnam wars showed obstructions in the coronary arteries. These obstructions are caused by **atherosclerosis**, which is a slow, progressive disease of the arteries that can originate in childhood.[4] It is characterized by the deposition of plaque beneath the lining of the artery (figure 2-4). Plaque consists of fatty substances, cholesterol, blood platelets, fibrin, calcium, and cellular debris. The atherosclerotic process is responsible for 80 percent of the coronary heart disease deaths in the United States. The lipid oxidation theory, which is the current theory of the development of atherosclerosis, is explained in the section dealing with cholesterol as a risk factor.

Chapter 2 Preventing Cardiovascular Disease   **37**

Wellness Across the Generations

Childhood Origins of Heart Disease

Behavior patterns established during childhood that increase the likelihood of coronary heart disease may and often do persist into adulthood. A physically inactive child is likely to become a physically inactive adult.[5] Only 50 percent of young people in the United States (ages 12 to 21 years) regularly participate in vigorous physical activity, and one-fourth report no physical activity at all.[4] Fifteen to 25 percent of children and adolescents are obese.[6] An estimated 6 million teenagers and 100,000 youngsters under the age of 13 are regular smokers.[7] Smoking rates among high school students rose from 27.5 percent in 1991 to 34.8 percent in 1995.[8] These are major risks that begin in childhood and continue into adulthood.

Attempts to prevent heart disease need to begin in childhood. Knowledgeable parents can serve as role models who practice, rather than just talk about, healthy behaviors. Active parents should be the strongest influence, but they are not the only influence. Schools need to offer quality physical education programs throughout the twelve years of precollege education, and communities should offer opportunities and provide facilities for active participation in games and recreational play.

Figure 2-4 Progressive Narrowing of a Normal Coronary Artery (Atherosclerosis)

Just the Facts

Heart Attack: The Warning Signs

The Warning Signs

- Uncomfortable pressure, fullness, a squeezing sensation as if a band were being tightened around the chest, pain in the center of the chest lasting longer than 2 minutes
- Pain that spreads to the shoulders, arms, or neck
- The above warning signs accompanied by dizziness, fainting, sweating, nausea, and shortness of breath.

What to Do If These Signs Appear

If you have chest discomfort lasting more than 2 minutes:

- Do not deny what may be occurring
- Call the emergency service or have a friend or family member drive you to the nearest hospital that has 24-hour emergency cardiac care
- Know in advance which hospitals have such service
- Prominently display in your home the telephone number of the emergency rescue service and also carry a copy with you.

As many as one-third of all heart attacks are silent; that is, they have no obvious signs or symptoms. Three to four million Americans experience cardiac **ischemia** without knowing it. Ischemia (reduced blood flow) occurs as the result of arterial disease or arterial spasms that restrict blood flow to any part of the body, including the heart.[1] Silent ischemia can and does initiate heart attacks without prior warning. However, the typical heart attack is obvious, and the symptoms are pronounced. See Just the Facts: Heart Attack: The Warning Signs.

Stroke (Brain Attack)

The majority of strokes (cerebrovascular accidents, or brain attacks) follow the same sequence of events that results in coronary heart disease. A stroke is essentially the result of diseased blood vessels that supply the brain. It shares the same risk factors as coronary heart disease, and it takes years to develop.

Strokes are caused by a **thrombus** (a clot that forms and occludes an artery supplying the brain) or an **embolus** (a clot that forms elsewhere in the body and fragments, dislodges, and is transported to one of the cerebral blood vessels that is too small for its passage). **Cerebral hemorrhage** (the bursting of a blood vessel in the brain caused by trauma, arterial brittleness, or aneurysm) is also a cause of stroke. An **aneurysm** is a weak spot in an artery that forms a balloonlike pouch that can rupture. It may be a congenital defect or the result of uncontrolled or poorly controlled hypertension.

Between 70 and 80 percent of all strokes are due to a thrombus or an embolus. Brain cells that were once supplied by these blood vessels die and do not regenerate. As a result, the functional losses that occur (e.g., paralysis on one side of the body, difficulty speaking) cannot be fully recovered. The fact that brain cells die also means that treatment will not be very effective. Many stroke victims are unable to return to a normal lifestyle unless the stroke was mild, in which case a full recovery is possible.

Strokes that are caused by hemorrhages result in a 50 percent mortality rate. Victims die from the pressure imposed by blood leaking into the brain. Those who survive this type of stroke are likely to recover more of their normal functions than are those whose strokes were caused by a blood clot. The blood that spills in and on the brain during a hemorrhagic stroke produces pressure that gradually abates as the blood is absorbed by the body. Function is regained as the pressure relents.

On many occasions a stroke is preceded by warning signs and signals days, weeks, or months before a major stroke. These must be recognized and then acted on so that prompt medical and lifestyle interventions may be instituted to prevent or delay a stroke.

Preventing a stroke is similar to preventing coronary heart disease. Both involve blood pressure and cholesterol control, smoking cessation, weight management, exercise, and proper nutrition. See Just the Facts: Stroke: The Warning Signs, which identifies the major warning signs.

Risk Factors for Heart Disease

The risk factors for cardiovascular disease have been categorized by the American Heart Association (AHA) as follows: (1) major risk factors that cannot be changed (increasing age, male gender, and heredity), (2) major risk factors that can be changed (elevated blood cholesterol levels, high blood pressure, cigarette smoking, physical inactivity, and obesity), and (3) other contributing factors (diabetes and stress) (figure 2-5).

These risk factors account for the majority of cardiovascular disease in the United States. However, there are many other factors that can be involved, some of which are backed by a sound and growing body of evidence. These include high serum homocysteine, lipoprotein (a), high blood fibrinogen, and high blood insulin levels. Other possible risk factors, supported by inconclusive evidence, include short stature, baldness, ear lobe creases, high serum uric acid level, and others. A few of the more important of these risk factors are covered later in this chapter.

Major Risk Factors That Cannot Be Changed

Age

Approximately 55 percent of all heart attacks occur in people who are 65 years of age or older. This age group accounts for more than 80 percent of fatal heart attacks.[1]

Male Gender

Until recently, the incidence of coronary heart disease among women was largely unexplored. Men have been the primary subjects in coronary heart disease and risk factor studies because of the high incidence of both among men. However, coronary heart disease is also the leading cause of death and disability among women, accounting for almost 250,000 deaths annually.[1] Women have less heart disease than men, particularly before menopause. See Wellness Across the Generations: Women and Coronary Disease: Pre- and Postmenopause.

An alarming trend in recent years is the increased incidence of heart attacks in premenopausal women

---

Just the Facts
Stroke: The Warning Signs

The American Heart Association suggests that people be familiar with the following warning signs:

- Temporary loss of speech or difficulty in speaking or understanding speech
- Unexplained dizziness, unsteadiness, or sudden falls
- Temporary dimness or loss of vision, particularly in one eye
- Sudden, temporary weakness or numbness of the face, arm, and leg on one side of the body
- Occurrence of a series of minor strokes, or transient ischemic attacks (TIAs)

Chapter 2 Preventing Cardiovascular Disease 39

Risk factors that cannot be changed

Increasing age

Male gender

Heredity

Risk factors that can be changed

Physical inactivity

High blood cholesterol

Smoking

High blood pressure

Obesity

Contributing risk factors

Diabetes

Stress

Figure 2-5 Cardiovascular Disease Risk Factors

Wellness Across the Generations

Women and Coronary Heart Disease: Pre- and Postmenopause

Heart attacks are relatively rare among premenopausal women because of the production and presence of estrogen (the female sex hormone responsible for the development of secondary sexual characteristics and the various phases of the menstrual cycle and essential for bone formation). Estrogen is also protective in that it lowers LDL cholesterol (the harmful form), raises HDL cholesterol (the protective form), and may increase blood flow to the heart.

During and after menopause, the production of estrogen decreases and eventually stops, and the protection from heart disease diminishes. Women tend to develop coronary heart disease about ten years later than men. By age 65 the risk for men and women equalizes.[10]

To maintain a lower risk after menopause women should consider estrogen replacement therapy (ERT), because this form of therapy can cut the risk of coronary heart disease in half. ERT is particularly beneficial for women who have had a previous heart attack or for those who are at high risk because of cigarette smoking, high blood pressure, high cholesterol, obesity, or physical inactivity. However, ERT may not be appropriate for all postmenopausal women because it increases the risk for breast cancer.

Women should make the decision regarding ERT replacement in consultation with their physicians who are aware of their heart disease risk and who know their family histories of breast cancer.

who have been smoking cigarettes long enough for it to affect their health, especially when combined with oral contraceptive use.

Heredity

According to the American Heart Association, "A tendency toward heart disease or atherosclerosis appears to be hereditary, so children of parents with cardiovascular disease are more likely to develop it themselves."[1] A history of first-degree male relatives (father, grandfather, and brothers) who have coronary heart disease or who died of coronary heart disease before the age of 55 or first-degree female relatives (mother, grandmother, and sisters) who have coronary heart disease or who died of coronary heart disease before the age of 65 indicates a strong familial tendency.[2] If the family history is positive, the modifiable risk factors must be controlled.

Although age, male gender, and heredity are major risks that are not under our direct control, we can modify their effects by living a wellness lifestyle. Abstaining from tobacco products; exercising regularly; controlling blood pressure, cholesterol, and body weight; managing stress; and maintaining a social support system can lessen the impact of these unchangeable risk factors.

Major Risk Factors That Can Be Changed

Cholesterol

Cholesterol is a steroid that is an essential structural component of neural tissue; it is used in the construction of cell walls and for the manufacture of hormones and bile (for the digestion and absorption of fats). A certain amount of cholesterol is required for good health, but high levels in the blood are associated with heart attacks and strokes.

The American Heart Association suggests that Americans reduce cholesterol consumption to less than 300 milligrams per day (300 mg/day), that fat intake be reduced to a maximum of 30 percent of the total calories consumed, and that saturated fat be reduced to no more than 10 percent of the total calories. Many authorities are convinced that limiting total fat and saturated fat is more important than being overly restrictive of cholesterol.

Data from 1987 to 1992 indicate that total fat consumption in the United States decreased by 6 percent, whereas saturated fat intake decreased by 11 percent. This parallels the decline in consumption of animal flesh and animal products.[11] Although this is a small step in the right direction, the fact is that the dietary intake of saturated fat remains too high, at 12 percent of total calories.[12] Many authorities recommend that saturated fat consumption make up no more than 8 percent of total calories. They also suggest that the most effective approach to lowering serum cholesterol is to reduce the intake of saturated fat in order to slow down the liver's production of cholesterol. At the same time, it is also a good idea to lower dietary cholesterol.

Americans have made substantial progress in reducing cholesterol consumption. The average cholesterol consumed by men and women respectively in 1960 was

HealthQuest Activities

- The *Heart Attack Risk* and *Cardiovascular Exploration* activities in Module 5 allow you to assess your risk for cardiovascular disease. In the first of these activities, *Heart Attack Risk*, answer the questions about your health history, behavioral practices, and knowledge about heart disease. *HealthQuest* will then provide the correct answers and point out any health risks indicated by your responses. In the *Cardiovascular Exploration* section, fill out all of the items and then click on the Show Me! button to find out your overall risk. You can get more specific feedback on each risk factor by clicking on the underlined words.

- Many young adults have difficulty understanding how cardiovascular disease affects quality of life. Heart disease seems only a distant possibility, but for many it can become all too real. To learn more, read about heart disease among women and minority groups in the *Social Perspectives* section. List several health choices that can increase the likelihood of developing cardiovascular disease, and explain how one's family history can affect the risk. Finally, describe what you would do if you observed someone having a heart attack.

704 mg/day and 493 mg/day.[13] By 1994, cholesterol intake had dropped to 376 mg/day for men and 259 mg/day for women.

Cholesterol is consumed in the diet (exogenous, or dietary cholesterol), but it is also manufactured by the body from saturated fats (endogenous). A normally functioning adult liver manufactures 1500 to 2500 mg of cholesterol daily.[14] The cells lining the small intestine provide another 500 mg daily, so the body is manufacturing up to 3000 mg/day.

If you add the typical dietary intake of 259 to 376 mg/day to this total, you can see that the body must process, use, or remove considerable amounts of cholesterol to prevent it from accumulating and clogging the arteries. The liver alone produces enough cholesterol to meet the body's needs. Therefore, consuming cholesterol is not necessary to maintain health. Table 2-1 lists some common foods that contain cholesterol and saturated fat.

A number of population studies during the last twenty years have indicated a positive relationship between serum cholesterol (the level of cholesterol circulating in the blood) and the development of coronary heart disease. The National Heart, Lung, and Blood Institute reviewed this evidence and concluded that high circulating levels of serum cholesterol cause heart disease.

Values of serum cholesterol above 200 milligrams per deciliter (mg/dl) of blood are higher than the average risk. Table 2-2 (on p. 45) shows the values of risk associated with total cholesterol (TC), LDL and HDL cholesterol (to be discussed shortly), and another serum lipid (blood fat), the triglycerides.

An important collaborative study involving twelve research centers throughout the United States provided clinical evidence implicating cholesterol as a culprit in coronary heart disease.[15] Half of a group of 3806 subjects was given a cholesterol-lowering drug, and the other half was given a placebo (a substance that looked like the drug but had no medicinal properties). The subjects were followed for approximately 7.4 years, at which time the data indicated that the drug group reduced their cholesterol levels by 13 percent, suffered 19 percent fewer heart attacks, and experienced 24 percent fewer fatal heart attacks. The incidence of coronary bypass surgery and angina were also significantly reduced. The researchers concluded that each 1 percent reduction in cholesterol level results in a 2 percent reduction in the risk of coronary heart disease.

A later follow-up of this study indicated that the reduction in coronary heart disease is probably closer to 3 percent for every 1 percent that cholesterol is lowered.[16] The strategies for lowering cholesterol in the blood are presented in Real-World Wellness: Strategies for Lowering Cholesterol.

The cholesterol carriers. The amount of cholesterol circulating in the blood accounts for only part of the total cholesterol in the body. Unlike sugar and salt, cholesterol does not dissolve in the blood, so it is transported by protein packages, which facilitate its solubility. These transporters are the lipoproteins that are manufactured by the body. They include the chylomicrons, very low-density lipoprotein (VLDL), intermediate-density lipoprotein (IDL), low-density lipoprotein (LDL), and high-density lipoprotein (HDL). Dietary cholesterol enters the body from the digestive system attached to the chylomicrons. The chylomicrons shrink as they give up their cholesterol to the cells of the body. The fragments that remain are removed by the liver and used to manufacture and secrete VLDLs, which are triglyceride-rich lipoproteins. The triglycerides represent 99 percent of the stored fats in the body. The VLDLs are degraded as their cargo of triglycerides is either used by the cells for energy or stored in adipose cells. The VLDL remnants may be removed by the liver or converted to LDLs (figure 2-6).

Table 2-1 Sources of Dietary Cholesterol and Saturated Fat

	Cholesterol (mg)*	Saturated Fat (g)**		Cholesterol (mg)*	Saturated Fat (g)**
Meats (3 oz.)			**Seafood (3 oz.)**		
Beef liver	372	2.5	Squid	153	.4
Veal	86	4.0	Oily fish	59	1.2
Pork	80	3.2	Lean fish	59	.3
Lean beef	56	2.4	Shrimp (6 large)	48	.2
Chicken (dark meat)	82	2.7	Clams (6 large)	36	.3
Chicken (white meat)	76	1.3	Lobster	46.4	.08
Egg	274	1.7	**Other items of interest**		
Dairy products (1 cup; cheese, 1 oz.)			Pork brains (3 oz.)	2,169	1.8
Ice cream	59	8.9	Beef kidney (3 oz.)	683	3.8
Whole milk	33	5.1	Beef hot dog (1)	75	9.9
Butter (1 tsp.)	31	7.1	Prime ribs of beef (3 oz.)	66.5	5.3
Yogurt (low fat)	11	1.8	Doughnut	36	4.0
Cheddar	30	6.0	Milk chocolate	0	16.3
American	27	5.6	Green or yellow vegetable or fruit	0	Trace
Camembert	20	4.3	Peanut butter (1 tbsp.)	0	1.5
Parmesan	8	2.0	Angel food cake	0	1.96
			Skim milk (1 cup)	4	.3
Oils (1 tbsp.)			Cheese pizza (3 oz.)	6	.8
Coconut	0	11.8	Buttermilk (1 cup)	9	1.3
Palm	0	6.7	Ice milk, soft (1 cup)	13	2.9
Olive	0	1.8	Turkey, white meat (3 oz.)	59	.9
Corn	0	1.7			
Safflower	0	1.2			

*There are 1000 mg in a gram.
**There are 28 g in an ounce and 454 g in a pound.

Real-World Wellness

Strategies for Lowering Cholesterol

My doctor told me that my cholesterol level is too high. How can I lower it to reduce my risk of having a heart attack or stroke?

First, establish a realistic goal, such as about how much you think you can lower your cholesterol. Second, identify the lifestyle changes that can lower cholesterol. Third, attempt to do all of the following that apply to you:

- Reduce your fat consumption to less than 30 percent of total calories (25 percent would be better).
- Reduce your saturated fat consumption to less than 10 percent of total calories (8 percent would be better).
- Reduce your dietary cholesterol to less than 300 mg/day (less than 200 mg/day would be better).
- Lose weight if you are overweight.
- Stop smoking cigarettes and/or stop using other tobacco products.
- Increase your consumption of soluble fiber, found in fruits, vegetables, and grains.
- Do aerobic exercise at least three to four times per week for at least 30 minutes each time.

If these strategies fail to normalize your cholesterol level in six months, you may have to consider taking cholesterol-lowering drugs.

Figure 2-6 Cholesterol Carriers

LDLs are the primary transporters of cholesterol and the most capable of producing atherosclerosis. Michael S. Brown and Joseph L. Goldstein won a 1985 Nobel Prize in medicine and physiology for discovering that the liver and the cells of the body have receptor sites that bind LDLs, removing them from circulation. The liver contains 50 to 75 percent of these sites; the remainder are in other cells of the body. When LDL concentrations are excessive, the liver sites become saturated, and further removal of them from the blood is significantly impeded. As a result, plasma levels of cholesterol rise, leading to the formation and development of atherosclerotic plaque.

The development of atherosclerosis in the coronary arteries is very complex. The *lipid oxidation theory* represents the latest thinking of the scientific community regarding the formation of plaque and therefore the growth and progress of atherosclerosis. This theory proposes that the initial event in the atherosclerotic process is an injury (lesion) that occurs to the inner lining of the arteries. Such injuries occur because of prolonged exposure to tobacco smoke, high blood pressure, elevated LDL cholesterol, diabetes mellitus, high amounts of serum homocysteine, and viral and bacterial infections.[3] These injuries, which occur at multiple sites, allow LDL cholesterol to infiltrate under the artery lining, where they become oxidized (come in contact with oxygen). Oxidized LDLs become toxic and trigger the body's immune system to destroy them. The process of destroying oxidized LDLs contributes to the formation of plaque. Generally, two to three decades after the atherosclerotic process begins, plaque has progressed to the point that one or more arteries become so narrowed that a blood clot or spasm occurs, shutting off blood supply to a portion of the heart muscle. The result is a heart attack. See figure 2-7 for an illustration of this process.

Heart attacks are rare when LDL values in the blood are below 100 mg/dl. A national panel of experts has developed guidelines for safe and unsafe levels of LDL, and these appear in table 2-2. A high circulating level of LDL cholesterol is positively related to cardiovascular disease. Weight loss, a diet low in saturated fat and total fat, exercise, and medication (if needed) will lower LDL levels in the blood.

HDLs are involved in reverse transport; that is, they accept cholesterol from the blood and tissues and transfer it to VLDLs and LDLs for transport to the

A. Normal artery

B. Fatty streak

C. Partially occluded vessel

D. Totally occluded vessel

A. When a lesion occurs, LDL-Cs infiltrate below the artery lining, where they become oxidized and toxic. Monocytes follow and engulf the toxic LDLs.

B. The monocytes swell with LDL-C and become bloated. Platelets stimulate the smooth muscle cells to grow. Monocytes become foam cells. The growth bulges into the artery opening (lumen) and is recognized as a fatty streak (the first noticeable sign of atherosclerosis).

C. The bulge (now plaque) continues to grow over decades and the artery channels continue to narrow.

D. Eventually a blood clot forms and stops blood flow to the heart muscle. The result is a heart attack and death of a portion of heart muscle.

Figure 2-7 Progression of Atherosclerosis and Coronary Artery Disease

liver, where it can be degraded, disposed of, or recycled. HDLs protect the arteries from atherosclerosis by clearing cholesterol from the blood. Cardiovascular health depends greatly on low levels of total cholesterol and LDLs and a high level of HDLs. Cigarette smoking, diabetes, elevated triglyceride levels, and anabolic steroids lower HDL, whereas physical exercise, weight loss, and moderate alcohol consumption raise it.

Moderate alcohol consumption (two drinks or less per day) increases HDL cholesterol levels. An alcoholic drink is defined as a 5-ounce glass of wine or a 12-ounce beer or 1½ ounces of 80-proof spirits. However, alcohol is a depressant that impairs judgment and removes inhibitions so that people under its influence behave in ways they ordinarily would not while sober. Alcohol consumption is not an acceptable way to raise HDL cholesterol.

Table 2-2 presents the current guidelines for HDL cholesterol levels in the blood. The higher the HDL, the greater the protection from cardiovascular disease. The average value for men is 45 mg/dl, and for women it is 55 mg/dl.[17] This biological difference in HDL levels between genders partly explains the lower incidence of heart disease in premenopausal women as compared

Table 2-2 Risk Profile—Lipid and Lipoprotein Concentrations

	Total Cholesterol (mg/dl)	LDL Cholesterol (mg/dl)	HDL Cholesterol (mg/dl)	Triglycerides (mg/dl)
High risk	≥245*	≥190	≤35†	≥1000
Moderate risk	221–244	160–189	36–44	500–999
Mild risk	201–220	130–159	45–54	250–499
Average risk	182–200	100–129	55–65	151–249
Low risk	<182‡	<100	≥65	≤150

*≥ Equal to or greater
†≤ Equal to or less
‡< Less than

Data are from a variety of sources, including the MRFIT study, NIH Consensus Conference, National Cholesterol Program, and Framingham Heart Study, as compiled by Goldberg, L., and D. L. Elliot. 1994. The use of exercise to improve lipid and lipoprotein levels. In *Exercise for Prevention and Treatment of Illness*, eds. L. Goldberg and D. L. Elliot. Philadelphia: F. A. Davis Co.

Table 2-3 Ratio of Total Cholesterol to HDL Cholesterol

Risk	Men	Women
Very low (one-half average)	<3.4	<3.3
Low risk	4.0	3.8
Average risk	5.0	4.5
Moderate risk (two times average)	9.5	7.0
High risk (three times average)	>23	>11

with men. After menopause, HDL levels in women begin to decrease, as does their protection provided by this subfraction of cholesterol. The ratio between total cholesterol (TC) and HDL (TC/HDL) should also be considered when the risk is interpreted. This ratio is determined by dividing TC by HDL (table 2-3).[17]

Another blood fat, the serum triglycerides, is involved in the development and progression of atherosclerosis. Average serum triglycerides, depending on age and gender, range from 50 mg/dl to 200 mg/dl. Table 2-2 identifies the risk associated with various serum triglyceride levels.

High serum triglycerides usually coexist with low HDL cholesterol, a proven risk factor for cardiovascular disease. Teasing out the independent effect of serum triglyceride levels has been difficult. But recent evidence has shown that high levels are a modest independent risk factor for heart disease and a very reliable predictor when coupled with low HDL cholesterol.[18]

Serum triglycerides greater than 190 mg/dl increase blood viscosity (blood thickness), resulting in sluggish blood flow. Viscous blood is more difficult to circulate, so oxygen and nutrients are not delivered as efficiently to the body's tissues, and these include the heart muscle.[19]

Table 2-2 shows the relative risk posed by high serum triglycerides. Levels below 150 mg/dl are in the low-risk category, but newer evidence suggests that an optimal level is below 100 mg/dl.[20]

A number of studies have shown that sedentary people with high triglycerides can reduce serum triglycerides by as much as 45 percent when they participate regularly in moderately intense exercise. Physically fit people metabolize serum triglycerides more effectively than do sedentary people and are able to clear these triglycerides from the blood more rapidly after a high-fat meal.[20]

Other strategies for lowering serum triglycerides include weight loss; reductions in dietary sugar, fat, and alcohol; and the substitution of fish for meat a couple of times during the week. Increasing fish consumption, as long as it is not fried, lowers the dietary intake of calories and saturated fat and increases the intake of omega-3 fatty acids, which tend to lower serum triglycerides.

Blood pressure

Blood pressure, which is recorded in millimeters of mercury (mmHg), is the force exerted against the walls of the arteries as blood travels through the circulatory system. Pressure is created when the heart contracts and pumps blood into the arteries. The arterioles (smallest arteries) offer resistance to blood flow, and if

Keeping your blood pressure under control helps keep your heart healthy.

Table 2-4 Classification of Blood Pressure for Adults Age 18 Years and Older

Category	Systolic (mmHg)	Diastolic (mmHg)
Normal	<130	<85
High normal	130–139	85–89
Hypertension		
Stage 1 (mild)	140–159	90–99
Stage 2 (moderate)	160–179	100–109
Stage 3 (severe)	180–209	110–119
Stage 4 (very severe)	≥210	≥120

the resistance is persistently high, the pressure rises and remains high. The medical term for high blood pressure is **hypertension**.

Hypertension is a silent disease that has no characteristic signs or symptoms, so blood pressure should be checked periodically. Blood pressure can be measured quickly with a sphygmomanometer. A cuff is wrapped around the upper arm and inflated with enough air to compress the artery, temporarily stopping blood flow. A stethoscope is placed on the artery below the cuff so that the sound of blood coursing through the artery can be heard when the air is released. The first sound represents the systolic pressure (the maximum pressure of blood flow when the heart contracts), and the last sound heard is the diastolic pressure (the minimum pressure of blood flow between heart beats). A typical pressure for young adults is 120/80. Pressures of 140/90 or greater are considered to be hypertensive.[1] The lower limit of normal is 100/60. From a health perspective, having a low to normal blood pressure and maintaining it as long as possible is advantageous.

Standards for classifying blood pressure in adults appear in table 2-4. This table represents the latest thinking among medical researchers about the stages of blood pressure values. All hypertensive values in the table represent an increased risk for cardiovascular and kidney disease. The higher the blood pressure, the greater the risk. The lower the blood pressure (within normal range), the better. For example, a 2 mmHg decrease in systolic blood pressure is estimated to reduce the risk of mortality from stroke by 6 percent and from coronary heart disease by 4 percent.[21]

Approximately 50 million American adults and children have high blood pressure, and 35,130 people die of its complications annually.[1] The cause of high blood pressure is not known in 90 to 95 percent of the cases. This is referred to as *essential hypertension*. *Essential* is a medical term that means "of unknown origin or cause." Essential hypertension cannot be cured, but it can be controlled. The other 5 to 10 percent of the cases of hypertension have a specific cause. If the cause can be determined and eliminated, blood pressure will return to normal.

The heart is adversely affected by uncontrolled or undiagnosed hypertension of long duration. Pumping blood for years against high resistance in the arteries increases the workload of the heart, and it becomes enlarged in response to the strain. The heart receives inadequate rest because the resistance to blood flow is consistently high, and this produces overly stretched muscle fibers. They progressively lose the ability to rebound. The result is that they contract less forcefully. At this point the heart loses its efficiency and weakens. If intervention does not occur early, congestive heart failure is inevitable. Hypertension also damages the arteries and accelerates atherosclerosis.

Hypertension is the most important risk factor for brain attacks (strokes) as well as a major risk for heart disease. More than 500,000 brain attacks occur every year. Certain segments of the population are at higher

Wellness on the Web Behavior Change Activities

What's Your Risk for Heart Disease?

In the battle to maintain a healthy heart, you have a powerful ally. The American Heart Association (AHA) is dedicated to educating and informing you on how to fight heart disease and stroke. Go to the AHA website at www.amhrt.org and complete the interactive risk assessment titled "What's Your Risk?" This assessment will show you what factors place you at greater risk for heart disease and allow you to take charge of your health by making more healthful lifestyle choices. Complete the 16 items and then click on the Submit button for your results. Which of your risk factors cannot be changed? Which can you change?

What Questions Should I Ask My Physician?

Often we tend to think of doctors as all-knowing gurus who can tell us everything we need to live a healthy life. The fact is, your relationship with your physician is really a partnership—and for best results, you need to know what to ask when you visit your doctor. The American Heart Association reminds you that, after making healthful lifestyle changes, your second-best friend in the fight against heart disease and stroke is your doctor. For help in formulating questions for this vital partner in your health care, go to the AHA website for women at http://women.americanheart.org/self_care/fs_doctor.html and read 10 questions you should ask your doctor at your next checkup. Help your physician help you live a healthier life!

Healthy Heart Workout Quiz

Attention couch potatoes: Physical inactivity is officially recognized as a major risk factor for cardiovascular disease by the American Heart Association! Your body was constructed for physical exertion—and actually thrives on it—whereas inactivity is debilitating. Go to the AHA website for women at http://women.americanheart.org/self_care/fs_fitness.html and take the "Healthy Heart Workout Quiz." After answering the 10 questions, click on the Submit button to receive your results. How much did you know about exercise and your heart?

---

risk, such as African-Americans, who have more than a 60 percent greater risk of death and disability from stroke than do whites; this is a direct result of pervasive hypertension.[22] Stroke mortality is highest in African-American females who were born before 1950 and in African-American males born after 1950.

Treatment for hypertension. Treatment for hypertension may include all or some of the following: weight loss, salt and alcohol restriction, calcium and potassium supplementation, voluntary relaxation techniques, exercise, and medication. Excess body weight increases the work of the heart because it must meet the nutrient demands of the extra tissue.

High salt intake increases the blood pressure in those who are salt sensitive. Estimates indicate that at least 30 percent of Americans are salt sensitive, but the actual number is probably higher. Salt is an acquired taste that can be modified. Curbing salt consumption while blood pressure is still normal cannot hurt and it may help.

Some calcium-deficient hypertensive people may normalize their blood pressure by taking calcium supplements. However, calcium supplementation does not work for all calcium-deficient hypertensive people, and it does not work for hypertensive people who are not calcium deficient.

Yoga, meditation, hypnotherapy, biofeedback, and other relaxation techniques can lower the pressure of hypertensive people. They can also reduce the pressure of normotensive people (those with normal blood pressure).[23] Meditating hypertensive people lowered their systolic pressure by 11 points and their diastolic pressure by 6 points more than did people in a control group who were counseled on the importance of losing excess weight, exercising regularly, cutting salt consumption, and drinking less alcohol.

Many people drink alcohol because it relaxes them, but ingestion of more than 2 ounces of alcohol per day raises blood pressure in some people. The same precautions regarding the use of alcohol and HDL cholesterol apply for hypertension.

The American College of Sports Medicine (ACSM) has developed a position paper on the relationship between exercise and hypertension.[24] Some of the more important conclusions follow:

1. Endurance exercises can reduce both systolic and diastolic pressures by 10 points each in people with mild essential hypertension (with systolic pressures between 140 and 180 mmHg and diastolic pressures between 90 and 105 mmHg).
2. Moderately intense endurance exercises lower the blood pressure as much as or more than vigorous exercise.
3. Endurance exercise training delays or prevents the onset of hypertension in people who are at high risk.

4. By itself, resistive or strength training does not seem to lower the blood pressure unless it is accompanied by aerobic training and is done in a circuit (circuit training is explained in Chapter 4).
5. Physically fit hypertensive people have a lower mortality rate than do physically unfit normotensive people.

The mechanisms through which exercise lowers blood pressure in hypertensive individuals are not fully understood. The probable mechanisms include the following:

1. Exercise contributes to weight loss, which in turn lowers blood pressure.
2. Aerobic training reduces resistance to blood flow in the arteries and at rest, lowering the force required to circulate blood.
3. Many hypertensive people have elevated levels of hormones that constrict blood vessels. Exercise metabolizes these, which results in less resistance to blood flow.
4. Exercise training sensitizes the cells to insulin, so less circulates in the blood. The kidneys respond by excreting sodium, which reduces the blood pressure.

Medications that control blood pressure have been developed. However, they have side effects that include weakness, leg cramps, stuffy nose, occasional diarrhea, heartburn, drowsiness, anemia, depression, headaches, joint pain, dizziness, impotence, and skin rash. The side effects are unique to the drugs being used to control blood pressure. Despite these side effects, many people find it easier to take the medicine than to make the difficult lifestyle changes that lower blood pressure. However, the effort to control blood pressure with medication should not negate the importance of controlling lifestyle factors that contribute to hypertension. Medicine and lifestyle efforts are not mutually exclusive—each contributes to blood pressure management.

Cigarette smoking/tobacco use

Many medical authorities consider cigarette smoking the most harmful of the preventable risk factors associated with chronic illness and premature death.[25] The American Cancer Society estimates that approximately 419,000 annual deaths are related to cigarette smoking.[25] In 1987, lung cancer became the leading cause of cancer death among women, replacing breast cancer. In 1997, 66,000 women died of lung cancer compared to 44,000 who died of breast cancer. Eighty-seven percent of all lung cancers in both sexes are directly related to cigarette smoking. Additionally, smoking accounts for 29 percent of all cancer deaths. Further, it is a major cause of heart disease and is associated with chronic bronchitis, emphysema, strokes, and other diseases.

Harmful products in cigarettes. Nicotine, carbon monoxide, and other poisonous gases, tars, and chemical additives for taste and flavor are the hazardous products in cigarettes. Carbon monoxide and nicotine have a devastating effect on the heart and blood vessels. Nicotine is an addictive stimulant that increases the resting heart rate, blood pressure, and metabolism. For this reason, it should be reclassified as a drug and placed under the jurisdiction of the Food and Drug Administration (FDA).

A brief summary of nicotine's effects on the cardiovascular system is found in Just the Facts: Nicotine. Carbon monoxide, a poisonous gas that is a by-product of the combustion of tobacco products, displaces oxygen in the blood because it has a greater attraction to hemoglobin. The diminished oxygen-carrying capacity of the blood is partly responsible for the shortness of breath that smokers experience with mild physical exertion.

Cigarettes and other tobacco products are not regulated by the FDA because tobacco is not classified as a food or drug. The tobacco industry is under no mandate to disclose the nature and type of chemicals that are added to tobacco products. Some of these additives are harmful. The public has a right to know, but the tobacco industry has successfully resisted attempts by government agencies and consumer groups to force disclosure.

The harmful effects of cigarette smoking are insidious and take time to appear. The medical profession measures the damage from smoking in pack years. Smoking one pack of cigarettes per day for fifteen years is equal to 15 pack years (15 years × 1 pack per day =

Just the Facts
Nicotine

Nicotine is a powerful stimulant that does the following:

- Increases LDL and lowers HDL levels
- Causes the platelets to aggregate, increasing the probability of arterial spasms
- Increases the oxygen requirement of cardiac muscle
- Constricts blood vessels
- Produces cardiac dysrhythmias (irregular heart beat)
- Is a causative agent in the 30% of coronary heart disease deaths related to smoking
- Increases the viscosity of the blood

15 pack years). Two packs per day for fifteen years is equal to 30 pack years (15 × 2 = 30). Medical problems become evident after 25 to 30 pack years.

The challenge of quitting. To quit the tobacco habit, you have to simultaneously break the addiction to nicotine and the psychological dependence on smoking. This involves changing behavior and effectively dealing with the social and situational stimuli that promote the desire to smoke. In a survey in 1984, 69 percent of smokers reported that they wanted to stop smoking.[26] Since 1964, more men than women have quit, more whites than African-Americans, and more non-Hispanics than Hispanics. More elderly people and more educated people also have higher quit rates.[27]

Complicating the effort to quit, particularly among young women, is the fear of gaining weight. Approximately 65 percent of those who quit do gain weight, but the physiological adaptations that occur may only account for a 7- to 8-pound weight gain. The physiological mechanisms responsible are probably associated with a slowing of metabolism, a slight increase in appetite, and slower transit time of food in the digestive system so that more is absorbed by the body. Weight gain beyond 8 pounds is probably caused by altered eating patterns rather than physiology. Food smells and tastes better when a person is not smoking. Food may substitute for a cigarette, especially during social activities. It may provide some of the oral gratification previously obtained from smoking, and it may relieve tension. Weight gain can be avoided by eating sensibly and exercising moderately and frequently.

As a group, smokers are 7 percent thinner than nonsmokers, but smokers tend to distribute more fat in the abdominal area.[28] The waist-to-hip ratio (WHR) is greater in smokers even though they are thinner. This fat distribution predisposes smokers to coronary heart disease, diabetes, stroke, and some forms of cancer.

Passive smoking and smokeless tobacco. Involuntary or passive smoking (inhaling the smoke of others) is associated with premature disease and death. Estimates indicate that 38,000 to 43,000 nonsmokers who are regularly exposed to environmental smoke die annually from smoking-related causes.[25] The majority of these (35,000 to 40,000) die from heart disease, and 3000 die from lung cancer. There is a dose-response effect. The more the nonsmoker is exposed to environmental smoke, the greater his or her risk for premature morbidity (illness) and mortality (death).

Children of smoking parents are more likely to experience a higher incidence of influenza, colds, bronchitis, asthma, and pneumonia. The impact of passive smoking on them can last a lifetime and may range from delayed physical and intellectual development to the hazards associated with prolonged exposure to carcinogenic substances.

An alarming trend is the escalating sale of smokeless tobacco products. Chewing tobacco and dipping snuff have become popular among high school and college men. The World Health Organization (WHO) has described the growing use of smokeless tobacco as a new threat to society. Nicotine is an addictive drug regardless of the method of delivery, and its effects are similar whether it is inhaled, as in smoking, or absorbed through the tissues of the oral cavity, as in dipping and chewing. The incidence of oral cancer may be 50 times higher among long-term users of smokeless tobacco products than among nonusers. Smokeless tobacco is addictive and deadly, and its use is rising among adolescent males.

Cigar sales in the country had been flat for twenty-five years until 1994, when sales began to increase as the result of a marketing campaign by the magazine *Cigar Aficionado*, cigar invitation-only dinners, and celebrity endorsements of cigar smoking, characterizing it as sophisticated and glamorous. Cigar smoking is no longer looked upon as the sole dominion of males; many women have taken up the habit. Cigar sales increased from 3.4 billion in 1993 to 5.1 billion in 1997.[29]

Cigars were not specifically included in the 1984 law that required tobacco companies to place labels on packages of cigarettes warning that they were hazardous to health. As a result, cigars carry no such warning label. This does not mean that cigar smoking is not harmful to health. See Just the Facts: Cigar Smoking—a Hazard to Health for the facts on cigar smoking.

Physical inactivity

Physical inactivity is finally being officially recognized as a major risk factor for cardiovascular disease by the American Heart Association.[1] The upgrading of physical inactivity, which appeared in the AHA's 1993 report, reflects the importance of participating in physical activities regularly. The AHA made the upgrade because the weight of the evidence that has been accumulating in the last few decades shows that exercise produces many important health benefits. This is good news for those who have been physically active, and it may motivate some sedentary people to become active.

Physical inactivity (hypokinesis) is debilitating to the human body. A couple of weeks of bed rest or chair rest produce muscle atrophy, bone demineralization, and decreases in aerobic capacity and maximum breathing capacity. Your body was constructed for and thrives on physical exertion.

Just the Facts

Cigar Smoking: A Hazard to Health

A common assumption is that cigar smoking is not as hazardous as cigarette smoking, because people usually don't inhale cigar smoke. The facts regarding the dangers of cigar smoking are as follows:

- Cigars contain nicotine, carbon monoxide, tars, and poisonous gases.
- Nicotine reaches the brain by being absorbed through the lining of the mouth rather than from the lungs, but the effect is the same. See Just the Facts: Nicotine for a summary of nicotine's harmful effects on the heart and blood vessels.
- Most of the same cancer-producing substances found in cigarettes are also present in cigars.
- Overall cancer deaths are 34 percent higher for men who smoke cigars than for men who do not.
- Cigar smokers have 4 to 10 times more risk of dying from mouth and throat cancers than do nonsmokers.

Two major reviews have shown that physical inactivity poses a significant risk for developing heart disease. In one review, the researchers critiqued forty-three studies and concluded that physical inactivity increased the risk for coronary heart disease by 1.5 to 2.4 times.[30] The risk associated with physical inactivity is similar to that of the other major risk factors. According to the Centers for Disease Control and Prevention, the need for regular exercise by the general public should be promoted as vigorously as efforts to control blood pressure, lower cholesterol, and stop smoking. A later review by another team of researchers concluded that inactive people have a 90 percent greater risk for developing coronary heart disease than do active people.[31]

With few exceptions, the results of later studies are consistent with the results of these two reviews. Some of the more recent studies have indicated a dose-response relationship between level of physical activity and cardiovascular disease.[32] This means that (1) men at high risk who regularly participate in light- to moderate-intensity physical activity expending about 1500 calories per week will likely lower their risk for coronary heart disease by about 25 percent to 50 percent, and (2) men who engage regularly in more intense physical activity (above the moderate level) lower their risk for coronary heart disease by 60 to 70 percent and experience greater longevity.

Several studies examined the effect on coronary heart disease on the level of physical fitness rather than on the total numbers of calories expended per week in physical activity. These studies corroborated the results of the calorie expenditure studies that physically fit people are less inclined to develop coronary heart disease than are unfit people. (Thus far, only one long-term study has included women in the subject population.[33])

In summary, people who are actively engaged in leisure-time or occupational physical activity as well as those who participate in physical activities for the purpose of developing fitness are at a lower risk of death from cardiovascular disease and all-cause mortality. Other major studies have supported the view that people who regularly engage in physical activities of moderate intensity have significantly fewer heart attacks and experience fewer deaths from all causes than do people who exercise little or not at all. Moderate activity was described as the equivalent of walking 1 to 2 miles per day for a total of 5 to 10 miles per week. The greatest health benefits were gained by those who expended 1500 to 2000 calories per week (15 to 20 miles of walking) in physical activity. A total of 17,000 men were followed for more than thirty years. Those who regularly walked, climbed stairs, or participated in sports activities decreased their risk from all causes of mortality. Those who expended a minimum of 500 calories per week (5 miles of walking or its equivalent) to a maximum of 3500 calories per week (35 miles of walking or its equivalent) experienced a progressive increase in longevity.

Investigators at the Cooper Institute for Aerobics Research[33] studied the relationship between physical fitness and mortality from all causes. The uniqueness of this study was twofold: first, the researchers measured the physical fitness levels of all subjects by treadmill testing, and second, more than 3000 of the 13,344 subjects were women. Because of their lower risk for cardiovascular disease, women have essentially been neglected as subjects in heart disease studies.

The results of this study indicated that a low physical fitness level increased the risk for both men and women of death from cardiovascular disease, cancer, and all other forms of disease. The difference in all-cause mortality was greatest between those who were in the moderately fit category and those in the low-fit category. The difference between the moderately fit and the highly fit was insignificant. For people who exercise regularly, the risk of dying from a heart attack is 35 to 55 percent less than it is for sedentary people.[34]

A study using only women as subjects investigated the physical fitness benefits versus the health benefits of three levels of walking intensity.[35] One group walked at 5 MPH, a second group walked at 4 MPH, and a third group walked at 3 MPH. The results showed that physical fitness improved on a predictable dose-response basis. The fastest walkers improved the most and the slowest walkers improved the least, but the cardiovascular risk was reduced equally among the three groups. Low-level exercise was as effective as the highest level in promoting cardiovascular health. Exercise for health does not have to be as strenuous as exercise for physical fitness.

The American College of Sports Medicine and the Centers for Disease Control and Prevention reacted to the results of these studies by jointly issuing a new recommendation for exercise for Americans. The new guideline states that "every U.S. adult should accumulate 30 minutes or more of moderate intensity physical activity on most, preferably all, days of the week."[36] This is a minimum guideline for exercise and was not intended to replace previous recommendations regarding more vigorous exercise for the purpose of improving physical fitness. Instead, the recommendation is directed at that 60 percent of our population who are sedentary or marginally active. Health professionals hope that the new recommendation will motivate physically inactive and underactive Americans to participate in a more active lifestyle.

The term *physical activity* refers to any physical movement that results in energy expenditure. Physical activity includes but is not limited to walking, climbing stairs, mowing the lawn (using a riding mower does not count), raking leaves without a blower, mopping and vacuuming floors, washing and waxing the car (by hand), dancing, and playing with children and grandchildren. Moderate intensity physical activity can be achieved by walking 3 to 4 miles per hour or through any other activity that burns as many calories as walking at those speeds.

People who consistently exercise above the moderate level not only receive the health benefits but also develop a higher level of physical fitness. Those who exercise in accordance with the new guidelines gain about the same health benefits as those who are more physically active, but they will not attain the same degree of physical fitness. That 60 percent of the population who are inclined to ignore the advice to exercise regularly can become part of the estimated 250,000 premature deaths per year that are attributed to a **sedentary** lifestyle.

The health and longevity returns from exercise and a physically active lifestyle are significant. Estimates indicate that longevity is increased by 1 minute for every minute spent walking and by 2 minutes for every minute spent jogging.[37] The potential for improving the health status of Americans through appropriate lifestyle behaviors is evident from estimates indicating that 60 percent of all deaths are premature and approximately 50 to 60 percent of all illness and disabilities are preventable.[38]

Obesity

Obesity strains the heart and co-exists with many of the modifiable risk factors that promote cardiovascular disease. Obese people who have no other risk factors are still more likely to develop heart disease or stroke. Obesity contributes to approximately 300,000 deaths annually in the United States. Not only is obesity associated with an increased risk for heart disease, but the manner in which fat is distributed in the body might also accentuate the risk.[39] Fat that accumulates in the upper half of the body (referred to as *visceral* or *central abdominal obesity*) is likely to be accompanied by high triglycerides, low HDL cholesterol, insulin resistance, and hypertension. This cluster of factors is called *syndrome X*, and it is associated with a significant increase in the likelihood of developing cardiovascular disease.

Obese people can lower their risk with a modest weight loss of 5 to 10 percent. This is a realistic, attainable goal. But the risk remains lower only if the loss of weight is maintained. Approximately 95 percent of people who lose weight regain it in a few years. Although dieting is the primary method for losing weight, regular exercise is the most effective method for maintaining the loss.

Other Contributing Factors

Diabetes mellitus

Diabetes mellitus is a metabolic disorder in which the body cannot make use of sugar (glucose) as a fuel. The hormone insulin must be produced and secreted into the bloodstream so that blood sugar can be transported into the cells. The cells have receptor sites to which insulin attaches, making the cell amenable to the entrance of sugar.

In type I diabetes, no insulin is produced, and so it must be injected daily. Type I, insulin-dependent diabetes mellitus (IDDM), usually occurs early in life. Type II, or non–insulin-dependent diabetes mellitus (NIDDM), occurs in middle-aged, overweight, sedentary adults. Excessive weight is a factor because it increases cellular resistance to insulin so that more insulin than normal is required to effect the passage of sugar from the blood to the cells. In contrast, exercise decreases insulin resistance, making cellular membranes more permeable to sugar. About 90 percent of all diabetes mellitus is of the type II variety. Data indicate that at least 75 percent of new cases of type II diabetes can be prevented through regular exercise and maintaining normal weight.[40]

Nurturing Your Spirituality

Can Stress and Depression Make You Sick?

A convincing body of evidence suggests that chronic anger, anxiety, loneliness, or depression can be catastrophic for people with coronary artery disease.[42] At the same time, emerging evidence shows that these same mood states and feelings in healthy people may increase the likelihood of developing heart disease in the future.

Scientists are beginning to unravel the connection between mood states and heart disease. Consistently high levels of stress hormones circulating in the bloodstream suppress the immune system by interfering with the normal repair and maintenance functions of the body. This increases one's vulnerability to infections and disease. Continuing high levels of cortisol and norepinephrine stimulate a prolonged fight or flight response that can eventually lead to wear and tear on the heart and arteries. Frequent and prolonged periods of stress increase blood pressure, and that usually leads to injuries of the artery walls. These injuries are the first step in the development and ultimate progression of atherosclerosis.[43] Data indicate that exaggerated responses to stress may be a triggering mechanism for heart attack and stroke.

Depression (prolonged sadness beyond a reasonable length of time) also stimulates the production of stress hormones. Depression that occurs later in life increases the risk of coronary heart disease in two ways: (1) by reducing blood flow to the heart in those whose blood vessels are narrowed and (2) by causing heart rhythm disturbances.[44]

Scientists have much to learn about the relationship between the heart and mind. Physicians are beginning to acknowledge that depression is a significant factor in producing cardiovascular complications for those who already have heart disease. The good news is that depression is treatable. Mild depression responds to regular exercise and voluntary relaxation techniques, both of which reduce the production of stress hormones. On the other hand, severe depression requires psychological counseling and medication plus regular exercise and relaxation training. Eighty percent of all people with severe depression respond to treatment.

Regular exercise promotes relaxation, reduces the response to stress, enhances emotional well-being, and lowers cardiac reactivity (high heart rate, blood pressure, and resistance to blood flow). Cardiac reactivity occurs when modest stressors produce physiological responses by the heart and circulatory system that are out of proportion to the stressor. If these occur frequently, the development of atherosclerosis may well be the result.

Exercise acts as a safety valve that enables people to "let off steam" in a constructive way. Jogging, swimming, cycling, weight training, racquetball, and other exercises focus our energies in worthwhile pursuits that rid the body of stress products that have accumulated. Exercise training, which is a physiological stressor, helps build tolerance to psychological and emotional stressors. In other words, the "physiological toughness" developed through exercise training enables us to cope more effectively with other types of stressors.[45]

Do stress and depression cause heart attacks? The answer is a qualified "yes." We should have a more definitive answer after a few more years of research.

Diabetes mellitus has numerous long-range complications. These primarily involve degenerative disorders of the blood vessels and nerves. Diabetics who die prematurely are usually the victims of cardiovascular lesions and accelerated atherosclerosis. The incidence of heart attacks and strokes is higher among diabetics than nondiabetics. In fact, diabetes increases the risk of coronary artery disease by 2 to 3 times the normal rate in men and 3 to 7 times the normal rate in women.

The arteries supplying the kidneys, eyes, and legs are particularly susceptible to atherosclerosis. Kidney failure is one of the long-term complications of diabetes. Diabetes is also the leading cause of blindness in U.S. adults. Impaired delivery of blood to the legs may lead to gangrene, necessitating amputation of the affected tissues. In addition to circulatory problems, degenerative lesions in the nervous system may result, leading to multiple diseases that result in dysfunction of the brain, spinal cord, and peripheral nerves. Unfortunately, medical science has been unable to identify the biological mechanisms responsible for these long-term vascular and neural complications. However, these complications can be mitigated by leading a balanced, well-regulated life, thereby keeping diabetes under control. Control includes dietary manipulation, exercise, weight control, rest, and medication if needed.

The landmark Physician's Health Study was the first major effort to show that exercise reduced the risk of developing type II diabetes. The physicians participating in the study who exercised vigorously five or more times per week had a 42 percent greater reduction in the incidence of type II diabetes than did those who exercised less than one time per week. The reduction in risk was particularly pronounced among those at greatest risk: the obese. The researchers concluded that at least 24 percent of all cases of type II diabetes were related to sedentary living. Even high-risk men (those who were overweight and had a parental history of diabetes) benefited from regular exercise. Every 500 calories burned per week in leisure-time physical activity reduced the risk of type II diabetes by 6 percent.[41]

Stress

Stress is difficult to define and quantify. Authorities agree that distress, or chronic stress, produces a complex array of physiological changes in the body. Together, these physiological events are called the *fight or flight response*. The hormones that are released by the body during these events produce the stress response. This includes (1) increases in heart rate, breathing rate, blood pressure; (2) the tendency for blood platelets to aggregate (clump together); (3) blood sugar rushing to the muscles to provide more energy; and (4) the activation of the immune system. The stress response represents a significant strain on the body.

Stressors (events or situations that cause stress) may be acute or chronic. Acute stressors are situational and temporary. Taking a midterm exam or making an oral presentation are examples of events that provoke acute stress. When such an event is over, the body returns, within a short time, to its prior state of balance and harmony. However, chronic stress (characterized by prolonged elevations of stress hormones and a general feeling of uneasiness that permeates one's life) presents a much more serious problem. Constant worry about work, finances, or relationships or persistent feelings of anger and isolation are examples of chronic stress. Is chronic stress a causative agent in the development of chronic diseases in general and heart disease specifically? See Nurturing Your Spirituality: Can Stress and Depression Make You Sick? (p. 52)

Prevention of Heart Disease

Preventing heart disease is much preferred to treating it after the fact. Prevention includes regular exercise, maintenance of optimal body weight, sound nutritional practices, abstinence from tobacco products, nonuse of alcohol (or use in moderation), and abstinence from drugs. Dealing with stress in constructive ways, removing oneself as much as possible from destructive and disease-producing environmental conditions, and having periodic medical examinations are other aspects of prevention. It is much better physically, psychologically, and economically to make the effort to enhance health now than to reject or ignore health promotion principles and treat disease later. It is never too late to change behavior. Even patients with coronary artery disease can benefit from lifestyle changes.

Until very recently, medical thinking indicated that established atherosclerotic plaques in the coronary arteries were there to stay. Progression of the disease seemed inevitable unless medical corrective procedures were employed. But evidence has surfaced indicating that reversal of the disease is possible with appropriate lifestyle behaviors.

Dean Ornish showed that comprehensive behavior changes are required to reverse established coronary artery disease. Ornish devised a program that included a vegetarian diet in which only 6.8 percent of the calories came from fat; 4.4 hours of moderate aerobic exercise per week; stress-management techniques consisting of stretching exercises, practicing of breathing techniques, meditation, progressive relaxation, and the use of imagery; smoking cessation; and attendance at regular group support meetings. The subjects in this study were evaluated against a control group who received "usual and customary" care.[46]

At the end of the first year, 82 percent of the subjects in the Ornish program showed regression of atherosclerosis compared with only 10 percent of the usual

Stress-relieving activities, such as meditation, soothe the spirit and may even lower your risk of heart disease and other chronic illnesses. How do you manage stress?

care group. Over the following four years, the Ornish subjects showed further regression, whereas the usual care group experienced progression of atherosclerosis.[47]

Other investigators have examined the effect of less stringent interventions than those advocated by the Ornish program on the regression of atherosclerosis. These attempts have been less successful than the Ornish program but more successful than the usual care program.

The main criticism of the Ornish program was that lifelong compliance would be difficult. Twenty-nine percent of the study participants dropped out during the last four years of the program. It is not easy to permanently change bad habits, but the hard work associated with following a low-fat diet, exercising consistently at a moderately intense level, and giving up smoking can make people with coronary artery disease feel better and may allow them to avoid surgery.

Refer to Assessment Activity 2-1 at the end of this chapter. Respond to each of the risk questions about factors to determine your risk status.

Other Possible Risk Factors

Iron-Enriched Blood

In 1992 a study completed in Finland found that men with high levels of iron (as measured by serum ferritin) also had a high probability of incurring heart problems. Since then, a number of studies completed in the United States have failed to confirm the high iron–high heart disease connection. In fact, these American studies found quite the opposite. Women with high iron levels were found to have half the heart disease risk as women with low iron stores, and men in the high iron group were 20 percent less likely to die of heart disease than were men with the lowest levels.[48] The rationale is that low iron levels lead to a reduction in oxygen-carrying hemoglobin so that less oxygen is transported to the tissues. It is entirely possible that the decrease in oxygen transport to the cells, including the cells of the heart, is responsible for the heart problems that occur with greater frequency in those who are iron deficient.

Now that you are aware of the major risk factors for heart disease, refer to Assessment Activities 2-1 and 2-2 to test your risk and your knowledge. Be as accurate as possible when providing the necessary information for Activity 2-1. Read the case study (Assessment 2-2) and respond to all of the questions.

Homocysteine

Homocysteine is an amino acid that is derived from food. Its function is to manufacture protein to build and maintain body tissues. Homocysteine is carried through the bloodstream, and under normal conditions, it is broken down into two other amino acids. When that breakdown does not occur, homocysteine levels rise to present a risk for heart disease. Several studies, including the Physician's Health Study and the Framingham Heart Study, showed that the probability of having a heart attack increases to 3 times the normal level in subjects with the highest homocysteine levels. This puts homocysteine on par with the other major risk factors for coronary artery disease.[49]

Homocysteine is measured in *micromoles*, which are based on molecular weight. The normal range is 4 to 15 micromoles per deciliter of blood. Heart attacks are more likely to occur to those whose levels are above 15.[50]

Homocysteine contributes to heart disease probably by damaging the inner lining of the arteries. The damage initiates the abnormal growth of smooth muscle cells, which in turn promotes the development and progression of atherosclerosis.

The good news is that homocysteine levels can be controlled with diet. The B vitamins (folic acid or folate, B_6, and B_{12}) are needed to split homocysteine into other amino acids. Folate is the most important of the three, but evidence indicates that optimal benefits occur when all three are available in appropriate amounts. The recommended daily amounts for these vitamins are 400 micrograms of folate, 6 micrograms of B_{12}, and 2 milligrams of B_6.

Lipoprotein (a) or Lp (a)

Lipoprotein (a) represents a group of particles that resemble LDL-C (the bad form of cholesterol). A high circulating level of Lp (a) in the blood may increase the risk for coronary artery disease and stroke, and although study results are not yet conclusive, they appear to be heading in that direction. Many scientists believe that high levels of Lp (a) promote the formation of blood clots and increase the ability of LDL-C to form plaque (the material that blocks arteries).

Lp (a) levels above 30 milligrams per deciliter of blood are considered high. Some medical researchers believe that high values of Lp (a) may be as dangerous to the heart as low levels of HDL-C (the good form of cholesterol).[51] Lp (a) levels are determined primarily by one's genetic composition. Low-fat diets and cholesterol-lowering drugs have little effect on Lp (a). Therefore, people with high levels of Lp (a) should concentrate on lowering LDL-C and total cholesterol, raising HDL, and keeping the other heart disease risk factors under control.

Medical Contributions

Diagnostic Techniques

Diagnosing cardiovascular disease is becoming more sophisticated. Diagnosis begins with a medical examination and patient history. This procedure may be supplemented with a variety of tests that may confirm or refute the physician's suspicions of the presence of cardiovascular disease. Exercise stress tests using a motor-driven treadmill with the patient hooked to an electrocardiogram (ECG) have gained popularity in the last ten years or so. Such noninvasive tests use surface electrodes on the chest that are sensitive to the electrical actions of the heart. Mechanical abnormalities of the heart produce abnormal electrical impulses that are displayed on the ECG strip. These are read and interpreted by the physician.

The treadmill "road tests" the heart as it works progressively harder to meet the increasing oxygen requirement as the exercise protocol becomes more physically demanding. This test is more accurate for men than women. The gender difference in response to the treadmill test is not completely understood, but it is believed that women's breasts and extra fat tissue interfere with the reception of electrical impulses by the chest electrodes.

In some cases a thallium treadmill test is required because it is more sensitive; however, it is also much more expensive. This involves the injection of radioactive thallium during the final minute of the treadmill test. Thallium is accepted, or taken up, by normal heart muscle but not by ischemic heart muscle. The absorption or nonabsorption of thallium can be seen on a television monitor. The thallium stress test increases diagnostic sensitivity to cardiovascular disease to approximately 90 percent.

Echocardiographpy is a safe, noninvasive technique that uses sound waves to determine the size of the heart, the thickness of the walls, and the function of the heart's valves. *Cardiac catheterization* is an invasive technique in which a slender tube is threaded from a blood vessel in an arm or leg into the coronary arteries. A liquid contrast dye that can be seen on X-ray film is injected into the coronary arteries. X-ray films are taken throughout the procedure to locate where and how severely the coronary arteries are narrowed.

Medical Treatment

A variety of drugs are used in cardiovascular therapies. These drugs lower blood pressure and cholesterol, minimize the likelihood of blood clotting, and dissolve clots during a heart attack.

Plain aspirin is proving to be a very effective drug in the fight against heart disease. Low-dose (one-fourth of a regular aspirin) aspirin therapy consisting of a single daily dose for those who have heart disease reduces the risk of having another heart attack or dying from a subsequent attack. Low-dose aspirin therapy is more effective when supplemented with a "booster" dose of one whole aspirin on the first and fifteenth of each month. Lastly, regular aspirin usage may prevent a first heart attack from occurring in apparently healthy people, but no one should take aspirin or any other drug without first consulting a physician.[52]

Surgical techniques have also affected the treatment of cardiovascular disease. *Coronary artery bypass surgery* is designed to shunt blood around an area of blockage by removing a leg vein and sewing one end of a leg vein into the aorta and the other end into a coronary artery below the blockage, thereby restoring blood flow to the heart muscle (figure 2-8).

The internal mammary arteries also are used for bypass grafts. In fact, many authorities consider these to be the ideal grafts. There are two internal mammary arteries, but the one in the left side of the chest is preferable because it is nearer to the coronary arteries. Many surgeons would rather not use both arteries in the same patient because the diminished flow of blood to the chest impairs healing of the surgical wound. Also, fashioning bypass grafts out of these arteries is time-consuming precision surgery, and there are only two of them and they don't reach all parts of the heart. The advantage is that 95 percent of them remain open ten years after surgery.

Balloon angioplasty uses a catheter with a doughnut-shaped balloon at the tip. The catheter is positioned at the narrow point in the artery, and the balloon is inflated, which cracks and compresses the plaque, stretches the artery wall, and widens the blood vessel to allow greater blood flow (figure 2-9). Laser angioplasty uses heat to burn away plaque if the catheter can be maneuvered into the correct position. This technology appears to be useful for patients with certain types of

Figure 2-8 Coronary Bypass Graft

56 **Wellness** Fundamental Concepts and Applications

Figure 2-9 Balloon Angioplasty

Figure 2-10 Coronary Stent

atherosclerotic narrowings or blockages. Coronary atherectomy, one of the newest techniques, uses a specially tipped catheter equipped with a high-speed rotary cutting blade to shave off plaque.

Catheterization techniques are also used to implant a coronary stent in a diseased artery. The stent is a flexible, metallic tube that functions like a scaffold to support the walls of diseased arteries, thus maintaining an open passage for blood flow (figure 2-10). Stents are positioned in such arteries by a catheter. When correctly positioned, a balloon inside the stent is inflated, causing the stent to expand. This action stretches the artery. Then the balloon is withdrawn, leaving the expanded stent behind to keep the blood vessel open.

This technique shows much promise, but there is a serious limitation associated with the procedure: It increases the risk of blood clots forming at the site of the stent. To counteract this risk, patients are given blood-thinning medications for two to three months following the stent's implantation, and then they are maintained on aspirin thereafter.

Artificial valves have been developed to replace defective heart valves, and these work quite well. Artificial (mechanical) hearts have not performed to expectation, however, because modern technology has not produced a device that can be powered internally. It appears that such a device is still a long way off.

Mechanical devices (left ventricular assist devices) have been used to aid the failing hearts of patients awaiting donor hearts. These devices take over the burden of pumping blood throughout the body and may keep patients alive for a month or more. Left ventricular assist devices suffer from the same power source problem as mechanical hearts.

Heart transplants have prolonged many lives. The outlook for patients has improved considerably because of the development and use of medicines to suppress the immune system in such patients and because of refinements in the prevention and early detection of the body's attempts to reject donor hearts. As a result, about 85 percent of transplant patients live longer than one year, and 65 percent survive for at least five years. In 1968, twenty-three heart transplants were performed; in 1995, about 2350 were performed.

Candidates for transplants are those whose hearts are irreversibly damaged with disease that does not respond to conventional treatment. Without a new heart, these people will die. The main problems associated with heart transplantation are insufficient numbers of donors, the difficulty of procuring compatible donor hearts, and the constant threat of organ rejection by the recipient.

Summary

- Approximately 1.5 million heart attacks occur each year, and 500,000 of these result in death.
- The heart is actually two pumps in one; the pulmonary pump, which sends deoxygenated blood to the lungs, and the systemic pump, which sends oxygenated blood to all tissues of the body.
- Blood plasma is a clear, yellowish fluid that makes up about 55 percent of the blood. The remaining 45 percent consists of blood solids—red blood cells, white blood cells, and blood platelets.
- Strokes are caused by a thrombus, an embolus, or a hemorrhage.
- Coronary heart disease is actually a disease of the coronary blood vessels that bring nourishment and oxygen to the heart.
- Many of the risk factors for heart disease originate in childhood.
- The treatment of heart disease includes the development of appropriate lifestyle habits and medical intervention.
- The major risk factors that cannot be changed are age, male gender, and heredity.
- The major risk factors that can be changed are elevated cholesterol levels, hypertension, cigarette smoking, physical inactivity, and obesity.
- The other contributing risk factors are diabetes mellitus and stress.
- Cholesterol is a steroid that is essential for many bodily functions, but too much circulating in the blood creates a risk for cardiovascular disease.
- Low-density lipoproteins are associated with the development of atherosclerotic plaque.
- High-density lipoproteins protect the arteries from the formation of plaque.
- Blood pressure is the force exerted against the walls of the arteries as blood is pumped from the heart and travels through the circulatory system.
- *Hypertension* is the medical term for high blood pressure.
- Cigarette smoking may be the most potent of the risk factors associated with chronic illness and premature death.
- Involuntary, or passive, smoking is associated with premature disease and death.
- Obesity is a major risk factor that often co-exists with many of the other risk factors for cardiovascular disease.
- Diabetes mellitus must be controlled to reduce the cardiovascular complications that accompany it.
- Regular exercise significantly reduces the risk for type II diabetes mellitus.
- Stress predisposes a person to illness and may hasten the disease process.
- Elevated levels of homocysteine and of Lp (a) in the blood are proving to be important risk factors for heart disease.
- Medical research has made a significant contribution to reducing the incidence of heart disease through the development of sophisticated technological advances in diagnosis and treatment.

Review Questions

1. Define *pulmonary pump* and *systemic pump* and discuss the function of each.
2. Describe the advent of heart disease in the United States.
3. Identify and describe the causes of stroke.
4. What is coronary heart disease? Discuss the treatment options that are available.
5. What are the risk factors for heart disease and how are they categorized by the AHA?
6. What is cholesterol? LDL? HDL?
7. What is the relationship between total cholesterol and HDL?
8. What is essential hypertension?
9. What ingredients in cigarettes increase the risk for cardiovascular disease? Describe their effect on the heart and blood vessels.
10. What is the risk associated with smokeless tobacco products?
11. Defend the proposition that a moderate level of exercise improves health and increases longevity.
12. What are the cardiovascular complications of diabetes mellitus?
13. How does stress contribute to cardiovascular disease?
14. Can heart disease be prevented or at least delayed? Identify the lifestyle behaviors that may be involved in the process.
15. Can atherosclerosis be reversed? Cite evidence to support your answer.
16. What contributions has the medical profession made to decreasing the death rate from heart disease?

References

1. American Heart Association: *1997 Heart and stroke—statistical update,* Dallas, 1997, American Heart Association.
2. Risk reduction, *Harvard Heart Letter* 5(11):1, 1995.
3. Squires, R. W. 1998. Coronary atherosclerosis. In *ACSM Resource Manual* (3d ed), ed. J. L. Roitman. Baltimore, Md.: Williams & Wilkins.
4. U.S. Dept. of Health and Human Services: Physical activity and health: a report of the surgeon general, Atlanta, 1996, U.S. Dept. of Health and Human Services, Centers for Disease Control and Prevention, National Center for Chronic Disease Prevention and Health Promotion.
5. Corbin, C. B., and R. P. Pangrazi. *Physical activity for children: a statement of guidelines,* NASE/AAHPERD, 1998.
6. Wardlaw G. M., P. M. Insel, and M. F. Seyler: *Contemporary nutrition: issues and insights,* St Louis, 1994, Mosby.
7. Bartecchi C. E. et al: The human cost of tobacco use, *New England Journal of Medicine* 330(13):907, 1994.
8. Up in smoke, *University of California at Berkeley Wellness Letter* 12(11):8, 1996.
9. Kannell W. B. et al: Epidemiology of acute myocardial infraction: the Framingham Study, *Medicine Today* 2:50, 1968.
10. Margolis S., S. C. Achuff. *Coronary heart disease.* Baltimore: 1998. The Johns Hopkins Medical Institutions.
11. Margolis, S., and L. J. Cheskin. 1998. *Weight Control.* Baltimore: The Johns Hopkins Medical Institutions.
12. Walsh, J. 1998. Low fat, no fat, some fat—high fat? Type of fat, not amount, may be key. *Environmental Nutrition* 21(4):1.
13. University of California at Berkeley. 1994. Fascinating facts. *University of California at Berkeley Wellness Letter* 10(6):1.
14. Lamb, L. 1992. Update on cholesterol and triglycerides. *Health Letter* 39(suppl.):1.
15. Editors. 1984. The lipid research clinics coronary primary prevention trial results. I. Reduction in incidence of coronary heart disease. *JAMA* 251:351.
16. LaRosa, J. C., et al. 1990. The cholesterol facts: A summary of the evidence relating dietary facts, serum cholesterol, and coronary heart disease: A joint statement by the American Heart Association and the National Heart, Lung, and Blood Institute. *Circulation* 81:1721.
17. Steen, S. N., and G. Butterfield. 1998. Diet and nutrition. In *ACSM Resource Manual* (3d ed.), ed. J. L. Roitman. Baltimore, Md.: Williams & Wilkins.
18. Harvard Medical School. 1998. Triglycerides emerge as a coronary risk factor. *Harvard Heart Letter* 8(11):6.
19. Tufts University. 1997. Why you know your triglyceride level. *Tufts University Health and Nutrition Letter* 15(5):3.
20. University of California at Berkeley. 1998. The ups and downs of triglycerides. *University of California at Berkeley Wellness Letter* 14(3):4.
21. National High Blood Pressure Education Program. 1993. *The Fifth Report of the Joint National Committee on Detection, Evaluation and Treatment of High Blood Pressure, National Heart, Lung, and Blood Institute, National Institutes of Health,* NIH publication no. 93-1088, Bethesda, Md.: National Institutes of Health.
22. U.S. Dept of Health and Human Services. 1988. *Healthy People 2010 objectives: Draft for public Comment.* Washington, D.C.: Office of Disease Prevention and Health Promotion.
23. Tufts University. 1997. Meditation lowers blood pressure as well as drugs. *Tufts University Diet and Nutrition Letter* 14(11):3.
24. ACSM. 1993. Physical activity, physical fitness, and hypertension. *Medicine and Science in Sports and Exercise* 25(10):1.
25. American Cancer Society. 1997. *Cancer Facts and Figures—1997,* Atlanta, Ga.: American Cancer Society.
26. Office on Smoking and Health, National Center for Chronic Disease Prevention and Health Promotion, CDC. 1996. Cigarette smoking among adults in the U.S., 1994. *MMWR* 45(27):588.
27. Centers for Disease Control and Prevention. 1994. CDC surveillance summaries. *MMWR* 43(SS-3).
28. U.S. Department of Health and Human Services. 1988. *The Health Consequences of Smoking—Nicotine Addiction, a Report of the Surgeon General.* Rockville, Md.: U.S. Department of Health and Human Services.
29. U.S. Department of Health and Human Services. 1998. *Progress Review—Tobacco, Prevention Report.* Washington, D.C.: Office of Disease Prevention and Health Promotion.
30. Powell, K. E. 1987. Physical activity and the incidence of coronary heart disease. *Annual Review of Public Health* 8:253.
31. Berlin, J. A., and G. A. Colditz. 1990. A meta-analysis of physical activity in the prevention of coronary heart disease. *American Journal of Epidemiology* 132:612.
32. Whaley, M. A., and L. A. Kaminsky. 1998. Epidemiology of physical activity, physical fitness, and selected chronic diseases. In *ACSM Resource Manual* (3d ed.), ed. J. L. Roitman. Baltimore, Md.: Williams & Wilkins.
33. Blair, S. N., et al. 1989. Physical fitness and all-cause mortality—a prospective study of healthy men and women. *JAMA* 262:2395.
34. Manson, J. E., et al. 1992. The primary prevention of myocardial infarction. *New England Medical Journal* 326:1406.
35. Duncan, J. J., et al. 1995. Women walking for health and fitness. *JAMA* 273:402.
36. Pate, R. R., et al. 1995. Physical activity and public health. *JAMA* 273:402.
37. Paffenbarger, R. S., and R. T. Hyde. 1986. Letter. *New England Journal of Medicine.* 315:400.
38. Pescatello, L. S., et al. 1994. Health care reform and the exercise professional. *ACSM Certified News* 4(2):1.
39. Gordon, N. F. 1998. Conceptional basis for coronary artery disease risk factor assessment. In *ACSM Resource Manual* (3d ed.), ed. J. L. Roitman. Baltimore, Md.: Williams & Wilkins.
40. Schardt, D., and S. Schmidt. 1996. How to avoid onset diabetes. *Nutrition Action Health Letter* 23(7):3.
41. Manson, J. E., et al. 1992. A prospective study of exercise and incidence of

diabetes among U.S. male physicians. *JAMA* 268:63.
42. Harvard University. 1998. Can stress make you sick? *Harvard Health Letter* 23(6):1.
43. Harvard University. 1998. Stress and atherosclerosis. *Harvard Health Letter* 23(4):8.
44. Harvard University. 1998. Grumpy old men: At risk for coronary disease? *Harvard Health Letter* 8(12):7.
45. Sime, W. E., R. S. Eliot, and E. E. Solberg. 1998. Stress and heart disease. In *ACSM Resource Manual* (3d ed.), ed. J. L. Roitman. Baltimore, Md.: Williams & Wilkins.
46. Ornish, D., et al. 1990. Can lifestyle changes reverse coronary heart disease? *The Lancet* 336:129.
47. Ornish, D., et al. 1993. Can lifestyle changes reverse atherosclerosis? Four-year results of the lifestyle heart trial. *Circulation* 88(suppl.):2064.
48. Editors. 1997. Iron's link to heart disease. *Healthnews* 3(3):7.
49. Harvard University. 1997. Evidence mounts for heart disease marker. *Harvard Health Letter* 22(11):1.
50. Mayo Clinic. 1977. Homocysteine. *Mayo Clinic Health Letter* 15(12):7.
51. University of California at Berkeley. 1997. Ask the experts. *University of California at Berkeley Wellness Letter* 14(3):7.
52. Hennekens, C. H., M. L. Dyken, and V. Fuster. 1997. Aspirin as a therapeutic agent in cardiovascular disease—a statement for healthcare professionals from the American Heart Association. *Circulation* 96:2757.

Suggested Readings

Harvard University. 1998. B vitamins and heart disease. *Harvard Health Letter* 23(12):8.

This article promotes the idea that a lack of vitamin B_6 may be a more important marker for heart disease than homocysteine levels in the blood. One major study suggests the possibility that heart attacks may produce an increase in homocysteine levels rather than the other way around. More research will clarify the roles of vitamin B_6 and homocysteine.

Tufts University. 1998. Different strokes—or no strokes at all—can improve fitness. *Tufts University Health and Nutrition Letter* 16(8):7.

This article extols the virtues of water exercise as an effective and safe means of improving one's level of physical fitness. Although swimming is appropriate for those who swim, other water activities may be used in place of swimming by those who do not.

University of California at Berkeley. 1998. Exercise does the trick. *University of California at Berkeley Wellness Letter* 15(1):2.

A short synopsis that examines the roles of exercise and diet in lowering cholesterol, total and LDL-C. It provides evidence to support combining dieting and exercise.

Brehm, B. A. 1998. Six tips for helping a friend kick the habit. *Fitness Management* 14(12):28.

This article tries to sensitize nonsmokers to the difficulty encountered by smokers who are trying to quit. The author provides six ways that nonsmokers can help smokers quit.

Gower, T. 1998. Rating the cholesterol busters. *Health* 12(8):120.

This article discusses natural ways to lower cholesterol. Natural ways include soy, soluble fiber, garlic, vitamin E, cholestin, and niacin.

Chapter 2 Preventing Cardiovascular Disease

Name _____ Date _____ Section _____

Assessment Activity 2-2

A Case Study of Bill M.

Directions: To determine your understanding of cardiovascular health and wellness, read the following case study and answer the accompanying questions. Bill, a 38-year-old man who is 5'8" tall and weighs 205 lb, has the following history:

- His father died of a heart attack at age 48 years; his grandfather died of a heart attack at age 52 years.
- His cholesterol level is 256 mg/dl, LDL is 172 mg/dl, and HDL is 40 mg/dl.
- His blood pressure is consistently in the 150/95 range.
- He smokes one pack of cigarettes per day.
- He drinks six to eight brewed cups of coffee daily.
- He eats two eggs with bacon or sausage and buttered toast daily.
- Meat is a major part of supper; he skips lunch.
- His favorite snacks are ice cream, buttered popcorn, and salted peanuts.
- He occasionally plays tennis on Sunday afternoons.
- He owns his own business and often works 55 to 60 hours per week.

Answer the following:

What are Bill's risk factors for coronary heart disease? _____

Which of these can he control? _____

What suggestions can you give him regarding his current diet? _____

_____

What effect may a change in diet have on his coronary risk profile? _____

_____

What suggestions can you make regarding Bill's need for exercise, and how might a change in his activity level affect his coronary risk profile? _____

_____

What are the risks associated with obesity? _____

_____

3

Increasing Cardiorespiratory Endurance

Key Terms

aerobic
aerobic capacity
cardiorespiratory endurance
cross-training
health-related fitness
hyperthermia
hypothermia
performance-related fitness

Objectives

After completing this chapter, you will be able to:
- Identify and define the health-related components of physical fitness.
- Discuss the principles of conditioning.
- Calculate your target heart rate for exercise by two different methods.
- Identify and discuss the health benefits of consistent participation in exercise.
- Describe the problems associated with exercise in hot and cold weather.

Goals for Behavior Change

- List three physical activities you normally do every week (exclusive of structured, planned exercise) and find and implement ways of making them more challenging.
- If you do not exercise regularly, list several factors that will motivate you to begin a cardiorespiratory endurance program. Begin a simple walking or other exercise program with these factors in mind.
- If you are physically active, list the main factors that will encourage you to improve the frequency, intensity, or duration of your activity. To help you stay motivated, post this list in a place where you will see it every day.
- Choose a piece of home exercise equipment that seems well suited to your exercise preferences and goals.

Technology has affected the lives of Americans by increasing productivity while simultaneously reducing and in some cases eliminating the amount of physical work for the labor force. Therefore, physical fitness for most of the population can no longer be attained on the job, and leisure hours represent the only time for its development. Literally dozens of physical activities, exercise regimens, sports, games, and household and other physical chores that may contribute to health enhancement and fitness development are available. These activities are sufficiently different from each other, running the gamut from low to high skill requirement, so that almost anyone can find one or two activities that are enjoyable, fun, and challenging. This chapter focuses on the principles and concepts that have evolved for developing cardiorespiratory endurance for the purposes of health enhancement and physical fitness.

The Components of Physical Fitness

Authorities do not agree on a definition of *physical fitness*, but most have endorsed the concept of performance-related and health-related fitness. **Performance-related fitness,** or sports fitness, consists of the following components: speed, power, balance, coordination, agility, and reaction time. These are essential for sports performance, but they may or may not contribute significantly to those activities performed for health enhancement (see the Just the Facts: What's the Difference?).

Speed is velocity, or the ability to move rapidly. *Power* is the product of force and velocity and the rate at which work is performed. *Balance,* or equilibrium, is the ability to maintain a desired body position either statically or dynamically. *Coordination* is the harmonious integration of the body parts to produce smooth, fluid motion. *Agility* is the ability to change direction rapidly. *Reaction time* is the time required (usually measured in hundredths of a second) to respond to a stimulus.

The components of **health-related fitness** are cardiorespiratory endurance, muscular strength, muscular endurance, flexibility, and body composition. In this text the exercise emphasis is on health-related fitness.

Performance-related and health-related fitness, although different, clearly are not mutually exclusive. For example, competitive athletes require an abundance of the performance-related components of fitness, but the nature of their sports may also require the simultaneous development of the health-related components. Athletes who play racquetball, tennis, basketball, soccer, and football fall within this category. Conversely, the same sports are appropriate for

Just the Facts
What's the Difference?

Components of Fitness
Health related
- Cardiorespiratory endurance
- Muscular strength
- Muscular endurance
- Flexibility
- Body composition

Performance related
- Speed
- Power
- Balance
- Coordination
- Agility
- Reaction time

Activities
Health related
- Walking
- Running
- Jogging
- Cycling
- Hiking
- Swimming
- Rope jumping
- Weight training
- Cross-country skiing

Performance related
- Racquetball
- Handball
- Squash
- Tennis
- Badminton
- Soccer
- Softball
- Basketball
- Football
- Water polo

health and fitness enthusiasts who prefer to achieve their goals through friendly competition.

However, the development and maintenance of health-related fitness do not necessarily depend on athletic ability or activities that are high in the performance components. Fitness for health purposes can be achieved with minimal psychomotor ability through activities such as walking, jogging, cycling, hiking, backpacking, orienteering, swimming, rope jumping, and weight training.

Such activities as these are self-paced; that is, the exerciser selects a pace that is relatively comfortable and that can be sustained for a minimum of 10 minutes. No competing opponent pushes the exerciser beyond his or her physiological limits.

Remember the adage "No pain, no gain?" Trying to comply with it has done more harm than good to sedentary people attempting to become physically active. The health benefits of exercise occur when exercise is somewhat uncomfortable but not painful. Only the most dedicated health enthusiasts and competitors can face exercise that constantly produces pain.

Although exercise for health enhancement should stress cardiorespiratory development, the other components of fitness should not be neglected. Flexibility exercises should be a part of warm-up and cool-down procedures. Flexibility exercises may be performed three to five times per week, and the best results occur during the cool-down period following the cardiorespiratory workout.[1] Stretching is most effective at this time because muscle temperature is elevated. Warm muscles respond well to stretching, and the likelihood of muscle injury is decreased as well. Resistance/strength training plays an important role and should be an integral part of a well-rounded fitness program.

As with all components of wellness, developing and sustaining an exercise program are the responsibilities of each individual. This text provides convincing evidence of the need for regular exercise and provides guidelines for initiating a sound program or reinforcement for those who are currently exercising.

Cardiorespiratory Endurance

Cardiorespiratory endurance is the ability to take in, deliver, and extract oxygen for physical work, that is, the ability to persevere at a physical task at a given intensity level. Cardiorespiratory endurance improves with regular participation in aerobic activities, such as speed walking, jogging, cycling, swimming, and cross-country skiing. The term **aerobic** literally means "with oxygen," but when applied to exercise, it refers to activities in which oxygen demand can be met continuously during performance. Aerobic performance depends on a continuous and sufficient supply of oxygen to burn the carbohydrates and fats needed to fuel such activities. In other words, someone performing aerobically has the capacity to sustain the intensity or the energy requirement for longer than a couple of minutes,[2] a phenomenon known as *steady state*. Steady state can be achieved only during aerobic exercise, and it represents a level of exertion that feels relatively comfortable to the exerciser. It is also referred to as a *pay as you go system* in that the oxygen cost of an activity is paid in full by the body during the activity.

Cardiorespiratory endurance is also referred to as **aerobic capacity,** or maximum oxygen consumption (VO_2 max). It is the most important component of physical fitness and is the foundation of total fitness.

The physiological changes that result from cardiorespiratory training are referred to as the *long-term* or *chronic effects of exercise*. The effects of training are measurable and predictable.

Heart Rate

A few months of aerobic training lowers the resting heart rate by 10 to 15 beats per minute (bpm).[3] It also lowers the heart rate for a given workload. For example, a slow jog may produce a heart rate of 165 beats per minute before training and 140 beats per minute after a few months of training. The trained heart is a stronger, more efficient pump that is capable of delivering the required blood and oxygen with fewer beats.

Stroke Volume

Stroke volume is the amount of blood that the heart can eject in one beat. Aerobic training increases the stroke volume by (1) increasing the size of the cavity of the ventricles, which results in more blood filling the heart, and (2) increasing the contractile strength of the ventricular wall, so contraction is more forceful and a greater amount of blood is ejected from the ventricles. The increase in stroke volume, both at rest and during exercise, is one of the primary effects of endurance training and one of the major mechanisms responsible for improvement in aerobic fitness.

Cardiac Output

Cardiac output is the amount of blood ejected by the heart in 1 minute. Cardiac output (Q) is the product of heart rate (HR) and stroke volume (SV) ($Q = HR \times SV$). Cardiac output increases with aerobic training during maximal effort—it does not increase at rest or during submaximal exercise. The reason that cardiac output does not change during rest or submaximal exercise is that the lowered resting heart rate compensates for the increase in stroke volume. What does change is the manner in which cardiac output is achieved. This is illustrated by the following example: An untrained 25-year-old man has a resting heart rate of 72 bpm and a stroke volume of 70 ml of blood per beat. His cardiac output at rest is calculated as follows:

$$Q = HR \times SV$$
$$= 72 \times 70$$
$$= 5040 \text{ ml } (5.0 \text{ L})$$

The same person after two years of aerobic training has the same cardiac output at rest, but it is achieved differently: The resting heart rate is now decreased to 55 bpm and the stroke volume is increased to 92 ml of blood per beat.

$$Q = 55 \times 92$$
$$= 5040 \text{ ml } (5.0 \text{ L})$$

The average cardiac output at rest is 4 to 6 liters of blood per minute. During maximal exertion, cardiac output reaches values of 18 to 20 liters of blood per minute for the average person but may reach as much as 40 liters per minute for large, well-conditioned athletes. What an incredible piece of work by an organ that weighs less than a pound! To put this in perspective,

HealthQuest Activities

- The *How Fit Are You?* exercise in Module 2 will help you determine your current level of fitness in four major areas: body composition, cardiorespiratory capacity, muscular strength, and flexibility. Complete the series of questions about how much you exercise, what types of training you do, how intensely you exercise, and your body size. After you complete the questions, *HealthQuest* will give you feedback in each of the four areas. Then develop an individual plan for improving or maintaining your current fitness level.

- The *Exercise Interest Inventory* in Module 2 allows you to rate your feelings about certain aspects of exercise. *HealthQuest* provides feedback about the activities and exercises you would most enjoy, based on your individual needs and preferences. First, write down the five fitness activities that you like best or in which you most often participate. After each one, indicate your motivation for engaging in that particular activity. For example, you could list "enjoyment," "habit," or "convenience." When you have completed the *Exercise Interest Inventory,* compare the two lists. Are there any surprises? What factors had you not considered to be influential in your choice of exercise?

imagine forty 1-liter cola bottles filled with blood. This is the amount that the hearts of some highly conditioned people can pump in 1 minute. Maximal cardiac output improves with training primarily because of the resulting increase in stroke volume.[3] Maximal heart rate is essentially unaffected by training; therefore, its influence on maximal cardiac output is relatively constant. However, maximal heart rate declines with age by about 1 bpm per year after age 20. Training cannot stop the decline; it can only slow the process somewhat.

Blood Volume

Aerobic training increases total blood volume, plasma volume (the liquid portion of the blood), and the blood solids (the red blood cells, white blood cells, and blood platelets). The increase is greatest in plasma volume, so the blood becomes more liquid. The increase in the ratio of plasma volume to red blood cell volume is an adaptation to exercise that lowers the viscosity, or thickness and stickiness, of the blood. This change decreases the resistance to blood flow, allowing it to circulate more easily through the blood vessels.

Blood is automatically shunted by the body to areas of greatest need. At rest, a significant amount is sent to the digestive system and kidneys. During vigorous exercise, as much as 85 percent of the blood is sent to the working muscles, reducing the amount sent to the digestive and urinary systems.[1]

Heart Volume

The muscles of the body respond to exercise by growing larger and stronger. As a muscular pump, the heart's volume and weight increase with endurance training. Training that lowers the resting heart rate stimulates greater filling of the ventricles, whose muscle fibers respond to the increased pool of blood by stretching. This produces a recoil effect in the muscle fibers that results in a stronger contraction with more blood ejected per beat. Continued training causes the ventricles to enlarge and grow stronger, so the weight and the size of the heart increase. The hypertrophied (enlarged) heart is a normal response to endurance training that has no long-term detrimental effects. In fact, although maintaining this effect for life is beneficial, several months of inactivity will reduce heart weight and size to pretraining levels. The atrophy (wasting away) associated with physical inactivity is inevitable.

Respiratory Responses

The chest muscles that support breathing improve in both strength and endurance with exercise. Vital capacity, which is the amount of air that can be expired maximally following a maximal inspiration, increases slightly. A corresponding decrease occurs in "dead space" air or residual volume, which is the amount of air remaining in the lungs after a maximal expiration.

Training substantially increases maximal pulmonary ventilation (the amount of air moved in and out of the lungs). Before training, the lungs can ventilate approximately 110 liters of air per minute. Pulmonary ventilation increases to about 135 liters of air following a few months of training. Highly trained athletes commonly ventilate 180 to 200 liters of air per minute.

Blood flow to the lungs, particularly to the upper lobes, appears to increase after training. This results in a larger and more efficient surface for the exchange of oxygen and carbon dioxide.

Metabolic Responses

Aerobic endurance training improves aerobic capacity by 5 to 25 percent in previously untrained, healthy adults. The magnitude of improvement is primarily dependent upon the initial level of physical fitness. The lower the fitness level, the greater the gain from aerobic training.[3] Rarely do improvements greater than 30 percent occur. When they do, they usually occur to those who also lose a large amount of body weight and fat.[4]

The improvement in aerobic capacity is the result of several physiological adaptations that increase the body's production of energy. First, adenosine triphosphate (ATP), the actual unit of energy for muscular contraction, is produced in greater quantities. The mitochondria, which are specialized organelles responsible for manufacturing ATP, respond to training by increasing in size and number to increase their output. Second, oxidative enzymes within the mitochondria that accelerate the production of ATP increase in quantity. Third, cardiac output and blood perfusion of the muscles performing the work increase. Fourth, training facilitates and increases the extraction of oxygen by the exercising muscles. These are some of the major adaptations that combine to enhance aerobic endurance.

Aerobic capacity (VO_2 max) is limited by heredity and is finite. The heredity component of VO_2 max is approximately 40 percent.[5] This represents a substantial influence on a given person's potential for aerobic performance. Therefore, the sensitivity of the VO_2 max response to aerobic training is to a significant degree dependent upon heredity. If those who inherit the genetic potential for endurance events also train diligently, they become capable of exceptionally high levels of performance. Diligent training with an average genetic potential results in average or slightly above average performance. Only a select few inherit the ability to produce world-class endurance performances. The majority of people are in the average category, but all can achieve their aerobic *potential* with training.

Aerobic capacity reaches a peak after six months to two years of steady endurance training. At this point, it levels off and remains unchanged for a number of years, even if training is intensified. However, aerobic performance continues to improve with harder training, because a higher percentage of the aerobic capacity can be maintained for a longer period. For example, six months of appropriate training may allow you to jog 3 miles at 60 percent of your aerobic capacity. Another year of harder training may allow you to run 3 miles at 85 percent of your capacity. Capacity has not changed during this time, but physiological adaptations have occurred that enable the body to function at progressively higher percentages of maximum capacity.

Aerobic capacity decreases with age. During adulthood, peak aerobic energy steadily declines by an average of about 1 percent per year between the ages of 25 and 75.[6] A significant portion of the decline is related to the lack of physical activity that accompanies aging: Those who are physically active throughout their lifetimes experience declines in aerobic capacity but not at the same rate as those who are inactive. See Wellness Across the Generations: Exercise Is for Everyone for more details about the impact of exercising on aging.

Wellness Across the Generations

Exercise Is for Everyone

The ability of the body to take in, transport, and extract oxygen for physical work and exercise declines with age. On the average, aerobic capacity declines by about 8 to 10 percent every decade after the age of 25 in both males and females. One of the major sources of this decline in the United States is the decreasing level of physical activity that tends to accompany aging. This trend toward inactivity also results in a loss of muscle weight, an increase in fat weight, and a decrease in metabolic rate, all of which contribute to the decline in aerobic capacity. Although physiological aging does lower aerobic capacity, at least 50 percent of the decline is due to "disuse atrophy" caused by inactivity.[7]

Biological aging cannot be stopped. We cannot live forever. However, exercise comes as close to an antiaging pill as anything else that is available. Even older people who have been sedentary for decades can benefit from aerobic exercise and weight training.

The beneficial outcomes of regular exercise for older people include an increase in energy, a favorable change in body composition (loss of fat, gain of muscle), an increase in muscular strength and endurance, an increase in metabolism, and significant improvements in cardiovascular and musculoskeletal health.[8] All of these changes translate into a higher quality of life and longevity.

Physically fit 60 and 70 year olds have the aerobic capacity of unfit 25 year olds.[8] All of this means that physically fit elderly people have the energy to live independently during their later years. The ability to perform the daily chores of living and to participate in an active lifestyle with energy to spare develops confidence that contributes to the enjoyment of life.

The effects of training persist as long as training continues. Training of moderate intensity may increase the VO_2 max by 10 to 20 percent. However, the VO_2 max returns to pretraining levels within a few months if training is discontinued.[9] Most of the decline occurs during the first month and slows down during the next two months. Fitness developed through years of continuous training can be lost in months if training is interrupted or discontinued. Highly conditioned athletes respond to detraining in a similar manner. In a study, subjects who suspended training for eighty-four days after ten years of active participation experienced a significant decline in aerobic capacity after three weeks of inactivity. They returned to pretraining levels in most fitness parameters by the end of the study. The exceptions to complete reversal were muscle capillary density and mitochondrial enzymes, which remained 50 percent higher than levels measured in sedentary control subjects. This study indicated that the results of inactivity are variable and affect some systems more quickly than others. Physical decline cannot be prevented with physical inactivity.

Three different methods for assessing your cardiorespiratory endurance are presented in the Assessments Activities. These include the Rockport Fitness Walking Test, the 1.5-Mile Run/Walk Test, and the 3-Minute Bench Step Test. Each is accompanied by norms, so you can compare your performance against the standards.

Cardiorespiratory Endurance and Wellness

Most Americans believe that exercise is good for them, but the majority cannot explain how or why. This section provides some of the answers.

Consistent participation in exercise is necessary to improve health status. Sporadic exercise does not promote physical fitness or contribute to health enhancement. In fact, infrequent participation increases the risk of sudden death during the time of exercise.[10] Physical inactivity is a major risk for coronary heart disease. The risk is approximately equal to that imposed by cigarette smoking, high blood pressure, and elevated serum cholesterol. Sixty percent of all adult Americans are inactive or marginally active. The number of physically inactive people exceeds the combined total of those who smoke, are hypertensive, or have high serum cholesterol.[10] Based on these numbers, promoting regular exercise for the general public should be an important priority of public health policy.

Coronary heart disease is rarely responsible for sudden cardiac death during or after exercise among people under the age of 30. Congenital heart defects or other cardiac abnormalities, such as faulty valves, enlarged hearts, and heart muscle disease, are the usual culprits for this age group. Most exertional deaths occur among older Americans and are due to coronary heart disease. A study by Harvard medical researchers found that heavy physical exertion, such as shoveling snow, gardening, walking fast, jogging, playing softball, and playing tennis, could trigger a heart attack.[11] For the physically unfit, the risk of incurring a heart attack during and in the first hour after strenuous exertion increased by 107 times. The risk for physically fit people increased only 2.7 times. These data applied equally to men and women.

The danger attributed to physical exertion is greatly diminished in people who exercise regularly. In fact, the benefits they receive from physical training far outweigh the minimal risk associated with one bout of strenuous exercise. A similar study conducted at the same time in Germany found amazingly similar results.[12]

One and one-half million heart attacks occur every year in the United States. The Harvard researchers concluded that 75,000 of these are exertional and they usually occur after strenuous exercise. Most of these heart attacks occur among those who are physically inactive and at high risk.[11] See Just the Facts: Exercise-Related Problems for some tips on reducing the hazards associated with regular exercise. Some selected health benefits of regular exercise are listed in table 3-1. If these benefits could be distilled and sold in pill form, the American public would line up to pay any reasonable price to attain them. And yet all of these benefits are readily available to anyone who is simply willing to commit the time and effort. While millions of people are exercising, 60 percent of the adult population is not.

Principles of Conditioning

Becoming familiar with the principles of exercise is necessary to maximize the results of a physical fitness program. Your objectives can be met through the appropriate manipulation of intensity, frequency, duration, overload, progression, and specificity. Setting of objectives, warm-up, cooldown, and careful selection of activity are important elements that add to the enjoyment and effectiveness of exercise.

Intensity

Intensity refers to the degree of vigorousness of a single session of exercise. In 1995, The American College of Sports Medicine (ACSM) and the Centers for Disease Control and Prevention (CDC) developed and promoted the following recommendation for exercise: Every U.S. adult should accumulate 30 minutes or more of moderately intense physical activity on most and preferably all days of the week.[13] The recommendation refers to *physical activity* rather than *exercise*. This is an umbrella term that includes many kinds of physical exertion, including structured exercise. *Moderate intensity* refers to walking at a 3 to 4 mile per hour pace (15 to 20 minutes per mile) or engaging in any activity that burns a similar number of calories at a similar rate. The 30 minutes of activity can be split up into two or three bouts of 10 to 15 minutes each throughout

Just the Facts

Exercise-Related Problems

Many health, fitness, and cosmetic benefits occur to those who exercise on a regular basis. Although they are outweighed by the benefits, risks are associated with such behavior. Despite precautions, injuries occasionally occur. Beginning exercisers are particularly susceptible to injury because of their lack of knowledge about training coupled with their misguided attempts to achieve their goals too quickly. The following suggestions should result in safer workouts:

1. Dress according to the weather: shorts, t-shirt, mesh baseball-type cap in warm weather; layers of light clothing, hat, gloves, ear protection, and windbreaker in cold weather.
2. Wear appropriate shoes for the activity in which you participate: jogging shoes, walking shoes, aerobic shoes, or cross-trainers. In general, exercise shoes should be one-half to three-quarters of an inch longer than your longest toe. There should also be room enough for the toes to spread out. The soles of most exercise shoes consists of three layers. The outer sole that contacts the floor or ground should be made of hard rubber. The next layer is the midsole, which protects the midfoot and toes. The last layer is made of a thick, spongy substance that absorbs most of the shock when the foot strikes the surface.
3. Warm up and cool down properly before and after exercise.
4. Exercise within your capacity—it should feel a little uncomfortable but not painful. According to the American College of Sports Medicine (ACSM), the initial stage of an exercise program should last four to six weeks at a low intensity (50 to 60 percent of the maximal heart rate or HR_{max}). Each exercise session should last for 12 minutes during the first week and increase by 2 minutes per week for the next 4 to 5 weeks. At this point, the exerciser is ready to increase the intensity, frequency, and duration of each session.
5. While following these simple guidelines reduces the possibility of incurring pain or injury, beginning exercisers may experience, as a result of overuse, shin splints, side stitch, blisters, chafing, muscle cramps, muscle soreness, achilles tendon injuries, and lower-back pain.
    a. Muscle soreness following exercise usually occurs among beginners who have yet to adapt to physical exertion or to those at any level of fitness who exceed their physical capabilities. Following the ACSM guidelines reduces exposure to muscle pain.
    b. Side stitches occur primarily among walkers and joggers. They consist of severe pain in the upper right quadrant of the abdomen. Side stitches may be caused by reduced blood flow to the diaphragm (a large, dome-shaped muscle that separates the abdominal cavity from the chest cavity), or they may be due to the collection of gas in the intestines. In either case, deep breathing and direct pressure applied with both hands at the site of the pain may provide relief. Sometimes, stopping the activity for a few minutes is required for the pain to subside.
    c. A common injury occurring among beginners is shin splints. Shin splints produce a burning pain that radiates along the inner surface of the large bones of the lower leg. These are nagging, painful injuries that are better prevented than treated. The causes of shin splints include training demands that exceed a person's capacity to perform. High-impact activities such as jogging or aerobics to music, poor-quality exercise shoes, hard exercise surfaces, and walking or jogging on hilly surfaces are other contributing causes. Treatment includes applications of ice, rest, wrapping or taping the affected shin, and placing heel lifts in the shoes.

---

the day. Table 3-2 provides a summary of the ACSM-CDC exercise principles and their application to the enhancement of health and physical fitness.

The recommendation for health enhancement is a minimum guideline designed to motivate and recruit that 60 percent of the population who are not physically active. It is not intended to lower the standard for those who currently exercise at a higher level or whose primary goal is the development of physical fitness. Programs designed primarily to improve health may not improve or may minimally improve physical fitness. It takes higher-intensity exercise to significantly improve physical fitness. Those who exercise for physical fitness purposes also derive health benefits in a two-for-one deal. It takes a slightly higher level of training to achieve both.

Table 3-1 Health-Related Benefits Associated with Regular Aerobic Exercise

Reduces the risk of cardiovascular disease
- Increases HDL cholesterol
- Decreases LDL cholesterol
- Favorably changes the ratios between total cholesterol and HDL-C and between LDL-C and HDL-C
- Decreases triglyceride levels
- Promotes relaxation; relieves stress and tension
- Decreases body fat and favorably changes body composition
- Reduces blood pressure, especially if it is high
- Makes blood platelets less sticky
- Decreases the incidence of cardiac dysrhythmias
- Increases myocardial efficiency
  1. Lowers resting heart rate
  2. Increases stroke volume
- Increases oxygen-carrying capacity of the blood
- Reduces the risk of colon cancer and breast cancer

Helps control diabetes
- Makes cells less resistant to insulin
- Reduces body fat

Develops stronger bones that are less susceptible to injury

Promotes joint stability
- Increases muscular strength
- Increases strength of the ligaments, tendons, cartilage, and connective tissue

Contributes to fewer lower-back problems

Acts as a stimulus for other lifestyle changes

Improves self-concept

Table 3-2 Summary of Exercise Principles for the Development of Physical Fitness and Health

Exercise Principles	To Develop and Improve Level of Physical Fitness (1998 Guidelines)	To Develop and Improve Health Status (1995 Guidelines)
Intensity	• 55/65 to 90% of HR_{max} • 55 to 64% of HR_{max} for sedentary beginners • 40/50 to 85% of the VO_2 or cardiac reserve	• Moderate (walking 3 to 4 MPH)
Frequency	• 3–5 days per week	• Most, preferably all, days of the week
Duration (time)	• 20–60 minutes at 60 to 90% of HR_{max} • 200–300 calories per exercise session	• 30 minutes or more in THR zone
Overload	• Should not exceed 10% of the previous workout	• NA*
Progression	• Based on physiological readiness • According to the schedule of overload	• NA
Specificity	• For competitors who are training for maximal performance	• NA

*not applicable

The intensity level recommended by the American College of Sports Medicine (ACSM) in 1990 for the purpose of developing physical fitness was 55/65 to 90 percent of the maximal heart rate (HR_{max}).[9] HR_{max} can be measured by a physical work capacity test on a treadmill or cycle ergometer. Because most people do not have access to such tests, HR_{max} can be estimated by subtracting age from 220. A 20-year-old person has an estimated HR_{max} of 200 beats per minute (220 − 20 = 200). This formula predicts rather than measures HR_{max}; therefore, a measurement error of approximately plus or minus 10 beats per minute is associated with its use.

After the HR_{max} has been determined, the target for exercise may be calculated. The target zone for exercise provides the desirable heart rate for the development of physical fitness. For the 20-year-old person whose HR_{max} is 200 beats per minute, the target zone for exercise is calculated as follows:

$$\begin{array}{r} 200 \text{ (estimated } HR_{max}) \\ \times\, 0.60 \text{ (60\% of } HR_{max}) \\ \hline 120 \text{ (lower-limit target)} \end{array}$$

$$\begin{array}{r} 200 \text{ (estimated } HR_{max}) \\ \times\, 0.90 \text{ (90\% of } HR_{max}) \\ \hline 180 \text{ (upper-limit target)} \end{array}$$

This 20-year-old person should exercise at a heart rate between 120 and 180 beats per minute, depending on objectives and level of fitness. The target for a person who has an average level of fitness is 150 to 160 beats per minute for exercise. The training effect occurs at heart rate levels below the maximum.

Another method for calculating exercise heart rate, the Karvonen formula, considers fitness level and resting heart rate. The training heart rate is calculated with this formula by using a percentage of the heart rate reserve (cardiac reserve), which is the difference between the HR_{max} and the resting heart rate. The best way to determine the resting heart rate for this method is to count your pulse rate for fifteen seconds while in the sitting position immediately after waking in the morning. You should repeat this for four to five consecutive days and average the readings for a relatively accurate representation of your resting heart rate. Next, you should estimate your level of fitness based on your exercise habits and select a category from table 3-3 to determine the appropriate exercise intensity level. If you cannot decide which category is the most appropriate, take one of the fitness tests at the end of this chapter. Your performance on these should place you in a category that reflects your physical fitness level.

The Karvonen formula is

$$THR = (MHR - RHR) \times TI\% + RHR$$

where *THR* is the training heart rate, or the heart rate that should be maintained during exercise, *MHR* is the maximum heart rate, *RHR* is the resting heart rate, and *TI%* is the training intensity (see table 3-3). Therefore the exercise heart rate for a 25 year old with a resting heart rate of 75 beats per minute and an average fitness level is calculated as follows:

$$\begin{array}{r} 220 \\ -\,25 \\ \hline 195 \text{ } (HR_{max}) \end{array}$$

$$\begin{aligned} THR &= (195 - 75) \times 0.70 + 75 \\ &= 120 \times 0.70 + 75 \\ &= 84 + 75 \\ &= 159 \end{aligned}$$

The training heart rate for this 25-year-old subject is 159 beats per minute. Assessment Activity 3-4 will enable you to determine your target heart rate for exercise.

Learning to take the pulse rate quickly and accurately is necessary to monitor exercise intensity by heart rate. Two of the most commonly used sites for taking the pulse rate are the radial artery on the thumb side of the wrist and the carotid artery at the side of the neck (figure 3-1). Use the first two fingers of your preferred hand to palpate the pulse. At the wrist, the pulse is located at the base of the thumb when the hand is held palm up. To find the carotid pulse, slide your fingers downward at the angle of the jaw below the earlobe to the side of the neck. You apply only enough pressure to feel the pulse, particularly at the carotid artery. Excessive pressure at this point stimulates specialized receptors that automatically slow the heart rate, leading to an underestimation of the rate actually achieved during exercise. The wrist is the preferred site for the *palpation* (examination by touch or feel) of the pulse rate. Measure the carotid pulse if you cannot feel your pulse at the wrist.

Locate and count the pulse rate immediately after exercise stops. Count the beats for ten seconds and multiply by 6 to get beats per minute. Start the count

Table 3-3 Guidelines for Selecting Exercise Intensity Level

Fitness Level	Intensity Level (%)
Low	60
Fair	65
Average	70
Good	75
Excellent	80–90

Figure 3-1 Sites for Taking a Pulse
The two sites for measuring pulse: *A*, location for taking a pulse at the carotid artery; *B*, location for taking a pulse at the wrist (radial artery).

by assigning a zero to the first beat that is felt or, as nurses do, start the count by assigning the first beat felt a value of 1. Regardless of which technique you use, be consistent in its application. Some practice is required to locate the pulse quickly and count it accurately.

Another method for monitoring the intensity of exercise is to rate your subjective perception of the effort. On some days, exercise seems easier than normal, and on other days it may seem more difficult.

Frequency

The *frequency* of exercise refers to the number of days of participation each week. The 1990 ACSM guidelines for improving physical fitness recommend that exercise be pursued three to five days per week for optimal results. Fewer than three days is an inadequate stimulus for developing fitness, and conversely, more than five days per week represents a point of diminishing returns from exercise and increases the likelihood of injury. Those who are exercising for health reasons and are following the 1995 guidelines are advised to engage in physical activities on most, preferably all, days of the week.

You can overdo exercise—too much results in staleness or overtraining. The signs of overtraining include the following:

- A feeling of chronic fatigue and listlessness
- Inability to make further fitness gains or regression of the level of fitness
- Sudden loss of weight
- An increase of 5 beats per minute in the resting heart rate
- Loss of enthusiasm for working out
- An increase in the risk for injury
- The occurrence of irritability, anger, and depression

Treatment requires that you cut back on training or stop completely for one to two weeks. When you resume exercise, it must be of lower intensity, frequency, and duration. You must rebuild and regain fitness gradually. Prevention is the best treatment for overtraining because people for whom exercise is a way of life are reluctant to discontinue training, even temporarily, for fear that they will lose their fitness edge. Convincing them that continuing to exercise is the worst possible action is extremely difficult.

Duration

Duration refers to the length of each exercise session. Intensity and duration are inversely related—the more intense the exercise, the shorter its duration. Intensity is always an important consideration for the development of physical fitness. Reducing the intensity somewhat while increasing the frequency and duration is the most beneficial method for health enhancement. In 1990, the ACSM recommended 20 to 60 minutes of continuous or noncontinuous aerobic activity.[1] The 1995 guidelines suggest the accumulation of 30 minutes or more of physical activity per day.[13]

Wellness on the Web Behavior Change Activities

How Hard Are You Training?
When you think of intensity, you think of hard work. In physical training, intensity refers to the degree of vigor you achieve in a single session of exercise. For cardiorespiratory endurance training, like running or power walking, you can measure intensity by using various heart-rate methods. One popular method is the Karvonen formula. Eoin Fahy, Ph.D., has a website dedicated to running at **www.home.connectnet.com/eoinf/index.html**. This site contains a special section you can use to estimate your training heart-rate zone using the Karvonen formula. From Dr. Fahy's home page, select "heart rate"; fill in your age, gender, and resting heart rate, and click "calculate." You'll find three different levels of training heart-rate ranges.

Why Exercise?
How do experts define physical fitness? There's no general agreement, but most authorities endorse the concept of performance-related and health-related fitness. Like all aspects of wellness, you as an individual are responsible for developing an exercise program and sticking with it. Taking this step is much easier when you understand the importance of exercise as an integral part of a quality lifestyle. Stephen Seiler, Ph.D, is an endurance sport enthusiast and exercise physiologist who has a strong interest in the physiology of performance and in the role of exercise as "preventive medicine." To enhance your understanding of exercise physiology as it relates to wellness, go to Dr. Seiler's website at **www.krs.hia.no/~stephens/index.html**. On his home page, select "Exercise Physiology—The Big Picture." Scroll down the list of topics and read more about a specific area of exercise physiology as it relates to your wellness and fitness goals.

The Key to Your Heart
When we say someone is "heartless," we're speaking figuratively, not literally, because every person most definitely has a heart. From the moment we're conceived until we draw our last breath, our heart works tirelessly to fuel the processes that give us life. In an average lifetime, the heart beats more than two and a half billion times without ever stopping to rest. Throughout history, this life-sustaining power has created an aura of mystery around the heart. Modern science has removed much of the mystery, but we continue to be fascinated and curious about this vital human organ. To explore the heart in detail, go to **www.sln.fi.edu/biosci/heart.html**. In "The Heart: An Online Exploration," you'll discover the complexities of the heart's development and structure. You'll have the opportunity to follow the blood as it circulates through the blood vessels and the various body systems. Most important, you'll learn how to keep your heart healthy and how to monitor your heart's health.

Another way to monitor duration is to calculate the number of calories expended per exercise session. The ACSM recommends that, if you expend 300 calories per exercise session, you exercise three times per week; if you expend only 200 calories per exercise session, you exercise four times per week. These guidelines are sufficient for health benefits to accrue, but for fitness purposes, they should be viewed as a minimal level of exercise. (Table 8-4 in Chapter 8 discusses the way to determine how long you need to engage in the activities of your choice to achieve these goals.)

Progression, Overload, and Specificity

As people attain a level of fitness that meets their needs and when further improvement is not desired, the program switches from developing fitness to maintaining it. At this point the principles of overload and progression may be set aside, but both are necessary for the improvement phase of fitness. *Overload* involves subjecting the body to unaccustomed stress. Challenging the body to periodically accept a slightly increased level of work forces it to adapt by attaining a higher level of fitness. Deciding when to impose each new challenge involves the principle of progression. The workload is increased only when the exerciser is ready to accept a new challenge. For aerobic exercise, target heart rate or perceived exertion may be used to establish criteria for scheduling the progression. For example, if you jog, swim, or cycle a certain distance, the exercise heart rate will decrease over time as your body adapts to training. When the exercise heart rate drops to a predetermined level or the effort required becomes quite comfortable, you should adjust the pace or distance to return to the original target zone. However, the new physical challenge should not exceed the current amount of exercise by more than 10 percent. This should ensure that the new workload is not excessive.

The principle of *specificity* of training suggests that the body adapts according to the specific type of stress placed on it. The muscles involved in any activity are the ones that adapt, and they do so in the specific way in which they are used. For example, jogging prepares you for jogging but is poor preparation for cycling. Cycling does not prepare you for swimming. Although

Just the Facts

Motivational Tips

Follow these tips to stay motivated to exercise:

- Exercise with a friend. Make sure both of you have compatible goals and are similar in fitness level. Friends can help each other sustain a program, particularly during busy times when the temptation to push exercise out of an already crowded schedule is quite high.
- Exercise with a group. Exchange ideas and literature about exercise with group members.
- Elicit the support of friends and family. Their support is a powerful source of reinforcement.
- Associate with other exercisers. They represent an enthusiastic, positive, and informative group—and their values are contagious.
- Join an exercise class or a fitness club. This gives you a place to go and meet people who want to exercise.
- Keep a progress chart. This will give you an objective account of your improvement.
- Exercise to music. Music makes the effort appear easier than it actually is.
- Set a definite time and place to exercise. This is particularly important during the early days of the program. Schedule exercise as you would any other activity of importance and then commit to the schedule.
- Participate in a variety of activities. Cross-training is excellent for the person who exercises for health or recreation.
- Do not become obsessive about exercise. Skipping exercise is not a good practice normally, but skipping is appropriate at times. Do not exercise when you are sick or overtired. Do not feel guilty about missing exercise for a day or two. Resume exercise as soon as you can.

---

these activities stress the cardiorespiratory system, they are sufficiently different that there is little fitness carry-over among them.

The principle of specificity is particularly important for competitive athletes. Competitors attempt to maximize the returns from their training effort; therefore, runners must train by running, swimmers must swim, and cyclists must cycle. The focus is on maximal improvement in one activity so that the body is trained in a specific manner. This locks athletes into regimented training programs, but noncompetitors who exercise for health and physical fitness reasons are not under such constraints. They can vary activities and prevent the boredom of participating in the same activity day after day, week after week. Cycling, jogging, swimming, racquetball, cross-country skiing, weight training, and other activities may be used in any combination or order for the development of physical fitness. This is the essence of **cross-training.** Not only does cross-training relieve boredom, it may reduce the incidence of injury because it does not stress the same muscles in the same way during every workout.

Cross-training has many advantages and is an excellent technique for attaining the health benefits of exercise. Variety, the major attraction of cross-training, can also be a disadvantage, however. By participating in many different activities, you seldom become proficient in any one. However, if the objective is physical fitness or health enhancement, proficiency is incidental.

Identifying goals provides some direction for the activities selected and the way the principles of exercise are to be manipulated to increase the probability of success. Only one or two major goals should be selected, and these should be as specific as possible so that an effective exercise program may be devised. Activities, objectives, and exercise principles must match.

When you have identified the objectives and know what you wish to achieve from the exercise program, identify the means for sustaining the program. Your resolve to exercise is shakiest during the early stages of the program, usually because people push untrained bodies beyond their limits. This results in sore muscles, stiffness, and possible injury. Consequently, the dropout rate is highest in the beginning of any exercise program. The irony is that the greatest return for the effort is attained during this phase. Some tips for sustaining that effort are presented in Just the Facts: Motivational Tips.

Other Exercise Considerations

Warming Up for Exercise

Warming up prepares the body for physical action. The process involves physical activities that gradually heat the muscles and elevate the heart rate. A brisk walk, slow jog, jogging or hopping in place, rope jumping, and selected calisthenics will raise the heart rate and increase muscle temperature. A person should break out in a sweat during the warm-up. This indicates that heart rate and body temperature have increased to some extent and the person is ready for more vigorous activity. The warm-up should last 5 to 10 minutes.

Increasing the heart rate gradually during the warm-up period is most important. This allows the circulatory system to adjust to the load. If the heart rate elevates suddenly, circulation cannot adjust rapidly enough to meet the oxygen and nutrient demands of the heart muscle. The effects of this lag time are abolished in about 2 minutes, but increasing the heart rate quickly can be hazardous even during those 2 minutes, particularly for those with compromised circulation. Even the healthy heart may be affected by eliminating the gradual phase of warm-up. One study showed that every one of forty-four healthy male subjects, ages 21 to 52 years, had normal electrocardiogram (ECG) responses to running on a treadmill when they were allowed a warm-up consisting of 2 minutes of easy jogging. However, 70 percent of the group developed abnormal ECG responses to the same exercise when they were not allowed to warm up.[14]

Warm-up may be specifically tailored to the activity to be performed. For example, joggers may warm up by slowly jogging the first 0.5 to 0.75 mile, gradually speeding up to the desired pace. Cyclists, swimmers, cross-country skiers, and rope skippers may use the same approach.

Passive warm-up techniques, such as massage, sauna baths, steam baths, hot showers, hot towels, and heating pads, should not be used as substitutes for an active warm-up. These techniques may precede an active warm-up if a person feels stiff and sore from the previous workout.

Stretching exercises may be performed after the warm-up is completed. At this point, muscle temperature is elevated so that stretching is more effective and muscle, tendon, and joint injuries are less likely to occur. Stretching is most effective during the cooldown period following the workout because (1) muscles are heated and receptive to stretching, and (2) muscles that have contracted repeatedly during exercise need to be stretched. Figures 5-1 through 5-8 in Chapter 5 illustrate some typical stretching exercises that may be used before and after the workout period.

Cooling Down from Exercise

The cooldown is as important as the warm-up. Cooldown should last 8 to 10 minutes and consist of two phases. The first phase involves approximately 5 minutes of walking or other light activities to prevent blood from pooling in the muscles that have been working. Light activity causes rhythmic contractions of the muscles, which in turn act as a stimulus to circulate blood from the muscles to the heart for redistribution throughout the body. This boost to circulation following exercise, often referred to as the *muscle pump,* is essential for recovery and shares some of the burden of circulation with the heart. The muscle pump effect does not occur if a period of inactivity follows exercise. An inactive cooldown forces the heart to work at a high rate to compensate for the reduced volume of blood returning to it because of blood pooling in the muscles. The exerciser runs the risk of dizziness, fainting, and more serious consequences associated with diminished blood flow to vital organs.

Light physical activity after exercise also speeds the removal of lactic acid that has accumulated in the muscles. *Lactic acid* is a fatiguing metabolite resulting from the incomplete breakdown of sugar. It is produced by exercise of high intensity or of long duration.

The second phase of cooldown should focus on the stretching exercises performed during the warm-up. Most participants find that stretching after exercise is more comfortable and more effective because the muscles are heated and more elastic.

Type of Activity

Many activities contribute to one or more components of health-related physical fitness. Activity selections should be based on objectives, skill level, availability of equipment, facilities, instruction, climate, and interest. Any rhythmic, continuous aerobic activity that uses large muscle groups and can be performed for an extended period of time is suitable for the attainment of health and fitness.

The President's Council on Physical Fitness and Sports (PCPFS) enlisted the aid of seven experts to evaluate fourteen popular physical activities for their contribution to physical fitness and general well-being. Although this assessment occurred several years ago, the ratings are as valid today as when they were originally conceived. A summary of these appears in table 3-4.

Selected sports have also been evaluated for their contribution to the health-related components of physical fitness. These appear in table 3-5. Lifetime sports (such as tennis, badminton, and racquetball) are more conducive to fitness development than are team sports (such as volleyball, soccer, softball, and basketball) because fewer players are needed. Ideally, fitness should be developed and maintained primarily through self-paced activities (for example, jogging, cycling, walking, and swimming), but the challenge inherent in sports may be necessary to sustain motivation for some people. Lifetime sports are challenging and fun, and they offer variety. However, fitness attained from these activities depends on skill level and a willingness to exert maximal effort in competition. The orthopedic demands of these activities may be greater than a sedentary beginner can tolerate. Quick stops and starts, bursts of high-intensity activity, sudden changes of direction, and rapid twists and turns place a great deal of

Table 3-4 Rating Fourteen Sports and Exercises

Exercise	Cardiorespiratory Endurance (Stamina)	Muscular Endurance	Muscular Strength	Flexibility	Balance	Weight Control	Muscle Definition	Digestion	Sleep	Total
Jogging	21*	20	17	9	17	21	14	13	16	148
Bicycling	19	18	16	9	18	20	15	12	15	142
Swimming	21	20	14	15	12	15	14	13	16	140
Skating (ice or roller)	18	17	15	13	20	17	14	11	15	140
Handball/squash	19	18	15	16	17	19	11	13	12	140
Skiing—nordic	19	19	15	14	16	17	12	12	15	139
Skiing—alpine	16	18	15	14	21	15	14	9	12	134
Basketball	19	17	15	13	16	19	13	10	12	134
Tennis	16	16	14	14	16	16	13	12	11	128
Calisthenics	10	13	16	19	15	12	18	11	12	126
Walking	13	14	11	7	8	13	11	11	14	102
Golf**	8	8	9	9	8	6	6	7	6	67*
Softball	6	8	7	9	7	7	5	8	7	64
Bowling	5	5	5	7	6	5	5	7	6	51

*The ratings are on a scale of 0 to 3; thus a rating of 21 is the maximum score that can be achieved (a score by 3 of all seven panelists). Ratings were made on the following basis: frequency, four times per week minimal; duration, 30 to 60 minutes per session.

**The rating was made on the basis of using a golf cart or caddy. If you walk the course and carry your clubs, the values improve.

Table 3-5 Rating Selected Sports

Sport	Cardiorespiratory Endurance	Muscular Strength/Endurance Upper	Muscular Strength/Endurance Lower	Flexibility	Body Composition
Badminton	M-H*	L	M-H	L	M-H
Football (touch)	L-M	L-M	M	L	L-M
Ice hockey	H	M	H	L	H
Racquetball	H	M	H	M	H
Rugby	H	M-H	H	M	H
Soccer	H	L	H	M	H
Volleyball	M	M	M	L-M	M
Wrestling	H	H	H	M-H	H

*H, high; M, medium; L, low. The values in this table are estimates that vary according to the skill and motivation of the participants.

stress on the musculoskeletal system. The physically fit can handle the aerobic and musculoskeletal requirements of active sports, but attempting to "play yourself into shape" is a mistake. With knowledge of the principles of exercise, warm-up, cooldown, and the contributions of various physical activities to physical fitness, you can design an exercise program using Assessment Activity 3-5. See Real-World Wellness: Choosing Fitness Equipment for the Home for helpful advice on exercising at home.

Environmental Conditions

People work and exercise in a variety of environmental conditions. Hot and cold weather produce unique problems for people who function outdoors. Their safety and comfort depend on their knowledge of the ways the body reacts to physical activity in different climatic conditions.

Heat is produced in the body as a by-product of metabolism. Physical activities significantly increase metabolism, generating more heat than normal. Heat must be dissipated efficiently, or heat may build up, resulting in **hyperthermia,** abnormally high body temperature that can cause illness or even death. *Heat exhaustion* is also a serious condition but not an imminent threat to life. It is characterized by dizziness, fainting, rapid pulse, and cool skin. Treatment includes immediate cessation of activity. The victim should be moved to a cool, shady place, placed in a reclining position, and given cool fluids to drink.

Heat stroke is a medical emergency and a threat to life. It is the most severe of the heat-induced illnesses. The symptoms include a high temperature (106° F or higher) and dry skin caused by the cessation of sweating. These symptoms are accompanied by delirium, convulsions, or loss of consciousness. The early warning signs include chills, nausea, headache, and general weakness. Victims of heat stroke should be rushed immediately to the nearest hospital for treatment.

Mechanisms of Heat Loss

Heat is lost from the body by conduction, convection, radiation, and evaporation of sweat. Conduction, convection, and radiation are mechanisms responsible for heat loss *and* heat gain. These three depend on the difference between the temperature of the body and that of the environment. These mechanisms do not function alone to effect heat loss or gain.

Conduction occurs when direct physical contact is made between objects of which one is cooler than the other. The greater the difference in temperature between the objects, the greater the transfer of heat. An example is entering an air-conditioned room from

Real-World Wellness

Choosing Fitness Equipment for the Home

I'm a working mother with two young children. My only chance to exercise is at home after the children have been put to bed. I'm most interested in purchasing a good piece of cardio equipment that will burn calories and increase my energy level. What advice can you give me for selecting such equipment?

Here are some helpful hints:

1. Some of the most effective cardio equipment includes motor-driven treadmills, stationary exercise bikes, stationary rowers, stair climbers, cross-country skiing machines, videotape aerobic workouts (with or without stepping benches), and jump ropes.
2. Selecting the right piece of equipment is important. Many well-intentioned home exercisers become bored with the equipment they purchase or find that it is not meeting their needs, so they quit exercising.
3. Try out a piece of equipment before buying it. Make sure it feels comfortable, is easy to use, and is the right size for you.
4. Give equipment the three-week test: Before making your purchase, borrow or rent the piece of equipment and use it three to five times per week for three weeks. At the end of three weeks, you should know whether you enjoy it well enough to use it regularly and whether it will meet your needs and goals. The best equipment in the world is useless unless you use it regularly.
5. Check the construction of equipment to make sure that it is sturdy. The machine should not rock or wobble, and it should perform smoothly.
6. Equipment that is made of lightweight sheet metal or has many plastic parts may not withstand regular use.
7. Do not buy the least expensive machine. Think of this purchase as a long-term investment. Usually a middle-of-the line product will do very well. These carry a ninety-day warranty for parts, and the warranty may be extended to also include service.
8. Shop at a reputable sports equipment store that has a knowledgeable sales staff who can answer your questions and help you make the appropriate choice.
9. Make sure that the store will deliver and set up the equipment.
10. If marketing and promotional claims made for the equipment sound too good to be true, they probably are.

outdoors on a summer day and sitting in a cool leather chair. Heat is lost through contact with the cooler chair.

Conductive heat loss occurs even more rapidly in water.[2] Water is not an insulator but a conductor. It absorbs several thousand times more heat than does air at the same temperature. Air is an excellent insulator but a poor conductor. This is the reason that sitting at poolside is more comfortable than sitting in the pool, even if the temperatures of air and water are equal.

Heat loss or gain by *convection* occurs when a gas or water moves across the skin. Heat is transferred from the body to the environment more effectively if a breeze is blowing. Convective heat loss in water is increased when a person is swimming rather than floating because of the increased movement of the water across the body. The same principle applies to running outdoors because of the air flow over the body.

Humans, animals, and inanimate objects constantly transmit heat by electromagnetic waves to cooler objects in the environment. This heat loss through *radiation* occurs without physical contact between objects. Heat is simply transferred on a temperature gradient from warmer objects to cooler ones.

Heat loss by radiation is very effective when the air temperature (ambient temperature) is well below skin temperature. This is one of the main reasons that outdoor exercise in cool weather is better tolerated than the same exercise in hot weather. Temperatures in the upper 80s and 90s often result in heat gain by radiation.

Evaporation of sweat is the main method of heat loss during exercise, and this process is most effective when the humidity is low. High humidity significantly impairs the evaporative process because the air is very saturated and cannot accept much moisture. If both temperature and humidity are high, losing heat is difficult by any of these processes. Under these conditions, adjusting the intensity and duration of exercise or moving indoors, where the climate can be controlled, may be beneficial.

Heat loss by evaporation occurs only when the sweat on the surface of the skin is vaporized—that is, converted to a gas. The conversion of liquid to a gas at the skin level requires heat supplied by the body. As liquid sweat absorbs heat from the skin, it changes to a gaseous vapor that is carried away by the surrounding air, resulting in the removal of heat generated from exercise. Small amounts of evaporative sweat remove large quantities of heat. For example, each pint of sweat that evaporates removes approximately 280 calories of heat. Beads of sweat that roll off the body do not contribute to the cooling process—only sweat that evaporates does.

Exercise in hot and humid conditions forces the body to divert more blood than usual from the working muscles to the skin in an effort to carry the heat accumulating in the deeper recesses to the outer shell. The net result is that the exercising muscles are deprived of a full complement of blood and cannot work as long or as hard. Exercise is therefore more difficult in hot and humid weather.

Heat loss by evaporation is seriously impeded when a person wears nonporous garments, such as rubberized and plastic exercise suits. These garments encourage sweating, but their nonporous nature does not allow sweat to evaporate. This practice is dangerous because it may easily result in heat buildup and *dehydration* (excessive water loss), leading to heat-stress illnesses. You should dress for hot-weather exercise by wearing shorts and a porous top. A mesh, baseball-type cap is optional. It is effective in blocking the absorption of radiant heat if you exercise in the middle of the day because the sun's rays are vertical. You do not need to wear a cap when exercising in the cooler times of the day or if the sun is not shining.

Guidelines for Exercise in the Heat

Guidelines for exercising in heat and humidity have been developed for road races, but these guidelines can be applied to any strenuous physical activity performed outdoors during warm weather. Ambient conditions are considered safe when the temperature is below 70° F and the humidity is below 60 percent. Caution should be used and people who are sensitive to heat and humidity should reconsider exercising when the temperature is greater than 80° F or the humidity is over 60 percent. People who are trained and heat acclimated can continue to exercise in these conditions, but they should be aware of the potential hazards and take precautions to prevent heat illness.

The keys to exercising without incident in hot weather are acclimating to the heat and maintaining the body's normal fluid level. The main consequence of dehydration (excessive fluid loss) is a reduction in blood volume. This results in sluggish circulation that decreases the delivery of oxygen to the exercising muscles. Lowered blood volume results in less blood that can be sent to the skin to remove the heat generated by exercise. If too much of the blood volume is lost, sweating stops and the body temperature rises, leading to heat stress illness. Heat illness is a serious problem that can be avoided by following these guidelines designed to preserve the body's fluid level:

- Estimating water loss:
  - Weigh yourself nude before and after exercise.
  - Towel off sweat completely after exercise and then weigh yourself.

In hot, humid weather, drinking water and wearing loose clothing help prevent hyperthermia and heat stress illnesses.

- Each pound of weight loss represents about 1 pint of fluid loss. Be sure to drink that and more after exercise. See Just the Facts: Fluid Consumption Before, During, and After Exercise.
- Other considerations:
  - Modify the exercise program by (1) working out during cooler times of day, (2) choosing shady routes where water is available, (3) slowing the pace or shortening the duration of exercise on particularly oppressive days, and (4) wearing light, loose, porous clothing to facilitate the evaporation of sweat.
  - Never take salt tablets. They are stomach irritants, they attract fluid to the gut, they sometimes pass through the digestive system undissolved, and they may perforate the stomach lining.
  - Exercise must be prolonged, produce profuse sweating, and occur over a number of consecutive days to reduce potassium stores. For the average bout of exercise, you do not need to worry about depleting potassium or make a special

Just the Facts

Fluid Consumption Before, During, and After Exercise

The American College of Sports Medicine[15] has issued the following recommendations about fluid consumption:

1. Make a special effort to drink plenty of fluid every day so that you will be fully hydrated prior to exercise.
2. For exercise lasting 60 minutes or less:
   - Drink a minimum of 1 pint (2 cups) of water about two hours prior to exercise
   - Start drinking soon after exercise begins and continue drinking at regular intervals in an effort to replace the fluid lost from sweating
   - Drink cool fluids (59° F to 72° F) flavored for palatability, because cool fluids do not interfere with stomach emptying, they do not cause stomach cramping, and they absorb some of the body's internal heat.
3. For intense exercise lasting 60 minutes or more:
   - Drink fluids that contain a small amount of carbohydrates (sugar: glucose, sucrose; starch: maltodextrin) and sodium on a regular basis
   - Regularly ingest carbohydrates to maintain blood glucose level and delay fatigue
   - Ingest sodium in very small amounts (0.5 to 0.75 gram per liter of fluid) to enhance taste and promote fluid retention
   - After the workout, continue drinking the same beverage until your thirst is satisfied and then drink some more.
4. Most exercisers are reluctant drinkers during workouts and do not drink enough to match the fluid they lose through sweating, but they should make a conscious effort to get enough fluid during exercise.
5. The general rule after exercise is to drink until you satisfy your thirst and then drink some more. The thirst mechanism of humans is a poor index of the body's need for fluid.
6. Water is an acceptable drink, but it may blunt the thirst drive before rehydration is complete. Therefore, find a tasty beverage that is noncarbonated, nonalcoholic, and caffeine free to drink after exercise. Homemade lemonade, fruit juices cut in half with water to reduce the concentration of sugar, and commercial sports drinks fit the bill very nicely.[8]

effort to replace it. The daily consumption of fresh fruits and vegetables, as suggested by the food pyramid, is all that is needed (see Chapter 6).
- Remember to use a sunscreen lotion when the weather is sunny or hazy. Be sure that the sunscreen you select has a sun-protection factor (SPF) of at least 15, and apply it liberally over exposed skin.

Guidelines for Exercise in the Cold

Problems related to exercise in cold weather include frostbite and **hypothermia** (abnormally low body temperature). *Frostbite* can lead to permanent damage or loss of a body part from gangrene. This can be prevented by adequately protecting exposed areas, such as fingers, nose, ears, facial skin, and toes. Gloves, preferably mittens or thick socks, should be worn to protect the fingers, hands, and wrists. Blood vessels in the scalp do not constrict effectively, so a significant amount of heat is lost if a head covering is not worn. A stocking-type hat is the best head covering because it can be pulled down to protect the ears. In very cold or windy weather, use surgical or ski masks and scarves to keep facial skin warm and to moisten and warm inhaled air.

All exposed or poorly protected flesh is vulnerable to frostbite when the temperature is low and the windchill high. Air temperature plus wind speed equals the windchill index. This value will help you know how to dress appropriately for outdoor exercise.

People often experience a hacking cough for a minute or two after physical exertion in cold weather. This is a normal response and should not cause alarm. Very cold, dry air may not be fully moistened when it is inhaled rapidly and in large volumes during exercise, so the lining of the throat dries out. When exercise is discontinued, the respiratory rate slows and the volume of inhaled air decreases, allowing enough time for the body to fully moisturize it. Coughing stops within a couple of minutes as the linings are remoistened.

Hypothermia is the most severe of the problems associated with outdoor activity in cold weather. Hypothermia occurs when body heat is lost faster than it can be produced. This can be a life-threatening situation.

Exercise in cold weather requires insulating layers of clothing to preserve normal body heat. Without this protection, body heat is quickly lost because of the large temperature gradient between the skin and environment. A layer or two of insulating clothing can be discarded if you get too hot.

Real-World Wellness

Exercising Safely in an Urban Environment

I live in a large city and like to jog outdoors in my neighborhood. How can I limit the risks associated with exercising in the heart of the city?

You can start by becoming familiar with the risks in order to avoid or lessen their impact. Some of the major hazards follow:

1. Traffic volume is one of the primary risks associated with jogging in a large city. This risk can be reduced by wearing reflective clothing, jogging during daylight hours, and jogging on the sidewalks rather than the streets. The best way to handle the problem is to find a nearby park or outdoor running track.
2. A second risk comes from air pollution, primarily carbon monoxide and ozone. The Centers for Disease Control and Prevention has identified outdoor exercisers as one group at high risk for the effects of ozone, carbon monoxide, and other air pollutants. Rapid, deep breathing during exercise results in inhaling more pollutants more deeply into the lungs. Some studies have shown that 30 minutes of jogging during heavy traffic conditions increased carbon monoxide levels in the blood to the equivalent of smoking half a pack of cigarettes.

   Carbon monoxide interferes with the delivery of oxygen to the body's tissues and, when inhaled in high quantities, can cause illness and death. Carbon monoxide emissions from cars, trucks, and buses are most prevalent during rush hours, so avoid jogging on busy streets during these times.

   Ozone causes lung inflammation and injury. The long-term effects of exercising in high ozone conditions are not known. Ozone tends to accumulate in the atmosphere after 10:00 A.M. It is heaviest during bright, sunny days because it is produced by the photochemical reaction of sunlight with hydrocarbons and nitrogen dioxide from motor vehicle exhaust.

   Jogging before the rush hour begins will (1) help control your exposure to motor vehicle emissions and (2) allow you to exercise prior to the buildup of ozone in the atmosphere.
3. Joggers and other outdoor exercises can be targets for crime. Carry no visible money or valuables, such as watches or jewelry. Carry an I.D. tag with your name and the telephone number of a family member or friend in case you are involved in an accident. Do not carry addresses, yours or your family's, in case you are mugged.

Hypothermia can occur even if the air temperature is above freezing.[16] The rate of heat loss for any temperature is influenced by wind velocity. Wind velocity increases the amount of cold air molecules that come in contact with the skin. The more cold molecules, the more effective the heat loss. The speed of walking, jogging, or cycling into the wind must be added to the speed of the wind to properly evaluate the impact of windchill.

You should wear enough clothing to stay warm but not so much as to induce profuse sweating. Knowing how much clothing to wear comes from experience exercising in different environmental conditions. Clothing that becomes wet with sweat loses its insulating qualities. It becomes a conductor of heat, moving heat from the body quickly and potentially endangering the exerciser.

If you exercise or work outdoors in cold weather, you may want to wear polypropylene undergarments. Polypropylene is designed to whisk perspiration away from the skin so that evaporative cooling does not rob heat from the body. You should wear a warm outer garment, preferably made of wool, over this material, If it is windy, wear a breathable windbreaker as the third, outer layer.

If you follow the guidelines for activity in hot and cold weather, you can usually participate quite comfortably all year long. Other hazards associated with outdoor exercise are discussed in Real-World Wellness: Exercising Safely in an Urban Environment.

Summary

- *Physical fitness* is defined in terms of performance-related and health-related fitness.
- Cardiorespiratory endurance is the most important component of health-related fitness.
- The long-term effects of physical training include modifications in heart rate, stroke volume, cardiac output, blood volume, heart volume, respiration, and metabolism.
- Aerobic capacity is finite, improves by 5 to 25 percent with training, and decreases with aging; this decrease is slower in those who are physically fit.
- The training effect is lost in stages if exercise is interrupted or discontinued.
- Exercise affects cholesterol levels, blood pressure, and triglyceride levels, may reduce the risks of diabetes mellitus and stress, and is an alternative method for quitting use of tobacco products.
- The principles of exercise can be manipulated to meet any exercise objective.
- Exercising by varying the activities per exercise session or during exercise sessions is cross-training.
- The heat generated by exercise is lost from the body by conduction, convection, radiation, and evaporation.
- Evaporation of sweat is the major mechanism for ridding the body of heat that develops during exercise.
- Hypothermia is the most severe problem associated with exercise in cold weather.

Review Questions

1. What are the physiological changes that occur from regular participation in aerobic exercise?
2. What are the health benefits that occur from regular participation in aerobic training?
3. Name and define the physiological changes that occur with exercise training.
4. Identify and define the principles of physical conditioning.
5. Define *cross-training* and give some examples.
6. Why should you warm up before exercise?
7. Identify and define the mechanisms of heat loss. Which of these is most important during exercise and why?
8. Describe fluid replacement before, during, and after exercise.

References

1. ACSM. 1998. The recommended quantity and quality of exercise for developing and maintaining cardiorespiratory and muscular fitness and flexibility in healthy adults. *Medicine and Science in Sports and Exercise* 30(6):975.
2. Foss, M. L., and S. T. Keteyian. 1998. *Fox's Physiological Basis for Exercise and Sport*. Boston: WCB/McGraw-Hill.
3. Franklin, B. A., and J. L. Roitman. 1998. Cardiorespiratory adaptations to exercise. In *ACSM's Resource Manual* (3d ed.), ed. J. L. Roitman. Baltimore, Md.: Williams & Wilkins.
4. Holly, R. G., and J. D. Shaffrath. 1998. Cardiorespiratory endurance. In *ACSM's Resource Manual* (3d ed.), ed. J. L. Roitman. Baltimore, Md.: Williams & Wilkins.
5. Blair, S. N., et al. 1995. Changes in physical fitness and all-cause mortality. *JAMA* 273:1093.
6. Williams, M. A. 1998. Human development and aging. In *ACSM's*

Resource Manual (3d ed.), Baltimore, Md.: Williams & Wilkins.
7. U.S. Dept. of Health and Human Services. 1996. *Physical Activity and Health: A Report of the Surgeon General.* Atlanta: U.S. Dept. of Health and Human Services, Centers for Disease Control and Prevention, National Center for Chronic Disease Prevention and Health Promotion.
8. Nieman, D. C. 1999. *Exercise Testing and Prescription.* Mountain View, Calif.: Mayfield Publishing Co.
9. Coyle, E. F. 1998. Deconditioning and retention of adaptations induced by endurance training. In *ACSM's Resource Manual* (3d ed.), ed. J. L. Roitman. Baltimore, Md.: Williams & Wilkins.
10. Beckman, S. 1998. Emergency procedures and exercise safety. In *ACSM's Resource Manual* (3d ed.), ed. J. L. Roitman. Baltimore, Md.: Williams & Wilkins.
11. Mittleman, M. A., et al. 1993. Triggering of acute myocardial infraction by heavy physical exertion. *New England Journal of Medicine* 329(23):1677.
12. Willich, S. N., et al. 1993. Physical exertion as a trigger of acute myocardial infarction. *New England Journal of Medicine* 329(23):1684.
13. Pate, R. R., et al. Physical activity and public health. A recommendation from the Centers for Disease Control and Prevention and the American College of Sports Medicine. *Journal of the American Medical Association* 273:402.
14. Barnard, R. J. et al. 1973. Cardiovascular responses to sudden strenuous exercise—heart rate, blood pressure, and ECG. *Journal of Applied Physiology* 34:833.
15. American College of Sports Medicine. 1996. Position paper on exercise and fluid replacement. *Medicine and Science in Sports and Exercise* 28:1.
16. Bernard, T. E. 1998. Environmental considerations: Heat and cold. In *ACSM's Resource Manual* (3d ed.), ed. J. L. Roitman. Baltimore, Md.: Williams & Wilkins.

Suggested Readings

Editors. 1998. Exercise and fracture risk. *Health News* 4(10):8.

Women who do aerobics or weight training or who play tennis at least two hours per week can expect to reduce the risk of hip and vertebral (spinal bones) fractures by one-third more than can inactive women. Exercise also helps women avoid falls by improving their strength, balance, and coordination.

Harvard University. 1998. An exercise prescription for older people. *Harvard Heart Letter* 8(5):1.

This article presents the principles of exercise and the precautions that should be taken by older people wanting to start an exercise program. It makes the case that age should not be a deterrent to aerobic and resistive exercises. Research is presented that documents the need for and the benefits that older people receive from regular participation in exercise.

Superko, H. R. 1998. The most common cause of coronary heart disease can be successfully treated by the least expensive therapy—exercise. *ACSM Certified News* 8(1):1.

Coronary artery disease is a metabolic disorder that has a strong genetic component, and its most common trait is a high amount of small LDL-C particles. This profile increases the risk three times above normal in males. But it successfully responds to regular exercise and loss of body weight.

Terbizan, D. J., and B. Straud. 1998. How Much Exercise? *Fitness Management* 14(9):32.

This article discusses the need for American adults to exercise and documents the reasons why. It also elaborates on the various goals that people attempt to meet through exercise and presents recommendations for their achievement, categorized in a five-level activity pyramid, from least intense to most intense: fat burning zone, heart healthy zone, aerobic zone, intense conditioning, and competitive zone.

Tufts University. 1998. How to stay young five years longer. *Tufts University Health and Nutrition Letter* 16(5):2.

Growing evidence indicates that middle-aged adults who exercise at least four hours per week, don't smoke, and remain lean are 50 percent more likely to live into their 70s than are sedentary, overweight smokers. Those who follow these lifestyle habits do not develop minor disabilities such as difficulty in walking or reaching for things until they reach the age of about 74. Overweight, nonexercising smokers begin experiencing these disabilities at age 69.

Chapter 3 Increasing Cardiorespiratory Endurance

Women

20- to 29-year-old women

30- to 39-year-old women

40- to 49-year-old women

50- to 59-year-old women

60-year-old and older women

Name _____   Date _____ Section _____

Assessment Activity 3-2

The 1.5-Mile Run/Walk Test

Directions: Select a measured course, preferably a running track, so that the starting and finishing points are at the same location for ease of timing and recording. Cover the distance as rapidly as possible to attain a realistic estimate of fitness level. You will perform better if you take the opportunity to practice running the course first so that you can learn how to pace yourself.

If you cannot run the entire distance, walk until you recover enough to continue running again. Allow a 5- to 10-minute warm-up before the test and an equal amount of time for cooling down after the test. Use the following charts to compare your performance with the norm.

Aerobic Physical Fitness Classification

Men

Fitness Category	13–19 Yrs.	20–29 Yrs.	30–39 Yrs.	40–49 Yrs.
Very poor	>15:31*	>16:01	>16:31	>17:31
Poor	12:11–15:30	14:01–16:00	14:46–16:30	15:36–17:30
Fair	10:49–12:10	12:01–14:00	12:31–14:45	13:01–15:35
Good	9:41–10:48	10:46–12:00	11:01–12:30	11:31–13:00
Excellent	8:37–9:40	9:45–10:45	10:00–11:00	10:30–11:30
Superior	<8:37	<9:45	<10:00	<10:30

*>, greater than; <, less than

Women

Fitness Category	13–19 Yrs.	20–29 Yrs.	30–39 Yrs.	40–49 Yrs.
Very poor	>18:31*	>19:01	>19:31	>20:31
Poor	16:55–18:30	18:31–19:00	19:01–19:30	19:31–20:00
Fair	14:31–16:54	15:55–18:30	16:31–19:00	17:31–19:30
Good	12:30–14:30	13:31–15:54	14:31–16:30	15:56–17:30
Excellent	11:50–12:29	12:30–13:30	13:00–14:30	13:45–15:55
Superior	<11:50	<12:30	<13:00	<13:45

Assessment Activity 3-3

The Bench Step Test

Directions: The equipment needed includes a sturdy 12-inch–high bench, a metronome, a stopwatch, and, if possible, a stethoscope. The metronome should be set at 96 beats per minute for a total of 24 cycles. One cycle consists of four steps as follows: up left foot, up right foot, down left foot, down right foot.

Step up and down in time with each beat of the metronome for 3 full minutes. At the end of the 3 minutes, sit down on the bench immediately. Start the pulse count within the first 5 seconds and continue for 1 full minute. Do not count for 15 seconds and multiply by 4, because the heart rate will be higher than the actual minute heart rate. The 1-minute postexercise heart rate is the score for the test. Refer to the following chart for scoring.

Postexercise 1-Minute Heart Rate (Beats per Minute)

Fitness Category	18–25 Yrs. Men	18–25 Yrs. Women	26–35 Yrs. Men	26–35 Yrs. Women	36–45 Yrs. Men	36–45 Yrs. Women
Excellent	70–78*	72–83	73–79	72–86	72–81	74–87
Good	82–88	88–97	83–88	91–97	86–94	93–101
Above average	91–97	100–106	91–97	103–110	98–102	104–109
Average	101–104	110–116	101–106	112–118	105–111	111–117
Below average	107–114	118–124	109–116	121–127	113–118	120–127
Poor	118–126	128–137	119–126	129–135	120–128	130–138
Very poor	131–164	141–155	130–164	141–154	132–168	143–152

*Count the pulse for 1 full minute after 3 minutes of stepping at 24 cycles/min. on a 12-inch bench.

Name _____ **Date** _____ **Section** _____

Assessment Activity 3-5

Design an Exercise Program

Directions: Design an exercise program for yourself. First, identify your goals (weight loss, health enhancement, improving your level of physical fitness, stress reduction, etc.) and second, respond accordingly to each of the following five items.

1. Activity or activities: _____
2. Frequency of exercise: _____
3. Intensity of exercise: _____
4. Duration of exercise: _____
5. Activity schedule: Place the activity or activities in the following weekly calendar with the suggested amount of time devoted to each activity.

Sunday	Monday	Tuesday	Wednesday	Thursday	Friday	Saturday

4

Building Muscular Strength and Endurance

Key Terms

anaerobic
atrophy
circuit resistance training (CRT)
concentric contraction
eccentric contraction
hypertrophy
isokinetic
isometric
isotonic
muscular endurance
muscular strength
variable resistance

Goals for Behavior Change

- Begin a strength-training program or improve the one in which you already participate.
- Supply your close family members with at least five health-related reasons they should participate in resistance training.
- Identify the parts of your body where you would like to make the greatest physical change and explain why.
- Identify some of the tasks or sports that you perform daily, weekly, or monthly that would be easier to do if you increased your strength.

Objectives

After completing this chapter, you will be able to do the following:

- Explain the benefits of resistance training for older people.
- Define the different types of muscle contraction.
- Identify the various systems of dynamic and static exercise training.
- Describe the limitations of isometric exercise training.
- Explain the advantages and disadvantages of circuit resistance training.
- Define each of the principles of resistance training.
- Explain the differences in strength between men and women.
- Describe the short- and long-term effects of anabolic steroid use.
- Describe the health benefits of resistance training.
- Describe the progressive resistance technique that increases muscle endurance.

Over the last decade, evidence has been steadily mounting of the growing importance of muscular development for health enhancement, fitness, and aesthetic purposes. The muscular system improves through resistive forms of exercises, such as weight training and calisthenics. Resistive exercises complement aerobic forms of exercise, because each uniquely contributes to health, physical fitness, and personal appearance. Both types of exercise are required for a well-rounded conditioning program, and together they produce optimum results.

Aerobic exercises, which improve cardiorespiratory function and enhance health status in many ways, are presented in Chapter 3. Resistance exercises also contribute to physiological and psychological health. In fact, many experts are convinced that resistance training is the only type of exercise capable of slowing, and possibly reversing, declines in muscle mass, bone density, and strength. Not long ago, these negative changes were considered to be the result of the aging process.[1]

The body contains more than 600 muscles, and 5 percent of these are located above the waist. All uscles, regardless of location, respond to the physio- ical law of use and disuse. "Use it or lose it" is an m that applies to all human beings during every e of the life cycle. Americans tend to become more tary as they age. The declining stimulation results rogressive shrinking and weakening of the

few exceptions—notably cross-country skiing, r nd swimming—aerobic activities provide lim- ite ation of upper body musculature. Sedentary livi ts the muscular system entirely and acceler- ates of muscle tissue and body strength. The need ce training was illustrated in a study of runne ten-year period. Runners who did no resistan suffered muscle atrophy in their upper bo maintaining muscle size in their legs.[2] Their h received little stimulation from jogging, decrea rcumference.

Jogging is u stimulate the arms at or above the threshold nee r muscular development or maintenance, but th ion of resistive exercises can. This is an example the two types of training complement each other

The Health Ber s of Resistance T ng

Irrefutable evidence prove rength training produces unique health benef ple of all ages as well as for those with vario f infirmities. The American College of Sports , The American Heart Association, and the Su neral's *Report on Physical Activity and Health* have all proclaimed and strongly supported the need for strength training for health enhancement and for improving quality of life. Strength training increases muscle mass and decreases the fat content of the body. The implications for weight loss and management are enormous, because muscle tissue is more metabolically active than is fat tissue. This means that the body burns more calories under any condition, including rest.[3]

An improvement in strength reduces the exerciser's heart rate and blood pressure while he or she is lifting weights. The practical application of these responses is that there is less stress on the heart when people lift or move moderately heavy objects in everyday life.[4]

Resistance training increases the strength and endurance of the antigravity muscles, improving posture and producing less stress on the lower back.[5] Stronger, more stable joints are better able to withstand physical stress or trauma.

Strength training also enables one to perform the functions of daily life with less effort. Actually, stronger muscles allow people to perform functional tasks that become more difficult as people age, such as getting in and out of a car, in and out of a bathtub, or up from an easy chair and climbing stairs. Dynamic forms of resistance training have a high degree of transferability to everyday activities.

An increase in leg strength helps those who have osteoarthritis (wear and tear arthritis) because stronger muscles absorb a greater share of the physical stress at joints. In effect, stronger muscles spare the joint structures from some of the weight-bearing activity. Rheumatologists (physicians who specialize in the diagnosis and treatment of arthritic conditions) often recommend weight training to their patients because it alleviates symptoms and strengthens the muscles, tendons, and ligaments that surround the joints.[1]

An improvement in leg strength also leads to better balance and decreases the likelihood of falling, which reduces the chances that a fracture might occur.[4] Osteoporosis is a disease characterized by the deterioration of the skeletal system. Bone mineral content decreases so that the bones become fragile and susceptible to fracture. Women are more prone to osteoporosis, but men are also affected as they age. People can protect the skeletal system by eating a nutritious diet and by participating regularly in weight-bearing and resistive exercise. Resistive exercises are versatile, having the capacity to stress all of the joints and the bones that articulate with them, and they produce lateral forces that increase the thickness and density of bones, so they have the potential to prevent osteoporosis.

The results brought about by resistance exercises allow people to live independently and with dignity as they age. Evidence indicates that Americans are living longer, and many will live with physical and functional limitations.[6] Illnesses occur with greater frequency and severity as we age, but much of the disability associated with aging is not due entirely to the aging process. Many authorities attribute at least 50 percent of these changes to "disuse atrophy."[7] The fact is that our typically sedentary lifestyles, which are more prevalent among the aging population than among any other group of Americans, are responsible for a significant number of these illnesses. Those who stimulate their muscles regularly, regardless of their age, do not experience the type of physical deterioration observed in those who are physically inactive. Recent research indicates that physical inactivity is responsible for the majority of age-related muscle loss.[1,8]

Strength training also produces an impressive array of psychological and emotional benefits, which include improvements in self-esteem and self-confidence.[3] It helps to improve the mood of mildly to moderately depressed individuals. Resistive exercise programs improve reaction time and may contribute to more restful sleep. Just the Facts: The Benefits of Resistance Training provides a summary of the positive outcomes that can be achieved through resistance training. Also see Wellness Across the Generations: Strength Training for Older Adults.

Many cardiac patients currently participate in strength development exercise. Substantial benefits may be gained at minimal risk.[9] Improving upper and lower body strength allows cardiac patients to perform everyday lifting activities with less effort and greater movement efficiency. Also, strength training may have a positive impact on cardiorespiratory endurance, hypertension, blood fat levels, and psychological well-being.

Anaerobic Exercise

Strength development exercises are **anaerobic**. *Anaerobic* literally means "without oxygen," and when applied to exercise, it refers to high-intensity physical activities in which oxygen demand is above the level that can be supplied during performance. Short-term supplies of fuel stored in the muscles provide the energy for anaerobic activities. As a result, these can only be sustained for several seconds. Sprinting 100 yards, lifting a heavy weight, and running up two or three flights of stairs are some examples of anaerobic activities.

Muscular Strength

Muscular strength is the maximum force that a muscle or muscle group can exert in a single contraction. It is best developed by some form of progressive resistance exercise, such as weight training with free weights (bar-bells and dumbbells) or single or multistation machine weights.

Muscular strength is developed best through high-intensity exercise. Lifting heavier loads a few times to fatigue produces larger gains than does lifting lighter loads many times to fatigue. Weight trainers speak of the amount of work accomplished in high-intensity exercise repetitions, sets, and terms of percentage of 1 repetition maximum (1 RM) for each exercise. A *repetition* is one complete lift of an exercise beginning with the starting position, moving the weight through a full range of motion, and returning to the starting position. Doing this ten times in a continuous fashion is referred to as *10 repetitions* or *10 reps,* and these 10 reps represent 1 *set* of that exercise. Repeating the entire sequence two more times completes *3 sets* of the exercise. One repetition maximum (1 RM) represents the heaviest load that can be lifted one time. Ten RM is a lighter load that can be lifted ten times but not eleven. In other words, maximum fatigue occurs on repetition number 10, thereby preventing repetition number 11.

Just the Facts

The Benefits of Resistance Training

Resistance training produces the following positive results:

- Increases muscle mass and decreases fat mass
- Increases strength and muscle endurance
- Increases basal metabolic rate (BMR)
- Develops the antigravity muscles (abdominal, lower back, hips, front and back of the thighs, both calves)
- Increases bone density (resulting in less risk of bone fracture)
- Improves dynamic balance (resulting in less risk of falling)
- Improves mobility, such as that necessary for walking and stair-climbing
- Improves reaction time
- Contributes to more restful sleep
- Helps to elevate the mood of mildly to moderately depressed people
- Improves body image, self-esteem, and self-confidence
- Improves the effectiveness of insulin in older adults
- Aids in weight loss and weight management
- May increase HDL cholesterol (the protective form)

Wellness Across the Generations

Strength Training for Older Adults

One of the realities of aging is muscle atrophy (decrease in size), resulting in a loss of strength, power, balance, and coordination. However, scientists have shown that a substantial amount of muscle loss is due to lack of appropriate physical activity rather than to the aging process. Engaging regularly in resistance exercises can build muscle, maintain muscle, and limit the loss of muscle tissue.

Inactive people can expect to lose approximately 50 percent of their muscle mass between 20 and 90 years of age.[10] This loss is accompanied by a 30 percent reduction in strength between 50 and 70 years of age. Data from the ongoing Framingham Study showed that 40 percent of female subjects 55 to 64 years of age, 45 percent of female subjects 65 to 74 years of age, and 65 percent of female subjects 74 to 85 years of age were unable to lift 10 pounds. The loss of muscle strength is most pronounced after age 70. Data show that muscle strength declines by approximately 15 percent per decade during the 60s and 70s and accelerates to 30 percent per decade thereafter.[10]

Because of this limitation, everyday functions taken for granted by the young become physical challenges, including opening bottle caps and jar lids, carrying groceries, and climbing stairs. If muscle atrophy progresses unabated, walking without assistance becomes very difficult if not impossible, and the likelihood of falling increases.

The good news is that the muscles of older people respond to training in much the same way as the muscles of young adults. In fact, older people may make greater gains because of their initial level of debility (weakness). Studies have shown that the elderly can double or even triple their strength level in as little as three to four months of strength training.[10] Strength training also seems to have profound anabolic (muscle-building) effects in elderly people.

Select a weight that is 80 to 90 percent of 1 RM if strength development is the primary goal. If you are a beginner, be extremely careful in establishing 1 RM for each exercise, because your musculoskeletal system is not trained to handle such loads. It is recommended that beginners skip the 1 RM method of weight selection and instead, through trial and error, find a weight that can be lifted for at least but not more than 8 to 10 reps. One RM for each exercise may be safely established after six weeks of training.

Muscle Contraction and Resistance Training

Muscle contraction is either static or dynamic. *Static contractions* (isometric) occur when muscles exert force but do not move (shorten or lengthen). *Dynamic contractions* (isotonic and isokinetic) involve muscle contractions that are either *concentric* (muscle shortening) or *eccentric* (muscle lengthening). See figure 4-1 for an illustration of each.

Some of the exercises commonly used to develop the major muscle groups of the body are shown in figures 4-2 to 4-17. The anatomical charts in figures 4-18 and 4-19 show the location of the muscles stressed in each exercise. These exercises are demonstrated on exercise machines and free weights, methods that are equivalent and work the same muscle groups.

See Assessment Activity 4-1 for a method of determining your strength based on body weight and gender.

Static Training (Isometrics)

Isometric contractions (in which muscle length is constant) occur when muscles produce tension but do not shorten, because the resistance is beyond the contractile force that can be generated by the exercising muscles. Examples of isometric contractions are pushing against a wall, pushing sideways or upward against a door jamb, and loading a weight machine with poundage that is beyond one's capacity to lift. See figure 4-20 for an illustration.

Optimal strength development from isometric contractions occurs with 5 to 10 sets of 6-second contractions at 100 percent of maximum force.

Isometric exercises are effective for developing strength, but this approach has some important limitations. The most serious of these is a higher than expected rise in exercise arterial blood pressure and an increased workload on the heart throughout the entire contraction. All-out straining isometric contractions should not be performed by people with heart and vascular disease. A second limitation is that strength developed isometrically is joint-angle specific. Maximum strength development occurs at the angle of contraction, with a training carryover of approximately 20 degrees in either direction from that angle.[11] To develop strength throughout the muscle's range of motion, you must perform isometric contractions at three different points in the range of motion.

Chapter 4 Building Muscular Strength and Endurance 101

Figure 4-1 Contractions
The two types of contractions: *A*, a concentric contraction; *B*, an eccentric contraction.

Figure 4-2 Biceps Curl
A: Start with your arms extended, palms up. *B*: Flex both arms, slowly move the weight through a full range of motion, and return to the starting position. The prime mover is the biceps brachii.

Figure 4-3 Biceps Curl (Free Weights)

Figure 4-4 Overhead Press

A: Sit upright with your hands approximately shoulder width apart. *B:* Slowly press the bar upward until your arms are fully extended, and lower to the starting position. Avoid an excessive arch in your lower back. The prime movers are the triceps and deltoid muscles.

Figure 4-5 Overhead Press (Free Weights)

Figure 4-6 Bench Press

A: Lie on your back with your knees bent and your feet flat on the bench to prevent arching your back. *B*: Slowly press the bar forward, fully extending your arms, and return to the starting position. The prime movers are the pectoralis major, triceps, and deltoid muscles.

Figure 4-7 Bench Press (Free Weights)

Figure 4-8 Abdominal Crunch

A: Sit upright with your chest against the pads, hands folded across your stomach. *B*: Slowly press forward through a full range of motion, and return to the starting position. The prime mover is the rectus abdominis muscle.

Figure 4-9 Abdominal Crunch (Mat Exercise)

Figure 4-10 Lower Back Extension
A: Place your thighs and back against the pads. *B*: Slowly press backward until your back is fully extended, and return to the starting position. The prime movers are the erector spine and gluteus maximus muscles.

Figure 4-11 Back Extension (Mat Exercise)

Because muscles cannot overcome the resistance in isometric training, measuring improvement is difficult, constituting another limitation of this system. Improvements in strength can be measured if exercisers have access to specialized equipment, such as dynamometers and tensiometers, that record the amount of force applied. Motivation for exercise is difficult to sustain without feedback.

Research indicates that isometric exercise systems are as effective as dynamic exercise systems for developing strength. The question is not which system is better but which system best satisfies the intended use for the newly acquired strength. The transferability of strength to occupational and leisure pursuits is very relevant.

Strength developed in the muscles is highly specific to the manner in which the muscles are trained. Muscles trained isometrically perform best when stressed isometrically; muscles trained dynamically perform best when stressed dynamically. There is some transfer of isometric training to everyday life. Carrying groceries, a baby, or any object in a fixed position or pushing and pulling objects requires isometric strength, but most movements are dynamic, and transfer is more widely applicable from dynamic systems of training.

Wellness Fundamental Concepts and Applications

Figure 4-12 Leg Press
A: Adjust the seat so that your legs are bent at approximately 90 degrees. *B*: Slowly extend your legs fully, and return to the starting position. The prime movers are the quadriceps and gluteus maximus muscles.

Figure 4-13 Half-Squat (Free Weights)

Figure 4-14 Hamstring Curl

A: Lie face down with your lower legs under the pads. *B*: Curl the weight approximately 90 degrees, and return to the starting position. The prime mover is the hamstring muscle group.

Dynamic Exercise

Dynamic exercises include **isotonic** (equal tension), variable resistance, free weights, and **isokinetic** (equal speed) exercises.

Isotonic training

Isotonic muscle contractions occur when muscles shorten and move the bones to which they are attached, resulting in movement around the joints. Isotonic movements consist of concentric and eccentric muscle contractions. The **concentric contraction** occurs when a muscle shortens as it develops the tension to overcome an external resistance. The **eccentric contraction** occurs when the muscle lengthens and the weight (resistance) is slowly returned to the starting position. When muscles contract eccentrically, they are resisting the force of gravity as they lengthen so that the weight is not allowed to free-fall. In general, muscles can produce about 40 percent more tension eccentrically than concentrically.[5] But no advantage exists for training programs that emphasize eccentric contractions. Research indicates that conventional isotonic programs develop as much strength and produce less of the delayed muscle soreness that is associated with eccentric contractions.

Figure 4-15 Hamstring Curl (Free Weights)

Figure 4-16 Chest Press
A: Keep your upper arms parallel to the floor, bend your elbows at 90 degrees, and place your hands on the handles.
B: Slowly push the bars until your elbows are pointing forward, and return to the starting position. The prime movers are the pectoralis major and deltoid muscles.

Figure 4-17 Lateral Supine Raises (Free Weights)

Isotonic exercises produce delayed muscle soreness twenty-four to forty-eight hours after a workout. Eccentric contractions cause microscopic damage to muscle fibers, their connective tissue, and the cell membranes.[12] Soreness occurs because the damaged tissues swell and apply pressure on the nerves. Delayed muscle soreness is more common among beginning exercisers, exercisers who attempt to overload too quickly, and those who change from one activity to another.

Stretching exercises, light workouts, or complete rest may be required to alleviate muscle soreness. Prevention is the best treatment. Prevention involves allowing enough time to adjust to a new routine (at least one month), overloading the muscles in small increments (not trying to do too much too fast), and exercising within capacity. Because muscle soreness may last forty-eight hours, those who use isotonic exercise systems are advised to exercise no more than every other day. This schedule ensures that the next bout of exercise will occur after soreness has abated.

Variable resistance training

Variable resistance exercise equipment was developed because isotonic exercises do not maximally stress muscles throughout their full range of motion. The maximum

Figure 4-18 Selected Muscles of the Body—Front View

Figure 4-19 Selected Muscles of the Body—Rear View

weight lifted isotonically is limited to the weakest point in the musculoskeletal leverage system. The weight appears lighter at some points in the joint movement and heavier at others. In reality, the weight itself is constant and the human bony leverage system changes.

Variable resistance equipment is designed to provide maximum resistance through the full range of motion. Universal Gym equipment accomplishes this by altering the lifter's leverage. Decreasing the leverage increases the resistance at points in the movement where the muscles are strongest. Nautilus equipment uses a system of cams to do the same. Variable resistance training challenges people to exert more force throughout the range of motion, which should result in greater returns. Whether variable resistance weight training is more effective than conventional weight training is yet to be resolved. Evidence indicates that it is as good and may be better, even though it varies the resistance imprecisely.

Free-weight training

Isotonic training with free weights (dumbbells and barbells) continues to be an appropriate method of strength development. Free-weight training provides many advantages. For athletes, it yields some flexibility in strength development because the movements are not confined to a track. Exercises can be selected or improvised to simulate the movements required by specific sports, allowing the development of the muscles that will be used in competition. Concurrently, ancillary musculature that plays a supporting or stabilizing role for the major muscles is also stimulated and developed.

For noncompetitors, free weights have several advantages. The equipment is inexpensive and versatile. A starter set of free weights typically costs less than $150. Free weights do not require much space, so the workout can occur in the home.

The main limitation of free-weight exercise is that this system does not provide maximum resistance throughout the full range of motion. A second limitation is the need for one or two spotters to assist with exercises such as the bench press and half-squats.

Isokinetic training

Isokinetic resistance training involves dynamic movements performed on exercise devices that produce maximum resistance throughout the full range of motion. The movement speed is preselected by the exerciser and

Just the Facts

Muscle Fiber Types

In humans, it appears that the total number of muscle fibers and the fiber type are set genetically and that both are fully established at birth. Current research indicates that the number of muscle fibers probably cannot be increased and the fiber type cannot be changed. If this theory is accurate, then the increases in muscle size resulting from training must be caused by hypertrophy (increase in size) of the existing fibers. Muscle hyperplasia (an increase in the number of muscle fibers) has been shown to occur in several species of animals through heavy resistance exercise. Muscle hyperplasia has not been verified in humans, but the possibility cannot be ruled out.

Muscles consist of three types of fibers: (1) type I or slow-twitch oxidative fibers (SO); (2) type IIa or fast-twitch, oxidative glycloytic fibers (FOG); and (3) type IIb or fast-twitch glycloytic fibers (FG). Each fiber type can be identified by its speed of contraction and the primary energy source that it uses. Slow-twitch oxidative fibers rely on the aerobic or oxygen system. These fibers are responsible for exercise and activities of an aerobic or endurance nature. The fast-twitch oxidative, glycloytic fibers (type IIa) contract faster than the type I fibers and are capable of using oxygen but not as efficiently as type I fibers. These fibers support exercises that require both aerobic and anaerobic energy. The fast-twitch glycloytic fibers (type IIb) have the fastest contractile speed of the three and support high-intensity anaerobic exercises.

Muscle fibers do not cross over—type I fibers remain slow-twitch and type II fibers remain fast-twitch, regardless of the type of training to which they are exposed. To produce a change in muscle fiber type requires a structural change in the motor nerve that supplies it with electrical impulses. A motor nerve stimulates either all slow-twitch or all fast-twitch fibers, and when the electrical impulse is delivered, all fibers in the motor unit contract.

The ratio between the fiber types also appears to be set genetically. Changing one fiber type to another under normal conditions is probably impossible, because the motor nerve that innervates (supplies nerve impulses to) the muscle determines its function.

The ratio of slow-twitch to fast-twitch muscle fibers can be determined by examining under a powerful microscope muscle biopsies from selected sites in the body. The muscle composition of world-class aerobic athletes (distance runners, cyclists, cross-country skiers) is predominately slow-twitch, whereas the muscle compositions of the world-class power or anaerobic event athletes (shot-putters, sprinters, power and Olympic weight lifters) is primarily fast-twitch. Knowing the ratio of fiber type could be important for these competitors, but it is relatively unimportant when one exercises for health reasons. Health enthusiasts can participate in a variety of activities with some degree of success and satisfaction regardless of fiber type.

---

remains constant throughout the movement. Isokinetic exercise theoretically improves on traditional and variable-resistance dynamic systems.[13] Isokinetic devices adjust the resistance to accommodate the force applied by the exerciser. The greater the application of force, the greater the resistance to movement supplied by the device. Maximum force applied through the full range of motion is countered with maximum resistance at all joint angles. This activates the greatest number of motor units and should produce greater gains in strength than other dynamic systems of exercise.

Circuit Resistance Training

Circuit resistance training (CRT) is very effective for people who wish to develop several fitness dimensions simultaneously. Muscular strength and endurance, changes in body composition, and improvement in cardiorespiratory endurance can be attained together.

A circuit usually consists of eight to fifteen exercise stations. The weight selected for each exercise station should equal 40 to 55 percent of the exerciser's capacity. The exerciser does as many repetitions as possible for 15 to 30 seconds at each station. The rest interval between exercise stations should equal the exercise time spent at each station. The circuit is repeated two to three times for a total elapsed time of 30 to 50 minutes per workout. As fitness improves, overload can be applied by (1) increasing the amount of weight at each station, (2) increasing the amount of exercise time at each station (up to 30 seconds), (3) decreasing the amount of rest between stations, or (4) any combination of these.

Figure 4-20 Isometric Contraction

An isometric contraction is a static contraction against an immovable object.

The CRT system is challenging, versatile, and fun. Exercise stations can be rearranged, exercises that develop similar muscle groups can be substituted for each other, and the order in which the circuit is traversed can be changed. Because relatively light weights are used, the likelihood of injury is reduced. Circuits can be set up in relatively small spaces. Machine weights are ideal for CRT because of the speed with which resistances can be changed, but free weights are adaptable to this system as well. The main limitation of CRT is that optimal gains in strength or cardiorespiratory endurance are difficult to achieve. Strength is most efficiently developed through lifting very heavy weights combined with a substantial rest period between sets. Cardiorespiratory endurance can best be achieved through rhythmic and continuous activities, such as jogging, cycling, cross-country skiing, and rowing, that are preformed for a minimum of 20 minutes per workout. An example of a circuit is presented in Just the Facts: Circuit Resistance Training.

Just the Facts

Circuit Resistance Training

The following is an example of a circuit. You should warm up before CRT and finish the workout with a cooldown.

Station 1	Leg presses or half-squats	15–30 secs.
Station 2	Bench presses	15–30 secs.
Station 3	Back hyperextensions	15–30 secs.
Station 4	Biceps curls	15–30 secs.
Station 5	Overhead presses	15–30 secs.
Station 6	Sit-ups or abdominal crunches	15–30 secs.
Station 7	Push-ups	15–30 secs.
Station 8	Lateral raises	15–30 secs.
Station 9	Hamstring curls	15–30 secs.
Station 10	Pull-ups	15–30 secs.

Muscular Endurance

Muscular endurance is the application of repeated muscular force against a submaximal resistance. Inflating a tire with a bicycle pump, walking up five flights of stairs, lifting a weight 20 times, and doing 50 sit-ups are some examples of activities that develop muscular endurance. It is developed by many repetitions against resistances that are considerably less than maximum.

Research has shown that the greatest effect on muscle endurance occurs with submaximal loads that can be lifted 20 or more times.[14] Programs that emphasize low resistance and high repetitions produce very limited improvement, if any, in *strength*. The primary stimulus of these programs is on the body's ability to supply blood and oxygen to the working muscles for them to contract on a repeated basis. Endurance exercises increase muscle capillarization and muscle myoglobin. An increase in muscle capillaries allows the muscles to accept more blood. The increase in oxygen carried by the capillaries is transferred to a greater quantity of myoglobin, which delivers it to the muscles. As with other types of isotonic resistance training programs, muscle endurance exercises should be performed no more than every other day.

Isometric or static muscle endurance is the ability to sustain or hold a submaximal contraction for a period of time.[5] Examples are carrying objects, such as groceries and other packages; pushing or pulling objects, such as a lawn mower; and carrying children.

Assessment Activity 4-2 presents a method of determining your muscular endurance. Assessment Activity 4-3 measures abdominal muscle endurance, and Assessment Activity 4-4 measures muscular strength and endurance with calisthenics.

Principles of Resistance Training

The principles of exercise—intensity, duration, frequency, overload, progression, and specificity—apply to resistance training as well as aerobic training. These principles were established over many years through research and experience. The current set of guidelines recommended for average healthy adults was published in 1998 by the American College of Sports Medicine (ACSM):[2]

> A minimum of eight to ten exercises involving the major muscle groups should be performed two to three days per week. A minimum of 1 set of 8 to 12 RM or to near fatigue should be completed by most participants; however, for older and more frail persons (approximately 50 to 60 years of age and above), 10 to 15 repetitions may be more appropriate.

These recommendations are minimum standards for weight training and are designed to motivate sedentary nonathletic adults to try this form of exercise. According to ACSM, more sets, heavier weights, and exercising three times per week produce greater results, but the additional time and effort required for more sets, greater frequency, and heavier weights probably exceed the interest of this population. Although this may be true, healthy American adults should be encouraged to exercise above these minimum recommendations.

Intensity

Intensity refers to the amount of weight used for a given exercise. It is probably the most important variable in resistance training, and it is the most important stimulus associated with the development of strength and muscle endurance.[14]

For muscular development and health enhancement, the intensity of resistance training may be set by selecting a weight (through trial and error) that can be lifted at least 8 times but no more than 12 times. This weight is probably 70 to 80 percent of a maximal effort.[10]

The intensity level for resistance exercise varies according to the training system used. Optimal strength development through isometrics involves maximal contractions, 5 to 10 sets with a total contraction time of 30 to 60 seconds. Optimal strength development

---

Wellness on the Web Behavior Change Activities

How Much Do You Know about Muscle Strength and Endurance?

"Being buff" and "getting ripped" are key goals of many body builders and other fitness enthusiasts. How important is muscle development for fitness, health, and aesthetic purposes? The body contains more than 600 muscles, and 65% of these are located above the waist. All muscles, regardless of location, respond to the physiological law of use and disuse. We Americans tend to become more sedentary as we age, and this decreased activity results in a progressive shrinking and weakening of the muscles. Go to Health-Line's website at www.health-line.com/articles/h19412dt.htm to take a quiz on muscle strength and endurance. Answer the 14 true-false questions to test your current knowledge. If you think an answer is true or mostly true, circle T. If you think an answer is false or mostly false, circle F. How much did you know?

How's Your Form?

There's more to weight training than building bulk. It's a gradual process, and speeding it up or failing to use appropriate techniques can definitely be hazardous to your health. To train safely and effectively, it's essential that you use the correct form and technique. The Global Health and Fitness (GHF) website offers instructions and video demonstrations for more than 100 different strength training exercises. Go to www.global-fitness.com and select "Exercise Instructions and Video Demonstrations." You'll find an anatomical map and a detailed explanation of each major muscle group, its exact location, functions and common activities that the muscle is used to perform, and the best strength training exercises for that muscle. Click on a muscle group and find a free sample video demonstration and exercise instruction for that group.

Customizing Your Strength Training Program

One person's ideal weight training program may be another's downfall. For optimal results, why not plan a customized program? Afraid it'll cost a fortune? Don't worry! The Global Health and Fitness website mentioned in Exercise 2 also provides strength training programs, customized and related to your experience and fitness level, goals and personal interests, and time commitment. At the GHF home page, select "Customized Exercise Programs." You can choose from a wide array of options to create just the right program for you.

through dynamic systems of exercise should include 3 to 5 sets of 4 RM to 6 RM per set, with at least 2 minutes' rest between sets, and this should be performed three times per week.[5] If muscle endurance is the primary goal, the workout should consist of 3 to 5 sets of 15 RM to 25 RM per set, with approximately 1 minute's rest between sets, performed three times per week.

Duration

The duration or length of each exercise session is dependent upon the number of exercises, repetitions, and sets, the amount of rest between sets, and the time available to the performer. The ACSM estimates that its minimum guidelines require about 20 minutes to complete. Conventional resistance programs (3 sets, 10 to 12 exercises, 8 to 12 reps) take about 50 minutes. Serious bodybuilding requires two to four hours in advanced weight training systems, six days per week. Availability of time and individual goals will dictate the length of workout.

Frequency

Frequency refers to the number of training sessions per week. Dynamic resistance exercises (isotonic and isokinetic) should be performed every other day (seven training sessions every two weeks) or three times per week (six training sessions every two weeks). Near-maximum gains in strength for novice weight trainers occur with these exercise frequencies.

Isometrics can be performed every day because muscle soreness does not result. However, for physiological and psychological reasons, you should designate two to three days of rest throughout the week.

Overload and Progression

The principle behind strength increase is straightforward—the muscles must be subjected periodically to greater resistance as they adapt to the previous resistance. This overload principle applies to all muscles regardless of the system of training.

Overload may be applied by progressively increasing the amount of weight lifted or the number of repetitions performed or by decreasing rest time between sets. An increase in the number of repetitions leads to increases in muscle endurance, an increase in the amount of weight lifted leads to an increase in muscle strength, and a decrease in rest time increases muscular and aerobic endurance.

The principle of progression relates to the application of overload. It dictates how much and when an increase in resistance, reps, or sets or a decrease in rest time should occur. For example, the application of overload in a strength development program featuring 6 RM is accomplished by increasing the load when the exerciser can perform more than six reps on more than one occasion. The added weight reduces the number of reps that can be performed. Continued training improves strength and increases the number of reps. Once again, when the exerciser can perform more than six reps on more than one occasion, the weight is increased. This cycle is repeated for as long as strength development is the goal.

Specificity

The principle of specificity reflects the body's response to exercise. The type of training dictates the type of muscle development. Training programs that emphasize high resistance and low repetitions increase muscle strength and size. The gains are the result of muscle **hypertrophy,** which is an increase in the diameter of muscle fibers, and the recruitment of more motor units.

Training programs that emphasize low resistance and a high number of repetitions develop muscle endurance. The high volume of work increases the blood and oxygen supply to the muscles by increasing capillary density and muscle myoglobin concentration.

The effectiveness of resistance training programs is based on the knowledgeable use of principles that guide such programs. However, other factors contribute to program effectiveness. These are found in Real-World Wellness: Other Important Considerations for Resistance Training.

Ergogenic Aids

Ergogenic aids are substances, techniques, or treatments that theoretically improve physical performance in addition to the effects of normal training. This discussion on ergogenic aids will be limited to a few of those that are reputed to accelerate muscle and strength development.

Many athletes and nonathletes alike take supplements of various types to accelerate muscle development. This short summary of a few of the many ergogenic aids suffices to show that some of these actually have performance-enhancing qualities, but many do not.

Protein Supplementation

The adult requirement for protein is 0.8 gram (g) per kilogram (1 kg = 2.2 lbs.) of body weight. Research has shown that resistance training may push this requirement to 1.6 to 1.8 g/kg of body weight.[15] Values such as these are easily obtained with the typical American diet, particularly for active people who tend to consume more calories than does the average adult. Protein in excess of these values has resulted in no further gains in strength, power, or muscle size.[16]

Real-World Wellness

Other Important Considerations for Resistance Training

In addition to the principles of resistance exercise, what factors should I consider to ensure the effectiveness and safety of my resistance training program?

Here are some other important factors for novice weight trainers:

- *Order of exercises:* Many people believe that large muscle exercises should precede small muscle exercises. This format allows one to train at a higher intensity level. Large muscle exercises such as half-squats or leg presses should be performed prior to hamstring curls; bench presses should precede triceps extensions. If small muscle group exercises precede large muscle exercises, fatigue (preexhaustion) is carried over to the large muscle exercises, which limits their effectiveness.

  Novice exercisers should not exercise the same muscles in consecutive exercises, because they are likely then to be less tolerant to the preexhaustion phenomenon that occurs from the buildup of lactic acid resulting from the previous exercise.

- *Rest intervals between sets:* The rest period depends upon the goals of training. For example, if the goal is strength development, the rest period between sets should be 2 to 3 minutes. If body building is the goal, the rest period should be 1 minute or less. If circuit training is the system used, the rest period between exercises should be 15 to 30 seconds.

- *Speed of movement:* For the general public, speed of movement should be relatively slow and controlled. It should take 2 to 3 seconds for the concentric contraction and the same amount of time for the eccentric concentration.

- *Multiple sets versus single sets:* Although 1 set of each exercise performed two to three days per week increases strength, it is a minimal effort. Doing 2 to 3 sets three times per week is better.

- *Breathing patterns:* Most important, never hold your breath during physical exertion because this produces an extraordinary rise in blood pressure. Breathe rhythmically during exertion. The suggested pattern of breathing during weight training is to exhale during concentric contractions, while muscles are shortening, and to inhale during eccentric contractions, while muscles are lengthening and while returning weights to starting positions.

- *Spotting:* Spotters are needed for certain exercises performed with free weights. These include multijoint exercises, in which weights must be returned to a rack on completion, and exercises during which weights need to be properly positioned. Half-squats and bench presses are examples of exercises requiring assistance.

- *Safety:* The chances of sustaining an injury from resistance training are relatively small, but as with all physical activities, the chance exists. Safety is enhanced by employing correct lifting techniques, making use of spotters, breathing properly, maintaining equipment in good working order, and wearing proper exercise clothing.

- *Full range of motion:* To develop strength throughout the full range of motion, exercising muscles must produce force through complete flexion and extension. Be careful not to hyperextend or overextend, which can result in injury.

Vitamins and Minerals

Physical performance is adversely affected by vitamin and mineral deficiencies. Those who have deficiencies can supplement their diets with the missing element or elements. However, the performance of well-nourished, physically active people is not improved through vitamin and mineral supplementation.

Creatine

Many, but not all, studies show that supplementing with creatine (an amino acid) may enhance performance in short-term, high-intensity activities such as resistance training. Creatine supplementation increases skeletal muscle creatine content for most people. It is particularly advantageous for strict vegetarians who eat no animal flesh and therefore have low levels as a result. Creatine supplementation promotes faster recovery from repetitive high-intensity exercises so that users can perform a higher volume of work than normal.[5]

Current evidence indicates that creatine supplementation is safe in the short-term, but long-term data are lacking. Creatine supplementation does not benefit the casual exerciser.

Ginseng

This herb has been used for centuries as a cure-all and energizer. Theoretically, it improves physical performance by combating fatigue. No credible scientific evidence supports this contention.

Chromium Picolinate

This mineral is purported to build muscle and promote weight loss. Deficiencies of chromium in the United States are rare. No good scientific evidence exists that chromium picolinate supplementation has the capacity to build muscle or enhance weight loss, but evidence indicates that it might be harmful to human cells.

Anabolic-Androgenic Steroids

Anabolic-androgenic steroids are hormones. Their anabolic properties contribute to muscle enlargement, while their androgenic properties produce masculinizing effects. They build muscle mass and strength, and as a result, they improve, in some people's estimation, physical appearance and physical performance.

Anabolic steroid use by nonathletes is on the rise. This is particularly true for young men. A nationwide survey of 3403 male high school seniors indicated that 6.6 percent of this group were current users or had previously been users of steroids and that 25 percent of the current users showed signs of dependency. According to this report, the improvement in physical appearance reputed to occur with steroid use accompanied by peer approval of those physical changes functioned as a powerful reinforcer for continued use.

Heavy steroid users were more likely than light users to take two or more steroids simultaneously and more apt to take these drugs by injection rather than in pill form. Injection as a method of delivery is highly characteristic of drugs that involve addiction. The steroid "hook" is insidious and powerful: 30 percent of the heavy users vowed that they would not discontinue steroid use if steroids were proved to cause liver cancer, 31 percent would not stop if they proved to cause heart attacks, and 39 percent would not stop if they proved to cause infertility.[17]

Although definitive evidence of the long-term effects of steroid use is not available, the potential for long-term harm is certainly real. Predicting how and when the effects of steroids will be manifested is impossible because people respond differently to these drugs as a result of differences in body chemistry. The steroid effect is complicated further by the fact that black market preparations contain additives, and some preparations are contaminated. The potential for harm is readily discernible; 80 to 90 percent of all steroids used are purchased through the black market. Table 4-2 presents some of the known and possible effects of steroid use.

Keeping a Daily Training Log

Beginning weight trainers should keep a daily log of their training activities. The advantages of keeping such a record far outweigh the minimal amount of bother, time, and effort required to make the entries during the workout. Each entry should be recorded during the rest period between sets.

Table 4-2 Overview of Anabolic Steroid Effects

Effects Supported by Strong Evidence

In Males and Females

Stunted growth when taken before puberty	Male-pattern baldness
	Deepening of the voice
Coronary artery disease	Menstrual irregularities (in women)
Low HDL cholesterol	
Sterility, low sperm count (in men)	Development of facial and body hair
Liver tumors and liver disease	Decreased breast size
	Clitoris enlargement (in women)
Death	
Acne	Fetal damage (when taken during pregnancy)
Water retention	
Oily, thickened skin	

Possible Effects

In Males and Females

Diarrhea	Bone pains
Muscle cramps	Impotence (in men)
Breast development (in men)	Sexual problems
	High blood pressure
Aggressive behavior	Kidney disease
Headache	Depression
Nausea	

Adapted from Nieman, D.C. 1999. *Exercise Testing and Prescription*. Mountain View, Calif.: Mayfield Publishing Co.

The advantages of maintaining a daily training log include the following:

- You will always know which exercises you performed and the amount of weight that was used for each.
- You will always know the number of repetitions and sets that you performed of each exercise.
- The training log provides an objective account of your improvement. You can compare the amount of weight you are currently lifting with the amount at the beginning of your training.
- The training log provides an accurate history.
- The training log is a motivating device that provides objective feedback of performance improvement.

A sample training log is shown in figure 4-21. A blank training log is given in Assessment Activity 4-5 for you to use to document your resistance training program. It will be helpful to make additional copies of this training log.

Name __Cathy Smith__ Starting date __Jan. 1, 1999__

Program objectives __To gain strength and muscle definition__

Exercise	Jan. 1 Resis. (lbs.)	Jan. 1 Reps	Jan. 1 Sets	Jan. 3 Resis. (lbs.)	Jan. 3 Reps	Jan. 3 Sets	Jan. 5 Resis. (lbs.)	Jan. 5 Reps	Jan. 5 Sets	Jan. 7 Resis. (lbs.)	Jan. 7 Reps	Jan. 7 Sets	Jan. 9 Resis. (lbs.)	Jan. 9 Reps	Jan. 9 Sets	Jan. 11 Resis. (lbs.)	Jan. 11 Reps	Jan. 11 Sets	Jan. 13 Resis. (lbs.)	Jan. 13 Reps	Jan. 13 Sets
1. Bench press	60	10	3																		
2. Biceps curl	25	10	3																		
3. Back extension	80	10	3																		
4. Leg press	150	10	3																		
5. Hamstring curl	30	10	3																		
6. Chest press	30	10	3																		
7. Abdominal crunch	—	25	3																		
8. Overhead press	35	10	3																		

Figure 4-21 Sample Training Log

Resistance (abbreviated as *Resis.*) refers to the amount of weight (in pounds) that is lifted or pressed. *Reps* (for *repetitions*) is the number of times the weight is lifted or pressed. *Sets* are the groups of reps.

Summary

- The physiological law of use and disuse applies to all human beings during all phases of the life cycle.
- The muscular systems of older adults are trainable and respond to resistance training with an increase in strength and muscle size.
- Muscular strength is the maximum force that a muscle or muscle group can exert in a single contraction.
- Dynamic exercises consist of concentric and eccentric muscle contractions.
- Isotonic exercises are dynamic in that muscles shorten and lengthen, producing movement around a joint.
- Variable resistance exercise equipment is designed to provide maximum resistance throughout the full range of motion.
- Circuit resistance training is a versatile system that allows a person to develop several fitness dimensions simultaneously.
- The principles of exercise—intensity, frequency, duration, overload, progression, and specificity—apply to resistance training. These can be manipulated to meet all muscle development objectives.
- The average man can generate 30 to 50 percent more force than the average woman.
- Anabolic steroids are performance-enhancing drugs that are harmful and illegal.
- Research in the last decade has shown that resistance training contributes to wellness in a variety of ways.
- Muscle endurance is the ability to apply repeated muscular force.

Review Questions

1. Define *muscular strength* and *muscular endurance*.
2. What are the differences among isometric, isotonic, isokinetic, and variable resistance exercises?
3. What are concentric and eccentric contractions?
4. What are the health benefits of participating in resistance exercise?
5. How do you account for the strength differences between men and women?
6. Name and define the principles of conditioning as they relate to resistance training.
7. What are the health consequences and physical performance benefits of steroid use?

References

1. Harvard University. 1998. Stay stronger longer with weight training. *Harvard Health Letter* 23(12):1.
2. American College of Sports Medicine. 1998. The recommended quantity and quality of exercise for developing and maintaining cardiorespiratory and muscular fitness, and flexibility in healthy adults. *Medicine and Science in Sports and Exercise* 30(6):975.
3. Bryant C. X., J. A. Peterson 1998. Strength for women through the stages of life. *Fitness Management* 14(7):36.
4. Bryant C. X., J. A. Peterson, and B. A. Franklin. 1998. Fountain of youth, *Fitness Management* 14(10): 44.
5. Nieman, D. C. 1999. *Exercise Testing and Prescription: A Health-Related Approach*. Mountain View, Calif.: Mayfield Publishing Co.
6. Modifica, M. 1998. Exercise and aging. *Fitness Management* 14(10):48.
7. U.S. Dept. of Health and Human Services. 1996. *Physical Activity and Health: A Report of the Surgeon General*. Atlanta: U.S. Dept of Health and Human Services, Centers for Disease Control and Prevention, National Center for Chronic Disease Prevention and Health Promotion.
8. Davis, A., et al. 1998. Strength, physical activity, and body mass index: Relationship to performance-based measure and activities of daily living among older Japanese women in Hawaii. *Journal of the American Geriatrics Society* 46:274.
9. Faigenbaum, A. D., and Y. Beniamini. 1997. The evaluation of muscular strength in cardiac patients. *ACSM Certified News* 7(2):1.
10. American College of Sports Medicine. 1998. Exercise and physical activity for older adults. *Medicine and Science in Sports and Exercise* 30(6):992.
11. Fleck, S. J., and W. J. Kraemer. 1997. *Designing resistance training programs*. Champaign, Ill.: Human Kinetics.
12. Foss, M. L., and S. J. Keteyian. 1998. *Fox's Physiological Basis for Exercise and Sport*. Boston: WCB/McGraw-Hill.
13. ACSM. 1995. *ACSM's Guidelines for Exercise Testing and Prescription*. Baltimore, Md.: Williams & Wilkins.
14. Kraemer, W. J., and J. A. Bush. 1998. Factors affecting the acute neuromuscular responses to resistance exercise. *ACSM's Resource Manual*. Baltimore, Md.: Williams & Wilkins.
15. Williams, M. H. 1998. *Nutrition for Health, Fitness, and Sport*. Dubuque, Iowa: WCB/McGraw-Hill.
16. Williams, M. H. 1998. Nutritional ergogenics and sports performances. *PCPFS Research Digest* 3(2): pp. 1–8.
17. Yesalis, C. E., S. P. Courson, and J. Wright. 1993. History of anabolic steroid use in sport and exercise. *Anabolic Steroids in Sport and Exercise*. Champaign, Ill.: Human Kinetics.

Suggested Readings

Baechle, T. R., and B. R. Groves. 1998. *Weight Training Steps to Success*. Champaign, Ill.: Human Kinetics.

This 192-page text, written by two respected authors, provides a step-by-step guide for beginning weight trainers. The text provides enough information for beginners to use to design their own valid programs of weight-training exercises. The text features more than 200 illustrations.

Westcott, W. L., and T. R. Baechle. 1998. *Strength Training Past 50*. Champaign, Ill.: Human Kinetics.

This text provides research-based guidelines, suggestions, and recommendations to help people 50 and older to develop and follow sound, effective, and safe strength-training programs.

Mann, C. 1998. *Built Hard*. Champaign, Ill.: Human Kinetics.

This text guides fitness enthusiasts who wish to enter the sport of bodybuilding. It also provides many insights for people who wish to improve their appearance. Contents include setting goals, cross-training, stretching, warming up, and developing all of the major muscles of the body.

Faigenbaum, A. D., and L. J. Micheli. 1998. Youth strength training, *The Fit Society* (spring): 1,8.

The authors provide evidence of the need for and effectiveness of weight training for adolescents. They also provide guidelines for proper resistance-training programs for this population.

Editors. 1998. Muscleing your way to independence. *Cardi Sense* 8(1): 1.

This article discusses the importance of maintaining muscle strength into our 60s, 70s, and 80s and demonstrates how elderly people can incorporate muscle-challenging activities into their daily tasks. The article also suggests how common objects in the home can be used in place of dumbbells to stimulate the muscles.

Name _____   Date _____   Section _____

Assessment Activity 4-1

Calculation of Strength (Selected Muscle Groups)

Directions: The calculation of strength by this method is expressed as the ratio of strength to body weight. The amount of weight accomplished for each lift is converted to a proportion of your body weight and is determined in the following manner:

1. Find your 1 RM for each of the following exercises: biceps curl (two arm), overhead press, bench press, half-squat or leg press, and hamstring curl.
2. Divide your 1 RM for each exercise by your body weight. For example, a 130-lb. woman performs a 1 RM bench press of 80 lbs. Her score is 80 ÷ 130 = 0.61. Turn to the chart for an interpretation of her score. Look under the Bench press column and note that her score of 0.61 is in the Average category. In this example, the woman has the following results on the five lifts: biceps curl = 0.28 (fair), standing press = 0.26 (fair), bench press = 0.61 (average), half-squat or leg press = 1.35 (good), and hamstring curl = 0.52 (good). These data are plotted in the first strength profile chart.
3. When you have computed a score for each of your lifts, turn to the strength profile charts. Plot your data in the blank chart provided.
4. Refer to figures 4-1 through 4-16 for a refresher on how to do these exercises.

Strength/Body Weight Ratio

Women

Biceps Curl	Overhead Press	Bench Press	Half-Squat or Leg Press	Hamstring Curl	Strength Category
0.45 and above	0.50 and above	0.85 and above	1.45 and above	0.55 and above	Excellent
0.38–0.44	0.42–0.49	0.70–0.84	1.30–1.44	0.50–0.54	Good
0.32–0.37	0.32–0.41	0.60–0.69	1.00–1.29	0.40–0.49	Average
0.25–0.31	0.25–0.31	0.50–0.59	0.80–0.99	0.30–0.39	Fair
0.24 and below	0.24 and below	0.49 and below	0.79 and below	0.29 and below	Poor

Men

Biceps Curl	Overhead Press	Bench Press	Half-Squat or Leg Press	Hamstring Curl	Strength Category
0.65 and above	1.0 and above	1.30 and above	1.85 and above	0.65 and above	Excellent
0.55–0.64	0.90–0.99	1.15–1.29	1.65–0.84	0.55–0.64	Good
0.45–0.54	0.75–0.89	1.00–1.14	1.30–1.64	0.45–0.54	Average
0.35–0.44	0.60–0.74	0.83–0.99	1.00–1.29	0.35–0.44	Fair
0.34 and below	0.59 and below	0.84 and below	Less than 1.0	0.34 and below	Poor

Strength Profile Charts

Example

	Biceps curl	Overhead Press	Bench Press	Half-Squat or Leg Press	Hamstring Curl
Excellent					
Good				■	■
Average			■		
Fair					
Poor	■	■			

Your Data

	Biceps curl	Overhead Press	Bench Press	Half-Squat or Leg Press	Hamstring Curl
Excellent					
Good					
Average					
Fair					
Poor					

Name _____   Date _____   Section _____

Assessment Activity 4-2

Muscular Endurance

Directions: Through trial and error, select a weight that you can use while performing 20 RM for each of the following exercises: bench press, leg extension or half-squat, biceps curl, and hamstring curl. For example, a male subject weighing 150 lbs. can perform 20 RM of 100 lbs. in the bench press. The score for this exercise is computed as follows:

$$\frac{100 \text{ lbs. (20 RM)}}{150 \text{ lbs.}} = 0.67 \text{ or } 67\%$$

Now look at the chart under Bench press and observe that a score of 67% is average. Perform each of the four exercises (20 RM) and calculate the muscle endurance scores following the example.

Muscle Endurance: Body Weight Ratio 20 RM

Men

Bench Press	Leg Extension or Half-Squat	Biceps Curl	Hamstring Curl	Strength Category
≥76%*	≥166%	≥50%	≥40%	Excellent
70%–75%	150%–165%	43%–49%	33%–39%	Good
60%–69%	133%–149%	37%–42%	27%–32%	Average
50%–59%	116%–132%	30%–36%	20%–26%	Fair
<50%	<116%	<30%	<20%	Poor

Women

Bench Press	Leg Extension or Half-Squat	Biceps Curl	Hamstring Curl	Strength Category
≥50%	≥115%	≥32%	≥38%	Excellent
42%–49%	100%–114%	23%–31%	31%–37%	Good
35%–41%	88%–99%	15%–22%	23%–31%	Average
27%–34%	77%–87%	12%–14%	15%–22%	Fair
<27%	<77%	<12%	<15%	Poor

*≥, equal to or greater than; <, less than.

Name _____ Date _____ Section _____

Assessment Activity 4-3

Abdominal Muscular Endurance—the Canadian Trunk Strength Test

Directions: The Canadian trunk strength test is an alternative to the conventional sit-up test to measure abdominal muscular endurance. It is not necessary or desirable to raise the trunk more than 30 degrees. Sit-ups beyond 30 degrees cause the abdomen to contract isometrically, so the hip flexors supply the power to raise the trunk above this level. The Canadian trunk strength test is performed in the following manner:

1. Lie on your back with knees bent 90 degrees.
2. Extend your arms so that the fingertips of both hands touch a strip of tape perpendicular to the body on each side.
3. Place two additional strips of tape parallel to the first two strips, 8 cm apart.
4. Curl up, sliding your fingertips along the mat until they touch the second set of tape strips, and then return to the starting position.
5. The curl up is slow, controlled, and continuous with a cadence of 20 curl ups/min. (3 secs./curl up).
6. A metronome provides the speed of movement. It is set at 40 beats/min. (curl up on one beat, down on the second).
7. Perform as many curl ups as you can up to a maximum of 75 without missing a beat. See figure 4-22 for a demonstration of the Canadian trunk strength test and then turn to the chart for an interpretation of your score.

Standards for the Canadian Trunk Strength Test

	Number Completed					
	Men—Age			**Women—Age**		
Strength Category	<35	35–44	>45	<35	35–44	>45
Excellent	60	50	40	50	40	30
Good	45	40	25	40	25	15
Marginal	30	25	15	25	15	10
Needs work	15	10	5	10	6	4

Figure 4-22 Canadian Trunk Strength Test

Chapter 4 Building Muscular Strength and Endurance **125**

Name _____ Date _____ Section _____

Assessment Activity 4-4

Assessing Muscular Strength and Endurance with Selected Calisthenic Exercises

Directions: The tests making up this assessment require minimal equipment and are easy to administer.

- *Chin-ups:* Grasp an overhead horizontal bar, hands shoulder-width apart, palms facing your body. On the upstroke your chin must go above the bar, and your arms must extend fully on the downstroke. Your legs must remain extended throughout the exercise and should not be used to thrust your body upward (figure 4-23).

- *Flexed-arm hang:* Perform this exercise if you cannot do chin-ups. Have someone assist you to the exercise position with your chin above the bar, palms facing away from your body. A stopwatch is started as soon as you assume this position and is stopped if you tilt your head back to keep your chin above the bar, if your chin touches the bar, or if your chin drops below the bar. Record the time to the nearest whole second (figure 4-24).

Figure 4-23 Chin-Ups

Figure 4-24 Flexed Arm Hang

Figure 4-25 Push-Ups

Figure 4-26 Modified Push-Ups

- *Push-ups:* Assume a prone position (face down) with your arms extended, hands on the floor under your shoulders. Keep your back and legs straight and your feet together. The person counting the push-ups should place a fist under your chest. Bend your elbows, lowering your chest until contact is made with the counter's fist, and then return to the starting position by straightening your arms. Repeat as many times as possible without resting to a maximum score of 46 push-ups (figure 4-25).
- *Modified push-ups:* Perform this exercise if you cannot do the standard push-up. The modified version is performed in the same manner as the standard push-up except that you support your body weight with your hands and knees. Do as many as you can without rest to a maximum of 24 (figure 4-26).

Muscular Strength and Endurance Standards

Chin-Ups	Flexed-Arm Hang (secs.)	Push-Ups	Modified Push-Ups	Strength Category
20 or more	30 or more	40 or more	24 or more	Excellent
15–19	24–29	32–39	14–23	Good
10–14	15–23	27–31	8–13	Average
6–9	9–14	20–26	2–7	Fair
5 or less	8 or less	19 or less	1 or less	Poor

Name _____ Date _____ Section _____

Assessment Activity 4-5

Resistance Training Log

Directions: Keep a record of your resistance fitness activities on the form provided. Make copies of this form for repeated uses.

Daily Training Log

Name _____ Starting date _____

Program objectives _____

Exercise	Date: Resis.* (lbs.)	Reps	Sets	Date: Resis. (lbs.)	Reps	Sets	Date: Resis. (lbs.)	Reps	Sets	Date: Resis. (lbs.)	Reps	Sets	Date: Resis. (lbs.)	Reps	Sets	Date: Resis. (lbs.)	Reps	Sets

*Resis, resistance; reps, repetitions.

129

5

Improving Flexibility

Key Terms

ballistic stretching
flexibility
goniometer
proprioceptive neuromuscular facilitation (PNF)
static stretching
stretch reflex

Objectives

After completing this chapter, you will be able to do the following:
- Define *flexibility*.
- Identify factors affecting flexibility.
- Distinguish among static, ballistic, and proprioceptive neuromuscular facilitation stretching.
- Assess and prescribe a personal flexibility program.
- Discuss the high incidence of neck pain, upper-back pain, and lower-back pain in the United States.
- Demonstrate proper lifting techniques for prevention of lower-back injury.

Goals for Behavior Change

- Begin participating regularly in a stretching program to improve flexibility.
- Identify some of the tasks or sports that you perform regularly for which being more flexible would be helpful.
- Practice correct lifting techniques when moving heavy objects.
- Modify your work or study area to lower the risk of neck and back pain.
- Try two safe ergogenic aids and analyze their effectiveness.

Flexibility and Wellness

Flexibility programs are planned, deliberate, and regularly performed sets of exercises designed to progressively increase the range of motion of a joint or series of joints.[1] Though often neglected, flexibility is an important component of health-related fitness.

Factors that limit joint movement include (1) the bony structure of the joints (the skeleton is established by heredity, but it can be harmed by trauma, disease, calcium deposits, etc.); (2) the amount of tissue (muscle and fat) around and adjacent to the joint; (3) the elasticity of muscles, tendons, and connective tissue; and (4) the skin (scar tissue from surgery or a laceration over a joint may limit movement). Other factors that influence flexibility are age, gender, and level and type of physical activity. Young people are more flexible than adults because tendons lose their elasticity with age. However, inactivity may play a greater role than the aging process in the loss of flexibility because muscles and other soft tissues lose elasticity when not used. Active individuals are usually more flexible than inactive people.[2] Women tend to be more flexible than men because the hormones that permit women's tissue to stretch during the childbirth process facilitate all body stretching.[3] The range of motion for most movements begins to decline in the mid-20s for men and women.[2] (Complete Assessment Activities 5-1 through 5-4 at the end of this chapter to determine your flexibility.)

Joint flexibility is important for several reasons. Inflexible muscles around the joints limit range of movement, eventually inhibiting activities of daily life. This phenomenon is most frequently seen in older people who have difficulty reaching down to tie their shoes or bending over to get a drink of water from a fountain. Lack of flexibility in the shoulders can affect performance of normal duties, such as changing an overhead light bulb or removing a can of vegetables from a cupboard.[4] Tight muscles may also contribute to joint deterioration by subjecting the bones to excessive pressure, causing pain and abnormalities in joint lubrication. Regular flexibility exercises can improve body posture. Flexibility exercises following aerobic activity reduce muscle soreness.[4]

According to the American College of Sports Medicine (ACSM), stretching exercises may prevent injuries.[5] The supporting data come primarily from observational studies, which are not as definitive as randomized, controlled clinical trials. But, even though scientific evidence does not strongly support flexibility training for injury prevention, sports medicine specialists advocate its use.[6] Based upon the available evidence as well as experience, flexibility exercises prevent injury and maintain a full range of joint motion.

Just the Facts
Benefits of Flexibility Training

Here are some of the positive outcomes of flexibility training:

- Reduction of stress and tension
- Muscle relaxation
- Improved fitness, posture, and symmetry
- Relief of muscle cramps
- Relief of muscle soreness
- Prevention of injury
- Reduced frequency of injury
- Return to full range of motion after an injury

Maintenance of flexibility is most important for the prevention of lower-back pain. For example, a sedentary lifestyle characterized by sitting for long periods leads to a loss of flexibility and increases the likelihood of lower-back injury. Flexibility of the hamstring muscles (a group of muscles in the back of the thighs) and the lower-back muscles contributes to good posture. Posture is also improved by the development of strong abdominal muscles and the maintenance of normal body weight. Extra body weight, particularly that which accumulates around the abdominal area, throws the body out of balance and applies a forward force on the lower (lumbar) spinal area, which places extra stress on the lower back.[7]

The benefits of flexibility training are summarized in Just the Facts: Benefits of Flexibility Training. See also Nurturing Your Spirituality: The Ancient Arts of Yoga and Tai Chi.

Developing a Flexibility Program

Flexibility can be improved by exercises that promote the elasticity of the soft tissues. Figures 5-1 through 5-8 demonstrate exercises that can maintain and improve the flexibility of the major body sites. These 10-minute exercises can be done every day, both before and after exercise, and also on days of rest from exercise.

When to Stretch

Stretching exercises can be included in the warm-up prior to exercise and in the cool-down period following

Nurturing Your Spirituality

The Ancient Arts of Yoga and Tai Chi

Medical health care training and delivery have been gradually adopting a more holistic view of treating patients. This holistic view recognizes the role of spirituality in the healing process. Johns Hopkins Medical School currently offers an elective course for its medical students on spirituality and healing.[12] The National Institutes of Health has awarded grants to a small number of medical schools to develop and promote courses on this subject.

At the same time that spirituality is making a medical comeback, Americans are searching for ways to alleviate stress, promote relaxation, and enhance health. Two physical arts that blend spirituality and health, tai chi and yoga, are gaining popularity.

Tai chi originated as a self-defense art, but it has evolved into a religious ritual, relaxation technique, and exercise program for people of all ages, including the very elderly. Tai chi features slow, balanced, low-impact movements that may reduce stress and improve flexibility, balance, and strength.[13] It requires concentration, controlled breathing, and balance while body weight is shifted as a person transitions from one movement to another. It is often referred to as *movement meditation*, because it promotes muscle relaxation through movement.

The potential benefits of tai chi include the following:

- Improved flexibility
- Physical therapy, because it may assist in recovery from injury
- Improved balance and coordination
- Improved strength, particularly of the lower body (buttocks, thighs, and calves)
- Improved posture
- Increased ability to relax
- Possible slight reduction in the resting blood pressure.

It takes years to become adept at tai chi, but several movements and positions can be learned with a few weeks of instruction.

Yoga originated in India about 6000 years ago. There are several types, but hatha yoga seems to be most popular among Americans. Hatha yoga features a system of exercises that promote physical fitness and mental well-being.[14]

Yoga is a Sanskrit word that means "union." Its practitioners strive for total union in experience that is, a union of physical, mental, and spiritual states. Achieving this union results in a calm, relaxed, tranquil attitude.

Research indicates that yoga's meditative characteristics may prevent or at least decrease the severity of psychosomatic illness. Psychosomatic illnesses are mind-body maladies. They are caused by negative mental states and attitudes that produce changes in body physiology that result in disease. Some common psychosomatic diseases are tension headaches, ulcers, asthma, stress, essential hypertension, impotence, back pain, and menstrual problems.

Master practitioners can, at will, influence bodily responses that are controlled by the autonomic nervous system, such as breathing rate, heart rate, and blood pressure. But it takes years of practice to achieve this level of control.

The exercises and body positions featured in yoga promote mobility and flexibility, but some of these positions are potentially unsafe. It is important to learn from an experienced instructor to minimize mistakes.

Practiced regularly, yoga may lower resting blood pressure, relieve mild depression, and contribute to strength and balance. Anecdotal evidence (evidence that comes from personal reports) also indicates that practitioners experience more energy and feel calmer and more focused.[14]

---

exercise and done on nonexercise days. Stretching prior to working out should occur only after the muscles have been warmed up with 5 to 10 minutes of brisk walking, slow jogging, riding a stationary bike, or similar activity. A gradual warm-up increases heart rate slowly and raises the temperature of muscles, tendons, and ligaments by increasing blood flow to these structures. Stretching after a warm-up is safer and more productive than stretching before: Stretching cold muscles increases the probability of incurring a soft tissue injury.[8] Warm up prior to stretching for approximately 10 minutes on the days of rest between workouts.

The highest payback from stretching comes at the end of an aerobic or resistive workout. During this time, the muscles are thoroughly warmed and capable of stretching maximally and safely. Also, the muscles that have been contracting and shortening vigorously and continuously during the workout should be systematically stretched and lengthened after the workout.

Types of Stretching

Muscles must contract for movement to occur. The contracting muscles are called *agonists* and are the prime movers. For an agonist to contract, shorten, and

Figure 5-1 Neck Stretches
Slowly bend your neck from side to side and front. Do not do head circles, because these require hyperextension (excessive extension) of the cervical (neck) area of the spinal column, which produces potentially harmful compression of the intervertebral disks.

Figure 5-2 Shoulder Stretch
A, gently pull your right arm behind your head and hold for 15 to 30 seconds. *B,* repeat with the other arm.

Chapter 5 Improving Flexibility 135

Figure 5-3 Chest and Shoulder Stretch
Stretch your arms to full extension with both palms on the floor and press your chest down to the floor. Hold 15 to 30 seconds and slowly release.

Figure 5-4 Back Stretch
A, cross your legs and lean forward, extending your arms to the front. *B*, hold for 15 to 30 seconds and slowly release.

Figure 5-5 Groin Stretch
A, place the soles of your feet together and lean forward. Hold 15 to 30 seconds. *B*, variation: push down gently on both knees and hold for 15 to 30 seconds.

136 Wellness Fundamental Concepts and Applications

Figure 5-6 Quadriceps Stretch

Lie on your side as shown. Bend the knee of your top leg, grasp your ankle with your free hand, and slowly pull your heel toward your buttocks until you feel the stretch in the muscles in the front of your thigh. Hold 15 to 30 seconds, roll over to the other side, and repeat with your other leg.

Figure 5-7 Hamstring Stretch

Place the sole of your left foot against the thigh of your extended right leg. Lean forward without bending the knee of your extended leg. Hold for 15 to 30 seconds and repeat with your other leg.

Figure 5-8 Calf and Achilles Tendon Stretch

Assume the position shown. Be sure the heel of your extended leg remains in contact with the floor and both feet are pointed straight ahead. Slowly move your hips forward until you feel the stretch in the calf of your extended leg. Hold 15 to 30 seconds and repeat with your other leg.

produce movement, a reciprocal lengthening of its *antagonist* must occur. For example, when the biceps muscle of the upper arm contracts, its opposite, the triceps muscle, must relax and lengthen. In this case the biceps is the agonist and the triceps is the antagonist, but the triceps becomes the agonist for movements that require it to contract, making the biceps the antagonist. Understanding these concepts is necessary to understanding stretching techniques.

Static stretching involves slowly moving to desired positions, holding them for 15 to 30 seconds, and then slowly releasing them. This method of stretching does not activate the **stretch reflex** (automatic or reflexive contraction of a muscle being stretched), so the muscle is essentially stretched without opposition.

The stretch reflex consists of two proprioceptors: the muscle spindle and the Golgi tendon organ. A *proprioceptor* is a sensory organ found in muscles, joints, and tendons that provides information regarding bodily movement and position. The *muscle spindle* is a receptor that is sensitive to changes in muscle length. The *Golgi tendon organ* is a receptor that is also sensitive to changes in muscle length but additionally responds to increases in muscle tension.[9]

Stretching the muscles also stretches their muscle spindles, which send volley sensory impulses, informing the brain that the muscles are being subjected to stretch. Impulses are sent back to the muscles, which cause them to contract reflexively, thus resisting the stretch. But if a muscle is stretched statically and the position is held for at least 6 seconds, the Golgi tendon organ responds to the change in length and tension by sending a volley of signals of its own to the brain via the spinal cord. Unlike the signals from the muscle spindle, those initiated by the Golgi tendon organ cause the antagonist muscle (the muscle being stretched) to relax reflexively. This protective mechanism allows the muscle to stretch through relaxation as the Golgi tendon organ nullifies or overrides the signals of the muscle spindle. Thus, stretching positions held for at least 6 seconds and preferably for 15 to 30 seconds allow muscles to lengthen and stretch with minimal chance of injury.

Static stretching should produce a feeling of mild discomfort but not pain. Static stretching (see figures 5-1 to 5-8) results in little or no muscle soreness, has a low incidence of injury, requires little energy, and can be done alone. For these reasons, static stretching is the preferred system for increasing flexibility.

These guidelines should be followed for safe and effective static stretching:

- Warm up for a few minutes before stretching by walking, slow jogging, doing light calisthenics, or doing some similar activity.
- Stretch to the point of mild discomfort.
- Do not stretch to the point of pain.
- Hold each stretch for 10 to 30 seconds minimum.
- Do not hold your breath during a stretch; breathe rhythmically and continuously.
- Move slowly from position to position.
- Perform each stretch at least four times.
- Stretch after the workout; this actually produces the greatest benefit because the muscles are warm and more amenable to stretching.
- Perform stretching exercises five to six times per week.[10]

Deliberate attempts to improve flexibility should occur throughout the life cycle. See Wellness Across the Generations: Flexibility Guidelines for Children and Older Adults for more specific information.

Proprioceptive neuromuscular facilitation (PNF) is another effective and acceptable stretching technique. It is more complex than most methods of stretching, but it is the most effective.[5,6,9] By combining slow passive movements (the force for passive movement is supplied by a partner) with maximal voluntary isometric contractions, you can bypass the stretch reflex stimulation that accompanies changes in muscle and tendon length.

All variations of PNF stretching require a partner and some combination of passive stretching and isometric contractions. Two of the common PNF

Wellness on the Web Behavior Change Activities

How's Your Flexibility?
Fitness isn't all about strength—it's also about a key but often neglected factor: flexibility. Flexibility is the ability to move your joints freely and without pain through a wide range of motion. Joint flexibility is important for several reasons. Inflexible muscles around your joints limit range of movement, eventually inhibiting your ability to perform daily living activities. Tight muscles may also contribute to joint deterioration by subjecting your bones to excessive pressure, causing pain and abnormalities in joint lubrication. How flexible should you be for your age and gender? Go to www.qctimes.webpoint.com/fitness/flextest.htm and complete the recommended test. When you're finished, click on "results" to see how well you did.

Go for the Stretch . . . and Then Some
Need more flexibility in your life? The best way to improve your flexibility is with exercises that promote the elasticity of your soft tissues. Stretching exercises alone may enhance your flexibility—but they may not be effective in reducing injury from exercise. To ensure flexibility, your best bet is a regimen of regular stretches plus exercises. Go to www.qctimes.webpoint.com/fitness/strindex.htm to find examples of exercises you can do to maintain flexibility in each area of your body.

Ready, Get Set, Stretch!
When you're set to stretch, visit the Global Health and Fitness (GHF) website to find exercise instructions and video demonstrations for more than 20 stretches. Go to www.global-fitness.com and select "Exercise Instructions and Video Demonstrations," and then click on "Flexibility Training." Each exercise description includes a video demonstration you can view on your computer screen. You can print out the beginning and midpoint images and take them to your health club, along with your customized 12-week strength training program and exercise and stretching instructions. Also available for viewing and printout are detailed instructions for each stretch that include a list of the specific muscle groups you'll be working, plus a list of alternative stretches that work the same muscle groups. Click on the "free sample" button for an explanation of each muscle group and instructions for the corresponding GHF flexibility training exercises.

Wellness Across the Generations

Flexibility Guidelines for Children and Older Adults

Flexibility peaks in the mid- to late 20s for men and women and declines thereafter in people who are not actively engaged in physical activities that include planned exercises for the purpose of maintaining or increasing range of motion. Evidence indicates that flexibility can be increased in healthy older adults who participate in aerobic activities supplemented with stretching exercises.[2] Physical activities such as walking and aerobic dance coupled with stretching exercises increases the range of motion of older adults.

Recommendations for improving the flexibility of children are somewhat different. Because children are more flexible than adults, 5 to 9 year olds need less time devoted to flexibility exercises than do older adults.[11] However, some formal stretching is required, and activities such as tumbling and climbing are suggested. For older children, ages 10 through 12, the amount of time spent on improving flexibility should be greater than that of younger children but less than that of adults. Children, especially boys, begin to lose flexibility at this age, so regular stretching exercises and physical activities, such as tumbling, that promote flexibility are recommended.

It is important to establish the habit of regularly stretching the muscles, tendons, and joints throughout one's lifetime. Stretching becomes even more important as we become older.

Figure 5-9 Contract-Relax (CR) Technique

Figure 5-10 Slow Reversal-Hold-Relax (SRHR) Technique

methods, contract-relax (CR) and slow reversal-hold-relax (SRHR), are presented in figures 5-9 and 5-10. For comparison, both figures exemplify stretching the hamstring group (muscles in the back of the thigh). The hamstrings are the antagonist muscle group, and the quadriceps muscles (muscles in the front of the thigh) are the agonists. For example, the CR method is performed as follows (figure 5-9):

- A partner gently pushes the upraised leg in the direction of arrow A. This movement passively stretches the antagonist (hamstrings).
- The subject follows this with a 6-second maximal contraction of the agonist (quadriceps).
- This is followed by another passive stretch of the hamstrings.

This is repeated twice with a few seconds of rest between sequences.

The SRHR method is performed in the following manner (figure 5-10):

- A partner gently pushes the upraised leg in the direction of arrow A.
- The subject then performs a 6-second maximal voluntary isometric contraction (MVIC) of the antagonists (hamstrings) against resistance supplied by the partner.
- The subject follows this with a 6-second maximal contraction of the agonists (quadriceps).
- This is followed by another passive stretch of the hamstrings.

This sequence is repeated twice with a few seconds of rest between exercises.

Although PNF appears to be the most effective stretching method for enhancing flexibility, it has some limitations. It requires a partner, it produces more pain and muscle stiffness, it requires more time, and it increases the risk of injury, particularly when used by novices.

Ballistic stretching uses dynamic movements or repetitive bouncing motions to stretch muscles. Each time a muscle is stretched in this manner, the muscle spindle (one of two receptors that make up the stretch reflex) located in that muscle is also stretched. It responds by sending a volley of signals to the central nervous system that order the muscle to contract, thus resisting the stretch. This is not only counterproductive—the muscle is forced to pull against itself—but also can lead to injury because the elastic limits of the muscle may be exceeded. Ballistic stretching is not recommended for flexibility development.

Flexibility Assessment

Measuring flexibility is rather difficult, and several instruments have been developed for this purpose. Probably the most widely used device is the **goniometer**. This is a protractorlike device that measures the range of motion of a specific joint. This method is an accurate means of assessing flexibility.[15] However, for the average person, assessing flexibility by using the goniometer is not practical.

Several tests are suitable for measuring flexibility when more sophisticated means cannot be used. (The directions and norms for these tests are provided in the assessment activities.) You should warm up and follow the rules for general stretching before taking the assessments.

Preventing Back and Neck Pain

All people experience tense muscles and muscle soreness in various parts of the body on an occasional basis. The neck, shoulder, and back are particularly susceptible to the types of pressures that cause pain. Sedentary lifestyles contribute to back pain; unfortunately 60 percent of Americans are sedentary or marginally active. Also contributing to neck and back pain are occupations that require workers to stand for long periods or to spend a significant amount of time sitting behind a desk, in front of a computer, or behind the wheel of an automobile. According to the Bureau of Labor Statistics, approximately 92,500 cases of occupational injuries and illnesses are due to repetitive motion. Typing or key entry, repetitive use of tools, and repetitive placing, grasping, or moving objects other than tools result in such injury.[16] Musculoskeletal problems are highly associated with these work-related physical tasks when the level of exposure is high. Performing unaccustomed physical work or engaging in unfamiliar sports also produces stress on the back and neck. Activities that require repetitive overhead reaching or extended sitting at a computer may produce pain and discomfort in the back, shoulders, and neck. The exercises in figures 5-1 through 5-4, coupled with a few minutes of moving about, may prevent or alleviate pain in these areas of the body.

These problems can be significantly lessened if (1) employers carefully design the layout of work stations, job methods, tools, and materials to reduce exposure to the physical factors related to performing repetitive tasks, and (2) employees become aerobically fit and engage in activities to promote muscle and joint flexibility.

Lower-back pain affects 80 to 90 percent of American adults at some point in their lives.[17] It is one of the main reasons people visit their primary care physicians even though 90 percent of people affected recover within a month.

The high incidence of lower-back pain is caused by the following: excess body weight, weak abdominal muscles, weak and inflexible back muscles, weak and inflexible hamstring muscles, poor posture, cigarette smoking, lifting objects incorrectly, work- or sports-related injuries, and diseases such as osteoarthritis and osteoporosis.

Excess body weight stresses the lower back by pulling the spinal column forward. This causes an excessive amount of arch in the lower back that results in poor alignment of the spine. As a result, obese people are more susceptible to lower-back problems than are normal-weight people.

Weak abdominal muscles, weak and inflexible back muscles, and tight hamstring muscles distort upright posture and tilt the pelvis forward, which increases stress on the lower back.[18] Figure 5-11 illustrates exercises that stretch the lower back and develop the abdominal muscles.

Smokers have a higher incidence of lower-back pain than do nonsmokers. Smoking appears to increase degenerative changes in the spine.

Figure 5-12 demonstrates correct and incorrect ways to lift a weight from the floor. Lifting correctly substantially lowers the risk of sustaining a lower-back injury. See Just the Facts: Tips for Preventing and Treating Back and Neck Pain.

The spinal column consists of thirty-three bones (the vertebrae) and represents the only bony connection between the upper and lower halves of the body. Although humans are born with thirty-three separate vertebrae, by adulthood five vertebrae of the sacrum fuse into one bone, and the four vertebrae of the coccyx also fuse into one bone, leaving a total of

140 Wellness Fundamental Concepts and Applications

Figure 5-11 Maintaining a Healthy Back

A, to develop the abdominal muscles, lie on your back in the position shown, and contract your abdominal muscles to force the lower back against the floor. Hold for 6 to 10 seconds. Relax and repeat 5 to 10 times.
B, to develop the abdominal muscles, lie on your back, cross your arms over your chest, and raise your shoulder blades off the floor as shown. Return to the starting position. Repeat 5 times and work up to 25.
C, to stretch the hamstrings, hips, and buttocks, raise one leg and extend the other. Reach up and grasp the upright leg below the calf. Alternate legs and work up to 20 repetitions with each.
D, to develop lower abdominal muscles, keep one leg bent with that foot flat on the floor. Raise the extended leg about 6 inches off the floor, and return to the starting position. Do 10 reps and repeat with the other leg. Work up to 25 reps.

Figure 5-12 How to Lift Objects

A, lifting an object from the floor with straight legs and a bent back places significant stress on the lower back, increasing the likelihood of injury. Notice the distance between the box being lifted and the body of the lifter. *B*, lifting an object from the floor with bent legs and a straight back allows the lifter to keep the box close to the body, which places the majority of stress on the legs rather than on the lower back.

Just the Facts

Tips for Preventing and Treating Back and Neck Pain

The following behaviors may help to alleviate or prevent back and neck pain:

- If you sit, stand, or work in one place for extended periods of time, periodically walk around for a few minutes and do some simple stretching exercises.
- If your job requires long periods of standing, you can reduce the stress on your lower back by placing one foot and then the other on a small stool for a few minutes at a time. This rounds the spine and reduces lower-back stress. You can also shift your weight from one foot to the other.
- If you drive for long periods of time, sit comfortably and make sure you can easily reach the dash, pedals, and steering wheel. You can also try placing a small pillow behind your lower back. Also, stop the vehicle every two to three hours to take a short stretch break
- Exercise regularly to develop the abdominal muscles and to stretch the back muscles.
- Stretch the back muscles and hamstrings at least three times per week.
- Maintain a healthy body weight.
- Bend at the knees while lifting objects so that your legs do most of the work.
- Do not smoke cigarettes, because they contribute to the degeneration of the spine.

---

twenty-four vertebral bones. See figure 5-13, which illustrates the shape and bony structure of the vertebral column.

Located between the bones of the spine are rings of tough fibrous tissue, the disks, which act as shock absorbers, keeping the vertebrae from rubbing against each other. The spinal column is S-shaped and consists of naturally occurring curves. When these curves are balanced, the body weight is evenly distributed and movement occurs fluidly. Misalignment in these regions applies substantial stress to the concave, or inner, side of the curves. The more pronounced the curves, the greater the stress because of the uneven distribution of weight on the bones and disks.

Approximately 90 percent of all back problems occur in the lumbar region (lower back) of the spine because that region carries the weight of the torso (the trunk of the human body). Fatigue causes the pelvis to tilt forward when a person is standing, increasing stress on the spinal column and its supporting structures. Wearing high-heeled shoes does the same thing.

Figure 5-13 The Vertebral Column

A, the complete column viewed from the left side. Note that the vertebrae of the sacrum are fused into one bone, and those of the coccyx have also fused into one bone. *B*, the vertebrae of the cervical curve from the right side.

Summary

- *Flexibility* refers to the range of motion at a joint or series of joints and is specific to each joint.
- Factors that influence flexibility of a joint are the bony structure, the amount of tissue at the joint, the skin, and the elasticity of the muscles, tendons, and ligaments at the joint.
- Flexibility is influenced by age, gender, and physical activity.
- The maintenance of flexibility of the hamstrings and lower back muscles is important in the prevention of lower-back pain.
- Normal body weight and good posture are also necessary for a healthy back.
- Ballistic stretching is counterproductive to improving joint elasticity and may contribute to injury.
- Static stretching is the recommended type of exercise. Stretches should be held for 15 to 30 seconds and repeated at least three times.
- Stretching should not be painful, only mildly uncomfortable.
- Stretching exercises can be performed daily.
- Proprioceptive neuromuscular facilitation is the most effective but most difficult form of stretching.
- Proprioceptive neuromuscular facilitation combines passive movement with isometric contractions.
- The goniometer is the most widely used device to measure flexibility.
- Lower-back pain is one of the most common reason for visiting a physician.
- Factors associated with lower-back and neck pain include excess weight, poor posture, inactivity, fatigue, weak abdominal muscles, wearing high heels, stress, cigarette smoking, weak, inflexible back and hamstring muscles, lifting objects incorrectly, work or sports injuries, and disease.

Review Questions

1. Explain why flexibility is such an important component of health-related fitness.
2. Discuss the steps to take when developing a flexibility program.
3. What concepts are necessary to understand about stretching?
4. Distinguish among static, ballistic, and PNF stretching.
5. Discuss the guidelines that should be followed for safe and effective stretching.
6. What factors are associated with lower-back and neck problems?
7. Describe the proper lifting technique for preventing back injury.
8. Discuss the role of repetitive movements in the development of upper-back and neck pain.
9. What can an employer and an employee do to reduce the potential for repetitive motion injuries?

References

1. Alter, M. J. 1996. *Science of Flexibility*. Champaign, Ill.: Human Kinetics.
2. ACSM. 1998. Position stand on exercise and physical activity for older adults. *Medicine and Science in Sports and Exercise* 30:6, 992.
3. Robergs, R. A., and S. O. Roberts. 1997. *Exercise Physiology*. St. Louis, Mo.: Mosby.
4. Tufts University. 1997. To stretch or not to stretch? *Tufts University Health and Nutrition Letter* 15(10):4.
5. ACSM. 1998. Position stand on the recommended quantity and quality of exercise for developing and maintaining cardiorespiratory and muscular fitness, and flexibility in adults. *Medicine and Science in Sports and Exercise* 30(6):975.
6. Nieman, D. C. 1999. *Exercise Testing and Prescription*. Mountain View, Calif.: Mayfield Publishing.
7. Bryant, C. X., and J. A. Peterson. 1998. Treating and preventing low back pain. *Fitness Management* 14(4):52.
8. University of California at Berkeley. 1998. The home stretch. *University of California at Berkeley Wellness Letter* 15(3):4.
9. Fredette, D. H. 1998. Exercise recommendations for flexibility and range of motion. In *ACSM Resource Manual* (3d ed.), ed. J. L. Roitman. Baltimore, Md.: Williams & Wilkins.
10. ACSM. 1995. *ACSM's Guidelines for Exercise Testing and Prescription*. Baltimore, Md.: Williams & Wilkins.
11. Corbin, C. B., and R. P. Pangrazi. 1998. *Physical Activity for Children: A Statement of Guidelines*. Reston, Va.: NASPE Publications.
12. Johns Hopkins University. 1998. Can Religion Be Good Medicine? *The Johns Hopkins Medical Letter* 10(9):3.
13. University of California at Berkeley. 1998. Tai chi: Smooth, balanced, low-impact. *University of California at Berkeley Wellness Letter* 15(2):6.
14. Harvard University. 1998. The ultimate mind-body workout. *Harvard Health Letter* 24(2):4.
15. Prentice, W. E. 1999. *Fitness and Wellness for Life*. Boston: WCB/McGraw-Hill.
16. U.S. Dept. of Health and Human Services and Office of Public Health and Science. 1998. *Healthy People 2010 Objectives: Draft for Public Comment*. Washington, D.C.: U.S. Dept. of Health and Human Services.
17. Harvard University. 1999. Fact and fiction about chiropractic. *Harvard Health Letter* 24(3):1.
18. Harvard University. 1998. Exercising options for a healthy back. *Harvard Health Letter* 23(11):4.

Suggested Readings

Alter, M. J. 1998. *Sport Stretch*. Champaign, Ill.: Human Kinetics.

This complete guide to developing and maintaining flexibility is applicable for both weekend warriors and serious athletes. It features step-by-step guidelines plus photos of 311 different stretching exercises.

Alter, M. J. 1996. *Science of Flexibility*. Champaign, Ill.: Human Kinetics.

For readers who want to move beyond the basics, this book discusses the following topics in some depth: factors that limit flexibility, methods for modifying limiting factors, controversial stretching exercises, and stretching for specific sports and health conditions.

Black, S. 1997. *The Supple Body: The Way to Fitness, Strength, and Flexibility*. Indianapolis, Ind.: Macmillan General Reference.

The premise of this book is that a fit body is one that is strong, flexible, and firm. This book guides the reader through a system of gentle exercises designed to achieve strength and flexibility. It includes color illustrations and 300 photos of exercises targeted to specific areas of the body.

Verna, C., S. Hosid, and J. Smolty. 1998. *The Complete Idiot's Guide to Healthy Stretching*. Aurora, Colo.: Alpha Books.

This text features more than 250 photographs illustrating stretching exercises for all parts of the body. It is useful for inactive people and athletes.

Chapter 5   Improving Flexibility   **145**

Name _____   Date _____   Section _____

Assessment Activity 5-1

Sit-and-Reach Test

The sit-and-reach test is used to measure hip flexor, lower-back, and hamstring flexibility. It is measured with a testing box that can be purchased or built. The box should be 12 inches high and have an overlap in front so that negative (minus) readings can be obtained when subjects are unable to reach their feet (the footline). For simplicity and standardization purposes, the footline is given a value of 0, with plus and minus readings given in inches.

Directions:
1. Warm up for 3 to 5 minutes before taking this test.
2. After warming up, remove your shoes and sit with both feet flat against the end board of the box with your legs fully extended and your knees locked.
3. Extend your arms forward as shown in the photo, one hand on top of the other with your fingertips perfectly even.
4. Bend forward from the waist as far as possible while sliding your hands along the scale.
5. Hold the maximum stretch for at least 1 second.
6. Perform three trials: The final score is the best of the three.
7. Lock your knees during all trials.
8. Use the following sit-and-reach test standards to interpret your score.

Trial 1: _____ inches

Trial 2: _____ inches

Trial 3: _____ inches

Sit-and-Reach Test Standards

Classification	Distance reached in inches (footline at 0)
Excellent	≥ 7*
Good	4.0–6.9
Average	0–3.9
Fair	−3.0– −0.25
Poor	≥−3.1

*≥ equal to or greater than

Name _____ Date _____ Section _____

Assessment Activity 5-2

Shoulder Flexion Test

Directions: The objective of the shoulder flexion test is to measure the deltoids and shoulder girdle. A measuring scale and straight edge are needed to perform this assessment. Begin by assuming a prone position with your arms fully extended. Your chin should remain in contact with the floor throughout the exercise. Grasp the straight edge with both hands and raise it as high as possible from the floor. The distance from the floor to the straight edge is measured as the height in inches. Repeat this assessment three times and record the best number in inches as the final score. See the following chart for your classification.

Trial 1: _____ inches

Trial 2: _____ inches

Trial 3: _____ inches

Shoulder Flexion Test Standard*

Classification	Men	Women
Excellent	26 or above	27 or above
Good	23–25	24–26
Average	18–22	19–23
Fair	13–17	14–18
Poor	12 or below	13 or below

*All scores are in inches. Use the best of three trials as the score.

Chapter 5 Improving Flexibility   149

Name _____   Date _____ Section _____

Assessment Activity 5-3

Sling Test

Directions: The purpose of this test is to determine the length and flexibility of your sling muscles (the extensor muscles of the back). If you have back problems or have had back surgery, consult a physician before attempting this test. This is a test and not an exercise, so it should not be used to increase flexibility.

Begin by lying on your back on the floor and bending both knees. Pull your right leg to your chest by tightly holding your knee with both hands. Straighten out your left leg and push it to the floor without letting your right leg move away from your chest.

A tester uses a ruler to measure the distance between the floor and back of the knee. Reverse your leg position and measure.

Sling Test Standards

Classification	Standard
Excellent	Able to hold one leg firmly against the chest with the other leg flat against the floor
Average	Able to hold one knee against the chest while the other knee is bent 2 to 4 inches off the floor
Fair	Able to hold the knee firmly against the chest while the other leg is 4 to 8 inches off the floor
Poor	Unable to pull one leg firmly against the chest without pain or discomfort and/or raising the other leg off the floor significantly (more than 8 inches)

Name _____   Date _____   Section _____

Assessment Activity 5-4

Trunk Extension

Directions: The purpose of this assessment is to measure the flexibility of the abdominal and hip flexor muscles. Begin the test by lying face down on the floor. Have a partner hold your legs as shown. Grasp your hands in the lower-back area, breathe in, lift your upper body as high off the floor as possible, and hold. A tester measures the distance between the floor and your chin. Repeat this two more times and record your best score. See the following chart for your classification.

Trial 1: _____ inches

Trial 2: _____ inches

Trial 3: _____ inches

Trunk Extension Assessment Standards*

Classification	Men	Women
Poor	16	17
Average	17–18	18–19
Good	19–21	20–23
Excellent	22	24

*Scores are in inches.

6

Forming a Plan for Good Nutrition

Key Terms

amino acids
antioxidants
botanicals
calorie
carotenoids
complex carbohydrates
Daily Values (DVs)
essential nutrients
fiber
folate
foodborne illness
Food Guide Pyramid (FGP)
food labels
free radicals
hydrogenation
legumes
minerals
monounsaturated fat
nutrient density
Olestra
phytochemicals
phytomedicinals
polyunsaturated fat
recommended dietary allowances (RDAs)
saturated fat
transfatty acids
vitamins
vitamin supplements

Goals for Behavior Change

- Decrease or increase your intake of the energy nutrients to meet dietary recommendations.
- Craft a nutrition profile that identifies your intake of essential nutrients and highlights your dietary strengths and shortcomings.
- Formulate a plan for implementing the *Dietary Guidelines for Americans* that addresses your dietary shortcomings.
- Identify and practice specific strategies for improving your diet.

Objectives

After completing this chapter, you will be able to do the following:

- Describe the functions and purposes of the essential nutrients.
- Discuss ways to apply the *Dietary Guidelines for Americans*.
- Explain the role of nutrients that are not classified as essential, such as fiber, phytochemicals, and botanicals, but that are thought to have unique health benefits.
- Determine your personal RDA for protein, carbohydrates, fat, and saturated fat.

Nutrition has captured the interest of Americans perhaps more than any other topic related to fitness and wellness. Whether concerning antioxidants or phytochemicals, homocysteine or cholesterol, omega-3 fatty acids or trans-fatty acids, HDLs or LDLs, nutrition issues make headlines in both scientific journals and popular magazines, and everybody seems to be an expert. So much is written by so many people that it is difficult to know what and whom to believe.

This chapter presents basic concepts of the science of *nutrition*, the study of nutrients and the way the body processes them, to guide you through the maze of nutrition information. The concepts presented here are within the framework of *Dietary Guidelines for Americans* and should provide you with a basis for sound nutritional planning.

Nutrition and Health

The relationship between nutrition and health has changed dramatically during the last fifty years. The deficiency diseases of the past, such as scurvy and rickets, have been replaced by diseases of dietary excess and imbalance. Chief among such excess is the disproportionate consumption of foods high in fat, often at the expense of foods high in complex carbohydrates, fiber, and other substances conducive to good health. Americans' dietary practices contribute substantially to the burden of preventable illness and premature death and are associated with four of the ten leading causes of death.[1] Coronary heart disease, stroke, and non–insulin-dependent diabetes mellitus have long been connected to nutrition. A growing body of research has also linked cancer to nutrition. It has been estimated, for example, that about 35 percent of all cancers are related to dietary factors, but a high intake of fruits and vegetables can cut cancer risk in half.[2]

Another important change in nutrition is the new attitude that previously established minimums for essential nutrients are insufficient to prevent today's major health problems. The **recommended dietary allowances (RDAs)** of essential nutrients were established to prevent acute deficiency diseases and to guide the consumption of the more than fifty nutrients necessary to meet the needs of nearly all healthy people in the population. Now the RDAs are being revised to prevent or delay the onset of chronic diseases. The RDA for vitamin C is a good example. An intake of 60 mg of vitamin C is considered adequate to prevent the deficiency disease scurvy. Studies today are investigating the potential additional benefits of 200 to 500 mg of vitamin C in preventing heart disease and cancer.

Also changing is the definition of *essential*. *Phytochemicals* (plant chemicals), *phytomedicinals* (plants with medicinal benefits), and *antioxidants* (compounds that generally prevent the oxidation of substances in food or the body) are the nutrients of the twenty-first century. A countless number of studies exploring the benefits of these nutrients may have dramatic effects on future dietary guidelines.

While the hallmark of the American diet is excess, the low intake of some nutrients also causes concern. Here are a few examples:

- 55 percent of Americans don't get enough calcium
- 11 percent of nonpregnant women and 9 percent of children between the ages of 1 and 2 are deficient in iron[1]
- Only 24 percent of the population consume two servings of fruits a day (including apples in apple pie)
- Americans average only one-third of a serving of dark green and deep yellow vegetables a day (about two bites' worth)[3]
- The lack of sufficient water intake is a universal problem that the American Medical Association (AMA) believes is a significant contributor to poor health[4]

Fortunately, improving your diet is not difficult. You don't have to give up your favorite foods to achieve a healthy diet. For many people, cutting back on less healthful foods and making small dietary changes may profoundly affect health and wellness. It is never too late to benefit from dietary improvements. The easy availability of many healthy options makes dietary improvement a realistic goal for most Americans.

Essential Nutrients

Food is made up of six classes of nutrients: carbohydrates, fat, protein, vitamins, minerals, and water. These nutrients are called **essential nutrients** because they cannot be made by the body and, therefore, must be supplied through the diet. Some experts list fiber as

Eating a variety of foods is the best way to ensure that your diet is nutritionally balanced. Have you tried an unfamiliar food lately?

a seventh nutrient, although technically some fibers are carbohydrates and are usually listed with the carbohydrates. Carbohydrates, fat, and protein are called *energy nutrients* because they provide energy (calories) to the body. Because they are needed in large amounts, they are also called *macronutrients*. Vitamins and minerals are called *micronutrients* because they are required in small amounts to regulate chemical processes. Water and fiber are nonnutrients and are also part of a healthy diet.

Calories

Food energy is expressed in kilocalories. A calorie is the amount of heat required to raise the temperature of a gram of water by 1° C. A kilocalorie equals 1000 calories of heat energy. Common reference to kilocalories usually excludes the prefix *kilo*, mainly for convenience. A gram of carbohydrates provides 4 calories (kilocalories) of energy, a gram of protein also provides 4 calories, a gram of fat provides 9 calories, and a gram of alcohol (which is not an essential nutrient) provides 7 calories.

The recommended diet for Americans emphasizes complex carbohydrates as the main source of energy. About 55 percent of calories should come from carbohydrates, with at least 45 percent of these from complex carbohydrates and no more than 10 percent from sugar. No more than 30 percent of calories should come from fat; 15 percent of calories should come from protein. The typical American diet, however, excluding alcohol, consists of 34 percent fat, 50 percent carbohydrates, and 16 percent protein[4] (figure 6-1). While significant improvements have been made, Americans' diets are still high in fat calories and low in carbohydrate calories. You can tell how your calorie sources compare with dietary recommendations by completing Assessment Activities 6-3 and 6-4.

Carbohydrates

Carbohydrates are sugars and starches obtained from plants. The simplest form of carbohydrates is sugar, also called *monosaccharide*. Monosaccharides include glucose and fructose (fruit sugar). Fructose is the sweetest of simple sugars. Disaccharides are double sugars, meaning that they are pairs of monosaccharides chemically linked. In this group of sugars are sucrose, or table sugar; lactose, or milk sugar; and maltose, or malt sugar.

Figure 6-1 Comparison of Recommended and Actual Diets

Both diets are for Americans 20 years and older and exclude alcohol. Recommendations for carbohydrates and protein are minimums; the recommendation for fat is a maximum. Carbohydrates include sugars.

Starches, also called *polysaccharides,* are **complex carbohydrates.** Starches are the preferred source of carbohydrates because the foods that contain them also supply fiber, vitamins, and minerals. A diet high in starch is likely to be lower in fat, especially saturated fat and cholesterol, lower in calories, and higher in fiber. An added benefit of starch consumption over simple sugar consumption is that it helps the body maintain a normal blood-sugar level through a slower, more even rate of digestion and glucose absorption. It takes one to four hours for the body to digest starch. This is one reason athletes involved in endurance activities, such as marathons, load up on complex carbohydrates before competition.

All carbohydrates are broken down in the intestine and converted in the liver into glucose. Glucose is blood sugar that is carried to cells, where it is used for energy. Glucose in excess of the body's need for energy is stored in limited amounts as glycogen in the muscles and the liver for future use; when glycogen stores are satisfied, glucose is converted to fat.

Many weight-conscious people mistakenly avoid starches, thinking that they are high in calories. Starch foods are often made fattening when they are prepared. For example, a baked potato without additives yields a modest 90 calories. Adding fat in the form of butter, sour cream, margarine, or cheese adds substantially to the calories of a potato.

Recommended carbohydrate intake

At least 55 percent of the calories in your diet should come from carbohydrates. Many experts believe this percentage should be much higher. An estimate of your carbohydrate intake can be determined by completing Assessment Activity 6-1.

Vegetables, fruits, and grain products are high in carbohydrates, vitamins, and minerals and generally low in fat, depending on how they are prepared and what is added to them at the table. Most Americans of all ages eat fewer than the recommended servings of these foods, even though they are associated with a lower risk of many chronic conditions.

All starchy foods are plant foods. Grains, such as rice, wheat, corn, millet, rye, barley, and oats, are the richest food source of starch. Legumes, including peanuts and dried beans, are another good source of starch. They also contain a significant amount of fiber and protein, both of which are discussed separately in this chapter.

Protein

Protein is different from carbohydrates and fats in that it contains nitrogen as well as carbon, hydrogen, and oxygen. Because of their unique chemical structures, proteins contain the basic materials that help the body form muscles, bones, cartilage, skin, antibodies, some hormones, and all enzymes.

The building blocks of protein are chemical structures called **amino acids.** There are approximately twenty amino acids: Eleven can be produced in the body, and nine must be supplied by the diet.[4] The latter are called *essential amino acid acids.* A *complete protein* is one that contains all the essential amino acids. A *high-quality protein* is a complete protein that contains the essential amino acids in amounts proportional to the body's need for them. Meat, fish, poultry, eggs, milk, and cheese are examples of high-quality, complete protein sources.

An *incomplete protein* does not contain all the essential amino acids in the proportions needed by the body. Generally, plant protein sources are incomplete. This fact has important implications for *vegans,* people who limit their diets to plant sources, because protein synthesis operates on the all-or-none principle. That is, the body cannot make partial proteins, only complete ones. If an amino acid is supplied by one source in a smaller amount than is needed, the total amount of protein made from the other amino acids will be limited. It is necessary to combine protein sources from cereal and grains with legumes to obtain all essential amino acids from plant sources. The practice of combining amino acids from various plant sources is called *protein complementing.*

One plant protein source unique among sources of amino acids is **legumes.** Legumes come from plants with seed pods that split on two sides when ripe, such as black-eyed peas, chickpeas (garbanzo beans), lentils, soybeans, and black, red, white, navy, and kidney beans. Legumes are low in calories, sodium, and fat and high in fiber and minerals. They are a nutritionally dense food (see table 6-1).

The most common legume crop in the world is the soybean.[6] The protein in soy is a complete protein—the most complete you can get from plant and vegetable sources—and just as good as animal protein.[7] Soybeans are high not only in protein but also in folate, omega-3 fatty acids, and minerals. In cultures in which soy is the main source of protein, rates of cardiovascular disease and some kinds of cancers are relatively low.[8] A possible reason for soy's benefits is that, by eating more soy, people consume fewer animal products. Another reason is that soy protein may change levels of certain hormones, which in turn may cause the liver to make less cholesterol. Soybeans also contain *phytoestrogens,* estrogenlike plant substances. Phytoestrogens unique to soybeans are called *isoflavones.* Isoflavones are thought to help prevent breast cancer by blocking natural estrogens.

Table 6-1 Comparison of Selected Legumes

	Calories	Protein (grams)	Fat (grams)	Iron (milligrams)	Calcium (milligrams)
Soybeans	86	14	8	4	88
Lentils	100	9	<1	3	19
Kidney beans	88	8	<1	3	25
Black beans	41	8	<1	2	25
Chickpeas	82	7	1	3	40

From American Dietetic Association. 1998. *Choosing Legumes: A Healthful and Versatile Food.* Available on-line at www.eatright.org/nfs45.html.

Soy is available in a variety of foods. Tofu, soy milk, soy nuts, and soy powder, which can be mixed into smoothies, scrambled into omelets, and baked into bread, are several examples.

Recommended protein intake

For most people, the recommended dietary allowance of protein is 0.36 grams per pound of body weight, or 54 grams for a 150-pound person and 72 grams for a 200-pound person. Growing children, pregnant or lactating women, and people recovering from illness require additional protein. Older adults may also need extra protein (see Wellness Across the Generations: Older Adults May Need More Protein). You can estimate your protein intake by completing Assessment Activity 6-1.

Exercise and other physical activities can change the body's need for protein (nutrition needs associated with physical activity are discussed separately in this chapter), but enough protein is usually already consumed. When more protein is consumed than is needed by the body, it is converted into energy or stored as fat. The body is less efficient at converting protein to energy than at converting carbohydrates to energy. High protein intake may cause the body to excrete calcium[10] and put excessive strain on the kidneys to excrete into the urine the excess nitrogen supplied by the protein. Although the kidneys of most healthy people can handle nitrogen excess easily, diseased kidneys have more difficulty. This is why people with kidney failure are placed on low-protein diets and why people who go on high-protein diets to lose weight (see Chapter 8) are encouraged to drink large quantities of water to flush the kidneys.

Wellness Across the Generations

Older Adults May Need More Protein

The only three groups of people once thought to require extra protein were growing children, pregnant women, and lactating (breast-feeding) women. Now researchers think more protein may be needed by a fourth group: adults 55 years old and older. Recent studies suggest that older adults who consume the RDA of protein lose more protein than they take in. As a result, they lose muscle mass and have a reduced concentration of immunoglobulin, a substance that protects against illness. With weakened immunity, there is a greater risk of contracting a disease or of requiring more time to recover from illness or surgery. An estimated 25 percent of older adults consume less than the RDA of protein.

Based on the results of their own and other studies, researchers at highly respected Tufts University[9] advise older men and women to eat about 0.45 grams of protein per pound of body weight. That adds up to 68 grams of protein a day for someone who weighs 150 pounds and 90 grams for someone who weighs 200 pounds.

Fat

Fats are oils, sterols (such as cholesterol), waxes, and other substances that are not water soluble. Fat is an essential component of all cells. Fats help synthesize and repair vital cell transport and absorb fat-soluble vitamins. Fat stored as adipose tissue provides insulation and a ready source of energy.

Basic fat facts

Fat, also called *lipid,* is a compound made by chemically bonding fatty acids to glycerol to form glycerides. When three fatty acids are hooked to glycerol, the fat compound is a triglyceride. Almost 95 percent of fat stored in the body is a triglyceride, with the remaining 5 percent consisting of other glycerides and cholesterol. Scientific literature usually refers to triglycerides when it discusses fat. The fatty acids that make up triglycerides can be saturated, monounsaturated, or polyunsaturated.

Chemically, fats are chains of carbon atoms strung together with hydrogen atoms. If a fat is a **saturated fat,** the carbon chain carries all the hydrogen atoms it can. If it is an unsaturated fat, there is room in the carbon chain for more hydrogen. If the fat is a **monounsaturated fat,** there is room for two hydrogen atoms. If the fat is a **polyunsaturated fat,** there is room for four hydrogen atoms. If it is highly polyunsaturated, there is room for many more hydrogen atoms.

Many people mistakenly assume that the word *polyunsaturated* on a food label means that the fat in the food is not saturated, but because of food-processing techniques, this assumption may be incorrect. If the words *hydrogenated* or *partially hydrogenated* are on the food label, the food contains varying amounts of saturated fat. Because fats are less stable, they are prone to spoilage. Consequently, for many foods, manufacturers use a chemical process called **hydrogenation,** in which hydrogen atoms are added to the unsaturated or polyunsaturated fats to make them more saturated and more resistant to spoilage. This process of hydrogenating food yields a new type of fat not found in nature called **transfatty acids** (see Just the Facts: How Much Transfatty Acid Is in Food?). Transfatty acids are saturated fats commonly found in margarine, fried fast foods, cookies, cakes, and many other foods made with shortening. Some scientists believe that transfatty acids, even those originating from a polyunsaturated food source, are as detrimental to health as saturated animal fat. High levels of these fats are less effective in lowering total and LDL cholesterol than are the liquid oils from which they are made. Also they seem to depress HDL cholesterol.[11]

Saturated and unsaturated fats can be differentiated by their appearance. Saturated fat is typically solid at room temperature. Lard, fat marbled in meat, and hardened grease from a skillet are good examples. Polyunsaturated fats are usually liquid at room temperature. Examples are safflower and corn oils. Solid vegetable shortenings are partially hydrogenated and have a soft consistency. Coconut oil, palm kernel oil, and palm oil are exceptions. They are vegetable oils and are liquid at room temperature, but they are among the most saturated of fats.

Fish oils are among the most unsaturated fats available. They are roughly twice as unsaturated as vegetable oils. They do not harden, even at low temperatures. Their unsaturation has created special interest in relation to heart disease. Fatty acids in cold-water seafood, such as salmon, mackerel, sardines, herring, anchovies, whitefish, bluefish, swordfish, rainbow trout, striped bass, Pacific oysters, and squid, consist of omega-3 fatty acids, which are thought to be effective in lowering cholesterol and triglyceride levels and reducing clot-forming rates, thereby reducing the risk of heart disease. Canadian health experts believe omega-3s are important enough that Canada has specific recommendations for how much of these people should eat every day.[12]

Olestra

Olestra is a synthetic fat that has the flavor and taste of real fat but contains no calories. It cannot be digested or absorbed and, therefore, passes through the digestive system unaltered. It was approved by the Food and Drug Administration in 1998 for use in snack foods.

While consumption of Olestra in small amounts is unlikely to cause problems in healthy adults, several side effects have been reported. Olestra can cause abdominal cramps and loose stools. It also inhibits the absorption of the fat-soluble vitamins A, D, E, and K and the absorption of carotenoids, substances thought to aid the immune system in warding off some cancers, heart disease, and eye problems. To counter the effects of Olestra on the absorption of important nutrients, some snack foods are fortified with fat-soluble vitamins.

Relying on fat substitutes like Olestra can help reduce fat in your diet. It is important to remember, however, that just because a product has less fat does not mean it is also low in calories. Experts speculate that the reduction in calories associated with low-fat foods made with Olestra is unlikely to reduce obesity significantly because Olestra is not yet used in foods that contribute the most fat to our diets—high-fat meats.[4] It will be years before the true effects of fat substitutes on the American diet are known.

Cholesterol

Cholesterol, a waxy substance that is technically a steroid alcohol found only in animal foods, is probably the most researched blood lipid. High levels of cholesterol are usually included among the major risk factors for cardiovascular disease. (For information on cholesterol, see Chapter 2.)

Just the Facts

How Much Transfatty Acid Is in Food?

To determine how much transfatty acid is in food, it is necessary to have a complete breakdown of the food's fat content. For example, a popular low–saturated fat margarine contains 10 grams of total fat, including 2 grams of saturated fat, 1.5 grams of polyunsaturated fat, and 2 grams of monounsaturated fat. Adding the amounts of these three fats and subtracting them from the total leaves about 4.5 grams unaccounted for. These grams probably represent transfatty acids. Because food labels don't always provide a complete breakdown of fat content, it is difficult to assess the amount of transfatty acids contained in a particular food. Food composition tables such as shown in table 6-2 and nutrition software such as those available with this text provide sufficient information to help you estimate transfatty acid content.

Table 6-2 Fat Content of Selected Foods

Food	Fat/(g)	Total*	Saturated	Monounsaturated	Polyunsaturated
Egg, whole, raw	5.01	64	19	25	8
Butter (pat)	11.4	100	67	31	4
Margarine, regular, hard (stick)	91.0	100	20	45	32
Cheese, cream (1 ounce)	9.9	90	57	25	3
Cheese, cheddar (1 cup)	37.5	74	47	20	2
Cheese, cottage (1 cup)	10.1	39	25	11	1
Milk, whole (1 cup)	8.2	49	30	14	2
Milk, skim (1 cup)	1.0	6	4	1	Trace[‡]
Frankfurter (2 ounces)	16.6	82	33	40	3
Bologna, pork (slice)	4.6	72	26	36	8
Flounder, baked (0.8 ounce)	1.9	9	Trace	Trace	Trace
Fish sticks (1 ounce)	3.4	39	10	18	10
Tuna, canned, oil-packed (3 ounces)	6.9	38	8	10	17
Tuna, canned, water-packed (3 ounces)	2.1	7	Trace	Trace	Trace
Ground beef (3 ounces)	19.2	65	25	28	3
Steak, broiled, sirloin (2 ounces)	4.89	56	24	26	2
Pork chop, broiled (3 ounces)	22.3	62	23	29	7
Chicken breast, fried, flour-coated (7 ounces)	17.4	36	10	14	8
Beans, navy (1 cup)	2.1	4	Trace	Trace	3
Potato (baked)	0.06	1	Trace	Trace	4
Potato chips (1.5 ounces)	13.0	61	16	11	31
Ice cream, vanilla, regular (1 cup)	22.5	48	28	14	2
Apple (raw, unpeeled)	0.5	6	1	Trace	2
Danish pastry	13.6	50	14	29	4

*includes undifferentiated fats

[†]rounded off to the nearest whole number

[‡]*Trace*, less than 0.9% of fat.

Recommended fat intake

To many people, *fat* has negative connotations and is viewed almost as a toxin, but as stated earlier, fat is an essential nutrient. During the first twelve months of life, fat is critical to the development of the brain, spine, and central nervous system. At least 50 percent of an infant's calories must come from fat.[13] However, the body's need for fat drops dramatically after the first year. Experts recommend a diet that includes a total fat intake of no more than 30 percent of total calories. That percentage is considered a maximum; many experts believe it is too high.

Fat intake in excess of 30 percent of total calories is consistently associated with heart disease. Saturated fat is the major dietary contributor to total blood cholesterol levels, even more than cholesterol intake. Many associations have also been made between dietary fat and certain types of cancer, notably breast, prostate, and colon cancer. Another health problem related to high fat intake is obesity. Very little energy is used to transfer fat from foods to fat storage; the body requires only 3 calories to store 100 calories of dietary fat as fat tissue, compared with 23 to 27 calories to digest 100 calories of carbohydrates. Fat also yields more than twice as many calories as do protein and carbohydrates.

Just how low should your fat intake be? If 30 percent is good, it might stand to reason that 20, 15, or 10 percent would be even better. Surprisingly, the answer is controversial. Research conducted by Dean Ornish (see Chapter 2) has shown that a very low-fat diet (10 percent of calories from fat) combined with quitting smoking, exercising, and reducing stress can reverse atherosclerosis. On the other hand, some studies have found that cutting fat intake too much may actually increase health risks. Researchers from the University of Washington investigated selected health effects of year-long diets containing either 30 percent, 26 percent, 22 percent, or 18 percent of daily calories from fat. Subjects on the lowest-fat diet showed a reduction in HDL cholesterol and a slight increase in triglycerides. These people had an increase in risk factors associated with heart disease. The optimal level of fat intake for reducing cholesterol was 26 percent.[14] Another study compared a very low-fat diet (10 percent of calories from fat) to a low-fat diet (26 percent of calories from fat). On average, both diets lowered cholesterol by 13 percent. But the very low-fat diet produced a 31 percent drop in HDLs ("good" cholesterol), whereas the decline in HDLs on the low-fat diet was just 13 percent. Also, triglyceride levels increased by 33 percent on the very low-fat diet, compared with 13 percent on the low-fat diet. The study concluded that a very low-fat diet can actually boost the danger of heart disease for some people.[5]

Experts offer several explanations of why diets low in total fat may actually increase heart disease risk. First, low-fat diets may be associated with diets high in carbohydrates.[5] Diets high in carbohydrates and low in fat elevate triglyceride levels and lower HDL levels. Second, low-fat diets may have a higher-than-normal ratio of saturated fat to other types of fat. Studies indicate that as long as saturated fat intake is low, the total fat content of a diet has no effect on heart disease risk. When saturated fats are replaced with unsaturated fats, HDL cholesterol declines only moderately, and triglyceride levels remain stable. In a fourteen-year study of 80,000 women, Harvard University researchers documented the relationship between dietary fat intake and heart disease.[15] They learned that the replacement of 5 percent of energy from saturated fat with energy from unsaturated fats reduced the risk of coronary heart disease by 42 percent. In addition, the replacement of 2 percent of energy from transfatty acids with energy from unhydrogenated fats reduced the risk by 53 percent. Researchers concluded that replacing saturated and transfatty acids with unhydrogenated monounsaturated and polyunsaturated fats is more effective in preventing heart disease than is reducing overall fat intake. It is possible that the important issue is not one of total fat; rather, it may be the type of fat that counts (see figure 6-2 for a comparison of dietary fats). Until the issue of quantity versus type is settled, the best advice is to reduce total fat intake to less than 30 percent and to concentrate on lowering saturated fat intake. Moderation is an important principle for fat intake just as it is for nutrition in general.

Most Americans have an excessive fat intake and are challenged to make changes in both the amount and type of fat eaten. Table 6-3 presents a quick reference of maximum fat intake for selected caloric intakes. You can estimate your personal maximum fat intake by completing Assessment Activity 6-2. You can also learn how fatty your eating habits are by completing Assessment Activity 6-5.

Saturated Fat. Experts agree that saturated fats need to be reduced in the American diet. Diets rich in saturated fats unquestionably increase the risk of heart disease and some cancers. Assessment Activity 6-2 will help you estimate your maximum saturated fat intake. It is recommended that no more than 8 percent of total calories come from saturated fat. This amounts to 9 grams per 1000 calories. Americans currently get 12 percent of their calories from saturated fat.[16] People with heart disease, diabetes, or a high LDL cholesterol level should restrict saturated fat intake to no more than 7 percent of total calories.[5]

Figure 6-2 Comparison of Dietary Fats

	Saturated	Monounsaturated	Polyunsaturated	Cholesterol (mg/tbsp)
Coconut oil	86	6	2	0
Palm kernel oil	81	11	2	0
Butter (fat)	66	30	4	33
Beef tallow	50	42	4	14
Palm oil	49	37	9	0
Lard	39	45	11	12
Chicken fat	31	22	47	11
Vegetable shortening	28	28	44	0
Cottonseed oil	27	54	19	0
Margarine	19	32	49	0
Peanut oils	19	46	30	0
Soybean oils	15	23	58	0
Olive oils	14	72	9	0
Corn oils	13	24	59	0
Sunflower oils	10	20	66	0
Safflower oils	9	12	74	0
Canola oils	6	62	32	0

Table 6-3 Maximum Fat and Saturated Fat Grams for Selected Caloric Intakes*

Daily Calorie Intake	Total Fat Grams per Day 30% Level	Total Fat Grams per Day 26% Level	Total Saturated Fat Grams per Day 10% Level	Total Saturated Fat Grams per Day 8% Level
1000	33	29	11	9
1500	50	43	17	13
2000	67	58	22	18
2500	83	72	28	22
3000	100	87	33	27

*If a person on a 1500-calorie diet wants to restrict fat intake to no more than 26% of calories, the limit is 43 grams (1500 × 0.26 – 390 total fat calories; 390 ÷ 9 = 43). Saturated fat intake at the 8% level is restricted to 13 grams (1500 × 0.08 = 120 saturated fat calories; 120 ÷ 9 = 13).

Monounsaturated Fat. Monounsaturated fats are liquid at room temperature and include olive oil, canola oil, and peanut oil. When monounsaturated fats are substituted for saturated fats, a person's blood fat profile usually improves and risk factors associated with heart disease and some forms of cancer are reduced. The recommendation for monounsaturated fats is 12 to 20 percent of total calories.[16] This amounts to 13 to 22 grams per 1000 calories.

Although the diet of people in Mediterranean countries is higher in fat than that of Americans, the incidence of heart disease and stroke in those countries is much lower. The main difference is that the Mediterranean diet is high in monounsaturated fat, usually from consumption of olive oil. This has prompted some scientists to suggest that Americans adopt this pattern of eating.

Polyunsaturated Fat. There are two main types of polyunsaturated (poly) fats: omega-6 and omega-3. The omega-6s make up 90 percent of poly fats in the American diet and come primarily from vegetable oils, such as soybean, corn, sunflower, and safflower oils. Omega-6 provides linoleic acid, an essential fatty acid. The omega-3s come primarily from seafood and provide linolenic acid, another essential fatty acid. The consumption of omega-6s and omega-3s is associated with cardiovascular benefits, including reduction of blood clotting, prevention of abnormal heart rhythms, and lowering of levels of total cholesterol and LDLs. Recommended intake of polyunsaturated fats is no more than 10 percent of total calories.[16] This amounts to 11 grams per 1000 calories.

Transfatty Acids. Transfatty acids start out as unsaturated fats but become like saturated fats because of the hydrogenation process. In high amounts, these fatty acids are associated with risk factors similar to those linked to saturated fats. Consumption of transfatty acids should be held to a minimum.

Vitamins

Vitamins are organic compounds (they contain carbon) that are necessary in small amounts for good health. The body can break vitamins down, but it cannot produce them, so vitamins have to be supplied in the diet. Unlike carbohydrates, fats, and proteins, vitamins yield no energy. Instead, some serve as catalysts that enable energy nutrients to be digested, absorbed, and metabolized. Some vitamins also interact with minerals. For example, vitamin C facilitates iron absorption, vitamin D improves calcium absorption, and thiamin requires the mineral magnesium to function efficiently.

Vitamins are either water soluble or fat soluble (see tables 6-4 and 6-5). Water-soluble vitamins include vitamin B complex and vitamin C. They are present in the watery components of food, distributed in the fluid components of the body, excreted in the urine, needed in frequent small doses, and unlikely to be toxic except when taken in megadoses (very large quantities).

Fat-soluble vitamins include vitamins A, D, E, and K and are found in the fat and oily parts of food. Because they cannot be dissolved and absorbed in the bloodstream, these vitamins must be absorbed into the lymph with fat and transported in lipoproteins. When consumed in excess of the body's need, fat-soluble vitamins are stored in the liver and fat cells. Their storage makes it possible for a person to survive for months or years without consuming them. At least three of the fat-soluble vitamins (A, D, and K) may even accumulate to toxic levels. Megadoses of these vitamins should be avoided.

Antioxidant vitamins

Three vitamins are classified as antioxidants—vitamins C, E, and the carotenoids. **Antioxidants** are protective substances because they help neutralize the activity of free radicals. **Free radicals** are naturally produced chemicals that arise from normal cell activity. Whenever the body uses oxygen or is exposed to a toxin, such as cigarette smoke, it forms free radicals. These unstable chemicals can damage cells throughout the body. They may damage a cell's DNA in ways that lead to cancer, interact with cholesterol in the bloodstream and form oxidized LDL (see Chapter 2), cause cataracts and rheumatoid arthritis, and be a factor in the physiological changes associated with the aging process. Anything that interferes with the destructive effects of free radicals offers a health advantage. Vitamins C and E and beta-carotene are believed to prevent the oxidation of cholesterol and other molecules linked to the diseases mentioned previously, most notably heart disease and cancer. A common cooking practice illustrates this antioxidant effect: Some foods like bananas, peaches, apples, and potatoes quickly turn brown when exposed to air. However, when such foods are dipped in lemon or orange juice, the vitamin C in the juice acts as an antioxidant and prevents browning.

Should Americans take supplements of antioxidant vitamins? Information from the research community is inconclusive. Until 1994 the evidence in support of vitamin supplements was so compelling that many scientists were beginning to believe that antioxidant vitamin supplements could be a highly effective, relatively inexpensive, and risk-free form of preventive medicine.

Interest in antioxidant supplements was dampened, however, with what is now referred to as the *Great Vitamin Scare of 1994*. That's when the six-year study on the effects of beta-carotene supplementation on more than 29,000 male smokers in Finland revealed that the incidence of cancer was 18 percent higher in the Finnish men who took the supplement than it was in those who didn't. Rather than lowering the incidence of cancer, beta-carotene supplementation appeared to increase the risk of cancer.

The results of the Finnish study are troubling and should not be dismissed. Clearly, more studies are needed. Despite all the promising leads, the value of antioxidant supplements in preventing disease is still unproven. It may be several years before large-scale studies provide more definitive conclusions. Even then it is unlikely that studies will ever establish a cause-and-effect relationship between antioxidants and

Table 6-4 Thirteen Essential Vitamins: Recommended Intake

Vitamins by Type	For Men	For Women	When Used as a Supplement
Fat-soluble vitamins			
1. Vitamin A	1000 RE (5000 IU)	800 RE (4000 IU)	*
2. Vitamin D	5 mcg (200 IU)	5 mcg: (200 IU)	400 IU
3. Vitamin E	10 mg (12–15 IU)	8 mg (12–15 IU)	200–400 IU
4. Vitamin K	70–80 mcg	60–65 mcg	Not recommended
Water-soluble vitamins			
5. Vitamin C (ascorbic acid)	60 mg	60 mg	100–200 mg
Vitamin B complex			
6. Thiamine (B-1)	1.2–1.5 mg	1.0–1.1 mg	Not recommended
7. Riboflavin (B-2)	1.4–1.7 mg	1.2–1.3 mg	Not recommended
8. Niacin	13–19 mg	13–19 mg	†
9. Pyridoxine (B-6)	2 mg	1.6 mg	‡
10. Pantothenic acid	4–7 mg	4–7 mg	Not recommended
11. Vitamin B-12	2 mcg	2 mcg	§
12. Biotin	30–100 mcg	30–100 mcg	Not recommended
13. Folate (folic acid)‖	400 mcg	400 mcg	#

*Vitamin A may be toxic in high doses. Beta-carotene supplements may increase lung cancer risk in smokers.
†Niacin may be prescribed in larger doses to lower cholesterol.
‡Pyridoxine megadoses may cause numbness.
§Strict vegetarians and adults over 60 years old may need vitamin B-12 supplements.
‖Folate comes from plants; folic acid is the human-made form used in vitamin pills and to fortify grains. Folic acid is twice as potent as folate (200 mcg of folic acid is roughly equivalent to 400 mcg of folate).
#Supplements of folate may be recommended before and during pregnancy.

From Margolis, S., and L. B. Wilder. 1998. *Nutrition and Longevity*. Baltimore, Md.: The Johns Hopkins Medical Institutions. Also from Tufts University. 1998. With age, calorie needs go down but nutrient needs go up. *Tufts University Health & Nutrition Letter* 16(10):4–5.

---

chronic diseases. There are too many factors to consider. For example, people who eat plenty of fruits and vegetables may also lead healthy lifestyles overall. Fruits and vegetables also contain thousands of plant chemicals (phytochemicals), many of which are just beginning to show promise against disease. Consequently, some scientists advocate patience until scientific consensus is reached, and they do not recommend taking supplements at this time. Other scientists believe that thousands of Americans may die prematurely of heart disease and cancer before a consensus develops and that the ground swell of evidence, despite some inconsistencies, supports taking antioxidants now, especially considering that only 36 percent of adults eat the recommended five to eight servings of fruits and vegetables each day.[1]

Presently there is only one strategy to combat disease that no scientist would dispute: Eat more produce. Fruits and vegetables are high in fiber and low in fat and contain hundreds of substances that have the potential to improve health—not just the few compounds that have been isolated and packaged as supplements. In all the research that has been done on diet, antioxidants, and disease, the strongest and most consistent pattern has been that eating a variety of fruits and vegetables produces benefits.

In preparing food for consumption it is important to remember that vitamin content is easily compromised. Improper storage, excessive cooking, and exposure to heat, light, and air may reduce the vitamin content in food.

Vitamin C

Vitamin C, also called *ascorbic acid*, is essential to the formation of collagen, a protein that is used to form all the connective tissues of your body. It is required in the breakdown and absorption of some amino acids and other minerals (such as iron) and in the formation of some hormones. It may also help the immune

Table 6-5 Vitamins: Food Sources and Wellness Benefits

Vitamins	Food Sources	Wellness Benefits
Fat-soluble vitamins		
1. Vitamin A	Liver, carrots, eggs, tomatoes, dark green and yellow-orange vegetables and some fruits	Healthy skin and mucous membranes, improved night vision, defense against infections; antioxidant benefits (from carotenoids)
2. Vitamin D	Fish oils and fortified milk; exposure to sunlight	Maintaining of blood levels of calcium and phosphorus; promotion of strong bones and teeth; possible reduction of risk of osteoporosis
3. Vitamin E	Plant oils (corn, soybean, safflower, etc.), nuts, seeds	Formation of red blood cells and utilization of vitamin K; antioxidant benefits
4. Vitamin K	Green vegetables, liver	Promotion of blood clotting; contribution to bone metabolism
Water-soluble vitamins		
5. Vitamin C (Ascorbic Acid)	Citrus fruits, green vegetables	Promotion of healthy gums and teeth; iron absorption; maintaining of normal connective tissues; help in wound healing; antioxidant benefits
Vitamin B complex		
6. Thiamine (B-1)	Whole grains, legumes, liver, nuts	Carbohydrate metabolism; nerve function
7. Riboflavin (B-2)	Dairy products, liver, enriched grains, spinach	Energy metabolism; production of red blood cells; improved health of skin and eyes
8. Niacin	Nuts, grains, meat, fish, tuna, mushrooms	Energy metabolism, fat synthesis, fat breakdown; lowering of cholesterol (when prescribed in large doses)
9. Pyridoxine (B-6)	Whole grains, meat, beans, nuts, fish, liver	Protein metabolism; possible immunity boost in the elderly; homocysteine metabolism
10. Pantothenic acid	Whole grains, dried beans, eggs, milk, liver	Energy metabolism; fat synthesis; production of essential body chemicals
11. Vitamin B-12	Animal foods, dairy products, seafood	Folate metabolism; nerve function; formation of red blood cells; homocysteine metabolism
12. Biotin	Cheese, egg yolks, mushrooms, grains	Glucose production; fat synthesis
13. Folate (folic acid)	Green leafy vegetables, liver, beans, grains, citrus fruits	DNA synthesis and protein metabolism; reduction of risk of certain birth defects; homocysteine metabolism

system prevent infections. As an antioxidant it may play a role in prevention of atherosclerosis and some forms of cancer.

Contrary to popular opinion, vitamin C does not prevent the common cold. Scientifically controlled studies reveal no difference in the incidence of colds among vitamin C users and nonusers. On a positive note, however, some studies suggest that large doses (about 2000 mg a day) can reduce the severity and duration of a cold's symptoms slightly. That much, however, might also cause diarrhea and kidney stones in susceptible people.[17]

The RDA of vitamin C is 60 mg, 70 mg during pregnancy, and 90 mg during lactation. For smokers the RDA is 100 mg because smoking appears to destroy some vitamin C. Advocates of increased vitamin C often recommend intakes of 200 mg or more.[4] Still, an intake of 200 mg/day can be achieved by food intake. Megadoses (2000 mg) of vitamin C offer little benefit to the body and may be harmful. As a water-soluble vitamin, doses in excess of the body's requirement are excreted through the kidneys. In other words, the body can only absorb so much. Side effects of large doses are diarrhea and abdominal discomfort. For those who absorb excess iron, supplements of vitamin C could be dangerous. Large intakes may also produce errors in the results of some diagnostic tests (such as the Hemoccult test which tests for blood in the intestines).

Antioxidant vitamins from foods like citrus fruits may help protect young and old alike from heart disease and cancer.

Carotenoids

More than 600 carotenoids are found in nature. They give fruits and vegetables their yellow, orange, and red colors. They're also abundant in dark green vegetables. Three of the major carotenoids (alpha-carotene, beta-carotene, and beta-cryptoxanthin) can be converted by the body into vitamin A and are referred to as *provitamin A*. Until recently, beta-carotene was thought to offer the most health-protecting antioxidant effect. However, after studies showed that the incidence of lung cancer increased in smokers who took beta-carotene supplements, researchers concluded that beta-carotene was not the main protector.

One carotenoid currently being studied for its antioxidant potency is lycopene, the predominant carotenoid in the blood and in the prostate gland in males. It cannot be converted to vitamin A, but it has twice the antioxidant potency of beta-carotene. Benefits attributed to lycopene are a reduced risk of some cancers, especially those of the digestive tract and the prostate. The best source of lycopene is tomatoes. Cooked tomatoes, such as those found in sauces, are a better source than raw tomatoes and tomato juice because heat ruptures plant cell walls, releasing the carotenoid. Also, lycopene is a fat-soluble substance, so some fat, like that found in pizza and most pasta sauces, is needed for it to be absorbed.[18]

Currently, carotenoid supplements, including beta-carotene and lycopene, are not recommended. Carotenoids interact with one another, and supplemental doses of one carotenoid may impair the absorption of others. Instead, eat a variety of vegetables and fruits to get a mix of carotenoids. Five servings a day of fruits and vegetables that are mostly yellow-orange, red, or dark green are recommended. It is likely that carotenoids are more beneficial to health when they are consumed together from food than when packaged separately, as in a supplement.

Vitamin E

Vitamin E is a fat-soluble vitamin and plays a role in the formation of red blood cells and maintenance of nervous tissues, and it aids in the absorption of vitamin A. Claims that vitamin E improves the skin, heals scars, prevents stretch marks, slows the aging process, and increases fertility are more folklore than fact.

The strongest evidence of the antioxidant benefits of vitamins exists for vitamin E.[7] Vitamin E is a potent antioxidant that attaches to LDL cholesterol and helps prevent damage from free radicals. Large-scale studies, involving tens of thousands of participants who were followed for an average of four to eight years, found that those who took vitamin E supplements were significantly less likely to develop coronary heart disease than were those who did not take supplements of vitamin E. Supplemental doses of 100 to 250 IU per day for at least two years resulted in a 37 and 44 percent decrease in heart disease risk for men and women, respectively.[5] The effect of consuming vitamin E from food versus obtaining comparable levels through supplements is difficult to determine because dietary vitamin E intake rarely reaches the 100 IU per day level, the minimum amount that appears to be protective. Vitamin E is found only in small amounts in a few foods. Low-fat diets are especially scarce in vitamin E.

Although these studies are impressive, there still is not enough evidence to recommend vitamin E supplements for the general population. Some experts warn of the dangers of tampering with the body's biochemistry; however, other experts recommend supplements of vitamin E because they believe it is not harmful and may be worthwhile. The people who stand to benefit the most from vitamin E supplements are those with coronary heart disease, diabetes, or high LDL cholesterol levels.[5] If you choose to take a supplement, select the natural form, rather than the synthetic, because it is absorbed more easily into the body. The label for natural vitamin E should read "d-alpha tocopherol."[19]

Folate, Vitamin B$_6$, Vitamin B$_{12}$

Folate is a part of the vitamin B complex and combines with vitamins B$_6$ and B$_{12}$ to form parts of DNA and RNA and to make heme, the iron-containing protein in red blood cells. These three also assist in the metabolism of amino acids. The terms *folate, folic acid,* and *folacin* are sometimes used incorrectly. Folate is the form that comes from plants; folic acid is the form found most often in your body and the form added to foods and supplements; *folacin* is a collective term for these and other forms of the vitamin. Folic acid is about twice as potent as folate. Vitamins B$_6$ and B$_{12}$ are plentiful in foods, and few people, with the possible exception of strict vegetarians, need to worry about deficiencies. With advancing age, some people have trouble producing stomach acids in sufficient quantities to separate vitamin B$_{12}$ from foods. They have no trouble absorbing B$_{12}$ from supplements because it is not attached to food, so older people may also need to supplement their diets with B$_{12}$. Good sources of these vitamins are meat products, dairy products, eggs, spinach, whole-wheat bread, and breakfast cereals.

Folate, as its name implies, is found in foliage—leafy vegetables, such as lettuce and spinach. It is also found in citrus fruits, whole-grain bread, and cereals. Of the three B vitamins mentioned here, folate is the one in which Americans are most likely to fall short.

Because folate has been associated with a reduction in the chances of neurological birth defects, such as spina bifida, a woman planning a pregnancy may be advised by her physician to eat foods rich in folate and possibly to take a supplement. In an effort to reduce the incidence of these birth defects, new food fortification guidelines were established in 1998 that require food manufacturers to fortify certain grain products, such as flour, bread, and cereal, with folic acid.

Current interest in folate was sparked by recent studies that demonstrated that people whose blood levels were low in folic acid had high homocysteine levels. *Homocysteine* is an amino acid that plays a role in the formation of two other amino acids, cysteine and methionine. To work properly, these amino acids require three B vitamins—folate, B$_6$, and B$_{12}$. If these vitamins are in short supply, homocysteine levels might rise.[4] High homocysteine levels are thought to increase the risk of heart disease (see Chapter 2). The compound has also been implicated in several other diseases, including cancer, diabetes mellitus, and neurological disorders.

The precise mechanism for the association between homocysteine levels and heart disease isn't clear. High concentrations of homocysteine are thought to make the artery walls sticky, promoting plaque formation. Whatever the reason, one thing appears clear: High homocysteine levels are associated with low folic acid levels. In the absence of folate, along with vitamins B$_6$ and B$_{12}$, homocysteine concentrations circulate unabated. There is speculation from the scientific community that during the next several years homocysteine levels might replace cholesterol as a major risk factor of heart disease.

The best way to lower homocysteine concentrations is to consume enough B vitamins. Emphasis should be on folate, which is more effective than B$_6$ and B$_{12}$.[5] Megadoses of folate should be avoided to prevent the possibility of a false negative for anemia (too few blood cells) caused by a vitamin B$_{12}$ deficiency. If you take folate supplements, tell your physician so that the appropriate tests can be ordered.

Vitamin supplements

Advertisements proclaim that vitamins provide energy, promote wellness, and prevent disease and that taking more results in more energy and better health. Consequently, 25 to 33 percent of all Americans take one or more **vitamin supplements** in multiple and single doses, in both natural and synthetic forms.[21] Vitamins do facilitate energy release from carbohydrates, fats, and proteins, but they do not provide energy. It is not possible to survive on water and vitamins.

The growing interest in vitamin supplements is primarily related to the antioxidant vitamins and folate. The relationship of these vitamins to health promotion and disease prevention, discussed previously, has sparked an unprecedented trend toward supplements. Despite this trend, however, strong definitive conclusions about supplements have not been advanced by the scientific community. The consensus among nutrition experts is that healthy adults who eat a variety of foods do not need them. These also advise that if you don't think you're getting enough vitamins in your food, taking a multivitamin pill with nutrients at RDA levels may offer some nutritional insurance, provided it is consumed in moderation and is not used as an excuse to eat a poor diet. According to the Center for Science in the Public Interest, if a supplement is needed, it is most likely to be folic acid, vitamin B$_{12}$, vitamin D, vitamin E, or calcium.[20] These supplements were identified because they are backed by years of supporting research and because Americans don't consume enough whole grains, fruits, and vegetables.

Although healthy people don't need vitamin supplements if they are eating a balanced diet, there are several situations[21] in which a vitamin or mineral supplement may be called for:

- **If you are age 65 or older,** you may need supplements of vitamins B_6, B_{12}, and D because of the difficulty in absorbing these vitamins with advancing age. Women, especially those not taking estrogen, may require more calcium and vitamin D to protect against osteoporosis.
- **If you are dieting,** consuming fewer than 1000 calories a day, you may benefit from a vitamin and mineral supplement.
- **If you have a disease** of the digestive tract, it may interfere with normal digestion and absorption of nutrients and justify your use of vitamin and mineral supplements.
- **If you smoke,** you may need vitamin C supplements.
- **If you drink excessive alcohol,** you may suffer from poor nutrition and the alcohol may interfere with the absorption and metabolism of vitamins.
- **If you are pregnant and lactating (breast-feeding),** supplements of folic acid, iron, and calcium may be recommended for you.
- **If you are a vegetarian** who eliminates most animal products from your diet, you may need additional vitamin B_{12}. Calcium and vitamin D supplements may also be warranted if your milk intake and sun exposure are limited.

Vitamin supplements are sometimes needed by people with irregular diets or unusual lifestyles or by people following certain weight-reduction regimens or strict vegetarian diets. In addition, infants and pregnant and lactating women may need supplements. When taken as supplements, vitamins should be viewed as medicine and, therefore, should be recommended by a physician.

When shopping for supplements, it is easy to be misled by advertising hype and inaccurate labels. Americans spend billions annually for vitamin, mineral, and herbal supplements. Much of this expenditure goes toward products with no scientifically proven health value. More than one-third of American investment in vitamins is wasted on pills and powders whose potency has expired or on items diluted by additives that do little more than boost prices. Consequently, it is important for consumers to be discriminating in their purchase of supplements (see Real-World Wellness: Consumer Tips for Vitamin Supplements).

Minerals

Minerals are simple but important nutrients. As inorganic compounds, they lack the complexity of vitamins, but they fulfill a variety of functions. For example, sodium and potassium affect shifts in body fluids, calcium and phosphorus contribute to the body's structure, iron is the core of hemoglobin (an oxygen-carrying compound in the blood), and iodine facilitates production of thyroxine (a hormone that influences metabolic rate).

There are twenty to thirty important nutritional minerals. Minerals should be consumed in smaller amounts than amounts of energy nutrients and water. Minerals that are present in the body and required in large amounts (more than 100 mg, or 0.02 teaspoon, per day) are called *major minerals* or *macrominerals*. They include, in descending order of prominence,

---

Real-World Wellness

Consumer Tips for Vitamin Supplements

Vitamin and mineral supplements seem to be everywhere. Thousands of products are stocked in health food stores, and even my local grocery store has a special health food section. Given all of the hype about supplements, what are some shopping tips to help me be a discriminating consumer?

The following advice[22] will help you get the best value when you shop for supplements:

- Shop for supplements that comply with strict scientific standards set by the U.S. Pharmacopoeia. These products carry the letters *USP* on the label.
- If you take a multivitamin/mineral supplement, shop for the bargain price. Select one that provides 100 percent of the RDAs with the exception of calcium, which is too bulky to be included in a multiple-vitamin pill.
- Calcium, which can be dissolved only in the stomach, is most effective when taken with food. Split calcium intake by consuming one-half of the supplement with breakfast and the other half with dinner.
- If you take antioxidants for their possible health benefits, shop by price.
- Look for an expiration date that shows how long the supplement should retain its potency.
- Avoid supplements that advertise "sustained release" of nutrients. The delayed release may prevent the nutrients from being absorbed.
- Don't pay extra for herbal ingredients. They have not been proven to enhance the body's use of supplements. About the only thing enhanced are store profits. The more money you spend on supplements, the more you tend to waste.
- Don't waste money on most health store recommendations. If you need a supplement, it's most likely to be calcium, a multivitamin, or an antioxidant.

calcium, phosphorus, potassium, sulfur, sodium, chloride, and magnesium. Major minerals contribute 60 to 80 percent of all inorganic material in the human body.

Minerals that are required in small amounts (less than 100 mg per day) are called *trace minerals* or *microminerals*. There are more than a dozen trace minerals, the best known being iron, zinc, and iodine (see Just the Facts: Minerals).

Some minerals are similar to water-soluble vitamins in that they are readily excreted by the kidneys, do not accumulate in the body, and rarely become toxic. Others are like fat-soluble vitamins in that they are stored and are toxic if taken in excess.

Minerals are different from vitamins; they are indestructible and require no special handling during food preparation. The only precautions that need to be taken are to avoid soaking minerals out of food and throwing them away in cooking water.

Major minerals are abundant in the diet; therefore, deficiencies are highly unlikely, especially if a variety of foods is included. If a deficiency in major minerals does occur, it is most likely to be a calcium deficiency, especially among women. Four out of five women ages 9 to 19, two out of three women ages 20 to 49, and three out of four women over 50 fall below the recommended allowance for calcium.[1] The RDA of calcium for adults 19 to 50 years old is 1000 mg, and 1200 mg is recommended for those 51 and older. Here are some tips for increasing your calcium intake:

- Try to consume as much calcium as possible from food. Skim milk and low-fat dairy products are excellent sources of calcium and are also fortified with vitamin D.
- Use calcium supplements to compensate for a calcium shortfall. Getting enough calcium from food requires consuming the equivalent of a quart of milk per day. As a result, many people benefit from an over-the-counter calcium supplement.
- Calcium is best absorbed in doses of 500 mg or less taken with meals.[2,3] The best type of calcium supplement is calcium carbonate, which is available in common antacids.
- Take calcium supplements with meals. Calcium is best dissolved and absorbed in stomach acids secreted during mealtime.
- Look for calcium-fortified foods. A cup of calcium-fortified orange juice, for example, contains about the same amount of calcium as a cup of milk and is absorbed more easily.
- Get the recommended intake of vitamin D. Vitamin D is necessary for the body to absorb calcium.
- If you're taking other supplements or medicines, check with your physician or pharmacist. Calcium can interfere with the absorption of iron, zinc, and certain medicines.
- If you have a history of kidney stones, exercise caution in taking large doses of calcium. High calcium intake might increase the risk of stone formation.

Just the Facts

Minerals

Here are some basic facts about minerals:

Major (Macro) Minerals
Types: calcium, phosphorus, potassium, sulfur, sodium chloride, and magnesium

Trace (Micro) Minerals
Types: iron, iodine, zinc, selenium, manganese, copper, molybdenum, cobalt, chromium, fluorine, silicon, vanadium, nickel, tin, cadmium

Minerals of Special Concern*

Calcium
Wellness benefits: contributes to bone and tooth formation, general body growth, maintenance of good muscle tone, nerve function, cell membrane function, and regulation of normal heart beat
Food sources: dairy products, dark-green vegetables, dried beans, shellfish
Deficiency signs and symptoms: bone pain and fractures, muscle cramps, osteoporosis

Iron
Wellness benefits: facilitates oxygen and carbon dioxide transport, formation of red blood cells, production of antibodies, synthesis of collagen, and use of energy
Food sources: red meat (lean), seafood, eggs, dried beans, nuts, grains, green leafy vegetables
Deficiency signs and symptoms: fatigue, weakness

Sodium[†]
Wellness benefits: essential for maintenance of proper acid-base balance and body fluid regulation; aids in formation of digestive secretions; assists in nerve transmission
Food sources: processed foods, meats, table salt
Deficiency signs and symptoms: rare

*Calcium and iron are of special concern because deficiencies are likely to exist, especially among women and children.
[†]Sodium is of concern because of potential for overconsumption.

Starting your day with low-fat dairy products, such as milk and yogurt, is a good way to add calcium to your diet.

Of the various trace minerals, iron is the most abundant. It is also one of concern to nutritionists because certain groups are at risk of having low iron levels. These include young children and early teens, menstruating women, and people with conditions that cause internal bleeding, such as ulcers or intestinal diseases.[21]

Iron deficiency in the diet is responsible for the most prevalent form of anemia in the United States. Iron deficiency hampers the body's ability to produce *hemoglobin*, a substance needed to carry oxygen in the blood. A lack of hemoglobin can cause fatigue and weakness and can even affect behavior and intellectual function. Proper infant feeding through use of iron-fortified milk or breast-feeding is the best safeguard against iron deficiency in infants. Among adolescents and adults, iron intake can be improved by increasing consumption of iron-rich foods, such as lean red meats, fish, certain kinds of beans, dried fruits, iron-enriched cereals and whole-grain products, and foods cooked in a cast-iron skillet. For some people, especially premenopausal women with inconsistent diets, iron supplements may be justified. In addition, consuming foods that contain vitamin C enhances the body's ability to absorb iron.

Iron deficiency is rare among healthy men and postmenopausal women. Even strict vegetarians can get iron in sufficient amounts by consuming legumes, dark-green leafy vegetables, and fortified breads and cereals. It is possible to get too much iron. Some studies report that high iron levels may be linked to heart disease, but the jury is still out on this issue. Also, some people have a rare genetic disorder called *hemochromatosis*, which permits an unhealthy buildup of iron. Iron overload may cause liver cancer, heart disease, diabetes, sterility, or other complications.

Zinc is another trace mineral that has received widespread publicity because of its link to the common cold. Early studies reported that zinc lozenges cured the cold within hours. More recent studies refute this claim and state that the one possible benefit is the shortening of the duration of a cold by about one day.

While zinc is essential for proper functioning of the immune system, too much can interfere with the body's use and absorption of other essential minerals, such as iron and copper. Also, excess zinc can lower HDL cholesterol.[24]

Water

Next to air, water is the substance most necessary for survival. Most everything in the body occurs in a water medium. Although people can live without vitamins and minerals for extended periods, death results within a few days without water.

Water makes up about 60 percent of the body's weight. Every cell in the body is bathed in water of the exact composition that is best for it. Even tissues that are not thought of as "watery" contain large amounts of water. For example, water makes up about 75 percent of brain and muscle tissues; bone tissue and fat tissue are about 20 percent water. As a rule, the bodies of men contain more water than do the bodies of women because men have more muscle tissue and muscle tissue holds more water than fat tissue, which is more prominent in the bodies of women.

Water performs many functions. It is vital to digestion and metabolism because it acts as a medium for chemical reactions in the body. It carries oxygen and nutrients to the cells through blood, regulates body temperature through perspiration, and lubricates the joints. It removes waste through sweat and urine, protects a fetus, and assists in respiration by moistening the lungs to facilitate intake of oxygen and excretion of carbon dioxide. It also assists with constipation relief and provides satiety, thus serving as a deterrent to the overconsumption of food.

Although most water intake comes from beverages, solid foods also make a significant contribution. Most fruits and vegetables are more than 80 percent water, meats are 50 percent water, bread is 33 percent water, and butter is approximately 15 percent water.

How much water should you drink? People are advised to drink 8 to 12 cups of fluids a day. Another general rule of thumb is to drink a quart of water for every 1000 calories expended.[25] More fluids are necessary before, during, and after physical activity (see Chapter 3). To determine when and how much fluid to drink, don't rely on thirst. If you're thirsty, the body has already lost too much fluid (see Real-World Wellness: How Can You Tell If You're Getting Enough Water?).

Plain tap water is the preferred source of fluid. Tap water has an advantage over bottled water in that it often contains fluoride, an additive that impedes tooth decay. Chlorine is another additive to municipal water supplies that provides a public health safeguard by destroying bacteria. Because it is added in such small quantities, fears about chlorine causing cancer are unsubstantiated. Another advantage of tap water over bottled water is that it is subjected to much more rigorous testing. Municipal water supplies, which are regulated by the Environmental Protection Agency, are tested every day for disease-causing microbes and chemical contaminants. Bottled water, which is regulated by the Food and Drug Administration, may or may not be tested.[26]

Under normal circumstances, too much water cannot be consumed because the body is efficient at getting rid of what it does not need. However, a sudden drinking binge in a short period early in the day will not satisfy the body's needs later; the excess will be excreted by the kidneys. Water consumption should occur throughout the day.

Other Nutrients with Unique Health Benefits

In addition to the six classes of essential nutrients, many other substances in food contribute to health. Three of the most notable ones are phytochemicals, botanicals, and fiber. Interest in these substances has given rise to two recent trends: the use of *nutraceuticals*, natural ingredients to promote and maintain health, and *chemoprevention*, the use of nutritional interventions to prevent diseases (such as cancer) by bolstering the immune system. New discoveries and recent developments in these areas have outpaced the scientific community's ability to monitor, test, and confirm various claims. Until these claims can be validated, the public should take a wait-and-see approach. While many of the chemical compounds in food promise to promote health or prevent disease, taken indiscriminately they may do more harm than good. The exception is fiber, for which most claims are backed by years of solid evidence. Some of the claims that have been studied and reported in the popular literature are highlighted here.

Phytochemicals

Phytochemicals are plant chemicals that exist naturally in all plant foods. Chemically they are not vitamins, minerals, fiber, or any of the energy nutrients. Rather they are the hundreds of thousands of active compounds found in small amounts in vegetables and fruits. Although phytochemicals have not been traditionally classified as essential nutrients, scientists believe that they might play an important role in preventing various diseases. For example, populations that consume higher amounts of fruits and vegetables have a lower risk of

---

Real-World Wellness

How Can You Tell If You're Getting Enough Water?

Experts say that thirst is not a good indicator of when and how much water to drink. If that's the case, how can I tell if I'm drinking enough water?

The following guidelines[25] will help you determine whether to increase your fluid intake.

- Check your urine. It should be clear or pale yellow. Dark-colored urine in small amounts is a sure sign that the body's fluid needs are not being met. (Note, however, that some medicines and vitamin supplements can also cause dark urine.)

- Needing to urinate every two to four hours is a signal that your fluid intake is appropriate. Sometimes people limit fluid intake to avoid trips to the bathroom. This is a mistake. The bladder adjusts to extra fluid intake.

- If you're eating lots of protein, your kidneys need extra water to flush out the waste products of protein metabolism.

- Consume at least 8 to 12 cups of fluid each day. Water is preferred because it is absorbed faster than any other beverage. Juices, milk, and foods that are liquid at room temperature also count. Five servings of fruits and vegetables yield about 2 cups of water. Even solid foods, such as meats and bread, provide water. Alcohol and caffeinated beverages (coffee, tea, and colas) don't count because they act as diuretics and increase the need for water.

cancer.[27] Some phytochemicals have a structure similar to the body's natural forms of estrogen. These compounds are called *phytoestrogens* (or *plant estrogens*), and when ingested by way of the diet, they may reduce the potentially harmful effect of the more potent, naturally occurring estrogens often associated with breast and prostate cancer.[4] Although phytochemicals have largely been studied for their role in cancer prevention, current research is exploring their relationship to many other diseases, including cardiovascular disease, osteoporosis, diabetes, and hypertension.

There is a great deal of excitement in nutrition and food sciences about the potential of phytochemicals in health promotion. The reported health benefits of several phytochemicals are highlighted in table 6-6. As scientists continue to isolate, identify, and study specific plant chemicals, it is likely that the place of such chemicals in disease prevention will become more important. Some experts speculate that phytochemicals will be the "vitamins for the twenty-first century."

Botanicals (Phytomedicinals) (Herbs)

Plants used medically are technically called **botanicals** or **phytomedicinals**. The popular literature usually refers to them as *herbs*. Herbs number in the thousands; however, only twenty to thirty are backed by well-conducted research studies similar to those used to test over-the-counter drugs in the United States[28] Herbs, however, are not regulated as drugs; instead, they are classified as dietary supplements. Consequently, there is considerable debate about their effectiveness and safety. The names, food sources, and health claims of several popular herbs are presented in Just the Facts: Some Common Herbs Sold as Nutritional Supplements. Herbs are not to be confused with hormone supplements, such as melatonin, DHEA (dehydroepiandrosterone), and DMSO (dimethylsulfoxide). Unlike herbs, which are extracted from plants, these are synthetic compounds. The purported health benefits of these hormones have not yet been proved.

If you decide to take an herb, here are some tips:

- Check with your physician before taking herbs, especially for serious conditions. Inform your physician of herbs you are taking, just as you would for prescribed medicines. There are many potential interactions with other supplements and medicines.
- Avoid using herbs if you are pregnant or nursing.
- Check the label for the abbreviation *USP*. This means that the manufacturer has met the stringent guidelines of the United States Pharmacopoeia, ensuring the quality, strength, purity, and consistency

Table 6-6 Health Benefits of Selected Phytochemicals

Phytochemical	Food Source	Possible Benefit
Allyl sulfide	Garlic, onions, leeks, chives	Decreases reproduction of tumor cells; facilitates excretion of carcinogens; blocks nitrite formation in stomach
Caffeic acid	Fruits	Facilitates excretions of carcinogens
Capsaicin	Hot peppers	Acts as an antioxidant; inhibits carcinogenesis
Coumarin	Citrus fruit, tomatoes	Prevents blood clotting; stimulates anticancer enzymes
Dithiolthione	Cruciferous vegetables	Stimulates anticancer enzymes
Phytoestrogen (isoflavones)	Soybeans, dried beans	Help prevent breast cancer by stopping the estrogen produced by the body from entering cells
Flavonoids	Fruits, vegetables, red wine, grape juice, green tea	Acts as an antioxidant
Phenolic acids (ellagic acid, ferulic acid)	Fruits, grains, nuts	Prevents DNA damage in cells; binds to iron, which may inhibit the mineral from creating free radicals; binds to nitrites in the stomach, preventing them from being converted into nitrosamines
Indoles, isothiocynates, sulforaphane	Cruciferous vegetables	Stimulates anticancer enzymes
Limonene	Citrus fruits	Stimulates anticancer enzymes
Phytic acid	Grains	Binds to iron, which may inhibit the mineral from creating cancer-causing free radicals

Just the Facts

Some Common Herbs Sold as Nutritional Supplements

Here are usual dosages and possible benefits and problems[29] of various herbs:

- **Bilberry** (*Vaccinium myrtillus*)
  Usual dosage: 240–480 mg dried berry extract of bilberry shrub
  Possible benefits: useful for simple diarrhea, varicose veins, hemorrhoids, glaucoma, night blindness, cataracts

- **Echinacea** (*Echinacea purpurea*)
  Usual dosage: 15–30 drops of tincture from purple coneflower extracts, up to five times a day
  Possible benefits: immune booster for colds, flus, and respiratory infections
  Potential problem: some allergic reactions reported in people with autoimmune disorders like lupus or multiple sclerosis

- **Feverfew** (*Tanacetum parthenium*)
  Usual dosage: 125 mg. of dried leaf extract
  Possible benefits: prevention and treatment of migraines and associated nausea
  Potential problem: a potential allergen for people sensitive to ragweed

- **Garlic** (*Allium sativum*)
  Usual dosage: 3 cloves of dietary garlic daily or 1 tsp. dried garlic powder, or in oil or pill form
  Possible benefits: may promote antibacterial, antifungal, and antiviral activity including those associated with the common cold; may have cardiovascular benefits
  Potential problem: in excess, possible interactions with other herbs and/or medicines

- **Ginger** (*Zingiber officinale*)
  Usual dosage: 500 mg
  Possible benefits: treatment of motion sickness, nausea, indigestion
  Potential problem: may aggravate gallstones, heartburn; acts as a blood thinner

- **Ginkgo** (*Ginkgo biloba*)
  Usual dosage: 120–160 mg from leaf extract of ginkgo tree, in divided doses
  Possible benefits: may improve memory and mental functioning; acts as an antioxidant; aids blood flow to the brain and to the legs
  Potential problem: acts as a blood thinner; may cause gastrointestinal upset, headaches, allergic skin reactions

- **Ginseng** (*Panax ginsing*)
  Usual dosage: 300 mg or one-half ginseng root extract in hot water
  Possible benefits: may enhance immunity
  Potential problem: may increase blood pressure; may cause headaches and skin problems

- **Saw palmetto** (*Serenoa repens*)
  Usual dosage: 320 mg of dried fruit extract from sabal in one to two doses
  Possible benefits: may improve urinary flow in men with enlarged prostate
  Potential problem: may cause inaccurate readings on (PSA) tests

- **St. John's Wort** (*Hypericum perforatum*)
  Usual dosage: 300 mg dried leaf and flower extract
  Possible benefits: may alleviate mild to moderate depression
  Potential problem: not useful for severe depression; may cause complications with prescription antidepressants

- **Valerian** (*Valeriana officinalis*)
  Usual dosage: 400–450 mg of extract 30 minutes before bedtime
  Possible benefits: treatment for insomnia, mild anxiety, restlessness
  Potential problem: may cause complications with sedatives or antidepressants

---

of the product. The letters *NF*, which stands for *National Formulary,* also ensure that the product meets minimum standards. Presently, only a handful of herbs have been subjected to review using USP standards.

- Do your homework. Read about the herb; ask your pharmacist for information. There are several Web sites that provide helpful information:

United States Pharmacopoeia: www.usp.org/did/mgrphs/botanica

American Botanical Council: www.herbalgram.org

The Herb Research Foundation: www.herbs.org

- Monitor your body's response. Start with a dose that is lower than that recommended. Stop taking an herb if you have an adverse reaction.

- Don't expect miracles. Herbs take longer to work than prescribed and over-the-counter medicines.
- Take specific herbs for specific needs. Avoid taking herbs continuously.

Fiber

One advantage of a high-starch diet is that it will likely be high in fiber unless the foods are refined or highly processed.

Fiber (formerly called *roughage*) is a general term that refers to the substances in food that resist digestion. The amount of fiber in a food is determined by its plant source and the amount of processing it undergoes. In general, the more a food is processed, the more the fiber is broken down or removed and the lower its fiber content.

There are two kinds of fiber: *soluble fiber* dissolves or swells in hot water, and *insoluble fiber* does not dissolve in water. Every plant food usually contains a mixture of fiber types.

Soluble fiber

Soluble fiber appears to have several favorable effects. Because it forms gel in water, it adds bulk and thickness to the contents of the stomach and may slow emptying, thus prolonging a sense of fullness which may help dieters control their appetites. Studies have shown that soluble fiber also lowers blood-cholesterol levels. Soluble fiber binds with certain digestive acids made from cholesterol in the liver and then escorts the acids away in the stool. The liver responds by drawing cholesterol from the blood to make more acids, which lowers blood cholesterol. According to most studies, LDL cholesterol drops from 3 to 7 percent when a person changes from a low-fiber diet to a high-fiber diet.[30] Diets high in carbohydrates and fiber, especially soluble fiber, improve blood-glucose control, lower insulin requirements, and decrease blood cholesterol and blood pressure in people with diabetes. Soluble fiber also slows the absorption of sugars from the small intestine, another benefit for those with type II (non–insulin-dependent) diabetes.[31]

Good sources of soluble fiber are fruits, vegetables, and grains. Specific fiber-rich foods are prunes, pears, oranges, apples, legumes, dried beans, cauliflower, zucchini, sweet potatoes, and oat and corn bran (table 6-7).

Insoluble fiber

Insoluble fiber adds bulk to the contents of the intestine. This speeds the transit time (time of passage) of a meal's remnants through the small and large intestines. This in turn appears to offer the following important health benefits:

Table 6-7 Fiber Content of Selected Foods

Food	Fiber (g)
Fruits	
Apple, with peel	4.2
Banana	3.3
Blackberries (1 cup)	9.7
Dates, chopped (1 cup)	15.5
Grapes	1.0
Orange	2.9
Peach, peeled	2.0
Pear, with skin	4.9
Prunes, dried, pitted (10)	13.5
Raisins, seedless (1 cup)	9.6
Breads	
Oatmeal (1 cup)	0.86
Pumpernickel (1 slice)	1.33
Rye (1 slice)	1.65
Wheat (1 slice)	1.40
Whole wheat (1 slice)	3.17
White (1 slice)	0.68
Cereals	
Bran Chex (2/3 cup)	5
Bran flakes (2/3 cup)	5
Cheerios (1 1/4 cup)	2
Corn flakes (1 cup)	1
Grapenuts (1 1/4 cup)	2
Raisin Bran (1/2 cup)	4
Rice Krispies (1 cup)	Trace
Shredded Wheat (1 biscuit)	3
Life (2/3 cup)	3
Vegetables	
Lima beans (1 cup)	9.2
Green beans (1 cup)	3.1
Cauliflower (1/2 cup)	1.3
Corn, canned (1/2 cup)	6.3
Garbanzo beans (1 cup)	8.6
Greens (1 cup)	2.9
Navy beans (1 cup)	16.5
Baked potato, with skin	4.4
Tomato	2.2
Carrot	2.0

- It helps prevent constipation because insoluble fiber attracts water into the digestive tract, thus softening the stool. Softer stools reduce the pressure in the lower intestine, creating less likelihood that rectal veins will swell and cause hemorrhoids.
- It stimulates muscle tone in the intestinal wall, which helps to prevent *diverticulosis*, a condition that occurs when the intestine bulges out into

pockets, possibly leading to *diverticulitis,* a condition in which the pockets become infected and sometimes rupture.
- It may reduce the risk of colon cancer. A shorter transit time reduces the exposure of the intestines to cancer-causing agents in the food. Insoluble fiber also stimulates the secretion of mucus in the colon. Mucus coats the colon wall and may provide a barrier that keeps cancer-causing agents from reaching the colon's cells.

The best source of insoluble fiber is wheat bran. Other good sources are whole grains, dried beans and peas, and most fruits and vegetables, especially those eaten with the skin.

If you are not accustomed to eating fiber-rich foods, gradually add them to your diet over four to six weeks, following these suggestions:[30]

- Eat whole-wheat bread rather than white bread.
- Look for whole grains, such as whole wheat, on food labels. Whole grains contain the entire seed of a plant, including the bran, germ, and endosperm. Foods that are "made with whole wheat flour" are mostly refined. Wheat flour and unbleached wheat flour are not whole grain.
- Add 2 to 3 tablespoons of 100 percent bran to low-fiber foods, such as breakfast cereal, pudding, and applesauce.
- Substitute brown rice, millet, and bulgur wheat for white rice and potatoes.
- Snack on popcorn instead of potato chips.
- Eat whole fruit instead of drinking juice.
- Use raspberries as a topping for ice cream and yogurt.
- Snack on an unpeeled apple or pear.
- Choose bran flakes over cornflakes.
- Top your salads and casseroles with a whole-grain cereal, such as shredded wheat.
- Eat the skin on your potato.
- Include beans in soups and vegetable salads.
- Eat oats, legumes, and fruits for insoluble fiber.

How much fiber?

Most Americans consume 16 grams of fiber per day.[4] The daily recommendation is 25 grams for a 2000-calorie diet and 30 grams for a 3000-calorie diet. Most Americans have trouble meeting this recommendation because of their heavy intake of meat products. Meat provides little or no fiber; consequently, only vegetarians are likely to get enough fiber. Eating naturally high-fiber foods, such as whole grains, fruits, vegetables, and beans, is a good way to increase fiber intake. Starting or ending the day with a high-fiber cereal is another convenient way to increase your consumption not only of fiber but also of many vitamins and minerals. Check the food labels which identify the amount of fiber per serving.

As with most other nutrients, fiber can be consumed in excess. Indiscriminate consumption of fiber may interfere with the body's ability to absorb other essential nutrients. A person who eats bulky foods but has only a small capacity may not be able to take in enough food energy or nutrients. A high intake of dietary fiber, such as 60 grams per day, also requires a high intake of water.[4]

Putting Nutrition to Work

Nutrition is a complex science and involves the study of thousands of nutrients and a countless number of possible interactions, all of which take place at the cellular level. Many of the results of nutritional practices, good or bad, take years or even decades to become apparent. Fortunately, it isn't necessary to be a biochemist to understand and follow nutritional practices that promote health and prevent the early onset of many health problems. The benchmark for developing a plan for good nutrition is the *Dietary Guidelines for Americans.* These guidelines, which were first published in 1980, are evaluated and revised every five years. The fourth and most recent version of these dietary guidelines[1] is listed here:

- Eat a variety of foods.
- Balance the food you eat with physical activity—maintain or improve your weight.
- Choose a diet with plenty of grain products, vegetables, and fruits.
- Choose a diet low in fat, saturated fat, and cholesterol.
- Choose a diet moderate in sugars.
- Choose a diet moderate in salt and sodium.
- If you drink alcoholic beverages, do so in moderation.

Eat a Variety of Foods

Variety is the first dietary guideline because it is the cornerstone of a healthy diet. Foods contain combinations of nutrients and other healthful substances, and no single food or food group can supply all of the RDAs of essential nutrients. For example, broccoli is loaded with vitamin C but contains no vitamin B_{12}; flounder provides vitamin B_{12} but no vitamin C. You should consume a variety of foods within each food group. Six flavors of gourmet ice cream are not what the experts have in mind when they recommend eating many different types of foods. It would be better to consume some low-fat milk, yogurt, cheese, and other dairy products over the course of several days than to focus on one dairy food. You can even have an occasional serving of gourmet ice cream. A diet that is

Chapter 6 Forming a Plan for Good Nutrition **175**

Wellness on the Web Behavior Change Activities

Put "Pyramid Power" to Work for You

When you want to plan a nutritionally balanced diet, your best bet is to eat a variety of foods according to the federal government's Food Guide Pyramid. You can use the Pyramid to determine how many servings from each food group to include in your diet; it's also a great way to ensure that you consume the recommended dietary allowances (RDAs) of essential nutrients each day. To use an interactive Food Guide Pyramid, go to www.nal.usda.gov:8001/py/pmap.htm. Place your mouse on any portion of the Pyramid and click to obtain a list of foods and the appropriate portions for each food group.

Food Facts—or Fiction?

Can you lose weight on a grapefruit diet? Does gelatin make your nails hard? Are some vegetables and fruits negative-calorie foods? Nutrition has captured the interest of Americans more than perhaps any other aspect of fitness and wellness. Whether it's HDLs or LDLs, fat or fiber, phytochemicals or vitamins, nutritional issues make headlines in both scientific journals and popular magazines, and everyone seems to be an expert. Go to Thrive's on-line food quiz at www.thriveonline.com/eats/dyngames/gen/eats.mythquiz.html to take a Food Fact or Fiction Quiz. Decide whether each statement is true or false, then press the "vote!" button to see how you scored. How well did you do?

Match Wits with the Sphinx

Go ahead—take the Food Guide challenge! Go to Thrive's on-line "Match Wits with the Sphinx" at www.thriveonline.com/eats/pyramid/index.html to challenge yourself on the interactive Food Guide Pyramid. Tour its fabulous pyramids and discover the answers to the world's oldest nutrition questions. You'll view the Food Guide Pyramid and its many layers for a rich variety of foods. You'll be challenged to unlock the secret of a healthy diet by clicking on the numbered layers. You'll also find out what constitutes a serving size for easy weight management and optimum health. What's more, a number of challenging questions are posed at each level to test your comprehension of important nutritional principles. Good luck on your discovery tour!

---

diverse is more likely to provide an adequate distribution of essential nutrients. It also helps to minimize exposure to toxins, both natural and synthetic, that may be present in one type of food.

Food guide pyramid

The best way to ensure variety in your diet is to use the Food Guide Pyramid (figure 6-3) as the foundation for food selection (see Real World Wellness: How Varied Is Your Diet?). The **Food Guide Pyramid** (**FGP**) portrays dietary guidelines in picture form and provides a structure for dietary planning by recommending the number of servings for each food group. The largest area of the pyramid is the base, which calls for six to eleven servings of grain products. Foods from this group make up about 40 percent of the daily diet. The next largest areas of the FGP are the fruit and vegetable groups. Together, grain products, fruits, and vegetables make up nearly three-fourths of the recommended diet. The top of the pyramid allows for a smaller number of servings from meat or meat substitutes and dairy products. About 25 percent of the servings in your daily diet should come from foods in these groups. No recommendations are given for the number of servings of fats, oils, and sweets. The advice is to consume these sparingly.

As helpful as the FGP is for meal planning, it has received some criticism. One important omission is any reference to fluid intake. This is a serious oversight because most Americans do not get enough water each day (see Real World Wellness: How Can You Tell If You're Getting Enough Water?). The American Medical Association (AMA) believes strongly that inadequate or inappropriate fluid intake is a significant contributor to poor health.[32] Another criticism is of its lack of guidance for people who don't eat a typical American diet. For that reason, other food pyramids have been developed that meet the needs of alternative diets, such as those of vegetarians. One such version is presented later in this chapter (see p. 180).

The FGP identifies a range of servings for the food groups. The number of servings that fits your needs depends on your required number of calories. Your calorie requirements depend on many factors, including age, gender, height, weight, activity level, health status, and pregnancy (see Wellness Across the Generations: The Nutrient Gap). Three calorie levels along with the corresponding recommended number of servings are presented in table 6-8.

Serving size

What counts as a serving depends on the food and how it is prepared. Sorting through serving sizes can be confusing. One ounce of a ready-to-eat cereal, for example,

Fats, oils, and sweets
Use sparingly.

KEY
☐ Fat (naturally occurring and added) ▽ Sugars (added)
These symbols show fats, oils, and added sugars in foods.

Milk, yogurt, and cheese
2–3 servings

Meat, poultry, fish, dry beans, eggs, and nuts
2–3 servings

Vegetables
3–5 servings

Fruits
2–4 servings

Bread, cereal, rice, and pasta
6–11 servings

Figure 6-3 Food Guide Pyramid
Children, teenagers, and adults under 25 years of age should choose three servings from the milk, yogurt, and cheese group.

Real-World Wellness

How Varied Is Your Diet?

I seem to choose the same foods every week in the cafeteria and to prepare only a limited number of dishes for dinner. Does my diet have enough variety?

Dietary Guidelines for Americans emphasizes variety, but just what is variety? Ten foods a day? Twenty? According to researchers at Tufts University,[33] people who average seventy-one to eighty-three foods over the course of fifteen days have more nutritious diets than those who choose fewer than fifty-eight items. Fortunately, you don't have to track your food selections for fifteen days to assess variety. Three days will suffice. Circle the following foods that you eat during the next three days. If you can circle twenty-eight, you are probably doing well. If your number is closer to fourteen, improving the variety of your food selections should become a goal.

- cheese
- ice cream/milk-based desserts
- milk
- yogurt
- other dairy
- beans and legumes
- beef
- eggs
- fish
- lamb, veal, game
- liver/organ meats
- nuts and seeds
- pork
- poultry
- processed meats
- green leafy vegetables
- orange and yellow vegetables
- potatoes and other root crops
- tomatoes and tomato products
- other vegetables
- berries
- citrus fruits
- fruit juices
- melons
- other fruit
- cold breakfast cereals
- hot breakfast cereals
- pasta
- rice
- white bread
- whole-wheat bread
- other grains
- candy
- margarine, butter, and oils
- salty snacks
- soft drinks
- sweet baked goods and desserts

Wellness Across the Generations
The Nutrient Gap

It has been estimated that as many as 25 percent of Americans 60 and older are malnourished. They do not suffer from nutritional diseases like scurvy or pellagra; rather, they consume insufficient amounts of key nutrients that have a direct effect on health and body function. Older adults usually expend less energy to meet the demands of their lifestyle than do their younger peers and therefore require fewer calories. This presents a dilemma because as their need for energy decreases, their need for nutrients increases or stays the same. Unfortunately, a decrease in caloric intake is usually associated with a decrease in key nutrients. There is a gap between what older adults need and what they get from food, as shown in the following chart:

Nutrient	What They Need (Age 50+)	How They're Doing	Why Adults Age 50+ Need It
Calcium	1200 mg	The average intake is 400–600 mg	The capacity to absorb calcium declines with age
Folate	400 µg	Only one-fourth of older adults get 400 µg	Reducing homocysteine levels becomes more important as heart disease risks increase
Riboflavin	1.1 mg, women 1.3 mg, men	Only one-third get enough	The body's need is the same throughout adulthood
Vitamin B_6	1.5 mg, women 1.7 mg, men	50–90% don't get enough	The body's metabolism changes with age
Vitamin B_{12}	2.4 µg	20% of adults over 60 and 40% over 80 are deficient	Increased difficulty in absorbing vitamin B_{12} comes with age
Vitamin D	_00 IU, ages 51–70; 600 IU, 71+	The average intake is 100–125 IU	Decreased ability of skin to synthesize vitamin D from sunlight comes with age
Protein	See Wellness Across the Generations: Older Adults May Need More Protein		

counts as a serving. This is equivalent to 1/2 cup of cooked cereal. One slice of bread is equivalent to one-half of a bagel. The fruit group is more confusing. One whole piece of fruit is the same as 1/2 cup of chopped fruit or 3/4 cup of fruit juice. The only sure way to determine serving size is to check food package labels. You can also refer to Just the Facts: What Counts as a Serving?

Moderation

Moderation is another important characteristic of the healthy diet. There is a place in the diet for almost any food if it is consumed prudently—the FGP doesn't label food "good" or "bad." Some foods do have a higher **nutrient density** than others, meaning they yield a higher ratio of nutrients to calories, but all foods contribute to nutrition (see Just the Facts: Nutrient Density). Moderation means exercising good judgment regarding quantity and frequency. It doesn't mean avoidance. The idea that a particular food is good or bad can be destructive to anyone trying to eat more healthfully. For example, a person with rigid attitudes who thinks that cheesecake is "bad" and then indulges in eating it might think, "I am bad, I have no willpower, and I am a weak person." The behavioral result might be a cheesecake binge, since the forbidden nature of the food makes it harder to resist. A more positive approach is to understand that cheesecake is not "bad" and that eating a slice does not make the eater a bad person.

Another reason for moderation is that even foods that are nutritionally dense can be consumed in excess. The interaction of the various substances in food can cause one nutrient to overpower or nullify the effects and benefits of another. The body's processes may be compromised or the nutrients in foods may interfere

Table 6-8 Nutrition Plan for Three Calorie Levels

	Calorie Level*		
	1600	2200	2800
Grain group servings	6	9	11
Vegetable group servings	3	4	5
Fruit group servings	2	3	4
Milk group servings†	2–3	2–3	2–3
Meat group servings‡	5	6	7
Total fat (g)	53	73	93
Percent fat calories	30	30	30
Total added sugars (tsp)§	6	12	18

*1600 calories is appropriate for many sedentary women and some older adults; 2200 calories is appropriate for most children, teenage girls, active women, and sedentary men (women who are pregnant or breast-feeding may need more). For teenage boys, many active men, and some very active women 2800 calories is appropriate.

†Women who are pregnant or breast-feeding, teenagers, and young adults to age 24 need 3 servings.

‡Meat group amounts are in total ounces.

§from candy, desserts, soft drinks, and other sweets

Just the Facts

What Counts as a Serving?

One way to estimate serving size when food labels aren't available is to use the parts of your hand. Here is how it's done:

- 1 thumb = 1 ounce of cheese
- 1 thumb tip = 1 teaspoon of foods such as mayonnaise, peanut butter, and sugar
- 3 thumb tips = 1 tablespoon
- 1 fist = 1 cup of pasta, rice, or vegetables
- 1 or 2 handfuls = 1 ounce of a snack food (1 handful of small foods, such as nuts, or 2 handfuls of larger foods, such as chips and pretzels)
- 1 palm (minus the fingers) = 3 ounces of meat, fish, or poultry

---

with the desired effects of medicines. Here are several examples of the negative effects of excessive consumption of various nutrients:

- Too much protein from animal sources may cause the body to lose extra calcium.[35]
- Botanicals such as garlic, ginger, and ginseng, when combined with vitamin E, fish oils, or blood thinning medicines (e.g., aspirin, Coumadin), may inhibit the blood-clotting mechanism of the body and cause internal bleeding.[36]
- Megadoses of vitamin A can cause birth defects.
- Megadoses of vitamin C can damage the cell's DNA, which can lead to cancer or heart problems. That is, large doses can negate vitamin C's normal antioxidant effect.[37] Large doses (2000 mg) can also cause diarrhea, nausea, abdominal cramps, and headache.[38]
- Excessive intake of vitamin D causes too much calcium to move from the bones to the blood and then to the urine through which it is excreted from the body.[39]
- High intake of folate may mask the symptoms of pernicious anemia, a condition associated with a vitamin B_{12} deficiency.
- Excess niacin may aggravate glucose intolerance associated with non–insulin-dependent diabetes.
- Foods high in vitamin K, such as broccoli, spinach, and turnip greens, may neutralize the effectiveness of blood-thinning medicines.
- Foods high in tyramine, such as cheese and sausage, can cause a sudden rise in blood pressure in people taking some antidepressant medicines.[40]

These examples are not meant to discourage your consumption of a particular food. Each food offers a unique contribution to health. Vitamin D, for instance, is required for calcium metabolism; however, too much of it may result in a depletion of calcium. Moderation is an important concept that applies to essential nutrients just as it applies to nutrients with bad reputations. Choosing foods from the FGP, with an emphasis on variety and moderation, not only satisfies the body's need for essential nutrients but also helps prevent problems associated with dietary excess.

Balance Food Intake with Physical Activity—Maintain or Improve Your Weight

The achievement and maintenance of a desirable body weight and composition are complex issues and are treated separately in this text. For a complete discussion of the principles of balancing food intake with physical activity for maintaining desirable body composition, refer to Chapters 7 and 8.

Just the Facts

Nutrient Density

A key strategy for eating well is to select foods that offer significant amounts of nutrients but small numbers of calories. If a particular food has a high ratio of nutrients to calories, it is a nutritionally dense food. You can determine the nutrient density of food by adding the percentages of the RDA for the essential nutrients and dividing by the number of calories per serving (see the following example). The higher the score, the higher the nutrient density. The concept of nutrient density can help the health-conscious and weight-conscious person make informed choices.

Calculating the Nutrient Density of Pizza (Cheese)

Calories	354
RDA %	
Protein	28%
Vitamin A	19%
Vitamin C	20%
Thiamin	25%
Riboflavin	29%
Niacin	19%
Calcium	33%
Iron	15%
Total	**188**

Nutrient density = 53% (188 ÷ 354 × 100)

Choose a Diet with Plenty of Grain Products, Vegetables, and Fruits

Grain products (bread, cereal, rice, and pasta) are emphasized in the FGP because they are rich in vitamins, minerals, complex carbohydrates, antioxidants, phytochemicals, and fiber. Most Americans of all ages eat fewer than the recommended number of servings from these three food sources.[1]

Clearly, the FGP emphasizes plant foods over animal products. This represents a dramatic change from the way many Americans eat. For example, in planning meals Americans often think first of the entrée, which is typically a meat dish. This is usually true whether we're eating at home or dining out. The FGP challenges us to reverse this approach by thinking of plant products first.

The vegetarian alternative

The importance of a plant-based approach to eating is evidenced by the fact that *Dietary Guidelines for Americans* now officially recognizes a vegetarian diet as a healthful and acceptable way of meeting all nutritional needs.[41] Some vegetarians avoid all animal products, including dairy products, poultry, eggs, and fish. Others include eggs and milk products but exclude fish, poultry, and red meat. There are many variations of vegetarian diet. The more common types are presented in table 6-9.

With the exception of vegans, most types of vegetarians have little trouble getting all of the essential nutrients, including protein. Milk products, eggs, fish, and poultry are sources of complete, high-quality protein. *Vegans,* who eat all-plant diets, need to be discriminating in their food selections because most plants are sources of incomplete protein. One notable exception, as mentioned earlier, is soy protein. Vegans who don't consume soy products need to combine complementary foods, such as grains and legumes, to obtain all of the essential amino acids.

The nutritional problem most likely to occur in a strict vegetarian diet is a deficiency in vitamin B_{12}, which occurs naturally only in animal products. Vegans can get vitamin B_{12} by taking a supplement or consuming food that has been fortified with B_{12}. Vitamin D is another potential problem to the vegan if he or she has limited exposure to the sun. Milk products, which are fortified with vitamin D, are about the only dietary source of vitamin D. However, the body can produce adequate amounts of this vitamin if the skin receives sufficient exposure to sunlight. During periods of limited sunlight exposure, vegans may need to take vitamin D supplements. Other essential nutrients richly supplied by animal products and thus of concern to vegans, such as riboflavin, iron, zinc, and calcium, can be easily derived from a variety of plant sources.

Figure 6-4, a food pyramid for ovolactovegetarians, presents a helpful plan for people trying to avoid meats. The recommended number of servings of grains, fruits, vegetables, and milk products is identical to the recommended amounts in the Food Guide Pyramid. The major difference is the exclusion of meat in favor of legumes, nuts, seeds, and eggs. Lactovegetarians can omit eggs from this pyramid.

Here are some practical tips for adding fruits, vegetables, and grains to the diet that should be helpful for people opting for a meatless meal, choosing to eat vegetarian for a day, or favoring vegetarianism as a lifestyle:

- Start off the day with fruit juice.
- Add fruit to a salad.
- Serve fruit for dessert.

Table 6-9 Types of Vegetarians

Type	What Is Excluded from Diet	What Is Included in Diet
Vegans	All animal products	Fruits, vegetables, grains, legumes, nuts, and seeds
Lactovegetarians	Eggs, fish, poultry, and meat	Milk products and fruits, vegetables, grains, legumes, nuts, and seeds
Ovolactovegetarians	Fish, poultry, and meat	Eggs (*ova*), milk products (*lacto*), plus fruits, vegetables, grains, legumes, nuts, and seeds
Pescovegetarians	Poultry and meat	Fish (*pesco*), eggs, milk products, fruits, vegetables, grains, legumes, nuts, and seeds
Pollovegetarians	Red meat	Poultry (*pollo*), fish, eggs, milk products, fruits, vegetables, grains, legumes, nuts, and seeds

Fats, oils, and sweets
Use sparingly.

These symbols show fats, oils, and added sugars in foods:
● Fat (naturally occurring and added)
▼ Sugars (added)

Milk, yogurt, and cheese
2–3 servings

Eggs,* legumes, nuts, and seeds
1–2 servings

Vegetables†
3–5 servings

Fruits
2–4 servings

Bread, cereal, rice, and pasta‡
6–11 servings

* Lactovegetarians can omit eggs from this pyramid.
† Include one dark green or leafy variety daily.
‡ One serving of a vitamin- and mineral-enriched cereal is recommended.
¶ Contains about 75 g of protein and 1650 calories.
‖ Base serving sizes on those listed for the Food Guide Pyramid.

Figure 6-4 Food Pyramid for Ovolactovegetarians¶

- Have a smoothie (blend fruit juice, ice, and a banana).
- Add fruit to cereal.
- Eat cereal as a snack.
- Eat vegetable snacks.
- Aim for a colorful plate, with dark-green, yellow, and red vegetables.
- Increase the number of vegetables in a salad by adding tomatoes, carrots, cucumbers, peppers, spinach, or broccoli.
- Eat a vegetable pizza.
- Make a soup with leftover vegetables.
- Eat an all-vegetable meal.
- Mix legumes with a salad.
- Try a new fruit or vegetable.
- Top fat-free frozen yogurt with low-fat granola and berries.
- Top salad with whole-wheat cereal.

A properly selected vegetarian diet has many health benefits (see Just the Facts: Health Benefits of a Vegetarian Diet). People who have health conditions associated with diets high in fat and saturated fat and low in folate, carotenoids, phytochemicals, and antioxidants stand to benefit from a plant-based diet.

Another strategy for increasing your consumption of grain products, vegetables, and fruits is to cultivate a taste for ethnic food. The typical diets of many other countries favor grains, fruits, and vegetables and place less emphasis on animal fats. However, watch out for the Americanization of ethnic foods. For example, the traditional Italian pasta dish comes with a tomato-based sauce containing small amounts of meat or meatballs on the side, served with crusty Italian bread or pizza with an extra-thick crust and a mere sprinkle of tomato sauce, herbs, and cheese. Americanized, the same dish comes with less pasta, more creamy sauces, and more meat, served with buttery garlic toast or pizza with a thin crust, pepperoni, sausage, olives, and extra cheese. For additional comparisons, see Just the Facts: Do You Eat Real Ethnic Food?

A diet that emphasizes the first two of the seven *Dietary Guidelines for Americans* will go a long way in helping to meet the remaining guidelines. A diverse diet with plenty of grains, fruits, and vegetables is usually low in fat, saturated fat, and cholesterol and moderate in sodium and sugars, depending on how the food is prepared and what is added to it at the table.

Choose a Diet Low in Fat, Saturated Fat, and Cholesterol

Some dietary fat is needed for good health. Fats supply energy and essential fatty acids and promote absorption of the fat-soluble vitamins. Whether from plant or animal sources, fat contains more than twice the num-

Just the Facts
Health Benefits of a Vegetarian Diet

As a group, vegetarians have lower morbidity and mortality rates from several chronic degenerative diseases than do nonvegetarians.[42] Typically, vegetarian diets are lower in fat and saturated fat and have higher concentrations of nutrients (vitamins, minerals, and phytochemicals) associated with health benefits. Here are some of the benefits of a vegetarian diet over a nonvegetarian diet:

- Lower cholesterol level
- Lower level of low-density lipoproteins
- Lower incidence of hypertension
- Fewer complications and lower mortality from type II diabetes mellitus
- Reduced incidence of lung, colorectal, and breast cancer
- Improved kidney function
- Reduction of coronary artery disease

ber of calories as its carbohydrate or protein equivalents. Fats are represented in the apex of the FGP; *Dietary Guidelines for Americans* calls for no servings of fat because the body's need for essential fatty acids is easily satisfied by foods in the other food groups. Perhaps one of the greatest shortcomings of the American diet is the abundance of fat. Compounding this problem is the reality that fat is usually consumed at the expense of fruits, vegetables, and grains. For many people, reducing both the amount and type of dietary fat eaten is a formidable challenge. Table 6-3 presents a quick reference of maximum fat intake for selected caloric intakes. You can estimate your personal maximum fat intake by completing Assessment Activity 6-2. You can learn how fatty your eating habits are by completing Assessment Activity 6-5.

Tips for reducing dietary fat

Here are some suggestions for reducing total dietary fat consumption, lowering saturated fat intake, and replacing saturated fats with unsaturated fats:

- Assess your fat intake. Complete the assessments at the end of this chapter along with those in *HealthQuest* to determine your fat intake. Compare your fat intake with the recommendations in table 6-3.

Just the Facts

Do You Eat Real Ethnic Food?

The typical diets of many other countries tend to contain more high-carbohydrate foods and fewer foods high in animal fats than does the common American diet. However, when ethnic foods are prepared in the United States, especially in restaurants, they are often "Americanized" by inclusion of larger portions of meat and cheese and addition of sauces. What follows are descriptions of some traditional, high-carbohydrate ethnic foods and their higher-fat Americanized versions. Which versions of these ethnic foods do you tend to eat?

Chinese
- Traditional: large bowl of steamed rice with small amounts of stir-fried vegetables, meats, and sauces as condiments
- Americanized: several stir-fried or batter-fried entrees in sauces, with a small bowl of fried rice on the side

Japanese
- Traditional: large bowl of steamed rice with broth-based soups containing rice noodles, vegetables, and small amounts of meat
- Americanized: tempura (batter-fried vegetables and shrimp), teriyaki chicken, oriental chicken salad with oil-based dressing

Italian
- Traditional: large mound of pasta with tomato-based sauce containing small amounts of meat or meatballs on the side, served with crusty Italian bread or pizza with an extra-thick crust and mere sprinkle of tomato sauce, herbs, and cheese
- Americanized: less pasta, more creamy sauces, and more meat, served with buttery garlic toast or pizza with a thin crust, pepperoni, sausage, olives, and extra cheese

Mexican
- Traditional: mostly rice, beans, warmed tortillas, and lots of hot salsa and chiles
- Americanized: crispy fried tortillas, extra ground beef, added cheese, sour cream, and guacamole (avocado dip)

German
- Traditional: large portions of potatoes, rye and whole-grain breads, stew with dumplings, and sauerkraut
- Americanized: fewer potatoes, less bread, more sausage and cheese

Middle Eastern
- Traditional: pita bread (round bread), pilaf (rice dish), hummus (chickpea dip), shaved slices of seasoned meat, diced vegetables, and yogurt-based sauces, all seasoned with garlic
- Americanized: meat kebabs, salads drenched in olive oil, less bread and pilaf

---

- Read labels and become familiar with the fat content of food. Try to identify foods that should be consumed in limited amounts; also identify foods that are low in fat (see table 6-2).
- Become familiar with sources of saturated, monounsaturated, and polyunsaturated fats (see figure 6-2).
- Check for the presence of transfatty acids by reading the fine print on food labels. Look for the words *hydrogenated* or *partially hydrogenated* to identify foods that should be consumed in limited amounts.
- Limit meat, seafood, and poultry to no more than 5 to 7 ounces per day.
- Eat chicken or turkey (without the skin) or fish instead of red meat in most meals.
- Substitute one or two meals of fish per week for red meats. Choose fish high in omega-3 fatty acids and low in saturated fat, such as Atlantic cod, haddock, salmon, shrimp, scallops, sardines, tuna, red snapper, and trout.
- Choose lean cuts of meat, trim all the visible fat, and throw away the fat that cooks out of the meat.
- Substitute meatless or low-meat main dishes for regular entrees.
- Substitute legumes for meat one or two times per week.
- Eat a vegetarian diet at least one day a week.
- Use no more than 5 to 8 teaspoons of fats and oils per day for cooking, baking, and preparing salads.
- Choose foods that contain fewer than 3 grams of fat per 100-calorie serving.
- Choose foods that contain less than 1 gram of saturated fat per 100-calorie serving.
- Use low-fat dairy products (whole milk has more than eight times the fat calories as skim milk).

Even if your weight is healthy, too many high-fat take-out dinners may mean too few fruits and vegetables.

- Substitute pureed fruit, such as applesauce, when cooking from a recipe that calls for cooking oil (equal substitution).
- Use soft margarine in place of hard margarine.
- Use liquid or spray margarine when possible.
- Serve dressings and condiments (for salads, potatoes, etc.) on the side. Try to cut these servings in half.
- Avoid fried foods. Substitute another cooking method (baking, grilling, broiling, or roasting) for frying.
- Eat more vegetables and fruits.
- Eat low-fat foods that have a high satiety value, such as whole grains and high-fiber foods.
- Substitute olive oil or canola oil for margarine, butter, or lard.
- Try to add diversity to your diet. Cultivate a taste for low-fat ethnic foods.
- Avoid a "forbidden fruit" approach to food selection. Any food can be enjoyed in moderation. If you consume an unusually high-fat food or meal, try to compensate with more prudent choices during the week.

Choose a Diet Moderate in Sugars

Sugars are carbohydrates. During digestion, all carbohydrates except fiber break down into sugars. Americans eat sugars in many forms, and most people enjoy the taste of sugars. Some sugars are used as natural preservatives, thickeners, and baking aids in foods. Most of the simple sugar eaten by Americans has been added to foods and beverages during processing and manufacturing. A food is likely to be high in sugars if one of the following terms is listed first or second in the ingredients list on a food label: brown sugar, corn sweetener, corn syrup, fructose, fruit juice concentrate, glucose (dextrose), high-fructose corn syrup, honey, invert sugar, lactose, maltose, molasses, raw sugar, sucrose (table sugar), or syrup. Many foods contain a combination of sugars.

Nutritionists recommend that sugar consumption be limited to 10 to 15 percent of total calories. On average, Americans get 18 percent of their calories from sugar. Intake of sugar by children may exceed 50 percent of total calories.[4]

The major health problem associated with a high sugar intake is dental caries (cavities). The main offenders are foods that are sweet and gummy. They stick to the teeth and supply bacteria with a steady source of carbohydrate from which to make acids that can dissolve tooth enamel. Foods that promote caries are termed *cariogenic*.

Contrary to popular belief, there is little or no evidence that high sugar intake causes hyperactivity in children, heart disease, diabetes, or obesity. If that were the case, most Americans would have all of these conditions. The major nutritional problem of a high-sugar diet occurs when sugar is substituted for more nutritionally dense foods. When this happens, the result may be insufficient vitamin and mineral intake.

Carbonated soft drinks are a major contributor to high-sugar diets. How much soda do you drink?

Choose a Diet Moderate in Salt and Sodium

Salt contains about 40 percent sodium by weight and is widely used in the preservation, processing, and preparation of foods. Sodium is an essential mineral, but it is one that Americans consume in excess. Average daily consumption of sodium is 4000 milligrams, which is eight times the minimum requirement of 500 milligrams (one-tenth of a teaspoon) and almost double the 2400 milligrams considered adequate.[43] The main health problems associated with consumption of too much sodium are hypertension, osteoporosis, and stomach cancer.[45] Of the three, hypertension, discussed in Chapter 2, is the most common problem. Sodium contributes to the development of osteoporosis because it pulls calcium from bones and causes the kidneys to excrete calcium. Sodium contributes to stomach cancer because it irritates the stomach lining, causing cells to replicate themselves, increasing the odds of cancer-cell initiation.

The majority of salt consumed is in the form of hidden salt added during the processing of food. Less than one third comes from the salt shaker.[44] Just how much salt is in a processed food can be determined by reading the package label.

Taste buds cannot always judge salt content. Some foods that taste salty may be lower in salt content than foods that do not. For example, peanuts taste salty because the salt is on the surface where the taste buds immediately detect it. However, cheese contains more salt than peanuts or potato chips, and chocolate pudding contains even more salt. To cut down on salt consumption, you should do the following:

- Avoid adding salt before tasting food.
- Add little or no salt to food at the table.
- Season food with sodium-free spices, such as pepper, allspice, onion powder, garlic, mustard powder, sage, thyme, and paprika.
- Avoid smoked meats and fish.
- Cut down on canned and instant soups.
- Read labels for sodium content, especially on frozen dinners or pizza, processed meat, processed cheese, canned or dried soup, and salad dressing. When shopping for canned and processed foods, select foods with no more than 200 mg of sodium per 100 calories.
- Eat plenty of fruits and vegetables high in potassium, calcium, and magnesium. These minerals may help keep blood pressure down.

Drink Alcoholic Beverages in Moderation

Dietary Guidelines for Americans recommends that alcoholic beverages be limited to one drink per day for women and two drinks per day for men.[5] (A drink is defined as 12 ounces of beer, 5 ounces of wine, or 1.5 ounces of 80-proof spirits.) The allowance for women is smaller because women, on average, are smaller than men, they have less muscle and, therefore, less water than men (so alcohol does not get diluted as well in their bodies), and they have less of an enzyme that breaks down alcohol before it reaches the bloodstream. A maximal level of alcohol consumption has not been set for women during pregnancy, so pregnant women and women who have a high chance of becoming pregnant should not use alcohol.

From a health perspective, alcohol has both advantages and serious risks. On the one hand, it is associated with drunk-driving injuries and deaths, cirrhosis of the liver, and a host of social ills caused by alcoholism. On the other hand, when consumed in moderate amounts as recommended by the *Dietary Guidelines*, it offers protection from heart disease and stroke in some people, even more so than does abstinence. Population studies show a 30 percent reduction in coronary risk among moderate drinkers, compared with abstainers. The data are similar in men and women and in various ethnic groups.[45]

Moderate consumption of alcohol is thought to be especially beneficial for people who are at risk for cardiovascular disease and stroke. Several theories have been advanced to explain this benefit: Alcohol may improve blood levels of high-density lipoproteins, and it may serve as a blood thinner by inhibiting the blood-clotting mechanism often associated with atherosclerosis. Contrary to popular belief, wine does not appear to offer any advantage over other forms of alcohol.

Regardless of alcohol's potential health benefits, experts don't recommend alcohol consumption for everyone. Some people have medical, religious, and personal reasons for abstaining. People with uncontrolled hypertension, liver disease, pancreatitis, or strong family histories of addiction should avoid alcohol. The same is true for women during pregnancy. Also, some medicines may have a potentiating effect when taken with alcohol. For women there is also some concern about the link between moderate consumption of alcohol and breast cancer. It is important to remember that the health benefits associated with alcohol come from a moderate level of consumption. Alcohol consumption in excess of that recommended in *Dietary Guidelines* can cause a variety of health problems that outweigh the potential benefits. As is the case with many health issues, moderation serves as the guiding principle for alcohol consumption.

Other Nutrition Issues of Concern

Nutrition and Pregnancy

Good nutrition is crucial to a successful pregnancy, and a healthy pregnancy starts before conception. Alcohol consumption, smoking, an inadequate diet, dietary excesses of some nutrients, drug abuse, and the interactions of a host of medicines are some of the factors that may threaten a pregnancy even before conception is known or confirmed. Poor health habits throughout pregnancy, especially during the first three months, can harm the mother and developing baby. Although genetic and environmental influences introduce some risk factors beyond the mother's control, there is a considerable amount of medical advice about weight gain and the nutritional needs unique to pregnant women.

Weight gain

Adequate weight gain for a mother is one of the best predictors of pregnancy outcome. A weight gain of 25 to 35 pounds yields optimal health for both mother and fetus if pregnancy lasts at least thirty-eight weeks. To accommodate the extra demands for energy, the expectant mother needs to increase her caloric intake by about 300 calories daily, particularly after the third month of pregnancy.[4] Inadequate weight gain can lead to many problems. It is important to monitor weight throughout the pregnancy. Large fluctuations in the recommended weight-gain pattern should be brought to the attention of the health care provider.

Nutrient needs

The RDAs for many nutrients increase during pregnancy:[4]

- The protein RDA increases by 10 to 15 grams daily.
- Extra vitamin D is needed to absorb and distribute extra calcium for developing fetal bones. Approximately 20 to 30 minutes of sun exposure several times a week, a quart of vitamin D–fortified milk, or a vitamin D supplement that contains 5 µg (200 IU) should suffice.
- Because of its role in DNA synthesis, folate is a crucial nutrient during pregnancy. The RDA for folate during pregnancy increases to 600 µg per day. Folate deficiencies have been linked to some neural tube birth defects, such as spina bifida. The increased need for folate can be achieved through the diet or a prenatal vitamin and mineral supplement.
- Iron intake should double during the final six months of pregnancy to achieve the RDA of 30 milligrams per day. The extra iron is needed to synthesize the additional hemoglobin required during pregnancy and to provide iron for the developing fetus. Women often need an iron supplement if their typical iron intake is marginal. Iron deficiencies during pregnancy may threaten the health of both the baby and the mother.
- Calcium is needed during pregnancy for skeletal and tooth development of the fetus, especially during the last three months, when growth of these tissues is most prolific. The RDA for calcium is 1300 mg. A prenatal supplement usually contains 200 mg of calcium.
- The zinc RDA increases 25 percent (to 15 milligrams) during pregnancy to satisfy the requirements for growth and development of the fetus. Foods rich in protein also supply zinc. Zinc deficiencies increase the chance of a low–birth-weight baby.
- Prenatal supplements may contribute to a successful pregnancy for some women and, with the possible exception of vitamin A, provide benefits that outweigh potential risks. Because of its role in cell differentiation, megadoses of vitamin A from both supplements and dietary sources are associated with birth defects, particularly when the vitamin A is consumed during the first three months of pregnancy. It is recommended that women set their limit of vitamin A according to the RDAs.

Slight modifications of the recommended servings in the Food Guide Pyramid should satisfy women's unique nutritional needs during pregnancy. The major differences involve adding a serving of food from two food groups: the milk group and the meat group. Women who practice either ovolactovegetarianism or lactovegetarianism generally do not have difficulty meeting their nutritional needs during pregnancy. Vegans, on the other hand, must plan their diets carefully to ensure adequate amounts of protein, vitamin D, vitamin B_6, iron, calcium, zinc, and vitamin B_{12}. Vegans need to increase their intake of grains, beans, nuts, and seeds to supply the required amounts of nutrients. Still, supplements of vitamin B_{12}, iron, and calcium along with a multipurpose prenatal supplement will probably also be necessary.[4]

Nutrition and Physical Activity

The relationship between physical activity and nutrition is obvious. The ability to engage in physical activity, whether it is low intensity and recreational or high intensity and competitive, is influenced by dietary intake. Conversely, nutritional needs change depending on the type, intensity, and duration of activity.

Nutrition and athletic performance are complex subjects involving not only the science of nutrition but also the sciences of biochemistry and physiology. While a presentation of the intricacies of sports nutrition is beyond the scope of this text, the following information should help you plan to meet your nutrient needs when you participate in regular physical activities.

Type of activity and energy source

The body's use of carbohydrates, fats, and protein for energy depends on the type of activity and the level of physical fitness. For high-intensity, anaerobic activities lasting for only a minute or less, such as a 100-yard sprint, carbohydrates are the major fuel source. For aerobic activities lasting from several minutes to four or five hours, a combination of carbohydrates, fats, and protein provides fuel for work. If the activity is intense, involving 75 percent or more of maximum oxygen consumption (such as of a runner trying to achieve a personal best in a 1-mile run), carbohydrates will be in greater demand. If the activity is moderately intense, using 40 to 60 percent of maximum (such as jogging or brisk walking), fats and carbohydrates are used evenly. If the activity lasts more than a few minutes and is less intense, using less than 30 percent of maximum (such as easy walking), fat becomes a major source of energy.[46] Energy from protein is minimal during most activities because protein functions as a fuel source primarily after carbohydrate fuel is depleted, such as might occur in activities of long duration (such as long-distance running), and then its contribution accounts for only about 10 percent of the energy. In general, carbohydrates are the main fuel source for both anaerobic and high-intensity aerobic activities; fat is the main fuel source for prolonged, low-intensity exercise; and protein is a minor fuel source, primarily for endurance activities.[4]

Recommended sources of energy

The diet of a physically active person should favor carbohydrates. The body is capable of converting carbohydrates to a usable form of energy more quickly and more efficiently than it can fats or protein. As a general rule, dietary intake of carbohydrates should account for 55 to 70 percent of the energy.[47] Tables 6-10 and 6-11 present some high-carbohydrate meal options that are appropriate as preactivity meals. An increase in carbohydrate intake should be accompanied by a decrease in fat intake. Fat should account for about 15 to 30 percent of energy, depending on the percentage of carbohydrate calories; protein should provide the remaining 15 percent.

Protein supplement

Many physically active people, especially athletes, have the mistaken notion that intense physical activities impose a greater than usual demand for protein. This idea

Table 6-10 Two High-Carbohydrate Preactivity* Meals

	Calories	Protein (grams)	Fat (grams)	Carbohydrate (grams)
Menu 1				
White bread, 2 slices	123	4	2	22
Peanut butter, 1 tbsp.	95	4	8	3
Grape jelly, 1 tbsp.	56	0	0	14
2% milk, 1 cup	125	8	5	12
Orange, 1 medium	60	1	0	15
Meal total:	459	17	15	66
Menu 2				
Vegetable lo mein (soft noodles with stir-fried vegetables), 2 cups	352	11	15	47
Fresh papaya, 1 cup	54	1	0	14
Herbal iced tea sweetened with honey, 12 oz.	56	0	0	13
Meal total:	462	12	15	74

*A preactivity meal should provide 1 to 4 grams of carbohydrate per kilogram of body weight, moderate amounts of protein, and small amounts of fat.

stems partly from the perception that, if a modest amount of a nutrient is good for you, large amounts must be even better and partly from the fact that protein is needed for the synthesis of new tissue. Both of these ideas can lead to mistaken conclusions. What athletes and others who are engaged in intense activities need is not extra protein but extra carbohydrates. The body's need for protein is biologically driven (see the previous discussion of recommended protein intake), and any excess in this amount is inefficiently converted to energy or stored as fat.

Two exceptions to this protein guideline occur for athletes engaged in endurance sports and athletes starting weight-training programs. The recommendations for protein range from 1.2 to 1.6 grams of protein per kilogram of body weight for the endurance athlete and 2.0 to 2.5 grams per kilogram of body weight for the weight-training athlete.[4] This represents a two- to threefold increase of the RDA for protein. Experts disagree about the importance of excessive protein intake for weight training.

Vitamins and minerals

Vitamin and mineral needs of the physically active person are about the same as those of the sedentary person. People who exercise usually eat more than sedentary people do and therefore get more vitamins and minerals as a matter of course. Contrary to popular belief, especially among athletes, there is no need to take vitamin and mineral supplements if adequate servings of food from the FGP are consumed. The American Medical Association, the American Dietetic Association, the American Institute of Nutrition, the Food and Nutrition Board, and the National Council Against Health Fraud have published position statements affirming that, with rare exception, there are no benefits of supplements that exceed the RDAs.[47] Megadoses of vitamins and minerals may, in fact, be counterproductive.

If a mineral deficiency occurs, it is most likely to involve iron and calcium, especially for women athletes. A deficiency of either of these minerals not only impairs athletic performance but also may lead to serious medical conditions. Dietary intake of these two minerals should be monitored regularly.

Fatty acids and activity

Most of the body's energy reserve is in its fat stores. When fat stores are broken down, fatty acids move through the bloodstream and enter muscle cells, where they are converted to energy. Well-trained muscles have a greater capacity to execute this conversion process and the ability to burn more fat. Thus, improved physical fitness causes more fat to be used for energy.[4,47] Also, the body's use of fat stores is affected by the duration of the activity. Prolonged activities (lasting more than 20 minutes) cause fat storage to be tapped for energy, particularly when the activity remains at a low-intensity level. Unlike carbohydrate stores, which are limited, an unlimited amount of fatty acids is available to sustain energy needs of low-intensity activities. Weight-conscious people interested in physical activity as a strategy for using fat, therefore, are better served by low-intensity to moderately intense activities that can be endured for a long period of time.

Fluid intake and activity

Consuming the right amount of fluids before, during, and after physical activity, which is addressed in Chapter 3, is crucial for the regulation of body temperature and the dissipation of heat.

Food Safety

Today, Americans face a paradox: We are urged to eat more fruits, vegetables, fish, and poultry but we are warned about contamination and **foodborne illness.** Recently, 25 million pounds of ground beef were recalled because of possible *E. coli* bacteria contamination; 200 Michigan schoolchildren developed stomach pains and jaundice from contaminated strawberries

Table 6-11 Convenient Preactivity Meals

Breakfast (McDonald's)	Energy content
Hot cakes with syrup and margarine	900 cal
Orange juice, 2 servings	67% from carbohydrates
English muffin (whole) with 2 tsp. margarine and 2 tsp. jam	(150 g)
• • •	
Cheerios, 3/4 cup	450 cal
Low-fat milk, 1 cup	82% from carbohydrates
Blueberry muffin	(92 g)
Orange juice, 1 serving	
Lunch or dinner (Wendy's)	
Chili, 8-oz. portion	900 cal
Baked potato with sour cream and chives	65% from carbohydrates
Chocolate Frosty, 10 oz.	(150 g)
• • •	
Grilled chicken sandwich	425 cal
Cola, 12 oz.	65% from carbohydrates
	(70 g)

that had been grown in Mexico; an outbreak of infectious diarrhea was traced to raspberries imported from Guatemala; dozens of cases of bloody diarrhea and one death were caused by a batch of organic apple juice made from California apples; and four children died from contaminated hamburgers cooked at a fast-food restaurant. Current estimates suggest that up to 33 million cases of foodborne illness occur in the United States each year, causing about 9,000 deaths.[46] These illnesses are difficult to prevent because they involve different kinds of organisms infecting foods of all types that are grown in many parts of the world.

Here is a short list of organisms that are common culprits of foodborne illnesses, along with their food sources and symptoms:

- *Staphylococcus* toxins are usually present in meats, poultry, egg products, tuna, potato and macaroni salads, and cream-filled pastries. Symptoms occur two to six hours after exposure and include diarrhea, vomiting, nausea, and abdominal cramps. Recovery normally takes place in twenty-four to thirty-six hours.
- *Salmonella* infections are associated with eggs, poultry, meat, dairy products, seafood, and fresh produce. Symptoms usually occur within six to forty-eight hours and include nausea, vomiting, abdominal cramps, diarrhea, fever, headache, and sometimes a rash. *Salmonella* infections may be quite serious, even fatal, in infants, the elderly, and the sick.
- *Clostridium botulinum,* usually referred to as *botulism,* occurs in an anaerobic environment, such as in canned goods, and affects low-acid foods like green beans, mushrooms, spinach, olives, and beef. Symptoms occur twelve to thirty-six hours after exposure and affect the central nervous system. Paralysis and death may follow. Infected food usually has an odor. Avoid canned goods that show any signs of damage.
- *Campylobacter jejuni* contamination is linked to raw and undercooked poultry, unpasteurized milk, and untreated water. Symptoms usually occur in two to five days and include diarrhea, fever, abdominal pain, nausea, headache, and muscle pain. Infections may last seven to ten days.
- *E. coli* O157:H7 is typically present in undercooked and raw ground beef, raw milk, lettuce, untreated water, and unpasteurized fruit juices. Symptoms include severe abdominal pain and cramping and diarrhea (first watery, then bloody).
- *Listeria monocytogenes* is associated with soft cheeses, poultry, fish, and raw meats and vegetables. The illness causes flulike symptoms, including fever, and may progress to fatal infections of the blood and central nervous system.
- *Hepatitis A virus* comes from contaminated fecal material from people who harvest, process, or handle food, including workers on farms, in food-processing plants, and in restaurants. Symptoms, which may not occur for several weeks, include fever, nausea, abdominal discomfort, and sometimes jaundice. The infection is usually mild, though symptoms can be severe.

With the exception of hepatitis A, the organisms listed are bacterial. For most of them, treatment consists of hydration and the administration of antibiotics. Other types of organisms are involved in foodborne illnesses. Parasites such as *Trichinella spiralis* (found in pork and wild game) and tapeworms (found in beef, pork, and fish) also infect many people. The same is true of fungi, which produce mold spores that yield toxins such as aflatoxin.

Most foodborne illnesses can be prevented by observing some basic rules for storing, handling, and preparing food. Following these simple rules represents a surprisingly formidable challenge to most Americans: According to recent surveys, only 1 percent of households would pass the inspection required of restaurants.[48] In your own home, follow these safety rules:

- Avoid cross-contamination: Do not prepare foods in an unclean sink and do not allow utensils that have come into contact with an unclean surface to touch food.
- Wash hands when first starting to handle food and after handling garbage or dirty dishes.
- Use separate cloths, sponges, and towels for washing dishes, wiping counters and tabletops, wiping hands, and drying clean dishes.
- Measure the temperature of cooked or held foods to make sure they're hot enough to destroy bacteria (see Just the Facts: How Hot Is Hot Enough?). Studies reveal that 50 percent of the public eat raw or undercooked eggs, 23 percent eat undercooked hamburger, and 17 percent eat raw clams and oysters.[49]
- Do not consume foods whose "use-by" dates have expired.
- Transfer leftovers from deep pots and casseroles to shallow pans before refrigeration in order to speed cooling (and thereby slow bacterial growth).
- Quickly freeze or refrigerate all ground meat and other perishable foods after shopping.
- Wash hands, utensils, and work areas with hot soapy water after contact with raw meat to keep bacteria from spreading. Also wash your hands after using the bathroom, diapering a child, using the telephone, handling garbage, or touching your face, your hair, or other people.
- Keep the refrigerator temperature below 40° F (37° F is optimal). Keep the freezer at or below 0° F.

Just the Facts

How Hot Is Hot Enough?

The only way you can be certain that food has been cooked thoroughly is to use a kitchen thermometer.[50] Visual cues, such as color or texture, aren't reliable indicators of a food's safety. When checking a meat's temperature, insert the thermometer in the deepest, thickest part without touching a bone. A thermometer's accuracy can be checked by placing it in boiling water. If it shows 212° F, it is accurate.

What follows are the minimum internal temperatures that various meat cuts must reach to be considered safe:

- Ground beef, veal, lamb, pork — 160° F
- Beef, veal, lamb (steaks, roasts, chops) — 145° F
- Pork (roasts, chops) — 160° F
- Ham
  - uncooked — 160° F
  - precooked — 140° F
- Poultry
  - ground chicken, turkey — 165° F
  - whole chicken, turkey — 180° F
  - breasts — 170° F
  - thighs, wings — 180° F
- Stuffing (cooked alone or in the bird) — 165° F
- Egg dishes, casseroles — 160° F
- Leftovers* — 165° F

*Reheated soups and gravies should be brought to a rolling boil. All other leftovers should be hot and steaming.

- Wash whole produce. This includes melons and citrus fruits before cutting them open, to prevent the transfer of bacteria from the fruit's skin to the edible part.
- Wash or sanitize cutting boards between each use.
- Store meat products in separate containers from fruits and vegetables.
- Flip steaks with tongs or a spatula rather than with a fork during cooking. Unlike ground beef, in which bacteria are mixed throughout the meat during the grinding process, steak harbors bacteria only on the surface. Sticking a fork into meat before it is cooked injects the interior with bacteria from the outside.
- Cook fish until it flakes with a fork.
- Put your sponge or scouring pad in the dishwasher every time you run it. Or microwave your sponge on high for thirty to sixty seconds.
- Don't store raw foods on the refrigerator shelf above ready-to-eat foods.
- Don't thaw frozen food on the kitchen counter or at room temperature. Thaw frozen food in the refrigerator or microwave.
- Don't eat hamburgers or any form of ground beef until the juices run yellow, with no trace of pink left. (The color of the meat isn't a reliable indicator of doneness. Check the juice.)
- Don't let juice from raw meat, poultry, or fish drip on your hands or any fresh foods in your grocery cart.
- Don't consume unpasteurized milk and juice or consume foods made with raw eggs.
- Don't use tasting utensils that have touched food under preparation.
- Don't grill, barbecue, broil, or pan-fry meats, poultry, or fish at extremely high temperatures. (Grills can reach temperatures in excess of 640° F. Ovens roast at a temperature of 350° F.) Cooking meats at high temperatures promotes the formation of heterocyclic amines, HCAs. HCAs are thought to be carcinogenic. Boiling, steaming, poaching, stewing, and microwaving do not produce HCAs.[51]
- Don't serve or transport cooked food on the plate used for raw meat.
- Don't store raw fish in your refrigerator for more than twenty-four hours. Raw poultry or ground beef will keep for one to two days and raw red meat for three to five.

Nutrition Strategies and Disease Prevention

This chapter emphasizes dietary practices that promote health and wellness, but the connections between food and disease must not be overlooked. Many of these connections have been referred to in the presentation of various nutrients and dietary guidelines, starting with the introduction to the chapter and ending with the previous section on food safety. Still, it is important to highlight some of the major diet and disease connections, with an emphasis on prevention. Remember that the interaction between food and disease is complex, and twenty to forty years may be needed to determine a relationship between disease and diet. With this in mind, here are some strategies[5] that may prevent or reduce the risks associated with several chronic conditions:

- *Heart disease.* Reduce saturated fat intake to no more than 8 percent of calories and total fat to no more than 30 percent and increase monounsaturated fat to 15 percent. Reducing fat consumption has the added advantage of lowering cholesterol levels. Cholesterol intake should be limited to 300 mg per day. Other strategies include reducing homocysteine levels by consuming plenty of folate, ingesting 25 grams of fiber, especially soluble fiber, and eating at least five servings of fruits and vegetables per day. Vitamin E supplements may also be helpful.

- *Hypertension.* Dietary strategies thought to be effective in reducing or preventing high blood pressure include limiting sodium intake to no more than 2400 mg, consuming potassium-rich fruits and vegetables, and obtaining calcium by eating two to three servings of low-fat dairy products per day.
- *Diabetes mellitus.* Strategies that apply to heart disease also apply to the management of blood sugar levels. Two additional tactics are to maintain a desirable weight, especially for people with non–insulin-dependent diabetes, and restrict intake of simple sugars and highly processed carbohydrates, such as white flour.
- *Osteoporosis.* Consume at least 1200 mg of calcium and 400 IU of vitamin D daily.
- *Cancer.* Many strategies that apply to heart disease also apply to cancer. In addition, consumption of cruciferous vegetables, such as cabbage, broccoli, brussels sprouts, and cauliflower, is thought to help prevent cancer of the gastrointestinal and respiratory tracts. Consumption of fruits and vegetables rich in carotenoids has been linked to a reduction in cancers of the ovaries, bladder, larynx, esophagus, and lung. Cancers of the stomach and esophagus are less common among people whose diets are rich in ascorbic acid, or vitamin C. To reduce the risks of breast cancer, limit alcohol consumption to fewer than seven drinks per week. The risks of colon cancer can be minimized by limiting the intake of red meat to two or three servings per week, consuming lean cuts of meat or no meat at all, and eating at least 25 grams of fiber, including insoluble fiber, per day. Prostate cancer risk can be reduced by following these guidelines and by eating several servings of cooked tomato products each week.

Food Labels

The FDA oversees the labeling of food products other than meat and poultry. With the passage of new label laws in 1992, virtually all processed and packaged foods are required to have uniform labels. These foods include processed meat and poultry, which are regulated by the USDA. Guidelines for voluntary labeling of raw vegetables and fruits and fish are also available and will likely be displayed in most supermarkets.

Food labels must indicate the manufacturer and the packer or distributor, declare the quantity of contents either by net weight or by volume, and list the common name of each ingredient in descending order of prominence. Information about those nutrients most closely associated with chronic disease risk factors—that is, the amount of total fat, saturated fat, cholesterol, sodium, sugar, dietary fiber, total carbohydrate, and protein—must also be included.

Labels are divided into two parts (figure 6-5) and present information according to generic standards called **Daily Values (DVs)**. Daily Values are benchmarks for evaluating the nutrient content of foods. They express this content as a percentage of a 2000-calorie diet (Recommended Dietary Allowances are not used as the standards because they are age and gender specific). Information in the top part of a label varies according to the contribution one serving of that food makes to the Daily Values listed in the bottom part of the label.

The DV standards located on the bottom panel are the same on all food labels and are based on two calorie levels: 2000 and 2500 (table 6-12). This means that total fat intake should be fewer than 65 grams for a 2000-calorie diet and fewer than 80 grams for a 2500-calorie diet. Dividing the nutrient content listed in the top panel by the DVs listed in the bottom panel yields the percent Daily Value for one serving. For example, a serving of Mac' n' Cheese contains 15 grams of fat, or 23 percent of the Daily Value of 65 g for a person on a 2000-calorie diet. With the application of simple arithmetic, you can calculate the Daily Value percents for any food with a breakdown of nutrient content.

Standard food labels are useful if daily caloric intake is approximately 2000 or 2500 calories and if the goal is to conform to minimum dietary recommendations. If your diet calls for significantly more or less of a nutrient, your DVs will differ. If that is the case, simply keep track of the total amount of a nutrient. For example, if you are on a 1500-calorie diet and are trying to limit fat intake to 20 percent, keep a running total of fat grams to determine when 33 g have been reached.

In the past, manufacturers often used labeling ploys to deceive consumers. Currently, laws limit labels to the following health claims:

- High-calcium foods may reduce the risk of osteoporosis.
- A diet low in saturated fat and cholesterol may lower the risk for heart disease.
- A low-fat diet may reduce the risk of some cancers.
- A low-sodium diet has been linked with reduced incidence of hypertension.

Figure 6-5 Food Label Showing Daily Values
Food labels provide information about those nutrients most associated with chronic disease risk factors.

Nutrition information is now required on virtually all processed food products.

The % Daily Value shows how a food fits into an overall daily diet but does not necessarily represent goals for diet planning. Upper limits are a better way to view the concept of 100% Daily Value, except for carbohydrate, dietary fiber, vitamins, and minerals.

Protein generally will not show a % Daily Value because determining % Daily Value would require expensive testing of protein quality of the product by the manufacturer.

Nutrition Facts
Serving Size 4.5 oz (126g/about 1/3 Box)
(Makes about 1 cup)
Servings Per Container about 2.5

Amount Per Serving	
Calories 410	
Calories from Fat 130	
	% Daily Value*
Total Fat 15 g	23%
Saturated Fat 9g	46%
Cholesterol 45mg	15%
Sodium 1160mg	48%
Total Carbohydrate 50g	17%
Dietary Fiber 2g	6%
Sugars 5g	
Protein 18g	

Serving size is set for various food products in household units by labeling laws. If you eat double the serving size listed, you need to double the % Daily Value and the calorie value. If you eat one-half the serving size shown, cut the % Daily Value and the calorie value in half.

Number of calories from fat.

% Daily Values are determined by dividing the nutrient content in one serving of the food by the Daily Values listed for the respective nutrient on the bottom panel.

Although the Dietary Guidelines recommend that Americans moderate their consumption of sugars, no specific recommendation for a maximum daily intake (in grams) has been made, so no Daily Value for sugars is available.

Table 6-12 Standardized Daily Values on Food Labels

	Calorie Levels	
	2000	2500
Total fat	< 65 g	< 80 g
Saturated fat	< 20 g	< 25 g
Cholesterol	< 300 mg	< 300 mg
Sodium	< 2400 mg	< 2400 mg
Total carbohydrates	300 g	375 g
Fiber	25 g	30 g

- High-fiber foods may reduce the risk of heart disease and certain forms of cancer.
- Vitamins A and C in fruits and vegetables may reduce the risk of some types of cancer.
- Folate may reduce the risk of neural tube birth defects.
- Fruits, vegetables, and grain products that contain fiber, particularly soluble fiber, may reduce the risk of coronary heart disease.
- Sugar alcohols (e.g., sorbitol, xylitol, mannitol) may reduce the risk of dental caries.
- Soluble fiber from whole oats may reduce the risk of coronary heart disease.
- Soluble fiber from psyllium seed husks may reduce the risk of coronary heart disease.

The FDA has defined commonly used words describing calories, sodium, sugar, fiber, fat, and cholesterol in food. For example, when the word *free* is highlighted on a package in reference to calories, it means that the product yields fewer than 5 calories per serving; in reference to sodium, it means the product contains fewer than 5 milligrams; and in reference to fat, it means the product contains less than 0.5 grams. When *light* or *lite* is used on a package label, it means that the product has one-third fewer calories or 50 percent less fat than a similar product. *Low calorie* foods can have no more than 40 calories per serving; *low-fat* foods can have no more than 3 grams of fat per serving. *Healthy* means that a food meets the criteria for low fat and low saturated fat, does not exceed maximum levels for sodium and cholesterol, and contains at least 10 percent Daily Value for at least one of the following: vitamins A and C, calcium, iron, protein, or fiber. The word *organic* now can be used only on raw products that are grown without added hormones, pesticides, or synthetic fertilizers and on processed foods that contain 95 percent organic ingredients.

Freshness dates have also been defined. Phrases such as *Best Before, Better If Used Before*, or *Best If Used By* tell how long food will retain its best flavor or quality. The food is still safe to eat after the printed date, but it might become stale or change somewhat in taste or texture. The *Expiration, Use By,* or *Use Before* date, which appears on refrigerated foods, provides the deadline for consumption. A product past its expiration date is no longer of sufficient quality and should not be eaten. The *Sell By* date is usually found on highly perishable foods with a particularly short shelf life, such as meat, milk, or bread. It indicates the last day the product should appear on a supermarket shelf. If stored properly, most foods will remain safe to eat for about a week after the *Sell By* date.[52]

Serving sizes are not standardized. Nevertheless, the FDA has set serving sizes for 139 food and drink categories according to information obtained from surveys of what people actually eat. Consequently, serving sizes are more realistic than ever before, and they permit comparison shopping.

Even with the improvements in label laws, the unwitting consumer can still be misled. A brand of margarine changed its name from *Brand . . . Light* to *Brand . . . Light Taste*—manufacturers can still use light to describe taste, texture, or color. The makers of a brand of brownie mix claim that it is low fat. But the fine print says that the low-fat designation pertains only to each serving of the mix. Once an edible brownie is created by adding vegetable oil, its fat-gram content more than triples. Some foods promise fruit or other ingredients but deliver only flavor. One brand of strawberry frozen yogurt has no real strawberries despite pictures on the label of real strawberries; a brand of blueberry pancakes has no berries. Clearly, although labels have improved dramatically during the past several years, they still fall short in several areas. Deception in old labels was more obvious; today's labels challenge consumers to apply a higher level of discrimination to sort between fact and fantasy.

Changes in American Eating Patterns

Changes in the American family are mirrored in the trend toward convenience-food eating. For many families, time is a precious commodity that has a dramatic influence on how, where, when, and what people eat. Family meals at home are being replaced by a quick-stop, eat-on-the-go trend. Dining out has become a part of the quintessential American lifestyle, with one of every three people eating away from home at any one mealtime.[53] Not only do many people eat away from home, but they also skip meals. For example, college students typically eat two meals a day and make up the difference by eating many snacks. One-fourth of adults skip breakfast, which is the appropriate meal to replace the carbohydrate stores used during the night's sleep.[4] It should be of little surprise, therefore, that midmorning sluggishness is a common mental and physical disposition of students and workers alike.

Snacking

Snacking refers to consuming food between the three main meals of the day. Most Americans have at least one snack per day, and snack foods represent one of the fastest-growing markets in the food industry. From a nutrition point of view, snacking is neither good or bad. The three meals a day standard is based more on social custom than on physiology. The key issue is not the time or frequency of eating but what is eaten. Nutritionally dense foods eaten as snacks are just as good for health as they are when consumed as meals. The converse is also true; foods low in nutrient density eaten at mealtime are just as worthless as when they are eaten as snacks. With the exception of foods restricted for medical reasons, all foods can contribute to a healthful diet. Problems occur when a person's diet is dominated by foods low in nutrient density. Rather than rule out snacking, consume snack foods that enhance wellness. The most direct way to improve snacking behavior is the most obvious one: Purchase and make nutritionally dense foods available (see Real World Wellness: Snack Ideas).

From a nutritional viewpoint, the criticisms of fast-food eating are the same as those of the rest of the American diet: too much fat, too many calories, too

> ### Real-World Wellness
>
> **Snack Ideas**
>
> *After completing a thorough three-day dietary analysis, I was surprised to learn that the key to improving my overall nutritional profile is to make changes in my snack food choices. My meals are fairly well balanced, but my snacks are typically high in fat, high in sodium, high in sugar, and just basically low in nutrient density. What are some examples of nutritionally dense snacks?*
>
> The following snacks are surprisingly flavorful and satisfying and will help you improve your overall nutrition:
>
> - Fresh raw vegetables served with a cottage cheese dip
> - Fresh fruit, prewashed and cut into bite-size pieces
> - Fruit dipped in yogurt
> - Bagels topped with reduced-fat cream cheese
> - Breadsticks
> - Air-popped popcorn seasoned with herbs
> - Frozen fruit-juice bars
> - Low-fat frozen yogurt
> - Pita chips with salsa
> - Pretzels
> - Rye crisps or rice cakes spread with a little peanut butter or low-fat cheese
> - Broth-based soup
> - Cereal (low sugar, low fat)
> - Shelled sunflower seeds
> - Gelatin with added fruit
> - English muffins
> - Flour tortillas with canned chili and grated low-fat cheese
> - Pita bread topped with spaghetti sauce and grated low-fat cheese
> - Fruit juice with added club soda
> - Hot cocoa (low sugar, low fat)
> - Milkshake made with low-fat milk and frozen fruit

much sodium, and not enough complex carbohydrates and fiber. The average meal of a cheeseburger, milk shake, and fries supplies about 1500 calories, 43 percent of which come from fat. Chicken and fish are just as fatty as other protein sources offered by fast-food restaurants because they are breaded and fried. Frying has the same effect on potatoes. Milk shakes get most of their calories from sugars. The Food Composition Table located in the appendix of this text along with nutrition software like HealthQuest provide detailed information that can be used to compare many fast-food menu items.

Eating at fast-food restaurants does not have to be a nutritionally worthless activity. Many restaurants are now aware that Americans are becoming more knowledgeable about the nutrient content of food and are demanding wholesome, safe, and nutritious foods. Consequently, there has been a trend toward more nutritious menus, including salad, pasta, and potato bars. Guided by good judgment in the choice of foods, an occasional meal at a fast-food chain does not have to compromise a well-balanced diet.

Prepackaged Convenience Dinners

Prepackaged convenience dinners have also become part of the American diet. Consumers spend billions of dollars a year on them, and food manufacturers are constantly turning out new lines. The challenge for health-conscious consumers is to determine which ones fit easily into a nutritious diet.

Prepackaged convenience dinners can be evaluated by applying the following criteria:

- There should be no more than and preferably fewer than 30 percent of calories from fat.
- There should be no more than 200 milligrams of sodium per 100 calories.
- They should meet at least 40 percent of the RDA for vitamins A and/or C.

Just because a dinner meets these criteria does not necessarily mean that it provides every nutrient. Some meals are likely to be deficient in some nutrients, so foods that will compensate must be added.

Planning a Nutrition Strategy for Wellness

It is not necessary to be a nutritionist to form a nutrition strategy that works for you. A nutrition plan will work only if it is personalized. Several strategies should be helpful in personalizing your nutrition plan.

Assess Your Nutrition

You should take an honest look at your eating choices and analyze your nutrition profile through Assessment Activities 6-3, 6-4, and 6-6 to determine whether you are doing the following:

- Eating a variety of foods every day from the Food Guide Pyramid
- Avoiding high-fat foods (more than the equivalent of 3 grams of fat per 100 calories)

Nurturing Your Spirituality

Enjoy Your Food—the Missing Dietary Guideline

The fast-paced, eat-on-the-run trend among Americans comes with a high price: Fewer and fewer people spend time preparing good, home-cooked meals, and even fewer use mealtime as a time for relaxing and social bonding. Other cultures recognize that mealtime is a key social time of the day and reflect this value in the dietary recommendations health experts offer their citizens:[54]

- In Japan, immediately following the guideline to avoid too much sodium comes the advice "Happy eating makes for a happy family life; sit down and eat together and talk; treasure family taste and home cooking."
- In Great Britain, the first guideline is "Enjoy your food."
- Korea tells its citizens to "Enjoy meals and keep harmony between diet and daily life."
- In Norway, people are told, "Food and joy equal health."
- In Vietnam, the advice is to "Serve a healthy family meal that is delicious and served with affection."

The greatest nutrition challenge for Americans may not be to reduce fat intake or cut back on sodium. It may be to construct a positive view of food and of mealtime. One highly respected nutrition publication reminds us, "Healthful eating is about more than eating the right mix of nutrients. It's also about sustaining well-being in a way that can't be measured on a blood test but that is just as important to overall health as vitamins and minerals.[54]

- Including sufficient fiber in the form of whole grains, dried beans, and fresh fruits and vegetables
- Consuming 8 to 12 cups of water (8 ounces each) daily
- Consuming no more than three or four high-sugar desserts or sweets each week
- Restricting your intake of high-salt foods, such as processed meats
- Consuming no more than one or two alcoholic drinks a day and not letting drinking interfere with your appetite

Make Small Adjustments

The principle of changing health behavior is that the smaller the change, the longer it lasts (see Chapter 1). For example, rather than vowing to abstain from eating ice cream, reduce the amount or number of servings at first and substitute a low-fat brand. If your diet is heavy in salt, you can gradually substitute sodium-free seasonings. If you have a sweet tooth, you can try low-sugar snacks. If you eat for fullness, you can prepare less food or leave food on your plate. You should plan an approach that builds on the cumulative effect of many small successes.

Think of balancing your diet over a long period rather than in just a day or a meal. Try to meet the dietary guidelines over several days or a week. For example, every meal does not need to contain less than 30 percent fat. Keep portions of favorite high-fat foods small, and limit other sources of fat. Check labels to get an idea of what nutrients you are consuming, but don't keep a calculator by your plate. If you eat foods from the Food Guide Pyramid, you will get all the vitamins, minerals, and protein you need.

Choose Foods for Wellness

Choosing foods for wellness means following the *Dietary Guidelines for Americans*. Your diet should

- Be low in saturated fat (maximum of 8 percent)
- Emphasize complex carbohydrates, such as bread, potatoes, and pasta
- Provide eight to twelve glasses of water throughout the day
- Provide iron and calcium
- Emphasize fresh fruits and vegetables
- Be low in sugar, salt, alcohol, and caffeine

Finally, make sure when choosing foods for wellness to enjoy what you eat (see Nurturing Your Spirituality: Enjoy Your Food—the Missing Dietary Guideline).

Summary

- The six classes of nutrients are carbohydrates, fat, protein, vitamins, minerals, and water. The nutrients that provide energy in the form of calories are carbohydrates, fat, and protein.
- The recommended diet for Americans in *Dietary Guidelines for Americans* emphasizes complex carbohydrates as the major source of energy. A diet high in complex carbohydrates is likely to be lower in fat, lower in calories, and higher in fiber.

- A complete protein is one that provides all of the amino acids in amounts proportional to the body's need for them. Protein sources from animals are complete proteins. Plant sources of complete protein, such as soy protein, come from the legume family.
- One of the greatest shortcomings of the American diet is its excessive intake of fat, especially saturated fat.
- The amount of saturated, monounsaturated, and polyunsaturated fat in foods varies considerably. Most food contains a mixture of these fats.
- The process of hydrogenation increases the saturated fat content of polyunsaturated and monounsaturated fats and yields small amounts of fat not found in nature called *transfatty acids*.
- Dietary fat intake should favor foods high in monounsaturated fats, such as olive oil, canola oil, and peanut oil.
- The consumption of antioxidant vitamins, especially in fruits and vegetables, is associated with a reduced risk of heart disease and cancer.
- Adequate folate consumption is thought to lower the concentration of homocysteine, an amino acid associated with an increased risk of heart disease.
- Two minerals of special concern today are calcium and iron. Most women fall short of the RDA for calcium. People at risk for low iron levels include young children, early teens, menstruating women, and people with health conditions that cause internal bleeding.
- People are advised to drink eight to twelve cups of fluids a day. Plain tap water is the preferred fluid.
- Phytochemicals are plant chemicals found naturally in foods. They play an important role in preventing many diseases.
- Many botanicals are thought to have health benefits. Because they are considered nutritional supplements and are not regulated with the same rigor as drugs, there is debate about their effectiveness and safety. Twenty to thirty botanicals are backed by well-conducted research.
- Insoluble fiber benefits the body by adding bulk to the stool, thus speeding the transit of food through the body, which reduces the chance of developing colon cancer, and lowering blood-cholesterol levels. Soluble fiber also benefits the body by lowering blood cholesterol levels.
- A good nutritional plan is one that consists of a variety of foods from the Food Guide Pyramid.
- A food is nutrient dense when it has a high ratio of nutrients to calories.
- Variety and moderation are principles that should most influence eating habits. There is room in the diet for any food as long as it is consumed in moderation in terms of both quantity and frequency.
- *Dietary Guidelines for Americans* officially recognizes a vegetarian diet as a healthful and acceptable way of meeting all of our nutritional needs.
- The health benefits of a vegetarian diet include a lower cholesterol level; lower levels of LDLs; reduced incidence of hypertension, lung, colorectal, and breast cancer; and fewer complications from non–insulin-dependent diabetes mellitus.
- Americans consume sugar and sodium in excessive amounts. The major health issue associated with high sugar intake is dental caries; for sodium it's hypertension.
- Moderate consumption of alcohol may be beneficial for some people who are at risk for cardiovascular disease and stroke.
- Pregnancy imposes a greater demand for some nutrients, including protein, vitamin D, folate, iron, calcium, and zinc.
- Carbohydrates are the main source of energy for both anaerobic and high-intensity aerobic activities; fat is the main energy source for prolonged, low-intensity exercise; and protein is a minor fuel source, primarily for endurance activities.
- The risk of foodborne illnesses can be reduced by preventing cross-contamination of food; by washing hands, fruits, produce, and meats; and by exercising caution in the way food is prepared and stored.
- Food labels provide helpful information about nutrients associated with the common chronic health problems of Americans as well as about essential nutrients.
- The criticisms of snacking and fast-food eating are the same as those of the rest of the American diet: too much fat, sodium, and sugar; too many calories; and not enough complex carbohydrates and fiber.
- Americans are challenged not only to eat more healthfully but also to construct a positive attitude about food and mealtimes.

Review Questions

1. What is meant by "Nutritional diseases of the past have been replaced by diseases of dietary excess and imbalance?"
2. What was the rationale for revising the Recommended Dietary Allowances for essential nutrients?
3. Identify three nutrients that most Americans do not consume in sufficient amounts.
4. How many calories are supplied by carbohydrates, fat, and protein? What percent of total calories should come from each of these sources? How does Americans' intake of energy nutrients compare with dietary recommendations?
5. Why are carbohydrates the preferred source of energy?
6. What is the difference between a high-quality, complete protein and a low-quality, incomplete protein?
7. What plant sources of protein are unique in that they are considered complete proteins?
8. What are the differences between saturated, monounsaturated, and polyunsaturated fats? What are some food sources of each? What percent of fat calories should come from each type?
9. What are transfatty acids? Why should they be avoided?
10. List five dietary practices that will help lower consumption of fat, especially saturated fat.

11. What are the similarities and differences between water-soluble and fat-soluble vitamins?
12. Which vitamins are classified as antioxidants? What is the relationship between antioxidants and health?
13. What role does folate play in preventing disease?
14. Identify three situations or circumstances that would justify use of a vitamin or mineral supplement.
15. What are phytochemicals? How are they different from botanicals? How do they contribute to health?
16. What two minerals are Americans most likely to be consuming in insufficient amounts? Which segments of the population are most likely to be affected?
17. Explain why thirst is not a good indicator of how much water to drink.
18. What are the major health benefits associated with insoluble fiber? soluble fiber?
19. What is the rationale for the assertion that variety and moderation are the most important principles for a healthy diet?
20. List three negative health effects associated with the excessive intake of nutrients considered good for health when taken in recommended amounts.
21. Distinguish between the different types of vegetarianism. Which types are most likely to require some form of vitamin or mineral supplementation? What are the health benefits of a vegetarian diet?
22. Identify four nutrients that pregnant women require in larger amounts than those in the RDAs.
23. How do the intensity and duration of physical activities affect the way the body uses carbohydrates, fat, and protein for energy? What type of physical activity is most conducive to burning fat calories?
24. List six things a person can do to help prevent unnecessary exposure to foodborne illnesses.
25. Distinguish between Recommended Dietary Allowances and Daily Values.
26. What are the main criticisms of snacking and fast-food eating?

References

1. U.S. Department of Health and Human Services. 1998. *Healthy People 2010 Objectives: Draft for Public Comment.* Washington, D.C.: U.S. Department of Health and Human Services, Office of Disease Prevention.
2. Liebman, B. 1998. Diet and cancer—the big picture. *Nutrition Action Health Letter* 25(10):1–7.
3. Tufts University. 1997. Report card for Americans' eating habits. *Tufts University Health and Nutrition Letter* 15(4):1.
4. Wardlaw, G. 1999. *Perspectives in Nutrition* (4th ed.). St. Louis, Mo.: WCB/McGraw Hill.
5. Margolis, S., and L. B. Wilder. 1998. *Nutrition and Longevity.* Baltimore, Md.: The Johns Hopkins Medical Institutes.
6. American Dietetic Association. 1998. *Choosing Legumes: A Healthful and Versatile Food.* Available on-line at www.eatright.org/nfs45.html.
7. Mayo Foundation for Medical Education and Research. 1997. Soy—a healthful diet addition. *Mayo Clinic Health Letter* 15(5):7.
8. Liebman, B. 1998. The soy story. *Nutrition Action Health Letter* 25(7):1–8.
9. Tufts University. 1997. Older adults may not be getting enough protein. *Tufts University Diet and Nutrition Letter* 14(11):2.
10. Editors. 1998. Meat-eaters need to bone up on calcium. *Environmental Nutrition* 21(4):1.
11. Editors. 1996. The truth about trans-fatty acids: Scientists can't agree on risk. *Environmental Nutrition* 19(2):1–6.
12. Tufts University. 1997. A type of fat we may need more of. *Tufts University Health and Nutrition Letter* 15(1):4–5.
13. Thomas, B. November 1998. Healthful diet for baby boils down to 'what' and 'when,' experts say. *The Commercial Appeal* 1:F3.
14. Harvard Medical School Publications Group. 1998. Dietary fat: How low should you go? *Harvard Health Letter* 23(3):6.
15. Hu, F. B., M. J. Stampfer, J. E. Manson, E. Rimm, G. A. Golditz, B. A. Rosner, C. H. Hennekens, and W. C. Willett. 1997. Dietary fat intake and the risk of coronary heart disease in women. *The New England Journal of Medicine* 337(21):1491–1499.
16. Editors. 1998. Low fat, no fat, some fat . . . high fat? Type of fat may be key. *Environmental Nutrition* 21(4):1–6.
17. Gershoff, S. N. (ed.). 1998. Vitamin C earns an "A" for health benefits. Do you get enough? *Environmental Nutrition* 21(6):1–4.
18. Forman, A. (ed.). 1997. As beta-carotene promises fade, focus turns to other carotenoids. *Environmental Nutrition* 20(6):1, 4.
19. Cooper, K. 1998. Cells under attack? Fight back! Antioxidants. *Diabetes Wellness Letter* A(1):7–8.
20. Liebman, B. 1998. Vitamins and minerals—what to take. *Nutrition Action Health Letter* 25(4):1, 3–7.
21. Mayo Foundation for Medical Education and Research. 1997. Vitamin and mineral supplements—sorting out fact from fiction amid a storm of controversy. *Mayo Clinic Health Letter* Supplement 15(6):1–8.
22. Rock, A. 1995. Vitamin hype: Why we're wasting $1 of every $3 we spend. *Money* 24(9):83–90.
23. Antinoro, L. 1997. A confusion of calcium supplements and drinks. *Environmental Nutrition* 20(1):5.
24. Schardt, D., and S. Schmidt. 1996. That zincing feeling. *Nutrition Action Health Letter* 23(3):10–11.
25. Antinoro, L. 1998. Dodging dehydration: Are you getting enough fluids? *Environmental Nutrition* 21(5):2.
26. Gottlieb, B. 1998. Tall tales from the table. *Health* 12(5):82–85.
27. Joyal, A. 1995. Those mighty phytos: Beyond the benefits of broccoli. *Environmental Nutrition* 18(11):1, 4.
28. Klausner, A. 1998. The herbal renaissance of the 90's: What's old is new again. *Environmental Nutrition* 21(4):1, 4–5.
29. Klausner, A. 1998. *EN's* herbal medicine cabinet: Top 10 herbs you can trust. *Environmental Nutrition* 21(5):1, 4–5.
30. Mayo Foundation for Medical Education and Research. 1996. Fiber—why

30. you need more, and good ways to get it. *Mayo Clinic Health Letter* 14(8): 4–5.
31. Foltz-Gray, D. 1997. The miracle of the loaves. *Health* 11(7):83–87.
32. Mermel, V. L. 1996. Eating from the bottom up: Using the food guide pyramid and the dietary guidelines. *Nutri News* (Fall):5.
33. Tufts University. 1997. Variety makes a better diet. *Tufts University Health and Nutrition Letter* 15(6):1, 6.
34. Tufts University. 1998. With age, calorie needs go down but nutrient needs go up. *Tufts University Health and Nutrition Letter* 16(10):4–5.
35. Editors. 1998. Meat eaters need to bone up on calcium. *Environmental Nutrition* 21(4):1.
36. Editors. 1997. The sometimes risky business of mixing herbs and medicines. *Environmental Nutrition* 20(10):7.
37. Lee, K., M. Mason, E. Strauss, P. Tucker, and P. Motte. 1998. Can large doses of vitamin C hurt me? *Health* 12(5):26.
38. Harvard Medical School Health Publishing Group. 1996. Too many vitamins. *Harvard Health Letter* 21(3):1–3.
39. Tufts University. 1997. Vitamin D toxicity may be widespread. *Tufts University Health and Nutrition Letter* 15(80):1.
40. Neergaard, L. November 22, 1998. Consumer group warns of food-drug interactions. *The Commercial Appeal* A10.
41. Editors. 1996. New dietary guidelines; second verse same as the first. *Environmental Nutrition* 19(20):3.
42. Messina, V. K., and K. I. Burke. 1998. *Position of the American Dietetic Association: Vegetarian Diets*. Available on-line at www.eatright.org/adap1197.html.
43. Terhus, M. 1996. To shake or not to shake: EN takes another look at salt. *Environmental Nutrition* 19(9):1, 4.
44. Liebman, B. 1996. Salt: The pressure is on. *Nutrition Action Health Letter* 23(7):6–9.
45. Klatsky, A. 1996. Sensible, safe, and beneficial alcohol drinking. *Nutri-News* (Fall):14–16.
46. Zuger, A. 1997. For safety's sake; scrub your produce. *Health News* 3(8):3–4.
47. Nieman, D. 1999. *Exercise Testing and Prescription—A Health Related Approach*. Mountain View, Calif.: Mayfield Publishing Co.
48. Gershoff, S. (ed.). 1998. If your kitchen were a restaurant, you'd fail inspection. *Tufts University Health and Nutrition Letter* 16(9):1.
49. Consumers Union. 1997. Food poisoning—how to protect yourself from pathogens. *Consumer Reports* 63(11):64–65.
50. Gershoff, S. (ed.). 1998. Why you need a kitchen thermometer. *Tufts University Health and Nutrition Letter* 16(4):6.
51. Schardt, D., and L. Corcoran. 1998. Beat the heat. *Nutrition Action Health Letter* 25(5):10–11.
52. Editors. 1997. Decoding the freshness dates on food labels. *Tufts University Health and Nutrition Letter* 15(9):3.
53. Platzman, A. 1998. Eating out fast, but healthfully; is it possible? *EN* finds out. *Environmental Nutrition* 21(7):1, 6.
54. Editors. 1998. The missing dietary guidelines; enjoy your food. *Tufts University Health and Nutrition Letter* 16(5):3.

Suggested Readings

Duyff, R. L. 1998. *The American Dietetic Association's Complete Food and Nutrition Guide*. Minnetonka, Mn.: Chronimed Pub.

This book presents clear, understandable information on the basics of metabolism and weight management, vegetarianism, nutrition for athletes, food allergies, and more. The section on eating during pregnancy and breastfeeding is helpful for any woman considering pregnancy. The book also discusses vitamin and mineral supplements and popular herbs.

Margolis, S., and L. B. Wilder. 1998. *Nutrition and Longevity*. Baltimore, Md.: The Johns Hopkins Medical Institutions.

This monograph was published as part of the highly respected *White Papers* for the lay public by The Johns Hopkins Medical Institution. It provides an update of the *Dietary Guidelines for Americans*, offering practical methods of implementation. It includes coverage of timely topics such as antioxidants, folate, and phytochemicals.

Reinhardt, M. W. 1998. *The Perfectly Contented Meat-Eater's Guide to Vegetarianism: A Book for Those Who Really Don't Want to Be Hassled About Their Diet*. New York: Continuum Pub. Group.

This entertaining, informative, thought-provoking book is not only for strict vegans but also for committed meat eaters and every type of eater in between. Sprinkled with humor, the text provides clever insights about vegetarianism and some good hints for meat eaters about getting used to not eating meat.

Rosenfeld, I. 1996. *Doctor, What Should I Eat? Nutrition Prescriptions for Ailments in Which Diet Can Really Make a Difference*. New York: Warner Books.

The author takes the position that almost every major medical condition is either caused by or affected by what a person eats. The book reviews all the findings about food and specific bodily breakdowns in alphabetical order, from acne to vaginal yeast infection. Topics include vitamin benefits, immune system boosters, sugar, antioxidants, and food remedies. The book identifies the right foods to treat or prevent scores of health care problems.

Wardlaw, G. M. 1999. *Perspectives in Nutrition* (4th ed.). St. Louis, Mo.: WCB/McGraw Hill.

This book provides in-depth, comprehensive information on all aspects of nutrition. It serves as an excellent introductory reference for the person interested in nutrition issues.

Assessment Activity 6-1

Assessing Your Carbohydrate and Protein RDA

Assessing Your Carbohydrate Intake Goal

Directions: Complete the following steps to determine your goal for carbohydrate intake in grams to meet the Recommended Dietary Guidelines of 55 percent of total calories from carbohydrate (including sugar and complex carbohydrate).

1. Caloric Intake

Your body weight multiplied by 15 equals caloric intake for body weight (approximate number of calories consumed daily, assuming that you are not in a weight-loss or weight-gain program):

_____ lbs. × 15 = _____ calories

2. Carbohydrate Calories

Your caloric intake multiplied by 55 percent equals recommended carbohydrate calories:

_____ calories × 55% = _____ carbohydrate calories

3. Carbohydrate (Grams)

Your recommended carbohydrate calories divided by 4 equals recommended carbohydrate in grams. Transfer this result to Assessment Activity 6-3, Part C, DRV column:

_____ calories ÷ 4 = _____ g

EXAMPLE: For a person weighing 185 pounds:

Body weight:	185 lbs.
	× 15
1. Caloric intake:	2775 Kcal
	× 0.55
2. Recommended carbohydrate calories:	1526 Kcal
	÷ 4
3. Recommended carbohydrates:	382 g

This amounts to approximately 14 ounces of carbohydrate (382 ÷ 28 = 14 ounces). (28 grams = 1 ounce)

Assessing Your Protein RDA

Directions: Adults under 55 require 0.36 grams of protein per pound of body weight. Some experts recommend that people 55 years old and older consume 0.45 grams per pound. For example, a 20-year-old person who weighs 150 pounds needs 54 grams of protein: 150 × 0.36 = 54. A 60-year-old person who weighs 150 pounds needs 67.5 grams: 150 × 0.46 = 67.5.

Complete the following steps to determine your RDA for protein:

Your weight:	_____ lbs.
≥ 55 years old:	× 0.45
< 55 years old:	× 0.36
Protein RDA:	_____ grams

Assessment Activity 6-2

Assessing Your Maximum Fat and Saturated Fat Intakes

Assessing Your Maximum Fat Intake

Directions: Complete the following steps to determine your estimated maximum fat intake in grams to stay within the dietary guidelines of 30 percent of total calories from fat.

1. Caloric Intake
Your body weight multiplied by 15 equals caloric intake for body weight (approximate number of calories consumed daily, assuming that you are not in a weight-loss or weight-gain program):

_____ lbs. × 15 = _____ calories

2. Maximum Fat Calories
Your caloric intake multiplied by 30 percent equals maximum fat calories:

_____ calories × 0.30 = _____ calories

3. Maximum Fat (Grams)
Your maximum fat calories divided by 9 equals maximum fat in grams. Transfer this result to Assessment Activity 6-3, Part C, DRV column:

_____ calories ÷ 9 = _____ g

EXAMPLE: For a person weighing 185 pounds:

Body weight:	185 lbs.
	× 15
1. Caloric intake:	2775 Kcal
	× 0.30
2. Maximum fat calories:	832.5 Kcal
	÷ 9
3. Maximum fat:	92.5 g

This amounts to approximately 3 ounces of fat (92.5 ÷ 28 = 3.3 ounces).

Assessing Your Maximum Saturated Fat Intake

Directions: Complete the following steps to determine your estimated maximum saturated fat intake in grams to stay within the dietary guidelines of 10 percent of total calories from fat.

1. Caloric Intake
Your body weight multiplied by 15 equals caloric intake for body weight (approximate number of calories consumed daily, assuming that you are not in a weight-loss or weight-gain program):

_____ lbs. × 15 = _____ calories

2. Maximum Saturated Fat Calories
Your caloric intake multiplied by 8 percent equals maximum saturated fat calories:

_____ calories × 0.08 = _____ calories

3. Maximum Saturated Fat (Grams)
Your maximum saturated fat calories divided by 9 equals maximum saturated fat in grams. Transfer this result to Assessment Activity 6-3, Part C, DRV column:

_____ calories ÷ 9 = _____ g

EXAMPLE: For a person weighing 185 pounds:

Body weight:	185 lbs.
	× 15
1. Caloric intake:	2775 Kcal
	× 0.08
2. Maximum saturated fat calories:	222 Kcal
	÷ 9
3. Maximum saturated fat:	24.7 g

This amounts to less than 1 ounce of saturated fat (24.7 ÷ 28 = 0.88 ounces).

Assessment Activity 6-3

Nutrient Intake Assessment

One way to determine if you are getting sufficient quantities of the proper nutrients is to keep a record of your diet. Ideally, this record will cover a time span of at least one week. However, in this exercise you are asked to assess your dietary selections for only one day. Therefore, choose a day that is representative of your overall nutritional practices. (Your instructor may ask you to conduct a two- or three-day assessment. In this case photocopy additional copies of the assessment forms as needed.)

Directions There are two options for completing this assessment: (1) use the NutriQuest software that accompanies the textbook or (2) analyze your diet manually by following the instructions and completing the forms in Assessment Activities 6-3 and 6-4. Whichever option you choose, record all of the foods and beverages that you consume during one day with the exception of vitamin or mineral supplements. Be specific regarding the amount eaten, how it is cooked, and so on. List condiments and seasonings, such as mustard, ketchup, and butter, and dressings and trimmings, such as lettuce, onions, marshmallows, and sugar. The more detailed your record, the more accurate it will be and the more you will learn from it. Remember, the quality of the results is dependent on the quality of the information entered. A carefully and thoroughly prepared dietary recall will yield a quite accurate nutritional profile.

Instructions for NutriQuest HealthQuest Once foods have been listed, you are ready to use the NutriQuest program to generate your personal nutrition assessment report. Follow the instructions for installing the program on your personal computer. Enter your new User Profile information. When you have completed data entry, print and arrange the results in the following order:

1. User profile with Instant Analysis information: recommended carbohydrate, fat, protein, total caloric intake, and BMI
2. Nutrient summary of macronutrients, vitamins, minerals (ABC button)
3. Nutrient spreadsheet (Spreadsheet button)
4. Food pyramid breakdown of servings for one day (Pyramid button)
5. Bar graph showing dietary intake analysis of nutrients and percent RDA (Bar graph button for RDA analysis)
6. Pie chart comparing breakdown of carbohydrates, fat, protein with recommendations (Left pie chart button)
7. Pie chart showing breakdown of fat (Right chart button)
8. Major source of nutrients for those vitamins and minerals that do not meet the RDAs in #2
9. Summary paragraph describing what you learned about your dietary strengths and deficiencies and what changes are needed to improve your nutrition profile

Instructions for Conducting a Manual Nutrition Assessment Complete Parts A, B, C, and D. Then proceed to Assessment Activity 6-4.

Part A: Recording Your Nutrient Intake

1. Use the following form to record your dietary selections for one day. Photocopy extra copies of the form as needed.
2. Refer to the Food Composition Table in the appendix and record appropriate values in the spaces provided. For foods not included in the appendix, refer to package labels, if available, to determine nutritive values.
3. Add the values for each nutrient and enter the result in the total column.

Foods for One Day: List in column headings. Photocopy extra copies as needed.

Nutrients								Total
Calories								
Protein (g)								
Carbohydrate (g)								
Fat (g)								
Cholesterol (mg)								
Saturated Fat (g)								
Sodium (mg)								
Potassium (mg)								
Iron (mg)								
Vitamin A (RE)								
Vitamin C (mg)								
Thiamin (mg)								
Riboflavin (mg)								
Niacin (mg)								
Calcium (mg)								
Fiber (g)								

Part B: Are You Meeting the RDA?

1. Transfer the values in the Total column in Part A to the Total column in Part B for the following nutrients.
2. Fill in the RDA column with your protein RDA results from Assessment Activity 6-1. For the remaining nutrients, look up your corresponding RDA in table 6-4.
3. Subtract the RDA from your totals and indicate your status in the appropriate column. A positive value means that you are meeting the RDA for that nutrient; a negative value means that you are deficient in that nutrient.
4. For nutrients with a negative value, identify several specific foods that will eliminate the deficiency. Refer to the Food Composition Table in the appendix.

Nutrient	Total	RDA	Status	Food Prescription
Protein		(Refer to Assessment Activity 6-1)		
Iron		15 mg (women) 10 mg (men)		
Vitamin A		4000 IU (women) 5000 IU (men)		
Vitamin C		60 mg		
Thiamin		1.0–1.1 mg (women) 1.2–1.5 mg (men)		
Riboflavin		1.2–1.3 mg (women) 1.4–1.7 mg (men)		
Niacin		13–19 mg		
Calcium		1000 mg (ages 19–50) 1200 mg (51+)		

Part C: Are You Meeting the DVs?

1. Transfer the values in the total column from part A to the total column in Part C for the following nutrients. (Refer to Assessment Activities 6-1 and 6-2 for your personal DV for fat, saturated fat, and carbohydrate.)

2. Compare the DV listed with your totals. Indicate your status by subtracting the DV value from your value. Note that some values are maximum and should not be exceeded; others are goals that serve as minimums.

Nutrient	Total	DV*	Status
Fat		(maximum)**	
Saturated fat		(maximum)**	
Cholesterol		300 mg (maximum)	
Sodium		2400 mg (maximum)	
Carbohydrate		(goal)***	
Fiber		25 g (goal)	
Potassium		3500 mg (goal)	

*DV based on 2000-calorie diet.
**See Assessment Activity 6-2
***See Assessment Activity 6-1

Part D: What Did You Learn?

Write a summary paragraph describing what you learned about your dietary strengths and deficiencies and what changes are needed to improve your nutrition profile.

Assessment Activity 6-4

How Does Your Diet Compare with the Recommended Diet?

Directions: The recommended guidelines suggest that carbohydrate calories should make up at least 55 percent of the diet (including complex carbohydrates and sugar), fat calories should be less than 30 percent, and protein calories should be 15 percent. The purpose of this assessment is to compare your diet with these recommendations. First convert your caloric intake to percentages as follows.

Percent Carbohydrate Calories Your carbohydrate intake (refer to total carbohydrate intake from Part I, Assessment Activity 6-3) multiplied by 4 equals your carbohydrate calories:

_____ g × 4 = _____ carbohydrate calories

Your carbohydrate calories divided by total calories (refer to Part I, Assessment Activity 6-3) multiplied by 100 equals percent carbohydrate calories:

_____ carbohydrate calories ÷ _____ total calories × 100 = _____%

Draw a bar on the graph to indicate percentage of carbohydrate calories.

EXAMPLE: For a person on a 2000-calorie diet who consumed 175 grams of carbohydrate:

175 × 4 = 700 carbohydrate calories
700 ÷ 2000 = 0.35
0.35 × 100 = 35%

Percent Protein Calories Your protein intake (refer to total protein intake from Part I, Assessment Activity 6-3) multiplied by 4 equals protein calories:

_____ g × 4 = _____ protein calories

Your protein calories divided by total calories (refer to Part I, Assessment Activity 6-3) multiplied by 100 equals percent protein calories:

_____ protein calories ÷ _____ total calories × 100 = _____%

Draw a bar on the graph to indicate percentage of protein calories.

EXAMPLE: For a person on a 2000-calorie diet who consumed 100 grams of protein:

100 × 4 = 400 protein calories
400 ÷ 2000 = 0.20
0.20 × 100 = 20%

Percent Fat Calories Your fat intake (refer to total fat intake from Part I, Assessment Activity 6-3) multiplied by 9 equals your fat calories:

_____ g × 9 = _____ fat calories

Your fat calories divided by total calories (refer to Part I, Assessment Activity 6-3) multiplied by 100 equals percent fat calories:

_____ fat calories ÷ _____ total calories × 100 = _____%

Draw a bar on the graph to indicate percentage of fat calories.

EXAMPLE: For a person on a 2000-calorie diet who consumed 100 grams of fat:

100 × 9   = 900 fat calories
900 ÷ 2000 = 0.45
0.45 × 100 = 45%

Example Profile The following graph shows the percentages for the example as the yellow bar below the recommended amount, which is shown as a red bar.

Protein	15%	Recommended
	20%	
Fat	30%	Recommended maximum
	45%	
Complex carbohydrates and sugar	45%	Recommended goal
	35%	

Percent: 10 20 30 40 50 60 70 80 90 100

Your Profile Complete the bars with amounts calculated for your diet:

Protein	15%	Recommended
Fat	30%	Recommended maximum
Complex carbohydrates and sugar	55%	Recommended goal

Percent: 10 20 30 40 50 60 70 80 90 100

Assessment Activity 6-5

Do You Have Fatty Habits?

Fat has earned a bad reputation because of the health problems it contributes to in high-fat diets. The following questionnaire will help you think about the amounts and types of fat that you generally eat. For each general type of food or food habit, circle the category that is more typical for your diet. If you never or almost never eat any items of a particular food type, just skip it.

Food Type/Habit	High Fat	Medium Fat	Low Fat
Chicken	Fried with the skin	Baked, broiled, or barbecued with the skin	Baked, broiled, or barbecued without the skin
Fat present on meats	Usually	Sometimes	Never
Fat used in cooking	Butter, lard, bacon grease, chicken fat	Margarine, oil	Nonstick cooking spray or no fat used
Additions to rice, bread, potatoes, vegetables, etc.	Butter, lard, bacon grease, chicken fat, coconut oil	Margarine, oil, peanut butter	Butter-flavored granules or no fat used
Pizza toppings	Sausage, pepperoni, extra cheese, combination	Canadian bacon	Vegetables such as peppers, onions, and mushrooms
Sandwich spreads	Mayonnaise or mayonnaise-type dressing	Light mayonnaise, oil and vinegar	Mustard, fat-free mayonnaise
Milk and milk products (e.g., yogurt)	Whole-milk and whole-milk products	Low-fat milk products and milk products	Skim milk and milk products
Sandwich side orders	Chips, potato salad, macaroni salad with creamy dressing	Coleslaw, pasta salad with clear dressing	Vegetable sticks, pretzels, pickle
Salad dressings	Blue cheese, Ranch, Thousand Island, other creamy type	Oil and vinegar, clear-base dressing	Oil-free dressing, lemon juice, flavored vinegar
Typical meat portion	6–8 oz. or more	4–5 oz.	2–3 oz.
Sandwich fillings	Beef or pork hot dogs, salami, bologna, pepperoni, cheese, tuna or chicken salad	Turkey hot dogs, 85% fat-free lunch meats, corned beef, peanut butter, hummus (chickpea paste)	95% fat-free lunch meats, roast turkey, roast beef, lean ham
Ground meats	Regular ground beef, sausage meat, ground meat, ground pork (about 30% fat)	Lean ground beef, ground chuck, turkey sausage meat (20–25% fat)	Ground turkey, extra-lean ground beef, ground round (about 15% fat)
Deep-fried foods (e.g., french fries, onion rings, fish or chicken patties, egg rolls, tempura)	Eat every day	Eat once a week	Eat once a month or never
Bread for sandwiches	Croissant	Biscuit	Whole wheat, French, tortilla, pita or pocket bread, bagel, sourdough, or English muffin
Cheeses	Hard cheeses (such as cheddar, Swiss, provolone, Jack, American, processed)	Part-skim mozzarella, part-skim ricotta, low-fat cheeses	Nonfat cheese, nonfat cottage cheese, no cheese
Frozen desserts	Premium or regular ice cream	Ice milk or low-fat frozen yogurt	Sherbet, Italian water ice, nonfat frozen yogurt, frozen fruit whip

Food Type/Habit	High Fat	Medium Fat	Low Fat
Coffee lighteners	Cream, liquid or powdered creamer	Whole milk	Low-fat or skim milk
Snacks	Chips, pies, cheese and crackers, nuts, donuts, chocolate, granola bars	Muffins, toaster pastries, unbuttered commercial popcorn	Pretzels, vegetable sticks, fresh or dried fruit, air-popped popcorn, bread sticks, jelly beans, hard candy
Cookies	Chocolate coated, chocolate chip, peanut butter, filled sandwich type	Oatmeal	Ginger snaps, vanilla wafers, graham crackers, animal crackers, fruit bars
Scoring	(_____ × 2) +	(_____ × 1) +	(_____ × 0) =

Total score: _____

Once you have completed the questionnaire, count the number of circles in each column and calculate your score as follows: Multiply the number of choices in the left-hand (high-fat) column by 2 and multiply the number of choices in the middle (medium-fat) column by 1; then add these two values together. Based on your total score, rate yourself as follows:

Less than 10   =Excellent fat habits
10 to 20   =Good fat habits
20 to 30   = Fat habits needing improvement
Over 30   = Very high-fat diet

If your score is 20 or higher, try to substitute more foods from the middle (medium-fat) column or, better still, the right (low-fat) column for foods in the left-hand (high-fat) column.

Chapter 6 Forming a Plan for Good Nutrition

Name _____ Date _____ Section _____

Assessment Activity 6-6

Eating Behaviors to Consider

Directions: Answer the following questions to reveal information about your eating habits, how you developed certain tastes, and your attitude about various foods:

1. When was the last time you tried a new food? What was the food? What were the circumstances? _____
   _____

2. What new foods have you learned to eat during the past year? _____
   _____

3. Name the foods that have been on your "will not try" list (that is, foods that you will not eat under any circumstances). _____

4. What special events do you celebrate in some way with food? _____

5. Where is your favorite place to eat? _____

6. If you were to go on an eating binge, what foods would you be most likely to eat? _____
   _____

7. Describe in detail your favorite meal. _____
   _____

8. Do you consider yourself a slow eater, moderately fast eater, or gulper? What do you think is responsible for your eating pattern? _____
   _____

9. To what extent, if any, are your eating habits related to stress? Emotions? _____
   _____

10. What do you consider to be your good eating habits? Poor eating habits? _____
    _____

Improving Body Composition

Key Terms

amenorrheic
body composition
body mass index (BMI)
obesity
overfat
overweight

Objectives

After completing this chapter, you will be able to do the following:

- Define *body composition*.
- Define *essential fat* and *storage fat*.
- Define and differentiate between *obesity* and *overweight*.
- Discuss the health implications of regionally distributed fat.
- Discuss the limitations of height/weight tables for weight management.
- Calculate body mass index and interpret the results.
- Describe hydrostatic weighing, bioelectrical impedance, and skinfold measurements as methods for determining body composition.

Goals for Behavior Change

- Use table 7-3 to calculate your body mass index and interpret your results.
- Make a commitment to either maintain your existing weight or select a healthier weight for yourself.
- Formulate a long-range plan to achieve or maintain an ideal body weight and improve your body composition.

The body is composed of fat mass and fat-free mass. **Body composition** is the ratio between the two. Fat-free weight includes all tissues—muscle, bone, blood, organs, fluids—exclusive of fat. Fat is found in the organs (such as the brain, heart, liver, and lungs) and adipose cells. Adipose cells are fat cells that are located subcutaneously (beneath the skin) and surrounding various body organs. They are an insulator against heat loss and a protection for the internal organs against trauma. The majority of body fat is found in adipose cells, where it acts as a vast storage depot for energy.

A certain amount of fat is required for normal biological functions. This is referred to as *essential fat*. Essential fat is located in the bone marrow, organs, muscles, and intestines; it is a component of cell-membrane structure as well as of brain and heart tissue. The amount of essential fat in the male and female bodies differs. Essential fat constitutes 3 to 5 percent of the total weight of men and 8 to 12 percent of the total weight of women.[1]

The higher female requirement for essential fat is directly related to fertility and childbearing. Women whose body fat drops below essential requirements such as gymnasts, ballerinas, long-distance runners and anorexics, often become **amenorrheic**; that is, they stop having a menstrual cycle. The period of infertility continues until they gain weight and their essential fat is restored. In both genders, essential fat represents a minimal threshold or lower limit for the maintenance of health.

Obesity

Obesity, or overfatness, is gender specific. For men, **obesity** is defined as body fat equal to or greater than 25 percent of total body weight, and for women, it is equal to or greater than 32 percent of total body weight.[2] These values are arbitrary because the point at which fat storage actually increases health risks has not been determined. Contributing further to the confusion is the fact that methods of assessing the amount of body fat are indirect, and each contains a degree of measurement error.

Acceptable body fat percentages have been derived from young adult subjects, and these standards have been applied to all age groups—age-specific standards have yet to be determined, and it is very possible that such standards will vary somewhat with age. The results of studies of young adults demonstrate that fat typically ranges from 20 to 30 percent for young females and 10 to 20 percent for young males.[1] These data have led many authorities to suggest that body fat values of 25 percent for females and 15 percent for males are quite acceptable.

However, more recent body fat health standards that are based on age and gender allow for an increase in percent body fat with age. This allowance amounts to a trade-off in risks for chronic diseases, especially for women. Low body fat among middle-aged women is associated with losses of bone mineral content, which can lead to osteoporosis and bone fractures. However, leanness or low body fat helps protect these women against heart disease. It is best for women to be lean enough to prevent heart disease yet not so lean as to risk the development of osteoporosis. This is particularly problematic for small-framed women, whose bone mineral content is already low. See tables 7-1 and 7-2 for recommended body fat percentages for women and men of different ages. See also Nurturing Your Spirituality: Setting Realistic Fitness and Weight-Loss Goals.

Overweight

Overweight refers to excessive weight for height without consideration of body composition. Because the term *overweight* makes no allowances for body

Table 7-1 Recommended Body Fat Percentages for Women

Age	Essential Fat %	Minimal Fat %	Recommended Fat %	Obese Fat %
Over 56	8–12	10–12	25–38	> 38
35–55	8–12	10–12	23–38	> 38
34 or younger	8–12	10–12	20–35	> 35

Adapted from Lohman, T. G., L. B. Houtkooper, and S. B. Going. 1997. Body composition assessment: Body fat standards and methods in the field of exercise and sports medicine. *ACSM Health Fitness Journal* 1:30.

Nurturing Your Spirituality

Setting Realistic Fitness and Weight-Loss Goals

Success in any endeavor requires the establishment of long-term goals. Goals that are challenging and worthwhile but not impossible to accomplish are the keys to success. For instance, it would be unrealistic to expect to run a marathon after a few months of sporadic training or to lose 30 pounds in one month and keep it off.

A more feasible approach is to set realistic short-term goals that can be accomplished relatively easily and quickly. The accomplishment of these will provide the feedback you need to stay on track and the reinforcement to continue the program.

Attainable, realistic goals for exercise should be consistent with the American College of Sports Medicine guidelines for exercise, and realistic weight loss should not exceed 1.5 to 2 pounds per week. People often throw themselves into exercise with a vengeance, as if to wipe out years of inactivity with a frenzied few weeks of activity. The same degree of impatience surfaces with weight-loss attempts.

The following guidelines increase the likelihood of succeeding with exercise and weight loss:

1. Genetics is responsible for 25 to 40 percent of all of the factors that determine how aerobically fit we may become.[3] We can all achieve our aerobic potential with regular exercise, but world-class endurance performances are beyond the reach of most of us. Exercise and enjoy it, be as good as you can, and be satisfied with a significant accomplishment. You should be encouraged to know that you are in the select 15 percent of the adult population who exercise regularly and vigorously.

2. Genetics is responsible for 30 to 50 percent of all of the factors that lead to overweight and obesity. Although this represents a substantial influence, authorities are convinced that overweight individuals inherit only the *tendency* to become overweight or obese.[4] Our physical activity patterns and eating habits determine whether genetic history becomes destiny.

3. For weight loss or physical fitness, participate in moderate physical activity (preferably low impact if you are a beginner) that builds exercise into your daily life, such as mowing the lawn, washing the car by hand, and climbing stairs instead of taking elevators, plus participate in a structured exercise program (walking, walking/jogging, cycling, swimming, aerobics, etc.). Thirty minutes or more of exercise per day, preferably five days per week, plus eating nutritious meals based on the Food Guide Pyramid will improve physical fitness and produce sensible weight loss that can be maintained for life.

4. Avoid the inflexible pursuit of artificial aesthetic ideals and aim for reasonable goals. Don't pressure yourself to achieve your goals too rapidly. Remember, healthy eating and sensible regular exercise are for a lifetime, not just a few weeks or months. Let the bodily changes that result from this lifestyle occur slowly, and you will be able to enjoy them for a lifetime.

Taking care of your body does not result in instant health. To make real changes in your lifestyle, you must change the way you think. You must do more than nurture your body; you must nurture your mind as well.

Table 7-2 Recommended Body Fat Percentages for Men

Age	Essential Fat %	Minimal Fat %	Recommended Fat %	Obese Fat %
More than 56	3–5	5	10–25	> 28
35–55	3–5	5	10–25	> 28
34 or younger	3–5	5	8–22	> 25

Adapted from Lohman, T. G., L. B. Houtkooper, and S. B. Going. 1997. Body composition assessment: Body fat standards and methods in the field of exercise and sports medicine. *ACSM Health Fitness Journal* 1:30.

Real-World Wellness

Practical Ways to Estimate Overweight and Obesity

What are some practical techniques I can use to determine whether I'm overweight or obese that don't require much time, a technician, or sophisticated measuring equipment?

Practical sources for measuring overweight and overfatness rely on subjective observations and other sensory information. These estimates do not quantify, in a real sense, the extent of the problem should one exist.

Our mirrors supply us with visual feedback. Stand naked in front of a full-length mirror and, as objectively as possible, observe the shape of your body, determine where fat has accumulated, and estimate the amount of muscle you have. Use a tape measure to measure the circumference of your waist and hips. Your hips should be larger than your waist. While you have the tape measure in your hands, measure the circumference of your ankle according to the directions in table 7-3. This will estimate your skeletal size or frame size. People with large frame sizes can carry more weight than can people of the same height with small frame sizes. Knowing your frame size may help you to more accurately interpret the results from the bathroom scale in conjunction with height/weight charts.

A few years ago the slogan "pinch an inch" became popular. If you can pinch an inch at various sites on the body, you are probably somewhat overweight.

The fit of your clothes will provide other clues. If your pants or dress size is increasing steadily, you are obviously gaining weight. Conversely, if the sizes are getting smaller, you are successfully losing weight, changing your body composition, or both. If you are not consciously trying to lose weight and don't need to lose but are doing so anyway, this could be a sign of emerging disease and should be evaluated by a physician.

There is always the feedback you receive from other people. They may tell you that you appear to have either gained or lost some weight. Their perceptions may or may not be correct, but your size has led them to their conclusions.

After all is said and done, remember this: About 40 percent of all men are dissatisfied with their appearance and two-thirds of young women between 13 and 19 years think they weigh too much. The fact is that millions of normal-weight Americans, particularly young women, are also attempting to lose weight.

We are preoccupied with thinness in the United States. Beauty is in the eye of the beholder, but the vision has been distorted by Madison Avenue's preoccupation with excessive leanness. We need to be realistic and understand that excessive leanness is not within the grasp of most people, nor should it be. Thinness does not always go hand in hand with robust health.

Table 7-3 Measurement of Ankles to Determine Body Frame Size

Measure the ankle at the smallest point above the two bones that protrude on each side of the ankle. The tape measure should be pulled very tightly. Read the tape measure in inches and see the table for an interpretation.

Gender	Small Frame	Medium Frame	Large Frame
Males	< 8 inches	8–9¼ inches	> 9¼ inches
Females	< 7½ inches	7½–8¾ inches	> 8¾ inches

---

composition, it is a poor criterion for determining the desirability of weight loss. For example, a well-muscled person may be overweight but lean in regard to body fat. By American social standards, such body mass is healthy, aesthetically pleasing, and desirable. It is also possible for a person to be well within the norms for total body weight but **overfat**; that is, such a person carries a large proportion of body weight in the form of fat rather than lean tissue. Overfat is unhealthy and unattractive according to American social standards.

See Real-World Wellness: Practical Ways to Estimate Overweight and Obesity.

Regional Fat Distribution

Deposition of fat varies among people. The amount of fat and the storage sites are influenced by heredity and gender (figure 7-1). After puberty, women generally deposit fat in the buttocks, hips, breasts, and thighs. These preferential sites are largely dictated by the female hormone estrogen.[4] This tendency is known as the *gynoid*, or feminine, pattern of fat deposition. Gynoid fat is not confined exclusively to women; a few men deposit fat in this configuration as well.

Because they produce very little estrogen, men usually deposit minimal amounts of fat in the female pattern. Instead, they primarily store fat in the abdomen,

Figure 7-1 Feminine Versus Masculine Deposition of Fat

lower back, chest, and nape of the neck. Some women store fat this way as well. After menopause, estrogen production decreases and the prevalence of android fat deposition increases.

Although the general claim is that android or upper body fat (sometimes called *central fat*) is harmful, newer evidence indicates that not all android fat is equal.[5] Intra-abdominal fat, which is stored deep within the abdominal cavity, carries a much higher risk than does subcutaneous abdominal fat, which is stored directly beneath the skin. Physical activity tends to reduce intra-abdominal fat as well as subcutaneous fat. Moderately intense physical activities, such as gardening and casual walking, may not improve one's cardiorespiratory endurance, but when coupled with modest caloric restriction, they can decrease abdominal fat.

The waist-to-hip ratio (WHR) is a simple method for determining the distribution of body fat. It requires an accurate measurement of the circumference of the waist at the narrowest point between the rib cage and the navel and of the hips at the largest circumference of the hip/buttocks region. The waist measurement is then divided by the hip measurement. The resulting value may be interpreted by comparing the WHR to the following standard:[6]

- Males: A WHR greater than 0.95 indicates an excessive amount of upper body fat. Acceptable levels are less than 0.95.
- Females: A WHR greater than 0.80 indicates an excessive amount of upper body fat. Acceptable levels are less than 0.80.

The WHR has been criticized for failing to recognize factors other than abdominal fat, such as skeletal size and muscle mass in the buttocks. An expert panel convened by the National Heart, Lung, and Blood Institute in 1998 concluded that a circumference measure of only the waist is more highly predictive of disease risk than is the WHR.[7] For males, a high waist circumference is greater than 40 inches, and for females it is greater than 35 inches. The power of waist circumference to predict heart disease is unaffected by height, and its predictive power is increased if combined with a body mass index greater than $25 kg/m^2$. Body mass index (BMI) is described in detail later in this chapter.

The masculine, or android, pattern of fat deposition is related to an increase in the risk for heart disease, stroke, type II diabetes, and some forms of cancer.[4] There are several reasons for this increased risk.

First, enzymes in abdominal adipose cells are very active, so fat moves in and out easily. In sedentary people, abdominal fat enters the bloodstream and is routed directly to the liver, where it becomes the raw material for the manufacture of very low-density lipoprotein (VLDL) triglycerides. Later these are converted to low-density lipoprotein cholesterol (LDL-C), and this increases the risk for cardiovascular disease. Conversely, active people direct abdominal fat to the muscles, where it is used as fuel for physical work.

Second, abdominal fat cells are larger than other fat cells. Large fat cells are associated with blood glucose (sugar) intolerance and excessive amounts of insulin in the blood. Such an environment is conducive to the development of type II diabetes because the cells' receptor sites become resistant to insulin. Higher than normal amounts of insulin must be secreted to transport sugar from the blood to the cells, but excessive insulin remains in the blood. The body's cells continue to resist insulin so blood sugar also remains high. This sequence of events is characteristic of glucose intolerance or poor regulation of sugar. Over the years these factors can lead to type II diabetes. A person does not have to be excessively overweight to be at risk for type II diabetes; it is enough that fat be concentrated in the abdominal region. This pattern of fat deposition increases the risk of developing type II diabetes 10 to 15 times.[8] Extra fat that accumulates in the hips (gynoid pattern) also increases the risk, but only 3 to 4 times.

Wellness on the Web Behavior Change Activities

What's Your BMI?

Body mass index (BMI) is definitely not everyone's favorite number. Why? Because it provides an acceptable estimate of the proportion of our body weight that's composed of fat. Although knowing your BMI is more fun if you're fit, don't be discouraged if you're not there yet—use this useful measure to help you achieve your desired level of fitness. Simply put, BMI is the ratio of body weight in kilograms to height in meters squared. There are several body mass index protocols, all of which represent attempts to adjust body weight to derive a height-free measure of body fat. Although BMI doesn't provide an estimate of percent body fat, it's far more useful than height/weight tables. Calculate your BMI easily and quickly by going to the "In Fitness and Health" website at www.phys.com/a_home/01home/home.htm and clicking on "Calculators." Select BMI, type in the information requested, then click on "calculate" to view your BMI.

Is There Really an "Ideal Weight"?

Your "ideal weight," if there is such a thing, depends on a host of factors: your gender, age, height, and frame size, to name the most prominent. Instead of agonizing over outdated height and weight tables published years ago by insurance companies, turn to the experts on the internet. You can calculate your ideal weight painlessly by going to the "In Fitness and Health" website mentioned above and clicking on "Calculators." Select "Ideal Weight," type in the information requested, then click on "calculate" and view your ideal weight.

Where's the "Beef"?

Do you have an android or a gynoid pattern of fat distribution? You can find out easily by determining your waist-to-hip ratio. Measure the circumference of your waist about ½ inch above the navel, and measure the circumference of your hips at the greatest protrusion of the buttocks. To find out what "shape" you're in, go to the "In Fitness and Health" website at www.phys.com/a_home/01home/home.htm and click on "Calculators." Select Health Risk and type in your age, gender, hip and waist measurements. Then click on "Calculate" and your fat distribution pattern will be calculated for you.

Third, excessive insulin in the blood interferes with the removal of sodium by the kidneys, possibly leading to hypertension. Concurrently, the high circulating level of insulin stimulates the overproduction of epinephrine and norepinephrine, both of which raise the blood pressure. This cluster of disorders—high blood pressure, high blood sugar (glucose intolerance), high blood lipids (cholesterol and triglycerides), and abdominal obesity—has deadly consequences. Researchers refer to this combination as *syndrome X* or *metabolic syndrome*.[9]

The good news about android fat is that it is more easily removed from the body than is fat stored in the gynoid pattern. People who store fat in the masculine pattern can usually lose it through exercise. Dietary restriction, although helpful, is often unnecessary. Fat stored in the feminine pattern, however, is highly resistant to removal from its storage depots. Losing gynoid fat usually requires calorie restriction and exercise. Even the best effort may not result in the removal of enough fat from the lower half of the body to satisfy the dieter. Lower-extremity fat is stubborn and much more difficult to lose than is upper-body fat.

Methods for Measuring Body-Weight Status

Height/Weight Tables

Optimal body weight is not necessarily reflective of optimal body composition. This fact was illustrated by a comparison of young and middle-aged men who were within 5 percent of their ideal weight as determined by height, weight, and frame-size charts. Although both groups were within the ideal range, the middle-aged subjects had twice the amount of fat as the young subjects.

Height/weight tables do not actually measure body composition. They simply act as a standard for total body weight based on height, body-frame size, and gender without regard to the composition of weight. These tables are therefore poor criteria for the establishment of weight-loss recommendations.

Body Mass Index

Another method for measuring body-weight status is to calculate **body mass index (BMI)**. Body mass index is the ratio of body weight in kilograms (kg) to height in meters (m) squared (BMI = wt [kg]/ht [m^2]). There are several body mass index protocols, all of which originate from height/weight measurements. These protocols represent an attempt to adjust body weight to derive a height-free measure of obesity. Although BMI does not provide an estimate of percent body fat and although BMI uses height/weight data, it is more useful than the height/weight tables,[3] and it can be used to compare population groups. It also correlates fairly well (r = 0.70) with percent fat derived from underwater weighing.[4]

In June 1998, the American Heart Association added *obesity* to its list of major controllable risk factors for heart disease.[10] Obesity is now viewed as a chronic disease that represents a "dangerous epidemic" in this country. Later that same month, The National Heart, Lung, and Blood Institute (NHLBI) issued its initial clinical recommendations on obesity. A panel of twenty-four experts commissioned by the NHLBI conducted an extensive review of the research literature on obesity and concluded that people with BMIs of 25.0 to 29.9 kg/m^2 should be classified as overweight.[11] The panel recommended that people whose BMIs fall in this category should attempt to lose weight if they have two or more weight-related risk factors for illness. These include high blood pressure, diabetes, impaired glucose tolerance, and a waist circumference of greater than 40 inches for men and greater than 35 inches for women.

People whose BMIs are 30 kg/m^2 and higher are considered to be obese, and the panel advises these people to make serious attempts to lose weight.[11] According to the new BMI guidelines, approximately 55 percent of American adults (97 million people) are too fat.

There are two major limitations to using BMI measurements: (1) the technique is misleading for people with greater than average muscle mass because it measures overweight rather than overfat, and (2) the results are difficult for the general public to interpret, and the average person does not know how to apply BMI values to weight loss. The first limitation is easily surmounted. People with large amounts of muscle tissue should be directed to use a technique such as skinfold measurements or underwater weighing to measure their body composition.

The second limitation is more challenging. Follow these guidelines to establish and interpret BMI measurement. First, calculate BMI, taking care to accurately measure weight and height.

Weigh yourself in the morning after voiding and prior to breakfast. Wear light clothing and no shoes. For the height measurement, take off your shoes and stand with your back against a flat wall with your heels, buttocks, shoulders, and head against it. Have another person establish your height by using an object that has a right angle, such as a carpenter's square, a textbook, a clipboard on edge, or any other rigid item that is rectangular and has a 90-degree angle. The person doing the measuring should place the right angle against the wall and slide it down to the top of your head, mark the wall at the bottom of the right angle, and use a tape measure to measure from the mark to the floor.

The simplest way to calculate BMI is to bypass the formula and to use table 7-4. Find your height in the left column and move across to your weight in the same row. The number at the top of this column is your BMI. For example, a man who is 71 inches tall and weighs 200 pounds has a BMI of 28 kg/m^2. This man is in the "overweight" category. How much weight would he need to lose if he wanted to achieve a BMI of 24 kg/m^2? He can easily calculate this from the table. Find the column with the desired BMI of 24 kg/m^2 and drop down in the table to the row with his height (71 inches). He should weigh 172 pounds to achieve a BMI of 24 kg/m^2. Then subtract his desired weight (172 pounds) from his current weight (200 pounds). He needs to lose 28 pounds to reach his goal. Turn to Assessment Activity 7-1 to calculate your BMI and your desired body weight.

Measurement of Body Fat

The only direct means to measure the fat content of the human body is to perform chemical analysis on cadavers. The information obtained from cadaver studies has been used to develop indirect methods for estimating fat content. Because these estimates are indirect, they contain some degree of measurement error and should be interpreted accordingly. These indirect methods are commonly used in exercise physiology laboratories and fitness and wellness centers. See Wellness Across the Generations: Body Composition of Children and Adolescents.

Selected Methods for Measuring Body Composition

Underwater Weighing

Underwater weighing, one of the most accurate of the measurement techniques, involves weighing subjects both on land and while they are completely submerged in water (figure 7-2).

Whole-body density is calculated from body volume according to Archimedes' principle of displacement. Several thousand years ago, Archimedes discovered that a body immersed in water loses an amount of weight equal to the weight of the displaced water. The loss of weight in water is directly proportional to the volume of the water that is displaced or the volume of the body that displaces that water. The density of bone and muscle is higher than that of water and tends to sink. The density of fat is lighter than water and tends to float. Therefore, people with more muscle mass weigh more in water than do those who have less.

Table 7-4 Calculating Body Mass Index (BMI)

Each entry gives the body weight in pounds for a person of a given height and BMI. Pounds have been rounded off. To use the table, find the appropriate height in the far-left column. Move across the row to a given weight. The number at the top of the column is the BMI for that height and weight.

BMI (kg/m^2)

Height (Inches)	19	20	21	22	23	24	25	26	27	28	29	30	35	40
						Body Weight (Pounds)								
58	91	96	100	105	110	115	119	124	129	134	138	143	167	191
59	94	99	104	109	114	119	124	128	133	138	143	148	173	198
60	97	102	107	112	118	123	128	133	138	143	148	153	179	204
61	100	106	111	116	122	127	132	137	143	148	153	158	185	211
62	104	109	115	120	126	131	136	142	147	153	158	164	191	218
63	107	113	118	124	130	135	141	146	152	158	163	169	197	225
64	110	116	122	128	134	140	145	151	157	163	169	174	204	232
65	114	120	126	132	138	144	150	156	162	168	174	180	210	240
66	118	124	130	136	142	148	155	161	167	173	179	186	216	247
67	121	127	134	140	146	153	159	166	172	178	185	191	223	255
68	125	131	138	144	151	158	164	171	177	184	190	197	230	262
69	128	135	142	149	155	162	169	176	182	189	196	203	236	270
70	132	139	146	153	160	167	174	181	188	195	202	207	243	278
71	136	143	150	157	165	172	179	186	193	200	208	215	230	286
72	140	147	154	162	169	177	184	191	199	206	213	221	258	294
73	144	151	159	166	174	182	189	197	204	212	219	227	265	302
74	148	155	163	171	179	186	194	202	210	218	225	233	272	311
75	152	160	168	176	184	192	200	208	216	224	232	240	279	319
76	156	164	172	180	189	197	205	213	221	230	238	246	287	328

Wellness Across the Generations
Body Composition of Children and Adolescents

The body composition of children changes during the growth process. It has been well established that obese children and adolescents have a higher probability of becoming obese adults than do normal-weight children and that dramatic changes in body fat and body composition can occur during the peripubertal years (the time before, during, and after puberty). The proportion of body fat in young children ranges from 10 to 15 percent, with boys toward the lower end and girls toward the upper.[12]

Body fat generally increases in adolescent boys and girls and continues to do so into young adulthood so that the percentage of fat in males increases to 15 to 20 percent, whereas that of females increases to 20 to 25 percent. As we age, the percentage of fat continues to increase while muscle mass decreases. By middle age, fat accumulation exceeds 25 percent of the total weight of many men and 30 percent of the total weight of many women. The reason is a growing disparity between energy intake (food consumption) and energy expenditure (level of physical activity). We become less active with age. Television, computers, automobiles, elevators, escalators, remote controls, golf carts, riding mowers, and a lack of quality physical education programs in the public schools have diminished the energy expended by American children and adults.

Skinfold measurements made on children and adolescents in the 1960s and 1970s have been compared with those made on similar subjects in the 1980s. A trend surfaced in this comparison, indicating that a systematic increase in body fat percentage had occurred during the interim.[13] For example, the incidence of obesity in the 6 to 11 age group increased from 17.6 to 27.1 percent. *The Surgeon General's Report on Physical Activity and Health* indicated that 15 to 25 percent of U.S. children are overweight.[14]

A study completed in 1992 examined the relationship between body fatness and health status among children and adolescents.[15] The risks for high blood pressure, high total and LDL cholesterol (the harmful form), and low HDL cholesterol (the protective form) were associated with body fat above 25 percent for men and 30 percent for women. These levels have subsequently been proposed as useful health standards for those who are between 6 and 18 years of age.

Figure 7-2 Underwater Weighing Apparatus
A, subject is in the ready position for underwater weighing. B, subject is being weighed.

Formulas have been developed that use weight on land and weight in water to determine the percent of the total weight that consists of fat.

Underwater weighing has an inherent error of measurement that can be minimized when the residual volume of air (the air left in the lungs after a maximal expiration) is accurately measured. If residual air is measured, the error is approximately 2.7 percent.[16] Accuracy also depends on the subject's ability to exhale maximally on each trial and to sit still while completely submerged for six to ten seconds.

The equipment required for underwater weighing includes an autopsy scale with a capacity of approximately 9 kg (about 20 lbs.). The scale is suspended over a tank of water that is at least 4 feet deep. The subject sits suspended chin-deep, exhales completely, and bends forward from the waist until entirely submerged. This position is maintained for 6 to 10 seconds to allow the scale to stabilize. Five to ten trials are required, and the underwater weight is attained by averaging the three heaviest readings. The subject's net underwater weight is calculated by subtracting the weight of the seat, its supporting structure, and a weight belt (if needed) from the gross underwater weight. Percent body fat can be calculated from body density by using appropriate formulas.

Bioelectrical Impedance Analysis

Bioelectrical impedance analysis (BIA) is a relatively new and simple method of determining body composition. The equipment is portable and computerized but fairly expensive. It is safe, noninvasive, quick, and convenient to use (figure 7-3). Additionally, it does not require a high degree of technical skill, it intrudes less on the subject's privacy than other methods, and it is generally more comfortable.

The most common application of BIA employs a harmless, low-level, single-frequency electric current. This current is passed through the body of the person being measured via electrodes attached to specific sites on the right hand and foot, as shown in figure 7-3. Impedance represents resistance to the transmission of an electrical current. Impedance is least in lean body tissues because of their high water content (approximately 73 percent water). Water is an excellent conductor of electricity. Conversely, fat contains only 14 to 22 percent water and is resistant to electrical flow.[1]

Figure 7-3 Bioelectrical Impedance Analysis

A major limitation of BIA is that it does not accurately estimate fat-free mass in very lean or very fat subjects. Body fatness is generally overestimated for lean subjects and underestimated in obese subjects.

Recent advances in BIA instrumentation have improved the technique.[1] The newer instruments use multiple electrical frequencies (MFBIA), which seem to be less susceptible to the hydration status of subjects. As a result, a better estimate of lean body mass can be achieved.

Bioelectrical impedance analysis is as accurate as skinfold measurements provided potential error sources are controlled.[1,16] The main sources of error are the hydration state of the subject and the prediction equation that is used. Hydration is affected by eating, drinking fluids, urination, and exercise, and it significantly influences the results. Technician error is relatively minor provided standard procedures for electrode placement and body position of the subject are followed. To reduce error, the temperature of the testing room should be comfortable, and the following guidelines should be given to subjects the day before they are scheduled for testing:

- No eating or drinking within four hours of the test
- No exercise within twelve hours of the test
- No urination within thirty minutes of the test
- No alcohol consumption within forty-eight hours of the test
- No diuretic medicines within seven days of the test

Skinfold Measurements

Skinfold measurements are one of the least expensive and most economical methods of measuring body composition. The cost of skinfold calipers can be as low as $10. Computerized models, however, can run as high as $600. The most accurate calipers maintain a constant jaw pressure of 10 g/mm² of jaw surface area.

Figure 7-4 Suprailium Skinfold Measurement
Take a diagonal fold above the crest of the ilium directly below the midaxilla (armpit).

The thumb and index finger are used to pinch and lift the skin and the fat beneath it. The caliper is placed beneath the pinch (figure 7-4 through 7-8). Tables 7-5 and 7-6 show how to convert the sum of millimeters of skinfold thickness to percentage of body fat. When performed by skilled technicians, skinfold measurements correlate quite well (0.80 or greater) with body density calculated from underwater weighing.[2]

Table 7-5 Percentage of Fat Estimated for Men (Sum of Chest, Abdomen, and Thigh Skinfolds)

Sum of Skinfolds (mm)	Under 23	23–27	28–32	33–37	38–42	43–47	48–52	53–57	Over 57
8–10	1.3	1.8	2.3	2.9	3.4	3.9	4.5	5.0	5.5
11–13	2.2	2.8	3.3	3.9	4.4	4.9	5.5	6.0	6.5
14–16	3.2	3.8	4.3	4.8	5.4	5.9	6.4	7.0	7.5
17–19	4.2	4.7	5.3	5.8	6.3	6.9	7.4	8.0	8.5
20–22	5.1	5.7	6.2	6.8	7.3	7.9	8.4	8.9	9.5
23–25	6.1	6.6	7.2	7.7	8.3	8.8	9.4	9.9	10.5
26–28	7.0	7.6	8.1	8.7	9.2	9.8	10.3	10.9	11.4
29–31	8.0	8.5	9.1	9.6	10.2	10.7	11.3	11.8	12.4
32–34	8.9	9.4	10.0	10.5	11.1	11.6	12.2	12.8	13.3
35–37	9.8	10.4	10.9	11.5	12.0	12.6	13.1	13.7	14.3
38–40	10.7	11.3	11.8	12.4	12.9	13.5	14.1	14.6	15.2
41–43	11.6	12.2	12.7	13.3	13.8	14.4	15.0	15.5	16.1
44–46	12.5	13.1	13.6	14.2	14.7	15.3	15.9	16.4	17.0
47–49	13.4	13.9	14.5	15.1	15.6	16.2	16.8	17.3	17.9
50–52	14.3	14.8	15.4	15.9	16.5	17.1	17.6	18.2	18.8
53–55	15.1	15.7	16.2	16.8	17.4	17.9	18.5	19.1	19.7
56–58	16.0	16.5	17.1	17.7	18.2	18.8	19.4	20.0	20.5
59–61	16.9	17.4	17.9	18.5	19.1	19.7	20.2	20.8	21.4
62–64	17.6	18.2	18.8	19.4	19.9	20.5	21.1	21.7	22.2
65–67	18.5	19.0	19.6	20.2	20.8	21.3	21.9	22.5	23.1
68–70	19.3	19.9	20.4	21.0	21.6	22.2	22.7	23.3	23.9
71–73	20.1	20.7	21.2	21.8	22.4	23.0	23.6	24.1	24.7
74–76	20.9	21.5	22.0	22.6	23.2	23.8	24.4	25.0	25.5
77–79	21.7	22.2	22.8	23.4	24.0	24.6	25.2	25.8	26.3
80–82	22.4	23.0	23.6	24.2	24.8	25.4	25.9	26.5	27.1
83–85	23.2	23.8	24.4	25.0	25.5	26.1	26.7	27.3	27.9
86–88	24.0	24.5	25.1	25.7	26.3	26.9	27.5	28.1	28.7
89–91	24.7	25.3	25.9	26.5	27.1	27.6	28.2	28.8	29.4
92–94	25.4	26.0	26.6	27.2	27.8	28.4	29.0	29.6	30.2
95–97	26.1	26.7	27.3	27.9	28.5	29.1	29.7	30.3	30.9
98–100	26.9	27.4	28.0	28.6	29.2	29.8	30.4	31.0	31.6
101–103	27.5	28.1	28.7	29.3	29.9	30.5	31.1	31.7	32.3
104–106	28.2	28.8	29.4	30.0	30.6	31.2	31.8	32.4	33.0
107–109	28.9	29.5	30.1	30.7	31.3	31.9	32.5	33.1	33.7
110–112	29.6	30.2	30.8	31.4	32.0	32.6	33.2	33.8	34.4
113–115	30.2	30.8	31.4	32.0	32.6	33.2	33.8	34.5	35.1
116–118	30.9	31.5	32.1	32.7	33.3	33.9	34.5	35.1	35.7
119–121	31.5	32.1	32.7	33.3	33.9	34.5	35.1	35.7	36.4
122–124	32.1	32.7	33.3	33.9	34.5	35.1	35.8	36.4	37.0
125–127	32.7	33.3	33.9	34.5	35.1	35.8	36.4	37.0	37.6

Table 7-6 Percentage of Fat Estimated for Women (Sum of Triceps, Suprailium, and Thigh Skinfolds)

Sum of Skinfolds (mm)	Under 23	23–27	28–32	33–37	38–42	43–47	48–52	53–57	Over 57
23–25	9.7	9.9	10.2	10.4	10.7	10.9	11.2	11.4	11.7
26–28	11.0	11.2	11.5	11.7	12.0	12.3	12.5	12.7	13.0
29–31	12.3	12.5	12.8	13.0	13.3	13.5	13.8	14.0	14.3
32–34	13.6	13.8	14.0	14.3	14.5	14.8	15.0	15.3	15.5
35–37	14.8	15.0	15.3	15.5	15.8	16.0	16.3	16.5	16.8
38–40	16.0	16.3	16.5	16.7	17.0	17.2	17.5	17.7	18.0
41–43	17.2	17.4	17.7	17.9	18.2	18.4	18.7	18.9	19.2
44–46	18.3	18.6	18.8	19.1	19.3	19.6	19.8	20.1	20.3
47–49	19.5	19.7	20.0	20.2	20.5	20.7	21.0	21.2	21.5
50–52	20.6	20.8	21.1	21.3	21.6	21.8	22.1	22.3	22.6
53–55	21.7	21.9	22.1	22.4	22.6	22.9	23.1	23.4	23.6
56–58	22.7	23.0	23.2	23.4	23.7	23.9	24.2	24.4	24.7
59–61	23.7	24.0	24.2	24.5	24.7	25.0	25.2	25.5	25.7
62–64	24.7	25.0	25.2	25.5	25.7	26.0	26.7	26.4	26.7
65–67	25.7	25.9	26.2	26.4	26.7	26.9	27.2	27.4	27.7
68–70	26.6	26.9	27.1	27.4	27.6	27.9	28.1	28.4	28.6
71–73	27.5	27.8	28.0	28.3	28.5	28.8	29.0	29.3	29.5
74–76	28.4	28.7	28.9	29.2	29.4	29.7	29.9	30.2	30.4
77–79	29.3	29.5	29.8	30.0	30.3	30.5	30.8	31.0	31.3
80–82	30.1	30.4	30.6	30.9	31.1	31.4	31.6	31.9	32.1
83–85	30.9	31.2	31.4	31.7	31.9	32.2	32.4	32.7	32.9
86–88	31.7	32.0	32.2	32.5	32.7	32.9	33.2	33.4	33.7
89–91	32.5	32.7	33.0	33.2	33.5	33.7	33.9	34.2	34.4
92–94	33.2	33.4	33.7	33.9	34.2	34.4	34.7	34.9	35.2
95–97	33.9	34.1	34.4	34.6	34.9	35.1	35.4	35.6	35.9
98–100	34.6	34.8	35.1	35.3	35.5	35.8	36.0	36.3	36.5
101–103	35.3	35.4	35.7	35.9	36.2	36.4	36.7	36.9	37.2
104–106	35.8	36.1	36.3	36.6	36.8	37.1	37.3	37.5	37.8
107–109	36.4	36.7	36.9	37.1	37.4	37.6	37.9	38.1	38.4
110–112	37.0	37.2	37.5	37.7	38.0	38.2	38.5	38.7	38.9
113–115	37.5	37.8	38.0	38.2	38.5	38.7	39.0	39.2	39.5
116–118	38.0	38.3	38.5	38.8	39.0	39.3	39.5	39.7	40.0
119–121	38.5	38.7	39.0	39.2	39.5	39.7	40.0	40.2	40.5
122–124	39.0	39.2	39.4	39.7	39.9	40.2	40.4	40.7	40.9
125–127	39.4	39.6	39.9	40.1	40.4	40.6	40.9	41.1	41.4
128–130	39.8	40.0	40.3	40.5	40.8	41.0	41.3	41.5	41.8

Age to Last Year

Figure 7-5 Chest Skinfold Measurement

Take a diagonal fold half the distance between the anterior axillary line and the nipple.

Figure 7-6 Thigh Skinfold Measurement

Take a vertical fold on the front of the thigh midway between the hip and the knee joint. The midpoint should be marked while the subject is seated.

Figure 7-7 Abdominal Skinfold Measurement

Take a vertical fold about 1 inch from the navel.

Figure 7-8 Triceps Skinfold Measurement

Take a vertical fold on the midline of the upper arm over the triceps, halfway between the acromion and olecranon processes (tip of the shoulder to the tip of the elbow). The arm should be extended and relaxed when the measurement is taken. All skinfold measurements should be taken on the right side. The calipers should be perpendicular to the fold. The photos do not reflect perpendicularity in order to show the site mark and the caliper face without the technician's hand in the way, obscuring both.

Determining Desired Body Weight from Body Fat

Calculating desirable body weight is a simple procedure when the percentage of body fat is known. The following example is for a 148-pound woman whose body fat is equal to 30 percent of her total body weight, based on her skinfold measurements. She wishes to reduce her body fat to 23 percent.

Find fat weight (FW) in pounds:

$$FW \text{ (lbs.)} = \frac{\text{Body weight (BW) (lbs.)} \times \% \text{ fat}}{100}$$
$$= \frac{148 \text{ lbs.} \times 30}{100}$$
$$= \frac{4440 \text{ lbs.}}{100}$$
$$= 44.4 \text{ lbs.}$$

Find lean weight (LW) in pounds:

$$LW \text{ (lbs.)} = BW - FW$$
$$= 148 \text{ lbs.} - 44.4 \text{ lbs.}$$
$$= 103.6 \text{ lbs.}$$

Find desirable body weight (DBW) in pounds:

$$DBW \text{ (lbs.)} = \frac{LW \text{ (lbs.)}}{1.0 - \% \text{ fat desired}}$$
$$= \frac{103.6 \text{ lbs.}}{1.0 - 0.23}$$
$$= \frac{103.6 \text{ lbs.}}{0.77}$$
$$= 134.5 \text{ lbs.}$$

The method for calculating desirable body weight based on percent body fat is relatively effective if the subject does the following:

- Exercises to maintain muscle tissue
- Loses no more than 1.5 pounds per week
- Is evaluated for body fatness two to three times during the weight-loss period
- Understands that indirect measurements of body fatness contain some error

Complete Assessment Activity 7-2 to determine your desirable body weight.

Summary

- Essential fat is necessary for normal biological function.
- Men carry 3 to 5 percent of their weight in the form of essential fat; women carry 8 to 12 percent of their weight as essential fat.
- *Obesity* is defined as overfatness.
- Men are obese when fat constitutes 25 percent or more of the body's weight, and women are obese when fat constitutes 32 percent or more of the body's weight.
- The majority of women store fat in the hips, buttocks, thighs, and breasts (gynoid fat).
- The majority of men store fat in the abdomen, lower back, chest, and nape of the neck (android fat).
- Height/weight tables are limited and poor instruments for weight-loss recommendations.
- Body mass index correlates fairly well with percent fat derived from hydrostatic weighing.
- A high body mass index correlates with hypertension, high total cholesterol, low HDL cholesterol, high serum triglycerides, and poor glucose tolerance.
- Bioelectrical impedance is a safe, quick, and relatively accurate method for assessing percent body fat.
- Skinfold measurements are one of the most economical methods of measuring body composition in terms of the cost of equipment and the time required to determine percent body fat.
- Underwater weighing is still considered the "gold standard" for measuring body composition.

Review Questions

1. What is essential fat and how is it distributed in men and women?
2. How would you define *obesity* and *overweight*?
3. At what level of fat deposition does obesity become a health hazard for men and women?
4. What are *gynoid obesity* and *android obesity*? Which is a greater health risk and why?
5. What are the limitations of height/weight tables for recommending weight loss?
6. What is body mass index and how is it classified for men and women?
7. How are underwater weighing, bioelectrical impedance, and skinfold measurements used to determine percent body fat?
8. How is healthy body weight determined when the percent body fat is known?

References

1. Going, S., and R. Davis. 1998. Body composition. In *ACSM's Resource Manual* (3d ed.), ed. J. L. Roitman. Baltimore, Md.: Williams & Wilkins.
2. ACSM. 1995. *ACSM's Guidelines for Exercise Testing and Prescription.* Baltimore, Md.: Williams & Wilkins.
3. Blair, S. N., et al. 1995. Changes in physical fitness and all-cause mortality. *JAMA* 273(14):1093.
4. Grilo, C. M., and K. D. Brownell. 1998. Interventions for weight management. In *ACSM's Resource Manual* (3d ed.), Baltimore, Md.: Williams & Wilkins.
5. Despres, J. P. 1997. Visceral obesity, insulin resistance, and dyslipidemia: Contribution of endurance exercise training to the treatment of plurimetabolic syndrome. *Exercise and Sport Sciences Reviews* 25: 271.
6. Bryant, C. X., and J. A. Peterson. 1998. Determining ideal body weight. *Fitness Management* 14(7):24.
7. NHLBI. 1998. *Obesity Education Initiative Expert Panel Clinical Guidelines on the Identification, Evaluation, and Treatment of Overweight and Obesity in Adults.* National Heart, Lung, and Blood Institute. Washington, D.C.
8. Bouchard, C., et al. 1993. Exercise, body fat, and the metabolic syndrome. *Medicine and Science in Sports and Exercise* 25:S1.
9. Gordon, N. F. 1998. Conceptual basis for coronary artery disease risk factor assessment. In *ACSM's Resource Manual* (3d ed.), ed. J. L. Roitman. Baltimore, Md.: Williams & Wilkins.
10. Harvard University. 1998. Guidelines call more Americans overweight. *Harvard Health Letter* 23(10):7.
11. Tufts University. 1998. Should fewer calories be in your future? *Tufts University Health and Nutrition Letter* 16(6):8.
12. Williams, M. A. 1998. Human development and aging. In *ACSM's Resource Manual* (3d ed.), ed. J. L. Roitman. Baltimore, Md.: Williams & Wilkins.
13. Robergs, R. A., and S. O. Roberts. 1997. *Exercise Physiology,* St. Louis, Mo.: Mosby.
14. U.S. Dept. of Health and Human Services. 1996. *Physical Activity and Health: A Report of the Surgeon General.* Atlanta: U.S. Dept. of Health and Human Services, Centers for Disease Control and Prevention, National Center for Chronic Disease Prevention and Health Promotion.
15. Williams, D. P., et al. 1992. Body fatness and risk for elevated blood pressure, total cholesterol, and serum lipoprotein ratios in children and adolescents. *American Journal of Public Health* 82:363.
16. Nieman, D. C. 1999. Exercise testing and prescription. Mountain View, Calif.: Mayfield Publishing.

Suggested Readings

Roche, A. F., S. B. Heymsfield, and T. G. Lohman, eds. 1996. *Human Body Composition.* Champaign, Ill.: Human Kinetics.

This book presents a full-scale treatment of the history and development of the techniques used to measure body composition. It describes the best and the most popular methods used.

Heyward, V. H., and L. M. Stolarczyk. 1996. *Applied Body Composition Assessment.* Champaign, Ill.: Human Kinetics.

This book, not for the casually interested reader, goes beyond the basics. It presents the scientific principles underlying some of the best and most popular techniques for measuring body composition.

Brown, J. E. 1999. *Nutrition Now.* Belmont, Calif.: West/Wadsworth.

A short chapter on body weight and body composition was written for those with little or no knowledge of these topics. The text covers in a very concise manner most popular techniques of measuring body composition.

Margolis, S., and L. J. Cheskin. 1998. *Weight Control.* Baltimore, Md.: The Johns Hopkins Medical Institutions.

Written for the layman, this book discusses methods for determining weight status and body composition and describes the advantages and disadvantages of using height/weight tables, body mass index, waist/hip ratio, underwater weighing, dual-energy X-ray absorptiometry (DEXA), and bioelectric impedance analysis. It is very informative, especially for beginners.

Howley, E. T., and B. D. Franks. 1997. *Health Fitness Instructor's Handbook.* Champaign, Ill.: Human Kinetics.

Chapter 9 covers body composition, discussing the impact of body weight and body composition on health status. It also describes in some detail many of the most effective and popular techniques for determining body composition.

Name _____ **Date** _____ **Section** _____

Assessment Activity 7-1

Using BMI to Estimate Body-Weight Status and Calculate Desirable Body Weight

Directions: Calculate your BMI:

1. Your body weight: _____ lbs.
2. Your height: _____ in.
3. Use the nomogram in table 7-4 to calculate your BMI.

   Your BMI: _____ kg/m²

4. Your desired BMI: _____ kg/m²
5. Once again, use the nomogram to calculate your desired body weight. Connect your desired BMI to your height and extend the line through the weight column.

   Your desired weight: _____ lbs.

6. Subtract your desired body weight from your current body weight to determine how much weight you need to lose or gain.

   Current weight – desired weight = weight to gain or lose

   _____ lbs. – _____ lbs. = _____ lbs.

Assessment Activity 7-2

Calculating Desirable Body Weight from Percent Body Fat

Directions: To find your desirable body weight, insert your current weight, percentage of body fat, and the desirable body fat that you wish to attain in the appropriate spaces. Then calculate fat weight, lean weight, and desirable body weight. Subtract desirable body weight from current weight. This figure tells you how much weight you must lose to achieve your desirable percentage of body fat.

Current weight = _____ lbs.

Current percentage of body fat = _____ %

Desirable body fat = _____ %

1. Fat weight

$$= \frac{\text{Body weight} \times \text{Percentage of fat}}{100}$$

= _____ lbs.

2. Lean weight
 = Body weight − Fat weight

 = _____ lbs.

3. Desirable body weight

$$= \frac{\text{Lean weight}}{1 - \text{Percentage of fat desired}}$$

= _____ lbs.

4. Amount of weight to lose = _____ lbs.

8

Achieving a Healthy Weight

Key Terms

anorexia nervosa
basal metabolic rate (BMR)
binge-eating disorder
body dysmorphic disorder (BDD)
bulimia
caloric deficit
caloric expenditure
caloric intake
diet resistance
fasting
hyperplasia
hypertrophy
overcompensatory eating
set point
thermogenic effect of food (TEF)
very-low–calorie diets (VLCDs)
weight cycling

Goals for Behavior Change

- Compare physical characteristics of your ideal body image with your actual body image.
- Estimate caloric expenditure for your basal metabolism and physical activity level.
- Adjust your caloric intake and physical activity as necessary to achieve a healthy weight.
- Formulate a plan for achieving a healthy weight.

Objectives

After completing this chapter, you will be able to do the following:

- Define *obesity* and *overweight*.
- Differentiate between hypertrophic and hyperplastic development of adipose cells.
- Identify and discuss the health aspects of obesity.
- Discuss biological and behavioral causes of obesity.
- Discuss the relationship of genetics, setpoint, overeating, and physical activity to body shape, fat distribution, and obesity.
- Define and identify *eating disorders* and their symptoms and treatment.
- Calculate the caloric cost of physical activities.
- Compare and contrast dieting and physical activity as strategies for weight management.
- Identify principles of weight management.

Theoretically, achieving a healthy weight is a simple issue: A person balances **caloric intake,** calories supplied by food, with **caloric expenditure,** calories expended by physical activity and metabolism. In practice, however, people vary considerably in their responses to both caloric intake and caloric expenditure. No two people have identical experiences with dieting or physical activity regimens. Some people who chronically face weight problems eat no more and sometimes less than their normal-weight peers. Conversely, some normal-weight people have voracious appetites and do not expend any more calories than their overweight peers.

How can this be explained? Are the differences due to heredity, metabolism, or errors in reporting food intake and physical activity expenditures? Although on the surface body weight appears to be a function of the basic laws of nature (caloric intake vs. caloric expenditure), in truth it is a complex issue that is still not fully understood by medical experts. For many people, self-improvement goals involving weight management are achievable and worthwhile. For others, formulating weight management goals means first constructing a realistic view of body image (see Nurturing Your Spirituality: Body Image Begins on the Inside). This chapter addresses some of the complexities of body weight issues and presents basic principles for achieving a healthy weight.

Americans' Obsession with Body Weight

Americans are preoccupied with their body weight. Books that offer creative but questionable advice for losing weight netted $141 million in sales in 1997.[2] The diet industry earns annual revenues of more than

Nurturing Your Spirituality

Body Image Begins on the Inside[1]

If you are unhappy with your body image, you are not alone. More than one-half of women and more than four of ten men are dissatisfied with their overall appearance; even more people are dissatisfied with their weight. Perceptions about body image are worse for young women. Almost two-thirds of girls and young women, ages 13 to 19, think they weigh too much. One-half of American women overestimate the sizes of their bodies.

Why are so many people unhappy with their body shapes or weights? Why do people tend to focus on their physical imperfections? Why does such a large discrepancy exist between the ways people see their own bodies and the ways others see them? Body image studies identify the following factors as being responsible for negative body images:

- Weight gain
- The media's preoccupation with thinness as the trademark for beauty
- Cultural pressures
- Disapproving messages from others
- Fluctuating moods
- Physical changes, such as pregnancy
- Chronic illness
- Childhood teasing
- Sexual abuse

What are the costs of an exaggerated negative body image? People who are deeply troubled about their appearance or preoccupied with selected physical "flaws" often limit their social activities; may not be assertive at work, school, or in personal relationships; may experience difficulty in forming a positive sexuality; may engage in high-risk behaviors; and often become victims of unrealistic fad diets. Extreme cases may involve a psychological disorder called *body dysmorphic disorder (BDD)*. People with this condition are so preoccupied with what they see as a disfiguring flaw that they shun social activities, including school and work.

Although self-improvement is a worthy goal for most people, when it comes to body image it is important to separate nature from nurture, heredity from environment. The challenge for many people with negative body images is to set realistic goals about what can be changed and to accept what can't be changed. Every one of us has a natural and unique size and shape. Our self-esteem depends on accepting the physical features that are unique to each of us. Changing what and how you think about your body can be healthier than constantly working to change your body weight and shape by diet and exercise. Having a positive body image is not just about losing weight or working with what is on the outside. It begins on the inside.

$33 billion by hawking far-out gadgets and gimmicks including lipo-slim briefs, which supposedly massage away cellulite; slimming insoles, shoe insoles that reportedly stimulate weight-loss acupressure points as you walk; and aroma pens, inhalants that come in banana, green apple, and peppermint claimed to squelch hunger pangs.[3,4,5] At any given time more than one-half of women and more than one-fourth of men are on a diet. Even children are getting the message that dieting is popular—50 percent of 9-year-old girls have dieted, although only 11 percent are overweight.[5,6] More than $30 billion a year are spent on gimmicks, gadgets, and strategies to trim, tuck, and tone waistlines.[2] Of adults, 50 million are dieting, and most of them are repeaters, averaging 2.3 diets per year.[3,4]

The evidence for this obsession can be found in advertisements and the news. Numerous television celebrities have engaged in special diet or weight-loss programs. Both the print and video media show countless numbers of advertisements that associate super svelte body images with almost every imaginable product. Consumers demand low-calorie versions of every consumable food, and much of this demand is motivated more by the desire to achieve an unobtainable physique than by health reasons. Consumers have been observed counting the number of calories even in a dose of laxatives. The phrase *calorie anxiety* applies to many Americans. Even health magazines and professional journals reinforce this preoccupation by featuring headlines of diet articles or diet studies on their covers. If some new diet finding is released by the scientific community, it will surely be headlined on national and local news shows and will quickly be followed by feature stories.

For some people the obsession with weight is so intense that it causes serious body-image problems, distorts their self-esteem, and eventually leads to eating disorders, such as anorexia nervosa, bulimia, and compulsive eating, three conditions that were almost unheard of twenty years ago. Extreme cases may involve a psychological disorder called **body dysmorphic disorder (BDD)**. BDD is an obsession with perceived flaws in physical appearance that is so extreme that it may disrupt a person's life and can lead to thoughts of suicide.[7]

The effects of weight obsession may be more subtle. Some people who are neither anorexic nor bulimic may develop aversive attitudes toward food, eating, and mealtime. Rather than serving as a source of pleasure and enjoyment, the eating experience becomes a constant test of willpower that rarely yields positive results. For too many people, attitudes about appearance, body weight, and food combined with the ubiquitous messages and body images promulgated by the media form a vicious cycle of guilt, denial, and unhappiness.

For example, the average height and weight of a contemporary fashion model is 5 feet 9 inches and 110 pounds. In contrast, the average height and weight of an American woman is 5 feet 4 inches and 142 pounds.[5] Only 10 percent of the population genetically fits models' height and weight zone.[8] The rest of the population is left with body images that are unobtainable and unrealistic. The challenge for many people is to break this cycle by constructing realistic views of their bodies, establishing positive attitudes toward food, and formulating realistic strategies to address the weight problem (see Assessment Activity 8-1).

Defining the Problem

For many Americans, weight loss is a healthy goal. Losing weight often means reducing the risk of developing common chronic health problems. However, many people who are not overweight and have good body composition try to lose weight. For them, losing weight offers no health benefits and may even be harmful.

The number of people who stand to benefit from weight loss is at an all-time high. New standards established by the National Institutes of Health define a healthy weight as a BMI equal to or more than 19 and less than 25. Being overweight is defined as having a BMI of 25 or higher; obesity is defined as having a BMI of 30 or higher. By these definitions, only 41 percent of U.S. adults 20 years or older are at a healthy weight—39 percent of males and 44 percent of females. Nearly one-fourth (22 percent) of U.S. adults are obese.[6] Both of these figures are significantly higher than comparison figures for each of the previous decades since data have been collected. Adults are not the only ones who are overweight. Eleven percent of all children and 10 percent of all adolescents are overweight or obese.[6] The dramatic increase in body weight has led some experts to proclaim that obesity is a chronic health condition of epidemic proportion. Obesity has been declared a disease by the National Institutes of Health (NIH); it has also been elevated to the status of a major risk factor for heart disease (see Chapter 2).

Americans are getting heavier for two obvious reasons: too much energy going in (as food) and too little energy going out (as exercise). The majority of Americans are sedentary; at the same time they are consuming more calories than they were fifteen years ago. Table 8-1 presents the calorie intakes for men and women between the ages of 16 and 39, based on the results of the *Third National Health and Nutrition Examination Survey (NHANES),* one of the major national surveys in the National Nutrition Monitoring and Related Research Program.[9]

Table 8-1 Average Calorie Intake* by Selected Age and Gender

Age	Men	Women
16–19 years	3097	1958
20–29 years	3025	1957
30–39 years	2872	1883
Combined average	2998	1933

*Average calorie intake for all age groups and both genders from 2 months to over 80 years is 2200.

Although BMI provides a basis for classifying levels of overweight and obesity, it is not without its limitations (see Chapter 7). It is also important to remember that BMIs of 25 and 30 (for overweight and obesity, respectively) are not precise points on a scale that when exceeded magically increase a person's risk for health problems. For example, although a BMI of 29.9 does not technically fall into the category of obesity, it is a very small step away from the "magic number" of 30, the cutoff point for obesity. For all practical purposes, a BMI of 29.9 carries the same risk of obesity as a BMI of 30.

Health Aspects of Obesity

In declaring obesity a disease, the NIH signaled a new approach toward obesity. Medical experts no longer regard being obese as a simple failure of willpower. Instead, obesity is considered a chronic disease, such as hypertension or diabetes. In 1994 weight-loss experts advocated "a conceptual housecleaning" in the way medical doctors and the general public think about weight.[10] The result is new knowledge and a different attitude about the causes and treatments of obesity.

One aspect of obesity that has not changed is its medical consequences. Morbidity occurs more frequently and with greater severity and mortality occurs at an earlier age among obese people than among those of normal weight.[6] In an extensive review of the scientific literature on obesity and health, a panel of twenty-four experts summoned by the National Heart, Lung, and Blood Institute proclaimed that obesity is second only to smoking as the largest cause of preventable death in the United States.[11]

Obesity is highly correlated with coronary heart disease and stroke. LDL cholesterol, which contributes to the development of atherosclerosis, is associated with obesity. According to the Framingham Heart Study, a 20 percent weight loss may reduce the risk of coronary heart disease by 40 percent.[12] One-third of all cases of hypertension are considered a result of obesity. Many hypertensive people experience a decline in systolic and diastolic blood pressures within the first two to three weeks of a weight-loss program.[12]

Obesity is also a major risk factor for some forms of cancer; it predisposes men to cancers of the colon, rectum, and prostate and women to cancers of the ovaries, uterus, and breasts.

Fifty percent of people with impaired glucose tolerance are overweight.[6] For people with a predisposition to type II diabetes, losing 10 pounds can reduce the chances of contracting the condition by 30 percent. For those who already have diabetes, a 5 percent weight loss can significantly improve the body's use of insulin and lower blood sugar levels.[12]

Obesity increases the risk of osteoarthritis. It intensifies symptoms in those who already have the disease.

Obesity is a prime risk factor for gallbladder disease. Obese individuals have a 3 to 7 times greater risk of gallstones, stones usually composed of cholesterol, than do normal weight people. Weight loss can reduce the risk of gallbladder disease, even though rapid weight loss temporarily increases gallstone formation.[12]

Obesity is a leading cause of sleep apnea, a condition characterized by loud snoring and brief halts in breathing (for about ten to thirty seconds at a time) during sleep. This condition is thought to be caused, in part, by the accumulation of fat tissue in the upper airway, which obstructs breathing. Sleep apnea can lead to daytime sleepiness and may also adversely affect heart function. A 10 to 15 percent weight reduction may relieve or even cure this condition.[12]

For some people, the first symptom of strain placed on the body by excess fat is shortness of breath. As fat accumulates, it crowds the space occupied by organs. Some people cannot sit comfortably because of fat accumulation in their abdomens. In a sitting position a person's lungs have limited space in which to expand.

Postsurgery complications occur more often in overweight people than in those who are not overweight. Wounds don't heal as well or as fast. Infections are more common.

In addition to suffering from medical hazards, it is not uncommon for obese people to suffer psychological stress, depression, social discrimination, and reduced income. They pay higher premiums for health insurance or are denied coverage. Obese children are often ridiculed by their slim peers. Armed forces personnel are forced out of the military if they gain weight beyond an acceptable level.

The link between obesity and chronic disease is well established, but evidence has emerged indicating that the *distribution* of fat is equally important to the development of disease. Studies have confirmed that abdominal fat is associated with a higher rate of heart attack and stroke than is fat distributed around the hips and thighs (see Chapter 7). Guidelines for doctors now suggest that, in addition to calculating BMI, they should assess waist circumference. A waist measurement of more than 40 inches in men and over 35 inches in women is considered a marker for risk in people with BMIs of 25.0 to 34.9.[11]

In summary, the medical community clearly concurs that the health risks and complications of obesity are associated with premature death. This is not necessarily the case for overweight, however. A twelve-year study of 324,135 adults found that the risk of dying associated with being overweight was relatively modest and declined as people grew older. By age 65 the increased risk was slight, and by age 74 it had disappeared. People who were moderately overweight but not obese had no increased risk of premature death.[12]

The response of medical experts to these findings has been mixed. Any increased risk of premature death, however slight, is reason enough to view excess weight as a serious health hazard. However, the dangers of excess weight may have been exaggerated, and for some people, the cure may be worse than the condition. Although controversy exists about the health effects of being overweight, maintaining a healthy weight is associated with good health.

Weight Loss: A New Attitude Emerges

The term *weight loss* lacks specificity and it is often used in such a way as to imply that indiscriminate weight loss—of body fluids, protein, and fat—is desirable. A more appropriate weight-related goal is to measure success by the amount of fat lost, not by weight loss. The term *weight loss* should be replaced by the more specific term *fat-weight loss*.

Until recently, advice to overfat people was imprecise. For example, the suggestion to "cut back on calories" reinforces the misconception that diet alone can lead to fat-weight loss. Successful weight management is rarely the result of following a diet or counting calories for a specific time period. Successful weight management usually requires a lifelong lifestyle change. The loss or gain of body weight, the development of fat cells, and the causes of obesity are complex issues related to the interaction of three factors—heredity, diet, and exercise.

Development of Obesity

The body consists of 30 to 40 billion adipose cells (fat cells) that provide storage space for extra energy. Adipose cells may be viewed as collapsible, thin-walled containers with unlimited storage capacities (figure 8-1). In prehistoric humans large fat stores developed when food was available in spring and summer, and this proved biologically advantageous when winters were long and harsh and food was scarce. Energy stored in fat cells could be tapped for use later. This is not the case today. Food is available year-round for most Americans and surplus fat storage is not advantageous.

Obesity occurs when adipose cells increase excessively in size (**hypertrophy**) or number (**hyperplasia**) or both. Obesity that results from an increase in the size of fat cells is hypertrophic, obesity that results from an increase in the number of fat cells is hyperplastic, and obesity that results from an increase in both is hypertrophic/hyperplastic.

Adipose cells follow a normal pattern of growth and development. When obesity develops in infancy or childhood (juvenile-onset obesity), more adipose cells develop, and each cell grows greatly, resulting in hypertrophic/hyperplastic obesity. When obesity develops in adulthood (adult-onset obesity), a normal number of adipose cells usually develops, but each cell contains a large amount of fat (see Just the Facts: Classification of Obesity). In extreme cases, adult-onset obesity can be both hyperplastic and hypertrophic.[14] Once developed, fat cells do not disappear in the adult state.

Adipose cells have a long lifespan. If adult obesity is both hypertrophic and hyperplastic, is it more difficult to lose weight than if adult obesity is due to hypertrophy alone? Some evidence indicates that an increased number of fat cells increases the body's reluctance to reduce fat stores. The needs of adipose cells may require that they store at least nominal amounts of fat. More fat cells would then result in more fat storage, complicating efforts to lose weight. The longer a person remains obese, the more difficult it is to correct the problem.

Gender differences in depositing fat become noticeable during and after puberty. Men distribute fat primarily in the upper half of the body, and women tend to deposit it in the lower half. The percentage of fat in the body reaches peak values during early adolescence for boys and then declines during the remainder of adolescent growth. Girls experience a continuous increase in the percentage of fat from the onset of puberty to age 18.

From approximately 2 years of age, obese children develop a greater number of fat cells than do children of normal weight, often as many as three times more.[15] Although it is widely believed that obese children become obese adults, only about one-third of obese preschoolers in fact do. The risk of adult obesity is greater for children and young adults who are obese at older ages. Overweight and obese children and adolescents represent only 21 percent of all children and

Figure 8-1 Adipose Cell Deposits

Adipose (fat) tissue can be deposited in many areas of the body. Losing fat and building lean muscle tissue boosts metabolism, reduces strain on the hips and knees, and may prevent lower-back pain.

Just the Facts

Classification of Obesity

There are several types of obesity, each resulting from different causes:

- Juvenile-onset obesity: Caused by an increase in both the number (hyperplastic) and size (hypertrophic) of fat cells
- Adult-onset obesity: Caused primarily by an increase in size of fat cells (hypertrophic)
- Other types of obesity: Caused by endocrine and/or genetic disorders, such as hypothyroidism, brain tumors, and Turner's syndrome

therefore do not account for the larger percent of obese adults. The large majority of obesity is thought to be adult-onset obesity.

Causes of Obesity

The laws of thermodynamics state that energy cannot be destroyed; it is used for work or converted into another form. Accordingly, the progressive accumulation of stored fat in the body is the result of consumption of more calories (energy) than are expended. Food energy in excess of the body's need results in storage of fat in adipose cells (figure 8-2). This relationship is demonstrated in almost all people. Excessive caloric intake and deficient energy expenditure are responsible for most obesity. What is more difficult to explain, however, is the difference among people's responses to the laws of energy conservation and expenditure. Two people may be overfed the same number of calories and yet differ in the amount of weight gained, even if their activity levels are held constant. What accounts for these differences? The answer suggests that obesity is a complex issue, involving both biological and behavioral theories.

Biological Theories

Age, metabolism, gender, disease, heredity, and set point are biological factors that influence body weight and obesity. As people age, their amount of muscle tends to drop, and fat accounts for a greater percentage of their body weight. Metabolism also slows naturally with age. Together these changes reduce calorie needs, often adding an extra pound a year after age 35.[1] Women usually have higher fat-to-muscle ratios than men because of the influence of hormones that are unique to fertility and the female reproductive system. Also men typically have higher muscle-to-fat ratios than women, which increases metabolism and caloric expenditure. Diseases that affect the thyroid gland may have a dramatic impact on body weight. An overactive thyroid gland (hyperthyroidism) increases the resting metabolic rate (RMR) and may cause weight loss. Conversely, an underactive thyroid gland (hypothyroidism) lowers RMR and may lead to overweight or obesity.

The two major biological explanations of obesity are heredity and setpoint. Although they are interrelated, they are discussed separately here.

Heredity

Studies of adoptees, identical twins, and fraternal twins help to reveal the influence of the genetic component on obesity. In classic longitudinal studies, researchers at the University of Pennsylvania examined the relative obesity and the body type of adults who had been adopted during childhood.[16] They classified 540 adoptees in the following categories: thin, median weight, overweight, and obese. They found that the subjects resembled their biological parents rather than their adoptive parents even though they learned and practiced the lifestyles of their adoptive parents.

The same research team from the University of Pennsylvania studied identical and fraternal male twins for more than twenty-five years.[17] Height, weight, and BMI were measured when the subjects entered the military and again twenty-five years later. Identical twins are excellent subjects for these studies because they have identical genetic makeups. Any physical differences that occur in one of a pair of identical twins can be attributed to environmental and/or lifestyle factors. The identical twins in this study were very similar in height, weight, and BMI when they entered the military and again twenty-five years later. Each member of the pair gained the same amount of weight at approximately the same time in life. The similarity in the identical twins was twice that observed in fraternal twins (twins who emanate from separate eggs and do not have identical genes).

The connection between heredity and obesity is also confirmed in studies that correlate the prevalence of childhood obesity with the prevalence of obesity in

Figure 8-2 Fat Storage

Fat can be manufactured in the body from any food and stored when caloric intake exceeds expenditure. Fat droplets travel to the liver from the stomach and intestines and then enter the circulatory system, where they are delivered to the cells and organs. Excess fats are stored in adipose tissue. When more energy is needed, fats are released from adipose cells. If the energy needs continue, the cells shrink.

parents. Eighty percent of children born to two obese parents will themselves become obese, compared to 40 percent of children born to one obese parent and 14 percent of children born to nonobese parents.[13]

Studies support the idea that obesity and fat deposition are significantly influenced by heredity. Approximately 33 percent of the reason a person weighs a certain amount is related to inherited factors.[12]

In addition to influencing body weight, heredity influences body shape. Body shape generally falls into one of three categories: ectomorph, endomorph, and mesomorph. Most people are a combination of all three with a tendency to be more like one or two of them. If a person's body shape strongly favors a particular classification, the person cannot realistically hope to attain another body type. It would be more appropriate for such a person to seek changes in body composition that reduce fat weight regardless of body-shape tendencies. Acceptance of one's natural shape along with its limitations is essential in constructing a realistic view of body weight. Rather than concentrating on weight or shape, the overweight or obese person would be better served by focusing on physical activity. According to Steven Blair, Director of the Cooper Aerobic Center in Dallas, physically fit obese people have a lower all-cause mortality (death from all causes) than do sedentary normal-weight persons.[18] In other words, it is possible to be obese and fit. Endomorphs with a BMI over 27 can negate the health risks associated with obesity through consistent participation in moderately intense physical activities.

Another factor that helps to explain the connection between heredity and obesity surfaced with the discovery of a protein that appears to control weight gain and loss. The protein is called *leptin* (from *leptos*, the Greek word for *thin*) and is made in fat cells by a gene called *ob* (for its connection with obesity), often referred to as the *fat gene*. Scientists hypothesize that obesity occurs for one of three reasons: (1) the gene fails to produce enough leptin, (2) the body's cells do not recognize leptin, or (3) the body develops a resistance to leptin. In experiments with mice, whose ob gene is nearly identical to human's, leptin injections caused the mice to lose weight, almost all of it fat. The mice also became more active and had higher metabolic rates during the treatment.[19] It is too early to know if the leptin connection is a true medical breakthrough or another false alarm, and experts warn against the idea that leptin is a magic bullet for weight loss. Even if human studies confirm the connection, leptin will still be a pharmaceutical adjunct to diet and exercise, not a replacement for them.

The set point theory

The set point theory of weight control also reflects the role of genetics. Proponents of this theory suggest that the body works to maintain a certain weight. More specifically, each person has an internal **set point** for fatness, sometimes called the *adipostat*, that seems to regulate the body by adjusting hunger, appetite, food intake, and energy expenditure. Researchers have demonstrated that human and animal subjects put on low-calorie or high-calorie diets lose and gain only to a certain level. When the diet ends, food consumption increases and they return to their approximate original weight.

How the body determines its set point is not known. One hypothesis is that the body is able to adjust its energy expenditure by varying how efficiently muscles burn calories. Researchers at New York's Rockefeller University discovered that a dieter's metabolism slows down after losing weight, so that doing the same amount of exercise at the new weight burns fewer calories.[20] The researchers found that, after losing 10 percent of their body weight, newly slimmer patients expended 15 percent less energy than expected for someone of similar size and body composition. The system also works in the other direction; when patients gained weight, their metabolisms increased 16 percent. After a quick weight gain, the metabolism speeds up to make muscle activity burn more calories, quickly bringing the body back to its normal weight—its set point. In other words, the body burns calories more slowly than normal when weight is lost and faster than normal when weight is gained. The body's metabolism adjusts in an effort to maintain the status quo. Whatever direction a person's weight goes, up or down, the body tends to resist that change.

Can a person change his or her set point? Proponents of the set point theory think that the set point does shift over time in response to behavioral factors: Eating a high-fat diet tends to raise the set point for fatness, and regular physical activity tends to lower it. This shift may be so slight and gradual as to go unnoticed for years.

Some proponents of the set point theory suggest that because some people are genetically programmed to have unwanted pounds, efforts to eliminate fat with diet, exercise, or both are doomed. The body can shut down its calorie-losing mechanism by lowering metabolism and can stimulate appetite to the point that a person must have food.

Other proponents of the set point theory argue that vigorous regular exercise brings about physiological changes in muscle that speed up metabolism and lower the set point, thereby lowering the level of fat the body will accept and defend. Exercise induces the body to stabilize at a lower body weight, which is precisely what dieters try to do. Unfortunately, there is no formula for calculating that a specific amount of exercise will result in the loss of a certain number of pounds.

Individual response to exercise varies in ways similar to the variations in response to dieting. Still, exercise seems to be the best way to overpower the body's set point.[23] This tendency is a classic case of a genetic inclination being modified through appropriate lifestyle behavior. It supports the idea that heredity (that is, obesity) is not destiny. Living a healthy life—through regular exercise and sound nutritional habits—cannot negate heredity, but it can modify it.

Behavioral Theories

Behavioral explanations of obesity include excessive caloric intake (overeating) and lack of physical activity (hypokinesis).

Overeating

The basic laws of nature require that calories be consumed before energy can be stored as excess weight. The body cannot make energy on its own. For the obese and overweight, therefore, caloric intake is an important issue.

Do obese people eat more than normal-weight people? This has been a controversial question and researchers are divided in their answer. Some studies show that obese people eat no more and sometimes less than normal-weight people.[21] Researchers would suggest that blaming obesity on a lack of willpower is unfair and oversimplifies the facts. They maintain that the body of the obese person is simply more efficient at converting calories to adipose cells for reasons beyond his or her control, such as genetic predisposition or higher setpoint for fatness. Stated another way, obese people may not eat more than normal-weight people; they just consume more calories than are required by their bodies.

Other researchers claim that obese people do eat more than normal-weight people; the problem, they argue, is a discrepancy in reporting of food intake. In one study, obese subjects underestimated their intake by 47 percent and overestimated physical activity by 51 percent.[12] According to these researchers, the phenomenon referred to as **diet resistance,** the inability to lose weight by dieting, has little to do with innate biological factors.

Although researchers are divided on the issue of overeating, they tend to agree that the abundance of food high in fat and calories is a major factor in the prevalence of obesity in the United States. In his review of the literature on obesity—a review that included more than 300 citations from the scientific literature—Nieman wrote, "Of all the current theories attempting to explain the epidemic of obesity in most Western societies, the high dietary fat intake hypothesis is most widely accepted by experts."[13] Overweight people tend to eat a higher-fat diet than do people of normal weight. Ounce for ounce, fat yields more than double the number of calories than protein or carbohydrates do (9 calories versus 4). This energy difference partially explains the relationship between dietary fat intake and weight gain. It is not a complete explanation because, in studies that hold the total number of calories constant and in which more calories are consumed than needed, subjects eating high-fat diets tend to store more excess calories as body fat than subjects eating lower-fat diets.[22] Calories from fat appear to be more readily converted to body fat than are calories from carbohydrate and protein.

Excess carbohydrates are converted to glycogen in the liver and muscle. The body can only store a limited amount of glycogen. This is not true for fat. Fat cells are distributed throughout the body. Whereas carbohydrate storage is carefully regulated, fat storage is not, allowing a high degree of expansion. The body's capacity to make and store fat may have served a useful purpose in earlier times when humans faced the constant threat of famines and when an energy reserve meant greater likelihood of survival. But given the sedentary lifestyles of most Americans, glycogen stores are rarely exhausted. The reality for too many people is that they burn carbohydrates and store fat.

Dietary fat also has less of a thermogenic effect than does carbohydrate or protein and can thus be easily stored as adipose tissue. The **thermogenic effect of food (TEF)** represents the amount of energy required by the body to digest, absorb, metabolize, and store nutrients. The body expends only 3 calories of energy to process 100 calories from fat compared with 25 calories to process 100 calories from carbohydrates (see Just the Facts: Dietary Fat Versus Dietary Carbohydrate). Between 10 percent and 15 percent of total body energy goes to support the TEF.[12] For example, after a meal containing 1000 calories, the body uses 100 to 150 calories just to process the meal. The TEF helps explain why studies consistently show that, when adults and children overeat and consume high amounts of dietary fat, they tend to gain weight. Conversely, when the intake of dietary fat is low and the intake of carbohydrate and fiber is high from nutrient-dense foods, desirable body weight is more readily achieved.[13] Cross-cultural comparisons confirm the dietary fat-obesity relationship. For example, Americans eat more than twice as much fat as the Chinese, yet the Chinese consume 20 percent more calories and there is little obesity in China.[13]

The high-fat theory of obesity leads to an important question: Can a person lose weight by simply focusing on fat calories? The answer depends on whether or not a reduction in fat calories is also accompanied by a reduction in total calories. Studies of the eating habits of

Just the Facts

Dietary Fat Versus Dietary Carbohydrate

Dietary fat promotes fat storage in the body. The body expends only 3 calories to convert an extra 100 calories of dietary fat to storage fat. Fat storage is accelerated if dietary fat is combined with simple sugar in the same meal, as in the combination of a hamburger with a sugared cola drink. Sugar triggers the release of extra insulin. Insulin activates fat cell enzymes that promote movement of fat from the blood to the fat cells.[23] Conversely, the ingestion of an extra 100 calories of complex carbohydrates requires that the body expend 25 calories to convert it to fat for storage. The conversion process for carbohydrates is more costly than that for fats and provides another reason for reducing fat consumption and increasing carbohydrate consumption.

Exercising with a friend is a fun way to stay active and keep your weight in check.

both men and women who consume low-fat products reveal that they often compensate by eating more snack and dessert foods high in sugar but low in fat so the use of low-fat foods becomes an excuse to eat more.[24] The idea that people can eat as much as they want as long as it is fat free appears to be more fantasy than fact. Although some researchers believe that fat is the main culprit associated with obesity; other experts emphasize calories. This helps to explain why Americans are getting heavier with each passing year, even though they are consuming a lower proportion of fat. Increased consumption of low-fat foods does not alone result in weight loss. Whereas eating low-fat foods is good for health and weight control, eating them in buffet-sized portions is not.

Lack of physical activity

Obesity is in large part caused by the sedentary lifestyle of most Americans. Scientific improvements have led to modern conveniences and labor-saving devices that decrease the need for physical activity. Advancements in technology make it possible to bank, shop, and even complete college courses without leaving the desktop computer. Less than 1 percent of the energy for operating factories comes from muscle power. Devices such as mechanized golf carts have made leisure activities less strenuous. Each new invention fosters a receptive attitude toward a life of ease. The mechanized way is generally the most expedient way in the time-oriented American society. Exercise for fitness is now separate from other parts of life. Even when people do exercise during their leisure time, their total daily energy expenditure still falls far short of what was typical several decades ago. The average sedentary person usually expends only 300 to 800 calories a day in physical activity, most of this through informal, unplanned types of movement.[13] Some experts believe that lack of physical activity is the distinguishing factor that separates the obese from those of normal weight.

The general decline in physical activity and fitness is correlated with the rise in obesity. More specifically, fitness is associated with increased BMR, improved body composition, preserved lean body mass during weight loss, lowered insulin levels, increased oxidative capacity of muscle tissues, larger amounts of glycogen stored in active muscles, and increased sensitivity to fat-mobilizing hormones that help to decrease body fat.[21] In the absence of exercise, the opposites of these factors work together to contribute to and exacerbate obesity.

Overweight people are usually less physically active than normal-weight people. Obese men informally walk an average of 3.7 miles per day, whereas normal-weight men walk 6 miles; obese women walk 2 miles per day, and normal-weight women walk 4.9 miles.[13]

To state that obese people are less physically active than normal-weight people is one thing; to claim that lack of physical activity causes obesity is quite different. Researchers are not clear which comes first: Does obesity lead to physical inactivity or does physical inactivity lead to obesity? The cause-and-effect nature of the relationship between these two factors has yet to be determined and is complicated by the fact that energy expenditure from exercise differs very little between the obese and the normal-weight. Because of their extra weight, the obese expend more energy when they participate in physical activity. In other words, even though they exercise less, they expend more energy in the course of activity. For this reason overeating is considered by most experts to be more important than inactivity as a determinant of obesity.[13] Still there is general agreement that exercise is vital to the success of weight maintenance. A statement included in a keynote speech delivered at the 1995 convention of the American College of Sports Medicine captures the essence of this dilemma: "The results of hundreds of studies reveal that while exercise in and of itself is not a major player in weight loss, it is the number one player in preventing weight gain."[25]

Dieting and Exercise: Strategies for Weight Maintenance or Weight Loss

To maintain weight, caloric intake must be balanced by caloric expenditure. To lose weight a person has to achieve a **caloric deficit** in which the number of calories burned exceeds the number of calories consumed. This is the basic principle of weight management. It is simple and straightforward, and it includes three obvious strategies: (1) restricting caloric intake by dieting, (2) increasing caloric expenditure through physical activity, and (3) a combination of dieting and physical activity. What is not so easy to explain is how two people can respond so differently to dieting and exercise weight-loss strategies. Complex forces, many of which are still not clearly understood, influence the success of weight-management/weight-loss efforts.

The loss of 1 pound of body fat requires a caloric deficit of 3500 calories. (The loss of 1 pound of adipose tissue yields more than 1 pound of body weight because fat storage includes some lean support tissue—muscle, connective tissues, blood supply, and other body components. A caloric deficit of 2700 calories results in a loss of 1 pound of body weight.)[14] A loss of 1 pound of body fat per week is a good goal and requires an average daily caloric deficit of 500 calories. A caloric deficit of more than 500 calories per day, unless medically supervised, borders on the extreme and is difficult to sustain over long periods of time. A loss of 2 pounds of body fat per week is considered a maximum goal.

Body fat loss in excess of 2 pounds per week is not practical for most people. For example, diets that promise a fat-weight loss of 10 pounds per week require a caloric deficit of 35,000 calories per week; that is an average of 7000 calories per day. For that kind of caloric deficit, a person would have to go to the extremes of fasting while running two marathons in one day. Weight loss in excess of a couple of pounds per week usually involves lean tissue weight, which should be retained, and fluid weight, which needs to be replaced to prevent health consequences ranging from dehydration to electrolyte imbalance.

A desirable long-term goal for a person needing to lose weight is 1 to 2 pounds per week until about 10 percent of excess weight is lost. The emphasis should be on a slow, steady weight loss rather than on a rapid weight loss. Once this goal is reached, the dieter should go into maintenance for about six months before attempting more weight loss.[14] For example, a 250-pound person should go into a six-month maintenance program after losing 25 pounds. This is a conservative approach to weight loss that is likely to yield health improvements while promoting a more stable, consistent body weight.

Dieting

Statistics show that dieting is the method of choice for most Americans trying to lose weight. Although dieting usually works only temporarily, most people who fail to maintain weight loss are willing to try again. Many people seek the miraculous diet that will transform them from fat to thin, preferably with minimal effort and in the shortest time possible.

The success rate of diet-only strategies is dismal. Only 5 percent of all dieters are successful in reducing to a target weight and maintaining the weight for more than five years. Typically, one-third of the weight lost during dieting is regained within the first year, and almost all weight lost is regained within three to five years.[14] Maintaining postdiet weight is one of the major failures of weight loss through dieting because dieters do not learn the habits and behaviors needed to remain at the new weight. As a result, they lose and regain weight many times in their lives. This pattern of repeated weight loss and gain, known as **weight cycling,** *yo-yo dieting,* and *seesaw approaches* to weight loss, is potentially harmful and counterproductive.

The consequences of weight cycling are numerous. The most immediate negative effect is rebound weight gain. Typically, weight gained after dieting includes not only the weight that was lost but additional weight as well. After years of yo-yo dieting, many dieters experience a weight gain pattern that takes on a stair-step effect, increasing in small but noticeable increments with each successive effort. In addition, the weight regained is in the form of adipose tissue, whereas the weight that was lost consisted of a mixture of adipose and muscle tissue. The net result of weight cycling is not only extra weight but also extra fat weight.

Weight cycling also increases the risk of death, especially from cardiovascular conditions. Researchers at Harvard University[26] studied data on 11,703 subjects over thirty years to see whether weight cycling had any effect on longevity. As expected, those whose weight remained stable had a lower mortality rate. However, those who lost weight were more likely to die than were those who gained weight. Men who gained more than 11 pounds were 36 percent more likely to die than were those whose weight remained stable. The men who lost more than 11 pounds, however, had a 57 percent higher chance of dying. The explanation proposed was that those who had lost 11 pounds over the decade had actually gained and lost an average of 100 pounds over their lifetimes. The stress of yo-yo dieting contributed to the higher death rates. With the high recidivism rate of dieters, the researchers concluded that it is probably better to remain slightly overweight than to weight cycle. This is not true, however, for people whose excessive body weight increases their risk for diabetes, high blood pressure, and high cholesterol levels. In a 1994 report of forty-three studies on the effects of weight cycling, researchers concluded that the health gains from a weight loss of as little as 5 to 10 pounds, even if temporary, outweigh the hazards of weight cycling for people with histories of these chronic conditions.[27] Still, experts agree that it is better to lose weight and keep it off.

The high recidivism rate of diet-only programs coupled with the negative effects of weight cycling seems to negate dieting as a strategy for losing weight. The cold reality, however, is that weight loss requires a caloric deficit, and limiting food intake is the most direct and immediate way to get results. The mistake people tend to make with most diet-only strategies is to set unrealistic goals. They want to lose too much weight and they want to lose it immediately. An ideal approach is to lose weight at the same rate as weight is gained. For most people this would involve a plan of modest dietary restrictions implemented over a period of months or years, rather than days or weeks. Weight-loss goals structured according to the guidelines mentioned are more likely to be successful.

In diet-only strategies, the caloric intake should not drop below 1200 per day in women or 1500 per day in men.[12] Gender differences in caloric intake are due to differences in physical activity patterns, metabolism (from more or less muscle tissue), and size. Because fat is more than twice as energy dense as carbohydrates, many experts recommend concentrating on limiting fat intake rather than on counting calories. If an eating plan calls for a caloric intake below 1200 calories for women and 1500 calories for men per day, discuss it with your health care provider. You may need to take vitamin and/or mineral supplements. One last caveat to people who are frustrated because they can't lose weight on a 1200- or 1500-calorie diet: If you can't lose weight at this caloric level, you probably don't need to lose weight. You might be better served by re-examining your reasons for losing weight.

In structuring a diet, it is important to observe the dietary recommendations in Chapter 6. Follow the Food Guide Pyramid by adjusting the number of servings while still maintaining the proportion of servings that come from grains, fruits, and vegetables. The diet should include common foods that fit into any social situation. Further, the plan should make provisions for relearning eating habits that will make weight loss permanent.

Very low–calorie diets

Very-low–calorie diets (VLCDs) are diets containing fewer than 800 calories a day. They are considered extreme diets (food is usually replaced with a powdered supplement) and should be viewed as a medical intervention. Typically, VLCDs are undertaken under medical supervision and administered in hospital/clinic settings for a period of three to four months and include counseling, behavior management, nutrition and dieting classes, and support groups. Often, they include an exercise program. Once the diet is completed, dieters on a VLCD gradually return to food intake.

VLCDs are usually recommended for people whose obesity is threatening to their health and who are unable to lose weight through dieting and exercise. People who have insulin-dependent diabetes mellitus, liver disease, kidney disease, or a history of heart disease are warned against this method of losing weight.

For people who can stay on them, VLCDs produce dramatic reductions in weight. Still, they are not a panacea. About 25 percent of people who start a VLCD drop out of the program. Like most extreme dieting programs, VLCDs have a high recidivism rate. As a result, VLCD programs are worthless without careful attention paid to long-term maintenance that incorporates newly learned eating patterns.[12]

Low-fat diets

Low-fat diets are potentially effective techniques for losing weight. With its high-caloric yield, low thermic effect, and almost unlimited capacity for storage, fat is a major threat to weight maintenance. Consequently, Americans are currently fixated on fat-free or low-fat foods. The assumption is that, if a food is low in fat, it is also low in calories. Only 7 percent of Americans are concerned about calories, compared with 60 percent who cite fat as public enemy number one.[28] As a result, although Americans are consuming fewer fat calories percentagewise, they are consuming more total calories from all sources and are getting heavier. (Actual fat intake remains the same as it was during the past ten years. Percentagewise, it dropped from 36 to 34 percent because of an increase in total calories consumed.[29]

Low-fat foods and overcompensatory eating

Although diet experts advocate restricting fat calories, low-fat diets have not been effective for many dieters because of **overcompensatory eating.** This occurs when the consumption of low-fat foods is accompanied by an increase in total calories. Researchers at Pennsylvania State University demonstrated this point when, on separate occasions, they gave a group of women two kinds of yogurt: One was labeled *high fat,* and one was labeled *low fat.* The ingredients were manipulated so that both kinds of yogurt had the same number of calories. A comparison group of women was given the same, but unlabeled, yogurt. Thirty minutes after consuming the yogurt, the women ate lunch. After eating the yogurt labeled *low fat,* subjects compensated by taking in more calories during lunch than they did when they consumed the yogurt labeled *high fat.* This pattern of overcompensatory eating was not observed for the comparison group who ate the unlabeled yogurt. The researchers concluded that, when the women ate yogurt labeled *low fat,* they rationalized that they could indulge more at lunch. When they didn't know what kind of yogurt they had eaten, they were more tuned in to their bodies' physical cues and naturally adjusted the amount they ate.[30]

The attitude that people can eat what they want, in unlimited quantities as long as it is fat free is wrong. Calories do count. Fat-free foods can help people lose weight if they are used properly, if they don't result in overcompensatory consumption of food, and if total calories are kept in line.

Low-fat diets and Olestra

The recent approval of Olestra (Olean) as a fat substitute is partly responsible for the proliferation of low-fat and fat-free foods. Many people unwittingly consume foods in large quantities thinking that, if it is fat-free, it is also calorie free. A fat-free product made with Olestra may turn out to have more total calories (from carbohydrates) than a companion product made with typical ingredients, including fat. For that reason it is important to check labels. The bottom line to look for is total calories. Diets high in Olestra also carry the risk of compromising the body's use of essential nutrients, such as fat-soluble vitamins. For some people the consumption of Olestra causes various abdominal symptoms (see Chapter 6).

Portion sizes and volume eating

Managing caloric intake is made more difficult today than in years past because of not only the increased availability of food but also the way food is marketed,

---

Wellness on the Web Behavior Change Activities

Get Off the Merry-Go-Round
For many of us, weight control and diet have a strong emotional component that sometimes causes us to make choices that aren't in our best interest. In reality, the diet-weight equation is simple and straightforward: To maintain weight, your caloric intake must be balanced by your caloric expenditure. To lose weight, you must achieve a caloric deficit in which the number of calories you burn exceeds the number of calories you consume. This is the basic principle of weight management. What's your "EQ," or exercise quotient? To find out, go to the Weightloss 2000 website at **www.weightloss2000.com/exer/exer_OI_howfit.htm** and take the quiz to see how much exercise you get each day. If you become just a little more active, you can shed unwanted pounds painlessly.

Boost Your Metabolism—Naturally!
Looking for the "magic bullet" for successful weight management? Magic or not, compelling evidence points to the importance of regular exercise in weight control and weight-loss maintenance. People who lose weight and keep it off almost always exercise daily. Studies that attempt to identify predictors of successful weight maintenance point to physical activity as one of the best markers for long-term success. Walking is considered an excellent form of exercise for shedding pounds. To calculate how many calories you just burned walking, go to the Healthy Ideas website at **www.healthyideas.com/walking/burn** and enter your weight and the duration of your walk, then select your approximate speed and click on "walk it off" to calculate your calories burned.

Eating Disorder Alert
In today's appearance-focused culture, we're all familiar with the terms anorexia nervosa, bulimarexia nervosa, and binge eating. Although these eating disorders differ markedly from each other in many respects, people who have them share a common trait: an intense fear of becoming overweight. Does this describe you? Whether the answer is yes or no, go to the Eating Disorders Recovery Group at **www.mirror-mirror.org/sub7.htm** to complete a self-test that will help you determine whether you may have an eating disorder. The questions presented involve behaviors and feelings that are common to persons who have eating disorders. Whatever your results, remember that you and no one else are the final judge of whether or not you have an eating disorder. If you think you do, you'll find help and support from a wide array of reputable sources.

packaged, and delivered. In trying to get a better value for the dollar, people think *bigger* and *more* are better. Food producers know this and use this approach to gain an advantage over the competition. *Supersized, all-you-can-eat, buffet style eating,* and *a meal in a sandwich* are some of the catch phrases used to increase business. When it comes to calories, the phrases are not all hype. A medium-size baked potato served at a fast-food restaurant weighs 7 ounces compared with the typical potato which weighs 4 ounces; a medium bagel weighs 4 ounces, double the size listed in food composition tables; a medium muffin is 6 ounces, triple the size of regular muffins; a double hamburger at one popular fast-food restaurant has almost three times the number of calories as its single hamburger counterpart; one casual dining restaurant offers a no-frills entree that weighs as much as the Manhattan *Yellow Pages.*

Signs in supermarkets can also encourage people to buy more food. A consumer planning to purchase one carton of ice cream is likely to return home with two cartons if the product is priced at two for $8 instead of at $4 each. When grocers suggest purchase of a specific number of items, shoppers are more likely to buy more than the one or two they intended to buy. Finally, portion size does not equate to serving size. When a restaurant serves an entree, it is likely to be on a larger plate or in a deeper bowl than those used in years past. Pasta bowls, for example, are popular because they are big. Some hold 40 ounces or 2½ pounds.

Do people actually eat more when food is packaged in larger quantities? In trying to answer this question, researchers gave either a 1- or 2-pound bag of M&Ms plus either a "medium" or "jumbo" movie theater–sized tub of popcorn to participants. On average, participants ate 112 M&Ms from the 1-pound bag and 156 from the 2-pound bag. Likewise, the average person ate roughly half a tub of popcorn, whether it was medium or jumbo, which held twice as much as the medium tub. The researchers concluded that people often eat about 50 percent more of pleasure-foods such as candy, chips, and popcorn when they come in bigger packages. With other foods, the increase is usually about 25 percent.[31]

Some common-sense approaches help people avoid overeating in spite of the gluttony of supersized portions of food. See Real-World Wellness: Practical Tips for Coping with Supersize Foods.

Real-World Wellness

Practical Tips for Coping with Supersize Foods

My friends and I enjoy eating out and prefer fast food or casual dining restaurants. The local restaurants provide some supersize bargains that fit a college budget. My problem is that I am a volume eater—I eat what is served, which is usually much more than I need and certainly more than is good for my waistline. But I live on a tight budget and refuse to throw away good food. What are some strategies that will help me manage my tendency for volume eating without being wasteful?

Here are some suggestions for volume purchasing without waste:

- Eat what you need, not necessarily what is served. Take the rest home.
- Share an entree, appetizer, or dessert. This saves calories and money. (Some restaurants add a surcharge for sharing meals.)
- Start each day with a plan. Think first in terms of your main meal and work around it. If you're planning a prime rib dinner, for example, favor vegetables and fruits for breakfast and lunch. One serving of prime rib is plenty of meat for one day.
- At a buffet, serve yourself small portions and eat slowly. Give your food time to digest. Emphasize vegetables and fruits in your food selections.
- Ask for a half order of an entree.
- Order only appetizers.
- When grocery shopping, plan ahead. Make a list of the amount or quantity of each item to buy. Stick to your list.
- If you're watching calories, learn what makes a serving. One small fistful of candy, french fries, or nuts is a serving. A portion of pasta, rice, or mashed potatoes is the size of your fist (see Chapter 6).
- Picture what you think is a reasonable serving before food is served. If more is served, take it home.

Popular diets

Many diets on the market are nutritionally sound, and many are not. Some are potentially hazardous, and many are based on faulty nutritional and physiological concepts. Some require that food be eaten in a certain order and severely restrict foods. Diets such as Jenny Craig come in premeasured servings. Some require medical supervision. Others impose unrealistic caloric restrictions, and still others make promises based more on fantasy than facts (table 8-2). The Food and Drug Administration (FDA) does not investigate every new fad diet, and many diet plans are published without the FDA's endorsement (see Just the Facts: Outlandish Weight-Loss Promises—What to Do). If a diet is published, it is usually because a publisher sees potential profits from its sales. Publishers know that the advice to "eat less fat and increase physical activity" will not sell books, but fad diets with secret ingredients or magic formulas will.

Because fad diets are unlikely to disappear, identifying some of the characteristics and marketing strategies used by diet promoters to appeal to unwitting consumers is helpful.[14] Fad diets

- Promote quick results
- Stress eating one type of food to the exclusion of others
- Emphasize gimmick approaches, such as eating food in a particular order
- Cite anecdotes and testimonials, usually involving well-known people
- Claim to be a panacea for everyone
- Often promote a secret ingredient
- Often recommend expensive supplements
- Rarely emphasize permanent changes in eating habits
- Usually show little concern for accepted principles of good nutrition (see Chapter 6)
- Are usually cynical about the evidence that comes from the scientific community

In general, dieting is an ineffective weight-management method. The expectation that temporary changes in eating habits will lead to permanent weight loss is unrealistic. Sensible and permanent dietary changes that depend on wise food choices are an excellent way to cut calories and a healthy way to eat. (Table 8-3 demonstrates how to reduce calories that come from fat and cholesterol by making appropriate substitutions.)

Diet Drugs

If recent history is a good predictor of the future, American dieters can anticipate a whole new arsenal of drug solutions for losing weight. Drugs that suppress appetite by stimulating the satiety center in the brain have helped many dieters lose weight temporarily. Drugs marketed under the names *fen-phen* (fenfluramine) and *redux* (dexfenfluramine) during the mid-1990s quickly sold in huge quantities. The popularity of these drugs did not last long, however, because of the plethora of side effects, including death, which eventually led to their withdrawal from the marketplace. Newer-appetite suppressant drugs such as Meridia (sibutramine) offer another pharmacologic solution for dieters. Although early studies of Meridia do not reveal the same side effects as those of its predecessors, the drug is not off the safety hook. Its short-term side effects are substantial and its long-term safety is a big unknown.[33]

Diet drugs are not intended for people who are overweight or marginally obese. Instead, they are intended for the management of severe obesity that does not respond to dieting and exercise regimens and for people whose obesity causes serious health risks that outweigh the possible risks of the medication. Unfortunately, many people are drawn to the quick-fix of a drug, and many physicians are willing to provide a prescription.

The reality, of course, is that drugs offer only a temporary solution. They do not correct the underlying cause of persistent weight gain. People who take weight-loss medications can anticipate the typical weight cycling effect of other dieting strategies with an added problem: Diet drugs are powerful medicines that tamper with the body's delicate balance of hormones and body chemicals. Except for the severely obese, long-term exposure to diet drugs creates harmful effects that may far outweigh the health benefits of fewer pounds of body weight.

Herbal Remedies

Herbal versions of prescription drugs used for losing weight are available in health food stores and many drugstores. Some herbs act as diuretics (chemicals that increase urine production), so they can help people lose water weight. Examples are buchu, celery seed, dandelion, juniper, parsley, and uva ursi. Diuretics are not effective for long-term weight loss because they trigger the body's thirst reflex to replace lost fluids. The body eventually adjusts to the continued use of diuretic herbs and retains water despite them.

Some herbs are stimulants that reportedly increase metabolism and suppress appetite. Examples are ephedra (in Chinese, *ma huang*) and caffeine. Ephedra (or ephedrine) is viewed as a natural form of fen-phen. To be effective, these herbs have to be taken in such large doses that they often cause unpleasant side effects such as insomnia, irritability, jitters, and elevated blood pressure. Ephedra has shown no weight-reduction benefits for mildly overweight people who simply want to lose 5 to 10 pounds.[34]

Another group of herbs produce a feeling of fullness. These are mucilaginous herbs: They absorb fluids, such as might occur in the stomach at mealtime, and expand substantially. The most notable herb in this group is psyllium. Psyllium seed is sold in bulk in herb shops and is also available in drugstores as the common bulk-forming laxative Metamucil. Studies of obese women taking psyllium before meals do not report any weight loss advantage.[34]

Hot, spicy herbs such as red pepper and mustard reportedly increase metabolism, which, in turn, causes more calories to be burned. Hot herbs also stimulate thirst. Researchers who observe weight-loss benefits from these herbs do not know if they are

Table 8-2 Popular Diets

Type	Description	Weight Loss	Health Drawbacks	Pros and Cons
Balanced (available in bookstores)				
Weight Watchers Quick Success Program (Weight Watchers International) Jane Fonda's New Workout & Weight Loss Program I Don't Eat (But I Can't Lose Weight) Complete University Medical Diet Jane Brody's Nutrition Book Fit or Fat Target Diet Popcorn Plus Diet Getting Thin Setpoint Diet Nautilus Diet Take Off Pounds Sensibly (TOPS) Overeaters Anonymous	Recommend 1000 or more calories/day; provide at least 50% carbohydrate, less than 30% fat, 15–20% protein; include variety of foods from all food groups; require regular exercise and lifestyle changes	1–2 lbs./week; promotion of permanent loss of fat, especially if combined with regular exercise	None (no side effects in healthy people); include adequate amount of food in all major food groups; no specialized medical supervisions necessary for healthy people	Provide variety and good nutrition; combined with exercise, can be used as a basis of lifelong weight control; no vitamin supplementation necessary; weight lost is fat, not muscle
High Carbohydrate				
Bloomingdale's Eat Healthy Diet Pritikin Permanent Weight Loss Manual	Involve varying calorie levels; encourage increasing carbohydrate intake to more than 60% of diet; can severely restrict protein and fat intake; often advocate positive lifestyle changes	Gradual or rapid, depending on caloric intake	May be too low in protein and require vitamin and mineral supplements	Safe and effective if protein level and caloric intake are adequate; may be so restrictive as to be difficult to maintain
Formula/Rx*				
HMR (Health Management Resources) Medifast Optifast	Suggest only 800 calories or fewer/day; require dieters to forgo food for about 12 weeks and eat only a protein supplement; after initial fast, gradually reintroduce food; may encourage exercise and lifestyle changes	Very rapid, 3 to 4 lbs./week; protein supplements said to reduce loss of muscle tissue; unknown whether dieters keep weight off	Can produce severe metabolic disturbances, heart beat irregularities, hair loss, dehydration, kidney problems, and sense of feeling cold; vitamins and mineral supplements required	Expensive, with costs as high as $500 per month; only for obese people (20% or more overweight), for those with a weight-related health problem, or for those who have failed on other diets; require close medical supervision

Category	Description	Weight Loss	Health Concerns	Other Concerns
Formula/OTC (over the counter) Nutrament Slender Slim Fast	May advocate fewer than 1000 calories/day; replace one or more meals with a low-calorie shake or food bar that contains some combination of protein, carbohydrates, fats, vitamins, minerals	Can be rapid, 3 or more lbs./week if daily caloric level falls below 1000; possible promotion of water and muscle loss; weight often regained	May be low in protein, carbohydrates, vitamins, or minerals; can be dangerous if used as sole source of nutrition	Teach reliance on patented products, not on sound, lifelong eating habits
Low carbohydrate/high protein *Dr. Atkins' Diet Revolution* *Complete Scarsdale Medical Diet* *Doctor's Quick Weight Loss Diet* (Stillman's "water diet") *The Zone/Protein Power/Healthy for Life*	Involve varying calorie levels; severely restrict carbohydrates such as bread, cereals, grains, starchy vegetables; maintains that carbohydrates cause an increase in insulin, which promotes fat accumulation	Rapid, 3 or more lbs./week; promotion of loss of water and muscle tissue; weight usually regained	Are usually unbalanced; may be very high in saturated fat and cholesterol; can cause fatigue, headaches, nausea, dehydration, and dizziness	Do not promote good eating habits; nutritional claims are unsound; not supported by scientific evidence
Very low calorie Diet Principal Rotation Diet	Suggest fewer than 1000 calories/day for part of diet or for its entirety; based on low-fat, high-carbohydrate foods	Rapid, 3 or more lbs./week; initial loss of water and muscle, not fat; weight usually regained	May be unbalanced and require vitamin and mineral supplements	Usually do not teach long-term good eating habits
Novelty diets *Beverly Hills Diet* Fit for Life Rice Diet Report Dr. Berger's Immune Power Diet Dr. Debetz Champagne Diet The Rotation Diet The Junk Food Diet Sun Sign Diet *The Diet Bible* The Love Diet	Usually involve fewer than 1000 calories/day; often make false claims that specific foods or combinations burn fat; suggest eating one type of food to exclusion of others	Can be rapid, depending on caloric intake; weight generally regained	Are unbalanced; may be dangerously low in protein; are often deficient in vitamins and minerals; can result in dizziness, diarrhea, gas, hair loss, brittle nails, and loss of vital muscle tissue	Are based on unsound nutritional guidelines; weight lost because of reduction in calories; can be dangerous; may be extremely restrictive and monotonous; may lead to bingeing
Company food programs Diet Center Jenny Craig Nutri/System Physician's Weight Loss Center	Involve portion-control by providing awareness of how much food yields various calorie levels; involve the purchase of prepackaged food; may include vitamin supplements and stringent dieting	Gradual or rapid, depending on degree of participation and caloric intake	May require vitamin supplements; set unrealistic expectations	Include some individual and group counseling, prepackaged foods are expensive; foster preoccupation with clothing sizes and ultra-thinness

*available through a physician or hospital-run program

Just the Facts

Outlandish Weight-Loss Promises—What to Do

Quick and unrealistic weight-loss schemes that promise outlandish results are common, and the number of fad diets promoted in print and video media exceeds the FDA's capacity to check claims and promises.[32] One newspaper recently published an advertiser's claim: "Lose 40 pounds by Christmas." The date of the advertisement was November 3, about seven weeks before Christmas. This ad was an example of blatantly misleading advertising. The responsibility for demonstrating "proof" rests with authors and publishers, who are often motivated more by profits than by credible and reliable information. What can the average consumer do if he or she is exposed to some outrageous claims?

- First and foremost, adopt an attitude of skepticism. If it sounds too good to be true, it probably is. No one diet device or pill can work miracles. Even respectable diet programs require you to eat less and exercise more.
- Call your local chapter of the Better Business Bureau to check claims and reputation before you enlist in a program or buy a product or gadget.
- Register a complaint with the source (newspaper, magazine, television station) of the advertisement.
- If you see a suspect ad, send it to NAD, Consumer Inquiries, 845 Third Avenue, 17th floor, New York, NY 10022.
- And remember, if you don't lose weight with a particular product, don't automatically blame yourself. You may have not failed; the product may have failed you.

from the herbs' effect on metabolism or if they cause people to fill up on water and, therefore, ingest fewer calories.

The view that herbs are safe because they come from nature is misleading. When packaged in large, concentrated doses and taken as pills or supplements, they should be viewed as drugs with potential side effects. From a medicinal point of view, a major shortcoming of herbs is that they are classified as supplements and, therefore, are not subjected to the same scientific testing as are FDA-approved drugs. Medical groups usually recommend that herbal weight-loss products be avoided, especially those containing ephedrine, until they are adequately tested.[35]

Fasting

Fasting, or complete starvation, has been practiced throughout history. Traditionally, people fasted for religious reasons. Although fasting is still used to achieve spiritual enlightenment by some people, a growing number of people fast for dubious physical reasons: to lose weight, to detoxify their bodies of impurities, and to cure everything from allergies to chronic diseases. The physical benefits of fasting have not been demonstrated in carefully planned studies. Most people who are in good health can tolerate a twenty-four-hour fast without a problem as long as they drink plenty of water. However, prolonged fasting can be harmful and even fatal.

Modified fasts that allow for fruit and vegetable juices in addition to water are generally safer. In terms of weight loss, however, fasting is not an effective strategy. Fasting, by its very nature, is an extreme action. Like any extreme diet plan, when this one is over, the weight returns. The one subjective benefit of fasting is that it may serve as a catalyst to help people create new health habits, gain a new appreciation for food, and learn how to distinguish hunger signals from cravings.[36] If you are healthy and still choose to fast, don't expect returns beyond a mental or spiritual lift. To be safe, don't fast for more than twenty-four hours and drink plenty of fluids. If you are taking medicines, consult your physician before fasting.[37]

Physical Activity

The optimal approach to weight loss combines mild caloric restriction with regular physical activity. Energy expenditure through physical activity should be increased at least 200 to 400 calories per day by increasing physical activity.[38] Together, physical activity and dieting should provide a caloric deficit of 300 to 1000 calories per day. This will lead to weight losses of ½ to 2 pounds per week and a 10 percent weight loss in six months.[13]

Use of calories

One of the obvious benefits of physical activity is that it burns calories. Calories are consumed according to body weight, so heavier people burn more calories per minute than do lighter people for the same activity. Table 8-4 presents the calorie consumption of some physical-fitness activities and a few common physical activities. To use it, multiply your body weight by the coefficient in the calories/min./lb. column and then

Table 8-3 Food Substitutions That Reduce Fat, Cholesterol, and Calories

Instead of eating . . .	Substitute . . .	To save*
1 croissant	1 plain bagel	35 calories, 10 g fat, 13 mg cholesterol
1 cup cooked egg noodles	1 cup cooked macaroni	50 mg cholesterol
1 whole egg	1 egg white	65 calories, 6 g fat, 220 mg cholesterol
1 oz. cheddar cheese	1 oz. part-skim mozzarella	35 calories, 4 g fat, 15 mg cholesterol
1 oz. cream cheese	1 oz. cottage cheese (1% fat)	74 calories, 9 g fat, 29 mg cholesterol
1 tsp. whipping cream	1 tbsp. evaporated skim milk, whipped	32 calories, 5 g fat
3.5 oz. skinless roast duck	3.5 oz. skinless roast chicken	46 calories, 7 g fat
3.5 oz. beef tenderloin, choice, untrimmed, broiled	3.5 oz. beef tenderloin, select, trimmed, broiled	75 calories, 10 g fat
3.5 oz. lamb chop, untrimmed, broiled	3.5 oz. lean leg of lamb, trimmed, broiled	219 calories, 28 g fat
3.5 oz. pork spare ribs, cooked	3.5 oz. lean pork loin, trimmed, broiled	157 calories, 17 g fat
1 oz. regular bacon, cooked	1 oz. Canadian bacon, cooked	111 calories, 12 g fat
1 oz. hard salami	1 oz. extra-lean roasted ham	75 calories, 8 g fat
1 beef frankfurter	1 chicken frankfurter	67 calories, 8 g fat
3 oz. oil-packed tuna, light	3 oz. water-packed tuna, light	60 calories, 6 g fat
1 regular-size serving french fries	1 medium-size baked potato	125 calories, 11 g fat
1 oz. oil-roasted peanuts	1 oz. roasted chestnuts	96 calories, 13 g fat
1 oz. potato chips	1 oz. thin pretzels	40 calories, 9 g fat
1 oz. corn chips	1 oz. plain air-popped popcorn	125 calories, 9 g fat
1 tbsp. sour-cream dip	1 tbsp. bottled salsa	20 calories, 3 g fat
1 glazed doughnut	1 slice angel-food cake	110 calories, 13 g fat, 21 mg cholesterol
3 chocolate sandwich cookies	3 fig bars	4 g fat
1 oz. unsweetened chocolate	3 tbsp. cocoa powder	73 calories, 13 g fat
1 cup ice cream (premium)	1 cup sorbet	320 calories, 34 g fat, 100 mg cholesterol

*The values listed are the most significant savings; smaller differences are not shown. Weights given for meats are edible portions.

---

multiply this value by the number of minutes spent participating in the activity. For example, to determine the calories expended by a 170-pound person who walks at 4.5 MPH for 30 minutes, do the following:

1. Multiply body weight by calories/min./lb.:

   170 lbs. × 0.048 calories/min./lb.
   = 8.16 calories/min.

2. Multiply calories/min. by the exercise time in minutes:

   8.16 calories/min. × 30 min. = 244.8 calories

If this person performs this exercise daily, 1 pound will be lost in approximately fourteen days or 25 pounds will be lost in one year, provided caloric intake is unchanged. The annual weight loss is calculated as follows:

3500 calories/lb. ÷ 245 calories/day = 14.29 days/lb.
365 days/year ÷ 14.29 days/lb. = 25.5 lbs./year

Follow the example in Assessment Activity 8-2 and apply the directions to your situation or to a hypothetical situation.

Aerobic exercises, such as walking and cycling, contribute significantly to weight loss. Minimal guidelines for maintaining fitness and losing weight require 300 calories per exercise session performed at least three times per week or 200 calories per session performed at least four times per week.[38] Added weight loss can be accomplished by increasing the length of each exercise session and/or the number of sessions per week. High-intensity activities burn extra calories, but low-intensity exercises are recommended to prevent injury. Complete Assessment Activity 8-4 to determine the number of minutes that you should devote to your favorite activities to burn a minimum of 300 calories.

Deconditioned people should start slowly and gradually progress to using 200 to 400 calories per exercise session. For many people, low-intensity, long-duration physical activity, such as walking, is optimal.

Table 8-4 Estimated Caloric Cost of Selected Activities

Activity	Calories/Min./Lb.*
Aerobic dance (vigorous)	0.062
Basketball (vigorous, full-court)	0.097
Bathing, dressing, undressing	0.021
Bed making (and stripping)	0.031
Bicycling (13 MPH)	0.071
Canoeing (flat water, 4 MPH)	0.045
Chopping wood	0.049
Cleaning windows	0.024
Cross-country skiing (8 MPH)	0.104
Gardening	
Digging	0.062
Hedging	
Raking	0 034
Weeding	0.038
Golf (twosome, carrying clubs)	0.045
Handball (skilled, singles)	0.078
Horseback riding (trot)	0.052
Ironing	0.029
Jogging (5 MPH)	0.060
Laundry (taking out and hanging)	0.027
Mopping floors	0.024
Peeling potatoes	0.019
Piano playing	0.018
Rowing (vigorous)	0.097
Running (8 MPH)	0.104
Sawing wood (crosscut saw)	0.058
Shining shoes	0.017
Shoveling snow	0.052
Snowshoeing (2.5 MPH)	0 060
Soccer (vigorous)	0.097
Swimming (55 yds./min.)	0.088
Table tennis (skilled)	0.045
Tennis (beginner)	0.032
Walking (4.5 MPH)	0.048
Writing while seated	0.013

*Multiply calories/min./lb. by your body weight in pounds and then multiply that product by the number of minutes spent in the activity.

For weight loss, all calories do not have to be expended in one exercise session. Three 15-minute walks in a day result in a substantial expenditure of energy. Any physical activity above the amount normally done in a day is a bonus for weight control. The cumulative effect of activities such as walking upstairs, mowing the lawn, and mopping floors can be combined with a structured exercise program to produce steady, safe weight loss.

Exercise stimulates metabolism

Basal metabolic rate (BMR) is the energy required to sustain life when the body is in a rested and fasted state. BMR is measured in calories and represents the energy needed to keep the heart, lungs, liver, kidneys, and all other organs functioning. More calories are used to maintain BMR than to perform any other function.

Metabolism is affected by age, gender, nervous system activity, secretions from endocrine glands, nutritional status, sleep, fever, climate, body surface area, and amount of muscle tissue. Because men have more muscle tissue than do women, their BMRs average 5 to 10 percent higher. See Assessment Activity 8-3 to learn how to estimate your BMR.

Muscle tissue stimulates metabolism. Therefore, physical activity is a key strategy for weight management. This is especially true for people as they get older (see Wellness Across the Generations: Age and Weight Gain Do Not Have to Go Together).

The key to weight control

Although scientifically controlled studies have not yet proven that physical activity is instrumental in losing weight, they provide compelling evidence of its importance in weight control and weight-loss maintenance. People who lose weight and keep it off almost always exercise daily. Studies that attempt to identify predictors of successful weight maintenance point to physical activity as one of the best markers for long-term success.[13] Researchers at the University of California at Davis found that 90 percent of women who had lost 20 pounds and kept it off for at least two years were avid exercisers; of the women who had regained the weight, only 35 percent were physically active. At the Baylor College of Medicine in Houston, another group of researchers put 160 obese adults on one of three year-long weight-loss programs: diet-only, exercise-only, or exercise and diet. Everyone lost weight. (The exercise and diet group lost the most). But two years later, the exercise-only participants were the only ones to keep the weight off.[39] Other large-scale studies that follow men and women in weight-loss programs for ten years consistently show that major weight gain is much more likely to occur in people who are sedentary than in those who are physically active.[13] Thus, although physical activity as a singular strategy has modest effects on weight loss, it is the key strategy for lifelong weight control. More importantly, moderate exercise improves health and reduces risk factors associated with morbidity and mortality for the obese just as it does for normal-weight people.

Wellness Across the Generations

Age and Weight Gain Do Not Have to Go Together

Weight gain is one experience people ages 25 to 65 have in common. From the time people embark on their professional careers until the time they start thinking about retirement, they often experience creeping weight gain, sometimes obesity. Often they blame the aging process. But is creeping obesity a function of biological factors that are part of the aging process, or are other factors involved? Rather than aging, it is more likely to be a higher standard of living that is responsible for such weight gain. A higher standard of living usually results in an easier, less active life. Improvements in standard of living go hand-in-hand with labor-saving devices that add convenience and, of course, save energy. Many experts believe that weight gain associated with increased age is a function of the subtle changes in metabolism caused by less muscle tissue, which is caused by less physical activity.

Metabolism is an important issue for the weight-conscious person, because 70 percent of our energy is expended to support basic life processes. Muscle tissue burns more energy at rest than does fat tissue, so changes in body composition that favor muscle tissue over fat tissue provide a calorie-burning advantage throughout the day. Conversely, changes in body composition that favor fat over muscle lower the body's metabolism and promote weight gain. Metabolism declines with age, primarily because of the physical inactivity and muscle loss that often accompany aging. The annual decrease in BMR beginning at 25 years of age, though imperceptible, has serious ramifications for weight management and accounts for a significant amount of the weight gained with age. The loss of muscle tissue is equal to 3 to 5 percent every decade after age 25. The subsequent decline in BMR produces changes in body composition. Exercise and physical activities are the keys to weight management because they increase or sustain muscle tissue, thus accelerating metabolism and using calories.

Exercise intensity and fat loss

In Chapter 6 a distinction is made between the intensity and duration of exercise and the accompanying use by the body of energy nutrients. In general, carbohydrates are the main source of energy for high-intensity exercise, and fat is the main source of energy for low-intensity exercise sustained for a prolonged time. (The body instinctively spares its protein reserve except when needed for activities of exceptional duration.) The fat-burning benefit of low-intensity exercise should be a source of encouragement for people trying to shed extra fat, making exercise a viable option for most people. Walking, gardening, yard work, housework, and golfing (assuming you're walking) burn fat calories.

Does this mean that high-intensity exercises are of little value as a weight-management strategy? The answer is no, because the overall goal is to create a caloric deficit, and calories count regardless of exercise intensity. Physically demanding activities such as

Strenuous physical activities that develop muscle, such as rock climbing, can also increase your metabolism.

jogging, running, rock climbing, swimming, cycling, and aerobics burn more total calories than do low-intensity activities if participation time is held constant; they just require a higher proportion of fuel from glycogen stores than from fat. Still, both energy sources are tapped. As pointed out by one fitness expert, if you burn 240 calories exercising for a half hour at a low intensity, 41 percent of those calories come from fat, giving you a fat loss of 96 calories. If you exercise for the same amount of time at a high intensity, you burn 450 calories, including 108 fat calories, even though the percentage of energy supplied by fat is only 24 percent.[40] The point of this example is not to discourage participation in low-intensity activities but only to suggest that, if you're in good health and enjoy vigorous exercise, you do not need to limit yourself to low-intensity exercise. Exercising on a consistent basis is the best strategy for managing weight, regardless of intensity level.

Regular Exercise Is the Key to Weight Management: Make It Fun

Whatever kind of exercise you do on a regular basis, it is the best strategy for weight management. If your motivation for exercise is based solely on external factors, such as losing weight or preventing disease, it is unlikely that exercise will become a permanent fixture in your lifestyle. Many experts believe that physical activity is more likely to become a lifestyle pattern if it is motivated by intrinsic factors, such as fun, pleasure, and feeling good. Losing weight is a good reason to start exercising, but you probably won't sustain exercise unless you learn to enjoy it and to value the way it makes you feel. People who are consistently physically active shift their focus from the outcome (weight loss) to the process of exercise itself. Regular exercisers want to work out because they like it and it makes them feel better.[41] (For tips on making exercise fun, see Nurturing Your Spirituality: Fun Is the Key to Regular Exercise for Weight Maintenance.) With this approach to exercise, even if weight loss is modest, overall health is improved.

It is easy to lose perspective when exercising for weight management. Remember that the primary determinant of health benefits is the total quantity of physical activity performed, rather than the type, duration, and intensity of the activity itself, regardless of weight status.[42]

Combining Dietary Modification and Exercise

Because caloric consumption and expenditure are involved in weight management, both should be manipu-

Nurturing Your Spirituality

Fun Is the Key to Regular Exercise for Weight Maintenance

Experts have shifted the paradigm of weight management from counting calories burned in exercise to promoting movement that is social, playful, and pleasurable. If exercise is fun, if it makes you feel good about yourself, and if it provides that mini-vacation each day (a time and place where nothing else interferes), it is more likely to be incorporated permanently into daily living. As noted by one expert, "Inner joy is the key to dutiful exercise. The body fails to persist if the soul is in rebellion."[43]

Do you want to move from an occasional dreaded workout to one that you look forward to on a regular basis? Here are some tips passed on by others who once were couch potatoes:

- First, examine your likes and dislikes. Think in terms of activities that are fun for you. These may be taking a stroll in a park, working in the flower garden, skating to class, or joining a fitness club.
- Build relationships with people who share your interests and goals. Workout partners often provide incentive and encouragement for working out.
- Tell people if you notice improvements in their energy level and in appearance after exercising. Not only will they feel better but so will you, and the compliment will likely be returned at some point.
- Join a fitness club or participate in a structured fitness program that will increase your repertoire of skills and activities.
- Find a comfortable workout environment with a supportive staff.
- Vary your activities. Variety is the antidote for boredom; cross-training is the key for many longtime exercisers.

lated to be effective. Combining sensible exercise and sensible changes in eating habits that can be maintained for life is the most effective approach to permanent weight management. Dieting alone can promote significant weight loss, but a substantial component of the weight loss may be lean tissue. Physical activity alone results in modest fat loss and an increase in lean body mass. Combination strategies involving both food restriction and physical activity meet the goals of

> ## Real-World Wellness
>
> **Behavioral Strategies for Reshaping Your Eating Habits**
>
> *In Chapter 1, I learned about intervention strategies for changing behavior. In this chapter I've learned about the importance of gaining control over the tendency to overeat. How can I apply behavioral principles from Chapter 1 to my goal of curbing overeating?*
>
> Try the following strategies:
>
> - Eat in a certain place—not in every room of your home.
> - Eliminate from your immediate environment all food that can be eaten without careful preparation.
> - Always eat at a carefully set place at the table and eat only one helping of planned foods.
> - Prepare only enough food for one meal.
> - Eat slowly.
> - Chew each bite twenty-five to fifty times.
> - Set down your utensils after every mouthful.
> - Partway through the meal, stop and relax without eating for two to three minutes.
> - Leave some food on your plate at each meal.
> - Plan to eat some meals alone. (There is a tendency to overeat in social situations.)
> - Eat a carefully balanced diet so that you are not deprived of a particular food element.

weight management most effectively: These strategies improve body composition by promoting weight loss, fat loss, and lean-tissue gain.

Behavioral Effects

Some evidence suggests that obese people are more likely than normal-weight people to eat in response to external cues. A clock that says it is suppertime; media messages advertising food and beverages; and the sight, sound, and aroma of food are more apt to elicit eating behavior in the obese. This tendency is the basis of the "externality" hypothesis: If people can learn to eat in response to external cues, they can also learn to recognize cues that stimulate eating behavior, substitute other behaviors for eating, and use techniques that decrease the amount of food eaten. As a result of this training the response to external cues should be reduced and replaced by attention to internal hunger signals. Many techniques have been developed over the past twenty years that may assist people in resisting the tendency to eat indiscriminately or to overeat. Generally, these techniques employ one or more of the following approaches:

1. *Self-monitoring:* A journal or daily log records food consumption, physical activities, and circumstances related to eating. In a recent study of dieters from two weeks before Thanksgiving until two weeks after New Year's, it was found that participants who were most consistent in monitoring food intake were also most successful in losing weight and keeping it off.[44]
2. *Control of precursors to eating:* The events and circumstances that elicit eating and overeating are identified.
3. *Control of eating:* Behavioral modification techniques are used to control, change, or modify specific eating behaviors. (See Real-World Wellness: Behavioral Strategies for Reshaping Eating Habits.)
4. *Reinforcement through the use of rewards:* Rewards tied to the achievement of behavioral goals are identified and used.

These techniques may be useful especially if they are combined with sensible food choices and exercise.

Eating Disorders

Anorexia nervosa (anorexia), *bulimarexia nervosa* (*bulimia*), and *binge-eating disorder* are eating disorders familiar to most Americans. Although they differ in key ways, they share a common factor: an intense fear of becoming overweight. Starvation is the primary strategy of the anoretic, but the bulimic gorges and then purges by vomiting or using diuretics and laxatives. Bulimics seldom starve to the point of emaciation; instead they are usually at or slightly above normal weight.[14] People may exhibit characteristics of anorexia and bulimia, severely limiting food intake and also purging. Such people are referred to as *anorexic-bulimic*. Most bulimics do not become anorexic, but many anorectics practice bulimic behavior.

Young females account for the majority of both disorders. Although the number of people who have full-blown bulimia or anorexia is small, symptoms of these disorders, such as induced vomiting and an extreme fear of gaining weight, are present in alarming numbers, especially among college students. Nearly one-fourth of college women and 14 percent of college men have been reported to engage in binge eating at least once a week.[13]

Anorexia Nervosa

The chief characteristic of **anorexia nervosa** is a refusal to maintain a minimally normal weight for age and height. Refusal to eat is the hallmark of the disease, regardless of whether other practices, such as binge-purge cycles, occur. Although specific causes of anorexia have not been identified, a combination of biological, social, and psychological factors contributes to the disorder. Support for an organic influence has centered on the hypothalamus (the portion of the brain reputed to house the appetite center) and the pituitary gland (the master gland of the body). Sociocultural theories focus on the compulsion of adolescent girls to become and remain lean. This exaggerated goal manifests itself at a time when girls are naturally depositing fat.

Anorexia is characterized by extreme weight loss, amenorrhea (absence of a menstrual period), and a variety of psychological disorders culminating in an obsessive preoccupation with the attainment of thinness. Fortunately, most anorectics recover fully after one experience with the disease. However, the longer a person practices anorexic behaviors, the slimmer the chance for recovery. Just the Facts: Criteria for Diagnosing Anorexia Nervosa lists the criteria that have been developed by the American Psychiatric Association for diagnosing anorexia.[45]

When confronted, anorectics typically deny the existence of a problem and the weight-loss behaviors that have resulted in their emaciated physical appearance. They also avoid medical treatment, refuse the well-intended advice of family and friends regarding professional assistance, and submit to treatment only under protest. Anorexia is a subtle disease, and anorectics become secretive in their behaviors. They are evasive, and many hide their disease in deep denial even while undergoing treatment, making the diagnosis especially difficult.

The course of treatment for anorexia is complex, involving a coordinated effort by several health care specialists. Hospitalization is often required because anorectics may have to be fed intravenously or by some other method if they cannot or will not eat. Medications that stimulate the appetite and medications that calm the patient are usually necessary. Nutritional counseling and psychological counseling—individual, group, and family—are integral components of treatment (see Real-World Wellness: Helping a Friend Overcome an Eating Disorder). Finally, behavior modification techniques are used to help change the perceptions and lifestyle of the anorectic. At this point, no single treatment has proved to be unusually successful in the treatment of anorectic patients.

Just the Facts
Criteria for Diagnosing Anorexia Nervosa

The American Psychiatric Association[45] has identified the following criteria for a diagnosis of anorexia nervosa:

- Weight change
  - unwillingness to maintain minimal normal body weight for the person's age and height
  - weight loss that leads to the maintenance of a body weight that is 15 percent below normal
  - failure to gain the amount of weight expected during a period of growth, resulting in a body weight that is 15 percent below normal
- Inordinate fear of gaining weight or becoming fat despite being significantly underweight
- Disturbed and unrealistic perceptions of body weight, size, or shape; feeling of being "fat" although emaciated; possible perception of one specific part of the body as "too fat"
- Absence of at least three menstrual cycles for women when they would normally be expected to occur (amenorrheic women have a normal menstrual cycle only during administration of hormone therapy)
- Rigid dieting; maintenance of rigid control in lifestyle; security found in control and order
- Rituals involving food and excessive exercise

Bulimia (Bulimarexia Nervosa)

Bulimia is characterized by alternate cycles of binge eating and restrictive eating. Binge eating is distinguished from ordinary overeating in that it involves the consumption of a large amount of food in a relatively brief period of time (that is, within a one- to two-hour period) and is accompanied by lack of control. Bingeing is nearly always done in private; in public, the bulimic tends to eat normal or even less than normal amounts. Unlike the occasional splurge almost everyone has, the bulimic becomes compulsive and habitual and often resorts to secretive eating. The psychological aftermath is guilt, shame, and self-disgust. Binges are usually followed by purging, primarily by self-induced vomiting supplemented with laxatives and diuretics. The physical and psychological ramifications of such a struggle include esophageal inflammation, erosion of tooth enamel caused by repeated vomiting, the possibility of electrolyte imbalances, and altered mood states, particularly anxiety and depression.

The diagnostic criteria for bulimia are given in Just the Facts: Criteria For Diagnosing Bulimia.[45] These criteria specify that, to be diagnosed a bulimic, a person must vomit at least twice a week for three months. Binge-purge cycles may occur daily, weekly, or in other

Real-World Wellness

Helping a Friend Overcome an Eating Disorder

I suspect a friend of mine is struggling with an eating disorder. How can I help without making matters worse? Are there some internet resources available?

Try doing the following:

- Talk to the person alone.
- Tell the person why you are concerned.
- Be nonjudgmental; ask clarifying questions; listen carefully.
- Offer to go with the person to talk to someone.
- Encourage her or him to verbalize feelings.
- Show how much you care by asking frequently how the person is doing.
- Show an interest in the person's life outside of eating.
- Enlist the help of a counselor if you think the disorder is severe; however, eating disorders are usually not emergency situations.
- Anticipate and accept that denial and anger are part of the illness.

Avoid doing the following:

- Threaten or challenge the person.
- Give advice about weight loss.
- Get into an argument.
- Try to keep track of the person's food consumption.
- Try to force the person to eat.
- Be patronizing by being overly caring.
- Try to be a hero or rescuer; the person may resent such efforts.

Here are some internet sites that serve as good resources:

- Eating Disorders Awareness and Prevention, Inc., at www.hometown.aol.com/edapinc/home.html
- National Eating Disorders Information Centre at www.nedic.on.ca
- American Dietetics Association at www.eatright.org
- The Center for Eating Disorders at www.eatingdisorder.org
- Pale Reflections Weekly Newsletter for Those with Eating Disorders at www.members.aol.com/paleref/index.html

Just the Facts

Criteria for Diagnosing Bulimia

The American Psychiatric Association[45] has identified the following criteria for a diagnosis of bulimia:

- Episodic secretive binge eating characterized by rapid consumption of large quantities of food in a short time; never overeating in front of others
- At least two eating binges per week for at least three months
- Loss of control over eating behavior while eating binges are in progress
- Frequent purging after eating; using techniques such as self-induced vomiting, laxatives, or diuretics; engaging in fasting or strict dieting; or engaging in vigorous exercise
- Constant and continual concern with body shape, size, and weight
- Erosion of teeth; swollen glands
- Purchase of syrup of ipecac

intervals. Bulimic behaviors range from binge eating frequently or from time-to-time, binge eating with a feeling of being unable to control food intake, severely restricting the diet between binge periods, and binge eating followed by purging. Purging in the form of laxatives, vomiting, diuretics, fasting, and excessive exercise follows in the hope that weight gain will be blunted. Because many people with bulimia engage in binge-purge practices in isolation and because bulimics are often not excessively thin, they cannot be diagnosed easily or by their appearance.

Bulimics are treated similarly to anorectics except that hospitalization is usually not required. In addition to nutritional and psychological counseling, treatment often includes antidepressive medication because bulimia is associated with clinical depression. Treatment focuses on correcting typical bulimic behaviors, such as "all-or-none" thinking: "If I'm not perfect, I'm a failure, so one slipup—one cookie—justifies a binge." Generally, psychotherapy aims primarily to help a person with self-acceptance and to be less concerned with body weight.[14]

Binge-Eating Disorder

Binge-eating disorder is similar to bulimia in two ways: (1) it involves eating large amounts of food in a short period of time, and (2) it is accompanied by a sense of lack of control regarding eating. It is different from bulimia in that it is not associated with compensatory behaviors, such as purging, fasting, and excessive exercise. When binge eating occurs on average at least two days a week for six months, it becomes an eating disorder. The American Psychiatric Association has identified additional criteria for this disorder[45] (See Just the Facts: Criteria for Diagnosing Binge-Eating Disorder.)

Underweight

A small number of people who are not anorectic or bulimic are naturally thin, and some of them are dissatisfied with their appearance. Being underweight presents as much of a cosmetic problem for affected people as obesity does for the obese person. Many underweight people find it more difficult to gain a pound than it is for obese people to lose one.

In their attempts to gain weight, many very lean people consume large quantities of food, particularly those that are rich in calories. Unfortunately, these foods are also high in fat and sugar. This eating pattern is unhealthy for anyone, regardless of body weight. The preferred approach is to combine muscle-building exercises with three well-balanced, nutritious meals supplemented by two nutritious snacks. The amount and type of weight gain should be closely monitored. Fat stores should not be increased unless the person is extremely thin and on the verge of dipping into stores of essential fat.

Principles of Weight Management: Putting It All Together

The best approach to weight management is the most obvious: maintaining a moderate lifestyle so that excess weight is not gained. In summary, the basic principles of weight maintenance and weight loss are the following:

1. Avoid the obsession with body weight. It is important to remember that body weight per se is not the most important issue; rather, body composition is. Modest weight gain distributed in the wrong places increases health risks. Conversely, significant weight gain in the form of muscle tissue enhances health and well-being. Women who had no weight problem when they were young can, with reasonable safety, add up to 15 pounds as they get older; most men who have had no weight problem can add up to 10 pounds.[46] Much greater weight gain, however, can lead to increased risk of early death and disability. You should consider losing weight if it becomes excessive or if you have a family history of disease that may be worsened by excess weight.

2. The most important factor in weight maintenance is physical activity. Americans weigh more now than ever before because of sedentary lifestyles. The challenge is either to sacrifice some labor-saving devices and their convenience or to consciously seek opportunities to impose extra physical demands on the body. This may mean choosing the stairs rather than the elevator or walking to class rather than driving. Participating in physical activities on a consistent basis is the best way to prevent excessive weight gain. It is also the best way to maintain weight loss over time. Almost all people who successfully lose weight and keep it off exercise daily. Exercise is the best way to overpower the body's set point for fatness.

Exercise is just as important to the chronically obese and overweight as it is to those who are trying to lose or maintain weight. Obese people who are fit enjoy the same health benefits as normal-weight people.

Just the Facts
Criteria for Diagnosing Binge-Eating Disorder

The American Psychiatric Association[45] has identified the following criteria for a diagnosis of binge-eating disorder:

- Recurrent episodes of eating an amount of food that is clearly larger than most people would eat in a similar circumstance
- Binge eating that occurs, on average, at least two days a week for six months
- A sense of lack of control over eating
- Binge eating associated with any three of the following:
  - eating large amounts of food when not feeling hungry
  - eating alone because of embarrassment over the amount of food eaten
  - eating much more rapidly than normal
  - eating far beyond comfort level
  - feeling guilty or depressed after eating

The ACSM recommends exercise that burns approximately 300 calories per session performed at least three times a week. This is equivalent to a 3-mile walk for most people. Remember, energy expenditure through exercise does not have to occur at one time. The effects of physical activity are cumulative and reinforce the value of activity spread throughout the day. The key issue in exercising is consistency and moderation. Plan an activity program that can be sustained one year and five years from now.

3. Follow the Food Guide Pyramid by eating nutrient-dense foods and stress consumption of complex carbohydrates. Calories from fat convert easily to fat, with only 3 percent being lost in the digestive process. By comparison, 25 percent of carbohydrate calories are lost in the process.

    Emphasize fiber in your diet. Because of fiber's high satiety value, people who eat a great deal of it usually consume fewer total calories at mealtime. An added benefit is that fiber may help block the digestion of some of the fat consumed with it. The less fat digested, the less absorbed in the bloodstream.[47]

4. Avoid volume eating. Calories count regardless of their source. The penchant to practice compensatory eating behavior may be especially common among people who choose low-fat and/or low-calorie products. People are eating food in larger quantities. Avoid buffet-style, all-you-can-eat restaurants. Practice behavioral strategies that make volume eating more difficult. And when eating low-fat or low-calorie foods, be aware of the tendency to overcompensate by eating more food. Remember, two servings of a low-fat food that contains 5 grams of fat yields 90 total fat calories and may actually exceed the number of fat calories in one serving of the regular, high-fat version.

5. Set realistic goals. Don't be misled by messages and advertisements that promise huge weight loss in a short period of time. Weight loss per week usually should not exceed 1 to 2 pounds. The ideal approach is to lose pounds at the same rate at which they were gained. In trying to set goals, ask yourself these questions: What is the least I have weighed as an adult, for at least a year? Based on past experiences what is the most weight I can expect to lose? Then, adjust your goals upward. Realize that people who succeed at maintaining a healthy weight almost never achieve their ideal. They become satisfied with a midpoint.[48]

6. Make a gradual lifestyle change. Such change represents a calm, deliberate approach rather than a frenetic "lose it now" attitude. A 200-pound person should exercise, reduce calories, and eat like a 180-pound person to become a 180-pound person. Once the weight is lost, the person cannot revert to the habits of a 200-pound person. A diet is only successful if the weight does not return.

7. Anticipate a plateau. During the first week of a diet, weight loss comes primarily from loss of protein, glycogen, and water but very little fat. As the body adjusts to a diet, fat loss increases. This adjustment takes about a week on a moderate diet and still longer when the diet is severe. Many dieters experience a plateau after about three to four weeks, not because they are suddenly cheating but because they have gained water weight while still losing body fat. If physically active, dieters may gain lean body mass and lose fat while maintaining weight. If weight loss is drastic during the early stages, it induces an adaptive response in the body that slows down metabolism. The body resists drastic change of any sort. Once its internal signals recognize a substantial reduction in caloric intake, it slows down to conserve fuel. After losing 20 to 30 pounds, expect to reach a stable plateau.

8. Avoid diet pills, special formula diets, all-you-can-eat diets, fat-burning concoctions, skin creams, and other fad diets. Some of these fads impose health risks, and others simply don't work or, if they do, their results are temporary and lead to weight cycling. The more extreme the diet, the less likely the weight loss will be permanent.

    The new generation of diet pills currently being investigated as a potential solution for the chronically obese should be viewed with caution. Even if such pills prove successful, they must be taken for life and they may have side effects as harmful to health as the extra weight. Many experts are reluctant to endorse a lifelong pharmaceutical solution to obesity.

9. Avoid very low-calorie diets. Such diets decrease BMR 10 to 20 percent, making weight loss success even harder. Results of four national surveys show that most people try to lose weight by eating 1000 to 1500 calories a day. Diets that cut calories to under 1200 (if you're a woman) or 1400 (if you're a man), however, do not allow enough food to be satisfying over the long haul.[15] A diet should minimize hunger and fatigue. Eating fewer than 1200 calories also makes it difficult to get minimal amounts of certain nutrients and promotes temporary loss of fluids rather than permanent loss of fat.

10. Develop an eating plan that includes easily obtained foods.

11. Develop a less rigid lifestyle, one that reduces the need to consciously control what is eaten. Maintaining weight loss is the antithesis of counting every calorie. In studies of children, researchers found that subjects who had the most body fat were those with the most controlling parents when it came to the amount of food eaten.[49] The studies found that children whose parents allowed them to be most spontaneous about food—eat when they were hungry and not necessarily finish all the food given to them—showed a natural instinct for regulating their own calories. Although parents are responsible for making sure children eat healthy food, children themselves are capable of figuring out how much to eat. The researchers concluded that these internal cues for food regulation, when interrupted by parents, may lead to overeating later in childhood and contribute to obesity later on. Parents are urged to relax control over the amount of food their children eat and to adopt a more flexible attitude toward their own dietary habits.

12. Avoid fasting and restrictive dieting. These practices often lead to a preoccupation with food, weight, and/or dieting. Dieting should allow people to attend parties, eat at restaurants, and participate in normal activities. People erroneously assume that if they have eaten just a little bit of a "forbidden" food, they have "crossed the line." Foods are neither "good" nor "bad." Labeling them as such often promotes a denial-guilt-preoccupation cycle in which one slight deviation from a diet or food choice is interpreted as a failure: A forbidden food is eaten (denial), a sense of relief from restraint leads to a binge, the binge leads to guilt and a feeling of failure, and both denial and guilt exacerbate the preoccupation. The preoccupation leads back to denial and the cycle continues. This cycle exerts considerable pressure on the dieter. To avoid the dissonance that comes with failure, the dieter often abandons attempts to lose weight. Given moderation and discretion, almost any food can be enjoyed. Food is one of life's pleasures, so you need not avoid any one food. If it is high in fat and calories, eat a small portion. If you do not deny yourself, you might not feel compelled to cheat.

13. Avoid meal skipping. One strategy that surprises some dieters with its effectiveness is eating frequent small meals and snacks. The more often a person eats, the less hungry that person feels and the less food that person will eat.[50] Eating five to six times a day—breakfast, a midmorning snack, lunch, an afternoon snack, dinner, and a before-bed snack—might require some retraining. Keep portions small and emphasize fruits and vegetables.

    Resist the temptation to skip breakfast. People who eat a healthy breakfast generally feel less hungry throughout the day. Recent studies suggest that breakfast eaters take in significantly less fat, less cholesterol, and more fiber over the course of a day than do people who skip breakfast. Breakfast eaters also tend to be leaner.[51]

14. Form a buddy system or join a support group. The support and encouragement of a friend or relative are often the difference between success and failure.

15. If you stop smoking, don't be discouraged by subsequent weight gain. If you are a heavy smoker, you can expect on average an increase in weight of 10 pounds. That's not enough to make most smokers obese. From a health perspective, you would have to gain 100 to 150 pounds after quitting to make your health risks as high as when you smoked.[51]

16. Don't indulge yourself in self-blame for past failures. View past dieting attempts objectively as a psychologist would. Focus more on what you learned from past experiences. Most people who are successful at maintaining weight loss are not successful in their first attempt. In studies that track dieters listed in the Weight Control Registry, 90 percent of them are repeaters. In some studies, nearly 60 percent of dieters were found to have made five attempts before achieving success.[52] Rather than blaming yourself, reflect on what you learned about yourself and what worked and didn't work.

17. Finally, accept yourself. Before trying to lose weight, determine how great a risk your weight poses to your health. People at risk for chronic conditions, such as hypertension and type II diabetes, for example, often improve dramatically with a modest weight loss. Some people, however, are overweight despite their best efforts to reduce. For such people, striving to attain a certain weight may be futile and even damaging to health. If a person was overweight throughout childhood, chances are that person will never be thin. Be realistic and aim for a healthy weight for you, not for an actor or actress. Everyone cannot be skinny. Everyone can try to be healthy.

Summary

- Americans' obsession with body weight is evidenced by the large number of women, men, and even children who are trying to lose weight at any given time.
- A healthy weight is defined as a BMI of 19.0 to 24.9. Overweight occurs with a BMI of 25 or over. Obesity occurs with a BMI of 30 or over. Only 41 percent of U.S. adults meet current standards for healthy weight.
- Obesity is a risk factor for coronary heart disease, stroke, hypertension, LDL cholesterol, some forms of cancer, impaired glucose tolerance, osteoarthritis, gallbladder disease, and sleep apnea.
- Obesity occurs when fat cells increase excessively either in size (hypertrophy) or in number (hyperplasia). Most obesity is adult-onset and caused by hypertrophy.
- Heredity and set point are the major biological factors associated with obesity.
- The development and distribution of body fat is under substantial genetic control.
- Physical activity is the best way to alter the body's set point for fatness.
- Overeating and lack of physical activities are the major behavioral explanations of obesity.
- Dietary intake of too much fat and too many calories is the major cause of obesity.
- Dietary fat has less of a thermogenic effect than do carbohydrate and protein and therefore is more efficiently and easily stored as fat tissue.
- The general decline in physical activity is highly correlated with the rise in obesity.
- Engaging in a physically active lifestyle is the best way to prevent weight gain.
- Approximately 70 percent of the energy liberated from food is expended to support BMR.
- Physical activity improves body composition, increases BMR, improves insulin sensitivity, and increases oxygen capacity and glycogen storage in muscles.
- Weight loss requires a caloric deficit in which food intake and exercise are manipulated so that caloric expenditure exceeds caloric intake.
- Complex forces influence the success of weight-loss efforts and help to explain why people respond so differently to similar dieting strategies.
- Low-fat diets often result in overcompensatory eating behaviors as a result of which the dieter ends up consuming more total calories.
- A desirable long-term goal for losing weight is 1 to 2 pounds per week until about 10 percent of excess weight is lost. A six-month maintenance period is suggested before more weight loss is attempted.
- Diet-only strategies should provide a loss of at least 1200 calories per day for women and 1500 for men.
- The optimal approach to weight loss combines mild caloric restriction with regular physical activity. Together these two strategies should provide a caloric deficit that does not exceed 500 to 1000 calories per day.
- A good physical activity prescription for weight loss is to manipulate exercise intensity and duration to burn 200 to 400 calories per session.
- Diet drugs are not intended for people who are simply overweight or only marginally obese. The harmful effects of long-term exposure to diet drugs may outweigh the health benefits of losing weight.
- Low-intensity exercises sustained for a prolonged period of time are effective in burning fat calories. However, regardless of intensity level, exercising on a consistent basis is the best strategy for managing weight.
- Anorexia, bulimia, and binge eating are three potentially destructive eating disorders with complex causes.

Review Questions

1. What evidence exists to support the idea that Americans are obsessed with weight control?
2. In terms of BMIs, what are the definitions of *healthy weight*, *overweight*, and *obesity*?
3. What is the pattern of growth of adipose cells from birth through puberty?
4. What health problems and chronic conditions are associated with obesity?
5. What is the relationship between obesity and morbidity and mortality?
6. What are the major biological and behavioral factors that help to explain obesity?
7. What evidence can you use to support the existence of an influential role of heredity in the development of obesity?
8. What does *set point* mean in reference to body shape and body weight? What strategy is best for altering a person's set point for fatness?
9. What dieting strategies need to be emphasized in weight-loss programs?
10. Compare and contrast dieting and exercise as strategies for (a) losing weight and (b) maintaining or preventing weight gain.
11. What is weight cycling?
12. Why is the thermogenic effect of food an important issue in weight management?
13. What is the relationship between BMR, physical activity, and body composition?
14. What are the signs and symptoms of anorexia, bulimia, and binge-eating disorder?
15. What are ten principles that should be considered when structuring an approach to weight management and/or weight loss?

References

1. Mayo. Foundation for Medical Education and Research. 1998. Body Image: What Do You See in the Mirror? Available on-line at www.mayohealth.org/mayo/9704/htm/body_ima.htm.
2. Consumers Union. 1998. Top selling diets: Lots of gimmicks, little solid evidence. *Consumer Reports* 63(1):60.
3. Tufts University. 1998. Sniffing your way to weight loss? *Tufts University Health and Nutrition Letter* 16(2):6.
4. Goldblatt, B. I. 1997. Advertisers get away with incredible weight-loss claims; how not to succumb. *Environmental Nutrition* 20(1):3.
5. Editors. 1996. Mission impossible. *People* 45(22):65.
6. U.S. Department of Health and Human Services. 1998. *Healthy People 2010 Objectives: Draft for Public Comment*. Washington, D.C.: U.S. Government Printing Office.
7. Lans, K. 1999. *When Minor Flaws Loom Large in the Mirror*. Available on-line at www.brown.edu/administration/george_street_Journal/v22/v22n5/dysmorph.html.
8. Womancomnetwork. 1998. *Imagetalk—Women's Wire on Body Image: Role Models?* Available on-line at www.womenswire.com/image/models2.html.
9. McDowell, M. A., et al. 1994. *Energy and Macro-Nutrient Intakes of Persons Ages 2 Months and Over in the United States: Third National Health and Nutrition Examination Survey, Phase I, 1988–91. Advanced Data from Vital and Health Statistics; No. 255*. Hyattsville, Md.: National Center for Health Statistics.
10. Harvard Medical School Publications Group, Inc. 1994. Losing weight, a new attitude emerges. *Harvard Health Letter* 4(7):1.
11. Harvard Medical School Publications Group, Inc. 1998. Guidelines call more Americans overweight. *Harvard Health Letter* 23(10):7.
12. Margolis, S., and L. Cheskin. 1998. *The Johns Hopkins White Papers: Weight Control*. Baltimore, Md.: The Johns Hopkins Medical Institutions.
13. Nieman, D. 1999. *Exercise Testing and Prescription—a Health Related Approach*. Mountain View, Calif.: Mayfield Publishing.
14. Wardlaw, G. M. 1999. *Perspectives in nutrition* (4th ed.). St Louis: WCB/McGraw-Hill.
15. Mayo Foundation for Medical Education and Research. 1994. Weight control—what works and why. *Mayo Clinic Health Letter* June (suppl.):1.
16. Stunkard, A., et al. 1986. An adoption study of human obesity. *New England Journal of Medicine* 314:193.
17. Stunkard, A., et al. 1986. A twin study of human obesity. *Journal of the American Medical Association* 256:51.
18. Blair, S. 1995. *The Health Hazards of a Sedentary Lifestyle*. Distinguished scholar presentation. Memphis: The University of Memphis.
19. Garnett, L. R. 1996. Is obesity all in the genes? *Harvard Health Letter* 21(6):1.
20. Leibel, R. L., M. Rosenbaum, and J. Hirsch. 1995. Changes in energy expenditure resulting from altered body weight. *New England Journal of Medicine* 332:621.
21. Hawks, S. R., and P. Richins. 1994. Toward a new paradigm for the management of obesity. *Journal of Health Education* 25(3):147.
22. Tufts University. 1997. On whether reduced-fat foods make reduced-fat bodies. *Tufts University Health and Nutrition Letter* 15(9):2.
23. Consumers Union. 1995. The facts about fats. *Consumer Reports* 60:389.
24. Massachusetts Medical Society. 1997. Low-fat, low sugar foods no guarantee of fewer calories. *HealthNews* 3(9):5.
25. Editors. 1995. Exercise won't usually help you lose weight, but . . . *Sports Medicine Digest* 17(10):1.
26. Editors. 1993. Do yo-yo dieters die young? *Health* 7(2):10.
27. Editors. 1995. Yo-yo diets aren't risky afterall. *Health* 9(1):18.
28. Flynn, M. E. 1995. Fat-free foods: A dieter's downfall? Studies show calories do count. *Environmental Nutrition* 18(4):1.
29. CSPI. 1994. Confusing fat. *Nutrition Action Health Letter* 21(4):4.
30. Liebman, B. 1997. Fooled by low-fat. *Nutrition Action Health Letter* 24(3):2.
31. Liebman, B. 1998. Supersize foods, supersize people. *Nutrition Action Health Letter* 25(6):6.
32. Goldblatt, B. I. 1997. Advertisers get away with incredible weight-loss claims; how not to succumb. *Environmental Nutrition* 20(1):3.
33. Environmental Nutrition, Inc. 1998. FDA clears diet drug, but safety an issue. *Environmental Nutrition* 21(1):3.
34. Nethealth, Inc. 1999. *Herbal Therapies*. Available on-line at www.weightloss2000.com/herbs/herbs_06_all.htm.
35. Mayo Foundation for Medical Education and Research. 1997. Weight-loss products: "Herbal" doesn't necessarily mean "safe." *Mayo Clinic Health Letter* 15(12):4.
36. Albertson, E. 1996. Fasting. *American Health* 15(6):65.
37. Environmental Nutrition, Inc. 1997. Fasting for health offers few benefits, questionable safety. *Environmental Nutrition* 20(5):7.
38. Roitman, J. L. 1998. *ACSM's Resource Manual for Guidelines for Exercise Testing and Prescription*. Baltimore, Md.: Lippincott, Williams & Wilkins.
39. Eller, D. 1997. The best way to lose weight. *Health* 11(4):34.
40. Brehm, B. 1996. Fat-burning: Getting down to the basics. *Fitness Management* 12(4):25.
41. White, D. 1999. Inner joy is key to dutiful exercise. *The Commercial Appeal* 160(4):C1.
42. Robison, J. 1997. Weight management: Shifting the paradigm. *Journal of Health Education* 28(1):28.
43. White, D. 1999. Inner joy is the key to dutiful exercise. *The Commercial Appeal* 160(4):C1–3.
44. Tufts University. 1998. Ever "forget" you're trying to eat less? Write it down. *Tufts University Health and Nutrition Letter* 16(8):8.
45. American Psychiatric Association. 1994. *Diagnostic and Statistical Manual of Mental Disorders* (4th ed.). Washington, D.C.: The Association.
46. Consumers Union. 1995. How much should you weigh? *Consumer Reports* 60:804.
47. Tufts University. 1998. Fiber cuts calories in more ways than one. *Tufts*

University Health and Nutrition Letter 16(2):3.
48. Manning, M. 1997. Imperfect beauty. *Health* 11(6):82.
49. Birch, L. L. 1995. Appetite and eating behavior in children. *Pediatric Clinicians of North America* 42:931.
50. Tufts University. 1998. Several small meals keep off body fat better than one or two large ones. *Tufts University Health and Nutrition Letter* 15(12):1.
51. Tufts University. 1996. If you want to quit smoking but fear the weight gain. *Tufts University Health and Nutrition Letter* 13(11):6.
52. Tufts University. 1998. What it takes to take off weight (and keep it off). *Tufts University Health and Nutrition Letter* 15(11):4.
53. Kolata, G. 1998. Study finds obesity doesn't hasten death to extent once thought. *The Commercial Appeal* 159(1):A4.

Suggested Readings

Abbas, M. A., and R. A. Abbas. 1998. *Beyond fen-phen: The secrets to modern, healthier, safer weight-loss.* Sytac Publishing.

This book explores the world of weight loss and obesity from diets, exercise, weight-loss medications, weight-reduction surgery, cosmetic surgery, and more. It is a comprehensive guide written for the overweight person struggling to lose weight.

Guay, M. 1998. *Don't Diet—Live It: Successful Weight Control for Real People who Enjoy Real Food.* Marietta, Ga.: White Papers Press.

This book maintains that the ultimate weight-control book only needs to contain four words: "Eat Less, Move More." Yet in our complicated society with its abundance of food, weight control is not that simple. Rather than offering a quick fix, the author provides a plan for those who are ready to make a permanent transition to a healthy lifestyle and lifelong weight control. There are no restrictive menus, no pills, no gimmicks but instead a sensible, flexible, achievable, and safe way to gain control of your lifestyle.

Hesse-Biber, S. 1997. *Am I Thin Enough Yet? The Cult of Thinness and the Commercialization of Identity.* Oxford: Oxford University Press.

This book discusses the preoccupation of American women with weight, analyzes the social, economic, and political pressures confronting women in a weight-obsessed society, and explains how women learn to equate thinness with beauty. It includes first-hand, intimate portraits of young women from a wide variety of backgrounds and draws on historical accounts from popular and scholarly sources to bring into focus the multitude of societal and psychological forces that compel American women to pursue the ideal of thinness at any cost.

Margolis, S., and L. Cheskin. 1998. *The Johns Hopkins White Papers: Weight Control.* Baltimore, Md.: The Johns Hopkins Medical Institutions.

Designed for the public, this monograph presents an overview of issues related to weight loss, compares popular weight-loss methods, describes medical conditions that may cause obesity, and outlines lifestyle treatments for weight loss. It is updated annually.

Nieman, D. 1999. *Exercise Testing and prescription—a Health Related Approach.* Mountain View, Calif.: Mayfield Publishing Co.

A chapter of this text is devoted to the relationship between physical activity and obesity. The author provides a comprehensive review of the literature on physical activity and obesity, citing more than 300 studies. Concepts, issues, and misconceptions are thoroughly discussed and researched.

Wardlaw, G. 1999. *Perspectives in Nutrition* (4th ed.). St. Louis: WCB/McGraw-Hill.

This comprehensive reference text on nutrition features chapters on dieting, weight control, and eating disorders.

Name _____   Date _____   Section _____

Assessment Activity 8-1

Assessing Your Body Image

Accepting those physical characteristics that are unique to you is an important first step to constructing a positive body image. In this assessment you will assess your body image from two perspectives: ideal and actual.

Directions: The following sets of bipolar adjectives relate to physical characteristics and appearance. Indicate your rating of these characteristics as follows:

1. Ideal body image: Circle the number that best represents how you would like your body to be in terms of each characteristic.
2. Actual body image: Put an X through the number that represents how you believe your body actually is in terms of each characteristic.

Body Image Characteristics

Graceful	1	2	3	4	5	6	7	8	9	10	Clumsy
Tall	1	2	3	4	5	6	7	8	9	10	Short
Slim	1	2	3	4	5	6	7	8	9	10	Fat
Large	1	2	3	4	5	6	7	8	9	10	Small
Attractive	1	2	3	4	5	6	7	8	9	10	Unattractive
Rugged	1	2	3	4	5	6	7	8	9	10	Delicate
Flabby	1	2	3	4	5	6	7	8	9	10	Muscular
Soft	1	2	3	4	5	6	7	8	9	10	Hard
Shapely	1	2	3	4	5	6	7	8	9	10	Unshapely
Weak	1	2	3	4	5	6	7	8	9	10	Strong
Well-proportioned	1	2	3	4	5	6	7	8	9	10	Poorly proportioned

Now answer the following questions:

1. Which characteristics of the ideal body image, if any, do you think can be achieved by dieting alone? By exercise alone?
2. How many of the items had a gap between the circles and the Xs?
3. On those items with a large gap, which characteristics of your actual body image actually can be changed?
4. What difference would it make if your body conformed to your "ideal body image?" Would it have any real influence on your relationships and your happiness?

From *Your Body Image*. Available on-line at **www.hc-sc.gc.ca/hppb/nutrition/pube/vtlk/vitlk13.htm.**

Name _____ Date _____ Section _____

Assessment Activity 8-2

Calculating Caloric Expenditure Through Exercise

Directions: This exercise illustrates the calculations used for determining weight loss through exercise. In the example in Part 1, a subject weighing 195 pounds wishes to lose 12 pounds by exercising 40 minutes per day five times per week. The form of exercise will be riding a bike at 13 MPH. Table 8-4 gives the appropriate coefficient (0.071) for this activity, and as previously mentioned there are 3500 calories in 1 pound of fat. Study this example and then apply it to the problem presented in Part II to answer the following questions:

- How many calories are expended per exercise session?
- How many pounds may be lost per week at this energy expenditure?
- How long will it take to lose 12 lbs.?

Part 1

1. Multiply body weight by the appropriate activity coefficient:
   195 lbs. × 0.071 = 13.8 calories/min.
   13.8 calories/min. × 40 min. = 552 calories

2. Multiply the number of calories expended per workout by the number of workouts per week:
   552 calories × 5 workouts/week = 2760 calories/week

   $$\frac{2760 \text{ calories/week}}{3500 \text{ calories/lb.}} = 0.79 \text{ lost/week}$$

3. Divide the total pounds you want to lose (12 lbs.) by the number of pounds lost per week:

   $$\frac{12 \text{ lbs.}}{0.79 \text{ lbs. lost/week}} = 15.2 \text{ weeks}$$

This subject would lose 12 pounds in fifteen weeks by riding a bike at 13 MPH for 40 minutes per day five times per week. Your weight-loss goals can be determined in the same way.

Part II

Now apply your knowledge of energy expenditure through exercise by solving the following problem. Jim weighs 220 pounds and wishes to lose 25 pounds by jogging at 5 MPH for 30 minutes per exercise session five days per week. Do the calculations to solve Jim's problem by following these steps:

1. Multiply body weight by the appropriate activity coefficient from table 8-4 for jogging 5 MPH.

   220 lbs. × _____ coefficient = _____ calories/min.

   _____ calories/min. × 30 min. = _____ calories

2. Multiply the number of calories expended per workout by the number of workouts per week:

   _____ calories × 5 workouts/week = _____

   _____ calories/week ÷ 3500 calories/lb. = _____ lbs. lost/week

3. Divide the total pounds to be lost by the number of pounds lost per week.

   25 lbs. ÷ _____ lbs. lost/week = _____ weeks

4. a. How many calories would Jim expend per exercise session? _____
   b. How many pounds will he lose per week at this energy expenditure? _____
   c. How many weeks will it take Jim to lose 25 pounds? _____

Coping with and Managing Stress

Key Terms

coping
distress
eustress
general adaptation ... (GAS)
...oneuroimmunology
...ion techniques
...essor

Objectives

After completing this chapter, you will be able to do the following:
- Define *stress*.
- Identify potential stressors.
- Describe the various types of stress.
- Describe the stages of the general adaptation syndrome (GAS).
- Explain the body's physiological response to stress.
- List the short- and long-term health effects of stress.
- Identify strategies that effectively deal with stress.

Goals for Behavior Change
- Identify your personal sources of stress.
- View stress as holding potential for personal growth.
- Develop a time-management plan.
- Select strategies for managing stress.
- Put into action a stress-management plan.

Stress profoundly affects people's lives. Everyone—students, businesspeople, parents, athletes—lives with stress. Stress is frequently viewed as an enemy. This is a misconception. Stress is often neither positive nor negative. How people deal with or react to what they perceive as stress is what determines its effect on their lives. As has been stated, "It is often said that stress is one of the most destructive elements in people's daily lives, but that is only a half truth. The way we react to stress appears to be more important than the stress itself."[1] The effects of stress can be either positive or negative. Positively used, stress can be a motivator for an improved quality of life. Viewed negatively, it can be destructive.

What is Stress?

Dr. Hans Selye was the first to define the term **stress** as the "nonspecific response of the body to any demands made upon it." It can be characterized by diverse reactions, such as muscle tension, acute anxiety, increased heart rate, hypertension, shallow breathing, giddiness, and even joy. From a positive perspective, stress is a force that generates and initiates action. Using Selye's definition, stress can accompany pleasant or unpleasant events. Selye referred to stress judged as "good" as **eustress**. This form of stress is the force that serves to initiate emotional and psychological growth. Eustress provides the experience of pleasure, adds meaning to life, and fosters an attitude that tries to find positive solutions to even complex problems. Eustress can accompany a birth, graduation, the purchase of a new car, the development of a new friendship, the accomplishment of a difficult task, and success in an area that previously produced anxiety. **Distress**, on the other hand, is stress that results in negative responses. Unchecked, negative stress can interfere with the physiological and psychological functioning of the body and may ultimately result in a disease or disability.[2]

Stress also provides humans with the ability to respond to challenges or dangers. It is vital to self-protection and also serves as a motivator that enhances human ability.

A **stressor** is any physical, psychological, or environmental event or condition that initiates the stress response (figure 9-1).

See Assessment Activity 9-2 to evaluate your own stress level in the different categories listed in figure 9-1.

What is considered a stressor for one person may not be a stressor for another. Speaking in front of a group may be stimulating for one person and terrifying for another. Some people experience extreme test anxiety and others feel very confident about written assessments. Fortunately, the stress response is not a genetic trait, and because it is a response to external conditions, it is subject to personal control. A person may not avoid taking a test, but he or she can apply techniques and take precautions that lessen the effects of the stress. For example, knowing the material thoroughly and engaging in deep breathing several minutes before a test helps dissipate anxiety. To maximize quality of life, people can find positive ways of coping with stress.

A stress response can enhance and actually increase the level of either mental or physical performance. This response is referred to as the *inverted-U theory*.[3] Not

Physical	Social	Intellectual	Emotional	Spiritual (values/morals)	Environmental	Occupational
Pathogens	Embarrassment	Mental fatigue	Uncontrolled anger	Guilt	Noise	Negative interaction with coworkers or supervisor
Drugs	Teasing	Overload	Unexpressed anger	Moral conflicts	Overcrowding	Deadline pressure
Smoking	Ridicule	Frustration	Inability to love	Lack of purpose	Poverty	Working overtime
Lack of sleep	Arguments	Mental stagnation	Lack of love	Lack of philosophy of life	Temperature	Difficulty balancing work with home life and school
Injury	Lack of social interaction		Poor self-esteem			
Sedentary lifestyle	Rejection					

→ Distress

Figure 9-1 Stressors That Can Create Distress

enough stress (hypostress) may result in a poorer effort, but too much stress can inhibit effort. There appears to be an optimal level of stress that results in peak performance (figure 9-2). Achievement of an appropriate level of stress depends on the person and the type of task. Table 9-1 lists some of the potentially positive outcomes associated with stress. Your body is constantly attempting to maintain a physiological balance. This balance is referred to as *homeostasis*. Any event or circumstance that causes a disruption (a stressor) in your body's homeostasis requires some type of adaptive behavior. Physiologically, whether a stressor is perceived as positive or negative, the body responds with the same three-stage process. This series of changes is known as the **general adaptation syndrome (GAS)**.[4] The three phases are alarm, resistance, and exhaustion (figure 9-3).

The *alarm* phase occurs when homeostasis is initially disrupted. The brain perceives a stressor and prepares the body to deal with it, a response sometimes referred to as the *fight-or-flight syndrome*. The subconscious appraisal of the stressor results in an emotional reaction. The emotional response stimulates a physical reaction that is associated with stress, such as the muscles becoming tense, the stomach tightening, the heart rate increasing, the mouth becoming dry, and the palms of the hands sweating.

The second stage is *resistance*. In this phase the body meets the perceived challenge through increased strength, endurance, sensory capacities, and sensory acuity. Hormonal secretions regulate the body's response to a stressor. Only after meeting and satisfying the demands of a stressful situation can the internal activities of the body return to normal. Girdano and George[5] argue that people have different levels of energy to deal with stressors. For short-term stressors, only a superficial level of energy is required, allowing deeper energy levels to be protected. Superficial levels of energy are readily accessible and easily renewable. Unfortunately, all stress cannot be resolved with superficial energy levels. When long-term or deep levels of stress are experienced, the amount of energy available is limited. If sufficient stress is experienced for an extended period, loss of adaptation can result. Although some scientists believe that energy stores may be genetically programmed, all people can replenish their energy stores through exercise, good nutrition, adequate sleep, and other positive behaviors.

When stressors become chronic or pervasive, the third phase, *exhaustion*, is reached. In exhaustion, energy stores have been depleted and rest must occur. Although weeks to years may pass before the effects of long-term stressors occur, if a person does not learn how to adequately deal with stress, exhaustion will result. At this point, stress may affect the stomach, heart, blood pressure, muscles, and joints. Fortunately, the effects of stressors can be completely or partially reversed when adequate management techniques are initiated. The earlier these management techniques are learned and used, the fewer problems result.

Figure 9-2 The Inverted-U Theory

Table 9-1 Positive Outcomes of Stress

Mental	Emotional	Physical
Enhanced creativity	Sense of control	High energy level
Enhanced thinking ability	Responsiveness to environment	Increased stamina
Greater goal orientation	Improved interpersonal relationships	Flexibility of muscles and joints
Enhanced motivation	Improved morale	Freedom from stress-related disease

Figure 9-3 The General Adaptation Syndrome (GAS)

Homeostasis	I. Alarm	II. Resistance	III. Exhaustion	Death	Recovery
All systems are reactive to everyday stressors in a balanced and healthful manner.	Stressor is perceived. Homeostasis slightly drops as the mind and body temporarily lose balance.	Adaptation resources are mobilized to combat stressor. Endocrine system comes into play.	Adaptation and energy stores are depleted. When replenished, body returns to homeostasis.	In extreme or chronic cases, exhaustion can become so pronounced that death can occur.	Stressful situations that are well or partially managed result in a complete or partial return to homeostasis and normal functioning.

Sources of Stress and Warning Signs

Most stressful situations fall into one of three categories: (1) harm and loss, (2) threat, and (3) challenge.[6] Examples of *harm-and-loss situations* are the death of a loved one, loss of personal property, physical assault, physical injury, and severe loss of self-esteem. *Threat situations* may be real or perceived and can range from being caught in traffic to being unable to perceive an event. Threatening events tax a person's ability to deal with everyday life. Threat stressors are any stressors that result in anger, hostility, frustration, or depression. *Challenge situations* are catalysts for either growth or pain. These stressors often involve major life changes and include such events as taking a new job, leaving home, graduating from college, and getting married. Challenge events are usually perceived as being good but involve stress because they disrupt homeostasis and require considerable psychological and physical adjustment.

Being aware of the mental and physical signals associated with stress is the beginning step in learning how to manage it. Assessment Activity 9-1 will aid you in identifying some of the major stressors. By using self-assessments to monitor for signs of stress, you can avoid excessive stress. The negative results of distress are shown in table 9-2. Indicators of excessive distress include the following:

- Chronic fatigue, migraine headaches, sweating, lower-back pain, sleep disturbances, weakness, dizziness, diarrhea, and constipation
- Harder and/or longer work or study while accomplishing less, an inability to concentrate, general disorientation
- Denial that there is a problem or troubling event
- Increased incidence of illness, such as colds and flu or constant worry about illness or becoming ill; overuse of over-the-counter drugs for the purpose of self-medication
- Depression, irritability, anxiety, apathy, an overwhelming urge to cry or run and hide, and feelings of unreality
- Excessive behavior patterns, such as spending too much money, drinking, breaking the law, and developing addictions
- Accident proneness
- Signs of reclusiveness and avoidance of other people
- Emotional tension, "keyed up" feeling, easy startling, nervous laughter, anxiety, hyperkinesia, and nervous tics

Table 9-2 Negative Results of Distress

Mental	Physical	Emotional
Short-term effects		
Poor memory	Flushed face	Irritability
Inability to concentrate	Cold hands	Disorganization
Low creativity	Gas	Conflicts
Poor self-control	Rapid breathing	Mood swings
Low self-esteem	Shortness of breath	Chronic sleep problems
	Dry mouth	Acid stomach
		Overindulgence in alcohol, drugs, food
Long-term effects		
Bouts of depression	Hypertension	Overweight/underweight
Mild paranoia	Coronary disease	Drug abuse
Low tolerance for ambiguity	Ulcers	Excessive smoking
Forgetfulness	Migraine/tension headaches	Ineffective use of work/leisure time
Inability to make decisions/quick to make decisions	Strokes	Overreaction to mild work pressure
	Allergies	

HealthQuest Activities

- The *How Stressed Are You?* activity in Module 1 allows you to look at several areas of your life (including money, school, relationships, and health) and identify stress caused by events and daily hassles. You can also rate your perceived stress level for each area. Use this feature to find out which area or areas generate the highest levels of stress for you.
- The *CyberStress* activity in Module 1 simulates a stress-filled day and can be used to help you assess your reactions to daily stressors. Choose the scenario that most closely matches your own. For example, if you work and go to school, you should check both on the preferences screen. As you are presented with stressful situations, choose the reaction that is closest to how you would react. At the feedback screen, print the screen showing your score. Then evaluate your experience by answering the questions in the *What Do You Think?* section.

Factors Generating a Stress Response

As mentioned earlier, the criteria for a stressful event and the response to that event for any person are unique to the individual. Figure 9-4 provides an overview of the complexity of the stress experience and some of the many moderating effects. For instance, a dysfunctional homelife (characterized by an alcoholic parent, a difficult divorce, or extreme poverty) may contribute to a personality that is more susceptible to difficult events, such as poor grades or a failed relationship. This combination of inadequate preparation for life along with an event that is perceived as personal failure is likely to lead to depression, anxiety, or anger. Conversely, a person whose background has fostered a deep sense of self-worth and meaningfulness will be able to better handle a difficult event and not perceive the event as a personal failure. Poor grades may be the result of poor study habits, an undiagnosed learning behavior, or inadequate sleep, and a failed relationship may be simply the result of a poor match, bad timing, or immaturity.

Physiological Responses to Stress

Stress abounds in life and can be experienced as the result of happy and unhappy events. Regardless of the stressor, each time a stressful event occurs, a series of neurological and hormonal messages are sent throughout the body.

The nervous system serves as a reciprocal network that sends messages between the awareness centers of the brain and the organs and muscles of the body. Part of this system is referred to as the *limbic system*. The limbic system contains centers for

Figure 9-4 Theoretical Framework of the Stress Experience

emotions, memory, learning relay, and hormone production and includes the pituitary gland, thalamus, and hypothalamus.

When a stressor is encountered, the body sends a message to the brain via the nervous system. The brain then synthesizes the message and determines whether it is valid or not. If a message is not verified by the brain as being threatening, the limbic system overrides the initial response and the body continues to function normally. If the initial response is translated as accurate and a stressor is detected, the body responds with some emotion (fear, joy, terror), and the hypothalamus begins to act.

The hypothalamus sends a hormonal message to the pituitary gland, which then releases a hormone (ACTH) that helps signal other glands in the endocrine system to secrete additional hormones, providing fuel to respond with the fight-or-flight reaction. Systolic blood pressure may rise 15 to 20 mmHg while fluid is retained. The adrenal cortex increases blood pressure to facilitate transportation of food and oxygen to active parts of the body.[7] Blood volume is increased.

The hypothalamus also sends a message to release the hormones epinephrine and norepinephrine, which initiate a variety of physiological changes. These changes include increased heart rate, increased metabolic rate, increased oxygen consumption, and the release of hormones called *endorphins,* which decrease sensations of pain.

The autonomic nervous system is responsible for a second major set of physiological responses. In reaction to a threat, the autonomic nervous system increases heart rate, strength of the skeletal muscles, mental activity, and basal metabolic rate; dilates the coronary arteries, pupils, bronchial tubes, and arterioles; and constricts the abdominal arteries. This system also returns the body to a normal, relaxed state.

Stress and the Immune System

The mind and body act on each other in remarkable ways. Our immune system is a part of the body's defense against illness and disease originating from factors and conditions both outside and inside our bodies. The immune system consists of a variety of mechanical and chemical defenses that serve to protect against such outside invaders as microorganisms, allergens, and other substances as well as inside factors such as

Everyday problems can trigger the stress response. What are your biggest stressors?

mutating cells or improperly functioning tissue. The immune system is a functional system rather than an organ system and, as a result, seems to be prone to the effects of stress when fighting off the situations and conditions previously mentioned.[8]

The biological link between emotions and disease and even death is quite strong. Mortality is three times higher in people with few close relationships than in those with numerous such relationships, and people with strong support groups have additional protection against life stressors. Death rates are higher for cancer patients with pessimistic attitudes. Illness is more common among people who feel locked into strife-ridden marriages. AIDS patients with healthy psyches seem better able to withstand disease.[9]

The immune function seems to be affected by the relationship between the brain and nervous system. This relationship among brain, nervous system, and immune response has been the outgrowth from the field of study called **psychoneuroimmunology (PNI)**. This relatively new medical discipline seeks to explain the connection between the brain, the nervous system, and the body's response to infections and deviated cell division. Several studies have shown that chronic stress suppresses the body's ability to initiate an effective immune response. This suppression is attributed to an increase in corticosteroids, which are produced during chronic stress. This increase in corticosteroid levels delays and weakens the immune response.[10] O'Leary found that chronic stress suppresses the immune system, particularly when the stress is associated with social disruption (leaving home for the first time), psychological depression (feeling "down" for prolonged periods of time), or some negative personality attribute (lack of self-confidence).[11] It has also been found that immunosuppression is associated with loneliness and feelings of hopelessness.[12] Recently, stress has been demonstrated to be associated with infertility.[13,14] No known specific reason exists for this correlation. Whether the stress is the result of infertility problems or another source, stress reduction intervention results in significant improvement in conception rates.

Because stress affects the immune system, the body becomes more susceptible to a multitude of ailments, from colds to cancer. Respiratory conditions, such as asthma, may become worse. The cardiovascular system reacts by constricting the blood vessels while increasing blood volume. The net result is a rise in blood pressure throughout a stress-ridden day. Multiple increases in blood pressure can eventually contribute to chronic high blood pressure. More forceful contraction of the heart elevates levels of free fatty acids, enhancing the development of clogged arteries leading to and including the heart itself. In extreme cases, sudden death can occur, especially for a person who has been experiencing high levels of uncontrolled stress for an extended period.

Headaches, including migraines, have long been associated with stress. Tension headaches are caused by involuntary contractions of the scalp, head, and neck muscles. Typical muscular reaction to stress is contracting or tensing. When chronic stress occurs, the body reacts by being constantly ready to respond, and the muscles become braced, always in a state of tension. More stress magnifies the tension the muscles are already undergoing. Increased muscular tension manifests itself in headaches, backaches, neckaches, and other pains. The smooth muscles that control internal organs also experience pains. More intense contractions can lead to stomachache, diarrhea, hypertension, heartburn, gastritis, diarrhea, bloating, inflammation of the pancreas, and blockage of the bile ducts.

Stress decreases saliva in the mouth, often making speaking awkward. Swallowing may become difficult, and the increase in stomach acids contributes to ulcer pain. People tend to perspire more, and electrical currents are transmitted more quickly across the skin. Skin conditions such as acne, psoriasis, herpes, hives, and eczema are exacerbated.

Wellness Across the Generations
Women's Changing Roles

As many families now have two-career households and more women work outside the home, it is natural to wonder if the double demands of household and worksite pose a threat to women's physical and psychological health. A recent study done at Duke University Medical Center by Linda Luecken and her colleagues, suggests that they do.

The study focused on 109 women with full-time clerical and customer-service jobs. Some had children and some did not. The results indicated that working women with children at home had higher levels of cortisol (a stress hormone thought to reflect high levels of distress), a greater lack of personal control, and more risk for cardiovascular disease than working women with no children. Both groups of women reported similar levels of work strain, but the working mothers reported higher levels of home strain, including greater demands and less control. This increased strain seemed to be caused by the reality that these women performed most of the child-rearing and household duties. Such chores as laundry, cleaning, cooking, chauffeuring, and homework more often fell to the women in the study than to their male partners.

Luecken and her colleagues estimated that working women with children have up to twenty-one hours more work per week than men have. They also found that working mothers have little chance to "unwind," so they have increased sympathetic nervous system arousal both during and after work. Even if male partners help with household duties, they often finish their duties with enough time to relax. The presence of a spouse or significant other did not significantly reduce the physiological and psychological consequences of stress on the working mother. Interestingly, higher income, ethnicity, and the number of children at home did not influence the level of stress.[21]

Here are some ways working mothers might balance the demands of work and household duties:

- Set limits. Schedule and honor your own time to relax. Learn to say "no."
- Make lists of your priorities, from most important to least important. Get done what is really important and let the rest go.
- Remember that perfection is the enemy of happiness.
- Team up with other parents to share the load: child care, dinner clubs, or shuttling.
- Pay attention to the moments of joy that parenting and connecting with a partner and friends have to offer.[22]

Stress also seems to affect the body's nutritional status. Individual nutritional patterns can also influence stress management efforts. For example, eating too much or too little, eating the wrong kinds of food, and overusing products such as caffeine or alcohol upset homeostasis. Diets high in fat, sugar, and processed foods place a heavy burden on various body systems. Ingesting too few calories can lead to the breakdown of lean tissue. To meet the demands of stress, you should maintain adequate nutrition through a balanced and varied diet. (Chapter 6 provides guidelines for developing a beneficial nutritional plan.) Table 9-3 provides some insight into the interactive natures of stress, nutritional status, and immunity.

Ultimately, no body system escapes the effects of stress. Long-term presence of certain stress-associated hormones in the brain damages receptors and cells found in the hippocampus. (The hippocampus sends messages when stress is occurring.) Because brain cells do not regenerate, these cells are lost forever. The effects of this loss are unknown, but indications are that eventually affected people become less able to respond to stress appropriately.[15] Assessment Activity 9-3 provides guidelines for identifying stress style and suggests relaxation activities.

Self-Esteem and Stress

How people feel about themselves and others and their perceptions of the stressors in their lives are part of the psychology of stress. Ability to cope with stress often hinges on impressions of how detrimental a stressor is and how adequately resources can deal with the situation. How much stress people feel themselves experiencing is closely associated with their own sense of self-esteem. Self-esteem includes beliefs and attitudes about changes, personal talent, skills, and one's ability to deal with the changes and challenges that inevitably occur in life. It is also the basis of self-efficacy and the locus of control (see Chapter 1). The most influential factor in determining response to stress may be people's own perceptions of themselves.

Table 9-3 Stress, Nutritional Status, and Immunity: An Interactive Effect

Although the mechanism is not completely understood, stress significantly affects nutritional status and therefore immunity. Several nutritional factors have implications for how your body responds to stress.

Energy
Stress can increase the body's basic caloric needs by as much as 200%. The stress hormones increase body heat production. When this heat is released, it is not available for cell metabolism. The caloric inefficiency induced by stress accounts for the increased need for energy intake.

Protein
Stress may increase the body's need for protein from 60% to as much as 500%. The integrity of the body's tissues, such as the skin and the tissue lining the mouth, lungs, and nose (called *mucosal tissue*), depends on adequate protein repair and maintenance of secretions of biochemicals that serve as protective agents. The formation of antibodies also requires protein.

Fats
Dietary fatty acids influence the synthesis of a group of fatty acid derivatives called *prostaglandins*. Prostaglandins stimulate or depress other cellular and immune functions in relation to stress.

Vitamins
Vitamin A functions to maintain healthy skin and mucous membranes. Individuals who are vitamin A–deficient have fewer mucous-secreting cells and those they do have produce less mucous—thus the protection provided by the mucous lining is diminished. Vitamin C has been shown to enhance the engulfing or "eating" actions of the immune cells called *macrophages*. If vitamin C is deficient, macrophages are less mobile and less able to consume disease-causing organisms. Deficiencies of vitamins A, B_{12}, and folate can impair production of the cells that enable antibody responses. Large doses of vitamin E have been associated with suppression of B cells, which are vital to the immune response. Finally, metabolic requirements for thiamin, riboflavin, and niacin are increased in response to a stressful situation.

Minerals
Deficiencies of zinc impair immune cell reproduction and responsiveness.

Wellness Across the Generations
The Time of Our Lives

Although middle age is often dreaded, the changes that inevitably occur as we grow older are not necessarily bad. In fact, more and more elderly adults report that the best time in their lives was not their youth, but rather their midlife years.

One recent study of this question involved more than 3000 people, each of whom answered more than 1100 questions. Researchers found that more than 70 percent of respondents viewed themselves as being in excellent health and felt their lives had purpose and meaning. In fact, nine of ten study participants said they had never experienced the proverbial midlife crisis. Most middle-aged people reported that they had been able to make the adjustment nesessary for life to remain rewarding. Most said that they did not have arthritis, backaches, skin problems, indigestion, constipation, depression, gum disease, high blood pressure, or migraines. And contrary to popular belief, most middle-aged women reported that menopause was a fairly benign experience.

One negative finding of the study is that middle-aged adults are not working very hard to maintain a high quality of life. In addition, respondents reported not having enough money and sex—probably two things lacking at any age, not just middle age. However, while sexual satisfaction was low, middle-aged adults seemed to be content overall with their marriages and relationships. Seventy-two percent said that their relationships were very good or excellent, and 90 percent felt that their relationships were unlikely to break up.

Finally, the survey found that by the time adults reached age 65, men felt an average of 12.6 years younger than their actual age and women felt 14.7 years younger than their actual age. As we grow older, our lives can become even more fulfilling, particularly if we can maintain a sense of control over our well-being by practicing healthful lifestyle habits. How can *you* ensure optimal health as you age?

Adapted from Johns Hopkins InteliHealth Online, www.intelihealth.com/IH?ihtIH?d=dm

Wellness on the Web Behavior Change Activities

What's Your Stress Index?
Over the last several years, the term "stress" has become a cultural cliché that's used to convey feelings of fatigue, burnout, tension, and discouragement, to name just a few. There's job stress, relationship stress, technological stress . . . and the list goes on. Cliché or not, though, we probably can all agree that, however we experience it, stress is real—and it can be extremely challenging to understand and manage. The destruction it causes can make our daily lives miserable. It can also affect every dimension of our health, sometimes severely. Strangely, we're not always aware that we're under stress. The signs and symptoms that can alert us to problems may be hard to recognize because we've become so accustomed to them. Want to quantify your stress level? The Canadian Mental Health Association has a 20-item checklist you can use to evaluate your stress index. Go to www.queendom.com/testjunkie.html and select "What is your stress index?" to complete the checklist, and then evaluate your results.

Are You Headed for Burnout?
When your stressors become chronic or pervasive, you've reached the third phase of the general adaptation syndrome: exhaustion. In the exhaustion phase, your energy stores have been depleted and rest is essential. This stage includes conditions like burnout, which occurs when highly committed people lose interest and motivation. Typically burnout affects hard-working, hard-driven people who become emotionally, psychologically, or physically exhausted. Cyberia Shrink has created a Burnout Inventory designed to evaluate your risk for burnout. Go to her website at www.queendom.com/burnout2.html and complete the 30 items. Read every statement carefully and indicate how often you feel that way or how often it applies to you. To obtain valid results, you need to answer all the questions. Click the "send" button. This inventory is scored on-line, so you'll receive your results on-screen. How did you fare?

What's Your Take on the World?
What's a severe stressor for one person may not be a stressor for another. Stress is often neither positive nor negative. How we deal with or react to what we perceive as stress is what determines its effect on our lives. Are you an optimist or a pessimist? Do you see the glass as half full or half empty? Your level of optimism can significantly affect how you respond to stressful situations. To determine your level of optimism or pessimism, go to www.psychtests.com/optimist.html and complete the "Optimism/Pessimism Inventory." How did you do?

Personality and Stress

Two physicians, Friedman and Roseman,[16] have written extensively about personality, cardiovascular disease, and stress. These researchers have described two stress-related personality types—type A and type B. Most people are neither type exclusively but fall somewhere between the two.

Type A personality is characterized by an urgent sense of time, impatience, competitiveness, aggressiveness, insecurity over status, and inability to relax. People with type A behavior characteristics are likely to be highly stressed. Type B people have a more unhurried approach to their lives. The type B personality does not become as upset at losing or not attaining a goal. Type B people also tend to set more realistic goals.[17] Researchers disagree on whether there is a possible relationship between the stress-prone type A personality and cardiovascular disease.[18]

In general, researchers believe that being a type A personality is not a problem if there is no underlying hostility. However, regardless of whether type A people are more susceptible to heart disease, they do experience more negative effects, such as tiredness and frustration, from short-term stress.

"Stress survivors"—people who have been found to handle stress successfully or have successful coping abilities—have several common characteristics. Psychologist Suzanna Kobasa[19] has isolated these attributes and characterized the type of person who exhibits them. A hardy personality tends to remain healthy even under extreme stress. Characteristics of a hardy personality or hardiness are challenge, commitment, and control (see Assessment Activity 9-5).

Challenge is the ability to see change for what it is—that is, not only inevitable but an opportunity for growth and development of unique individual abilities. *Commitment* is delineated by a strong sense of inner purpose. It is necessary to want to succeed in order to achieve success. Commitment is the ability to become really involved while maintaining the discernment to know when dedication and desire are harmful. *Control* is the recognition that one has power over one's own life and attitudes. People who have a sense of control act in situations rather than react to them.

Dealing with Stress

All events in life precipitate a reaction. How people react or respond to situations differs. **Coping** is the attempt to manage or deal with stress. Coping is independent of outcome—it does not necessarily result in success.

Dealing successfully with stress may require using a variety of techniques (see Real-World Wellness: Guidelines for Dealing with Stress). Because stress-related responses are based primarily on mental perceptions, coping strategies that achieve desirable results may need to originate in a change in attitude or outlook. If specific situations or people are perceived as disruptive, one solution is to avoid them, for example.

Although there are no easy answers, there is always some kind of answer or solution. When dealing with a stressor reaches a point where it seems there are no solutions, the tension from the situation becomes increasingly detrimental. It may then become necessary to consider changing attitudes, goals, and values.

Seeking the help of a professional counselor is frequently beneficial when attempting to resolve particularly stressful situations. Assessment Activity 9-4 identifies ways to recognize some of the positive and negative behaviors that can be used to deal with stress.

Learning about and using relaxation techniques can help alleviate or even prevent detrimental effects associated with stress. Engaging in positive self-talk and relabeling negative experiences (viewing difficulties as "challenges" rather than as problems, for example) are positive steps in reducing stress-related disorders. Eating well, taking time to enjoy life, laughing, exercising, and living in the present all reduce stress. People can handle stress effectively when they work on developing all of their abilities to the fullest, when they develop lifestyles that are compatible with personal values, and when they develop realistic expectations for themselves. Working toward these goals is the way to establish a wellness lifestyle (see Real-World Wellness: Marta's Day).

Successful coping includes being aware of incidents and situations that you might perceive as being stressful. Recognition of stressors means being aware of how your body responds to stress. Recognition requires continuous monitoring of your body and mind for evidence of excessive stress.

Successful coping takes real effort. One suggestion is to focus on the signals your body is sending when experiencing stress and then to think back to the event or situation that might have triggered those feelings. Another suggestion is to recreate a recent event that has been stressful. After visualizing the episode, write down six ways that the outcome could have been different—three ways it could have been worse and three ways it could have been better. The latter will increase awareness of how to better handle similar situations in the future. A last suggestion is to try something new. The idea is that you be challenged and meet that challenge successfully. Trying something new and meeting the challenge reinforces your sense of being able to deal with life successfully.[19]

Relaxation Techniques

The ultimate goal in stress coping and management is to reduce the negative effects of stress. Different **relaxation techniques** have proved successful. Brief descriptions of various techniques follow. If you are interested in pursuing the use of these techniques further, you can

---

Real-World Wellness
Guidelines for Dealing with Stress

Being in school can be so overwhelming. I have many classes, extracurricular activities, and a pile of homework each night. How can I balance it all?

Following are guidelines for effectively dealing with potential harmful stress:

- **Schedule time effectively.** Practice good time-management techniques by using time wisely. This means taking time out for yourself every day and scheduling work when you are usually at your peak ability (see Assessment Activity 9-5).
- **Set priorities.** Know what is important to you. Do not attempt to work on four or five projects simultaneously. Keep your efforts focused on one or two major items.
- **Establish realistic goals.** Goals must be achievable. Do not establish impossible expectations and then become frustrated when they are not accomplished as quickly as you would like. Write down long-range goals and then establish checks for keeping yourself on track and monitoring progress. Short-term goals help you see how you are moving toward your goal and provide rewards as you advance toward success.
- **See yourself as achieving the goals.** Visualize yourself as being successful. Go over in your mind what it will look and feel like to accomplish a goal.
- **Give yourself a break.** Take time every day to exercise and relax.

Real-World Wellness

Marta's Day

This semester I've been getting up late for class, putting off studying, and eating poorly. I'm feeling very stressed out, and my grades have begun to suffer. What can I do to get out of this downward spiral?

Here is an analysis of Marta's day including her stress responses to events in her day and suggestions for other ways to react.

Event	Marta's Stress Response	A Better Approach
Morning: Is late rising for first class; stayed up late studying the night before	Skips first class to study for exam; misses notes from that class and cannot contact friend to see if she can use her notes; skips breakfast	Begin studying for a test a few days before the exam; do not attempt to cram everything into one night; get a good night's rest and get up early to review your notes; eat breakfast and attend first class.
Is late for test	Stays home too long and gets caught in traffic; arrives late for the test; does not have a full hour to complete the test	Leave early to allow for traffic and parking problems; be on time to concentrate on the test and have time to relax a few minutes.
Lunch	Skips lunch—has a soft drink and potato chips	Have a nutritionally balanced meal in a relaxing atmosphere; go with a friend just to chat.
Afternoon: Is late for work because had to return overdue library book	Rushes to library; has to pay fine; has to stand in line at the library for 15 minutes	Write down when books are due and return them on time; use a daily calendar to plan activities and allot time to take care of personal business.
Evening: Watches TV until midnight; neglects to study for test the day after tomorrow	Is too tired and "stressed out" to study so just watches TV all evening; has a hamburger and soda for dinner	Take a short nap after work and have a nutritious meal; plan the evening so that some time is spent watching TV and some is spent studying; go to bed early so you can get to school on time and rested.
Next morning: Gets up late for class again	Begins the same cycle of feeling tired and pressured and being late	Analyze current time constraints to determine where more time needs to be allotted and how to develop a more efficient plan (see Assessment Activities 9-5 and 9-6).

find more information about them in books or on tapes. These books and tapes can be purchased at bookstores or may be found at your library.

Deep Breathing

Deep breathing is the most basic technique used in relaxation and is often the foundation for other methods. The primary benefit of this technique is that it can be done anywhere and anytime. It is beneficial to practice deep breathing several times a day. The methodology consists of completely filling the lungs when breathing so that the abdomen expands outward. Begin by taking a deep breath and then exhaling slowly through the mouth. A hand can be placed on the stomach to ensure that it is fully expanded. If the stomach does not rise, the breath is not deep enough or the abdomen is being held too tightly. Repeat this cycle several times and then rest quietly for 3 to 5 minutes.

Progressive Muscle Relaxation

Progressive muscle relaxation creates awareness of the difference between muscular tension and a relaxed state. This is a three-step process that begins with tensing of a muscle group and noticing how the tension feels. Next, make a conscious effort to relax the tension and notice that feeling. The third phase consists of concentrating on the differences between the two sensations. Beginning at either the head working down or at

> **Real-World Wellness**
>
> **Progressive Muscle Relaxation**
>
> *When I'm uptight, my muscles get so tense that I can't relax. What can I do to loosen them again?*
>
> There are numerous progressive muscle relaxation activities. The exercises are frequently structured by a facilitator. Some exercises begin with the feet, hands, or face, but because of space constraints, only the relaxing of the face will be described here. You can add the other parts of the body by recording the entire process on audiotape and listening to the tape as often as desired—usually once a day or two to three times a week. Take your time (3 to 4 minutes) for each area of the body.
>
> - Assume a comfortable position and concentrate on the instructions. You may find it beneficial to lie down or sit in a comfortable chair.
> - Close your eyes.
> - Allow all your muscles to relax and feel loose and heavy. Take several deep breaths.
> - Wrinkle your forehead and hold for 6 seconds.
> - Notice the feelings.
>   - Relax; allow the forehead to become smooth
>   - Notice the feeling of relaxation.
> - Frown with your eyes, forehead, and scalp and hold for 6 seconds.
>   - Experience the sensation of tension.
>   - Relax the muscles.
>   - Notice the feelings of relaxation.
> - Keeping your eyes closed, clench your jaw and push your teeth together.
>   - Hold for 6 seconds.
>   - Notice the tension.
>   - Relax your jaw and allow your lips to part slightly.
> - Now press your tongue against the roof of your mouth and feel the tension.
>   - Hold for 6 seconds.
>   - Allow your tongue to return to its normal position, experiencing the sensation of relaxation.
> - Now press your lips together as tightly as possible.
>   - Hold for 6 seconds.
>   - Relax and notice the feelings of relaxation over your lips.
> - Using the same principles, gradually move through the body from the shoulders to the arms, hands, fingers, back, chest, abdomen, hips, legs, ankles, feet, and toes.

the feet working up, tense and relax all major muscle groups (see Real-World Wellness: Progressive Muscle Relaxation).

Autogenics

Autogenics is the use of self-suggestion to produce a relaxation response. Autogenics begins with a deep breath and a conscious effort to relax. This technique may follow a progression from head to feet or feet to head. Repeat the phrase "My arm feels heavy and warm" several times before moving on to the next muscle group. You can repeat other phrases that carry a calming message such as "I am completely calm and relaxed." End the session by thinking, "I am refreshed and alert." Autogenics takes practice, time, and commitment and should be practiced twice a day for about 10 minutes. Commercial tapes may help guide people wanting to learn autogenics (see Real-World Wellness: Performing Autogenic Training).

Meditation

Meditation can be approached from a variety of perspectives. As a stress-reduction technique its purpose is to help the practitioner temporarily tune out the world and to invoke relaxation. During a meditation session, the person meditating concentrates or focuses his or her attention on a *mantra*, or particular word or sound, while attempting to eliminate all outside distractions.

Begin by taking a comfortable position on a couch or in a chair. Take several deep breaths, slowly inhaling and exhaling. Shut your eyes or softly focus them on an object so that the details are blurred. Concentrate all your thoughts on a word or phrase that you have selected to use, such as *peace* or *relax*, while continuing to breathe slowly and deeply.[20] The relaxation response can also be initiated by counting breaths backward from 100 or by imagining a white light that slowly travels throughout your body, letting in light and energy while expelling tension and fear. Many commercial meditation tapes are available.

Visualization

Visualization (imagery) is a form of relaxation that uses the imagination. Begin by finding a comfortable position, shut your eyes, and take several deep breaths. Several variations of visualization can then be used. You can imagine a tranquil scene, such as a beach on a sunny day or a valley with a stream or forest, and then

Real-World Wellness

Performing Autogenic Training

I'm looking for a practical technique I can use to reduce my stress. I know it's important to relax, but I have a hard time relaxing sometimes. Merely telling myself to relax doesn't work. What can I do to help myself relax?

Autogenic training is a form of hypnosis that helps the practitioner develop images of warmth and relaxation. With practice, autogenic training can increase peripheral blood flow and reduce muscle tension. *Autogenic* means "self-generating." The technique is a type of self-hypnosis that utilizes deep breathing and conjures images through a series of phrases to evoke the relaxation response. Here are guidelines for practicing autogenics:

- Either sitting or lying down, begin by taking five to six deep breaths and contract any muscles that are tense.
- Repeat to yourself, "My breathing is slow and even, my breathing is smooth and rhythmic."
- Continue with the deep breathing and imagine you are on a warm, sunny beach with the waves moving in and over your body, generating a warm and relaxed feeling.
- Feel the waves move over your stomach, hips, back, legs, and feet.
- Repeat to yourself, "I am relaxed, I am calm, I am quiet. My breathing is smooth and rhythmic. My heartbeat is calm and regular."
- Starting with your right arm, repeat the following as the breathing continues slowly and regularly: "My right arm and hand are heavy and warm." Continue with your left arm.
- Focus on both arms and repeat the phrase, "My arms and hands are heavy and warm."
- Move the focus to your legs and feet and repeat, "My legs and feet are heavy and warm." Focus on the right side, the left side, and finally both legs at the same time.
- As you proceed through the session, visualize the waves of warmth and relaxation washing over your entire body. Continue to breath slowly and deeply.
- As you prepare to wrap up the session, continue to breathe deeply and slowly and begin to get back in touch with where you are. Tell yourself you are warm, safe, secure, and relaxed.
- Count down from 5:
  4. Take a deep breath and visualize the room.
  3. Take a deep breath and begin to stretch.
  2. Take a deep breath and slowly open your eyes.
  1. You are mentally alert and ready to get back to your activity. You are fully awake.

---

place yourself in the scene. Imagine all of the scene's sights, sounds, smells, and feelings. People suffering from a terminal illness frequently imagine scenes in which their immune system attacks or destroys their disease, or they envision themselves as healthy and disease free. People who want to make major life changes, such as losing weight or stopping smoking, can envision themselves slim or not smoking or imagine themselves in trouble situations such as a situation in which you are tempted to overeat or smoke. Then people can envision themselves making wise choices or not engaging in undesirable behaviors. Visualization can also be used to improve athletic performance. Tapes are available that can assist people in learning how to develop this technique.

Biofeedback

Biofeedback, which is based on scientific principles, is designed to enhance awareness of body functions—it is an educational tool. Sensory equipment demonstrates subtle body changes, such as increases or decreases in skin temperature, muscle contraction, and brain wave variations. This biofeedback, or feedback on biological processes, enables people to become aware of what is happening in their bodies when stressed and learn how to control tensions through awareness of sensations that are relaxing. After a few sessions, people should begin to recognize and thereby alter their typical bodily responses to situations that serve as stressors for them.

Massage Therapy

In recent years massage therapy has become an acceptable form of stress reduction and a healing alternative. Some people consider today's American society to be in the midst of a "touch famine." Appropriate touching is lacking even though we recognize the need for physical interaction. Babies who are not handled can actually die from this type of deprivation. Although adults are not likely to respond so extremely to lack of touch, the need to be touched does not disappear with age. Research findings indicate that massage can promote physical relaxation and well-being. Certified massage therapists are licensed by the American Massage Therapy Association.[24]

Music

The power of music is undisputed. A strong beat and rhythmic music instill in almost all people of any age the desire to respond by moving or dancing. Quiet music soothes by causing people to breathe more deeply, stilling turbulent emotions, reducing metabolic response, and calming the autonomic nervous system.

Humor

Laughter is a powerful stress-reducing agent. A deep laugh temporarily raises pulse rate and blood pressure and tenses the muscles. After a good laugh, however, pulse rate and blood pressure actually go down and the muscles become more relaxed. Laughter works in two ways. Being able to laugh at a situation reminds you that life is seldom perfect or predictable. Laughing helps keep events in perspective. Laughing also works to reinforce a positive attitude. Laughing or even smiling can actually improve mood.

Time Management

A major contributor to stress is the pressure associated with time constraints. By effectively using time, you can eliminate a great deal of stress. For the college student, effective use of time is crucial, especially when the student is working and attending school at the same time. Procrastination can add to stress and undermine academic work, personal relationships, and work efforts. Good time management including appropriate prioritizing, scheduling, and the completion of personal responsibilities can contribute to feelings of personal satisfaction.

Certain behaviors or habits can unnecessarily rob you of time:[25]

1. **Workaholism.** *Workaholism* is spending excessive amounts of time working, even though the activity may not be productive. Generally, people who engage in workaholic behavior like to work long hours and do not use time-saving techniques. They also may become overinvolved in unimportant tasks that eat away at their time, requiring them to use extra time to accomplish important tasks.
2. **Time juggling.** Time jugglers constantly overschedule themselves, often making promises to be in more than one place at a time. Because it is frequently impossible to do several things at once or be in two places at the same time, this behavior often results in the neglecting of important activities.
3. **Procrastination.** Procrastinators consistently put off until later things that could just as easily be done now. Some procrastinators choose the simplest of two tasks to do now to avoid the really important ones until the last possible minute, when the pressure is on.
4. **Perfectionism.** Perfectionists go beyond trying to do their best to achieve perfection. Because standards of perfection vary from one person to the next, this behavior rarely results in a sense of accomplishment, and the inability to achieve impossible goals contributes to feelings of dissatisfaction and failure.
5. **Yesism.** *Yesism* is the inability to tell anyone "no." Extremely nice people often suffer from this condition because they don't like to disappoint others or they fear being rejected, even if saying "yes" ends up only costing them.

Although difficult to overcome, many of the aforementioned characteristics can be moderated if you are determined to do so. Here are some suggestions for appropriate use of your time:

1. Write down realistic goals and priorities. Assess current activities to determine whether they are essential, important, or trivial. Ask yourself the question "When does the task have to be completed?" Write down the priorities for the next day before going to sleep each night and rank them in order. This strategy provides you with a night to "sleep on them." You can then approach them systematically, according to need, the next day.
2. Develop a time framework. To help alleviate stress, establish the amount of time to be spent on each activity. Some tasks cannot be completed in a day's time. If this is the case, estimate the days or weeks required to complete the task. This is especially important in accomplishing long-term commitments. Allotting blocks of time each day of each week helps to alleviate the extreme pressure of completing a difficult task in a short time. For example, if a term paper is due at the end of a semester, you can spend a certain number of hours each week working on the paper. You can establish goals for the completion of the paper and devise rewards for yourself each time you achieve a goal. Another strategy is to study for each course every day by allotting a specific time to read and review the subject material covered in each class.
3. Know where and when you can best complete a task. Know the circumstances under which you function best. Is it easier for you to concentrate if you work in the library or the dorm room? Where will you have the fewest interruptions? Do you concentrate best in the morning, afternoon, or evening?
4. Establish priorities. To find time for everything that must be done, you have to know your priorities. Divide tasks into those that must be done

immediately, those that can wait a brief time, and those that are not essential. Once you have established priorities, start with the highest priority item and work through the list.

5. Ask for help if responsibilities become overwhelming. Say "no" when there are too many tasks to handle. Do not feel guilty about saying "no"; this only adds more stress. For example, if sorority or fraternity demands are too great, either ask others to share the workload or refuse the responsibility.
6. Take a break. Every day should provide for fun, leisure, time alone, and relaxation. Make the most of every day. Schedule in time every day for yourself.

Assessment Activity 9-6 is a prioritization worksheet to help you organize your tasks. Assessment Activity 9-7 provides you with a log. Use it to record your daily activities for several days to a week. Then review it and see if you are spending your time as effectively as you thought or if you have overscheduled what you can do in a twenty-four–hour period. This can provide you with a basis for devising improved time-management plans.

Exercise

Because the fight-or-flight syndrome stimulates the body into action, exercise is a logical method of responding to that physiological command. Exercise has been found to directly affect the brain chemistry. Studies have shown an increase in endorphin levels after an easy or a strenuous run.[26] (Endorphins are natural pain killers that function to help alleviate sensations of pain and stimulate a positive response from the immune system.) Exercise is a positive stressor (eustressor) and, when properly used, seems to offset the adverse effects of distress.[24] Studies have demonstrated that exercise reduces the severity of the stress response, shortens the recovery time from the stressor, and diminishes vulnerability to stress-related disease. The higher the fitness level, the more beneficial the exercise in reducing stress. (The recommended types of exercise programs are discussed in Chapter 3.)

A correctly designed exercise program produces beneficial physiological responses and can induce psychological effects that serve to reduce anxiety, promote feelings of accomplishment, and evoke muscle relaxation.

Many people consider stretching a means of invoking feelings of relaxation, and stretching is also associated with reduced tension. Moderate levels of exertion are frequently considered most beneficial for most people. (A moderate-level activity is a walk at the rate of approximately 3 miles an hour.) Excessive or addictive exercise habits can have the reverse effect and actually contribute to feelings of tension and irritability. When

Exercise is a great way to reduce anxiety, increase positive feelings, and relieve stress.

engaging in exercise as a stress-reduction technique, strive to find the level that creates the greatest sense of well-being upon completion.

Selecting a Stress-Reducing Technique

No single stress-reduction technique automatically reduces stress for everyone. People are comfortable with and enjoy different activities, and personal preference is what determines long-term use. When dealing with stress, you must first become aware that a stress response is occurring. People are frequently unaware that the reason they are always tired or irritable or have body aches is they are experiencing stress's negative effects. Second, you find the stress-reduction techniques that work best for you. Usually, more than one approach is required, depending on the person and his or her type of stress response. Any technique that helps create a sense of relaxation, provides personal time,

Nurturing Your Spirituality

Enjoying Healthy Pleasures

Certain lifestyle patterns have detrimental effects upon our well-being and quality of life: not exercising, smoking, drinking to excess, not wearing a seat belt, and eating poorly. However, just as important as avoiding lifestyle patterns that can negatively affect quality of life is appreciating the joys, thrills, delights, and happiness that are part of our lives. The idea is to minimize the negative and maximize the positive in our lives. Pleasure has gotten a bad name and we have become almost phobic about enjoying ourselves and having fun. In their book *Healthy Pleasures*, Ornstein and Sobel[23] point out that, even though certain negative habits and addictions are unhealthy, we also must seek to feel good mentally and emotionally. We need to seek enjoyment to enhance our survival. Ornstein and Sobel emphasize that no better way exists to ensure healthy, life-saving behaviors than to make them pleasurable. From eating to reproduction to caring for others, pleasure can guide us to better health. Doing what feels good is often beneficial for health and survival.

A pleasurable experience can be as simple as taking time to enjoy a sunset, smell the air after a rain shower, napping for half an hour in the afternoon, making a kind comment to a stranger or friend, or letting go of anger toward another human being. Seeking out pleasure may involve giving ourselves positive self-talks, looking for humor, and hanging out with happy people. Enjoying our gifts of pleasure is powerful medicine and can be contagious. It is cheap and effective, and its only side effect is a happy life. The following website provides a storehouse of information on the importance of adding pleasure to your life: **www/arise.org**.

---

and allows you to gain control can lead to a happier, healthier, more enjoyable life. Third, the best form of stress management is the prevention of negative effects before they become unmanageable. Well-thought-out, prudent lifestyle decisions based on knowledge of health behaviors and understanding of your own needs and expectations may be the best contribution you can make to your own stress-management plan.

Summary

- Stress is the nonspecific response of the body to any demands on it.
- Anything that creates stress is a stressor.
- Stressors may generate eustress (good stress) or distress (bad stress).
- The general adaptation syndrome (GAS) explains how the body responds to a stressor. The three stages of GAS are alarm, resistance, and exhaustion.
- The stress response can enhance physical and mental performance. This is referred to as the *inverted-U theory*.
- Whether positive or negative, a stressful event always produces a series of neurological and hormonal messages that are sent through the body.
- The responses to stress can be physiological (cardiovascular, gastrointestinal, musculoskeletal), psychological (causing depression, anxiety, anger), or behavioral (generating an inability to work, arguments).
- The immune system can be compromised as the result of prolonged stress, resulting in increases of susceptibility to comunicable diseases and chronic conditions.
- High stress has been associated with infertility problems.
- People's perceptions of stress are associated with self-esteem, self-efficacy, and locus of control.
- People who deal effectively with stress seem to view stressful situations as opportunities for growth, have a sense of inner purpose, and view themselves as having power over their lives.
- Coping is the effort(s) made to manage or deal with stress.
- Many techinques—including autogenics, deep breathing, visualization, muscle relaxation, meditation, massage, biofeedback, exercise, yoga, music, and humor—can help reduce stress.
- Effective time management can be a key to stress reduction.

Review Questions

1. What is stress? What are stressors?
2. What are the stages the mind and body go through when exposed to a stressor?
3. What are some potential signals that a person is experiencing chronic stress and what are the possible effects?
4. What factors influence how a person perceives and copes with stress?
5. Define *hardiness* and how it may help a person effectively deal with stress.
6. What are some guidelines for handling stress positively?
7. Discuss various stress-reducing techniques.

References

1. Siegal, B. S. 1988. *Love, Medicine and Miracles*. New York: Perennial Library.
2. Selye, H. 1975. *Stress Without Disease*. New York: New American Library.
3. Hanson, P. G. 1986. *The Joy of Stress*, Kansas City, Kans.: Andrews, McMeel & Parker.
4. Selye, H. 1978. *The Stress of Life* (rev. ed.). New York: McGraw-Hill.
5. Girdano, D., and E. George Jr. 1989. *Controlling Stress and Tension*. Englewood Cliffs, N.J.: Prentice Hall.
6. Folkman, S. 1984. Personal control and stress and coping processes: A theoretical analysis. *Journal of Personal and Social Psychology* 46:839.
7. Seward, B. L. 1994. *Managing Stress*. Boston: Jones and Bartlett.
8. Blonna, R. 1996. *Coping with Stress in a Changing World*. St. Louis: Mosby.
9. Gelman, D., and M. Hager. November 7, 1988. Body and soul. *Newsweek* 88.
10. Glaser, R., et al. 1987. Stress-related immune suppression: Health implications. *Brain Behavior-Immunity* 1(1):7.
11. O'Leary, A. 1990. Stress, emotion, and human immune function. *Psychology Bulletin* 108(3):363.
12. Pellitier, K., and D. Herzing. 1988. Psychoneuroimmunology: Toward a mind-body model: A critical review. *Advances* 5(1):27.
13. Domar, A., and H. Dreher. 1996. *Healing Mind, Healthy Woman: Using the Mind-Body Connection to Manage Stress and Take Control of Your Life*. New York: Henry Holt.
14. Domar A., P. Zuttermeister, and R. Friedman. 1997. *The Relationship Between Distress and Conception in Infertile Women*. Paper presented at the Annual Meeting of the American Society of Reproductive Medicine, Cincinnati, Ohio.
15. Greenberg, J. 1990. *Stress Management*. Dubuque, Iowa: Wm. C. Brown.
16. Friedman, M., and R. Roseman. 1984. *Type A Behavior and Your Heart*: New York: Alfred A Knopf.
17. Flannery, R. B. 1987. Toward stress-resistant persons: A stress management approach to the treatment of anxiety. *American Journal of Preventive Medicine* 3(1):25.
18. Fischman, J. 1987. Type A on trial. *Psychology Today* 21(2):42.
19. Kobasa, S. 1984. How much stress can you survive? *American Health* 5(7):64.
20. Benson, H. 1985. *The Relaxation Response*, New York: Berkley.
21. Luecken, L. J., et al. 1997. Stress in employed women: Impact of marital status and children at home on neurohormonal output and home strain. *Psychosomatic Medicine* 59:352.
22. Light, K. C. 1997. Stress in employed women: A women's work is never done if she's a working mom. *Psychosomatic Medicine* 59:360.
23. Sobel, D. S., and R. Ornstein. 1989. *Healthy Pleasures*. Reading, Mass.: Addison Wesley.
24. Lamb, L. E. 1992. Understanding stress. *Health Letter* 39(suppl.):12.
25. Crews, D., and D. Landers. 1987. A meta-analytic review of aerobic fitness and reactivity to psychosocial stressors. *Medicine and Science of Sports Exercise* 19:5114.
26. Appenzeller, D., et al. 1980. Neurology of endurance training versus endorphins. *Neurology* 30:418.

Suggested Readings

Williams, V., and R. Williams. 1998. *Lifeskills*. New York: Times Books.

This review of the research on relationships and health goes on to describe a systematic self-help program to build better relationships to strengthen physical well-being. Eight basic life skills are described.

Schiraldi, G. R. 1997. *Conquer Anxiety, Worry and Nervous Fatigue: A Guide to Greater Peace*. Ellicott City, Md.: Chevron Publishing Corporation.

The purpose of this book is to help readers learn to recognize and understand the symptoms of worry and anxiety. It provides a guide to stress-management strategies, including relaxation, rational thinking, confiding past trauma, solution-focused problem solving, meditation, proper sleep, nutrition, exercise, time management, assertiveness training, building self-esteem, and strengthening spiritual commitment.

Maskach, C., and M. Leiter. 1997. *The Truth About Burnout: How Organizations Cause Personal Stress and What To Do About It*. San Francisco: Jossey-Bass Publishers.

The authors encourage employees and managers to view the problems of burnout as an opportunity to address the major contributing pressures, such as exhaustion, cynicism, and ineffectiveness at work. The book is based on the real-world experiences of the authors working with companies to prevent and deal with burnout.

Chapter 9 Coping with and Managing Stress **291**

Name _____ Date _____ Section _____

Assessment Activity 9-1

Life Stressors

The following stress scale was developed by Miller and Rahe. It includes positive and negative events, since both require adaptation. Research has confirmed that stress can have a significant impact on physical and emotional health. The total score on this self-test offers you insight into your risk for illness as a result of recent life events. Stressful changes won't necessarily harm you; the potential for damage rests in how you handle stress.

Directions: To determine the possible impact of various recent changes in your life, circle the "stress points" listed that you experienced during the past year.

Health
An injury or illness that
- kept you in bed a week or more or sent you to the hospital — 74
- did not require long bed rest or hospitalization — 44

Major dental work — 26
Major change in eating habits — 27
Major change in sleeping habits — 26
Major change in your usual type or amount of recreation — 28

Work
Change to a new type of work — 51
Change in your work hours or conditions — 35
Change in your responsibilities at work
- to more responsibilities — 29
- to fewer responsibilities — 21

Home
Major change in living conditions — 26
Change in residence
- within the same town/city — 25
- to a different town/city/state — 47

Change in family get-togethers — 25
Major change in health or behavior of family member — 55
Marriage — 50
Pregnancy — 67
Miscarriage or abortion — 65
Addition of a new family member
- through birth of a child — 66
- through adoption of a child — 65
- through a relative moving in — 59

Spouse beginning or ending work — 46
Changes at work involving
- promotion — 31
- demotion — 42
- transfer — 32

Troubles at work
- with your boss — 29
- with coworkers — 35
- with persons under your supervision — 35
- involving other issues or people — 28

Major business adjustment — 60
Retirement — 52
Loss of job
- due to being laid off from work — 68
- due to being fired from work — 79

Correspondence course to help you in your work — 18

Personal and Social
Change in personal habits — 26
Beginning or ending school or college — 38
Change of school or college — 35
Change in political beliefs — 24
Change in religious beliefs — 29
Change in social activities — 27
Vacation trip — 24
New close personal relationship — 37
Engagement to marry — 45
Girlfriend or boyfriend problems — 39
Sexual difficulties — 44
Child leaving home
- to attend college — 41
- to marry — 41
- for other reasons — 45

Change in the marital status of your parents
- through divorce — 59
- through remarriage — 50

Change in arguments with spouse — 50
In-law problems — 38
Separation from spouse
- due to work — 53
- due to marital problems — 76

Divorce — 96
Birth of grandchild — 43
Death of spouse — 119
Death of
- child — 123
- brother or sister — 102
- parent — 100

Financial
Major change in finances
- through increased income — 38
- through decreased income — 60
- through investment or credit difficulties — 56

Loss or damage of personal property — 43

Moderate purchase	20
Major purchase	37
"Falling out" of a close personal relationship	47
Accident	48
Minor violation of the law	20
Being held in jail	75
Death of a close friend	70
Major decision about your immediate future	51
Major personal achievement	36
Foreclosure on a mortgage or loan	58

Total score: _____

Interpreting your score: Add up your points. A total score of 250 to 500 is considered a moderate amount of stress. If you score higher than that, you may face an increased risk of illness. If your scores is lower than 250, consider yourself fortunate.

From Miller and Rahe. 1997. Life changes scaling for the 1990s. *Journal of Psychosomatic Research* 43.

Name _____ Date _____ Section _____

Assessment Activity 9-6

Time-Management Worksheet

Directions: What follows is a prioritizing worksheet. Copies can be made for the different days of the week, or you can develop your own format. First, make a list of all the things you absolutely, positively have to get done today, no matter what! There should be very few things on this list. If the list runs longer than two or three items, you need to rethink what is really essential to do and what it is you would really *like* to do. There is a difference.

Must Do List

1. _____
2. _____
3. _____

Things That Are Important But Not Necessary

1. _____
2. _____
3. _____
4. _____
5. _____
6. _____

Other Things I Would Like to Get Done

1. _____
2. _____
3. _____
4. _____
5. _____
6. _____

Approximate how much time you think each activity will take. Some people like to spend an hour on one project and then switch to another; other people like to work continuously on one project until it is complete. Obviously your preference will affect your scheduling of work and the amount of time you allot. Your best friend may not work in the same way you do. That's okay. You need to prioritize your own list and set your own goals and timetable. Be sure to schedule time for yourself regularly. It is vital to your stress management.

Me time:_____

Activity: _____

Time allotment:_____

Name _____ Date _____ Section _____

Assessment Activity 9-7

Analyzing Your Use of Time

Managing your time effectively can significantly contribute to your feeling of being in control of your life. A by-product of this sense of control is reduced stress and tension; with effective time management you will be able to meet daily demands with less effort. Since the basis of change is recognizing that there needs to be a change and then determining the areas in your life that require change, a good way to begin meeting your time management needs is to analyze how you are currently managing your time.

Directions: Make several copies of this log and keep track of your time for a week. Include all your activities—from classes to meals to driving time to conversations with friends. At the end of the day and week, rate each hour as to how important the activities that occurred during that time were. Taking time to relax, talk to friends, and be alone are considered important to total well-being and should not be discounted.

Daily Log

Time	Activities	Where	Essential, important, or trivial
6:00–7:00 AM			
7:00–8:00			
8:00–9:00			
9:00–10:00			
10:00–11:00			
11:00–12:00			
12:00–1:00 PM			
1:00–2:00			
2:00–3:00			
3:00–4:00			
4:00–5:00			
5:00–6:00			
6:00–7:00			
7:00–8:00			
8:00–9:00			
9:00–10:00			
10:00–11:00			
11:00 PM–6:00 AM			

Analyzing Your Log

1. What activities did you find to be the most productive for you? Which were the least productive? _____

2. Where were your most productive activities performed? Your unproductive activities? _____

3. What time of day did you find to be the most productive for you—morning, afternoon, or evening? _____

The analysis should be based on the full week's activities. You are looking for patterns of behavior that provide the best effects for you. You may find that you work best at home or in the dormitory in the afternoons or at the library in the evenings. Using this assessment, try to find the best patterns of achievement for you.

Food Composition Table

Modified from Wardlaw GM, Insel PM: *Perspectives in nutrition*, ed 3, New York, 1996, The McGraw-Hill Companies.

Code	Name	Amount	Unit	Grams	Kilocalories	Carbohydrates (g)	Protein (g)	Fat (g)
11001	ALFALFA SEEDS, SPROUTED, FRESH	½	CUP	16.5	5	1	1	0
12067	ALMONDS, TOASTED, UNBLANCHED	½	CUP	71.0	418	16	14	36
19294	APPLE BUTTER	1	TBSP.	18.0	33	9	0	0
9400	APPLE JUICE, UNSWEETENED	¾	CUP	185.8	87	22	0	0
9003	APPLES, FRESH, W/ SKIN	1	MEDIUM	138.0	81	21	0	0
9020	APPLESAUCE, SWEETENED	½	CUP	127.5	97	25	0	0
9019	APPLESAUCE, UNSWEETENED	½	CUP	122.0	52	14	0	0
9024	APRICOTS, CND, JUICE PACK	½	CUP	124.0	60	15	1	0
9022	APRICOTS, CND, WATER PACK	½	CUP	121.5	33	8	1	0
9032	APRICOTS, DRIED, SULFURED	¼	CUP	32.5	77	20	1	0
9021	APRICOTS, FRESH	3	MEDIUM	106.0	51	12	1	0
11015	ASPARAGUS, CND	½	CUP	121.0	23	3	3	1
11011	ASPARAGUS, FRESH	½	CUP	67.0	15	3	2	0
11019	ASPARAGUS, FRZ, CKD	½	CUP	100.0	28	5	3	0
9037	AVOCADOS, FRESH	1	MEDIUM	201.0	324	15	4	31
10124	BACON	1	SLICE	6.0	35	0	2	3
10131	BACON, CANADIAN-STYLE, GRILLED	1	SLICE	21.0	39	0	5	2
62528	BACON, TURKEY	1	SLICE	14.0	25	0	3	2
18001	BAGELS, PLAIN	1	3½ IN.	71.0	195	38	7	1
19400	BANANA CHIPS	1	OUNCE	28.4	147	17	1	10
9040	BANANAS, FRESH	1	MEDIUM	114.0	105	27	1	1
6150	BARBECUE SAUCE	½	CUP	125.0	94	16	2	2
15187	BASS, FRESHWATER, CKD, DRY HEAT	3	OUNCE	85.1	124	0	21	4
16006	BEANS, BAKED, CND. VEGETARIAN	½	CUP	127.0	118	26	6	1
16007	BEANS, BAKED, CND. W/BEEF	½	CUP	133.0	161	22	8	5
16008	BEANS, BAKED, CND. W/ FRANKS	½	CUP	128.5	182	20	9	8
16009	BEANS, BAKED, CND. W/ PORK	½	CUP	126.5	134	25	7	2
16315	BEANS, BLACK, CKD	½	CUP	86.0	114	20	8	0
11056	BEANS, GREEN, CND	½	CUP	68.0	14	3	1	0
11052	BEANS, GREEN, FRESH	½	CUP	55.0	17	4	1	0
11061	BEANS, GREEN, FZN	½	CUP	67.5	18	4	1	0
16029	BEANS, KIDNEYS, CND	½	CUP	128.0	104	19	7	0
16073	BEANS, LIMA, CND	½	CUP	120.5	95	18	6	0
11040	BEANS, LIMA, FZN	½	CUP	90.0	95	18	6	0
16039	BEANS, NAVY CND	½	CUP	131.0	148	27	10	1
16044	BEANS, PINTO, CND	½	CUP	120.0	94	17	5	0
16103	BEANS, REFRIED, CND	½	CUP	126.5	135	23	8	1
13347	BEEF, CORNED, BRISKET, CKD	3	OUNCE	85.1	213	0	15	16
13355	BEEF, CURED, PASTRAMI	3	OUNCE	85.1	297	3	15	25
13357	BEEF, CURED, SAUSAGE, SMOKED	3	OUNCE	85.1	265	2	12	23
13358	BEEF, CURED, SMOKED, CHOPPED	3	OUNCE	85.1	105	2	17	4
13360	BEEF, CURED, THIN-SLICED	3	OUNCE	85.1	151	5	24	3
13300	BEEF, GROUND, EXTRA LEAN, PAN-FRIED	3	OUNCE	85.1	217	0	21	14
13307	BEEF, GROUND, LEAN, PAN-FRIED	3	OUNCE	85.1	234	0	21	16
13312	BEEF, GROUND, REGULAR, BROILED	3	OUNCE	85.1	246	0	20	18
13314	BEEF, GROUND, REGULAR, PAN-FRIED	3	OUNCE	85.1	260	0	020	19
13327	BEEF, LIVER, CKD, PAN-FRIED	3	OUNCE	85.1	185	7	23	7
13004	BEEF, STEAKS AND ROASTS, CKD, 1/4 IN. FAT	3	OUNCE	85.1	259	0	22	18
7043	BEEF, THIN SLICED	1	SLICE	4.2	7	0	1	0
11081	BEETS, CKD	½	CUP	85.0	37	8	1	0
18009	BISCUITS, PLAIN OR BUTTERMILK	1	EACH	35.0	127	17	2	6
9050	BLUEBERRIES, FRESH	½	CUP	72.5	41	10	0	0
9055	BLUEBERRIES, FROZEN, SWEETENED	½	CUP	115.0	93	25	0	0
10126	BOLOGNA	1	SLICE	23.0	57	0	4	5
12078	BRAZILNUTS, DRIED, UNBLANCHED	½	CUP	70.0	459	9	10	46
19167	BREAD PUDDING	1	CUP	252.0	423	62	13	15
18080	BREAD STICKS, PLAIN	1	STICK	10.0	41	7	1	1
18020	BREAD, BANANA	1	SLICE	60.0	203	33	3	7
18024	BREAD, CORNBREAD	1	PIECE	65.0	173	28	4	5
18025	BREAD, CRACKED-WHEAT	1	SLICE	25.0	65	12	2	1

Food Composition Table

Saturated Fat (g)	Monounsaturated Fat (g)	Polyunsaturated Fat (g)	Fiber (g)	Cholesterol (g)	Folate (g)	Vitamin A (RE)	Vitamin B$_6$ (mg)	Vitamin B$_{12}$ (μg)	Vitamin C (mg)	Vitamin E (mg)	Riboflavin (mg)	Thiamin (mg)	Calcium (mg)	Iron (mg)	Magnesium (mg)	Niacin (mg)	Phosphorus (mg)	Potassium (mg)	Sodium (mg)	Zinc (mg)
0	0	0	0	0	6	3	0	0	1	-	0	0	5	.2	4	.1	12	13	1	.2
3	23	8	8	0	45	0	.1	0	0	-	.4	.1	201	3.5	216	2	390	549	8	3.5
-	-	-	0	0	0	0	0	0	0	-	0	0	1	0	1	0	1	16	0	0
0	0	0	-	0	0	0	.1	0	77	0	0	0	13	.7	6	-	13	221	6	.1
0	0	0	4	0	4	7	.1	0	8	.8	0	0	10	.2	7	.1	10	159	0	.1
0	0	0	2	0	1	1	0	0	2	-	0	0	5	.4	4	.2	9	78	4	.1
0	0	0	1	0	1	4	0	0	1	-	0	0	4	.1	4	.2	9	92	2	0
0	0	0	2	0	2	210	.1	0	6	-	0	0	15	.4	12	.4	25	205	5	.1
0	0	0	2	0	2	157	.1	0	4	-	0	0	10	.4	9	.5	16	233	4	.1
0	0	0	3	0	3	235	.1	0	1	-	0	0	15	1.5	15	1	38	448	3	.2
0	0	0	3	0	9	277	.1	0	11	-	0	0	15	.6	8	.6	20	314	1	.3
0	0	0	2	0	116	64	.1	0	22	-	.1	.1	19	2.2	12	1.2	52	208	472	.5
0	0	1	0	86	39	.1	0	9	-	26	.1	.1	14	.6	12	.8	38	183	1	3
0	0	0	-	0	135	82	0	0	24	-	.1	.1	23	.6	13	1	55	218	4	.6
5	19	4	12	0	124	123	.6	0	16	-	.2	.2	22	2.1	78	3.9	82	1204	20	.8
1	1	1	0	5	0	0	.1	2	-	0	0	1	.1	1	.4	20	29	96	.2
1	1	1	0	12	1	0	.1	.2	5	-	0	.2	4	1.5	62	82	325	.4
1	-	-	-	10	-	0	-	-	0	-	-	-	0	0	-	-	-	-	170	-
0	0	0	1	0	16	0	0	0	0	-	.2	.4	53	2.5	21	3.2	68	72	379	.6
8	1	0	2	0	4	2	.1	0	2	-	0	0	5	.4	22	.2	16	152	2	.2
0	0	0	3	0	22	9	.7	0	10	.3	.1	.1	7	.4	33	.6	23	451	1	.2
0	1	1	1	0	5	109	.1	0	9	-	0	0	24	1.1	22	1.1	25	217	1019	.2
1	2	1	0	74	14	30	.1	2	2	-	.1	.1	88	1.6	32	1.3	218	388	77	.7
0	0	0	6	0	30	22	.2	0	4	-	.1	.2	64	.4	41	.5	132	376	504	1.8
2	2	0	-	29	58	28	.1	0	2	-	.1	.1	60	2.1	33	1.3	108	426	632	1.6
3	4	1	9	8	39	19	.1	0	3	-	.1	.1	62	2.2	36	1.2	134	302	553	2.4
1	1	0	7	9	46	23	.1	0	3	-	0	.1	67	2.2	43	.6	137	391	524	1.8
0	0	0	-	0	128	1	.1	0	0	-	.1	.2	23	1.8	60	.4	120	305	204	1
0	0	0	1	0	22	24	0	0	3	-	0	0	18	.6	9	.1	13	74	171	.2
0	0	0	2	0	20	37	0	0	9	-	.1	0	20	.6	14	.4	21	115	3	.1
0	0	0	2	0	6	36	0	0	6	-	0	0	30	.6	14	.3	16	76	9	.4
0	0	0	-	0	63	0	.1	0	2	-	.1	.1	35	1.6	40	.6	134	329	444	.7
0	0	0	6	0	61	0	.1	0	0	-	0	.1	25	2.2	47	.3	89	265	405	.8
0	0	0	-	0	14	15	.1	0	5	-	0	.1	25	1.8	50	.7	101	370	26	.5
0	0	0	7	0	82	0	.1	0	1	-	.1	.2	62	2.4	62	.6	176	377	587	1
0	0	0	4	0	72	0	.1	0	1	-	.1	.1	44	1.9	32	.4	110	361	499	.8
1	1	0	7	0	106	0	.1	0	8	-	.1	.1	58	2.2	49	.6	106	497	536	1.7
5	8	1	0	83	5	0	.2	1.4	14	-	.1	0	7	1.6	10	2.6	106	123	964	3.9
9	12	1	0	79	6	0	.2	1.5	3	-	.1	.1	8	1.6	15	4.3	128	194	1044	3.6
10	11	1	0	57	3	0	.1	1.6	10	-	.1	0	6	1.5	11	2.7	89	150	962	2.4
2	2	0	0	39	7	0	.3	1.5	18	-	.1	.1	7	2.4	18	3.9	154	321	1070	3.3
1	1	0	0	35	9	0	.3	2.2	12	-	.2	.1	9	2.3	16	4.5	143	365	1224	3.4
5	6	1	0	69	8	0	.2	1.7	0	-	.2	.1	6	2	18	4	136	265	60	4.6
6	7	1	0	71	8	0	.2	1.9	0	-	.02	0	9	1.9	17	4.1	135	254	65	4.4
7	8	1	0	77	8	0	.2	2.5	0	-	.2	0	9	2.1	17	4.9	145	248	71	4.4
8	8	1	0	76	8	0	.2	2.3	0	-	.2	0	9	2.1	17	5	145	255	71	43
2	1	1	0	410	187	9125	1.2	95.1	20	-	3.5	.2	9	5.3	20	12.3	392	310	90	4.6
7	8	1	0	75	6	0	.3	2.1	0	-	.2	.1	9	2.2	19	3.1	173	266	53	5
0	0	0	0	2	0	0	0	.1	1	-	0	0	0	.1	1	.2	7	18	60	.2
0	0	0	1	0	68	3	.1	0	3	-	0	0	14	.7	20	.3	32	259	65	.3
1	2	2	-	0	2	0	0	0	0	-	.1	.1	17	1.2	6	1.2	151	78	368	.2
-	-	-	2	0	5	7	0	0	9	-	0	0	4	.1	4	.3	7	65	4	.1
-	-	-	2	0	8	5	.1	0	1	-	.1	0	7	.4	2	.3	8	69	1	.1
2	2	0	0	14	1	0	.1	.2	8	-	0	.1	3	.2	3	.9	32	65	272	.5
11	16	17	4	0	3	0	.2	0	0	-	.1	.7	123	2.4	158	1.1	420	420	1	3.2
6	5	2	-	166	33	164	.2	-	2	-	.6	.2	287	2.8	48	1.6	275	564	582	1.3
0	0	0	-	0	3	0	0	0	0	-	.1	.1	2	.4	3	.5	12	12	66	.1
2	3	2	-	26	7	14	.1	.1	1	-	.1	.1	11	.8	8	.9	34	79	119	.2
1	1	2	-	26	12	35	.1	.1	0	-	.2	.2	162	1.6	16	1.5	110	96	428	.4
0	0	0	1	0	10	0	.1	0	0	-	.1	.1	11	.7	13	.9	38	44	135	.3

Appendix

Code	Name	Amount	Unit	Grams	Kilocalories	Carbohydrates (g)	Protein (g)	Fat (g)
18342	BREAD, DINNER ROLL, PLAIN	1	EACH	35.0	105	18	3	3
18347	BREAD, DINNER ROLL, WHEAT	1	EACH	33.0	90	15	3	2
18029	BREAD, FRENCH OR VIENNA	1	SLICE	25.0	69	13	2	1
18033	BREAD, ITALIAN	1	SLICE	30.0	81	15	3	1
18035	BREAD, MIXED-GRAIN	1	SLICE	26.0	65	12	3	1
18037	BREAD, OAT BRAN	1	SLICE	30.0	71	12	3	1
18041	BREAD, PITA, WHITE, ENRICHED	1	PITA	60.0	165	33	5	1
18042	BREAD, PITA, WHOLE-WHEAT	1	PITA	64.0	170	35	6	2
18044	BREAD, PUMPERNICKEL	1	SLICE	32.0	80	15	3	1
18046	BREAD, PUMPKIN	1	SLICE	60.0	199	31	2	8
18047	BREAD, RAISIN	1	SLICE	26.0	71	14	2	1
18060	BREAD, RYE	1	SLICE	32.0	83	15	3	1
18064	BREAD, WHEAT (INCLUDES WHEAT BERRY)	1	SLICE	25.0	65	12	2	1
18069	BREAD, WHITE	1	SLICE	25.0	67	12	2	1
11091	BROCCOLI, CKD	½	CUP	78.0	22	4	2	0
11093	BROCCOLI, FRZ, CHOPPED, CKD	½	CUP	92.0	26	5	3	0
18151	BROWNIES	1	EACH	56.0	227	36	3	9
11099	BRUSSELS SPROUTS, CKD	½	CUP	78.0	30	7	2	0
62601	BUFFALO (CHICKEN) WINGS	4	EACH	91.0	190	2	18	12
18351	BUNS, HAMBURGER OR HOT DOG, MIXED-GRAIN	1	EACH	43	113	19	4	3
18350	BUNS, HAMBURGER OR HOT DOG, PLAIN	1	EACH	43.0	123	22	4	2
4146	BUTTER, W/ SALT	1	PAT	5.0	36	0	0	4
1145	BUTTE,R W/O SALT	1	PAT	5.0	36	0	0	4
1002	BUTTER, WHIPPED	1	TBSP.	11.0	79	0	0	9
11110	CABBAGE, CKD	½	CUP	75.0	17	3	1	0
11749	CABBAGE, FRESH	1	CUP	70.0	17	4	1	0
18096	CAKE, CHOCOLATE, W/ CHOCOLATE FROSTING	1	SLICE	64.0	235	35	3	10
18110	CAKE, FRUITCAKE	1	PIECE	43.0	139	26	1	4
18113	CAKE, GERMAN CHOCOLATE, W/ FROSTING	1	SLICE	111.0	404	55	4	21
18119	CAKE, PINEAPPLE UPSIDE-DOWN	1	SLICE	115.0	367	58	4	14
18120	CAKE, POUND	1	SLICE	28.4	110	14	2	6
18133	CAKE, SPONGE	1	SLICE	3.0	110	23	2	1
18139	CAKE, WHITE, W/ FROSTING	1	SLICE	74.0	264	42	4	9
18140	CAKE, YELLOW, W/ CHOCOLATE FROSTING	1	SLICE	64.0	243	35	2	11
18141	CAKE, YELLOW, W/ VANILLA FROSTING	1	SLICE	64.0	239	38	2	9
11655	CARROT JUICE, CND	¾	CUP	184.5	74	17	2	0
11125	CARROTS, CKD	½	CUP	78.0	35	8	1	0
11124	CARROTS, FRESH	1	MEDIUM	60.0	26	6	1	0
11131	CARROTS, FRZ, CKD	½	CUP	73.0	26	6	1	0
12585	CASHEWS, DRY ROASTED	½	CUP	68.5	393	22	10	32
15235	CATFISH, CHANNEL, FARMED, CKD, DRY HEAT	3	OUNCE	85.1	129	0	16	7
15011	CATFISH, FRIED	3	OUNCE	85.1	195	7	15	11
11935	CATSUP	1	TBSP.	15.0	16	4	0	0
11135	CAULIFLOWER, FRESH	½	CUP	50.0	13	3	1	0
11138	CAULIFLOWER, FRZ, CKD	½	CUP	90.0	17	3	1	0
11144	CELERY, CKD	½	CUP	75.0	14	3	1	0
11143	CELERY, FRESH	½	CUP	60.0	10	2	0	0
8183	CEREALS, WHOLE WHEAT HOT NATURAL CEREAL	1	CUP	242.0	150	33	5	1
1150	CHEESE SPREAD, PAST. PROCESSED, AMERICAN	2	OUNCE	56.7	165	5	9	12
1147	CHEESE, AMERICAN, PASTEURIZED PROCESSED	2	OUNCE	56.7	213	1	13	18
1004	CHEESE, BLUE	1½	OUNCE	42.5	150	1	9	12
1005	CHEESE, BRICK	1½	OUNCE	42.5	158	1	10	13
1006	CHEESE, BRIE	1½	OUNCE	42.5	142	0	9	12
1008	CHEESE, CARAWAY	1½	OUNCE	42.5	160	1	11	12
1009	CHEESE, CHEDDAR, AMERICAN DOMESTIC	1½	OUNCE	42.5	171	1	11	14
1011	CHEESE, COLBY	1½	OUNCE	42.5	167	1	10	14
1015	CHEESE, COTTAGE, LOWFAT, 2% FAT	1½	OUNCE	42.5	38	2	6	1
1017	CHEESE, CREAM	1½	OUNCE	42.5	148	1	1	15
62554	CHEESE, CREAM, FAT FREE	2	TBSP.	35.0	35	2	5	0
62553	CHEESE, CREAM LIGHT	2	TBSP.	32.0	70	2	3	5

Food Composition Table

Saturated Fat (g)	Monounsaturated Fat (g)	Polyunsaturated Fat (g)	Fiber (g)	Cholesterol (g)	Folate (g)	Vitamin A (RE)	Vitamin B6 (mg)	Vitamin B12 (μg)	Vitamin C (mg)	Vitamin E (mg)	Riboflavin (mg)	Thiamin (mg)	Calcium (mg)	Iron (mg)	Magnesium (mg)	Niacin (mg)	Phosphorus (mg)	Potassium (mg)	Sodium (mg)	Zinc (mg)
1	1	0	1	0	11	0	0	0	0	-	.1	.2	42	1.1	8	1.4	41	47	182	.3
1	1	0	-	0	5	0	0	0	0	-	.1	.1	58	1.2	14	1.3	39	44	112	.3
0	0	0	1	0	8	0	0	0	0	-	.1	.1	19	.6	7	1.2	26	28	152	.2
0	0	0	1	0	9	0	0	0	0	-	.1	.1	23	.9	8	1.3	31	33	175	.3
0	0	0	2	0	12	0	.1	0	0	-	.1	.1	24	.9	14	1.1	46	53	127	.3
0	0	1	1	0	8	0	0	0	0	-	.1	.2	20	.9	9	1.4	32	34	122	.3
0	0	0	1	0	14	0	0	0	0	-	.2	.4	52	1.6	16	2.8	58	72	322	.5
0	0	1	5	0	22	0	.1	0	0	-	.1	.2	10	1.8	44	1.8	115	109	340	1
0	0	0	2	0	11	0	0	0	0	-	.1	.1	22	.9	17	1	57	67	215	.5
1	2	4	-	26	7	334	0	0	1	-	.1	.1	11	1	8	.8	32	55	188	.2
0	1	0	1	0	9	0	0	0	0	-	.1	.1	17	.8	7	.9	28	59	101	.2
0	0	0	2	0	16	0	0	0	-	-	.1	.1	12	.9	13	1.2	40	53	211	.4
0	0	0	1	0	10	0	0	0	0	-	.1	.1	26	.8	12	1	38	50	133	.3
0	0	0	1	0	9	0	0	-	0	-	.1	.1	27	.8	6	1	24	20	135	.2
0	0	0	2	0	39	108	.1	0	58	-	.1	0	36	.7	19	.4	46	228	20	.3
0	0	0	3	0	52	174	.1	0	37	-	.1	.1	47	.6	18	.4	51	166	22	.3
2	5	1	1	10	7	11	0	.1	0	-	.1	.1	16	1.3	17	1	57	83	175	.4
0	0	0	3	0	47	56	.1	0	48	-	.1	.1	28	.9	16	.5	44	247	16	.3
-	-	-	-	100	-	60	-	-	1	-	-	-	24	.4	-	-	-	-	900	-
	1	0	2	0	12	0	0	0	0	-	.1	.2	41	1.7	21	1.9	52	65	197	.5
0	1	0	-	0	12	0	0	0	0	-	.1	.2	60	1.4	9	1.7	38	61	241	.3
3	1	0	0	11	0	38	0	0	0	.1	0		1	0	0	0	1	1	1	0
3	1	0	0	11	0	38	0	0	0	.1	0	0	1	0	0	0	1	1	41	0
6	3	0	0	24	0	83	0	0	0	-	0		3	0	0	0	3	3	91	0
0	0	0	2	0	15	10	.1	0	15	-	0	0	23	1	6	.2	11	73	6	.1
0	0	0	-	0	40	9	.1	0	36	-	0	0	33	.4	11	.2	16	172	13	.1
3	6	1	2	29	5	18	-	.1	0	-	.1	0	28	1.4	22	.4	78	128	214	.4
0	2	1	2	2	1	8	0	0	0	-	0	0	14	.9	7	.3	22	66	116	.1
5	9	5	-	53	4	23	0	.1	0	-	.1	.1	53	1.2	19	1.1	173	151	369	.5
3	6	4	-	25	8	75	0	.1	1	-	.2	.2	138	1.7	15	1.4	94	129	367	.4
3	2	0	-	63	3	44	0	.1	0	-	.1	0	10	.4	3	.4	39	34	113	.1
0	0	0	-	39	5	17	0	.1	0	-	.1	1	27	1	4	.7	52	38	93	.2
2	4	2	-	1	5	12	0	.1	0	-	.2	.1	96	1.1	9	1.1	69	70	242	.2
3	6	1	1	35	5	17	0	.1	0	-	.1	.1	24	1.3	19	.8	103	114	216	.4
2	4	3	-	36	6	12	0	.1	0	-	0	.1	40	.7	4	.3	92	34	220	.2
0	0	0	1	0	7	4751	.4	0	16	-	.1	.2	44	.8	26	.7	77	539	54	.3
0	0	0	3	0	11	1915	.2	0	2	-	0	0	24	.5	10	.4	23	177	51	.2
0	0	0	2	0	8	1688	.1	0	6	-	0	.1	16	.3	9	.6	26	194	21	.1
0	0	0	3	0	8	1292	.1	0	2	-	0	0	20	.3	7	.3	19	115	43	.2
6	19	5	2	0	47	0	.2	0	0	-	.1	.1	31	4.1	178	1	336	387	438	3.8
2	4	1	0	54	6	13	.1	2.4	1	-	.1	.4	8	.7	22	2.1	208	273	68	.9
3	5	3	-	69	14	7	.2	1.6	0	-	.1	.1	37	1.2	23	1.9	184	289	238	.7
0	0	0	0	0	2	15	0	0	2	-	0	0	3	.1	3	.2	6	72	178	0
0	0	0	1	0	29	1	.1	0	23	-	0	0	11	.2	8	.3	22	152	15	.1
0	0	0	2	0	37	2	.1	0	28	-	0	0	15	.4	8	.3	22	125	16	.1
0	0	0	1	0	17	10	.1	0	5	-	0	0	32	.3	9	.2	19	213	68	.1
0	0	0	1	0	17	8	.1	0	4	-	0	0	24	.2	7	.2	15	172	52	.1
-	-	-	-	0	27	0	.2	0	0	-	.1	.2	17	1.5	53	2.2	167	172	564	1.2
8	4	0	0	31	4	107	.1	.2	0	-	.2	0	319	.2	16	.1	496	137	921	1.5
11	5	1	0	54	4	164	0	.4	0	-	.2	0	349	.2	13	0	252	92	369	1.7
8	3	0	0	32	15	97	.1	.5	0	-	.2	0	224	.1	10	.4	165	109	592	1.1
8	4	0	0	40	9	128	0	.5	0	-	.1	0	286	.2	10	.1	192	58	238	1.1
7	3	0	0	43	28	77	.1	.7	0	-	.2	0	78	.2	9	.2	80	65	268	1
8	4	0	0	40	8	123	0	.1	0	-	.2	0	286	.3	9	.1	208	40	293	1.3
9	4	0	0	45	8	129	0	.4	0	-	.2	0	307	.3	12	0	218	42	264	1.3
9	4	0	0	40	8	117	0	.4	0	-	.2	0	291	.3	11	0	194	54	257	1.3
1	0	0	0	4	6	9	0	.3	0	-	.1	0	29	.1	3	.1	64	41	173	.2
9	4	1	0	47	6	186	0	.2	0	-	.1	0	34	.5	3	0	44	51	126	.2
0	-	-	-	5	-	100	-	-	0	-	-	-	120	0	-	-	-	-	180	-
4	-	-	-	15	-	80	-	-	0	-	-	-	48	8	-	-	-	-	150	-

309

Appendix

Code	Name	Amount	Unit	Grams	Kilocalories	Carbohydrates (g)	Protein (g)	Fat (g)
62579	CHEESE, FAT FREE SLICES, WHITE	1	SLICE	21.3	30	2	5	0
62578	CHEESE, FAT FREE SLICES, YELLOW	1	SLICE	21.3	30	2	5	0
1019	CHEESE, FETA	1½	OUNCE	42.5	112	2	6	9
1156	CHEESE, GOAT, HARD TYPE	1½	OUNCE	42.5	192	1	13	15
1159	CHEESE, GOAT, SOFT TYPE	1½	OUNCE	42.5	114	0	8	9
1022	CHEESE, GOUDA	1½	OUNCE	42.5	152	1	11	12
1025	CHEESE, MONTEREY	1½	OUNCE	42.5	159	0	10	13
1028	CHEESE, MOZZARELLA, PART SKIM MILK	1½	OUNCE	42.5	108	1	10	7
1026	CHEESE, MOZZARELLA, WHOLE MILK	1½	OUNCE	42.5	120	1	8	9
1161	CHEESE, MOZZARELLA, SUBSTITUTE	1½	OUNCE	42.5	105	10	5	5
1032	CHEESE, PARMESAN, GRATED	1	TBSP.	5.0	23	0	2	2
1035	CHEESE, PROVOLONE	1½	OUNCE	42.5	149	1	11	11
1037	CHEESE, RICOTTA, PART SKIM MILK	1½	OUNCE	42.5	59	2	5	3
1036	CHEESE, RICOTTA, WHOLE MILK	1½	OUNCE	42.5	74	1	5	6
1038	CHEESE, ROMANO	1½	OUNCE	42.5	164	2	14	11
1040	CHEESE, SWISS, DOMESTIC	1½	OUNCE	42.5	160	1	12	12
1044	CHEESE, SWISS, PASTEURIZED PROCESSED	2	OUNCE	56.7	189	1	14	14
18148	CHEESECAKE, NO-BAKE TYPE	1	SLICE	80.0	219	28	4	10
9072	CHERRIES, SWEET, CND, JUICE PACK	½	CUP	125.0	67	17	1	0
9070	CHERRIES, SWEET, FRESH	½	CUP	72.5	52	12	1	1
9076	CHERRIES, SWEET, FROZEN, SWEETENED	½	CUP	129.5	115	29	1	0
18308	CHERRY PIE	1	SLICE	125.0	325	50	3	14
19033	CHEX MIX	1	CUP	42.5	181	28	5	7
5283	CHICKEN SALAD SANDWICH SPREAD	3	OUNCE	85.1	170	6	10	11
5054	CHICKEN, BACK, MEAT ONLY, CKD, FRIED	3	OUNCE	85.1	245	5	26	13
5055	CHICKEN, BACK, MEAT ONLY, CKD, ROASTED	3	OUNCE	85.1	203	0	24	11
5050	CHICKEN, BACK, MEAT & SKIN, CKD, FRIED, FLR	3	OUNCE	85.1	282	6	24	18
5051	CHICKEN, BACK, MEAT & SKIN, CKD, ROASTED	3	OUNCE	85.1	255	0	22	18
5063	CHICKEN, BREAST, MEAT ONLY, CKD, FRIED	3	OUNCE	85.1	159	0	28	4
5064	CHICKEN, BREAST, MEAT ONLY, CKD, ROASTED	3	OUNCE	85.1	140	0	26	3
5059	CHICKEN, BREAST, MEAT & SKIN, CKD, FRIED, FLR	3	OUNCE	85.1	189	1	27	8
5060	CHICKEN, BREAST, MEAT & SIN, CKD, ROASTED	3	OUNCE	85.1	168	0	25	7
5044	CHICKEN, DARK MEAT, MEAT ONLY, CKD, FRIED	3	OUNCE	85.1	203	2	25	10
5045	CHICKEN, DARK MEAT, MEAT ONLY, CKD, ROASTED	3	OUNCE	85.1	174	0	23	8
5036	CHICKEN, DARK MEAT, MEAT & SKIN, CKD, FRIED, FLR	3	OUNCE	85.1	242	3	23	14
5037	CHICKEN, DARK MEAT, MEAT & SKIN, CKD, ROASTED	3	OUNCE	85.1	215	0	22	13
5072	CHICKEN, DRUMSTICK, MEAT ONLY, CKD, FRIED	3	OUNCE	85.1	166	0	24	7
5073	CHICKEN, DRUMSTICK, MEAT ONLY, CKD, ROASTED	3	OUNCE	85.1	146	0	24	5
5068	CHICKEN, DRUMSTICK, MEAT & SKIN CKD, FRIED, FLR	3	OUNCE	85.1	208	1	23	12
5069	CHICKEN, DRUMSTICK, MEAT & SKIN, CKD, ROASTED	3	OUNCE	85.1	184	0	23	9
5081	CHICKEN, LEG, MEAT ONLY, CKD, FRIED	3	OUNCE	85.1	177	1	24	8
5082	CHICKEN, LEG, MEAT ONLY, CKD, ROASTED	3	OUNCE	85.1	162	0	23	7
5077	CHICKEN, LEG, MEAT & SKIN, CKD, FRIED, FLR	3	OUNCE	85.1	216	2	23	12
5078	CHICKEN, LEG, MEAT & SKIN, CKD, ROASTED	3	OUNCE	85.1	197	0	22	11
5097	CHICKEN, THIGH, MEAT ONLY, CKD, FRIED	3	OUNCE	85.1	185	1	24	9
5098	CHICKEN, THIGH, MEAT ONLY, CKD, ROASTED	3	OUNCE	85.1	178	0	22	9
5093	CHICKEN, THIGH, MEAT & SKIN, CKD, FRIED, FLR	3	OUNCE	85.1	223	3	23	13
5094	CHICKEN, THIGH, MEAT & SKIN, CKD, ROASTED	3	OUNCE	85.1	210	0	21	13
5106	CHICKEN, WING, MEAT ONLY, CKD, FRIED	3	OUNCE	85.1	179	0	26	8
5107	CHICKEN, WING, MEAT ONLY, CKD, ROASTED	3	OUNCE	85.1	173	0	26	7
5102	CHICKEN, WING, MEAT & SKIN, CKD, FRIED, FLR	3	OUNCE	85.1	273	2	22	19
5103	CHICKEN, WING, MEAT & SKIN, CKD, ROASTED	3	OUNCE	85.1	247	0	23	175
16058	CHICKPEAS, CND	½	CUP	120.0	143	27	6	1
16059	CHILI W/BEANS, CND	½	CUP	127.5	143	15	7	7
19183	CHOCOLATE PUDDING	1	CUP	298.1	396	68	8	12
15158	CLAMS, CKD, BREADED AND FRIED	3	OUNCE	85.1	172	9	12	9
15160	CLAMS, CND, DRAINED SOLIDS	3	OUNCE	85.1	126	4	22	2
19219	COCONUT CREAM PUDDING	1	CUP	280.0	291	50	9	7
15016	COD, ATLANTIC, CKD, DRY HEAT	3	OUNCE	85.1	89	0	19	1
15017	COD, ATLANTIC, CND	3	OUNCE	85.1	89	0	19	1

Saturated Fat (g)	Monounsaturated Fat (g)	Polyunsaturated Fat (g)	Fiber (g)	Cholesterol (g)	Folate	Vitamin A (RE)	Vitamin B$_6$ (mg)	Vitamin B$_{12}$ (µg)	Vitamin C (mg)	Vitamin E (mg)	Riboflavin (mg)	Thiamin (mg)	Calcium (mg)	Iron (mg)	Magnesium (mg)	Niacin (mg)	Phosphorus (mg)	Potassium (mg)	Sodium (mg)	Zinc (mg)
0	-	-	0	0	-	40	-	-	0	-	-	-	120	0	-	-	-	18	310	-
0	-	-	0	0	-	40	-	-	0	-	-	-	120	0	-	-	-	18	310	-
6	2	0	0	38	14	54	.2	.7	0	-	.4	.1	209	.3	8	.4	143	26	475	1.2
10	3	0	-	45	2	663	0	.1	0	-	.5	.1	381	.8	23	1	310	20	147	.7
6	2	0	0	20	5	578	.1	.1	0	-	.2	0	60	.8	7	.2	109	11	156	.4
7	3	0	0	48	9	74	0	.7	0	-	.1	0	298	.1	12	0	232	51	348	1.7
8	4	0	0	38	8	108	0	.4	0	-	.2	0	317	.3	11	0	189	34	228	1.3
4	2	0	0	25	4	75	0	.3	0	-	.1	0	275	.1	10	0	197	36	198	1.2
6	3	0	0	33	3	102	0	.3	0	-	.1	0	220	.1	8	0	158	29	159	.9
2	3	1	0	0	5	186	0	.3	0	-	.2	0	259	.2	17	.1	248	193	291	.8
1	0	0	0	4	0	9	0	.1	0	-	0	0	69	0	3	-	40	5	93	.2
7	3	0	0	29	4	112	0	.6	0	-	.1	0	321	.2	12	.1	211	59	372	1.4
2	1	0	0	13	6	48	0	.1	0	-	.1	0	116	.2	6	0	78	53	53	.6
4	2	0	0	22	5	57	0	.1	0	-	.1	0	88	.2	5	0	67	44	36	.5
7	3	0	0	44	3	60	0	.5	0	-	.2	0	452	.3	17	0	323	37	510	1.1
8	3	0	0	39	3	108	0	.7	0	-	.2	0	409	.1	15	0	257	47	111	1.7
9	4	0	0	48	3	130	0	.7	0	-	.2	0	438	.3	17	0	432	122	777	2
6	3	1	2	34	14	79	0	.2	0	-	.2	.1	138	.4	15	.4	187	169	304	.4
0	0	0	1	0	5	16	0	0	3	-	0	0	17	.7	15	.5	27	164	4	.1
0	0	0	2	0	3	15	0	0	5	-	0	0	11	.3	8	.3	14	162	0	0
0	0	0	1	0	5	25	0	0	1	-	.1	0	16	.5	13	.2	21	258	1	.1
3	7	3	1	0	10	-	.1	0	1	-	0	0	15	.6	10	.3	36	101	308	.2
-	-	-	0	0	6	6	.7	5.3	20	-	.2	.7	15	10.5	27	7.2	80	114	432	.9
3	3	5	0	26	4	36	.1	.3	1	-	.1	0	9	.5	9	1.4	28	156	321	.9
4	5	3	0	79	8	25	.3	.3	0	-	.2	.1	22	1.4	21	6.5	150	213	84	2.4
3	4	3	0	77	6	24	.3	.3	0	-	.2	.1	20	1.2	19	6	140	202	82	2.3
5	7	4	-	76	7	31	.3	.2	0	-	.2	.1	20	1.4	20	6.2	141	192	77	2.1
5	7	4	0	75	5	84	.2	.2	0	-	.2	.1	18	1.2	17	5.7	131	179	74	1.9
1	1	1	0	77	3	6	.5	.3	0	-	.1	.1	14	1	26	12.6	209	235	67	.9
1	1	1	0	72	3	5	.5	.3	0	-	.1	.1	13	.9	25	11.7	194	218	63	.9
2	3	2	-	76	3	13	.5	.3	0	-	.1	.1	14	1	26	11.7	198	220	65	9
2	3	1	0	71	3	23	.5	.3	0	-	.1	.1	12	.9	23	10.8	182	208	60	.9
3	4	2	0	82	8	20	.3	.3	0	-	.2	.1	15	1.3	21	6	159	215	82	2.5
2	3	2	0	79	7	19	.3	.3	0	-	.2	.1	13	1.1	20	5.6	152	204	79	2.4
4	6	3	-	78	7	26	.3	.3	0	-	.2	.1	14	1.3	20	5.8	150	196	76	2.2
4	5	3	0	77	6	49	.3	.2	0	-	.2	.1	13	1.2	19	5.4	143	187	74	2.1
2	3	2	0	80	8	15	.3	.3	0	-	.2	.1	10	1.1	20	5.2	158	212	82	2.7
1	2	1	0	79	8	15	.3	.3	0	-	.2	.1	10	1.1	20	5.2	156	209	81	2.7
3	5	3	-	77	7	21	.3	.3	0	-	.2	.1	10	1.1	20	5.1	150	195	76	2.5
3	4	2	0	77	7	26	.3	.3	0	-	.2	.1	10	1.1	20	5.1	149	195	77	2.4
2	3	2	0	84	8	17	.3	.3	0	-	.2	.1	11	1.2	21	5.7	164	216	82	2.5
2	3	2	0	80	7	16	.3	.3	0	-	.2	.1	10	1.1	20	5.4	156	206	77	2.4
3	5	3	-	80	7	24	.3	.3	0	-	.2	.1	11	1.2	20	5.6	155	198	75	2.3
3	4	3	0	78	6	33	.3	.3	0	-	.2	.1	10	1.1	20	5.3	148	191	74	2.2
2	3	2	0	87	8	18	.3	.3	0	-	.2	.1	11	1.2	22	6.1	169	220	81	2.4
3	4	2	0	81	7	17	.3	.3	0	-	.2	.1	10	1.1	20	5.5	156	202	75	2.2
3	5	3	-	82	7	25	.3	.3	0	-	.2	.1	12	1.3	21	5.9	159	202	75	2.1
4	5	3	0	79	6	41	.3	.2	0	-	.2	.1	10	1.1	19	5.4	148	189	71	2
2	3	2	0	71	3	15	.5	.3	0	-	.1	0	13	1	18	6.2	139	177	77	1.8
2	2	2	0	72	3	15	.5	.3	0	-	.1	0	14	1	18	6.2	141	179	78	1.8
5	8	4	-	69	3	32	.3	.2	0	-	.1	0	13	1.1	16	5.7	128	151	65	1.5
5	6	4	0	71	3	40	.4	.2	0	-	.1	0	13	1.1	16	5.7	128	156	70	1.5
0	0	1	5	0	80	2	.6	0	5	-	0	0	38	1.6	35	.2	108	206	359	1.3
3	3	0	6	22	29	43	.2	0	2	-	.1	.1	60	4.4	57	.5	196	465	666	2.6
2	5	4	3	9	9	33	.1	0	5	-	.5	.1	268	1.5	63	1	238	537	385	1.3
2	4	2	-	52	15	77	.1	34.2	9	-	.2	.1	54	11.8	12	1.8	160	277	310	1.2
0	0	0	0	57	24	145	.1	84.1	19	-	.4	.1	78	23.8	15	2.9	287	534	95	2.3
5	1	0	-	20	11	140	.4	.7	2	-	.4	.1	316	.6	45	.3	249	445	456	1
0	0	0	0	47	7	12	.2	.9	1	-	.1	.1	12	.4	36	2.1	117	208	66	.5
0	0	0	0	47	7	12	.2	.9	1	-	.1	.1	18	.4	35	2.1	221	449	185	.5

Food Composition Table 311

Appendix

Code	Name	Amount	Unit	Grams	Kilocalories	Carbohydrates (g)	Protein (g)	Fat (g)
18104	COFFEECAKE	1	SLICE	63.0	263	29	4	15
11159	COLESLAW	½	CUP	64.0	44	8	1	2
11162	COLLARDS, CKD	½	CUP	64.0	17	4	1	0
11161	COLLARDS, FRESH	1	CUP	36.0	11	3	1	0
11164	COLLARDS, FRZ. CHOPPED, CKD	½	CUP	85.0	31	6	3	0
20092	CORN, CKD	½	CUP	70.0	88	20	2	1
11901	CORN, SWEET, WHITE, CKD	½	CUP	82.0	89	21	3	1
11905	CORN, SWEET, WHITE, CND	½	CUP	82.0	66	15	2	1
11906	CORN, SWEET, WHITE, CND, CREAM STYLE	½	CUP	128.0	92	23	2	1
11900	CORN, SWEET, WHITE, FRESH	½	CUP	77.0	66	15	2	1
11168	CORN, SWEET, YELLOW, CKD	½	CUP	82.0	89	21	3	1
11174	CORN, SWEET, YELLOW, CND, CREAM STYLE	½	CUP	128.0	92	23	2	1
11167	CORN, SWEET, YELLOW, FRESH	½	CUP	77.0	66	15	2	1
15137	CRAB, ALASKA KING, CKD, MOIST HEAT	3	OUNCE	85.1	82	0	16	1
15138	CRAB, ALASKA KING, IMITATION	3	OUNCE	85.1	87	9	10	1
18216	CRACKERS, CRISPBREAD, RYE	1	EACH	10.0	37	8	1	0
18217	CRACKERS, MATZO, PLAIN	1	EACH	28.4	112	24	3	0
18219	CRACKERS, MATZO, WHOLE-WHEAT	1	EACH	28.4	100	22	4	0
18220	CRACKERS, MELBA TOAST, PLAIN	1	EACH	5.0	20	4	1	0
18229	CRACKERS, RITZ	1	EACH	3.0	15	2	0	1
18226	CRACKERS, RYE, WAFERS, PLAIN	1	EACH	25.0	84	20	2	0
18228	CRACKERS, SALTINES	1	EACH	3.0	13	2	0	0
18232	CRACKERS, WHEAT, REGULAR	1	EACH	2.0	9	1	0	0
9078	CRANBERRIES, FRESH	½	CUP	47.5	23	6	0	0
9080	CRANBERRY JUICE BOTTLED	¾	CUP	189.4	108	27	0	0
14240	CRANBERRY-APRICOT JUICE DRINK, BOTTLED	¾	CUP	183.4	117	30	0	0
15243	CRAYFISH, FARMED, CKD, MOIST HEAT	3	OUNCE	85.1	74	0	15	1
18238	CREAM PUFFS, SHELL, W/ CUSTARD FILLING	1	EACH	130.0	335	30	9	20
1067	CREAM SUBSTITUTE, NONDAIRY, LIQUID	1	TBSP.	15.0	20	2	0	1
1069	CREAM SUBSTITUTE, NONDAIRY, POWERED	1	TSP.	2.0	11	1	0	1
1049	CREAM, HALF AND HALF, CREAM AND MILK	1	TBSP.	15.0	20	1	0	2
1053	CREAM, HEAVY WHIPPING	1	TBSP.	15.0	52	0	0	6
1052	CREAM, LIGHT WHIPPING	1	TBSP.	15.0	44	0	0	5
1050	CREAM, LIGHT, COFFEE OR TABLE	1	TBSP.	15.0	29	1	0	3
1054	CREAM, WHIPPED, PRESSURIZED	1	TBSP.	3.0	8	0	0	1
18239	CROISSANTS, BUTTER	1	MEDIUM	57.0	231	26	5	12
18242	CROUTONS, PLAIN	1	CUP	30.0	122	22	4	2
18243	CROUTONS, SEASONED	1	CUP	40.0	186	25	4	7
11205	CUCUMBERS, FRESH	½	CUP	52.0	7	1	0	0
18245	DANISH PASTRY, CHEESE	1	EACH	71.0	266	26	6	16
18246	DANISH PASTRY, FRUIT	1	EACH	71.0	263	34	4	13
18247	DANISH PASTRY, NUT	1	EACH	65.0	280	30	5	16
9087	DATES, DOMESTIC, NATURAL AND DRY	½	CUP	89.0	245	65	2	0
18251	DOUGHNUTS, CHOCOLATE, SUGARED OR GLAZED	1	EACH	42.0	175	24	2	8
18253	DOUGHNUTS, FRENCH CRULLERS, GLAZED	1	EACH	41.0	169	24	1	8
18255	DOUGHNUTS, GLAZED	1	EACH	60.0	242	27	4	14
18248	DOUGHNUTS, PLAIN	1	EACH	47.0	198	23	2	11
18249	DOUGHNUTS, PLAIN, CHOCOLATE-COATED OR FROSTED	1	EACH	43.0	204	21	2	13
18250	DOUGHNUTS, PLAIN, SUGARED OR GLAZED	1	EACH	45.0	192	23	2	10
18254	DOUGHNUTS, W/ CREME FILLING	1	EACH	85.0	307	26	5	21
18256	DOUGHNUTS, W/ JELLY FILLING	1	EACH	85.0	289	33	5	16
18257	ECLAIRS, CUSTARD-FILLED W/ CHOCOLATE GLAZE	1	EACH	62.0	162	15	4	10
19168	EGG CUSTARDS	1	CUP	282.0	296	30	14	13
1142	EGG SUBSTITUTE, FROZEN	1	CUP	240.0	384	8	27	27
1143	EGG SUBSTITUTE, LIQUID	1	CUP	251.0	211	2	30	8
1057	EGGNOG	1	CUP	254.0	342	34	10	19
11210	EGGPLANT, CKD	½	CUP	48.0	13	3	0	0
11209	EGGPLANT, FRESH	½	CUP	41.0	11	2	0	0
1128	EGGS, CHICKEN, WHOLE, CKD, FRIED	1	LARGE	46.0	92	1	6	7
1129	EGGS, CHICKEN, WHOLE, CKD, HARD-BOILED	1	LARGE	50.0	78	1	6	5

Saturated Fat (g)	Monounsaturated Fat (g)	Polyunsaturated Fat (g)	Fiber (g)	Cholesterol (g)	Folate (g)	Vitamin A (RE)	Vitamin B₆ (mg)	Vitamin B₁₂ (μg)	Vitamin C (mg)	Vitamin E (mg)	Riboflavin (mg)	Thiamin (mg)	Calcium (mg)	Iron (mg)	Magnesium (mg)	Niacin (mg)	Phosphorus (mg)	Potassium (mg)	Sodium (mg)	Zinc (mg)
4	8	2	2	20	20	18	0	.1	0	-	.1	.1	34	1.2	14	1.1	68	77	221	.5
0	0	1	-	5	17	52	.1	0	21	-	0	0	29	.4	6	.2	20	116	15	.1
-	-	-	1	0	4	175	0	0	8	-	0	0	15	.1	4	.2	5	84	10	.1
-	-	-	1	0	4	120	0	0	8	-	0	0	10	.1	3	.1	4	61	7	0
-	-	-	-	0	65	508	.1	0	22	-	.1	0	179	1	26	.5	23	213	43	.2
0	0	0	3	0	4	4	0	0	0	-	0	0	1	.2	25	.4	53	22	0	.4
0	0	0	5	0	38	0	0	0	5	-	.1	.2	2	.5	26	1.3	84	204	14	.4
0	0	0	2	0	57	0	.1	0	6	-	.1	0	4	.5	22	1.2	65	172	365	.7
0	0	0	2	0	35	0	0	0	5	-	0	.2	2	.4	28	1.3	69	208	12	.3
0	0	0	2	0	38	18	0	0	5	-	.1	.2	2	.5	26	1.3	84	204	14	.4
0	0	0	2	0	40	13	0	0	7	-	.1	0	4	.7	16	1	53	160	265	.3
0	0	0	2	0	57	13	.1	0	6	-	.1	0	4	.5	22	1.2	65	172	365	.7
0	0	0	2	0	35	22	0	0	5	-	0	.2	2	.4	28	1.3	69	208	12	.3
0	0	0	0	45	43	8	.2	9.8	6	-	0	0	50	.6	54	1.1	238	223	912	6.5
0	0	1	0	17	1	17	0	1.4	0	-	0	0	11	.3	37	.2	240	77	715	.3
0	0	0	2	0	2	0	0	0	0	-	0	0	3	.2	8	.1	27	32	26	.2
0	0	0	1	0	4	0	0	0	0	-	.1	.1	4	.9	7	1.1	25	32	1	.2
0	0	0	3	0	10	0	0	0	0	-	.1	.1	7	1.3	38	1.5	86	90	1	.7
0	0	0	0	0	1	0	0	0	0	-	0	0	5	.2	3	.2	10	10	41	.1
0	0	0	0	0	0	0	0	0	0	-	0	0	4	.1	1	.1	7	4	25	0
0	0	0	-	0	11	1	.1	0	0	-	.1	.1	10	1.5	30	.4	84	124	199	.7
0	0	0	0	0	1	0	0	0	0	-	0	0	4	.2	1	.2	3	4	39	0
0	0	0	0	0	0	0	0	0	0	-	0	0	1	.1	1	.1	4	4	16	0
-	-	-	2	0	1	2	0	0	6	-	0	0	3	.1	2	0	4	34	0	.1
-	-	-	-	0	0	0	0	0	67	-	0	0	6	.3	4	.1	4	34	4	.1
0	-	-	0	0	1	84	0	0	0	-	0	0	17	.3	6	.2	9	112	4	.1
0	0	0	0	117	9	13	.1	2.6	0	-	.1	0	43	.9	28	1.4	205	202	82	1.3
5	8	5	-	174	20	259	.1	.5	0	-	.4	.2	86	1.5	16	1.1	142	150	443	.8
0	1	-	0	0	0	1	0	0	0	-	0	0	1	0	0	0	10	29	12	0
1	0	0	0	0	0	0	0	0	0	-	0	0	0	0	0	0	8	16	4	0
1	0	0	0	6	0	16	0	0	0	-	0	0	16	0	2	0	14	19	6	.1
3	2	0	0	21	1	63	0	0	0	-	0-	0	10	0	1	0	9	11	6	0
3	1	0	0	17	1	44	0	0	0	-	0	0	10	0	1	0	9	15	5	0
2	1	0	0	10	0	27	0	0	0	-	0	0	14	0	1	0	12	18	6	0
0	0	0	0	2	0	6	0	0	0	-	0	0	3	0	0	0	3	4	4	0
7	3	1	2	43	16	78	0	.2	0	-	.1	.2	21	1.2	9	1.2	60	67	424	.4
0	1	0	2	0	7	0	0	0	0	-	.1	.2	23	1.2	9	1.6	34	37	209	.3
2	4	1	2	1	16	2	0	0	0	-	.2	.2	38	1.1	17	1.9	56	72	495	.4
0	0	0	0	0	7	11	0	0	3	-	0	0	7	.1	6	.1	10	75	1	.1
5	8	2	-	32	18	44	0	.2	0	-	.2	.1	25	1.1	11	1.4	77	70	320	.6
3	7	2	1	15	11	11	-	.1	3	-	.,2	.2	33	1.3	11	1.4	63	59	251	.4
4	8	4	1	30	18	9	.1	.1	1	-	.2	.1	61	1.2	21	1.5	72	62	236	.6
-	-	-	7	0	11	4	.2	0	0	-	.1	.1	28	1	31	2	36	580	3	3
2	5	1	1	24	7	11	0	.1	0	-	0	0	89	1	14	.2	68	50	143	.2
2	4	1	-	5	3	-	0	0	0	-	.1	.1	11	.6	5	.6	50	32	141	.1
3	8	2	1	4	13	-	0	.1	0	-	.1	.2	26	1.2	13	1.7	56	65	205	.5
2	5	4	1	17	4	8	0	.1	0	-	.1	.1	21	.9	9	.9	126	60	257	.3
4	7	2	1	25	7	13	0	.2	0	-	0	.1	15	1.1	17	.6	87	49	184	.3
2	5	1	-	14	5	1	0	.1	0	-	.1	.1	27	.5	8	.7	53	46	181	.2
6	11	3	-	20	12	7	0	.1	0	-	.1	.3	21	1.6	17	1.9	65	68	263	.7
4	9	2	-	22	14	7	0	1	1	-	.1	.3	21	1.5	17	1.8	72	67	249	.6
3	4	2	-	79	9	118	0	.2	0	-	.2	.1	39	.7	9	.5	66	73	209	.4
7	4	1	-	245	28	169	.1	.9	1	-	.6	.1	316	.8	39	.2	319	431	217	1.5
5	6	15	0	5	39	324	.3	.8	1	-	.9	.3	175	4.8	36	.3	172	512	479	2.4
2	2	4	0	3	37	542	0	.7	0	-	.8	.3	133	5.3	22	.3	304	828	444	3.3
11	6	1	0	149	2	203	.1	1.1	4	-	.5	.1	330	.5	47	.3	278	420	138	1.2
0	0	0	1	0	7	3	0	0	1	-	0	0	3	.2	6	.3	11	119	1	1
0	0	0	1	0	8	3	0	0	1	-	0	0	3	.1	6	.2	9	89	1	.1
2	3	1	0	211	17	114	.1	.4	0	-	.2	0	25	.7	5	0	89	61	612	.5
2	2	1	0	212	22	84	.1	.6	0	-	.3	0	25	.6	5	0	86	63	62	.5

Food Composition Table 313

Code	Name	Amount	Unit	Grams	Kilocalories	Carbohydrates (g)	Protein (g)	Fat (g)
1131	EGGS, CHICKEN, WHOLE, CKD, POACHED	1	LARGE	50.0	75	1	6	5
1132	EGGS, CHICKEN, WHOLE, CKD, SCRAMBLED	½	CUP	110.0	183	2	12	13
18260	ENGLISH MUFFINS, MIXED-GRAIN (INCLUDES GRANOLA)	1	EACH	66.0	155	31	6	1
18258	ENGLISH MUFFINS, PLAIN	1	EACH	57.0	134	26	4	1
18264	ENGLISH MUFFINS, WHEAT	1	EACH	57.0	127	26	5	1
18170	FIG BARS	1	EACH	16.0	56	11	1	1
15027	FISH FILLETS AND STICKS, FRIED	3	OUNCE	85.1	231	20	13	10
15029	FOUNDER, CKD, DRY HEAT	3	OUNCE	85.1	100	0	21	1
18269	FRENCH TOAST, MADE W/ LOWFAT (2%) MILK	1	SLICE	65.0	149	16	5	7
9103	FRUIT SALAD JUICE PACK	½	CUP	124.5	62	16	1	0
9102	FRUIT SALAD, WATER PACK	½	CUP	122.5	37	10	0	0
18173	GRAHAM CRACKERS, PLAIN OR HONEY	1	EACH	70	30	5	0	1
19015	GRANOLA BARS, HARD, PLAIN	1	EACH	28.4	134	18	3	6
19020	GRANOLA BARS, SOFT, PLAIN	1	EACH	28.4	126	19	2	5
9135	GRAPE JUICE, CND OR BOTTLED, UNSWEETENED	¾	CUP	189.4	116	28	1	0
9124	GRAPEFRUIT JUICE, CND, SWEETENED	¾	CUP	187.0	86	21	1	0
9123	GRAPEFRUIT JUICE, CND, UNSWEETENED	¾	CUP	185.2	70	17	1	0
9404	GRAPEFRUIT JUICE, PINK, FRESH	¾	CUP	185.3	72	17	1	0
9128	GRAPEFRUIT JUICE, WHITE, FRESH	¾	CUP	185.3	72	17	1	0
9116	GRAPEFRUIT, FRESH, WHITE	1	MEDIUM	136.0	45	11	1	0
9120	GRAPEFRUIT, SECTIONS, CND, JUICE PACK	½	CUP	124.5	46	11	1	0
9119	GRAPEFRUIT, SECTIONS, CND, WATER PACK	½	CUP	122.0	44	11	1	0
9131	GRAPES, AMERICAN TYPE, FRESH	½	CUP	46.0	29	8	0	0
6114	GRAVY, AU JUS, CND	¼	CUP	59.6	10	1	1	0
6527	GRAVY, UNSPECIFIED TYPE	¼	CUP	65.4	22	4	1	0
15032	GROUPER, CKD, DRY HEAT	3	OUNCE	85.1	100	0	21	1
15037	HALIBUT, CKD, DRY HEAT	3	OUNCE	85.1	119	0	23	3
15196	HALIBUT, GREENLAND, CKD, DRY HEAT	3	OUNCE	85.1	203	0	16	15
7032	HAM AND CHEESE LOAF (OR ROLL), LUNCH MEAT	1	SLICE	28.4	73	0	5	6
7031	HAM SALAD SPREAD	1	TBSP.	15.0	32	2	1	2
7028	HAM, EXTRA LEAN, APPX 5% FAT	1	SLICE	28.4	37	0	5	1
62626	HAMBURGER PATTY, MEATLESS	1	EACH	90.0	140	8	18	4
20030	HOMINY, CND, WHITE	½	CUP	80.0	58	11	1	1
20330	HOMINY, CND, YELLOW	½	CUP	80.0	58	11	1	1
19296	HONEY	1	TBSP.	21.0	64	17	0	0
7022	HOT DOG, BEEF	1	EACH	57.0	180	1	7	16
7024	HOT DOG, CHICKEN	1	EACH	45.0	116	3	6	9
62605	HOT DOG, FAT FREE	1	EACH	50.0	40	2	7	0
7025	HOT DOG, TURKEY	1	EACH	45.0	102	1	6	8
16137	HUMMUS, FRESH	½	CUP	123.0	210	25	6	10
18270	HUSH PUPPIES	1	EACH	22.0	74	10	2	3
19270	ICE CREAM, CHOCOLATE	½	CUP	66.0	143	19	3	7
19090	ICE CREAM, FRENCH VANILLA, SOFT-SERVE	½	CUP	66.5	143	15	3	9
19271	ICE CREAM, STRAWBERRY	½	CUP	66.0	127	18	2	6
19095	ICE CREAM, VANILLA	½	CUP	66.0	133	16	2	7
19088	ICE MILK, VANILLA	½	CUP	66.5	92	15	3	3
19096	ICE MILK, VANILLA, SOFT SERVE	½	CUP	66.5	84	14	3	2
62547	ICED TEA, BOTTLED, ALL FLAVORS	1	CUP	236.6	118	29	0	0
19297	JAMS AND PRESERVES	1	TBSP.	20.0	48	13	0	0
19300	JELLIES	1	TBSP.	19.0	51	13	0	0
9148	KIWIFRUIT, FRESH	1	MEDIUM	76.0	46	11	1	0
17225	LAMB, GROUND, CKD, BROILED	3	OUNCE	85.1	241	0	21	17
17002	LAMB, MEAT AND FAT, CKD	3	OUNCE	85.1	250	0	21	18
4002	LARD	¼	CUP	51.3	462	0	0	51
11247	LEEKS, CKD	½	CUP	5.20	16	4	0	0
11246	LEEKS, FRESH	½	CUP	52.0	32	7	1	0
19380	LEMON PUDDING	1	CUP	298.1	373	75	0	9
9150	LEMONS, FRESH, W/O PEEL	1	MEDIUM	58.0	17	5	1	0
11252	LETTUCE, ICEBERG, FRESH	1	CUP	56.0	7	1	1	0
11253	LETTUCE, LOOSELEAF, FRESH	1	CUP	56.0	10	2	1	0

Food Composition Table

Saturated Fat (g)	Monounsaturated Fat (g)	Polyunsaturated Fat (g)	Fiber (g)	Cholesterol (g)	Folate (g)	Vitamin A (RE)	Vitamin B₆ (mg)	Vitamin B₁₂ (μg)	Vitamin C (mg)	Vitamin E (mg)	Riboflavin (mg)	Thiamin (mg)	Calcium (mg)	Iron (mg)	Magnesium (mg)	Niacin (mg)	Phosphorus (mg)	Potassium (mg)	Sodium (mg)	Zinc (mg)
2	2	1	0	212	18	95	.1	.4	0	-	.2	0	25	.7	5	0	89	60	140	.6
4	5	2	0	387	33	215	.1	.8	0	-	.5	.1	78	1.3	13	.1	187	152	308	1.1
0	1	0	-	0	23	1	.1	0	0	-	.2	.3	129	2	29	2.4	98	103	275	.6
0	0	1	-	0	21	0	0	0	0	-	.2	.3	99	1.4	12	2.2	76	75	264	.4
0	0	0	-	0	22	0	.1	0	0	-	.2	.2	101	1.6	22	1.9	66	106	218	.6
0	1	0	1	0	2	1	0	0	0	-	0	0	10	.5	4	.3	10	33	56	.1
3	4	3	0	95	15	26	.1	1.5	0	-	.2	.1	17	.6	21	1.8	154	222	495	.6
0	0	0	0	58	8	9	.2	2.1	0	-	.1	.1	15	.3	49	1.9	246	293	89	.5
2	3	2	-	75	15	86	0	.2	0	-	.2	.1	65	1.1	11	1.1	76	87	311	.4
0	0	0	-	0	3	756	0	0	4	-	0	0	14	.3	10	.4	17	1454	6	.2
0	0	0	-	0	3	54	0	0-	2	-	0	0	9	.4	6	.5	11	96	4	.1
0	0	0	0	0	1	0	0	0	0	-	0	0	2	.3	2	.3	7		42	.1
1	1	3	2	0	7	4	0	0	0	-	0	.1	17	.8	27	.4	79	95	83	.6
2	1	2	1	0	7	0	0	.1	0	-	0	.1	30	.7	21	.1	65	92	79	.4
0	0	0	0	0	5	2	.1	0	0	-	.1	0	17	.5	19	.5	21	250	6	.1
0	0	0	0	0	19	0	0	0	50	-	0	.1	15	.7	19	.6	21	303	4	.1
0	0	0	0	0	19	2	0	0	54	.1	0	.1	13	.4	19	.4	20	283	2	.2
0	0	0	-	0	19	82	.1	0	70	-	0	.1	17	.4	22	.4	28	300	2	.1
0	0	0	0	0	19	2	.1	0	70	-	0	.1	17	.4	22	.4	28	300	2	.1
0	0	0	1	0	14	1	.1	0	45	-	0	.1	16	.1	12	.4	11	201	0	.1
0	0	0	0	0	11	0	0	0	42	-	0	0	19	.3	14	.3	15	210	9	.1
0	0	0	0	0	11	0	0	0	27	-	0	0	18	.5	12	.3	12	161	2	.1
0	0	0	1	0	2	5	.1	0	2	-	0	0	6	.1	2	.1	5	88	1	0
0	0	0	-	0	1	0	0	.1	1	-	0	0	2	.4	1	.5	18	48	30	.6
0	0	0	0	0	1	0	0	0	0	-	0	0	9	.1	3	.2	12	16	356	.1
0	0	0	0	40	9	43	.3	.6	0	-	0	.1	18	1	31	.3	122	404	45	.4
0	1	1	0	35	12	46	.3	1.2	0	-	.1	.1	51	.9	91	6.1	242	490	59	.5
3	9	1	0	50	1	15	.4	.8	0	-	.1	.1	3	.7	28	1.6	179	293	88	.4
2	3	1	0	16	1	7	.1	.2	.7	-	.1	.2	16	.3	5	1	72	83	381	.6
1	1	0	0	6	0	0	0	.1	1	-	0	.1	1	.1	2	.3	18	22	137	.2
0	1	0	0	13	1	0	.1	.2	7	-	.1	.3	2	.2	5	1.4	62	99	405	.5
2	-	1	5	0	-	0	-	-	0	-	-	.3	96	1.5	-	4	-	-	380	7.5
0	0	0	2	0	1	0	0	0	0-	0	0	0	8	.5	13	0	28	7	168	.8
0	0	0	-	0	1	9	0	0	0	-	0	0	8	.5	13	0	28	7	168	.8
-	-	-	0	0	0	0	0	0	0	-	0	0	1	.1	0	0	1	11	1	0
7	8	1	0	35	2	0	.1	.9	14	-	.1	0	11	.8	2	1.4	50	95	585	1.2
2	4	2	0	45	2	17	.1	.1	0	-	.1	0	43	.9	5	1.4	48	38	617	.5
0	0	0	0	15	0	0	-	-	0	-	-	-	0	.2	-	-	-	-	460	-
3	3	2	0	48	4	0	.1	.1	0	-	.1	0	48	.8	6	1.9	60	81	642	1.4
2	4	4	6	0	73	2	.5	0	10	-	.1	.1	61	1.9	36	.5	138	214	300	1.4
0	1	2	1	10	4	9	0	0	0	-	.1	.1	61	.7	5	.6	42	32	147	.1
4	2	0	-	22	11	79	0	.2	0	-	.1	0	72	.6	19	.1	71	164	50	.4
5	2	0	-	61	6	102	0	.3	1	-	.1	0	87	.1	8	.1	77	118	41	.3
-	-	-	-	19	8	51	0	.2	5	-	.2	0	79	.1	9	.1	66	124	40	.2
4	2	0	0	29	3	77	0	.3	0	-	.2	0	84	.1	9	.1	69	131	53	.5
2	1	0	0	9	4	31	0	.4	1	-	.2	0	92	.1	10	.1	72	140	57	.3
1	1	0	0	8	4	19	0	.3	1	-	.1	0	104	0	9	.1	80	147	47	.4
0	-	-	0	0	0	0	-	-	0-	-	-	-	0	0	-	-	-	-	10	-
0	0	0	0	0	7	0	0	0	2	-	0	0	4	.1	1	0	2	15	8	0
-	-	-	0	0	0	0	0	0	0	-	0	0	2	0	1	0	1	12	7	0
-	-	-	3	0	-	14	-	0	74	-	0	0	20	.3	23	.4	30	252	4	-
7	7	1	0	82	16	0	.1	2.2	-	.1	.2	.1	19	1.5	20	5.7	171	288	69	4
8	8	1	0	82	15	0	.1	2.2	0	-	.2	.1	14	1.6	20	5.7	160	264	61	3.8
20	23	6	0	49	0	0	0	0	0	.6	0	0	0	0	0	0	0	0	0	.1
0	0	0	-	0	13	3	.1	0	2	-	0	0	16	.6	7	.1	9	45	5	0
0	0	0	1	0	33	5	.1	0	6	-	0	0	31	1.1	15	.2	18	94	10	.1
1	4	3	-	0	0	0	0	0	0	-	0	0	6	.2	3	0	15	3	417	.1
0	0	0	2	0	6	2	0	0	31	-	0	0	15	.3	5	.1	9	80	1	0
0	0	0	1	0	31	18	0	0	2	-	0	0	11	.3	5	1	11	88	5	.1
0	0	0	1	0	28	106	0	0	10	-	0	0	38	.8	6	.2	14	148	5	.2

Appendix

Code	Name	Amount	Unit	Grams	Kilocalories	Carbohydrates (g)	Protein (g)	Fat (g)
11251	LETTUCE, ROMAINE, FRESH	1	CUP	56.0	9	1	1	0
15148	LOBSTER, NORTHERN, CKD, MOIST HEAT	3	OUNCE	85.1	83	1	17	1
62533	MACARONI AND CHEESE	1	CUP	111.9	360	44	1	13
20100	MACARONI, CKD, ENRICHED	1	CUP	140.0	197	40	7	1
20400	MACARONI, CKD, UNENRICHED	1	CUP	140.0	197	40	7	1
20106	MACARONI, VEGETABLE, CKD, ENRICHED	1	CUP	134.0	172	36	6	0
20108	MACARONI, WHOLE-WHEAT, CKD	1	CUP	140.0	174	37	7	1
62535	MANGO JUICE	¾	CUP	179.9	66	16	-	0
9176	MANGOS, FRESH	½	CUP	82.5	54	14	0	0
4128	MARGARINE, IMITATION (APPX 40% FAT)	1	TSP.	4.8	17	0	0	2
4132	MARGARINE, REGULAR, W/ SALT ADDED	1	TSP.	4.7	34	0	0	4
4130	MARGARINE, SOFT, W/ SALT ADDED	1	TSP.	4.7	34	0	0	4
11256	MARINARA SAUCE	½	CUP	125.0	85	13	2	4
19303	MARMALADE, ORANGE	1	TBSP.	20.0	49	13	0	0
19116	MARSHMALLOWS	1	CUP	46.0	146	37	1	0
4018	MAYONNAISE	1	TBSP.	14.7	57	4	0	5
62610	MAYONNAISE, FAT FREE	1	TBSP.	15.0	10	3	0	0
62609	MAYONNAISE, LIGHT	1	TBSP.	15.0	25	1	0	2
9181	MELONS, CANTALOUPE, FRESH	1	WEDGE	80.0	28	7	1	0
9183	MELONS, CASABA, FRESH	1	WEDGE	164.0	43	10	1	0
9184	MELONS, HONEYDEW, FRESH	1	WEDGE	129.0	45	12	1	0
19120	MILK CHOCOLATE	1	BAR	44.0	226	26	3	13
19126	MILK CHOCOLATE COATED PEANUTS	1	OUNCE	28.4	147	14	4	9
19127	MILK CHOCOLATE COATED RAISINS	1	OUNCE	28.4	111	19	1	4
19132	MILK CHOCOLATE W/ ALMONDS	1	BAR	41.0	216	22	4	14
1110	MILK SHAKES, THICK CHOCOLATE	1	CUP	345.4	410	73	11	9
1111	MILK SHAKES, THICK VANILLA	1	CUP	345.4	386	61	13	10
1088	MILK, BUTTERMILK	1	CUP	245.0	99	12	8	2
1103	MILK, CHOCOLATE DRINK, LOWFAT, 2% FAT	1	CUP	250.0	179	26	8	5
1102	MILK, CHOCOLATE DRINK, WHOLE	1	CUP	250.0	208	26	8	8
1095	MILK, CND, CONDENSED, SWEETENED	¼	CUP	76.3	245	42	6	7
1082	MILK, LOWFAT, 1% FAT	1	CUP	244.0	102	12	8	3
1079	MILK, LOWFAT, 2% FAT	1	CUP	244.0	121	12	8	5
1085	MILK, SKIM	1	CUP	245.0	86	12	8	0
1077	MILK, WHOLE, 3.3% FAT	1	CUP	244.0	150	11	8	8
1078	MILK, WHOLE, 3.7% FAT	1	CUP	244.0	157	11	8	9
18274	MUFFINS, BLUEBERRY	1	LARGE	65.0	180	31	4	4
18279	MUFFINS, CORN	1	LARGE	65.0	198	33	4	5
18283	MUFFINS, OAT BRAN	1	LARGE	65.0	176	31	5	5
18273	MUFFINS, PLAIN	1	LARGE	65.0	192	27	4	7
18287	MUFFINS, WHEAT BRAN	1	LARGE	65.0	184	27	5	8
11261	MUSHROOMS, CKD	½	CUP	78.0	21	4	2	0
11264	MUSHROOMS, CND, DRAINED SOLIDS	½	CUP	78.0	19	4	1	0
11260	MUSHROOMS, FRESH	½	CUP	35.0	9	2	1	0
20113	NOODLES, CHINESE, CHOW MEIN	½	CUP	22.5	119	13	2	7
20310	NOODLES, EGG, CKD, ENRICHED	½	CUP	80.0	106	20	4	1
20510	NOODLES, EGG, CKD, UNENRICHED	½	CUP	80.0	106	20	4	1
20112	NOODLES, EGG, SPINACH, CKD, ENRICHED	½	CUP	80.0	106	19	4	1
20115	NOODLES, JAPANESE, SOBA, CKD	½	CUP	57.0	56	12	3	0
15058	OCEAN PERCH, ATLANTIC, CKD, DRY HEAT	3	OUNCE	85.1	103	0	20	2
4053	OIL, OLIVE	1	TBSP.	13.5	119	0	0	14
4042	OIL, PEANUT	1	TBSP.	13.5	119	0	0	14
4058	OIL, SESAME	1	TBSP.	13.6	121	0	0	14
4044	OIL, SOYBEAN	1	TBSP.	13.6	121	0	0	14
4034	OIL, SOYBEAN, (HYDR)	1	TBSP.	13.6	121	0	0	14
4543	OIL, SOYBEAN, (HYDR) & CTTNSD	1	TBSP.	13.6	121	0	0	14
4518	OIL, VEGETABLE, CORN	1	TBSP.	13.6	121	0	0	14
4582	OIL, VEGETABLE, CANOLA	1	TBSP.	13.6	121	0	0	14
4501	OIL, VEGETABLE, COCOA BUTTER	1	TBSP.	13.6	121	0	0	14
4502	OIL, VEGETABLE, COTTONSEED	1	TBSP.	13.6	121	0	0	14

Food Composition Table

Saturated Fat (g)	Monounsaturated Fat (g)	Polyunsaturated Fat (g)	Fiber (g)	Cholesterol (g)	Folate (g)	Vitamin A (RE)	Vitamin B₆ (mg)	Vitamin B₁₂ (μg)	Vitamin C (mg)	Vitamin E (mg)	Riboflavin (mg)	Thiamin (mg)	Calcium (mg)	Iron (mg)	Magnesium (mg)	Niacin (mg)	Phosphorus (mg)	Potassium (mg)	Sodium (mg)	Zinc (mg)
0	0	0	1	0	767	146	0	0	13	-	.1	.1	20	.6	3	.3	25	162	4	.1
0	0	0	0	61	9	22	.1	2.6	0	-	.1	0	52	.3	30	.9	157	299	323	2.5
8	-	-	16	40	-	100	-	-	0	-	-	-	240	1.5	-	-	-	-	1029	-
0	0	0	2	0	10	0	0	0	0	-	.1	.3	10	2	25	2.3	76	43	1.	.7
0	0	0	2	0	10	-	0	0	0	-	0	0	10	.7	25	.6	76	43	1	.7
0	0	0	6	0	8	7	0	0	0	-	.1	.2	15	.7	25	1.4	67	42	8	.6
0	0	0	6	0	7	0	.1	0	0	-	.1	.2	21	1.5	42	1	125	62	4	1.1
-	-	-	-	0	-	0	-	-	30	-	-	-	0	0	-	-	-	-	18	-
0	0	0	1	0	-	321	.1	0	23	.9	0	0	8	.1	7	.5	9	129	2	0
0	1	1	0	0	0	48	0	0	0	.2	0	0	1	0	0	0	1	1	46	0
1	2	1	0	0	0	47	0	0	0	.4	0	0	1	0	0	0	1	2	44	0
1	1	2	0	0	0	47	0	0	0	.3	0	0	1	0	0	0	1	2	51	0
1	2	1	-	0	17	120	.3	0	16	-	.1	.1	22	1	30	2	44	530	786	.3
-	-	-	0	0	7	1	0	0	1	-	0	0	8	0	0	0	1	7	11	0
-	-	-	0	0	0	0	0	0	0	-	0	0	1	.1	1	0	4	2	22	0
1	1	3	0	4	1	12	0	0	0	.6	0	0	2	0	0	0	4	1	104	0
0	-	-	0	0	-	0	-	-	0	-	-	-	0	0	-	-	-	1	105	-
0	-	-	-	5	0	0	-	-	0	-	-	-	0	0	-	-	-	5	130	-
-	-	-	1	0	14	258	.1	0	34	.1	0	0	9	.2	9	.5	14	247	7	.1
-	-	-	1	0-	-	5	-	0	26	-	0	.1	8	.7	13	.7	11	344	20	-
-	-	-	1	0	-	5	.1	0	32	-	0	.1	8	.1	9	8	13	350	13	-
8	4	0	2	10	3	21	0	.2	0	-	.1	0	84	.6	26	.1	95	169	36	.6
4	4	1	1	3	2	0	.1	.1	0	-	0	0	29	.4	26	1.2	60	142	12	.5
2	1	0	1	1	1	2	0	.1	0	-	0	0	24	.5	13	.1	41	146	10	.2
7	6	1	3	8	5	6	0	.2	0	-	.2	0	92	.7	37	.3	108	182	30	.5
6	3	0	1	36	17	73	.1	1.1	0	-	.8	.2	456	1.1	55	.4	435	774	383	1.7
7	3	0	0	41	23	97	.1	1.8	0	-	.7	.1	505	.3	41	.5	398	631	330	1.3
1	1	0	0	9	12	20	.1	.5	2	-	.4	.1	285	.1	27	.1	219	371	257	1
3	1	0	4	17	12	142	.1	.8	2	-	.4	.1	284	.6	33	.3	254	422	150	1
5	2	0	4	30	12	72	.1	.8	2	-	.4	.1	280	.6	33	.3	251	417	149	1
4	2	0	0	26	9	62	0	.3	2	-	.3	.1	216	.1	20	.2	193	284	97	.7
2	1	0	0	10	12	144	.1	.9	2	-	.4	.1	300	.1	34	.2	235	381	123	1
3	1	0	0	18	12	139	.1	.9	2	-	.4	.1	297	.1	33	.2	232	377	122	1
0	0	0	0	4	13	149	.1	.9	2	-	.3	.1	302	.1	28	.2	247	406	126	1
5	2	0	0	33	12	76	.1	.9	2	-	.4	.1	291	.1	33	.2	228	370	120	.9
6	3	0	0	35	12	83	.1	.9	4	-	.4	.1	290	.1	33	.2	227	368	119	.9
1	2	1	2	20	10	-	0	.4	1	-	.1	.1	37	1	10	.7	128	80	291	.3
1	2	2	-	33	22	23	.1	.1	0	-	.2	.2	48	1.8	24	1.3	185	45	339	.5
1	1	3	5	0	12	-	.1	0	0	-	.1	.2	41	2.7	102	.3	244	330	255	1.2
1	2	4	2	25	8	26	0	.1	0	-	.2	.2	130	1.6	11	1.5	99	79	304	.4
1	2	4	-	21	34	163	.2	.1	5	-	.3	.2	122	2.7	51	2.6	185	207	382	1.8
0	0	0	2	0	14	0	.1	0	3	-	.2	.1	5	1.4	9	3.5	68	278	2	.7
0	0	0	2	0	10	0	0	0	0	-	0	.1	9	.6	12	1.2	51	101	332	.6
0	0	0	0	0	7	0	0	0	1	-	.2	0	2	.4	4	1.4	36	130	1	.3
1	2	4	1	0	5	2	0	0	0	-	.1	.1	5	1.1	12	1.3	36	27	99	.3
0	0	0	-	26	6	5	0	.1	0	-	.1	.1	10	1.3	15	1.2	55	22	132	.5
0	0	0	-	26	6	5	0	.1	0	-	0	0	10	.5	15	.3	55	22	132	.5
0	0	0	2	26	17	11	.1	.1	0	-	.1	.2	15	.9	19	1.2	46	30	10	.5
0	0	0	-	0	4	0	0	0	0	-	0	.1	2	.3	5	.3	14	20	34	.1
0	1	0	0	46	9	12	.2	1	1	0	.1	.1	117	1	33	2.1	236	298	82	.5
2	10	1	0	0	0	0	0	0	0	1.6	0	0	0	.1	0	0	0	0	0	0
2	6	4	0	0	0	0	0	0	0	1.6	0	0	0	0	0	0	0	0	0	0
2	5	6	0	0	0	0	0	0	0	.2	0	0	0	0	0	0	0	0	0	0
2	3	8	0	0	0	0	0	0	0	1.5	0	0	0	0	0	0	0	0	0	0
2	6	5	0	0	0	0	0	0	0	1.1	0	0	0	0	0	0	0	0	0	0
2	4	7	0	0	0	0	0	0	0	1.7	0	0	0	0	0	0	0	0	0	0
2	3	8	0	0	0	0	0	0	0	2	0	0	0	0	0	0	0	0	0	0
1	8	4	0	-	0	0	0	0	0	-	0	0	0	0	0	0	0	0	0	0
8	4	0	0	0	0	0	0	0	0	.2	0	0	0	0	0	0	0	0	0	0
4	2	7	0	0	0	0	0	0	0	4.8	-	0	0	0	0	0	0	0	0	0

Appendix

Code	Name	Amount	Unit	Grams	Kilocalories	Carbohydrates (g)	Protein (g)	Fat (g)
405	OIL, VEGETABLE, PALM	1	TBSP.	13.6	121	0	0	14
4513	OIL, VEGETABLE, PALM KERNEL	1	TBSP.	1.6	118	0	0	14
4510	OIL, VEGETABLE, SAFFLOWER, LINOLEIC	1	TBSP.	13.6	121	0	0	14
4511	OIL, VEGETABLE, SAFFLOWER, OLEIC	1	TBSP.	13.6	121	0	0	14
4584	OIL, VEGETABLE, SUNFLOWER	1	TBSP.	13.6	121	0	0	14
11279	OKRA, CKD	½	CUP	80.0	26	6	1	0
11278	OKRA, FRESH	½	CUP	50.0	19	4	1	0
11281	OKRA, FRZ, CKD	½	CUP	92.0	34	8	2	0
11280	OKRA, FRZ, UNPREPARED	½	CUP	71.3	21	5	1	0
10161	OLIVE LOAF, LUNCH MEAT	1	SLICE	28.4	67	3	3	5
9194	OLIVES, RIPE, CANNED (JUMBO-SUPER COLLOSSAL)	1	JUMBO	8.3	7	0	0	1
9193	OLIVES, RIPE CANNED (SMALL-EXTRA LARGE)	1	SMALL	3.2	4	0	0	0
11282	ONIONS, FRESH	½	CUP	79.9	30	7	1	0
9206	ORANGE JUICE, FRESH	¾	CUP	186.0	84	19	1	0
9215	ORANGE JUICE, FROM CONCENTRATE	¾	CUP	186.4	84	20	1	0
9200	ORANGES, FRSH	1	MEDIUM	131.0	62	15	1	0
15168	OYSTER, EASTERN, BREADED AND FRIED	3	OUNCE	85.1	168	10	7	11
15170	OYSTER, EASTERN, CND	3	OUNCE	85.1	59	3	6	2
18390	PANCAKES, BUTTERMILK	1	4 IN.	9.5	22	3	1	1
18293	PANCAKES, PLAIN	1	4 IN.	9.5	22	3	1	1
18300	PANCAKES, WHOLE-WHEAT	1	4 IN.	44.0	92	13	4	3
9226	PAPAYAS, FRESH	1	MEDIUM	304.0	119	30	2	0
11808	PARSNIPS, CKD, W/SALT	½	CUP	78.0	63	15	1	0
11299	PARSNIPS, CKD, W/O SALT	½	CUP	78.0	63	15	1	0
11298	PARSNIPS, FRESH	½	CUP	66.5	50	12	1	0
20321	PASTA, CKD, ENRICHED, W/ADDED SALT	½	CUP	70.0	99	20	3	0
20121	PASTA, CKD, ENRICHED, W/O ADDED SALT	½	CUP	73.0	99	20	3	0
20094	PASTA, FRESH-REFRIGERATED, PLAIN, CKD	½	CUP	73.0	96	18	4	1
20096	PASTA, FRESH-REFRIGERATED, SPINACH, CKD	½	CUP	73.0	95	18	4	1
20097	PASTA, HOMEMADE, MADE W/EGG, CKD	½	CUP	73.6	96	17	4	1
20098	PASTA, HOMEMADE, MADE W/O EGG, CKD	½	CUP	73.6	91	18	3	1
20127	PASTA, SPINACH, CKD	½	CUP	70.0	91	18	3	0
20125	PASTA, WHOLE-WHEAT, CKD	½	CUP	70.0	87	19	4	0
9251	PEACH NECTAR, CND/W/O ADDED VIT C	¾	CUP	186.4	101	26	1	0
9238	PEACHES, CND, JUICE PACK	½	CUP	124.0	55	14	1	0
9240	PEACHES, CND, LIGHT SYRUP PACK	½	CUP	125.5	68	18	1	0
9237	PEACHES, CND, WATER PACK	½	CUP	122.0	29	7	1	0
9246	PEACHES, DRIED, SULFURED	¼	CUP	40	96	25	1	0
9236	PEACHES, FRESH	1	MEDIUM	87.0	37	10	1	0
9250	PEACHES, FROZEN, SLICED, SWEETENED	½	CUP	125.0	118	30	1	0
16097	PEANUT BUTTER, CHUNK STYLE, W/SALT	2	TBSP.	32.3	190	7	8	16
16098	PEANUT BUTTER, SMOOTH STYLE, W/SALT	2	TBSP.	32.3	190	7	8	16
16088	PEANUTS, ALL TYPES, CKD, BOILED, W/SALT	½	CUP	31.5	100	7	4	7
16090	PEANUTS, ALL TYPES, DRY-ROASTED, W/SALT	½	CUP	73.0	427	16	17	36
16390	PEANUTS, ALL TYPES, DRY-ROASTED, W/O SALT	½	CUP	73.0	427	16	17	36
16087	PEANUTS, ALL TYPES, FRESH	½	CUP	73.0	414	12	19	36
16089	PEANUTS, ALL TYPES, OIL-ROASTED, W/SALT	½	CUP	72.0	418	14	19	35
16389	PEANUTS, ALL TYPES, OIL-ROASTED, W/O SALT	½	CUP	72.0	418	14	19	35
9340	PEARS, ASIAN, FRESH	1	MEDIUM	122.0	51	13	1	0
9254	PEARS, CND, JUICE PACK	½	CUP	124.0	62	16	0	0
9253	PEARS, CND, WATER PACK	½	CUP	122.0	35	10	0	0
9252	PEARS, FRESH	1	MEDIUM	166.0	98	25	1	1
11300	PEAS, EDIBLE-PODDED, FRESH	½	CUP	72.5	30	5	2	0
11305	PEAS, GREEN, CKD	½	CUP	80.0	67	13	4	0
11308	PEAS, GREEN, CND	½	CUP	85.0	59	11	4	0
11304	PEAS, GREEN, FRESH	½	CUP	72.5	59	10	4	0
11313	PEAS, GREEN, FRZ, CKD	½	CUP	80.0	62	11	4	0
12142	PECANS, DRIED	½	CUP	54.0	360	10	4	37
11329	PEPPERS, HOT CHILI, GREEN, CND	1	EACH	73.0	18	4	1	0
11670	PEPPERS, HOT CHILI, GREEN, FRESH	1	EACH	45.0	18	4	1	0

Saturated Fat (g)	Monounsaturated Fat (g)	Polyunsaturated Fat (g)	Fiber (g)	Cholesterol (g)	Folate (g)	Vitamin A (RE)	Vitamin B₆ (mg)	Vitamin B₁₂ (μg)	Vitamin C (mg)	Vitamin E (mg)	Riboflavin (mg)	Thiamin (mg)	Calcium (mg)	Iron (mg)	Magnesium (mg)	Niacin (mg)	Phosphorus (mg)	Potassium (mg)	Sodium (mg)	Zinc (mg)
7	5	1	0	0	0	0	0	0	0	2.6	0	0	0	0	0	0	0	0	0	-
11	2	0	0	0	0	0	0	0	0	-	0	0	0	0	0	0	0	0	0	-
1	2	10	0	0	0	0	0	0	0	4.7	0	0	0	0	0	0	0	0	0	0
1	10	2	0	0	0	0	0	0	0	4.7	0	0	0	0	0	0	0	0	0	0
1	11	1	0	-	0	0	0	0	0	-	0	0	0	0	0	0	0	0	0	0
0	0	0	2	0	37	46	.1	0	13	-	0	.1	50	.4	46	7	45	258	4	.4
0	0	0	1	0	33	33	.1	0	11	-	0	.1	41	.4	29	.5	32	152	4	.3
0	0	0	3	0	134	47	0	0	11	-	.1	.1	88	.6	47	.7	42	215	3	.6
0	0	0	2	0	105	33	0	0	9	-	.1	.1	58	.4	31	.5	30	150	2	.4
2	2	1	0	11	1	6	.1	.4	.2	-	.1	.1	31	.2	5	.5	36	84	421	.4
0	0	0	-	0	0	3	0	0	0	-	0	0	8	.3	0	0	0	1	75	0
0	0	0	-	0	0	1	0	0	0	-	0	0	3	.1	0	0	0	0	28	0
0	0	0	1	0	15	0	.1	0	5	.2	0	0	16	.2	8	.1	26	125	2	.2
0	0	0	0	0	56	37	.1	0	93	.1	.1	2	20	.4	20	.7	32	372	2	.1
0	0	0	0	0	82	15	.1	0	73	-	0	.1	17	.2	19	.4	30	354	2	.1
0	0	0	3	0	40	28	.1	0	70	.3	.1	.1	52	.1	13	.4	18	237	0	.1
3	4	3	-	69	12	77	.1	13.3	3	-	.2	.1	53	5.9	49	1.4	135	208	355	74.1
1	0	1	0	47	8	77	.1	16.3	4	-	.1	.1	38	5.7	46	1.1	118	195	95	77.4
0	0	0	-	6	1	3	0	0	0	-	0	0	15	.2	1	.1	13	14	50	.1
0	0	0	-	6	1	5	0	0	0	-	0	0	21	.2	2	.1	15	13	42	.1
1	1	1	-	27	9	28	-	.1	0	-	.2	.1	110	1.4	20	1	164	123	252	.5
0	0	0	5	0	116	85	.1	0	188	-	.1	.1	73	.3	30	1	15	781	9	.2
0	0	0	-	0	45	0	.1	0	10	-	0	.1	29	.5	23	.6	54	286	192	.2
0	0	0	-	0	45	0	.1	0	10	-	0	.1	29	.5	23	.6	54	286	8	.2
0	0	0	3	0	44	0	.1	0	11	-	0	.1	24	.4	19	.5	47	249	7	.4
0	0	0	-	0	5	-	0	0	0	-	.1	.1	5	1	13	1.2	38	22	70	.4
0	0	0	0	0	5	-	0	0	0	-	.1	.1	5	1	13	1.2	38	22	1	.4
0	0	0	-	24	5	4	0	.1	0	-	.1	.2	4	.8	13	.7	46	18	4	.4
0	0	0	-	24	13	10	.1	.1	0	-	.1	.1	13	.8	18	.7	42	27	4	.5
0	0	0	-	30	14	13	0	.1	0	-	.1	.1	7	.9	10	.9	38	15	61	.3
0	0	0	-	0	13	0	0	0	0	-	.1	.1	4	.8	10	10	29	14	54	.3
0	0	0	-	0	8	11	.1	0	0	-	.1	.1	21	.7	43	1.1	76	41	10	.8
0	0	0	3	0	4	0	.1	0	0	-	0	.1	11	.7	21	.5	62	31	2	.6
0	0	0	1	0	3	48	0	0	10	-	0	0	9	.4	7	.5	11	75	13	.1
0	0	0	1	0	4	47	0	0	4	-	0	0	7	.3	9	.7	21	159	5	.1
0	0	0	1	0	4	44	0	0	3	-	0	0	4	.5	6	.7	14	122	6	.1
0	0	0	1	0	4	65	0	0	4	-	0	0	2	.4	6	.6	12	121	4	.1
0	0	0	3	0	0	86	0	0	2	-	.1	0	11	1.6	17	1.8	48	398	3	.2
0	0	0	2	0	3	47	0	0	6	-	0	0	4	.1	6	.9	10	171	0	.1
0	0	0	2	0	4	35	0	0	118	-	0	0	4	.5	6	.8	14	162	7	.1
3	8	5	2	0	30	0	.1	0	0	-	0	0	13	.6	51	4.4	102	241	157	.9
3	8	5	2	0	25	0	.1	0	0	-	0	0	11	.5	51	4.2	104	233	154	.8
1	3	2	3	0	23	0	0	0	0	-	0	.1	17	.3	32	1.7	62	57	237	.6
5	10	11	8	0	106	0	.2	0	0	5.7	.1	.3	39	1.6	128	9.9	261	480	593	2.4
5	18	11	6	0	106	0	.2	0	0	-	.1	.3	39	1.6	128	9.9	251	480	4	2.4
5	18	11	6	0	175	0	.3	0	0	6.1	.1	.5	67	3.3	123	8.8	274	515	13	2.4
5	18	11	7	0	91	0	.2	0	0	5	.1	.2	63	1.3	133	10.3	372	491	312	4.8
5	18	11	7	0	91	0	.2	0	0	-	.1	.2	63	1.3	133	10.3	372	491	4	4.8
0	0	0	4	0	10	0	0	0	5	-	0	0	5	0	10	.3	13	148	0	0
0	0	0	2	0	1	1	0	0	2	-	0	0	11	.4	9	.2	15	119	5	.1
0	0	0	2	0	1	0	0	0	1	-	0	0	5	.3	5	.1	9	65	2	.1
0	0	0	4	0	12	3	0	0	7	-	.1	0	18	.4	10	.2	18	208	0	.2
0	0	0	2	0	30	10	.1	0	44	-	.1	.1	31	1.5	17	.4	38	145	3	.2
0	0	0	4	0	51	48	.2	0	11	-	.1	.2	22	1.2	31	1.6	94	217	2	1
0	0	0	3	0	38	65	.1	0	8	-	.1	.1	17	.8	14	.6	57	147	186	.6
0	0	0	4	0	47	46	.1	0	29	.1	.1	.2	18	1.1	24	1.5	78	177	4	.9
0	0	0	4	0	47	54	.1	0	8	-	.1	.2	19	1.3	23	1.2	72	134	70	.8
3	23	9	4	0	21	7	.1	0	1	-	.1	.5	19	1.2	69	.5	157	212	1	3
0	0	0	1	0	7	45	.1	0	50	-	0	0	5	.4	10	.6	12	137	856	.1
0	0	0	1	0	11	35	.1	0	109	-	0	0	8	.5	11	.4	21	153	3	.1

Appendix

Code	Name	Amount	Unit	Grams	Kilocalories	Carbohydrates (g)	Protein (g)	Fat (g)
11820	PEPPERS, HOT CHILI, RED, CND	1	EACH	73.0	18	4	1	0
11819	PEPPERS, HOT CHILI, RED, FRESH	1	EACH	45.0	18	4	1	0
11632	PEPPERS, JALAPEÑO, CND	¼	CUP	34.0	8	2	0	0
11333	PEPPERS, SWEET, GREEN, FRESH	1	MEDIUM	74.0	20	5	1	0
11821	PEPPERS, SWEET, RED, FRESH	1	MEDIUM	74.0	20	5	1	0
11951	PEPPERS, SWEET, YELLOW, FRESH	1	MEDIUM	74.0	20	5	1	0
11945	PICKLE RELISH, SWEET	1	TBSP.	15.0	29	5	0	0
11941	PICKLE, CUCUMBER, SOUR	1	SLICE	7.0	1	0	0	0
11937	PICKLE, CUCUMBER, DILL	1	SLICE	6.0	1	0	0	0
11940	PICKLE, CUCUMBER, SWEET	1	SLICE	6.0	7	2	0	0
9273	PINEAPPLE, JUICE, CND	¾	CUP	187.6	105	26	1	0
9268	PINEAPPLE, CND, JUICE PACK	½	CUP	125.0	75	20	1	0
9267	PINEAPPLE, CND, WATER PACK	½	CUP	123.0	39	10	1	0
9266	PINEAPPLE, FRESH	1	SLICE	84.0	41	10	0	0
12652	PISTACHIO, DRY ROASTED	½	CUP	64.09	388	18	10	34
9282	PLUMS, CND, PURPLE, JUICE PACK	½	CUP	126.0	73	19	1	0
9281	PLUMS, CND, PURPLE, WATER PACK	½	CUP	124.5	51	14	0	0
9279	PLUMS, FRESH	1	MEDIUM	66.0	36	9	1	0
19034	POPCORN, AIR-POPPED	1	CUP	8.0	31	6	1	0
19036	POPCORN, CAKES	1	CAKE	10.0	38	8	1	0
19038	POPCORN, CARAMEL-COATED, W/PEANUTS	1	CUP	35.2	141	28	2	3
19039	POPCORN, CARAMEL-COATED, W/O PEANUTS	1	CUP	35.2	152	28	1	5
19040	POPCORN, CHEESE-FLAVOR	1	CUP	11.0	58	6	1	4
19035	POPCORN, OIL-POPPED	1	CUP	11.0	55	6	1	3
19408	PORK SKINS, BARBECUE-FLAVOR	1	OUNCE	28.4	153	0	16	9
19041	PORK SKINS, PLAIN	1	OUNCE	28.4	155	0	17	9
10193	PORK, BACKRIBS	3	OUNCE	85.1	315	0	21	25
10127	PORK, BRAUNSCHWEIGER	3	OUNCE	85.1	305	3	11	27
10220	PORK, GROUND, CKD	3	OUNCE	85.1	253	0	22	18
10154	PORK, HAM AND CHEESE LOAF OR ROLL	3	OUNCE	85.1	220	1	14	17
10147	PORK, HAM PATTIES, GRILLED	3	OUNCE	85.1	291	1	11	26
10148	PORK, HAM SALAD SPREAD	3	OUNCE	85.1	184	9	7	13
10185	PORK, HAM, CND, EXTRA LEAN AND REG, ROASTED	3	OUNCE	85.1	142	0	18	7
10140	PORK, HAM, CND, REGULAR (APPROX 13% FAT), ROASTED	3	OUNCE	85.1	192	0	17	13
10134	PORK, HAM, EXTRA LEAN (5% FAT), ROASTED	3	OUNCE	85.1	123	1	18	5
10133	PORK, HAM, EXTRA LEAN (5% FAT), UNHEATED	3	OUNCE	85.1	111	1	16	4
10183	PORK, HAM, EXTRA LEAN AND REG, ROASTED	3	OUNCE	85.1	140	0	19	7
10182	PORK, HAM, EXTRA LEAN AND REG, UNHEATED	3	OUNCE	85.1	138	2	16	7
10151	PORK, HAM, MEAT AND FAT, ROASTED	3	OUNCE	85.1	207	0	18	14
10153	PORK, HAM, MEAT ONLY, ROASTED	3	OUNCE	85.1	134	0	21	5
10136	PORK, HAM, REGULAR (11% FAT), ROASTED	3	OUNCE	85.1	151	0	19	8
10135	PORK, HAM, REGULAR (11% FAT), UNHEATED	3	OUNCE	85.1	155	3	15	9
10172	PORK, SMOKED LINK SAUSAGE, GRILLED	3	OUNCE	85.1	331	2	19	27
10089	PORK, SPARERIBS, MEAT AND FAT, CKD, BRAISED	3	OUNCE	85.1	338	0	25	26
10221	PORK, TENDERLOIN, MEAT AND FAT, CKD, BROILED	3	OUNCE	85.1	171	0	25	7
10223	PORK, TENDERLOIN, MEAT ONLY, CKD, BROILED	3	OUNCE	85.1	159	0	26	5
19042	POTATO CHIPS, BARBECUE-FLAVOR	1	OUNCE	28.4	139	15	2	9
19421	POTATO CHIPS, CHEESE-FLAVOR	1	OUNCE	28.4	141	16	2	8
19422	POTATO CHIPS, LIGHT	1	OUNCE	28.4	134	19	2	6
19411	POTATO CHIPS, PLAIN, SALTED	1	OUNCE	28.4	152	15	2	10
19811	POTATO CHIPS, PLAIN, UNSALTED	1	OUNCE	28.4	152	15	2	10
19043	POTATO CHIPS, SOUR-CREAM-AND-ONION-FLAVOR	1	OUNCE	28.4	151	15	2	10
11672	POTATO PANCAKES, HOME-PREPARED	1	OUNCE	28.4	77	8	2	4
11414	POTATO SALAD	½	CUP	125.0	179	14	3	10
19415	POTATO STICKS	1	OUNCE	28.4	148	15	2	10
11843	POTATOES, AU GRATIN, HOME-PREPARED	½	CUP	122.5	162	14	6	9
11363	POTATOES, BAKED, W/O SKIN	1	MEDIUM	202.0	188	44	4	0
11674	POTATOES, BAKED, W/SKIN	1	MEDIUM	202.0	220	51	5	0
11365	POTATOES, BOILED, CKD IN SKIN	1	MEDIUM	202.0	176	41	4	0
11367	POTATOES, BOILED, CKD, W/O SKIN	1	MEDIUM	202.0	174	40	3	0

Food Composition Table

Saturated Fat (g)	Monounsaturated Fat (g)	Polyunsaturated Fat (g)	Fiber (g)	Cholesterol (g)	Folate (g)	Vitamin A (RE)	Vitamin B₆ (mg)	Vitamin B₁₂ (μg)	Vitamin C (mg)	Vitamin E (mg)	Riboflavin (mg)	Thiamin (mg)	Calcium (mg)	Iron (mg)	Magnesium (mg)	Niacin (mg)	Phosphorus (mg)	Potassium (mg)	Sodium (mg)	Zinc (mg)
0	0	0	1	0	7	868	.1	0	50	-	0	0	5	.4	10	.6	12	137	856	.1
0	0	0	1	0	11	484	.1	0	109	-	0	0	8	.5	11	.4	21	153	3	.1
0	0	0	-	0	5	58	.1	0	4	-	0	0	9	1	4	.2	6	46	497	.1
0	0	0	1	0	16	422	.2	0	141	.5	0	0	7	.3	7	.4	14	131	1	.1
0	0	0	2	0	16	422	.2	0	141	.5	0	0	7	.3	7	.4	14	131	1	.1
-	-	-	-	0	19	18	.1	0	136	-	0	0	8	.3	9	.7	18	157	1	.1
0	0	0	-	0	0	2	0	0	0	-	0	0	0	.1	1	0	2	4	122	0
0	0	0	0	0	0	1	0	0	0	-	0	0	0	0	0	0	1	2	85	0
0	0	0	0	0	0	2	0	0	0	-	0	0	1	0	1	0	1	7	77	0
0	0	0	0	0	0	1	0	0	0	-	0	0	0	0	0	0	1	2	56	0
0	0	0	0	0	43	0	.2	0	20	-	0	.1	32	.5	24	.5	15	251	2	.2
0	0	0	1	0	6	5	.1	0	12	-	0	.1	17	.3	17	.4	7	152	1	.1
0	0	0	1	0	6	1	.1	0	9	-	0	.1	18	.5	20	.4	9	132	1	.2
0	0	0	1	0	6	2	.1	0	9	-	0	.1	18	.5	22	.4	5	156	1	.1
4	23	5	7	0	38	15	.2	0	5	-	.2	.3	45	2	83	.9	305	621	499	.9
0	0	0	1	0	3	127	0	0	4	-	.1	0	13	.4	10	.6	19	194	1	.1
0	0	0	1	0	3	113	0	0	3	-	.1	0	9	.2	6	.5	16	157	1	.1
0	0	0	1	0	1	21	.1	0	6	-	.1	0	3	.1	5	.3	7	114	0	.1
0	0	0	1	0	2	2	0	0	0	-	0	0	1	.2	10	.2	24	24	0	.3
0	0	0	0	0	2	1	0	0	0	-	0	0	1	.2	16	.6	28	33	29	.4
0	1	1	1	0	6	2	.1	0	0	-	0	0	23	1.4	28	.7	45	125	104	.4
1	1	2	2	2	1	4	0	0	0	-	0	0	15	.6	12	.8	29	38	73	.2
1	1	2	1	1	5	5	0	.1	0	-	0	0	12	.2	10	.2	40	29	98	.2
1	1	1	1	0	2	2	0	0	0	-	0	0	1	.3	12	.2	27	25	97	.3
3	4	1	-	33	9	52	0	0	0	-	.1	0	12	.3	0	1	62	51	756	.2
3	4	1	-	27	0	11	0	.2	0	-	.1	0	9	.2	3	.4	24	36	521	.2
9	11	2	-	100	3	3	.3	.5	0	-	.2	.4	38	1.2	18	3	166	268	86	2.9
9	13	3	0	133	37	3589	.3	17.1	8	-	1.3	.2	8	8	9	7.1	143	169	972	2.4
7	8	2	0	80	5	2	.3	.5	1	-	.2	.6	19	1.1	20	3.6	192	308	62	2.7
6	8	2	0	48	3	20	.2	.7	21	-	.2	.5	49	.8	14	2.9	215	250	1142	1.7
9	12	34	0	61	3	0	.1	.6	0	-	.2	.3	8	1.4	9	2.8	86	208	904	1.6
4	6	2	0	31	1	0	.1	.6	5	-	.1	.4	7	.5	9	1.8	102	128	776	.9
2	3	1	0	35	4	0	.3	.7	19	-	.2	.8	6	.9	17	4.3	188	299	908	2
4	6	2	0	53	4	0	.3	.9	12	-	.2	.7	7	1.2	14	4.5	207	304	800	2.1
2	2	0	0	45	3	0	.3	.6	18	-	.2	.6	7	1.3	12	3.4	167	244	1023	2.4
1	2	0	0	40	3	0	.4	.6	22	-	.2	.8	6	.6	14	4.1	185	298	1215	1.6
2	3	1	0	48	3	0	.3	.6	19	-	.2	.6	7	1.2	16	4.5	211	308	1178	2.2
2	3	1	0	45	3	0	.3	.7	23	-	.2	.8	6	.8	15	4.3	201	253	1087	1.7
5	7	2	0	53	3	0	.3	.5	-	-	.2	.5	6	.7	16	3.8	182	243	1010	2
2	2	1	0	47	3	0	.4	.6	-	-	.2	.6	6	.8	19	4.3	193	269	1129	2.2
3	4	1	0	50	3	0	.3	.6	19	-	.3	.6	7	1.1	19	5.2	239	348	1276	2.1
3	4	1	0	48	3	0	.3	.7	24	-	.2	.7	6	.8	16	4.5	210	282	1120	1.8
10	12	3	0	58	4	0	.3	1.4	2	-	.2	.6	26	1	16	3.9	138	286	1276	2.4
9	11	2	0	103	3	3	.3	.9	-	-	.3	.3	40	1.6	20	4.7	222	272	79	3.9
2	3	1	-	80	5	2	.4	.8	1	-	.3	.8	4	1.2	30	4.3	247	378	54	2.5
2	2	0	-	80	5	2	.4	.9	1	-	.3	.8	4	1.2	31	4.4	251	384	55	2.5
2	2	5	1	0	24	6	.2	0	10	-	.1	.1	14	.5	21	1.3	53	357	213	.3
2	2	3	-	1	0	2	.1	0	15	-	0	0	20	.5	21	1.4	85	433	213	.3
1	1	3	-	0	8	0	.2	0	7	-	.1	.1	6	.4	25	2	55	494	139	0
3	3	3	1	0	13	0	.2	0	9	-	.1	0	7	.5	19	1.1	47	361	168	.3
3	3	3	-	0	13	0	.2	0	9	-	.1	0	7	.5	19	1.1	47	361	2	.3
3	2	5	1	2	18	6	.2	.3	11	-	.1	.1	20	.5	21	1.1	50	377	177	.3
1	1	2	1	27	7	4	.1	.1	6	-	0	0	7	.4	9	.6	31	223	144	.2
2	3	5	-	85	8	41	.2	0	12	-	.1	.1	24	.8	19	1.1	65	317	661	.4
3	2	5	1	0	11	0	.1	0	13	-	0	0	5	.6	18	1.4	49	351	71	.3
4	3	1	-	18	10	47	.2	0	12	-	.1	.1	146	.8	24	1.2	138	485	530	.8
0	0	0	3	0	18	0	.6	0	26	-	0	.2	10	.7	51	2.8	101	790	10	.6
0	0	0	5	0	22	0	.7	0	26	-	.1	.2	20	2.7	55	3.3	115	844	16	.6
0	0	0	4	0	20	0	.6	0	26	-	0	.2	10	.6	44	2.9	89	766	8	.6
0	0	0	4	0	18	0	.5	0	15	-	0	.2	16	.6	40	2.7	81	663	10	.5

Appendix

Code	Name	Amount	Unit	Grams	Kilocalories	Carbohydrates (g)	Protein (g)	Fat (g)
11370	POTATOES, HASHED BROWN	½	CUP	78.0	119	6	2	11
11657	POTATOES, MASHED, HOME-PREPARED	½	CUP	105.0	81	18	2	1
11671	POTATOES, O'BRIEN, HOME-PREPARED	½	CUP	97.0	79	15	2	1
11844	POTATOES, SCALLOPED	½	CUP	122.5	105	13	4	5
19047	PRETZELS, HARD, PLAIN, SALTED	1	OUNCE	28.4	108	22	3	1
19814	PRETZELS, HARD, PLAIN, UNSALTED	1	OUNCE	28.4	108	22	3	1
19050	PRETZELS, HARD, WHOLE-WHEAT	1	OUNCE	28.4	103	23	3	1
9294	PRUNE JUICE, CND	¾	CUP	191.8	136	33	1	0
9289	PRUNES, DEHYDRATED	¼	CUP	33.0	112	29	1	0
9293	PRUNES, DRIED, STEWED, W/ADDED SUGAR	¼	CUP	59.5	74	20	1	0
9292	PRUNES, DRIED, STEWED, W/O ADDED SUGAR	¼	CUP	53.0	57	15	1	0
9291	PRUNES, DRIED, UNCOOKED	¼	CUP	40.3	96	25	1	0
11429	RADISHES, FRESH	½	CUP	58.0	10	2	0	0
11431	RADISHES, ORIENTAL, CKD	½	CUP	73.5	12	3	0	0
11432	RADISHES, ORIENTAL, DRIED	½	CUP	58.0	157	37	5	0
11430	RADISHES, ORIENTAL, FRESH	½	CUP	44.0	8	2	0	0
9297	RAISINS, GOLDEN SEEDLESS	½	CUP	72.5	219	58	2	0
9299	RAISINS, SEEDED	½	CUP	72.5	215	57	2	0
9298	RAISINS, SEEDLESS	½	CUP	72.5	218	57	2	0
9302	RASPBERRIES, FRESH	½	CUP	61.5	30	7	1	0
9306	RASPBERRIES, FROZEN RED, SWEETENED	½	CUP	125.0	129	33	1	0
62536	RAVIOLI, BEEF	1	CUP	243.9	230	36	9	5
62537	RAVIOLI, CHEESE	1	CUP	243.9	220	38	9	3
62557	RED BEANS AND RICE	2	OUNCE	56.7	189	40	8	1
19051	RICE CAKES, BROWN RICE, PLAIN	1	CAKE	9.0	35	7	1	0
19816	RICE CAKES, BROWN RICE, PLAIN, UNSALTED	1	CAKE	9.0	35	7	1	0
19193	RICE PUDDING	1	CUP	298.1	486	66	6	22
20037	RICE, BROWN, LONG-GRAIN, CKD	½	CUP	97.5	108	22	3	1
20045	RICE, WHITE, LONG-GRAIN, CKD	½	CUP	79.0	103	22	2	0
20049	RICE, WHITE, LONG-GRAIN, INSTANT, ENRICHED	½	CUP	82.5	81	18	2	0
20053	RICE, WHITE, SHORT-GRAIN, CKD	½	CUP	93.0	121	27	2	0
20057	RICE, WHITE, W/PASTA, CKD	½	CUP	101.0	123	22	3	3
15232	ROUGHY, ORANGE, CKD, DRY HEAT	3	OUNCE	85.1	76	0	16	1
62541	SALAD DRESSING, BLUE CHEESE	2	TBSP.	32.0	90	5	1	7
62542	SALAD DRESSING, BLUE CHEESE, FAT FREE	2	TBSP.	35.0	50	12	1	0
4120	SALAD DRESSING, FRENCH	2	TBSP.	31.3	134	5	0	13
62545	SALAD DRESSING, FRENCH, FAT FREE	2	TBSP.	35.0	50	12	0	0
4020	SALAD DRESSING, FRENCH, LO FAT	2	TBSP.	32.5	44	7	0	2
4114	SALAD DRESSING, ITALIAN	2	TBSP.	29.4	137	3	0	14
62543	SALAD DRESSING, ITALIAN, FAT FREE	2	TBSP.	31.0	10	2	0	0
4021	SALAD DRESSING, ITALIAN, LO CAL	2	TBSP.	30.0	32	1	0	3
62539	SALAD DRESSING, RANCH	2	TBSP.	29.0	170	2	0	18
62540	SALAD DRESSING, RANCH, FAT FREE	2	TBSP.	35.0	50	11	0	0
4015	SALAD DRESSING, RUSSIAN	2	TBSP.	30.7	151	3	0	16
4022	SALAD DRESSING, RUSSIAN, LOW CAL	2	TBSP.	32.5	46	9	0	1
4016	SALAD DRESSING, SESAME SEED	2	TBSP.	30.7	136	3	1	14
4017	SALAD DRESSING, THOUSAND ISLAND	2	TBSP.	31.3	118	5	0	11
4023	SALAD DRESSING, THOUSAND ISLAND, LO CAL	2	TBSP.	30.7	49	5	0	3
62544	SALAD DRESSING, THOUSAND ISLAND, FAT FREE	2	TBSP.	35.0	45	11	0	0
4135	SALAD DRESSING, VINEGAR AND OIL	2	TBSP.	31.3	140	1	0	16
15209	SALMON, ATLANTIC, WILD, CKD, DRY HEAT	3	OUNCE	85.1	155	0	22	7
15212	SALMON, PINK, CKD, DRY HEAT	3	OUNCE	85.1	127	0	22	4
62546	SALSA	2	TBSP.	33.0	20	5	0	0
15088	SARDINE, ATLANTIC, CND IN OIL	3	OUNCE	85.1	177	0	21	10
6313	SAUCE, WHITE	½	CUP	131.9	120	11	5	7
11439	SAUERKRAUT, CND, SOL & LIQ	½	CUP	118.0	22	5	1	0
7003	SAUSAGE, BEERWURST, PORK	1	SLICE	23.0	55	0	3	4
7006	SAUSAGE, BOCKWURST	1	LINK	65.0	200	0	9	18
7013	SAUSAGE, BRATWURST	1	LINK	85.0	256	2	12	22
7089	SAUSAGE, ITALIAN, CKD	1	LINK	83.0	268	1	17	21

Saturated Fat (g)	Monounsaturated Fat (g)	Polyunsaturated Fat (g)	Fiber (g)	Cholesterol (g)	Folate (g)	Vitamin A (RE)	Vitamin B6 (mg)	Vitamin B12 (μg)	Vitamin C (mg)	Vitamin E (mg)	Riboflavin (mg)	Thiamin (mg)	Calcium (mg)	Iron (mg)	Magnesium (mg)	Niacin (mg)	Phosphorus (mg)	Potassium (mg)	Sodium (mg)	Zinc (mg)
4	5	1	2	-	6	0	.2	0	4	-	0	.1	6	.6	16	1.6	33	250	19	.2
0	0	0	2	2	9	20	.2	0	7	-	0	.1	27	.3	19	1.2	50	314	318	.3
1	0	0	-	4	8	55	.2	0	16	-	.1	.1	35	.5	17	1	49	258	210	.3
2	2	1	-	7	11	23	.2	0	13	-	.1	.1	70	.7	23	1.3	77	463	410	.5
0	0	0	1	0	24	0	0	0	0	-	.2	.1	10	1.2	10	1.5	32	41	486	.2
0	0	0	1	0	24	0	0	0	0	-	.2	.1	10	1.2	10	1.5	32	41	82	.2
0	0	0	-	0	15	–0	.1	0	0	-	.1	.1	8	.8	9	1.9	35	122	58	.2
0	0	0	2	0	1	0	.4	0	8	-	.1	0	23	2.3	27	1.5	48	529	8	.4
0	0	0	-	0	1	58	.2	0	0	-	.1	0	24	1.2	21	1	37	349	2	.2
0	0	0	2	0	0	17	.1	0	2	-	.1	0	12	.6	11	.4	20	186	1	.1
0	0	0	3	0	0	16	.1	0	2	-	.1	0	12	.6	11	.4	19	177	1	.1
0	0	0	3	0	1	80	.1	0	1	-	.1	0	21	1	18	.8	32	300	2	.2
0	0	0	1	0	16	1	0	0	13	-	0	0	12	.2	5	.2	10	135	14	.2
0	0	0	1	0	13	0	0	0	11	-	0	0	12	.1	7	.1	18	209	10	.1
0	0	0	-	0	171	0	.4	0	0	-	.4	.2	365	3.9	99	2	118	2027	161	1.2
0	0	0	1	0	12	0	0	0	10	-	0	0	12	.2	7	.1	10	100	9	.1
0	0	0	3	0	2	3	.2	0	2	-	.1	0	38	1.3	25	.8	83	541	9	.2
0	0	0	5	0	2	0	.1	0	4	-	.1	.1	20	1.9	22	.8	54	598	20	.1
0	0	0	3	0	2	1	.2	0	2	-	.1	.1	36	1.5	24	.6	70	544	9	.2
0	0	0	4	0	16	8	0	0	15	.2	.1	0	14	.4	11	.6	7	93	0	.3
0	0	0	5	0	32	7	0	0	21	-	.1	0	19	.8	16	.3	21	142	1	.2
2	-	-	4	20	-	150	-	-	2	-	-	-	0	1.5	-	-	-	-	1150	-
1	-	-	4	15	-	60	-	-	1	-	-	-	24	1.5	-	-	-	-	1280	-
0	-	-	7	0	-	99	-	-	6	-	-	.2	48	1.5	-	2.8	-	-	786	-
0	0	0	0	0	2	0	0	0	0	-	0	0	1	.1	12	.7	32	26	29	.3
0	0	0	0	0	2	0	0	0	0	-	0	0	1	.1	12	.7	32	26	2	.3
3	10	8	-	3	9	104	.1	.6	1	-	.2	.1	155	.9	24	.5	203	179	253	1.5
0	0	0	2	0	4	0	.1	0	0	-	0	.1	10	.4	42	1.5	81	42	5	.6
0	0	0	0	0	2	0	.1	0	0	-	0	.1	8	.9	9	1.2	34	28	1	.4
0	0	0	0	0	3	0	0	0	0	-	0	.1	7	.5	4	.7	12	3	2	.2
0	0	0	-	0	2	0	.1	0	0	-	0	.2	1	1.4	7	1.4	31	24	0	.4
1	1	1	4	1	7	0	.1	.1	0	-	.1	.1	8	.9	12	1.8	37	42	574	.3
0	1	0	0	22	7	20	.3	2	0	-	.2	-	-	-	-	-	-	-	30	-
4	-	-	0	10	-	0	-	-	0	-	-	-	24	0	-	-	-	-	470	-
0	-	-	0	0	-	0	-	-	0	.4	-	-	0	0	-	-	-	-	340	-
3	3	7	0	18	1	6	0	0	0	1.6	0	0	3	.1	0	0	4	25	428	0
0	-	-	0	0	-	100	-	-	0	-	-	-	0	0	-	-	-	-	300	-
0	0	1	0	2	0	0	0	0	0	.3	0	0	4	.1	0	0	5	26	256	.1
2	3	8	0	0	1	7	0	0	0	1.5	0	0	3	.1	0	0	1	4	231	0
0	-	-	0	0	-	0	-	-	0	-	-	-	0	0	-	-	-	-	290	-
0	1	2	0	2	0	0	0	0	0	.3	0	0	1	.1	0	0	2	5	236	0
3	-	-	0	5	-	0	-	-	0	-	-	-	0	0	-	-	-	-	270	-
0	-	-	0	0	-	0	-	-	0	.6	-	-	0	0	-	-	-	-	310	-
2	4	9	0	6	3	63	0	.1	2	1.8	0	0	6	.2	0	.2	11	48	266	.1
0	0	1	0	2	1	5	0	0	2	.1	0	0	6	.2	0	0	12	51	282	0
2	4	8	-	0	0	63	0	0	0	1.5	0	0	6	.2	0	0	11	48	307	0
2	3	6	1	8	2	30	0	.1	0	1.3	0	0	3	.2	1	0	5	35	219	0
0	1	2	0	5	2	29	0	.1	0	.3	0	0	3	.2	0	0	5	35	307	0
0	-	-	0	0	-	0	-	-	0	-	-	-	0	0	-	-	-	-	300	-
3	5	8	0	0	0	0	0	0	0	1.3	0	0	0	0	0	0	0	2	0	0
1	2	3	0	60	25	11	.8	2.6	0	-	.4	.2	13	.9	31	8.6	218	534	48	.7
1	1	1	0	57	4	35	.2	2.9	0	-	.1	.2	14	.8	28	7.3	251	352	73	.6
0	-	-	0	0	-	80	-	-	4	-	-	-	0	0	-	-	-	-	240	-
1	3	4	0	121	10	57	.1	7.6	0	-	.2	.1	325	2.5	33	4.5	417	338	430	1.1
3	2	1	-	17	8	46	0	.5	1	-	.2	0	212	.1	132	.3	128	222	398	.3
0	0	0	3	0	28	2	.2	0	17	-	0	0	35	1.7	15	.2	24	201	780	.2
1	2	1	0	14	1	0	.1	.2	7	-	0	.1	2	.2	3	.7	24	58	285	.4
7	8	2	0	38	4	4	.1	.5	0	-	.1	.3	10	.4	12	2.7	95	176	718	1
8	10	2	0	51	2	0	.2	.8	1	-	.2	.4	37	1.1	13	2.7	127	180	473	2
8	10	3	0	65	4	0	.3	1.1	2	-	.2	.5	20	1.2	15	3.5	141	252	765	2

Food Composition Table **323**

Appendix

Code	Name	Amount	Unit	Grams	Kilocalories	Carbohydrates (g)	Protein (g)	Fat (g)
7037	SAUSAGE, KIELBASA, KOLBASSY	1	LINK	85.0	264	2	11	23
7038	SAUSAGE, KNOCKWURST	1	LINK	68.0	209	1	8	19
7075	SAUSAGE, LINK, PORK AND BEEF	1	LINK	68.0	228	1	9	21
16107	SAUSAGE, MEATLESS	1	LINK	25.0	64	2	5	5
7057	SAUSAGE, PEPPERONI	1	SLICE	5.5	27	0	1	2
7059	SAUSAGE, POLISH-STYLE	1	EACH	227.0	740	4	32	65
7064	SAUSAGE, PORK, LINKS OR BULK, CKD	1	LINK	13.0	48	0	3	4
7072	SAUSAGE, SALAMI, BEEF AND PORK, DRY	1	SLICE	10.0	42	0	2	3
7068	SAUSAGE, SALAMI, BEEF, CKD	1	SLICE	23.0	60	1	3	5
7074	SAUSAGE, SMOKED LINK, PORK	1	LINK	68.0	265	1	15	22
15092	SEA BASS, CKD, DRY HEAT	3	OUNCE	85.1	105	0	20	2
12036	SEEDS, SUNFLOWER, DRIED	½	CUP	72.0	410	14	16	36
12537	SEEDS, SUNFLOWER, DRY ROASTED, W/SALT ADDED	½	CUP	64.0	372	15	12	32
12538	SEEDS, SUNFLOWER, OIL ROASTED, W/SALT ADDED	½	CUP	67.5	415	10	14	39
12539	SEEDS, SUNFLOWER, TOASTED, W/SALT ADDED	½	CUP	67.0	415	14	12	38
14346	SHAKE, CHOCOLATE	1	CUP	226.4	288	46	8	8
14428	SHAKE, STRAWBERRY	1	CUP	226.4	256	43	8	6
14347	SHAKE, VANILLA	1	CUP	226.4	251	41	8	7
11640	SHALLOTS, FREEZE-DRIED	½	CUP	7.2	25	6	1	0
11677	SHALLOTS, FRESH	½	CUP	79.9	58	13	2	0
19097	SHERBET, ALL FLAVORS	1	CUP	192.0	265	58	2	4
15150	SHRIMP, CKD, BREADED AND FRIED	3	OUNCE	85.1	206	10	18	10
15151	SHRIMP, CKD, MOIST HEAT	3	OUNCE	85.1	84	0	18	1
15149	SHRIMP, FRESH	3	OUNCE	85.1	90	1	17	1
15102	SNAPPER, CKD, DRY HEAT	3	OUNCE	85.1	109	0	22	1
62599	SORBET, ALL FLAVORS	½	CUP	90.0	100	25	0	0
6474	SOUP, BEAN W/BACON	1	CUP	264.9	106	16	5	2
6007	SOUP, BEAN W/HAM	1	CUP	243.0	231	27	13	9
6406	SOUP, BEAN W/HOT DOGS	1	CUP	250.0	187	22	10	7
6404	SOUP, BEAN W/PORK	1	CUP	253.0	172	23	8	6
6008	SOUP, BEEF BROTH OR BOUILLON	1	CUP	240.0	17	0	3	1
6547	SOUP, BEEF MUSHROOM	1	CUP	244.0	73	6	6	3
6409	SOUP, BEEF NOODLE	1	CUP	244.0	83	9	5	3
6070	SOUP, BEEF, CHUNKY	1	CUP	240.0	170	20	12	5
6402	SOUP, BLACK BEAN	1	CUP	247.0	116	20	6	2
6478	SOUP, CAULIFLOWER	1	CUP	256.1	69	11	3	2
6411	SOUP, CHEESE	1	CUP	247.0	156	11	5	10
6480	SOUP, CHICKEN BROTH OR BOUILLON	1	CUP	244.0	22	1	1	1
6417	SOUP, CHICKEN GUMBO	1	CUP	244.0	56	8	3	1
6549	SOUP, CHICKEN MUSHROOM	1	CUP	244.0	132	9	4	9
6419	SOUP, CHICKEN NOODLE	1	CUP	241.0	75	9	4	2
6018	SOUP, CHICKEN NOODLE, CHUNKY	1	CUP	240.0	175	17	13	6
6485	SOUP, CHICKEN RICE	1	CUP	252.8	61	9	2	1
6022	SOUP, CHICKEN RICE, CHUNKY	1	CUP	240.0	127	13	12	3
6425	SOUP, CHICKEN VEGETABLE	1	CUP	241.0	75	9	4	3
6024	SOUP, CHICKEN VEGETABLE, CHUNKY	1	CUP	240.0	166	19	12	5
6412	SOUP, CHICKEN W/DUMPLINGS	1	CUP	241.0	96	6	6	6
6423	SOUP, CHICKEN W/RICE	1	CUP	241.0	60	7	4	2
6015	SOUP, CHICKEN, CHUNKY	1	CUP	251.0	178	17	13	7
6426	SOUP, CHILI BEEF	1	CUP	250.0	170	21	7	7
6027	SOUP, CLAM CHOWDER, MANHATTAN STYLE	1	CUP	240.0	134	19	7	3
6230	SOUP, CLAM CHOWDER, NEW ENGLAND	1	CUP	248.0	164	17	9	7
6034	SOUP, CRAB	1	CUP	244.0	76	10	5	2
6201	SOUP, CREAM OF ASPARAGUS	1	CUP	248.0	161	16	6	8
6210	SOUP, CREAM OF CELERY	1	CUP	248.0	164	15	6	10
6216	SOUP, CREAM OF CHICKEN	1	CUP	248.0	191	15	7	11
6243	SOUP, CREAM OF MUSHROOM	1	CUP	248.0	203	15	6	14
6246	SOUP, CREAM OF ONION	1	CUP	248.0	186	18	7	9
6253	SOUP, CREAM OF POTATO	1	CUP	248.0	149	17	6	6
6256	SOUP, CREAM OF SHRIMP	1	CUP	248.0	164	14	7	9

Food Composition Table

Saturated Fat (g)	Monounsaturated Fat (g)	Polyunsaturated Fat (g)	Fiber (g)	Cholesterol (g)	Folate (g)	Vitamin A (RE)	Vitamin B_6 (mg)	Vitamin B_12 (μg)	Vitamin C (mg)	Vitamin E (mg)	Riboflavin (mg)	Thiamin (mg)	Calcium (mg)	Iron (mg)	Magnesium (mg)	Niacin (mg)	Phosphorus (mg)	Potassium (mg)	Sodium (mg)	Zinc (mg)
8	11	3	0	57	4	0	.2	1.4	18	-	.2	.2	37	1.2	14	2.4	126	230	915	1.7
7	9	2	0	39	1	0	.1	.8	18	-	.1	.2	7	.6	7	1.9	67	135	687	1.1
7	10	2	0	48	1	0	.1	1	13	-	.1	.2	7	1	8	2.2	73	129	643	1.4
1	1	2	1	0	7	16	.2	0	0	-	.1	.6	16	.9	9	2.8	56	58	222	.4
1	1	0	0	4	0	0	0	.1	0	-	0	0	1	.1	1	.3	7	19	112	.1
23	31	7	0	159	5	0	.4	2.2	2	-	.3	1.1	27	3.3	32	7.8	309	538	1989	4.4
1	2	0	0	11	0	0	0	.2	0	-	0	.1	4	.2	2	.6	24	47	168	.3
1	2	0	0	8	0	0	.1	.2	3	-	0	.1	1	.2	2	.5	14	38	186	.3
2	2	0	0	15	0	0	0	.7	4	-	0	0	2	.5	3	.7	26	52	270	.5
8	10	3	0	46	3	0	.2	1.1	1	-	.2	.5	20	.8	13	3.1	110	228	1020	1.9
1	0	1	0	45	5	54	.4	.3	0	-	.1	.1	11	.3	45	1.6	211	279	74	.4
4	7	24	8	0	164	4	.6	0	1	-	.2	1.6	84	4.9	255	3.2	508	496	2	3.6
3	6	21	4	0	152	0	.5	0	1	-	.2	.1	45	2.4	83	4.5	739	544	499	3.4
4	7	26	5	0	158	3	.5	0	1	-	.2	.2	38	4.5	86	2.8	769	326	407	3.5
4	7	25	-	0	159	0	.5	0	1	-	.2	.2	38	4.6	86	2.8	776	329	411	3.6
5	2	0	-	29	8	52	.1	.8	1	-	.6	.1	256	.7	38	.4	231	453	220	.9
4	-	-	-	25	7	66	.1	.7	2	-	.4	.1	256	.2	29	.4	226	412	188	.8
4	2	0	-	25	7	72	.1	.8	2	-	.4	.1	276	.2	27	.4	231	394	186	.8
0	0	0	-	0	8	404	.1	0	3	-	0	0	13	.4	7	.1	21	119	4	.1
0	0	0	-	0	27	998	.3	0	6	-	0	0	30	1	17	.2	48	267	10	.3
2	1	0	-	10	8	27	.1	.2	8	-	.1	0	104	.3	15	.2	77	184	88	.9
2	3	4	-	151	7	48	.1	1.6	1	-	.1	.1	57	1.1	34	2.6	185	191	293	1.2
0	0	0	0	166	3	56	.1	1.3	2	-	0	0	33	2.6	29	2.2	117	155	191	1.3
0	0	1	0	129	3	46	.1	1	2	-	0	0	44	2	31	2.2	174	157	126	.9
0	0	1	0	40	5	30	.4	3	1	-	0	0	34	.2	31	.3	171	444	48	.4
0	-	-	1	0	-	0	-	-	12	-	-	-	0	0	-	-	-	-	10	-
1	1	0	9	3	8	5	0	0	1	-	.3	.1	56	1.3	29	.4	90	326	927	.7
3	4	1	11	22	29	396	.1	.1	4	-	.1	.1	78	3.2	46	1.7	143	425	972	1.1
2	3	2	-	12	30	87	.1	.1	1	-	.1	.1	87	2.3	47	1	165	477	1092	1.2
2	2	2	9	3	32	89	0	.1	2	-	0	.1	81	2	46	.6	132	402	951	1
0	0	0	0	0	5	0	0	.2	0	-	.1	0	14	.4	5	1.9	31	130	782	0
1	1	0	-	7	10	0	0	.2	5	-	.1	0	5	.9	10	1	34	154	942	1.5
1	1	0	1	5	4	63	0	.2	0	-	.1	.1	15	1.1	5	1.1	46	100	952	1.5
3	2	0	1	14	13	262	.1	.6	7	-	.2	.1	31	2.3	5	2.7	120	336	866	2.6
0	1	0	4	0	25	49	.1	0	1	-	.1	.1	44	2.1	42	.5	106	274	1198	1.4
0	1	1	-	0	3	0	0	.2	3	-	.1	.1	10	.5	3	.5	51	105	843	.3
7	3	0	-	30	5	109	0	0	0	-	.1	0	141	.7	5	.4	136	153	958	.6
0	0	0	0	0	2	12	0	0	0	-	0	0	15	.1	5	.2	12	24	1484	0
0	1	0	2	5	15	0	.1	0	5	-	0	0	24	.9	5	.7	24	76	954	.4
2	4	2	-	10	0	112	0	0	0	-	.1	0	29	.9	10	1.6	27	154	942	1
1	1	1	1	7	2	72	0	.1	0	-	.1	.1	17	.8	5	1.4	36	55	1106	.4
1	3	2	4	19	5	122	0	.3	0	-	.2	.1	24	1.4	10	4.3	72	108	850	1
0	1	0	1	3	1	0	0	.1	0	-	0	0	8	0	0	.4	10	10	981	.1
1	1	1	1	12	4	586	0	.3	4	-	.1	0	34	1.9	10	4.1	72	108	888	1
1	1	1	1	10	5	265	0	.1	1	-	.1	0	17	.9	7	1.2	41	154	945	.4
1	2	1	-	17	12	600	.1	.2	6	-	.2	0	26	1.5	10	3.3	106	367	1068	2.2
1	3	1	1	34	2	53	0	.2	0	-	.1	0	14	.6	5	1.8	60	116	860	.4
0	1	0	1	7	1	65	0	.1	0	-	0	0	17	.7	0	1.1	22	101	815	.3
2	3	1	2	30	5	131	.1	.3	1	-	.2	.1	25	1.7	8	4.4	113	176	889	1
3	3	0	9	12	17	150	.2	.3	4	-	.1	.1	42	2.1	30	1.1	147	525	1035	1.4
2	1	0	3	14	9	329	.3	7.9	12	-	.1	.1	67	2.6	19	1.8	84	384	1001	1.7
3	2	1	1	22	10	40	.1	10.2	3	-	.2	.1	186	1.5	22	1	156	300	992	.8
0	1	0	1	10	15	51	.1	.2	0	-	.1	.2	66	1.2	15	1.3	88	327	1235	1.5
3	2	2	1	22	30	84	.1	.5	4	-	.3	.1	174	.9	20	.9	154	360	1042	.9
4	2	3	1	32	8	67	.1	.5	1	-	.2	.1	186	.7	22	.4	151	310	1009	.2
5	4	2	0	27	8	94	.1	.5	1	-	.3	.1	181	.7	17	.9	151	273	1047	.7
5	3	5	0	20	10	37	.1	.5	2	-	.3	.1	179	.6	20	.9	156	270	1076	.6
4	3	2	1	32	12	67	.1	.5	2	-	.3	.1	179	.7	22	.6	154	310	1004	.6
4	2	1	0	22	9	67	.1	.5	1	-	.2	.1	166	.5	17	.6	161	322	1061	.7
6	3	0	0	35	10	55	.4	1	1	-	.2	.1	164	.6	22	.5	146	248	1037	.8

Code	Name	Amount	Unit	Grams	Kilocalories	Carbohydrates (g)	Protein (g)	Fat (g)
6501	SOUP, CREAM OF VEGETABLE	1	CUP	260.1	107	12	2	6
6036	SOUP, GAZPACHO	1	CUP	244.0	56	1	9	2
6037	SOUP, LENTIL W/HAM	1	CUP	248.0	139	20	9	3
6440	SOUP, MINESTRONE	1	CUP	241.0	82	11	4	3
6039	SOUP, MINESTRONE, CHUNKY	1	CUP	240.0	127	21	5	3
6493	SOUP, MUSHROOM	1	CUP	253.0	96	11	2	5
6445	SOUP, ONION	1	CUP	241.0	58	8	4	2
6249	SOUP, PEA, GREEN	1	CUP	254.0	239	32	13	7
6451	SOUP, PEA, SPLIT W/HAM	1	CUP	253.0	190	28	10	4
6050	SOUP, PEA, SPLIT W/HAM, CHUNKY	1	CUP	240.0	185	27	11	4
6359	SOUP, TOMATO	1	CUP	248.0	161	22	6	6
6461	SOUP, TOMATO BEEF W/NOODLE	1	CUP	244.0	139	21	4	4
6463	SOUP, TOMATO RICE	1	CUP	247.0	119	22	2	3
6499	SOUP, TOMATO VEGETABLE	1	CUP	253.0	56	10	2	1
6465	SOUP, TURKEY NOODLE	1	CUP	244.0	68	9	4	2
6466	SOUP, TURKEY VEGETABLE	1	CUP	241.0	72	9	3	3
6064	SOUP, TURKEY, CHUNKY	1	CUP	236.0	135	14	10	4
6500	SOUP, VEGETABLE BEEF	1	CUP	253.1	53	8	3	1
6067	SOUP, VEGETABLE, CHUNKY	1	CUP	240.0	122	19	4	4
6468	SOUP, VEGETARIAN VEGETABLE	1	CUP	241.0	72	12	2	2
1056	SOUR CREAM	1	TBSP.	12.0	26	1	0	3
62556	SOUR CREAM, FAT FREE	1	TBSP.	16.0	13	3	1	0
1074	SOUR CREAM, IMITATION, NONDAIRY, CULTURED	1	TBSP.	14.4	30	1	0	3
62555	SOUR CREAM, LIGHT	1	TBSP.	16.0	16	1	1	1
6134	SOY SAUCE	1	TBSP.	18.0	10	2	1	0
11455	SPAGHETTI SAUCE	½	CUP	124.5	136	20	2	6
11458	SPINACH, CKD	½	CUP	90.0	21	3	3	0
11461	SPINACH, CND, DRAINED SOLIDS	½	CUP	107.0	25	4	3	1
11457	SPINACH, FRESH	1	CUP	56.0	12	2	2	0
11464	SPINACH, FRZ, CKD	½	CUP	95.0	27	5	3	0
11642	SQUASH, SUMMER, CKD	½	CUP	90.0	18	4	1	0
11641	SQUASH, SUMMER, FRESH	½	CUP	65.0	13	3	1	0
11644	SQUASH, WINTER, BAKED	½	CUP	102.5	40	9	1	1
11643	SQUASH, WINTER, FRESH	½	CUP	58.0	21	5	1	0
11953	SQUASH, ZUCCHINI, BABY, FRESH	1	MEDIUM	11.0	2	0	0	0
9316	STRAWBERRIES, FRESH	½	CUP	74.5	22	5	0	0
9320	STRAWBERRIES, FROZEN, SWEETENED	½	CUP	127.5	122	33	1	0
9318	STRAWBERRIES, FROZEN, UNSWEETENED	½	CUP	74.5	26	7	0	0
11508	SWEET POTATOES, BAKED IN SKIN	½	CUP	100.0	103	24	2	0
11510	SWEET POTATOES, BOILED, W/O SKIN	½	CUP	164.0	172	40	3	0
11659	SWEET POTATOES, CANDIED	½	CUP	113.4	155	32	1	4
11514	SWEET POTATOES, MASHED	½	CUP	127.5	129	30	3	0
11511	SWORDFISH, CDK, DRY HEAT	3	OUNCE	85.1	132	0	22	4
19348	SYRUP, CHOCOLATE, FUDGE-TYPE	1	TBSP.	21.0	73	12	1	3
19349	SYRUP, CORN, DARK	1	TBSP.	20.0	56	15	0	0
19351	SYRUP, CORN, HIGH-FRUCTOSE	1	TBSP.	19.0	53	14	0	0
19350	SYRUP, CORN, LIGHT	1	TBSP.	20.0	56	15	0	0
19353	SYRUP, MAPLE	1	TBSP.	20.0	52	13	0	0
19128	SYRUP, PANCAKE, LO CAL	1	TBSP.	20.0	33	9	0	0
19360	SYRUP, PANCAKE, W/2% MAPLE	1	TBSP.	20.0	53	14	0	0
19113	SYRUP, PANCAKE, W/BUTTER	1	TBSP.	20.0	59	15	0	0
18360	TACO SHELLS, BAKED	1	MEDIUM	13.0	61	8	1	3
9221	TANGERINE JUICE, FRESH	¾	CUP	185.2	80	19	1	0
9219	TANGERINES, CND, JUICE PACK	½	CUP	124.5	46	12	1	0
9220	TANGERINES, CND, LIGHT SYRUP PACK	½	CUP	126.0	77	20	1	0
9218	TANGERINES, FRESH	1	MEDIUM	84.0	37	9	1	0
19218	TAPIOCA PUDDING	1	CUP	298.1	355	58	6	11
6112	TERIYAKI SAUCE	1	TBSP.	18.0	15	3	1	0
16126	TOFU, FRESH, FIRM	1	OUNCE	28.4	41	1	4	2
16127	TOFU, FRESH, REGULAR	1	OUNCE	28.4	22	1	2	1

Food Composition Table

Saturated Fat (g)	Monounsaturated Fat (g)	Polyunsaturated Fat (g)	Fiber (g)	Cholesterol (g)	Folate (g)	Vitamin A (RE)	Vitamin B₆ (mg)	Vitamin B₁₂ (µg)	Vitamin C (mg)	Vitamin E (mg)	Riboflavin (mg)	Thiamin (mg)	Calcium (mg)	Iron (mg)	Magnesium (mg)	Niacin (mg)	Phosphorus (mg)	Potassium (mg)	Sodium (mg)	Zinc (mg)
1	3	1	1	0	8	3	0	.1	4	-	.1	1.2	31	.5	10	.5	55	96	1170	.3
0	1	1	4	0	10	20	.1	0	3	-	0	0	24	1	7	.9	37	224	1183	.2
1	1	0	-	7	50	35	.2	.3	4	-	.1	.2	42	2.7	22	1.4	184	357	1319	.7
1	1	1	1	2	16	234	.1	0	1	-	0	.1	34	.9	7	.9	55	313	911	.7
1	1	0	2	5	31	434	.2	0	5	-	.1	.1	60	1.8	14	1.2	110	612	864	1.4
1	2	2	1	0	5	0	0	.3	1	-	.1	.3	66	.5	5	.5	76	200	1020	.1
0	1	1	1	0	15	0	0	0	1	-	0	0	27	.7	2	.6	12	67	1053	.6
4	2	1	3	18	8	58	.1	.4	3	-	.3	.2	173	2	56	1.3	239	376	1046	1.8
2	2	1	-	8	3	46	.1	.3	2	-	.1	.1	23	2.3	48	1.5	213	400	1007	1.3
2	2	1	4	7	5	487	.2	.2	7	-	.1	.1	34	2.1	38	2.5	178	305	965	3.1
3	2	1	0	17	21	109	.2	.4	68	-	.2	.1	159	1.8	22	1.5	149	449	932	.3
2	2	1	1	5	7	54	.1	.2	0	-	.1	.1	17	1.1	7	1.9	56	220	917	.8
1	1	1	1	2	14	77	.1	0	15	-	0	.1	22	.8	5	1.1	35	331	815	.5
0	0	0	1	0	10	20	.1	0	6	-	0	.1	8	.6	20	.8	30	104	1146	.2
1	1	0	1	5	2	29	0	.1	0	-	.1	.1	12	1	5	1.4	49	76	815	.6
1	1	1	0	2	5	243	0	.2	0	-	0	0	17	.8	5	1	41	176	906	.6
1	2	1	-	9	11	715	.3	2.1	6	-	.1	0	50	1.9	24	3.6	104	361	923	2.1
1	0	0	1	0	8	23	.1	.3	1	-	0	0	13	.9	23	.5	35	76	1002	.3
1	2	1	1	0	17	588	.2	0	6	-	.1	.1	55	1.6	7	1.2	72	396	1010	3.1
0	1	1	0	0	11	301	.1	0	1	-	0	.1	22	1.1	7	.9	34	210	822	.5
2	1	0	0	5	1	23	0	0	0	-	0	0	14	0	1	0	10	17	6	0
0	-	-	-	3	-	30	-	-	0	-	-	-	36	0	-	-	-	-	18	-
3	0	0	0	0	0	0	0	0	0	-	0	0	0	.1	1	0	6	23	15	.2
1	-	-	-	5	-	18	-	-	0	-	-	-	22	0	-	-	-	27	9	-
0	0	0	0	0	0	3	0	0	0	-	0	0	3	.4	6	.6	20	32	1029	.1
1	3	2	4	0	27	153	.4	0	14	-	.1	.1	35	.8	30	1.9	45	478	618	.3
0	0	0	2	0	131	737	.2	0	9	-	.2	.1	122	3.2	78	.4	50	419	63	.7
0	0	0	-	0	105	939	.1	0	15	-	.1	0	136	2.5	81	.4	47	370	29	.5
0	0	0	2	0	109	376	.1	0	16	-	.1	0	55	1.5	44	.4	27	312	44	.3
0	0	0	3	0	102	739	.1	0	12	-	.2	.1	139	1.4	66	.4	46	283	82	.7
0	0	0	1	0	18	26	.1	0	5	-	0	0	24	.3	22	.5	35	173	1	.4
0	0	0	1	0	17	13	.1	0	10	-	0	0	13	.3	15	.4	23	127	1	.2
0	0	0	3	0	29	365	.1	0	10	-	0	.1	14	.3	8	.7	21	448	1	.3
0	0	0	1	0	13	235	0	0	7	-	0	.1	18	.3	12	.5	19	203	2	.1
0	0	0	-	0	2	5	0	0	4	-	0	0	2	.1	4	.1	10	50	0	.1
0	0	0	2	0	13	2	0	0	42	.1	0	0	10	.3	7	.2	14	124	1	.1
0	0	0	2	0	19	3	0	0	53	-	.1	0	14	.8	9	.5	17	125	4	.1
0	0	0	2	0	13	3	0	0	31	.2	0	0	12	.6	8	.3	10	110	1	.1
0	0	0	3	0	23	2182	.2	0	25	-	.1	.1	28	.4	20	.6	55	348	10	.3
0	0	0	4	0	18	2796	.4	0	28	-	.2	.1	34	.9	16	1	44	302	21	.4
2	1	0	-	9	13	475	0	0	8	-	0	0	29	1.3	12	.4	29	214	79	.2
0	0	0	-	0	14	1929	.3	0	7	-	.1	0	38	1.7	31	1.2	66	268	96	.3
1	2	1	0	43	2	35	.3	1.7	1	-	.1	0	5	.9	29	10	287	314	98	1.3
1	1	1	0	3	1	5	0	.1	0	-	0	0	21	.3	10	0	36	45	27	.2
-	-	-	0	0	0	0	0	0	0	-	0	0	4	.1	2	0	7	9	31	0
-	-	-	0	0	0	0	0	0	0	-	0	0	0	0	0	0	0	0	0	0
-	-	-	0	0	0	0	0	0	0	-	0	0	1	0	0	0	0	1	24	0
-	-	-	0	0	0	0	0	0	0	-	0	0	13	.2	3	0	0	41	2	.8
-	-	-	0	0	0	0	0	0	0	-	0	0	0	0	0	0	9	1	40	0
-	-	-	0	0	0	0	0	0	0	-	0	0	1	0	0	0	2	1	12	0
0	0	0	-	1	0	3	0	0	0	-	0	0	0	0	0	0	2	1	20	0
0	1	1	1	0	1	5	0	0	0	-	0	0	21	.3	14	.2	32	23	48	.2
0	0	0	0	0	9	78	.1	0	57	-	0	.1	33	.4	15	.2	26	330	2	.1
0	0	0	1	0	6	106	.1	0	43	-	0	.1	14	.3	14	.6	12	166	6	.6
0	0	0	1	0	6	106	.1	0	25	-	.1	.1	9	.5	10	.6	13	98	8	.3
0	0	0	2	0	17	77	.1	0	26	-	0	.1	12	.1	10	.1	8	132	1	.2
2	5	4	0	3	12	0	.3	.3	2	-	.3	.1	250	.7	24	.9	236	310	352	.8
0	0	0	0	0	4	0	0	0	0	-	0	0	5	.3	11	.2	28	41	690	0
0	1	1	1	0	8	5	0	0	0	-	0	0	58	3	27	.1	54	67	4	.4
0	0	1	0	0	4	3	0	0	0	-	0	0	30	1.5	29	.1	27	34	2	.2

Code	Name	Amount	Unit	Grams	Kilocalories	Carbohydrates (g)	Protein (g)	Fat (g)
16129	TOFU, FRIED	1	OUNCE	28.4	77	3	5	6
11954	TOMATILLOS, FRESH	1	MEDIUM	34.0	11	2	0	0
11540	TOMATO JUICE, CND, W/ SALT	¾	CUP	183.0	31	8	1	0
11886	TOMATO JUICE, CND, W/O SALT	¾	CUP	183.0	31	8	1	0
11533	TOMATOES, CND, STEWED	½	CUP	127.5	33	8	1	0
11537	TOMATOES, CND, W/ GREEN CHILIES	½	CUP	120.5	18	4	1	0
11531	TOMATOES, CND, WHOLE, REG PK	½	CUP	120.0	24	5	1	0
11529	TOMATOES, FRESH	1	MEDIUM	123.0	26	6	1	0
11527	TOMATOES, GREEN, FRESH	1	MEDIUM	123.0	30	6	1	0
11955	TOMATOES, SUN-DRIED	¼	CUP	13.5	35	8	2	0
11956	TOMATOES, SUN-DRIED, PACKED IN OIL	¼	CUP	27.5	59	6	1	4
62538	TORTELLINI, BEEF	1	CUP	257.9	230	46	5	1
19057	TORTILLA CHIPS, NACHO-FLAVOR	1	OUNCE	28.4	141	18	2	7
19424	TORTILLA CHIPS, NACHO-FLAVOR, LIGHT	1	OUNCE	28.4	126	20	2	4
19056	TORTILLA CHIPS, PLAIN	1	OUNCE	28.4	142	18	2	7
19058	TORTILLA CHIPS, RANCH-FLAVOR	1	OUNCE	28.4	139	18	2	7
18363	TORTILLAS, CORN	1	MEDIUM	25.0	56	12	1	1
18364	TORTILLAS, FLOUR	1	MEDIUM	35.0	114	19	3	2
15219	TROUT, CKD, DRY HEAT	3	OUNCE	85.1	162	0	23	7
15241	TROUT, RAINBOW, FARMED, CKD, DRY HEAT	3	OUNCE	85.1	144	0	21	6
15116	TROUT, RAINBOW, WILD, CKD, DRY HEAT	3	OUNCE	85.1	128	0	19	5
15128	TUNA SALAD	3	OUNCE	85.1	159	8	14	8
15183	TUNA, LIGHT MEAT, CND IN OIL	3	OUNCE	85.1	168	0	25	7
15184	TUNA, LIGHT MEAT, CND IN WATER	3	OUNCE	85.1	111	0	25	0
15185	TUNA, WHITE MEAT, CND IN OIL	3	OUNCE	85.1	158	0	23	7
15186	TUNA, WHITE MEAT, CND IN WATER	3	OUNCE	85.1	116	0	23	2
15221	TUNA, YELLOWFIN, CKD, DRY HEAT	3	OUNCE	85.1	118	0	25	1
5297	TURKEY, BOLOGNA	1	SLICE	21.0	42	0	3	3
7079	TURKEY BREAST MEAT	1	SLICE	21.0	23	0	5	0
5287	TURKEY LUNCH MEAT	1	SLICE	28.4	36	0	5	1
5296	TURKEY ROAST, ROASTED	3	OUNCE	85.1	132	3	18	5
5291	TURKEY ROLL, LIGHT AND DARK MEAT	3	OUNCE	85.1	127	2	15	6
5290	TURKEY ROLL, LIGHT MEAT	3	OUNCE	85.1	125	0	16	6
5299	TURKEY SALAMI	1	SLICE	28.4	56	0	5	4
5294	TURKEY THIGH, PREBASTED, MEAT & SKIN, CKD, ROASTED	3	OUNCE	85.1	134	0	16	7
5190	TURKEY, BACK, MEAT & SKIN, CKD, ROASTED	3	OUNCE	85.1	207	0	23	12
5192	TURKEY, BREAST, MEAT & SKIN, CKD, ROASTED	3	OUNCE	85.1	161	0	24	6
5188	TURKEY, DARK MEAT, CKD, ROASTED	3	OUNCE	85.1	159	0	24	6
5184	TURKEY, DARK MEAT, MEAT & SKIN, CKD, ROASTED	3	OUNCE	85.1	188	0	23	10
5306	TURKEY, GROUND, CKD	3	OUNCE	85.1	200	0	23	11
5194	TURKEY, LEG, MEAT & SKIN, CKD, ROASTED	3	OUNCE	85.1	177	0	24	8
5186	TURKEY, LIGHT MEAT, CKD, ROASTED	3	OUNCE	85.1	134	0	25	3
5182	TURKEY, LIGHT MEAT, MEAT & SKIN, CKD, ROASTED	3	OUNCE	85.1	168	0	24	7
5168	TURKEY, MEAT ONLY, CKD, ROASTED	3	OUNCE	85.1	145	0	25	4
5166	TURKEY, MEAT & SKIN, CKD, ROASTED	3	OUNCE	85.1	177	0	24	8
5288	TURKEY, THIN SLICED	3	OUNCE	85.1	94	0	19	1
5196	TURKEY, WING, MEAT & SKIN, CKD, ROASTED	3	OUNCE	85.1	195	0	23	11
11565	TURNIPS, CKD	½	CUP	78.0	14	4	1	0
11564	TURNIPS, FRESH	½	CUP	65.0	18	4	1	0
18328	VANILLA CREAM PIE	1	SLICE	126.0	350	41	6	18
19201	VANILLA PUDDING	1	CUP	298.1	388	65	7	11
17089	VEAL, MEAT AND FAT, CKD	3	OUNCE	85.1	196	0	26	10
17091	VEAL, MEAT ONLY, CKD	3	OUNCE	85.1	167	0	27	6
11578	VEGETABLE JUICE CND	¾	CUP	181.5	34	8	1	0
11581	VEGETABLES, MIXED, CND	½	CUP	81.5	38	8	2	0
11584	VEGETABLES, MIXED, FRZ	½	CUP	91.0	54	12	3	0
18392	WAFFLES, BUTTERMILK	1	EACH	75.0	217	25	6	10
18367	WAFFLES, PLAIN	1	EACH	75.0	218	25	6	11
18403	WAFFLES, PLAIN, FROZEN, TOASTED	1	EACH	33.0	87	13	2	3
15223	WHITEFISH, CKD, DRY HEAT	3	OUNCE	85.1	146	0	21	6

Food Composition Table

Saturated Fat (g)	Monounsaturated Fat (g)	Polyunsaturated Fat (g)	Fiber (g)	Cholesterol (g)	Folate (g)	Vitamin A (RE)	Vitamin B$_6$ (mg)	Vitamin B$_{12}$ (µg)	Vitamin C (mg)	Vitamin E (mg)	Riboflavin (mg)	Thiamin (mg)	Calcium (mg)	Iron (mg)	Magnesium (mg)	Niacin (mg)	Phosphorus (mg)	Potassium (mg)	Sodium (mg)	Zinc (mg)
1	1	3	1	0	8	0	0	0	0	-	0	0	105	1.4	17	0	81	41	5	.6
-	-	-	1	0	2	4	0	0	4	-	0	0	2	.2	7	.6	13	91	0	.1
0	0	0	1	0	36	102	.2	0	33	-	.1	.1	16	1.1	20	1.2	35	403	661	.3
0	0	0	1	0	36	102	.2	0	33	+	.1	.1	16	1.1	20	1.2	35	403	18	.3
0	0	0	+	0	7	70	0	0	17	+	0	.1	42	.9	.15	.9	26	305	324	.2
0	0	0	-	0	11	47	.1	0	7	-	0	0	24	.3	13	.8	17	129	483	.2
0	0	0	1	0	9	72	.1	0	18	-	0	.1	31	.7	14	.9	23	265	196	.2
0	0	0	1	0	18	76	.1	0	23	.4	.1	.1	6	.6	14	.8	30	273	11	.1
0	0	0	2	0	11	79	.1	0	29	-	0	.1	16	.6	12	.6	34	251	16	.1
0	0	0	2	0	9	12	0	0	5	-	.1	.1	15	1.2	26	1.2	48	463	283	.3
1	2	1	-	0	6	35	.1	0	28	-	.1	.1	13	.7	22	1	38	430	73	.2
0	-	-	9	15	-	150	-	-	4	-	-	-	96	1.5	-	-	-	-	770	-
1	4	1	2	1	4	12	.1	0	1	-	.1	0	42	.4	23	.4	69	61	201	.3
1	3	1	-	1	7	12	.1	0	0	-	.1	.1	45	.5	27	.1	90	77	284	-
1	4	1	2	0	3	6	.1	0	0	-	.1	0	44	.4	25	.4	58	56	150	.4
1	4	1	-	0	5	8	.1	0	0	-	.1	0	40	.4	25	.4	68	69	174	.4
0	0	0	1	0	4	6	.1	0	0	-	0	0	44	.4	16	.4	79	39	40	.2
0	1	1	1	0	4	0	0	0	0	-	.1	.2	44	1.2	9	1.3	43	46	167	.2
1	4	2	0	63	13	16	.2	6.4	0	-	.4	.4	47	1.6	24	4.9	267	394	57	.7
2	2	2	0	58	20	73	.3	4.2	3	-	.1	.2	-	.3	27	7.5	226	375	36	.4
1	1	2	0	59	16	13	.3	5.4	2	-	.1	.1	-	.3	26	4.9	229	381	48	.4
1	2	4	0	11	6	23	.1	1	2	-	.1	0	14	.9	16	5.7	151	151	342	.5
1	3	2	0	15	5	20	.1	1.9	0	-	.1	0	11	1.2	26	10.5	265	176	43	.8
0	0	0	0	15	4	20	.3	1.9	0	-	.1	0	10	2.7	25	10.5	158	267	43	.4
1	2	3	0	26	4	20	.4	1.9	0	-	.1	0	3	.6	29	9.9	227	283	43	.4
1	1	1	0	36	3	20	.4	1.9	0	-	0	0	3	.5	29	4.9	227	241	43	.4
0	0	0	0	49	2	17	.9	.5	1	-	0	.4	18	.8	54	10.2	208	484	40	.6
1	1	1	0	21	1	0	0	.1	0	-	0	0	18	.3	3	.7	28	42	184	.4
0	0	0	0	9	1	0	.1	.4	0	-	0	0	1	.1	4	1.7	48	58	301	.2
0	0	0	0	16	2	0	.1	.1	0	-	.1	0	3	.8	5	1	54	92	282	.8
2	1	1	0	45	4	0	.2	1.3	-	-	.1	0	4	1.4	19	5.3	208	253	578	2.2
2	2	2	0	47	4	0	.2	.2	0	-	.2	.1	27	1.1	15	4.1	143	230	498	1.7
2	2	1	0	36	3	0	.3	.2	0	-	.2	.1	34	1.1	14	6	156	213	416	1.3
1	1	1	0	23	1	0	.1	.1	0	-	0	0	6	.5	4	1	30	69	285	.5
2	2	2	0	53	5	0	.2	.2	0	-	.2	.1	7	1.3	14	2	145	205	372	3.5
4	4	3	0	77	7	0	.3	.3	0	-	.2	0	28	1.9	19	2.9	161	221	62	3.3
2	2	2	0	63	5	0	.4	.3	0	-	.1	0	18	1.2	23	5.4	179	245	54	1.7
2	1	2	0	72	8	0	.3	.3	0	-	.2	.1	27	2	20	3.1	174	247	67	3.8
3	3	3	0	76	8	0	.3	.3	0	-	.2	0	28	1.9	20	3	167	233	65	3.5
3	4	3	0	87	6	0	.3	.3	0	-	.1	0	21	1.6	20	4.1	167	230	91	2.4
3	2	2	0	72	8	0	.3	.3	0	-	.2	.1	27	2	20	3	169	238	65	3.6
1	0	1	0	59	5	0	.5	.3	0	-	.1	.1	16	1.1	24	5.8	186	259	54	1.7
2	2	2	0	65	5	0	.4	.3	0	-	.1	.1	16	1.1	24	5.8	186	259	54	1.7
1	1	1	0	65	6	0	.4	.3	0	-	.2	.1	18	1.2	22	5.3	177	242	54	1.7
2	3	2	0	70	6	0	.3	.3	0	-	.1	.1	21	1.5	22	4.6	181	253	60	2.6
0	0	0	0	35	3	0	.3	1.7	0	-	.1	0	22	1.5	21	4.3	173	238	58	2.5
3	4	3	0	69	5	0	.4	.3	0	-	.1	0	6	.3	17	7.1	195	236	1217	1
0	0	0	2	0	7	0	.1	0	9	-	0	0	20	1.2	21	4.9	168	226	52	1.8
0	0	0	1	0	9	0	.1	0	14	-	0	0	17	.2	6	.2	15	105	39	.2
5	8	4	-	78	14	107	.1	.4	1	-	.3	0	25	.4	4	.1	220	45	197	.1
2	5	4	0	21	0	18	0	.3	0	-	.4	.2	113	1.3	16	1.2	131	159	328	.7
4	4	1	0	97	13	0	.3	1.3	0	.3	.3	.1	19	1	22	6.8	203	276	74	4
2	2	1	0	100	14	0	.3	1.4	0	.4	.3	.1	20	1	24	7.2	213	287	76	4.3
0	0	0	1	0	38	212	.3	0	50	-	.1	.1	20	.8	20	1.3	31	350	662	.4
0	0	0	-	0	19	949	.1	0	4	-	0	0	22	.9	13	.5	34	237	121	.3
0	0	0	5	0	17	389	.1	0	3	-	.1	.1	23	.7	20	.8	46	154	32	.4
2	3	5	-	50	11	26	0	.2	0	-	.3	.2	137	1.6	14	1.5	124	128	451	.6
2	3	5	-	52	11	49	0	.2	0	-	.3	.2	191	1.7	14	1.6	143	119	383	.5
0	1	1	-	8	12	120	.3	.8	0	-	.2	.1	77	1.5	7	1.5	139	42	260	.2
1	2	2	0	65	14	33	.3	.8	0	-	.1	.1	28	.4	36	3.3	294	345	55	1.1

Code	Name	Amount	Unit	Grams	Kilocalories	Carbohydrates (g)	Protein (g)	Fat (g)
15131	WHITEFISH, SMOKED	3	OUNCE	85.1	92	0	20	1
20089	WILD RICE, CKD	½	CUP	82.0	83	17	3	0
62552	YOGURT, FROZEN, FAT FREE	½	CUP	67.0	100	22	4	0
62604	YOGURT, FRUIT, FAT FREE	1	CUP	248.0	233	48	10	0
62627	YOGURT, FRUIT, FAT FREE, LIGHT	1	CUP	248.0	110	19	10	0
1121	YOGURT, FRUIT, LOWFAT, 10 G PROTEIN PER 8 OZ.	1	CUP	227.0	231	43	10	2
62603	YOGURT, PLAIN, FAT FREE	1	CUP	248.0	120	17	13	0
1119	YOGURT, VANILLA, LOWFAT, 11 G PROTEIN PER 8 OZ.	1	CUP	227.0	194	31	11	3

RESTAURANTS, INCLUDING FAST FOOD (QUICK SERVICE)

Code	Name	Amount	Unit	Grams	Kilocalories	Carbohydrates (g)	Protein (g)	Fat (g)
32391	ARBY'S-BEEF'N CHEDDAR SANDWICH	1	EACH	194.0	443	30	35	20
32400	ARBY'S-CHICKEN BREAST FILLET SANDWICH	1	EACH	204.0	547	53	26	28
32413	ARBY'S-CURLY FRIES	1	EACH	99.2	337	43	4	18
32405	ARBY'S-FISH FILLET SANDWICH	1	EACH	221.0	526	50	23	27
32411	ARBY'S-FRENCH FRIES	1	EACH	70.9	246	30	2	13
32406	ARBY'S-HAM'N CHEESE SANDWICH	1	EACH	170.1	411	38	24	19
32390	ARBY'S-REGULAR ROAST BEEF	1	EACH	155.9	388	38	25	16
32393	ARBY'S-SUPER ROAST BEEF	1	EACH	241.0	516	51	26	23
32410	ARBY'S-TURKEY SUB	1	EACH	277.0	599	54	33	28
34858	BURGER KING-BACON DOUBLE CHEESEBURGER	1	EACH	202.0	613	29	34	40
34856	BURGER KING-CHEESEBURGER	1	EACH	134.7	360	35	18	16
34857	BURGER KING-DOUBLE CHEESEBURGER	1	EACH	191.4	537	32	33	30
34855	BURGER KING-HAMBURGER	1	EACH	122.9	310	35	16	12
34841	BURGER KING-SALAD W/HOUSE DRESSING	1	EACH	176.0	159	8	3	13
34846	BURGER KING-SALAD W/REDUCED-CALORIE ITALIAN	1	EACH	176.0	42	7	2	1
34859	BURGER KING-WHOPPER	1	EACH	283.5	684	54	28	39
21002	FAST FOOD-BISCUIT W/EGG	1	EACH	136.0	316	24	11	20
21003	FAST FOOD-BISCUIT W/EGG AND BACON	1	EACH	150.0	458	29	17	31
21004	FAST FOOD-BISCUIT W/EGG AND HAM	1	EACH	192.0	442	30	20	27
21005	FAST FOOD-BISCUIT W/EGG AND SAUSAGE	1	EACH	180.0	581	41	19	39
21007	FAST FOOD-BISCUIT W/EGG, CHEESE, AND BACON	1	EACH	144.0	477	33	16	31
21008	FAST FOOD-BISCUIT W/HAM	1	EACH	113.0	386	44	13	18
21009	FAST FOOD-BISCUIT W/SAUSAGE	1	EACH	124.0	485	40	12	32
21010	FAST FOOD-BISCUIT W/STEAK	1	EACH	141.0	455	44	13	26
21001	FAST FOOD-BISCUIT, PLAIN	1	EACH	74.0	276	34	4	13
21027	FAST FOOD-BROWNIE	1	EACH	60.0	243	39	3	10
21060	FAST FOOD-BURRITO W/BEANS	1	EACH	108.5	224	36	7	7
21061	FAST FOOD-BURRITO W/BEANS AND CHEESE	1	EACH	93.0	189	27	8	6
21062	FAST FOOD-BURRITO W/BEANS AND CHILI PEPPERS	1	EACH	102.0	206	29	8	7
21063	FAST FOOD-BURRITO W/BEANS AND MEAT	1	EACH	115.5	254	33	11	9
21064	FAST FOOD-BURRITO W/BEANS, CHEESE, AND BEEF	1	EACH	101.5	165	20	7	7
21065	FAST FOOD-BURRITO W/BEANS, CHEESE, AND CHILI PEPPERS	1	EACH	167.0	329	42	17	11
21066	FAST FOOD-BURRITO W/BEEF	1	EACH	110.0	262	29	13	10
21067	FAST FOOD-BURRITO W/BEEF AND CHILI PEPPERS	1	EACH	100.5	213	25	11	8
21068	FAST FOOD-BURRITO W/BEEF, CHEESE, AND CHILI PEPPERS	1	EACH	152.0	316	32	20	12
21069	FAST FOOD-BURRITO W/FRUIT (APPLE OR CHERRY)	1	EACH	74.0	231	35	3	10
21100	FAST FOOD-CHEESEBURGER, LARGE, DOUBLE PATTY	1	EACH	258.0	704	40	38	44
21098	FAST FOOD-CHEESEBURGER, LARGE, SINGLE PATTY	1	EACH	219.0	563	38	28	33
21097	FAST FOOD-CHEESEBURGER, LARGE, SINGLE PATTY W/BCN & COND	1	EACH	195.0	608	37	32	37
21096	FAST FOOD-CHEESEBURGER, LARGE, SINGLE PATTY, PLAIN	1	EACH	185.0	609	47	30	33
21095	FAST FOOD-CHEESEBURGER, REGULAR, DOUBLE PATTY	1	EACH	228.0	650	53	30	35
21091	FAST FOOD-CHEESEBURGER, REGULAR, SINGLE PATTY	1	EACH	154.0	359	28	18	20
21089	FAST FOOD-CHEESEBURGER, REGULAR, SINGLE PATTY, PLAIN	1	EACH	102.0	319	32	15	15
21011	FAST FOOD-CHEESEBURGER, TRIPLE PATTY, PLAIN	1	EACH	304.0	796	27	56	51
21103	FAST FOOD-CHICKEN FILLET SANDWICH W/CHEESE	1	EACH	228.0	632	42	29	39

Saturated Fat (g)	Monounsaturated Fat (g)	Polyunsaturated Fat (g)	Fiber (g)	Cholesterol (g)	Folate (g)	Vitamin A (RE)	Vitamin B₆ (mg)	Vitamin B₁₂ (μg)	Vitamin C (mg)	Vitamin E (mg)	Riboflavin (mg)	Thiamin (mg)	Calcium (mg)	Iron (mg)	Magnesium (mg)	Niacin (mg)	Phosphorus (mg)	Potassium (mg)	Sodium (mg)	Zinc (mg)
0	0	0	0	28	6	48	.3	2.8	0	-	.1	0	15	.4	20	2	112	360	867	.4
0	0	0	1	0	21	0	.1	0	0	-	.1	0	2	.5	26	1.1	67	83	2	1.1
0	-	-	0	-	20	-	-	0	-	-	-	96	0	-	-	-	-	70	-
0	0	0	0	7	-	0	-	-	0	-	-	-	438	0	-	-	-	423	153	-
0	0	0	0	5	-	0	-	-	15	-	-	-	420	.2	-	-	-	510	160	-
2	1	0	0	10	21	25	.1	1.1	1	-	.4	.1	345	.2	33	.2	271	442	133	1.7
0	0	0	0	5	-	0	-	-	4	-	.2	-	480	0	-	-	0	600	170	-
2	1	0	0	11	24	30	.1	1.2	2	-	.5	.1	389	.2	37	.2	306	498	149	1.9

10	4	4	1	85	45	64	.4	2.3	1	.4	.5	.4	202	5.6	44	6.5	442	380	1801	6
6	11	11	2	101	35	17	.7	.4	0	2.9	.4	.5	123	3.9	51	16.4	322	366	1130	1.9
7	8	2	-	0	-	-	-	-	-	-	.1	.1	16	.8	-	1.9	-	724	167	-
7	9	11	-	44	-	-	-	-	1	-	.3	.3	72	2.1	-	5.3	-	450	872	-
3	6	5	-	0	-	-	-	-	4	-	-	.1	-	.6	-	1.9	-	240	114	-
7	8	2	1	68	83	112	.2	.6	3	1.3	.6	.4	151	3.8	19	3.1	177	338	899	1.6
4	8	2	1	58	45	71	.3	1.4	2	.2	.3	.4	61	4.7	35	6.6	268	354	888	3.8
9	8	6	2	41	42	0	.5	4.4	0	.4	.6	.6	118	6.6	60	9.7	414	518	822	11
6	7	8	-	82	-	-	-	-	-	-	.4	.5	94	3.2	-	9.4	-	-	1432	-
17	15	6	1	115	32	74	.4	3.4	8	1.6	.4	.3	162	4.1	39	8.4	386	480	833	6.6
-	-	-	-	-	-	-	-	-	-	-	-	-	-	-	-	-	-	-	705	-
14	12	2	2	111	34	111	.3	2	7	2	.3	.2	210	3.3	34	5.5	339	383	947	4.5
-	-	-	-	-	-	-	-	-	-	-	-	-	-	-	-	-	-	-	560	-
-	-	-	-	11	-	-	-	-	25	-	0	0	352	.1	95	.2	592	402	293	.1
-	-	-	-	0	-	-	-	-	25	-	0	0	320	.1	105	.2	472	390	430	.1
18	15	2	3	113	34	209	.3	3.1	14	4.2	0	0	113	6.5	54	5.6	339	565	1075	5.8
6	8	4	-	233	30	178	.1	.7	0	-	.3	.3	154	3.1	20	.7	185	160	654	1.1
10	13	6	-	353	30	53	.1	1	3	-	.2	.1	189	3.7	24	2.4	239	251	999	1.6
8	11	5	-	300	33	240	.3	1.2	0	-	.6	.7	221	4.6	31	2	317	319	1382	2.2
15	16	4	-	302	40	164	.2	1.4	0	-	.5	.5	155	4	25	3.6	490	320	1141	2.2
11	14	3	-	261	37	166	.1	1.1	2	-	.4	.3	164	2.5	20	2.3	459	230	1260	1.5
11	5	1	-	25	8	34	.1	0	0	-	.3	.5	160	2.7	23	3.5	554	197	1433	1.6
14	13	3	1	35	9	14	.1	.5	0	-	.3	.4	128	2.6	20	3.3	446	198	1071	1.6
7	11	6	-	25	11	16	.2	.9	0	-	.4	.4	116	4.3	27	4.2	204	234	795	2.7
9	3	1	-	5	6	24	0	.1	0	-	.2	.3	90	1.6	9	1.6	260	87	584	.3
3	4	3	-	10	4	2	0	.2	3	-	.1	.1	25	1.3	16	.6	88	83	153	.6
3	2	1	-	2	59	16	.2	.5	1	-	.3	.3	56	2.3	43	2	49	327	493	.8
3	1	1	-	14	41	119	.1	.4	1	-	.4	.1	107	1.1	40	1.8	90	248	583	.8
4	3	0	-	16	59	10	.1	.6	1	-	.4	.2	50	2.3	36	2.2	57	290	522	1.7
4	4	1	-	24	37	32	.2	.9	1	-	.4	.4	53	2.4	42	2.7	70	328	668	1.9
4	2	1	-	62	30	75	.1	.5	3	-	.4	.2	65	1.9	25	1.9	70	205	495	1.2
6	4	1	-	78	72	190	.2	1	3	-	.6	.3	144	3.8	48	3.8	142	402	1024	3
5	4	0	-	32	20	14	.2	1	1	-	.5	.1	42	3	41	3.2	87	370	746	2.4
4	3	0	-	27	18	23	.2	.6	1	-	.4	.2	43	2.2	30	2.5	70	249	558	2.2
5	5	1	-	85	29	56	.2	1	2	-	.6	.3	111	3.9	35	4.2	158	333	1046	4
5	3	1	-	4	4	37	.1	.5	1	-	.2	.2	16	1.1	7	1.9	15	104	212	.4
18	17	5	-	142	49	54	.4	3.4	1	-	.5	.4	240	5.9	52	7.2	395	596	1148	6.7
15	13	2	-	88	28	129	.3	2.6	8	1.2	.5	.4	206	4.7	44	7.4	311	445	1108	4.6
16	14	3	-	111	33	80	.3	2.3	2	-	.4	.3	162	4.7	45	6.6	400	332	1043	6.8
15	13	2	-	96	39	148	.3	2.5	0	-	.6	.5	91	5.5	39	11.2	422	644	1589	6.6
13	13	6	-	93	34	84	.3	2.1	3	2	.4	.6	169	4.7	36	8.3	349	390	921	4.1
9	7	1	-	52	22	71	.2	1.2	2	-	.2	.3	182	2.6	26	6.4	216	229	976	2.6
6	6	2	-	50	27	37	.1	1	0	-	.4	.4	141	2.4	21	3.7	196	164	500	2.4
22	22	3	-	161	52	85	.6	5.9	3	-	.6	.6	283	8.3	61	11.5	541	821	1213	10.9
12	14	10	-	78	46	128	.4	.5	3	-	.5	.4	258	3.6	43	9.1	406	333	1238	2.9

Food Composition Table **331**

Appendix

Code	Name	Amount	Unit	Grams	Kilocalories	Carbohydrates (g)	Protein (g)	Fat (g)
21101	FAST FOOD-CHICKEN FILLET SANDWICH, PLAIN	1	EACH	182.0	515	39	24	29
21037	FAST FOOD-CHICKEN NUGGETS PLAIN	1	EACH	17.0	48	3	3	3
21038	FAST FOOD-CHICKEN NUGGETS, W/BARB. SAUCE	1	EACH	17.0	43	3	2	2
21039	FAST FOOD-CHICKEN NUGGETS, W/HONEY	1	EACH	17.0	49	4	2	3
21040	FAST FOOD-CHICKEN NUGGETS, W/MUST. SAUCE	1	EACH	17.0	42	3	2	2
21041	FAST FOOD-CHICKEN NUGGETS W/SWEET AND SOUR	1	EACH	17.0	45	4	2	2
21042	FAST FOOD-CHILI CON CARNE	1	CUP	253.0	256	22	25	8
21070	FAST FOOD-CHIMICHANGA, W/BEEF	1	EACH	174.0	425	43	20	20
21071	FAST FOOD-CHIMICHANGA, W/BEEF AND CHEESE	1	EACH	183.0	443	39	20	23
21030	FAST FOOD-CHOCOLATE CHIP COOKIES	1	BOX	55.0	233	36	3	12
21043	FAST FOOD-CLAMS, BREADED AND FRIED	3	OUNCE	85.1	333	29	9	20
21128	FAST FOOD-CORN ON THE COB W/BUTTER	1	EACH	146.0	155	32	4	3
21045	FAST FOOD-CRAB, SOFT-SHELL, FRIED	1	EACH	125.0	334	31	11	18
21011	FAST FOOD-CROISSANT W/EGG AND CHEESE	1	EACH	127.0	368	24	13	25
21012	FAST FOOD-CROISSANT W/EGG, CHEESE, AND BACON	1	EACH	129.0	413	24	16	28
21013	FAST FOOD-CROISSANT W/EGG, CHEESE AND HAM	1	EACH	152.0	474	24	19	34
21014	FAST FOOD-CROISSANT W/EGG, CHEESE, AND SAUSAGE	1	EACH	160.0	523	25	20	38
21015	FAST FOOD-DANISH PASTRY, CHEESE	1	EACH	91.0	353	29	6	25
21016	FAST FOOD-DANISH PASTRY, CINNAMON	1	EACH	88.0	349	47	5	17
21017	FAST FOOD-DANISH PASTRY, FRUIT	1	EACH	94.0	335	45	5	16
21104	FAST FOOD-EGG AND CHEESE SANDWICH	1	EACH	146.0	340	26	16	19
21018	FAST FOOD-EGG, SCRAMBLED	2	EGGS	94.0	199	2	13	15
21074	FAST FOOD-ENCHILADA W/CHEESE	1	EACH	163.0	319	29	10	19
21075	FAST FOOD-ENCHILADA W/CHEESE AND BEEF	1	EACH	192.0	323	30	12	18
21076	FAST FOOD-ENCHIRITO W/CHEESE, BEEF, AND BEANS	1	EACH	193.0	344	34	18	16
21019	FAST FOOD-ENG. MUFFIN W/BUTTER	1	EACH	63.0	189	30	5	6
21020	FAST FOOD-ENG. MUFFIN W/CHEESE AND SAUSAGE	1	EACH	115.0	393	29	15	24
21021	FAST FOOD-ENG. MUFFIN W/EGG, CHEESE, AND CAN. BACON	1	EACH	146.0	383	31	20	20
21022	FAST FOOD-ENG. MUFFIN W/EGG, CHEESE, AND SAUSAGE	1	EACH	165.0	487	31	22	31
21047	FAST FOOD-FISH FILLET, BATTERED AND FRIED	1	EACH	91.0	211	15	13	11
21105	FAST FOOD-FISH SANDWICH W/TARTAR SAUCE	1	EACH	158.0	431	41	17	23
21106	FAST FOOD-FISH SANDWICH W/TARTAR SAUCE AND CHEESE	1	EACH	183.0	523	48	21	29
21023	FAST FOOD-FRENCH TOAST W/BUTTER	1	SLICE	67.5	178	18	5	9
21031	FAST FOOD-FRIED PIE, FRUIT (APPLE, CHERRY, OR LEMON)	1	EACH	85.0	266	33	2	14
21077	FAST FOOD-FRIJOLES W/CHEESE	3	OUNCE	85.1	115	15	6	4
21116	FAST FOOD-HAM AND CHEESE SANDWICH	1	EACH	146.0	352	33	21	15
21117	FAST FOOD-HAM, EGG, AND CHEESE SANDWICH	1	EACH	143.0	347	31	19	16
21114	FAST FOOD-HAMBURGER, DOUBLE PATTY W/COND AND VEG	1	EACH	226.0	540	40	34	27
21111	FAST FOOD-HAMBURGER, DOUBLE PATTY W/CONDIMENTS	1	EACH	215.0	576	39	32	32
21110	FAST FOOD-HAMBURGER, DOUBLE PATTY, PLAIN	1	EACH	176.0	544	43	30	28
21113	FAST FOOD-HAMBURGER, LARGE, SINGLE PATTY W/COND & VEG	1	EACH	218.0	512	40	26	27
21112	FAST FOOD-HAMBURGER, LARGE, SINGLE PATTY, PLAIN	1	EACH	137.0	426	32	23	23
21108	FAST FOOD-HAMBURGER, SINGLE PATTY W/CONDIMENTS	1	EACH	107.0	275	33	14	10
21107	FAST FOOD-HAMBURGER, SINGLE PATTY, PLAIN	1	EACH	90.0	275	31	12	12
21115	FAST FOOD-HAMBURGER, TRIPLE PATTY W/CONDIMENTS	1	EACH	259.0	692	29	50	41
21119	FAST FOOD-HOT DOG W/CHILI	1	EACH	114.0	296	31	14	13
21120	FAST FOOD-HOT DOG W/CORN FLOUR COATING (CORNDOG)	1	EACH	175.0	460	56	17	19
21118	FAST FOOD-HOT DOG, PLAIN	1	EACH	98.0	242	18	10	15
21028	FAST FOOD-ICE MILK, VANILLA, SOFT-SERVE W/CONE	1	EACH	103.0	164	24	4	6
21078	FAST FOOD-NACHOS W/CHEESE	3	OUNCE	85.1	260	27	7	14
21079	FAST FOOD-NACHOS W/CHEESE AND JALAPENO PEPPER	3	OUNCE	85.1	253	25	7	14
21080	FAST FOOD-NACHOS W/CHEESE, BEANS, GROUND BEEF	3	OUNCE	85.1	190	19	7	10
21081	FAST FOOD-NACHOS W/CINNAMON AND SUGAR	3	OUNCE	85.1	462	49	6	28
21130	FAST FOOD-ONION RINGS, BREADED AND FRIED	1	EACH	10.0	33	4	0	2
21048	FAST FOOD-OYSTERS, BATTERED OR BREADED, AND FRIED	3	OUNCE	85.1	225	24	8	11
21025	FAST FOOD-PANCAKES W/BUTTER AND SYRUP	1	EACH	74.0	166	29	3	4
21049	FAST FOOD-PIZZA W/CHEESE	1	SLICE	63.0	140	21	8	3
21050	FAST FOOD-PIZZA W/CHEESE, SAUSAGE, AND VEGETABLES	1	SLICE	79.0	184	21	13	5
21051	FAST FOOD-PIZZA W/PEPPERONI	1	SLICE	71.0	181	20	10	7
21131	FAST FOOD-POTATO, BAKED W/CHEESE SAUCE	1	EACH	296.0	474	47	15	29

Food Composition Table

Saturated Fat (g)	Monounsaturated Fat (g)	Polyunsaturated Fat (g)	Fiber (g)	Cholesterol (g)	Folate (g)	Vitamin A (RE)	Vitamin B₆ (mg)	Vitamin B₁₂ (μg)	Vitamin C (mg)	Vitamin E (mg)	Riboflavin (mg)	Thiamin (mg)	Calcium (mg)	Iron (mg)	Magnesium (mg)	Niacin (mg)	Phosphorus (mg)	Potassium (mg)	Sodium (mg)	Zinc (mg)
9	10	8	-	60	29	31	.2	.4	9	-	.2	.3	60	4.7	35	6.8	233	353	957	1.9
1	1	0	0	10	2	5	.1	.1	0	-	0	0	3	.2	3	1.1	34	42	90	.2
1	1	0	-	8	4	6	0	0	0	-	0	0	3	.2	3	.9	28	42	108	.1
1	1	0	-	9	2	4	0	0	0	-	0	0	3	.2	3	1	30	38	79	.2
1	1	0	-	8	2	4	0	0	0	-	0	0	3	.2	3	.9	29	37	103	.1
1	1	0	-	8	2	10	0	0	0	-	0	0	3	.2	3	.9	28	36	89	.1
3	3	1	-	134	30	167	.3	1.1	2	-	1.1	.1	68	5.2	46	2.5	197	691	1007	3.6
9	8	1	-	9	31	16	.3	1.5	5	-	.6	.5	63	4.5	63	5.8	124	586	910	5
11	9	1	-	51	33	126	.2	1.3	3	-	.9	.4	238	3.8	60	4.7	187	203	957	3.4
5	5	1	-	12	16	15	0	.1	1	.4	.2	.1	20	1.5	17	1.4	52	82	188	.3
5	8	5	-	65	7	27	0	.8	0	-	.2	.2	15	2.3	23	2.1	176	196	617	1.2
2	1	1	-	6	44	96	.3	0	7	-	.1	.2	4	.9	41	2.2	108	359	29	.9
4	8	5	-	45	20	4	.2	4.5	1	-	.1	.1	55	1.8	25	1.8	131	163	1118	1.1
14	8	1	-	216	37	255	.1	.8	0	-	.4	.2	244	2.2	22	1.5	348	174	551	1.8
15	9	2	-	215	35	120	.1	.9	2	-	.3	.3	151	2.2	23	2.2	276	201	889	1.9
17	11	2	-	213	36	117	.2	1	11	-	.3	.5	144	2.1	26	3.2	336	272	1081	2.2
18	14	3	-	216	38	109	.1	.9	0	-	.3	1	144	3	24	4	290	283	1115	2.1
5	16	2	-	20	15	13	.1	.2	3	-	.2	.3	70	1.8	15	2.5	80	116	319	.6
3	11	2	-	27	14	5	.1	.2	3	-	.2	.3	37	1.8	14	2.2	74	96	326	.5
3	10	2	-	19	15	24	.1	.2	2	-	.2	.3	22	1.4	14	1.8	69	110	333	.5
7	8	3	-	291	37	181	.1	1.1	1	-	.6	.3	225	3	22	2.1	302	188	804	1.6
6	6	2	0	400	53	252	.2	.9	3	.9	.5	.1	54	2.4	13	.2	227	138	211	1.6
11	6	1	-	44	34	186	.4	.7	1	-	.4	.1	324	1.3	51	1.9	134	240	784	2.5
9	6	1	-	40	192	142	.3	1	1	-	.4	.1	228	3.1	83	2.5	167	574	1319	2.7
8	7	0	-	50	253	133	.2	1.6	5	-	.7	.2	218	2.4	71	3	224	560	1251	2.8
2	2	1	-	13	17	33	0	0	1	.1	.3	.3	103	1.6	13	2.6	85	69	386	.4
10	10	3	-	59	18	86	.1	.7	1	-	.3	.7	168	2.3	24	4.1	186	215	1036	1.7
9	7	2	-	234	44	158	.2	.8	1	.6	.5	.5	207	3.3	34	3.9	320	213	784	1.8
12	13	3	-	274	54	172	.2	1.4	1	-	.5	.8	196	3.5	30	4.5	287	294	1135	2.4
3	2	6	-	31	51	11	.1	1	0	-	.1	.1	16	1.9	22	1.9	156	291	484	.4
5	8	8	-	55	44	30	.1	1.1	3	.9	.2	.3	84	2.6	33	3.4	212	340	615	1
8	9	9	-	68	31	97	.1	1.1	3	1.8	.4	.5	185	3.5	37	4.2	311	353	939	1.2
-	-	-	-	58	15	73	0	.2	0	-	.2	.3	36	.9	8	2	73	88	257	.3
7	6	1	-	13	4	33	0	.1	1	.4	.1	.1	13	.9	8	1	37	51	325	.2
2	1	0	-	19	57	36	.1	.3	1	-	.2	.1	96	1.1	43	.8	89	308	449	.9
6	7	1	-	58	72	76	.2	.5	3	.3	.5	.3	130	3.2	16	2.7	152	291	771	1.4
7	6	2	-	246	43	149	.2	1.2	3	-	.6	.4	212	3.1	26	4.2	346	210	1005	2
11	10	3	-	122	27	11	.5	4.1	1	-	.4	.4	102	5.9	50	7.6	314	570	791	5.7
12	14	3	-	103	45	4	.4	3.3	1	-	.4	.3	92	5.5	45	6.7	284	527	742	5.8
10	12	2	-	99	37	0	.3	2.9	0	1.3	.4	.3	86	4.6	37	8.3	234	363	554	5.7
10	11	2	-	87	37	33	.3	2.4	3	-	.4	.4	96	4.9	44	7.3	233	480	824	4.9
8	10	2	-	71	32	0	.2	2.1	0	-	.3	.3	74	3.6	27	6.2	175	267	474	4.1
4	4	2	-	43	17	13	.1	.8	3	.4	.3	.3	51	2.5	22	4.7	110	215	564	2.1
4	5	1	-	35	25	0	.1	.9	0	.5	.3	.3	63	2.4	19	3.7	103	145	387	2
16	18	3	-	142	31	16	.6	4.9	1	-	.5	.3	65	8.3	54	11	394	785	712	10.7
5	7	1	-	51	50	6	0	.3	3	-	.4	.3	19	3.3	10	3.7	192	166	480	.8
5	9	3	-	79	60	37	.1	.4	0	-	.7	.3	102	6.2	18	4.2	166	263	973	1.3
5	7	2	-	44	29	0	0	.5	0	-	.3	.2	24	2.3	13	3.6	97	143	670	2
4	2	0	-	28	5	52	.1	.2	1	.4	.3	.1	153	.2	15	.3	139	169	92	.6
6	6	1	-	14	8	69	.2	.6	1	-	.3	.1	205	1	42	1.2	208	129	614	1.3
6	6	2	-	35	8	196	.2	.4	0	-	.2	.1	259	1	45	1.2	164	122	724	1.2
4	4	2	-	7	13	156	.1	.3	2	-	.2	.1	128	.9	32	1.1	129	151	600	1.2
14	9	3	-	31	6	9	.1	1.3	6	-	.3	.1	66	2.3	15	3.1	26	61	343	.5
1	1	0	-	2	1	0	0	0	0	0	0	0	9	.1	2	.1	10	16	52	0
3	4	3	-	66	8	66	0	.6	.3	-	.2	.2	17	2.7	14	2.7	120	111	414	9.6
2	2	1	-	19	11	22	0	.1	1	.4	.2	.1	41	.8	16	1.1	152	80	352	.3
2	1	0	-	9	59	74	0	.3	1	-	.2	.2	117	.6	16	2.5	113	110	336	.8
2	3	1	-	21	27	101	.1	.4	2	-	.2	.2	101	1.5	18	2	131	179	382	1.1
2	3	1	-	14	53	55	.1	.2	2	-	.2	.1	65	.9	9	3	75	153	267	.5
11	11	6	-	18	27	228	.7	.2	26	-	.2	.2	311	3	65	3.3	320	1166	382	1.9

Code	Name	Amount	Unit	Grams	Kilocalories	Carbohydrates (g)	Protein (g)	Fat (g)
21132	FAST FOOD-POTATO, BAKED W/CHEESE SAUCE AND BACON	1	EACH	299.0	451	44	18	26
21133	FAST FOOD-POTATO, BAKED W/CHEESE SAUCE AND BROCCOLI	1	EACH	339.0	403	47	14	21
21134	FAST FOOD-POTATO, BAKED W/CHEESE SAUCE AND CHILI	1	EACH	395.0	482	56	23	22
21135	FAST FOOD-POTATO, BAKED W/SOUR CREAM AND CHIVES	1	EACH	302.0	393	50	7	22
21136	FAST FOOD-POTATO, FRENCH FRIED IN BEEF TALLOW	1	LARGE	115.0	359	44	5	19
21137	FAST FOOD-POTATO, FRENCH FRIED IN BEEF TALLOW AND VEG OIL	1	LARGE	115.0	358	44	5	19
21138	FAST FOOD-POTATO, FRENCH FRIED IN VEGETABLE OIL	1	LARGE	115.0	355	44	5	19
21139	FAST FOOD-POTATOES, MASHED	½	CUP	120.0	100	19	3	1
21026	FAST FOOD-POTATOES, HASHED BROWN	½	CUP	72.0	151	16	2	9
21122	FAST FOOD-ROAST BEEF SANDWICH W/CHEESE	1	EACH	176.0	473	45	32	18
21121	FAST FOOD-ROAST BEEF SANDWICH, PLAIN	1	EACH	139.0	346	33	22	14
21052	FAST FOOD-SALAD, W/O DRESSING	½	CUP	69.3	11	2	1	0
21053	FAST FOOD-SALAD, W/O DRESSING, W/CHEESE AND EGG	½	CUP	72.3	34	2	3	2
21054	FAST FOOD-SALAD, W/O DRESSING, W/CHICKEN	½	CUP	72.7	35	1	6	1
21055	FAST FOOD-SALAD, W/O DRESSING, W/PASTA AND SEAFOOD	½	CUP	139.0	126	11	5	7
21056	FAST FOOD-SALAD, W/O DRESSING, W/SHRIMP	½	CUP	78.7	35	2	5	1
21058	FAST FOOD-SCALLOPS, BREADED AND FRIED	1	EACH	24.0	64	6	3	3
21059	FAST FOOD-SHRIMP, BREADED AND FRIED	1	OUNCE	28.4	79	7	3	4
21123	FAST FOOD-STEAK SANDWICH	1	EACH	140.0	315	36	21	10
21124	FAST FOOD-SUBMARINE SANDWICH W/COLDCUTS	1	EACH	228.0	456	51	22	19
21125	FAST FOOD-SUBMARINE SANDWICH W/ROAST BEEF	1	EACH	216.0	410	44	29	13
21126	FAST FOOD-SUBMARINE SANDWICH W/TUNA SALAD	1	EACH	256.0	584	55	30	28
21032	FAST FOOD-SUNDAE, CARAMEL	1	EACH	155.0	304	49	7	9
21033	FAST FOOD-SUNDAE, HOT FUDGE	1	EACH	158.0	284	48	6	9
21034	FAST FOOD-SUNDAE, STRAWBERRY	1	EACH	153.0	268	45	6	8
21082	FAST FOOD-TACO	1	LARGE	263.0	568	41	32	32
21083	FAST FOOD-TACO SALAD	½	CUP	66.0	93	8	4	5
21084	FAST FOOD-TACO SALAD W/CHILI CON CARNE	½	CUP	87.0	97	9	6	4
21088	FAST FOOD-TOSTADA, W/GUACAMOLE	1	OUNCE	28.4	39	3	1	3
21085	FAST FOOD-TOSTADA, W/BEANS AND CHEESE	1	EACH	144.0	223	27	10	10
21086	FAST FOOD-TOSTADA, W/BEANS, BEEF, AND CHEESE	1	EACH	225.0	333	30	16	17
21087	FAST FOOD-TOSTADA, W/BEEF AND CHEESE	1	EACH	163.0	315	23	19	16
40349	HARDEE'S-BIG CHEESE	1	EACH	141.8	495	28	30	30
40350	HARDEE'S-BIG DELUXE	1	EACH	248.1	675	46	31	41
40356	HARDEE'S-BIG FISH SANDWICH	1	EACH	191.4	514	49	20	26
40353	HARDEE'S-BIG ROAST BEEF	1	EACH	163.0	365	39	22	13
40351	HARDEE'S-BIG TWIN	1	EACH	141.8	369	28	19	20
40358	HARDEE'S-BISCUIT	1	EACH	78.0	275	35	5	13
40348	HARDEE'S-CHEESEBURGER	1	EACH	100.6	335	29	17	17
40357	HARDEE'S-CHICKEN FILLET	1	EACH	191.4	510	42	27	26
40347	HARDEE'S-HAMBURGER	1	EACH	100.1	305	29	17	13
40354	HARDEE'S-HOT DOG	1	EACH	50.0	346	26	11	22
40355	HARDEE'S-HOT HAM & CHEESE	1	EACH	141.8	376	37	23	15
40352	HARDEE'S-ROAST BEEF SANDWICH	1	EACH	141.8	323	39	19	11
44118	JACK IN THE BOX-BACON CHEESEBURGER	1	EACH	242.0	705	41	35	45
44101	JACK IN THE BOX-BREAKFAST JACK	1	EACH	126.0	313	29	19	14
44141	JACK IN THE BOX-CHEESECAKE	1	EACH	99.0	309	29	8	18
44115	JACK IN THE BOX-JUMBO JACK	1	EACH	222.0	497	41	25	26
44116	JACK IN THE BOX-JUMBO JACK W/CHEESE	1	EACH	242.0	559	40	28	31
44136	JACK IN THE BOX-REGULAR FRENCH FRIES	1	EACH	109.0	351	45	4	17
44135	JACK IN THE BOX-SMALL FRENCH FRIES	1	EACH	68.0	219	28	3	11
47265	K.F.C.-COLONEL'S CHICKEN SANDWICH	1	EACH	166.0	482	39	21	27
47261	K.F.C.-FRENCH FRIES	1	EACH	77.0	244	31	3	12
47260	K.F.C.-MASHED POTATOES AND GRAVY	1	EACH	98.0	71	12	2	2
47239	K.F.C.-ORIGINAL RECIPE CENTER BREAST	1	EACH	103.0	261	9	25	15
47240	K.F.C.-ORIGINAL RECIPE DRUMSTICK	1	EACH	57.0	169	5	12	12
47241	K.F.C.-ORIGINAL RECIPE THIGH	1	EACH	95.0	324	11	16	24
47237	K.F.C.-ORIGINAL RECIPE WING	1	EACH	53.0	172	5	12	11
48204	MCDONALD'S-BACON, EGG AND CHEESE BISCUIT	1	EACH	153.0	432	32	18	26
48174	MCDONALD'S-BIG MAC	1	EACH	215.0	560	43	25	32

Food Composition Table

Saturated Fat (g)	Monounsaturated Fat (g)	Polyunsaturated Fat (g)	Fiber (g)	Cholesterol (g)	Folate (g)	Vitamin A (RE)	Vitamin B₆ (mg)	Vitamin B₁₂ (μg)	Vitamin C (mg)	Vitamin E (mg)	Riboflavin (mg)	Thiamin (mg)	Calcium (mg)	Iron (mg)	Magnesium (mg)	Niacin (mg)	Phosphorus (mg)	Potassium (mg)	Sodium (mg)	Zinc (mg)
10	10	5	-	30	30	173	.7	.3	29	-	.2	.3	308	3.1	69	4	347	1178	972	2.2
9	8	4	-	20	61	278	.8	.3	48	-	.3	.3	336	3.3	78	3.6	346	1441	485	2
13	7	1	-	32	51	174	.9	.2	32	-	.4	.3	411	6.1	111	4.2	498	1572	699	3.8
10	8	3	-	24	33	278	.8	.2	34	-	.2	.3	106	3.1	69	3.7	184	1383	181	.9
9	8	1	-	21	38	3	.3	.1	6	-	0	.2	18	1.6	38	2.6	153	819	187	.6
8	8	2	-	16	38	3	.3	.1	6	-	0	.2	18	1.6	38	2.6	153	819	187	.6
6	9	3	-	0	38	3	.3	.1	6	-	0	.2	18	1.6	38	2.6	153	819	187	.6
1	0	0	-	2	10	12	.3	.1	0	-	.1	.1	25	.6	22	1.4	66	353	272	.4
4	4	0	-	9	8	3	.2	0	5	.1	0	.1	7	.5	16	1.1	69	267	290	.2
9	4	4	-	77	40	46	.3	2.1	0	-	.5	.4	183	5.1	40	5.9	401	345	1633	5.4
4	7	2	-	51	40	21	.3	1.2	2	-	.3	.4	54	4.2	31	5.9	239	316	792	3.4
0	0	0	-	0	26	79	.1	0	16	-	0	0	9	.4	8	.4	27	119	18	.1
1	1	0	-	33	28	38	0	.1	3	-	.1	0	33	.2	8	.3	44	124	40	.3
0	0	0	-	24	23	32	.1	.1	6	-	0	0	12	.4	11	2	57	149	70	.3
1	2	3	-	17	33	213	.1	.6	13	-	.1	.1	24	1.1	17	1.2	68	200	524	.6
0	0	0	-	60	29	26	0	1.3	3	-	.1	0	20	.3	13	.4	53	135	163	.4
1	2	0	-	18	7	7	0	.1	0	-	.1	0	3	.3	5	0	49	49	153	.2
1	3	0	-	35	8	6	0	0	0	-	.2	0	14	.5	7	0	60	32	250	.2
3	4	2	-	50	62	31	.3	1.1	4	-	.3	.3	63	3.5	34	5	204	360	547	3.1
7	8	2	-	36	55	80	.1	1.1	12	-	.8	1	189	2.5	68	5.5	287	394	1651	2.6
7	2	3	-	73	45	50	.3	1.8	6	-	.4	.4	41	2.8	67	6	192	330	845	4.4
5	13	7	-	49	56	41	.2	1.6	4	-	.3	.5	74	2.6	79	11.3	220	335	1293	1.9
5	3	1	0	25	12	68	0	.6	3	.9	.3	.1	189	.2	28	.9	217	318	195	.8
5	2	1	0	21	9	57	.1	.6	2	.7	.3	.1	207	.6	33	1.1	228	395	182	.9
4	3	1	0	21	18	58	.1	.6	2	.8	.3	.1	161	.3	24	.9	155	271	92	.7
17	10	1	-	87	37	226	.4	1.6	3	-	.7	.2	339	3.7	108	4.9	313	729	1233	6
2	2	1	-	15	13	26	.1	.2	1	-	.1	0	64	.8	17	.8	48	139	254	.9
2	2	1	-	2	21	71	.2	.2	1	-	.2	.1	82	.9	17	.8	51	130	295	1.1
1	1	0	-	4	12	24	0	.1	0	-	.1	0	46	.2	8	.2	25	71	87	.4
5	3	1	-	30	75	85	.2	.7	1	-	.3	.1	210	1.9	59	1.3	117	403	543	1.9
11	4	1	-	74	97	173	.2	1.1	4	-	.5	.1	189	2.5	68	2.9	173	491	871	3.2
10	3	1	-	41	15	96	.2	1.2	3	-	.6	.1	217	2.9	64	3.1	179	572	897	3.7
-	-	-	-	-	-	-	-	-	-	-	-	-	-	-	-	-	-	-	1251	-
-	-	-	-	-	-	-	-	-	-	-	-	-	-	-	-	-	-	-	1063	-
-	-	-	-	-	-	-	-	-	-	-	-	-	-	-	-	-	-	-	314	-
6	6	2	1	55	29	0	.3	3	0	.2	.4	.4	80	4.5	40	6.6	280	389	1071	7.4
9	7	4	1	45	28	14	.2	1.9	2	.7	.3	.2	66	3.3	29	5.5	161	229	475	3.8
-	-	-	-	-	-	-	-	-	-	-	-	-	-	-	-	-	-	-	650	-
-	-	-	-	-	-	-	-	-	2	-	.3	.5	-	-	-	5.5	-	-	789	-
-	-	-	-	-	-	-	-	-	-	-	-	-	-	-	-	-	-	-	360	-
-	-	-	-	-	-	-	-	-	2	-	.6	.6	-	-	-	6.4	-	-	682	-
-	-	-	-	-	-	-	-	-	-	-	-	-	-	-	-	-	-	-	744	-
-	-	-	-	-	-	-	-	-	-	-	-	-	-	-	-	-	-	-	1067	-
5	5	2	1	44	25	0	.3	2.6	0	.2	.4	.3	70	3.9	35	5.7	244	323	908	6.5
15	16	9	-	113	-	70	-	-	8	-	.5	.2	200	2.8	-	8.4	-	-	1240	-
5	5	3	-	190	-	138	.1	1.1	3	-	.5	.4	184	2.6	25	5.3	323	198	1080	1.9
9	7	2	-	63	-	-	-	-	-	-	.2	0	88	.3	-	1.9	-	-	2.8	-
10	11	2	-	72	-	67	.3	2.4	4	-	.3	.4	121	4.1	40	10.5	236	444	1023	3.8
13	11	2	-	98	-	196	.3	2.7	4	-	.3	.5	243	4.1	44	10.1	366	444	1482	4.3
4	7	-	-	0	-	-	-	-	26	-	0	.2	-	.7	-	3.6	-	-	194	-
3	7	-	-	0	-	-	-	-	16	-	-	.1	-	.4	-	2.3	-	-	121	-
6	4	9	1	47	29	14	.6	.3	0	2.3	.3	.4	100	3.1	41	10.6	261	297	1060	1.5
3	7	1	-	2	-	-	-	-	16	-	.1	.2	-	.3	-	1.9	-	-	139	-
1	0	0	-	-	-	-	-	-	0	-	0	-	16	.2	-	1.1	-	-	339	-
4	4	2	0	87	4	15	.6	.4	0	.5	.1	.1	16	1.2	31	14	238	265	603	1.1
2	3	2	-	59	5	14	.2	.2	0	.4	.1	0	7	.7	13	3.4	99	130	268	1.7
6	6	3	0	103	8	28	.3	.3	0	.5	.2	.1	13	1.4	23	6.5	176	224	549	2.4
3	6	2	-	59	-	-	-	-	-	-	.1	0	24	.3	-	2.9	-	-	383	-
8	16	2	1	248	18	157	.2	.6	0	1.5	.3	.4	181	2.6	30	2.5	442	232	1206	1.7
10	20	2	-	103	21	106	.3	1.8	2	-	.4	.5	256	4	38	6.8	314	237	950	4.7

Appendix

Code	Name	Amount	Unit	Grams	Kilocalories	Carbohydrates (g)	Protein (g)	Fat (g)
48205	MCDONALD'S-BISCUIT W/SPREAD	1	EACH	75.0	260	32	5	13
48170	MCDONALD'S-CHEESEBURGER	1	EACH	116.0	310	30	15	13
48187	MCDONALD'S-CHEF SALAD	1	EACH	265.0	215	7	20	12
48181	MCDONALD'S-CHICKEN MCNUGGETS	1	EACH	18.5	45	3	3	3
48226	MCDONALD'S-CHOCOLATE LOWFAT MILK SHAKE	1	EACH	294.1	321	66	11	2
48189	MCDONALD'S-CHUNKY CHICKEN SALAD	1	EACH	255.0	143	5	23	3
48198	MCDONALD'S-EGG MCMUFFIN	1	EACH	135.0	284	27	18	11
48201	MCDONALD'S-ENGLISH MUFFIN W/SPREAD	1	EACH	58.0	170	26	5	4
48175	MCDONALD'S-FILLET O' FISH	1	EACH	141.0	437	38	14	26
48188	MCDONALD'S-GARDEN SALAD	1	EACH	189.0	50	6	4	2
48169	MCDONALD'S-HAMBURGER	1	EACH	102.0	255	30	12	9
48209	MCDONALD'S-HASH BROWN POTATOES	1	EACH	53.0	130	15	1	7
48210	MCDONALD'S-HOTCAKES W/MARGARINE AND SYRUP	1	EACH	174.0	440	74	8	12
48180	MCDONALD'S-LARGE FRENCH FRIES	1	EACH	122.0	400	46	6	22
48176	MCDONALD'S-MCCHICKEN	1	EACH	187.0	415	39	19	20
48223	MCDONALD'S-MCDONALDLAND COOKIES	1	EACH	56.7	290	47	4	9
48179	MCDONALD'S-MEDIUM FRENCH FRIES	1	EACH	97.0	320	36	4	17
48171	MCDONALD'S-QUARTER POUNDER	1	EACH	166.0	410	34	23	20
48207	MCDONALD'S-SAUSAGE BISCUIT	1	EACH	118.0	420	32	12	28
48203	MCDONALD'S-SAUSAGE BISCUIT W/EGG	1	EACH	175.0	505	33	19	33
48199	MCDONALD'S-SAUSAGE MCMUFFIN	1	EACH	135.0	345	27	15	20
48200	MCDONALD'S-SAUSAGE MCMUFFIN W/EGG	1	EACH	159.0	430	27	21	25
48208	MCDONALD'S-SCRAMBLED EGGS	1	EACH	100.0	140	1	12	10
48190	MCDONALD'S-SIDE SALAD	1	EACH	106.0	30	4	2	1
48178	MCDONALD'S-SMALL FRENCH FRIES	1	EACH	68.0	220	26	3	12
48227	MCDONALD'S-STRAWBERRY LOWFAT MILK SHAKE	1	EACH	294.1	320	67	11	1
48225	MCDONALD'S-VANILLA LOWFAT MILK SHAKE	1	EACH	294.1	320	60	11	1
52366	PIZZA HUT-CHEESE PIZZA, HAND TOSSED	1	SLICE	70.0	259	28	17	10
52359	PIZZA HUT-CHEESE PIZZA, PAN	1	SLICE	70.0	246	29	15	9
53322	PIZZA HUT-CHEESE PIZZA, THIN'N CRISPY	1	SLICE	70.0	199	19	14	9
52363	PIZZA HUT-PEPPERONI PIZZA, THIN'N CRISPY	1	SLICE	70.0	207	18	13	10
52370	PIZZA HUT-PEPPERONI PERSONAL PAN PIZZA	1	EACH	250.0	675	76	37	29
52367	PIZZA HUT-PEPPERONI PIZZA, HAND TOSSED	1	SLICE	70.0	250	25	14	12
52360	PIZZA HUT-PEPPERONI PIZZA, PAN	1	SLICE	70.0	270	31	15	11
52365	PIZZA HUT-SUPER SPRM PIZZA, THIN'N CRISPY	1	SLICE	70.0	232	22	15	11
52362	PIZZA HUT-SUPER SUPREME PIZZA, PAN	1	SLICE	70.0	282	27	17	13
52369	PIZZA HUT-SUPER SUPREME, HAND TOSSED	1	SLICE	70.0	278	27	17	13
52371	PIZZA HUT-SUPREME PERSONAL PAN PIZZA	1	EACH	250.0	647	76	33	28
52368	PIZZA HUT-SUPREME PIZZA, HAND TOSSED	1	SLICE	70.0	270	25	16	13
52361	PIZZA HUT-SUPREME PIZZA, PAN	1	SLICE	70.0	295	27	16	15
52364	PIZZA HUT-SUPREME PIZZA, THIN'N CRISPY	1	SLICE	70.0	230	21	14	11
62559	SUBWAY-BMT, ON ITALIAN ROLL	1	12 IN.	213.0	982	83	44	55
62561	SUBWAY-CLUB SANDWICH, ON ITALIAN ROLL	1	12 IN.	213.0	693	83	46	22
62562	SUBWAY-COLD CUT COMBO, ON ITALIAN ROLL	1	12 IN.	184.0	853	83	46	40
62564	SUBWAY-HAM AND CHEESE, ON ITALIAN ROLL	1	12 IN.	184.0	643	81	38	18
62565	SUBWAY-MEAT BALL SANDWICH, ON ITALIAN ROLL	1	12 IN.	215.0	918	96	42	44
62567	SUBWAY-ROAST BEEF, ON ITALIAN ROLL	1	12 IN.	184.0	689	84	42	23
62569	SUBWAY-SEAFOOD, ON ITALIAN ROLL	1	12 IN.	210.0	986	94	29	57
62571	SUBWAY-SPICY ITALIAN, ON ITALIAN ROLL	1	12 IN.	213.0	1043	83	42	63
62572	SUBWAY-STEAK AND CHEESE, ON ITALIAN ROLL	1	12 IN.	213.0	765	83	43	32
58318	TACO BELL-BEAN BURRITO	1	EACH	206.0	387	63	15	14
58319	TACO BELL-BEEF BURRITO	1	EACH	206.0	431	48	25	21
58321	TACO BELL-BURRITO SUPREME	1	EACH	198.0	440	55	20	22
62585	TACO BELL-LIGHT 7-LAYER BURRITO	1	EACH	276.0	440	67	19	9
62583	TACO BELL-LIGHT BEAN BURRITO	1	EACH	198.0	330	55	14	6
62586	TACO BELL-LIGHT BURRITO SUPREME	1	EACH	248.0	350	50	20	8
62584	TACO BELL-LIGHT CHICKEN BURRITO	1	EACH	170.0	290	45	12	6
62587	TACO BELL-LIGHT CHICKEN BURRITO SUPREME	1	EACH	248.0	410	62	18	10
62582	TACO BELL-LIGHT CHICKEN SOFT TACO	1	EACH	120.0	180	26	9	5
62575	TACO BELL-LIGHT SOFT TACO	1	EACH	99.0	180	19	13	5

Food Composition Table

Saturated Fat (g)	Monounsaturated Fat (g)	Polyunsaturated Fat (g)	Fiber (g)	Cholesterol (g)	Folate (g)	Vitamin A (RE)	Vitamin B₆ (mg)	Vitamin B₁₂ (µg)	Vitamin C (mg)	Vitamin E (mg)	Riboflavin (mg)	Thiamin (mg)	Calcium (mg)	Iron (mg)	Magnesium (mg)	Niacin (mg)	Phosphorus (mg)	Potassium (mg)	Sodium (mg)	Zinc (mg)
3	9	1	1	1	6	0	0	.1	0	1.8	.1	.2	75	1.3	14	1.5	168	100	730	.7
5	8	1	-	50	18	118	.1	.9	2	.5	.2	.3	199	2.3	21	3.9	177	223	750	2.1
6	6	1	-	120	-	385	-	-	13	-	.3	.3	240	1.4	-	3.4	-	-	459	-
1	2	0	-	9	-	-	-	-	-	-	0	0	-	.1	-	1.3	-	-	97	-
1	1	0	-	10	-	92	-	-	0	-	.5	.1	333	.8	-	.4	-	-	241	-
1	2	1	1	80	28	373	.6	.6	20	11	.2	.2	35	1	38	8.7	262	445	235	3
4	6	1	1	221	43	147	.2	.8	1	1.8	.3	.5	250	2.7	32	3.6	312	208	724	1.8
2	2	1	2	9	51	37	.1	-	0	.1	.1	.3	151	1.6	12	2.5	60	74	285	.4
5	10	11	1	50	20	44	.1	.8	-	-	.1	.3	164	1.8	27	2.7	227	149	1023	.9
1	1	0	-	65	-	900	-	-	21	-	.1	.1	32	.8	-	.4	-	-	70	-
3	5	1	-	37	-	40	-	-	2	-	.2	.3	80	1.5	-	3.8	-	-	490	-
1	4	2	-	0	-	-	-	-	1	-	-	.1	-	.8	-	-	-	-	330	-
2	5	5	-	8	-	40	-	-	-	-	.3	.3	80	1	-	2.9	-	-	685	-
5	15	2	-	0	-	-	-	-	15	-	-	.2	-	.6	-	2.9	-	-	20	-
4	9	7	-	50	-	20	-	-	2	-	.2	.9	120	1.5	-	8.6	-	-	830	-
1	7	1	-	0	-	-	-	-	-	-	.2	.2	-	1	-	1.9	-	-	300	-
4	12	2	-	0	-	-	-	-	12	-	-	.2	-	.4	-	2.9	-	-	150	-
8	11	1	-	84	-	40	-	-	4	-	.3	.4	120	2	-	6.7	-	-	645	-
8	17	3	-	44	-	-	-	-	-	-	.2	.5	64	1	-	3.8	-	-	1040	-
10	20	3	-	260	-	60	-	-	-	-	.3	.5	80	2	-	3.8	-	-	1210	-
7	11	2	-	57	-	40	-	-	-	-	.3	.5	160	1.5	-	4.8	-	-	770	-
8	14	3	-	270	-	100	-	-	-	-	.4	.5	200	2	-	4.8	-	-	920	-
3	5	2	-	425	-	100	-	-	-	-	.3	.1	48	1	-	-	-	-	290	-
0	1	0	-	33	-	800	-	-	12	-	.1	.1	16	.4	-	-	-	-	35	-
3	8	5	-	0	-	-	-	-	9	-	-	.2	-	.2	-	1.9	-	-	110	-
1	1	0	-	10	-	60	-	-	-	-	.5	.1	280	-	-	.4	-	-	170	-
1	1	0	-	10	-	60	-	-	-	-	.5	.1	280	-	-	-	-	-	170	-
7	3	-	-	28	-	50	-	.3	5	-	.2	.2	300	1.5	32	2.6	220	198	638	2.3
5	5	-	-	17	-	45	-	.3	4	-	.3	.3	252	1.5	26	2.5	188	160	470	2
5	3	-	-	17	-	35	-	.3	2	-	.2	.2	264	.9	21	2.3	188	131	434	1.8
5	5	-	-	23	-	35	-	.3	3	-	.2	.2	180	.9	19	2.5	148	144	493	1.7
13	17	-	-	53	-	120	-	.4	10	-	.7	.6	584	3.2	53	7.8	360	408	1335	3.8
6	5	-	-	25	-	50	-	.3	4	-	.3	.3	176	1.4	26	2.7	156	208	634	1.9
5	7	-	-	21	-	50	-	.3	4	-	.2	.3	208	1.8	25	2.6	176	203	564	2.1
5	5	-	-	28	-	50	-	.4	4	-	.2	.3	184	1.4	26	2.6	168	232	668	2.3
6	7	-	-	28	-	60	-	.4	5	-	.3	.4	216	1.9	32	3	188	266	724	2.7
7	6	-	-	27	-	55	-	.4	6	-	.3	.4	176	1.9	33	3.5	168	258	824	2.4
11	17	-	-	49	-	120	-	.5	11	-	.7	.6	416	3.7	53	7.6	320	487	1313	3.8
6	7	-	-	28	-	55	-	.4	6	-	.3	.4	192	2.3	35	3.4	184	289	735	2.9
7	8	-	-	24	-	60	-	.4	5	-	.4	.4	200	1.4	33	2.9	184	290	832	2.8
6	6	-	-	21	-	50	-	.3	5	-	.2	.3	172	1.7	30	2.6	160	272	664	2.3
20	24	7	5	133	63	67	.5	2.3	5	5.1	.3	.3	64	4.3	66	5.1	308	917	3139	6.1
7	8	4	5	84	47	74	.6	1	20	1.3	.3	.5	58	3.1	66	12.5	384	971	2717	2.5
12	15	10	5	166	39	87	.2	1.2	17	.9	.3	.4	227	2.9	28	3.8	315	876	2218	2.7
7	8	4	5	73	45	174	.3	.8	17	3.8	.4	.5	304	2.2	50	3.6	527	834	1710	2.8
17	17	4	3	88	35	72	.4	3.2	19	1	.4	.3	78	5	47	9.4	263	1210	2022	6.2
8	9	4	5	83	54	58	.4	2	5	4.4	.3	.2	55	3.7	57	4.4	266	910	2288	5.3
11	15	28	-	56	91	107	.3	6.5	5	2.5	.4	.5	230	4.4	32	7	336	641	2027	5.3
23	28	7	5	137	-	-	-	-	-	-	-	-	-	-	-	-	-	-	880	2282	-
12	12	4	6	82	36	119	.4	2.5	6	.8	.5	.3	231	4.2	43	5.1	456	909	1556	6.8
4	-	2	3	9	-	-	-	-	53	-	2	.4	190	4	-	2.8	-	495	1148	-
8	-	2	2	57	-	-	-	-	2	-	.3	.4	150	3	-	3.2	-	380	1311	-
8	-	2	3	33	-	-	-	-	26	-	2.1	.4	190	4	-	3.6	-	501	1181	-
-	-	-	-	5	-	350	-	-	5	-	-	-	300	2.5	-	-	-	-	1130	-
-	-	-	-	5	-	300	-	-	2	-	-	-	120	2	-	-	-	-	1340	-
-	-	-	-	25	-	600	-	-	9	-	-	-	96	1.5	-	-	-	-	1160	-
-	-	-	-	30	-	200	-	-	4	-	-	-	72	1.5	-	-	-	-	900	-
-	-	-	-	65	-	250	-	-	5	-	-	-	72	1.5	-	-	-	-	1190	-
-	-	-	-	30	-	150	-	-	5	-	-	-	48	.8	-	-	-	-	570	-
4	-	1	2	25	-	40	-	-	0	-	.2	.4	48	.6	-	2.8	-	196	554	-

Appendix

Code	Name	Amount	Unit	Grams	Kilocalories	Carbohydrates (g)	Protein (g)	Fat (g)
62581	TACO BELL-LIGHT SOFT TACO SUPREME	1	EACH	128.0	200	23	14	5
62574	TACO BELL-LIGHT TACO	1	EACH	78.0	140	11	11	5
62588	TACO BELL-LIGHT TACO SALAD	1	EACH	464.0	330	35	30	9
62580	TACO BELL-LIGHT TACO SUPREME	1	EACH	106.0	160	23	14	5
58328	TACO BELL-MEXICAN PIZZA	1	EACH	223.0	575	40	21	37
58325	TACO BELL-NACHOS	1	EACH	106.0	346	37	7	18
58323	TACO BELL-NACHOS BELL GRANDE	1	EACH	287.0	649	61	22	35
58329	TACO BELL-PINTOS' N CHEESE	1	EACH	128.0	190	19	9	9
58337	TACO BELL-SALSA	1	EACH	10.0	18	4	1	0
58314	TACO BELL-SOFT TACO	1	EACH	92.0	225	18	12	12
58313	TACO BELL-TACO	1	EACH	78.0	183	11	10	11
58332	TACO BELL-TACO SALAD	1	EACH	575.0	905	55	34	61
58333	TACO BELL-TACO SALAD W/O SHELL	1	EACH	520.0	484	22	28	31
58316	TACO BELL-TOSTADO	1	EACH	156.0	243	27	9	11
61273	WENDY'S-BIG CLASSIC	1	EACH	251.0	480	44	27	23
62322	WENDY'S-BKD POTATO W/BACON AND CHEESE	1	EACH	380.0	510	75	17	17
61287	WENDY'S-BKD POTATO W/BROCCOLI AND CHEESE	1	EACH	411.0	450	77	9	14
62524	WENDY'S-BKD POTATO W/CHEESE	1	EACH	383.0	550	74	14	24
61281	WENDY'S-CHICKEN CLUB SANDWICH	1	EACH	220.0	520	44	30	25
61285	WENDY'S-FRENCH FRIES, BIGGIE	1	EACH	170.0	450	62	6	22
61284	WENDY'S-FRENCH FRIES, MEDIUM	1	EACH	136.0	360	50	5	17
61283	WENDY'S-FRENCH FRIES, SMALL	1	EACH	91.0	240	33	3	12
61301	WENDY'S-FROSTY DAIRY DESSERT, MEDIUM	1	EACH	321.8	460	76	12	13
61271	WENDY'S-PLAIN SINGLE	1	EACH	133.0	350	31	25	15
61272	WENDY'S-SINGLE W/EVERYTHING	1	EACH	219.0	440	36	26	23

Food Composition Table

Saturated Fat (g)	Monounsaturated Fat (g)	Polyunsaturated Fat (g)	Fiber (g)	Cholesterol (g)	Folate (g)	Vitamin A (RE)	Vitamin B₆ (mg)	Vitamin B₁₂ (µg)	Vitamin C (mg)	Vitamin E (mg)	Riboflavin (mg)	Thiamin (mg)	Calcium (mg)	Iron (mg)	Magnesium (mg)	Niacin (mg)	Phosphorus (mg)	Potassium (mg)	Sodium (mg)	Zinc (mg)
-	-	-	-	25	-	100	-	-	2	-	-	-	48	.6	-	-	-	-	610	-
4	-	1	1	20	-	40	-	-	0	-	.1	.1	0	0	-	1.2	-	159	276	-
-	-	-	-	50	-	1200	-	-	27	-	-	-	120	1.5	-	-	-	-	1610	-
-	-	-	-	20	-	100	-	-	2	-	-	-	0	0	-	-	-	-	340	-
11	-	10	3	52	-	-	-	-	31	-	.3	.3	257	4	-	3	-	408	1031	-
6	-	2	1	9	-	-	-	-	2	-	.2	-	191	1	-	.6	-	159	399	-
12	-	3	4	36	-	-	-	-	58	-	.3	.1	297	3	-	2.2	-	674	997	-
4	-	1	2	16	-	-	-	-	52	-	.2	.1	156	1	-	.4	-	384	642	-
0	-	0	0	0	-	-	-	-	-	-	.1	-	36	1	-	-	-	376	376	-
5	-	1	2	32	-	-	-	-	1	-	.2	.4	116	2	-	2.8	-	196	554	-
5	-	1	1	32	-	-	-	-	1	-	.1	.1	84	1	-	1.2	-	159	276	-
19	-	12	4	80	-	-	-	-	75	-	.6	.5	320	6	-	4.8	-	673	910	-
14	-	2	3	80	-	-	-	-	74	-	.4	.2	290	4	-	3.2	-	612	680	-
4	-	1	2	16	-	-	-	-	45	-	.2	.1	180	2	-	.6	-	401	596	-
7	8	7	-	75	-	60	-	-	12	-	.3	.5	120	3.5	-	6.7	-	500	850	-
4	3	8	-	15	-	100	-	-	36	-	.2	.5	80	2.5	-	6.7	-	1370	1170	-
2	3	7	-	0	-	200	-	-	60	-	.1	.3	80	2.5	-	4.8	-	1310	450	-
8	6	7	-	30	-	150	-	-	36	-	.2	.3	240	2	-	3.8	-	1210	640	-
6	7	9	-	75	-	20	-	-	9	-	.4	.6	80	8	-	15.2	-	470	980	-
5	15	1	-	0	-	-	-	-	12	-	.1	.3	16	.8	-	3.8	-	950	280	-
4	12	1	-	0	-	-	-	-	9	-	0	.2	16	.6	-	2.9	-	760	220	-
2	8	1	-	0	-	-	-	-	6	-	0	.2	-	.4	-	1.9	-	510	150	-
7	3	1	-	55	-	100	-	-	-	-	1	.2	320	.8	-	.8	-	830	260	-
6	7	2	-	70	-	-	-	-	-	-	.2	.4	80	3	-	5.7	-	280	510	-
7	7	7	-	75	-	60	-	-	9	-	.2	.4	80	3	-	6.7	-	430	850	-

Glossary

abstinence to refrain completely from engaging in a particular behavior.

acesulfame nonnutritive sweetener that is 200 times sweeter than sucrose and marketed as "sunette" in many food products.

Acquired Immunodeficiency Syndrome (AIDS) viral destruction of the immune system, causing loss of ability to fight infections.

acute illness an illness that occurs suddenly, often has no identifiable cause, is usually treatable, and often disappears in a short time.

addiction a pathological need for a substance that has life-damaging potential.

addictive behavior behavior that is excessive, compulsive, and psychologically and physically destructive.

adipose cells fat cells.

adrenocorticotropic hormone (ACTH) hormone released by the hypothalamus during periods of stress that initiates various physiological responses.

aerobic literally "with oxygen"; when applied to exercise, refers to activities in which oxygen demand can be supplied continuously by individuals during performance.

aerobic capacity maximum oxygen consumption.

alcohol socially acceptable drug.

alcoholism disease in which an individual loses control over drinking; inability to refrain from drinking.

alternative medicine body of therapies that are not taught in the U.S. medical schools and are generally unavailable from doctors or hospitals.

amenorrheic cessation of menstruation.

amino acids chemical structures that form protein.

anabolic steroids drugs closely related to testosterone that increase muscle mass in humans.

anaerobic literally "without oxygen"; when applied to exercise, refers to high-intensity physical activities in which oxygen demand is greater than the amount that can be supplied during performance.

android deposition of fat that is characteristic of men; fat tends to accumulate in the abdomen and upper body.

aneurysm weak spot in an artery that forms a balloonlike pouch that can rupture

angina chest pain that is the result of ischemia (see **ischemic**).

anorexia nervosa serious illness of deliberate self-starvation with profound psychiatric and physical components.

antioxidants compounds that block the oxidation of substances in food or the body (vitamins C and E and beta-carotene are examples).

arthritis inflammatory disease of the joints.

asymptomatic without symptoms.

atherosclerosis slow, progressive disease of the arteries characterized by the deposition of plaque on the inner lining of arterial walls.

ATP adenosine triphosphate, the actual unit of energy used for muscular contraction.

atrophy a decrease in the size of organ, muscles, and body tissues from disease or disuse.

autogenics form of suggestion that precipitates relaxation.

autoimmune disease disease in which the immune system fails to recognize its own body parts and produces antibodies against them to the point of causing injury.

autonomic nervous system part of the nervous system that is concerned with control of involuntary bodily functions.

avoidance a behavioral strategy that emphasizes eliminating circumstances associated with undesirable behavior.

ballistic stretching repetitive contractions of agonist muscles to produce very quick, rapid stretches of antagonist muscles.

balloon angioplasty surgical procedure that involves the insertion of a catheter with a balloon at the tip used to compress fatty deposits and plaque against the walls of the artery.

basal cell carcinoma the most common type of skin cancer. It grows slowly and usually does not metastasize (spread).

basal metabolic rate (BMR) number of calories needed to sustain life.

behavior assessment process of counting, recording, observing, measuring, and describing behavior.

behavior substitution lifestyle change technique in which an incompatible behavior is substituted for a behavior being altered.

behavioral contract a written agreement in a lifestyle-change program.

benign noncancerous; refers to a growth that is unable to spread.

binge drinking consuming five or more drinks in a single session at least once during the previous two weeks, with the intent to become intoxicated.

binge-eating disorder practice of eating large amounts of food in a short period of time.

biofeedback educational tool used to provide information about an individual's physiological actions.

blood alcohol concentration (BAC) percentage of alcohol content in the blood.

body composition amount of lean versus fat tissue in the body.

body dysmorphic disorder (BDD) a psychiatric disorder characterized by a preoccupation with perceived imperfections in physical appearance that cause the person to withdraw from social activities.

body mass index (BMI) the ratio of body weight in kilograms to height in meters squared.

botanicals plants that are thought to have medicinal properties (also called *herbs* and *phytomedicinals*).

bulimia eating disorder characterized by episodes of secretive binge eating and purging.

Caesarean section delivery surgical removal of the fetus through the abdominal wall.

caffeine a stimulant that increases the heart rate.

caloric expenditure calories expended by physical activity and metabolism.

caloric intake calories supplied by food.

calorie short for *kilocalorie*, which is the unit of measurement for food energy. A calorie is the amount of heat required to raise the temperature of 1 gram of water 1 degree Centigrade.

cancer group of diseases characterized by uncontrolled, disorderly cell growth.

cannabinoids chemicals found only in marijuana.

cannabis sativa Indian hemp plant from which marijuana and hashish are derived.

carbon monoxide a colorless, tasteless, odorless gas that is the product of incomplete combustion of carbon-containing fuels.

carcinogens substances that cause cancer or enable the growth of cancer cells; cancer-causing agents.

carcinoma cancer of a body surface or body cavity, such as cancer of the breast, lung, skin, stomach, testis, or uterus.

cariogenic refers to the promotion of dental caries, or cavities.

cardiac dysrhythmia irregular heart rate that is sometimes intractable.

cardiac output amount of blood ejected by the heart in 1 minute.

cardiorespiratory endurance ability to take in, deliver, and extract oxygen for physical work.

catheterization the process of examining the heart by introducing a thin tube (catheter) into a vein or an artery and passing it into the heart.

cause and effect in medical research, the type of a relationship in which one variable is scientifically proved to cause a certain effect.

cerebral hemorrhage bursting of a blood vessel in the brain.

chemoprevention nutritional intervention to prevent diseases, such as cancer, by bolstering the immune system.

chemotherapy use of drugs and hormones to treat various cancers.

child abuse physical, emotional, or sexual mistreatment of a child.

chlamydia one of the most common sexually transmitted diseases.

cholesterol steroid that is an essential structural component of neural tissue and cell walls and is required for the manufacture of hormones and bile.

chronic disease a disease that usually begins gradually and persists for an indefinite period of time, usually months or years.

chronic effects of exercise the physiological changes that result from cardiorespiratory training.

circuit resistance training (CRT) a total of 8 to 15 exercises are usually used in a circuit. The exerciser goes through the circuit three times with minimum rest between exercise stations.

cocaine a stimulant used in powdered form.

cognitive dissonance an internal conflict that occurs when a person's behaviors are inconsistent with his or her beliefs, values, or knowledge.

communicable diseases diseases that can be transmitted from one person to another.

complete protein protein that contains all the essential amino acids.

complex carbohydrates polysaccharides, including starch and fiber.

concentric contraction shortening of the muscle as it develops the tension to overcome an external resistance.

condyloma warts on the genitalia.

contraindication reason for not prescribing a drug or treatment.

control group in health research, the group receiving no treatment.

coping effort(s) made to manage or deal with stress.

coronary artery bypass surgery procedure involving the removal of a leg vein that is used as a shunt around the blocked area in the coronary artery.

countering the substitution of a new behavior for an undesirable one.

crack smokable form of cocaine that is extremely dangerous and very addictive.

Crohn's disease a type of inflammatory bowel disease whose cause is unknown. Crohn's disease is characterized by frequent and intense diarrhea, abdominal pain, gas, fever, and rectal bleeding.

cross-training the attainment of physical fitness by participating in a variety of activities regularly.

crude fiber residue of plant food following chemical treatment in the laboratory.

cunnilingus oral sex performed on the female genitalia.

Daily Values (DVs) provides nutritional guidelines for ingestion of carbohydrate, fat, saturated fat, cholesterol, sodium, potassium, and dietary fiber.

deceptive advertising advertising that misleads consumers by overstating or exaggerating the performance of a product.

deductible amount paid by a patient before being eligible for benefits from an insurance company.

defensive medicine practice of prescribing medical tests to protect doctors against malpractice lawsuits.

dehydration excessive loss of body water.

delta-9-tetrahydrocannabinol (THC) major psychoactive drug found in marijuana.

depressants known as sedatives and tranquilizers; these agents slow the central nervous system.

designer drugs illegally manufactured drugs that mimic controlled substances.

diabetes mellitus metabolic disorder involving the pancreas and the failure to produce insulin; a risk factor for cardiovascular disease.

diagnostic laboratory tests tests conducted for specific symptoms during a physical examination.

dietary fiber residue of plant food after digestion in the human body. One gram of crude fiber equals 2 to 3 grams of dietary fiber.

diet resistance the inability to lose weight by dieting.

disability insurance insurance that pays for income lost because of the inability to work due to an illness or injury.

distress form of stress that results in negative responses.

diuretics substances that increase water output and body's need for water.

diverticulitis infection of the diverticula of the intestines.

diverticulosis condition of having saclike swellings (diverticula) in the walls of the intestines.

double-blind study type of health research in which neither the researcher nor the subjects know who is receiving an experimental treatment.

drug chemical substance that has the potential to alter the structure and functioning of a living organism.

eccentric contraction the lengthening of a muscle as the weight or resistance is returned to the starting position.

echocardiography noninvasive technique that uses sound waves to determine the shape, texture, and movement of the valves of the heart.

ectomorph body shape characterized by thin body frame.

elderly abuse physical, emotional, sexual, or medical abuse of an elderly person. Most often the abuser is an adult child of the victim.

electrocardiograph (ECG) device for recording electrical variations in action of the heart muscle.

embolus mass of undissolved matter in the blood or lymphatic vessels that detaches from the vessel walls.

endomorph body shape characterized by rounded physical features and large body frame.

endorphins mood-elevating, pain-killing substances produced by the brain.

energy nutrients nutrients, such as carbohydrates, fat, and protein, that provide a source of energy for the body.

environmental dimension of wellness comprises aspects of wellness that improve quality of life in the community, including laws and agencies that safeguard the physical environment.

epidemiological studies population studies that observe the health habits and diseases of large numbers of people.

epinephrine hormone produced by the adrenal medulla that speeds up body processes.

essential fat fat that is indispensable for individuals to function biologically and necessary to support life.

essential hypertension high blood pressure caused by unknown reasons.

essential nutrients nutrients that cannot be made by the body and must be supplied in the diet.

ethyl alcohol intoxicating agent in alcoholic drinks; colorless liquid with a sharp, burning taste.

eustress stress judged as "good" positive stress or stress that contributes to positive outcomes.

exclusion medical services that are not covered by an insurance policy.

experimental group in health research, the group receiving some form of experimental treatment.

false negative test results that incorrectly show a person is healthy when an abnormality actually exists.

false positive test results that incorrectly show an abnormality when a person is actually healthy.

family practitioner medical doctor who serves as a general practitioner for an individual or a family.

fasting complete starvation; avoidance of food consumption.

fat mixture of triglycerides.

fellatio oral sex performed on the male genitalia.

fiber substances in food that resist digestion; formerly called *roughage*.

fight-or-flight syndrome initial phase of the general adaptation syndrome (GAS); when a stressor is encountered, the body responds by preparing to stand and fight or run away depending on the situation; also called the *alarm phase* of the GAS.

fixed indemnity benefits specified amounts that are paid by an insurance company for particular medical procedures.

flexibility range of motion at a joint.

fraternal twins twins who emanate from separate eggs and do not have identical genes.

freebasing smoking liquefied cocaine.

free radicals naturally produced chemicals that arise from cell activity.

fructose fruit sugar.

general adaptation syndrome (GAS) series of physiological changes that occur when a stressor is encountered; the GAS is conceived of as having three phases: alarm, resistance, and exhaustion.

genital warts warts on the genitalia.

glucose primary source of energy used by the body; blood sugar.

glyceride general term for fat compounds, including triglyceride, monoglyceride, and diglyceride.

Golgi tendon organ a proprioceptor that responds to muscle stretch and tension.

goniometer a protractor-like instrument used to measure the flexibility of various joints.

gonorrhea bacterial disease that is sexually transmitted and can lead to serious complications if left untreated, including sterility and scarring of the heart valves.

gynoid fat deposition characteristic of females, in whom fat tends to accumulate on the hips and thighs.

hardiness label used in describing a particular type of personality that tends to remain healthy even under extreme stress; the three components of hardiness are challenge, commitment, and control.

hashish resin from the *cannabis sativa* plant that can be smoked to alter mood; a frequently abused drug.

hate crimes crimes directed at individuals or groups solely because of their racial, ethnic, or religious background, sexual orientation, or other differences from the perpetrator.

headache a common discomfort that is often caused by distress, tension, and anxiety; may be the result of injury or brain disease.

health balancing of the physical, emotional, social, and spiritual components of personality in a manner that is conducive to optimal well-being and a higher quality of existence.

health-behavior gap discrepancy between what people know and what they actually do regarding their health.

health care providers people and facilities such as physicians and hospitals that provide health care services.

health fatalism in health information the view that new information cannot be believed or trusted because it will inevitably be refuted.

health insurance a contract between an insurance company and an individual or a group for the payment of medical care costs.

health maintenance organization (HMO) prepaid group insurance program that provides a full range of medical services.

health-promoting behaviors things done to maintain and improve one's level of wellness.

health promotion art and science of helping people change their lifestyle to move toward a higher state of wellness.

health-related fitness components of fitness that include cardiorespiratory endurance, muscular strength, muscular endurance, flexibility, and body composition.

health risk appraisals questionnaires used to provide information about health habits, lifestyle, and medical history.

heat exhaustion serious heat-related condition characterized by dizziness, fainting, rapid pulse, and cool skin.

heat stroke heat-related medical emergency characterized by high temperature (106° F or higher) and dry skin and accompanied by some or all of the following: delirium, convulsions, and loss of consciousness.

hemoglobin substance in blood that carries oxygen.

hepatitis B one of five types of viral hepatitis. Hepatitis B is the most serious type and can be transmitted sexually.

herbs see *botanicals*.

herpes simplex virus (HSV) virus responsible for herpes genitalis, a sexually transmitted disease.

highly polyunsaturated fat fatty acid composed of triglycerides in which the carbon chain has room for many hydrogen atoms.

homeostasis state of balance or constancy; the body is continually attempting to maintain homeostasis.

homicide the intentional taking of another person's life; murder.

homocysteine amino acid that is thought to increase the risk of heart disease.

homogeneous group group of subjects with similar characteristics.

hypertrophy increase in the size of organs and muscle tissue.

human immunodeficiency virus (HIV) virus that is the source of AIDS.

human papilloma virus (HPV) causative agent of condyloma (genital warts).

hydrogenation process of adding hydrogen to unsaturated fatty acid to make it more saturated.

hyperglycemia high blood sugar.

hyperplasia increase in the number of cells.

hypertension high blood pressure.

hyperthermia excessive buildup of heat in the body.

hyperthyroidism disease caused by an overactive thyroid gland.

hypertrophy increase in the size of a cell.

hypokinesis physical inactivity.

hypothalamus part of the limbic system that contains the center for many bodily functions; in stressful situations the hypothalamus releases specific hormones to elicit appropriate bodily responses.

hypothermia cold weather-related condition that results in abnormally low body temperature.

hypothyroidism disease caused by an underactive thyroid gland.

iatrogenic disease condition caused as a result of receiving medical care.

identical twins twins who emanate from the same egg.

immunization a vaccine or other preparation administered to prevent disease.

immunotherapy in relation to cancer, technique for stimulating the body's immune system to destroy cancer cells.

implied consent nonverbal authorization of a medical procedure such as a cooperation during the administration of tests.

incomplete protein protein that does not contain all the essential amino acids in the proportions needed by the body.

infarction death of heart muscle tissue.

inflammatory bowel disease a variety of diseases that cause inflammation of the intestines. The two most common types are Crohn's disease and ulcerative colitis.

influenza commonly called *flu*; caused by a virus.

informed consent legal provision requiring patient's authorization of any medical procedure, therapy, or treatment.

inhalants substances that cause druglike effects when inhaled.

insoluble fiber fiber that does not dissolve in water; comes from wheat bran and vegetables.

insulin hormone secreted by the pancreas that increases the use of glucose by the tissues of the body.

intensity degree of vigorousness of a single bout of exercise.

internist medical doctor specializing in internal medicine and sometimes serving as a primary care physician.

ischemia diminished supply of blood to the heart muscle.

isoflavones Phytoestrogens in soybeans that are thought to help prevent breast cancer by blocking natural estrogens.

isokinetic method for developing muscular strength that involves a constant rate of speed and changes in the amount of weight resistance.

isometric use of static contractions to develop strength.

isotonic method for developing muscular strength that involves a variable rate of speed and a constant weight resistance.

lactic acid metabolite formed in muscles as a result of incomplete breakdown of sugar.

lactose simple sugar; milk sugar.

lactovegetarian a person who eats plant foods and dairy products but excludes eggs, fish, poultry, and meat from their diet.

leptin a protein made in fat cells that controls weight gain and loss.

leukemia cancer of the blood-forming tissues, including the bone marrow and spleen.

life insurance insurance that pays a death benefit.

limbic system large, C-shaped area that contains the centers for emotions, memory storage, learning relay, and hormone production (the pituitary gland, thalamus, and hypothalamus).

lipid class of nutrients more commonly referred to as *fat*.

lipoprotein fat-carrying protein.

locus of control perspective from which an individual views life. Individuals with an *internal* locus-of-control believe that their decisions make a difference and that they have control over their lives. People with *external* locus-of-control see themselves as "victims" and consider other people, situations, and conditions as being the controlling factors in their lives.

low-calorie diet diet that limits intake to 800 to 1000 calories a day; results in atrophy of heart muscle.

lymphoma cancer that develops in the lymphatic system, including the neck, armpits, groin, and chest.

macronutrients nutrients required by the body in large amounts. Usually refers to the energy nutrients: protein, fat, and carbohydrates.

mainstream smoke smoke that is inhaled and exhaled by smoker.

major minerals those minerals required in large amounts (more than 5 grams a day).

malignant cancerous; refers to a growth that has the ability to spread to other areas of the body.

Glossary

mammography x-ray examination of the breast to detect cancer.

marijuana comes from the cannabis plant.

megadose large doses, usually in the form of supplements.

melanoma a dangerous form of skin cancer that has a strong tendency to spread to other areas of the body.

mesomorph body shape characterized by a muscular, athletic body build.

metabolism all chemical reactions that occur within the cells of the body.

metastasis process by which cancerous cells spread from their original location to another location in the body.

micronutrients nutrients required by the body in small amounts. Usually refers to vitamins and minerals.

migraine headaches headaches characterized by throbbing pain that can last for hours or days, sometimes accompanied by nausea and vomiting. Migraines are thought to be the result of dilation of blood vessels in the head.

minerals inorganic compounds in food necessary for good health.

mitochondria the cell's "powerhouse."

moderate calorie diet diet that limits caloric intake to 1300 to 1600 calories a day.

monounsaturated fat fatty acid composed of triglycerides in which the carbon chain has room for two hydrogen atoms.

morbidity incidence of disease and/or sickness.

mortality incidence of death.

muscular endurance application of repeated muscular force developed by many repetitions against resistances considerably less than maximum.

muscular strength maximal force that a muscle or muscle group can exert in a single contraction.

myocardial infarction heart attack; death of heart muscle tissue.

narcotics powerful painkillers.

negative reinforcers avoidance of something unpleasant.

neoplasm abnormal mass of cells; also called a *tumor*; can be benign or malignant.

neutraceuticals natural ingredients intended to promote and maintain health.

newsgroup a location on the internet where electronic messages related to a medical topic are posted.

nicotine addictive substance and alkaloid poison found in tobacco.

nucleoside analogs a combination of drugs (AZT& ddI) that seems to prevent the development of opportunistic infections associated with AIDS.

nutrient substance found in food that is required by the body.

nutrient density ratio of nutrients to calories; also called the *index of nutritional quality*.

nutrition science that deals with the study of nutrients and the way the body ingests, digests, absorbs, transports, metabolizes, and excretes these nutrients.

obesity excessive amount of storage fat.

ob gene a gene found in fat cells that produces leptin. Also called the "fat gene."

occupational dimension of wellness comprises aspects of wellness that help achieve a balance between work and leisure in a way that promotes health and a sense of personal satisfaction.

Olestra a synthetic fat that has the flavor and taste of real fat but yields no calories.

omega-3 fatty acids type of fatty acid found in cold-water seafood and thought to lower the risks of heart disease.

oncogene cancer-causing gene.

osteoarthritis most common form of arthritis characterized by the deterioration of articular cartilage that covers the gliding surfaces of the bones in certain joints.

osteophyte another name for a bone spur.

osteoporosis progressive decrease in the mineral content of bone, making bones brittle.

overcompensatory eating an eating pattern characterized by overconsumption of low-fat foods, which causes an increase in total caloric intake.

overfat may or may not be within normal guidelines for weight but with an excessive ratio of fat compared with lean tissue.

overweight excessive weight for one's height without regard for body composition.

ovolactovegetarian a person who eats plant foods, eggs, and dairy products but excludes fish, poultry, and meat from the diet.

partner abuse physical or emotional abuse committed by an adult against his or her partner.

passive smoking inhalation of environmental cigarette smoke by a nonsmoker.

pathogen disease-producing organism.

pelvic inflammatory disease (PID) chronic condition of infection in the uterus, fallopian tubes, and upper reproductive areas; the leading cause of infertility in women.

performance-related fitness sports fitness; composed of speed, power, balance, coordination, agility, and reaction time.

periodic examination physical exam in which tests and assessments are prescribed according to risk factors.

pescovegetarian a person who eats plant foods, eggs, dairy products, and fish but excludes red meat from the diet.

phytochemicals plant chemicals that exist naturally in foods.

phytoestrogen plant hormone (estrogen) that exists naturally in foods.

phytomedicinals see *botanicals*.

placebo inactive substance, such as a fake drug.

pollovegetarian a persons who eats plant foods, eggs, dairy products, fish, and poultry but excludes red meat.

polyunsaturated fat fatty acid composed of triglycerides in which the carbon chain has room for four or more hydrogen atoms.

positive reinforcers rewards earned for achieving goals in a lifestyle-change program.

preferred providers organization (PPO) a group of private practitioners who sell their services at reduced rates to insurance companies.

preventive health behaviors health practices associated with the promotion of wellness and the prevention of sickness and death.

primary care physician medical doctor who is responsible for an individual's overall health.

primary site (reference to cancer) original site of cancer cell formation.

proprioceptive neuromuscular facilitation (PNF) consists of several stretching techniques that involve some combination of contraction and static stretching and holding agonist and antagonist muscle groups.

prospective study an epidemiological study in which researchers predict possible disease relationships and patterns among groups of people.

protease inhibitor inhibits the enzyme protease, which allows HIV to develop.

protein complementing practice of combining plant protein with cereal/grain protein to provide complete protein.

psychoactives drugs that can alter feelings, moods, and/or perceptions.

psychosomatic diseases diseases (physical symptoms) caused by psychological and emotional stressors.

psychoneuroimmunology (PNT) a medical discipline whose philosophy rests on the connections among brain function, the nervous system, and the body's response to infection and abnormal cell division.

radiotherapy use of radiation to either destroy cancer cells or destroy their reproductive mechanism so they cannot replicate.

RDA acronym for recommended dietary allowances.

reactance motivation a behavioral response to force or coersion in which behavior is the opposite of that intended (e.g., a child refuses to eat a particular food because of parental force).

recidivism the tendency to revert to original behaviors/conditions after completing a behavioral change program.

recommended dietary allowances (RDA) daily recommended intakes of nutrients for normal, healthy people in the United States.

reference daily intakes (RDI) represents minimum standards for essential nutrients and replaces the U.S. recommended daily allowance established in 1968.

relaxation techniques techniques used in coping with and managing stress.

reliability extent to which health studies yield consistent results.

reminders a behavioral strategy used to formulated action goals.

residual volume amount of air remaining in the lungs after expiration.

retrospective study an epidemiological study in which researchers review previously gathered data to identify possible disease relationships and patterns among groups of people.

reward deficiency syndrome a variety of disorders that have in common the traits of impulsiveness, addiction, and compulsiveness.

rheumatoid arthritis most crippling form of arthritis, characterized by inflammation of the joints, pain, swelling, and deformity.

risk factors conditions that threaten wellness and increase the chances of contracting a disease.

road rage overly aggressive driving that includes physical or verbal assault against another driver after a traffic dispute.

saccharides refers to sugars (general term).

safer sex a pattern of behavior in which steps are taken to protect oneself and one's partner from pregnancy and infection with HIV and sexually transmitted diseases. These steps can include using condoms or dental dams and having periodic medical tests and examinations.

sarcoma cancer of a connective tissue, such as bone and muscle.

saturated fat fatty acid composed of triglycerides in which all the fatty acids contain the maximum number of hydrogen atoms.

scientifically controlled study a study conducted in a controlled setting that involves a treatment (experimental) group and a placebo (control) group.

secondary site refers to the location of cancer cells after they have spread from the primary site.

sedentary physically inactive.

selective health examination specific test used in response to specific symptoms or for diagnosing a specific problem.

self-care movement toward individuals taking increased responsibility to prevent or manage certain health conditions.

self-efficacy people's belief in their ability to accomplish a specific task or behavior; that belief then affects the outcome of the task or behavior; the theory that individuals who expect to succeed

tend to succeed and those who expect to fail tend to fail.

self-help approach to lifestyle change that assumes individuals can plan and execute their own plans.

set point theory theory that the body has a preference for maintaining a certain amount of weight and defends that weight quite vigorously.

sexually transmitted diseases (STDs) diseases spread through sexual contact, such as AIDS, chlamydia, gonorrhea, and herpes.

shaping up a behavioral strategy in which a person acclimates to desired behaviors in small increments

sidestream smoke smoke given off by burning tobacco products.

skinfold measures method for determining the amount of body fat by using skin calipers.

sleep apnea a condition characterized by loud snoring and brief periods during which breathing ceases.

soluble fiber fiber that dissolves in water; comes from fruit pectins and oat bran.

squamous cell carcinoma the second most common type of skin cancer. It rarely spreads to other areas, but it grows more quickly than basal cell carcinoma.

starch plant polysaccharides composed of glucose and digestible by humans.

static stretching passive stretching of antagonist muscles by slowly stretching and holding a position for 15 to 30 seconds.

statistical relationship an association between two or more variables or events.

statistical significance the probability that a study's findings are reliable and are not due to chance.

stimulants drugs that speed up the central nervous system.

stimulus control technique in lifestyle management involving the elimination and/or manipulation of stimuli related to a specific behavior.

stress nonspecific response of the body to any demands made on it.

stressor any physical, psychological, or environmental event or condition that initiates the stress response.

stretch reflex the myotatic reflex.

stroke volume amount of blood that the heart can eject in one beat.

subliminal advertising technique in which messages, words, and symbols are embedded or hidden in advertisements.

sucrose table sugar.

syndrome X combination of high blood pressure, high blood sugar, high blood lipids, and abdominal obesity.

syphilis a sexually transmitted disease.

tar black, sticky, dark fluid composed of thousands of chemicals and found in tobacco.

tension headaches most common kind of headache; caused by involuntary contractions of the scalp, head, and neck muscles and may be precipitated by anxiety, stress, and allergic reactions.

thermogenic effect of food (TEF) the amount of energy required by the body to digest, absorb, metabolize, and store nutrients.

thrombus stationary blood clot; can occlude an artery supplying the brain.

trace minerals those minerals required in small amounts.

transfatty acids saturated fat found in processed food that has been hydrogenated.

transmit time the time it takes food to move through the body.

triglyceride compound composed of carbon, hydrogen, and oxygen with three fatty acids.

tropical oils oils that come from the fruit of coconut and palm trees.

ulcerative colitis chronic inflammation of the colon lining. The symptoms are the same as those of Crohn's disease, but the only area affected is the colon lining.

unintentional injury any injury that occurs as a result of an accident or reckless behavior.

unsaturated fat fatty acid composed of triglycerides in which the carbon chain has room for more hydrogen atoms.

validity extent to which the research design of a health study permits the assertion of certain health claims.

variable resistance provides increasing resistance as a weight is lifted through the full range of motion.

vegan a person whose diet is limited to plant foods. Also called a *strict vegetarian*.

viral hepatitis inflammation of the liver caused by one or more viruses.

visualization a form of meditation that makes use of the imagination.

vital capacity amount of air that can be expired after a maximum inspiration.

vitamin supplements natural and synthetic compounds taken orally to supplement the vitamins consumed in food.

vitamins organic compounds in food necessary for good health.

weight cycling potentially harmful pattern of repeated weight loss and weight gain.

wellness engaging in activities and behaviors that enhance quality of life and maximize personal potential.

Credits

Chapter 1: Page 5: © Jim Pickerell/Tony Stone Images; **p. 11:** © Gregg Adams/Tony Stone Images; **p. 16:** © Jurgen Reisch/Tony Stone Images

Chapter 2: Page 46: © Spencer Grant/Photo Edit; **p. 53:** © Gary A. Conner

Chapter 3: Page 81: © Michael Newman/Photo Edit

Chapter 4: Fig. 4.20: © The McGraw-Hill Companies, Inc./Stewart Halperin, photographer

Chapter 6: Page 154: © Matthew Klein/Photo Researchers, Inc.; **p. 165:** © Stewart Cohen/Tony Stone Images; **p. 169:** © Chris Harvey/Tony Stone Images; **p. 183** (left) © Ian O'Leary/Tony Stone Images; (right): © John Eastcott/Yva Momatiuk/The Image Works

Chapter 8: Page 242: © Myrleen Cate/Tony Stone Images; **p. 253:** © Oli Tennent/Tony Stone Images

Chapter 9: Page 279: © David Oliver/Tony Stone Images; **p. 288:** © Lori Adamski Peek/Tony Stone Images

Index

A
Abdominal crunch, 104
Abdominal fat, and risk of illness, 217–218, 236–237
Abdominal muscular endurance, assessment of, 123
Accidents, death from, 7
Achilles tendon stretch, 136
Action stage, self-help approach, 17–18
Acute illness, meaning of, 7
Adenosine triphosphate (ATP), and cardiorespiratory training, 69
Advertising, subliminal advertising, 12
Aerobic capacity
   and cardiorespiratory training, 69
   genetic factors, 215
   limitations to, 69
   meaning of, 67
Aerobic exercise. *See also* Cardiorespiratory training
   health benefits, 72
African Americans
   and hypertension, 46–47
Age. *See also* Children; Older adults
   and cardiovascular disease, 38
   and weight gain, 239, 253
Agonists, 133
Alcohol use
   and HDL levels, 44
   health benefits, 184
   health risks from, 184
Amino acids, 156
Anabolic-androgenic steroids, negative health effects, 115
Anaerobic exercise. *See also* Resistance training
   meaning of, 99
Aneurysm, and stroke, 38
Anger, health effects of, 5–6
Anorexia nervosa, 255–256
   diagnostic criteria for, 256
Antagonists, 136
Antioxidants, 162–163
Arteries, and circulation, 34
Art therapy, and health, 5
Aspirin, heart disease prevention, 55
Atherosclerosis
   and cholesterol level, 36, 43–44
   lipid oxidation theory, 43
   progression of, 36, 44
Autogenics, steps in, 285, 286

B
Back extension, 105
Back pain
   causes of, 139
   prevention of, 139–141
Back stretch, 135
Ballistic stretching, 139
Balloon angioplasty, 55–56
Basal metabolic rate (BMR)
   and age, 253
   exercise effects, 252
B complex vitamins, 163, 164, 166
   food sources of, 164
   functions of, 164
   recommended intake, 163
Behavior
   influences on, 12
   resistance motivation, 12
Behavior change
   assessment for, 16
   contracting, 18
   countering strategies for problem behaviors, 18
   goal setting for, 17
   resistance to, 12, 15–16
   self-help approach, 15–19
   shaping up, 18
Bench press, 103–104
Bench step test, 91
Beta carotene, 165
Biceps curl, 101, 102
Bilberry, 172
Binge-eating disorder, 257–258
   diagnostic criteria for, 258
Bioelectrical impedance analysis (BIA), 221–222
Biofeedback
   health uses of, 5
   stress management, 286
Birth defects, reducing with folate, 166, 185
Blood
   circulation of, 34–35
   components of, 35
Blood pressure, 45–48
   high/low readings, 46
   hypertension, 46–48
   measurement of, 46
Blood volume, and cardiorespiratory training, 68
Body composition
   meaning of, 214
   obesity, 214
   overfat, 216
   overweight, 214, 216
   regional fat distribution, 216–218
Body composition assessment
   bioelectrical impedance analysis (BIA), 221–222
   skinfold measurements, 222–225
   underwater weighing, 219, 221
Body dysmorphic disorder, 234, 235
Body fat
   and children/adolescents, 220
   desirable weight calculated from, 226, 231
   recommendations for men, 215
   recommendations for women, 214
Body fat distribution, 216–218
   feminine pattern of, 216–217, 218
   masculine pattern of, 217
   and risk of illness, 217–218
   waist-to-hip ratio, 217
Body image
   assessment of, 265
   negative image, factors in, 234
Body mass index (BMI), 218–219
   assessment of, 229
   for overweight and obesity, 235
   table for calculation of, 220
Body shape, genetic factors, 240
Body weight
   American preoccupation with, 234–235
   caloric intake/caloric expenditure balance, 234
   desirable weight calculation, 226, 231
   genetic factors, 215
   increases for adult Americans, 235–236
Body weight assessment
   body mass index (BMI), 218–219
   direct measurement, 219
   height/weight tables, 218
Brain
   stress response, 278

Index

Breathing
    deep breathing, 284
    and resistance training, 114
Bulimia, 256–257
    diagnostic criteria for, 257
B vitamins, cardiovascular disease prevention, 54

C

Calcium, 168–169
    food sources of, 168
    functions of, 168
    supplements, 168
Calf stretch, 136
Calisthenic exercises, muscular strength assessment, 125–127
Caloric deficit, and weight loss, 243
Calories
    burning and weight loss, 250–252
    caloric cost and common activities, 252
    caloric cost and common activities assessment, 271
    definition of, 155
    expenditure through exercise assessment, 267
    recommended intake, 155
Campylobacter jejuni, cause and signs of, 188
Canadian trunk strength test, 123
Cancer
    dietary strategies for, 190
    and obesity, 236
Carbohydrates, 155–156
    assessing intake, 199
    complex, 156
    pre-exercise meals, 186–187
    recommended intake, 156
    simple, 155
Carbon monoxide
    detection in home, 307
Cardiac catheterization, 55
Cardiac output, and cardiorespiratory training, 67–68
Cardiorespiratory endurance, 67–76
    definition of, 67
    and wellness, 70
Cardiorespiratory training, 67–70
    and blood volume, 68
    and cardiac output, 67–68
    and heart rate, 67
    and heart volume, 68
    metabolic responses to, 68–70
    respiratory responses to, 68
    and stroke volume, 67
Cardiovascular disease
    coronary heart disease, 36–37
    diagnosis of, 54–55
    medical treatment of, 55–57
    statistics on, 34
    stroke, 37–38
Cardiovascular disease prevention
    B vitamins, 54
    diet, 53–54, 189–190
    iron-enriched blood, 54
    lipoprotein (a), 54
Cardiovascular disease risk, 36, 38–53
    and abdominal fat deposition, 217
    age, 38

blood pressure, 45–48
cholesterol level, 40–45
cigarette smoking, 48–49
diabetes mellitus, 51–53
genetic factors, 40
homocysteine, 54
male gender, 38, 40
obesity, 51, 236
physical inactivity, 49–51
stress, 53
very low fat diets, 160
Cardiovascular system
    circulation, 34–35
    heart, 34–35
Carotenoids, 165
Cerebral hemorrhage, and stroke, 38
Challenge, meaning of, 282
Chest press, 108
Chest stretch, 135
Children
    body fat, 220
    lifestyle of, 37
    obesity, 237
Cholesterol, 40–45
    and atherosclerosis, 36, 43–44
    and coronary heart disease, 41
    dietary sources of, 42
    lowering, strategies for, 42, 190
    suggested daily consumption, 40
    transport of, 41, 43
Chromium picolinate, 114–115
Chronic disease
    meaning of, 7
Cigarette smoking
    cardiovascular disease risk, 48–49
    cardiovascular effects of, 49
    death from, 10
    passive smoking, 49
Cigarette smoking cessation, 49
Cigar smoking, 49, 50
Circuit resistance training, 110–111
Circulation, 34–35
Cities, exercise tips, 82
Clostridium botulinum, cause and signs of, 188
Cognitive dissonance, meaning of, 15
Cold temperature and exercise, 82–83
    frostbite, 82
    hypothermia, 82–83
    precautions, 82–83
Commitment, meaning of, 282
Concentric muscle contraction, 100, 101, 107
Congenital heart defects, 36, 70
Congestive heart failure, 36
Contemplation stage, self-help approach, 15
Contracting, behavior change, 18
Cool down, exercise, 77
Coping. *See also* Stress management
    coping style assessment, 297–298
    guidelines for, 283
Coronary artery bypass surgery, 55
Coronary heart disease, 36–37
    and childhood behavior patterns, 37
    forms of, 36

heart attack, 37–38
risk factors, 36
Creatine supplementation, 114
Cross-training, benefits of, 76
Cycling, weight cycling, 243–244

D

Daily log, resistance training, 115–116, 129
Daily Values (DV), food labels, 190, 191
Dance therapy, and health, 5
Death, leading causes of, 7, 10
Deep breathing, for relaxation, 284
Dehydration, prevention and exercise, 80–82
Depression, and illness, 52
Diabetes mellitus
    and abdominal fat deposition, 217–218
    cardiovascular disease risk, 51–53
    complications of, 52
    dietary strategies for, 190
    and obesity, 236
    stress, and illness, 52
    Type I, 51–52
    Type II, 52–53
Diet. *See also* Nutrients; Nutrition
    disease prevention strategies, 189–190
    nutritional assessment, 193–194
    prepackaged convenience foods, 193
    small adjustments, value of, 194
    snacking, 192–193
Dietary fat, 157–162
    assessing intake, 201, 209–210
    and athletic activity, 187
    and cholesterol, 158
    fat content of foods, chart of, 159
    fish oils, 158
    high-fat theory of obesity, 241–242
    monounsaturated fat, 158
    oils, fat content comparison, 161
    polyunsaturated fat, 158, 162
    recommended intake, 160–162
    saturated fat, 158, 160–162
    stress effects on, 281
    synthetic fat, 158
    transfatty acids, 158, 159, 162
Dietary Guidelines for Americans, 174, 184, 194
Diet drugs, 247
Dieting, 243–247
    diet-only programs, 243–244
    fad diets, 246–247
    low-fat diets, 244–245
    and overcompensatory eating, 245
    and oversized food portions, 245–246
    popular diets, listing of, 248–249
    very-low-calorie diets, 244
Diet resistance, 241
Disaccharides, 155
Distress, definition of, 274
Duration
    aerobic exercise, 74–75
    resistance training, 113
Dynamic contractions, muscle, 100

E

Eating behaviors
  assessment of, 211
  changing, strategies for, 255
Eating disorders, 235
  anorexia nervosa, 255–256
  binge-eating disorder, 257–258
  bulimia, 256–257
  underweight, 258
Eccentric muscle contraction, 100, 101, 107
Echinacea, 172
Echocardiography, 55
E. coli, cause and signs of, 188
Elderly. *See* Older adults
Embolus, and stroke, 37–38
Emotional arousal, meaning of, 15
Emotional wellness, and physical health, 4–6
Endorphins, 278
Energy, stress effects on, 281
Energy nutrients, 155
Environment, impact on wellness, 6–7
Epinephrine, stress response, 278
Ergogenic aids
  anabolic-androgenic steroids, 115
  chromium picolinate, 114–115
  creatine supplementation, 114
  ginseng, 114
  protein supplementation, 113
Essential nutrients. *See* Nutrients
Estrogen
  and body fat distribution, 216–217
  heart disease prevention, 40
Ethnic foods, traditional compared to Americanized, 182
Eustress, meaning of, 274
Exercise
  and basal metabolic rate (BMR), 252
  and cold weather, 82–83
  cool down, 77
  cross-training, 76
  effects on hypertension, 48
  energy and nutrition, 186–187
  fitness equipment, 79
  and fluid consumption, 81–82
  fun, importance of, 254
  health benefits of, 52
  and hot weather, 79–82
  motivational tips, 76
  overtraining, 74
  safety tips, 71
  sports activities, 78
  for stress management, 288
  types of activities, 77–79
  in urban environment, 82
  warm up, 76–77
  and weight loss, 250–254
Exercise principles, 70–76
  duration, 74–75
  frequency, 74
  intensity, 70, 73–74
  overload, 75
  specificity, 75–76

F

Fad diets, 246–247
Fasting, and weight loss, 250
Fat-soluble vitamins, 162, 163, 164
Fen-phen, 247
Feverfew, 172
Fiber, 173–174
  health benefits, 174–175
  insoluble fiber, 173–174
  recommended intake, 174
  soluble fiber, 173
  sources of, 173, 174
Fight or flight, stress response, 53, 275
Fish oils, 158, 162
Fitness assessment
  bench step test, 91
  and exercise program design, 95
  heart rate calculation, 93
  1.5-mile run/walk test, 89
  Rockport Fitness Walking Test, 85–87
Fitness equipment, buying guidelines, 79
Flexibility assessment
  goniometer, 139
  shoulder flexion test, 147
  sit-and-reach test, 145
  sling test, 149
  trunk extension, 151
Flexibility training. *See also* Stretching exercises
  benefits of, 132
Fluid consumption, and exercise, 81–82, 187
Folate
  food sources of, 164, 166
  functions of, 164, 166
  in pregnancy, 166, 185
Foodborne illness, 187–189
  cooking guidelines, 189
  prevention of, 188–189
  types of, 188
Food Guide Pyramid, 175–176
  illustration of, 176
  serving size, 175, 177
Food labels
  claims allowed on, 190–191
  Daily Values (DV), 190, 191
  example of, 191
  FDA information specification, 192
Free radicals
  antioxidant protection, 162–163
  formation of, 162
Free-weight training, 109
Frequency
  aerobic exercise, 74
  resistance training, 113
Frostbite, 82

G

Gallbladder disease, and obesity, 236
Garlic, 172
Gender differences
  cardiovascular disease risk, 38, 40
  fat deposition, 216–217, 237
General adaptation syndrome, phases of, 275–276
Genetic factors
  aerobic capacity, 215
  body shape, 240
  body weight, 215
  cardiovascular disease risk factors, 40
  diabetes mellitus, 405
  obesity, 239–240
Ginger, 172
Ginkgo, 172
Ginseng, 114, 172
Goal setting
  as coping strategy, 283
  realistic goals, 17
  weight loss, 215
Goniometer, 139
Groin stretch, 135

H

Half-squat, 106
Hamstring curl, 107
Hamstring stretch, 136
Hardy personality, assessment of, 299
Headaches
  and stress, 279
Health behavior, assessment of, 31
Health disparities
  Healthy People 2010 on, 8–9
  and population groups, 7
Health-related fitness, meaning of, 66
Healthy People 2000, 8
Healthy People 2010, on health disparities, 8–9
Heart
  anatomy of, 34–35
  and circulation, 35
Heart attack, 37–38
  estrogen as protection, 40
  heart damage from, 36
  risk assessment, 61–63
  silent, 37
  after strenuous exercise, 70
  warning signs, 37
Heart rate
  calculation of, 73–74, 93
  and cardiorespiratory training, 67
Heart transplant, 56–57
Heart volume, and cardiorespiratory training, 68
Hearty personality, characteristics of, 282
Height/weight tables, 218
Hepatitis A, cause and signs of, 188
Herbs, 171–173
  listing of common herbs, 172
  precautions in use, 171–173
  weight loss remedies, 247, 250
High-density lipoproteins, 43–44
  guidelines for levels of, 45
  increasing, 44
  protective effects of, 44
  and very low fat diet, 160
Homeostasis, 275
Homocysteine
  cardiovascular disease risk, 54, 166
  reduction of levels, 166, 190
Hot weather and exercise, 79–82
  heat loss, types of, 80
  prevention of, 80–82

Index

Hydrogenation, 158
Hyperplasia, fat cells, 237
Hypertension, 46–48
   and abdominal fat deposition, 218
   and cardiovascular system damage, 46
   dietary strategies for, 190
   essential hypertension, 46
   and obesity, 218, 236
   risk factors, 45–47
   treatment of, 47–48
Hypertrophy
   fat cells, 237
   muscle, 113
Hypnosis
   autogenics, 285, 286
   health uses of, 5
Hypothalamus, and stress response, 278
Hypothermia, 82–83

I
Imagery, and health, 5
Immune system, and stress, 278–280
Intellectual wellness, importance of, 6
Intensity
   aerobic exercise, 70, 73–74
   resistance training, 112–113
Internet
   wellness sites, 14
Iron, 168, 169
   deficiency, 169
   food sources of, 168, 169
   functions of, 168
   levels and cardiovascular disease, 54
Ischemia, 37
Isoflavones, 156
Isokinetic training, 109–110
Isometric exercises, 100–107
   limitations of, 100
Isotonic training, 107–108

K
Karvonen formula, heart rate calculation, 73

L
Lactic acid, 77
Lactovegetarians, 180
Lateral supine raises, 108
Leg press, 106
Legumes, 156–157
   nutritional benefits of, 156–157
Lifestyle
   assessment inventory, 23–29
   of children and adolescents, 37
   lifting objects, guidelines for, 140
Limbic system, functions of, 277–278
Lipid oxidation theory, 43
Lipoprotein (a), cardiovascular disease prevention, 54
Listeria monocytogenes, cause and signs of, 188
Locus of control, health locus of control assessment, 29
Low-density lipoproteins, 43
   safe/unsafe levels, 43, 45

Low-fat diet, 181–183
   fat content in, 160
   fat reduction tips, 181–183, 251
   heart disease risk, 160
   and overcompensatory eating, 245
   and weight loss, 244–245
LSD (lysergic acid diethylamide), 347
Lycopene, 165

M
Macronutrients, 155
Maintenance stage, self-help approach, 19
Massage therapy, stress management, 286
Meditation
   and health, 5
   steps in, 285
   stress management, 285
Mediterranean diet, 161–162
Men, and cardiovascular disease risk, 38, 40
Meridia, 247
Metabolic syndrome, 218
Metabolism, exercise effects, 252
Micronutrients, 155
Middle age, life satisfaction survey, 281
Minerals, 167–169
   and athletic activity, 187
   calcium, 168–169
   iron, 168, 169
   major minerals, 167–168
   in pregnancy, 185
   sodium, 168
   trace minerals, 168
   zinc, 169
Monosaccharides, 155
Monounsaturated fat, 158
   recommended intake, 161
Motivation, tips for exercise, 76
Movement meditation, benefits of, 133
Muscle contractions
   agonists and antagonists, 136
   concentric and eccentric, 100, 101, 107
   dynamic contractions, 100
   static contractions, 100
Muscles
   fiber types, 110
   front/rear views of, 109
   hypertrophy, 113
Muscle soreness, and strength training, 108
Muscular endurance
   assessment of, 121
   best exercises for, 111
Muscular strength, development of, 99–100
Muscular strength assessment
   abdominal muscular endurance, 123
   with calisthenic exercises, 125–127
   for muscular endurance, 121
   strength/body weight ratio, 119–120
Music
   music therapy, 5
   stress management, 286–287
Myocardial infarction, 36. *See also* Heart attack

N
Nautilus equipment, 109
Neck pain, prevention of, 139–141
Neck stretches, 134
Nicotine, cardiovascular effects of, 49
Nutrient intake assessment, 203–205
Nutrients
   and calories, 155
   carbohydrates, 155–156
   dietary fat, 157–162
   excessive consumption, examples of, 178
   fiber, 173–174
   and food variety, 174–175
   herbs, 171–173
   minerals, 167–169
   nutrient density, 177, 179
   phytochemicals, 170–171
   protein, 156–157
   vitamins, 162–167
   water, 169–170
Nutrition
   and alcohol consumption, 184
   essential nutrients, 154–155
   Food Guide Pyramid, 175–176
   low-fat diet, 181–183
   moderation and healthy diet, 177–178
   in pregnancy, 185
   relationship to physical activity, 185–187
   salt, 184
   stress effects on, 281
   sugar, limiting intake, 183
   and variety of foods, 174–175, 176
   vegetarian diet, 179–181
Nutritional assessment
   carbohydrate intake, 199
   dietary fat, 201, 209–210
   eating behaviors, 211
   nutrient intake, 203–205
   protein intake, 199
   for recommended dietary intakes, 207–208

O
Obesity
   and age, 239
   cardiovascular disease risk, 51, 236
   classification of, 238
   definition of, 214
   development of, 237
   diet resistance, 241
   genetic factors, 239–240
   health risks of, 236–237
   high-fat theory of, 241–242
   and physical inactivity, 242–243
   set point theory, 240–241
Occupational wellness, importance of, 6
Oils, fat content of, 161
Older adults
   flexibility guidelines for, 138
   malnutrition of, 177
   nutritional requirements of, 177
   protein intake, 157
   and resistance training, 100
Olestra, 158, 245
Omega-3 fatty acids, 158, 162

Omega-6 fatty acids, 162
1.5–mile run/walk test, 89
Osteoporosis
  dietary strategies for, 190
Overcompensatory eating, and dieting, 245
Overfat, meaning of, 216
Overhead press, 102–103
Overload
  aerobic exercise, 75
  resistance training, 113
Overtraining, signs of, 74
Overweight, definition of, 214, 216
Ovolactovegetarians, 180

P

Parasites, foodborne, 188
Passive smoking, 49
Perfectionism, problem of, 287
Performance-related fitness, meaning of, 66
Personality traits
  hardy personality, 299
Pescovegetarians, 180
Physical activity. *See also* Exercise
  benefits of, 13, 50–51
  caloric cost of common activities, 252
  relationship to nutrition, 185–187
  use of term, 51
Physical Activity and Health, 11
Physical fitness
  cardiorespiratory endurance, 67–76
  health-related fitness, 66
  performance-related fitness, 66
Physical inactivity
  cardiovascular disease risk, 49–51
  and obesity, 242–243
Phytochemicals, 170–171
  food sources of, 171
  health benefits, 171
  types of, 171
Phytoestrogens, 156, 171
Pollovegetarians, 180
Polysaccharides, 156
Polyunsaturated fat, 158, 162
  recommended intake, 162
  types of, 162
Potentiating effect, meaning of, 333
Prayer, and health, 5
Precontemplation stage, self-help approach, 15
Pregnancy
  diet and nutritional needs in, 185
  folate in, 166, 185
  vitamins/minerals in, 185
  weight gain in, 185
Prepackaged convenience foods, 193
  supersized portions, 246
Preparation stage, self-help approach, 16–17
Procrastination, problem of, 287
Progression
  aerobic exercise, 75
  resistance training, 113
Progressive muscle relaxation, 284–285
  steps in, 285

Proprioceptive neuromuscular facilitation (PNF), 137–139
  guidelines for, 138
Protein, 156–157
  amino acids, 156
  assessing intake, 199
  complete and incomplete, 156
  legumes, 156–157
  and older adults, 157
  recommended intake, 157
  stress effects on, 281
Protein supplementation, 113, 186–187
Psychoneuroimmunology (PNI)
  study of, 279
Psychotherapy, and health, 5

Q

Quadriceps stretch, 136

R

Recidivism, meaning of, 16
Recommended dietary allowances (RDAs), 154
Redux, 247
Relaxation methods, 283–285
  deep breathing, 284
  and hypertension, 47
  progressive muscle relaxation, 284–285
Repetition, in resistance training, 99, 112–113
Resistance motivation, meaning of, 12
Resistance training
  circuit resistance training, 110–111
  daily log, 115–116, 129
  exercises, illustrations of, 101–108
  free-weight training, 109
  health benefits of, 98–99
  increasing effectiveness, tips for, 114
  isokinetic training, 109–110
  isometric exercises, 100–107
  isotonic training, 107–108
  muscle soreness, 108
  and older adults, 100
  performance aids. *See* Ergogenic aids
  variable resistance training, 108–109
Resistance training principles
  duration, 113
  frequency, 113
  intensity, 112–113
  overload, 113
  progression, 113
  specificity, 113
Rheumatic heart disease, 36
Rockport Fitness Walking Test, 85–87

S

St. John's wort, 172
Salmonella infections, cause and signs of, 188
Salt intake
  and hypertension, 47
  limiting, tips for, 184
Saturated fat, 158, 160–162
  recommended intake, 160
Saw palmetto, 172

Self-efficacy
  and health, 6
  meaning of, 6
Self-esteem
  components of, 280
  and stress, 280
Self-help approach, 12–19
  action stage, 17–18
  basis of, 13
  contemplation stage, 15
  maintenance stage, 19
  precontemplation stage, 15
  preparation stage, 16–17
  termination stage, 19
Serum triglycerides, and heart disease, 45
Serving size
  examples of, 178
  meaning of, 175, 177
Set point theory, obesity, 240–241
Shaping up, behavior change, 18
Shin splints, causes of, 71
Shoes, athletic, 71
Shoulder flexion test, 147
Shoulder stretch, 134
Side stitches, causes of, 71
Skinfold measurements, 222–225
Sleep apnea, and obesity, 236
Sling test, 149
Smokeless tobacco, 49
Snacking, 192–193
  healthful snacks, 193
Social health, importance of relationships, 4
Sodium
  functions of, 168
  limiting intake, 47, 184
Soybeans, health benefits, 156–157
Specificity
  aerobic exercise, 75–76
  resistance training, 113
Spine, vertebral column, illustration of, 142
Spirituality
  aspects of, 3–4
  and physical health, 5
Sports, fitness rating for, 78
Spotting, and resistance training, 114
Staphylococcus, cause and signs of, 188
Static contractions, muscle, 100
Static stretching, 136–137
  guidelines for, 137
Strength assessment. *See* Muscular strength assessment
Strength training. *See* Resistance training
Stress
  assessment of, 291–295
  cardiovascular disease risk, 53
  dealing with. *See* Stress management
  definition of, 274
  general adaptation syndrome phases, 275–276
  good stress, 274
  and immune system, 278–280
  negative effects of, 276–277
  and nutrition, 281
  physiological effects of, 53, 275, 277–278

and self-esteem, 280
stressful situations, categories of, 276
stress-related personality types, 282
stress style, 295
Stress management
 autogenics, 285
 biofeedback, 286
 coping tips, 283
 exercise, 288
 massage therapy, 286
 meditation, 285
 music, 286–287
 pleasurable experiences as, 289
 relaxation methods, 283–285
 time management, 287–288
 visualization, 285–286
Stressors
 definition of, 274
 individual reactions to, 274
 life stressor assessment, 291–292
 types of, 53, 274
Stress tests, 55
Stretching exercises, 67
 ballistic stretching, 139
 for cooldown, 77
 illustrations of, 134–136
 proprioceptive neuromuscular facilitation (PNF), 137–139
 static stretching, 136–137
Stretch reflex, 136
Stroke, 37–38
 causes of, 37–38, 46
 prevention of, 38
 warning signs, 38
Stroke volume, and cardiorespiratory training, 67
Subliminal advertising, 12
Sugar, limiting intake, 183
Support groups
 value of, 5
Syndrome X, 51, 218

T
Tai chi, benefits of, 133
Tapeworms, foodborne, 188
Termination stage, self-help approach, 19
Thermogenic effect of food, 241
Thrombus, and stroke, 37–38
Thyroid gland, and body weight, 239
Time juggling, problem of, 287
Time management, 287–288
 guidelines, 287–288
 time robbers, 287
 use of time analysis, 303–304
 worksheet for, 301–302

Transfatty acids, 158, 159, 162
Transtheoretical Model of Behavior Change, and self-help approach, 13
Treadmill test, 55
Trunk extension test, 151
Type A personality, 282
Type B personality, 282

U
Underwater weighing, 219, 221
Underweight, 258
Universal Gym, 109

V
Valerian, 172
Variable resistance training, 108–109
Vegans, 179
Vegetarian diet, 179–181
 deficiency problems of, 180
 dietary strategies, 179, 181
 food pyramid for, 180
 forms of, 180
 health benefits, 181
 in pregnancy, 185
Very-low-calorie diets, 244
Visualization, stress management, 285–286
Vitamin A
 carotenoids, 165
 food sources of, 164
 recommended intake, 163
Vitamin C
 food sources of, 164
 functions of, 163–164, 164
 recommended intake, 163, 164
Vitamin D
 and calcium, 168
 functions of, 164
 recommended intake, 163
Vitamin E
 food sources of, 164
 functions of, 164, 165
 recommended uses, 165
Vitamin K
 food sources of, 164
 functions of, 164
 recommended intake, 163
Vitamins, 162–167. *See also* individual vitamins
 antioxidants, 162–163
 and athletic activity, 187
 deficiency and vegetarian diet, 180
 fat-soluble vitamins, 162, 163, 164
 functions of, 162
 for older adults, 177
 in pregnancy, 185

shopping tips, 167
stress effects on, 281
supplements, recommended use, 166–167
water soluble vitamins, 162, 163, 164

W
Waist-to-hip ratio, body fat distribution, 217
Warm up, exercise, 76–77
Water, 169–170
 and exercise, 81–82, 187
 functions of, 169
 recommended intake, 170
Water soluble vitamins, 162, 163, 164
Weight cycling, 243–244
Weight gain
 and high fat intake, 160
 and pregnancy, 185
 and quitting smoking, 49
Weight loss
 and caloric deficit, 243
 and calories burned, 250–252
 cycling, 243–244
 diet drugs, 247
 dieting, 243–247
 estimation of, 216
 fasting, 250
 herbal remedies, 247, 250
 and physical activity, 250–254
 predictors of success, 252, 254–255, 258–260
 realistic goal setting, 215
Wellness
 benefits of, 2
 and cardiorespiratory endurance, 70
 challenges to, 9–11
 components of, 3–7
 self-help approach, 12–19
 steps in, 9
Women
 coping with work/home stress, 280
 estrogen, protective effects, 40
Workaholism, 287

Y
Yesism, problem of, 287
Yoga
 benefits of, 133
 and health, 5

Z
Zinc, 169
 stress effects on, 281